CONSTRUCTING MEANING

Teaching Language and Literacy K–8

Sixth Edition

CONSTRUCTING MEANING

Teaching Language and Literacy K–8

Sixth Edition

Joyce Bainbridge
UNIVERSITY OF ALBERTA

Rachel Heydon
WESTERN UNIVERSITY

WITH A CHAPTER ON MULTILITERACIES BY
Kathryn Hibbert

NELSON
EDUCATION

Constructing Meaning: Teaching Language and Literacy K–8, Sixth Edition

by Joyce Bainbridge and, Rachel Heydon, with a chapter on multiliteracies by Kathryn Hibbert

VP, Product and Partnership Solutions:
Anne Williams

Publisher:
Lenore Taylor-Atkins

Marketing Manager:
Terry Fedorkiw

Content Development Manager:
Courtney Thorne

Photo Researcher:
Karen Hunter

Permissions Coordinator:
Karen Hunter

Production Project Manager:
Christine Gilbert

Production Service:
Cenveo Publishing Services

Copy Editor:
Marcia Gallego

Proofreader:
Pushpa V. Giri

Indexer:
BIM Publishing Services

Design Director:
Ken Phipps

Managing Designer:
Franca Amore

Interior Design:
Cathy Mayer

Cover Design:
Cathy Mayer

Cover Image:
Hero Images/Getty Royalty Free

Compositor:
Cenveo Publisher Services

Library and Archives Canada Cataloguing in Publication Data

Bainbridge, Joyce, 1944-, author
     Constructing meaning: teaching language and literacy K-8 / Joyce Bainbridge, University of Alberta, Rachel Heydon, Western University; with a chapter on multiliteracies by Kathryn Hibbert.
—Sixth edition.

Includes bibliographical references and index.
ISBN 978-0-17-658078-0 (paperback)

1. Language arts (Elementary).
2. English language—Study and teaching (Elementary). I. Heydon, Rachel, 1971-, author II. Title.

LB1575.8.B34 2016   372.6'044
C2015-904540-1

BRIEF TABLE OF CONTENTS

CONTENTS

CHAPTER 4 Early Literacy 106

CHAPTER 5 The Nature and Assessment of Reading 151

CHAPTER 12 **Responding to Literature 410**

ABOUT THE AUTHORS

Joyce Bainbridge

Joyce is professor emerita, Department of Elementary Education, and former vice dean of the Faculty of Education at the University of Alberta. She received her M.A. and Ed.D. at the University of Northern Colorado. The recipient of teaching and research awards, she taught university courses in language and literacy education for many years, and continues to teach educational research courses. She is the author of two textbooks and many journal articles.

Rachel Heydon

Rachel is professor and program chair of curriculum studies and studies in applied linguistics, Faculty of Education, Western University. She holds a Ph.D. in Curriculum, Teaching, and Learning from the Ontario Institute for Studies in Education, University of Toronto. Dr. Heydon coordinates the pre-service elementary language arts courses at Western and teaches literacy and curriculum theory courses at the graduate level. She is associate editor of the *Journal of Curriculum Studies*, co-editor of the journal *Language and Literacy*, a former president of the Language and Literacy Researchers of Canada, and author of many publications about curriculum, early childhood, literacy, and teacher professional learning in literacy.

Kathryn Hibbert

Kathryn, author of the multiliteracies chapter, is an associate professor, Faculty of Education at Western University. Her research interests pertain to the scholarship of teaching and learning, the pedagogy of multiliteracies, and the pedagogical potential of virtual learning environments. Dr. Hibbert takes a socio-cultural approach to learning about the nature of literacy in both school settings and professional practice settings, and the policies, decisions, and practices that inform them.

PREFACE

Research has consistently shown that children and youth develop their language and literacy abilities through interacting meaningfully with people in their daily lives—at storytime, in talk with peers, when searching for information, and while at play. When learners are in school, they use language in purposeful ways across the curriculum. Learning is enhanced through interactions with educators, families, peers, and other people both within and outside the school context. In the school setting, educators play a crucial role in maximizing learners' language and literacy acquisition. They serve as strong models, providing a stimulus for thinking and exploring ideas. They put multiliteracies into action.

This sixth edition of *Constructing Meaning* is an introduction to teaching K to 8 language and literacy from an integrated, social constructivist perspective. This perspective draws heavily on multiliteracies theory, which highlights the multiple modes, media, discourses, and languages through which people communicate. The pedagogies we suggest promote critical literacies, and in this edition we strive to be explicitly sensitive to what literacy means today and the kinds of demands this places on educators and learners. Throughout the book, we discuss and illustrate the various ways in which rapidly evolving communication technologies and learner demographics have radically changed literacy from even a generation ago. These are exciting times for language and literacy educators and learners, and we have tried to offer many ways for pre- and in-service educators to capitalize on this excitement by helping to support learners' literacy learning in all their teaching.

In keeping with the first five editions, we provide a comprehensive yet accessible pedagogical framework grounded in our theoretical approach. This framework can provide beginning and even experienced educators with a range of ideas related to different areas of language and literacy education.

There are some major changes in this edition. First of all, we have reordered the sequence of some chapters to align the book more closely with the structure of language and literacy education courses taught in faculties of education. Second, we have created more streamlined content to emphasize what is most important in language and literacy education and to promote contemporary and enduring trends in the field. Throughout our revisions for the sixth edition, we have maintained the structural and organizational strategies that proved successful in past editions. For instance, we continue to introduce each chapter with a graphic organizer that provides readers with an overview of topics and subtopics to be considered, and we present scenarios of educator practice. Definitions of terms in boldface type are presented in the Glossary at the end of the book. Included in many chapters are book lists, examples of teaching/learning activities, and samples of learners' reading, writing, visual representations, and oral language. We end each chapter with a summary and a short annotated list of professional resources for readers who wish to pursue an area further. We rely heavily on web resources, frequently including them in our lists of suggested professional resources for educators. The Appendix contains publishing information for all the children's and young adult books mentioned in the chapters, along with additional titles, both fiction and nonfiction, that we recommend for learners at various grade levels.

Our goal in **Chapter 1** is to situate Canadian language and literacy teaching and learning and set up all subsequent discussions in the book. We contemplate literacy teaching today and highlight issues of learner diversity and definitions of literacy. All of this leads into the introduction of our theoretical framework, complete with an overview of pedagogical strategies, before we turn to you, as educator, and identify some of the things that educators need to grapple with in their curricular conversation on how and what to teach. In this chapter, like the others, we invite readers to reflect on their beliefs, practices, and experiences in a bid to help educators become critically reflective professional decision makers.

Chapter 2 is a companion to Chapter 1, following upon the big ideas of how to design language and literacy programs to address the funds of knowledge and needs of all learners. We structure the chapter by forwarding key pedagogical decisions that educators need to make. We then go on to suggest ways that learners, time, and space can be organized to maximize learning in different contexts, as always highlighting the work of real educational practitioners in relation to the research literature. The chapter concludes with a section on families as partners.

Given the notion that "literacy floats on a sea of talk" (Britton, 1972, p. 58), in **Chapter 3** we describe the structure of language and explore how language functions in different social contexts and in the learning process, in particular. We suggest how to enhance listening and speaking in classrooms and how to assess learners' oral language abilities.

The focus of **Chapter 4** is early literacy. In this chapter, we begin by describing an early years classroom that operates from an emergent literacy curriculum. We then consider the nature of early childhood literacy. We provide suggestions for assessing young children's literacy acquisition and for planning appropriate programs to be responsive to their knowledge, interests, and needs. We end the chapter by describing specific instructional strategies to promote young children's language and literacy practices and learning.

Reading is the focus of **Chapters 5** through 7. In **Chapter 5** we begin by describing various theoretical perspectives on reading and strategies for assessing what learners know, can do, and value. In **Chapters 6** and 7, we suggest specific instructional techniques to support learners in becoming lifelong, purposeful, and strategic readers.

In **Chapter 8** we focus on the role of literacy in learning across the curriculum. We describe strategies for reading in the content areas, teaching text structures, and reading and researching information, as well as working with journal writing, learning logs, research reports, and study skills.

Chapters 9 and **10** are devoted to teaching writing. In **Chapter 9**, we examine forms of writing, the process of composing, and guidelines for implementing a writing workshop. **Chapter 10** deals with strategies for assessing learners' writing as well as for teaching the conventional aspects of writing (spelling, grammar, and handwriting).

Chapter 11 addresses the literature available for children and young adults, and provides lists of books for learners in K to 8, with a heavy emphasis on Canadian content and social justice issues.

Chapter 12 addresses the importance of responding to literature through a range of activities; it also suggests ways to organize response groups, journals, drama, multimedia, and the visual arts. The chapter discusses how to select literature for learners' reading pleasure and for classroom use.

In **Chapter 13**, Kathryn Hibbert explores new media. She offers some insights to help educators as they expand their definitions of literacy teaching and learning to include accessing, creating, and redesigning multiple forms of text. The approach utilizes multiple communication channels and modes of delivery, acknowledging the diverse cultural and social settings of today's classrooms.

INSTRUCTOR RESOURCES

The **Nelson Education Teaching Advantage (NETA)** program delivers research-based instructor resources that promote student engagement and higher-order thinking to enable the success of Canadian students and educators. Visit Nelson Education's **Inspired Instruction** website at **http://www.nelson.com/inspired/** to find out more about NETA.

The following instructor resources have been created for *Constructing Meaning: Teaching Language and Literacy K–8*, sixth edition. Access these ultimate tools for customizing lectures and presentations at **http://www.nelson.com/instructor**.

NETA PowerPoint

Microsoft® PowerPoint® lecture slides for every chapter have been created by Luigi Iannacci of Trent University. There is an average of 15 slides per chapter featuring the information included in key figures and tables from *Constructing Meaning: Teaching Language and Literacy K–8*, Sixth Edition. NETA principles of clear design and engaging content have been incorporated throughout, making it simple for instructors to customize the deck for their courses.

Image Library

This resource consists of digital copies of figures, short tables, and photographs used in the book. Instructors may use these jpegs to customize the NETA PowerPoint or create their own PowerPoint presentations.

NETA Instructor Guide

This resource to accompany *Constructing Meaning: Teaching Language and Literacy K–8*, Sixth Edition has been prepared by Luigi Iannacci of Trent University. This guide contains suggested classroom activities, a chapter summary, discussion questions, and a list of additional resources to give instructors the support they need to engage their students within the classroom.

CourseMate

CourseMate includes:

- an interactive ebook that includes note-taking and highlighting functionality
- interactive teaching and learning tools, including:
  - o quizzes
  - o flashcards
  - o videos
  - o suggested books for the classroom
  - o additional resources
  - o and more

ACKNOWLEDGMENTS

We thank all the K to 8 learners, educators, undergraduate students, graduate students, and colleagues who have helped us understand the nature of the teaching and learning of language and literacy during our years as learners, teachers, and researchers. Particular appreciation is expressed to the educators who took the time to write and talk to us about their classroom experiences and to the learners who provided samples of their reading, writing, and oral language.

We acknowledge the significant contribution of Kathryn Hibbert, who developed Chapter 13: New Media. Kathy's expertise and experience in this area has deeply enriched the book.

We are grateful for the involvement and contributions of several others, too: Dawn Ford, who assisted us with the photographs, and Elisabeth Davies, Emma Cooper, Wambui Gichuru, Lori McKee, and Joelle Nagle from Western University for their research assistance. On a personal note, Rachel extends her deep appreciation to Oliver Cavanaugh for always helping to make language new again.

We also appreciate the valuable comments and suggestions from instructors at our own and other universities, as well as from the following reviewers selected by Nelson Education: Jim Chevalier, University of Windsor; Roswita Dressler, University of Calgary; Lynne Wiltse, University of Alberta; and the late Mary Clare Courtland, Lakehead University, who was a long-time scholar of language and literacy education and a friend to many of us in the field. We will miss her keen insight and advice.

Finally, we thank the editorial staff at Nelson Education for encouraging us to write a sixth edition of this book and for providing advice and support during its development.

Joyce Bainbridge
Rachel Heydon

Introduction to Language and Literacy Teaching and Learning

LITERACY IN CONTEMPORARY TIMES

- The Dimensions of Language and Literacy
- Defining Literacy
- Multiliteracies
- Implications for Language and Literacy Education
- Critical Reflection
- Critical Literacy
- Literacy and Identity

MULTILITERACIES PEDAGOGIES

- Cambourne's Conditions for Learning: A Starting Point for Language and Literacy Teaching

INTRODUCTION TO TEACHING LANGUAGE AND LITERACY

FACTORS THAT MEDIATE TEACHERS' LANGUAGE AND LITERACY PLANNING

- What to Teach?
- What Do the Documents Say? Language and Literacy Learning in Canadian Classrooms
- Who Are the Learners in Front of Us?

INSTRUCTIONAL COMPONENTS OF MULTILITERACIES PEDAGOGIES

- Instructional Component Considerations

EDUCATORS' HISTORIES AS STUDENTS AND BELIEFS

Teacher candidates

MARCO'S JOURNEY TOWARD BECOMING A LANGUAGE AND LITERACY TEACHER

Bright and energetic, Marco, whose mother tongue is Italian, came to his Bachelor of Education program with an undergraduate degree in psychology and experience as a web designer for a parenting magazine: a strong foundation for a language and **literacy** teacher! Yet when he entered his first language arts education course, Marco confessed, "At first I was a little afraid of this course because I didn't think I had a lot to give in the language arts curriculum." We got to know Marco, and learned about the origins of his hesitation. In an interview about his own literacy development in response to a "graphic life map" (see readwritethink.org) he'd made to represent the high and low points in his literacy life history, Marco explained,

> I was never a big reader.... As a child, I left [Canada] and I went to Uruguay for four years, so my language halted for a while. I had a new language, a new culture, and a new way of communicating with people, and so, I think that kind of set me back a bit, then [just] when I excelled in Spanish, we came back [to Canada]. I was taking ESL classes [but], I was never really successful with language academically, so it was kind of a back burner, I have to do it because they're making me do it. I was never really excited about language or about reading or writing. It was just, very minimal and I wasn't very successful until after university and then things started picking up.

Marco's past schooling experiences did not take advantage of his language and literacy knowledge, and they left him with a limited view of literacy. For instance, at the beginning of his course, Marco believed literacy was just about reading. He explained that the literacy instruction he had received at school consisted mainly of reading, which meant trying to "get the words right." As his teacher preparation progressed, however, Marco came to some insights.

> I've realized I do have a lot and slowly … I'm starting to understand that language [arts] is more than just teaching [learners] to read and write.... we all communicate and … all that is language arts.... I thought that I had nothing, but I … realized, wow I do have a lot more to give, and a lot of strengths in the area.*

By the end of the language arts course Marco saw that literacy involves the various ways that people communicate, including those ways that use **new media**. This insight was so exciting to him that he posted the following in the course's online discussion in response to a conversation on using technology in the classroom:

> What a GREAT idea …! As most of you know, I'm all about bringing tech and the Internet into the classroom.... Each one of our students needs to be able to know how to interact and interpret this new world.... The possibilities make my

---

* R. Heydon & K. Hibbert. "'Relocating the Personal' to engender critically reflective practice in pre-service literacy teachers." *Teaching and Teacher Education*, Vol. 26, Issue 4, May 2010, pp. 796–804.

brain tingle. Think of a *Literature Circle* with Molly's class in [Toronto], Judy's class in [Victoria], Connie's class in [Charlottetown] and my class here in [town]! I'm not kidding when I say I would give my baby toe for a SMART Board!"*

Marco's enthusiasm came when he learned that his knowledge and expertise in the digital world (e.g., web design and classroom technology such as interactive whiteboards) were important parts of language and literacy education. He also learned that his experience as a **culturally and linguistically diverse (CLD)** learner lent him a sensitivity toward his students who were learning English, and that when this was combined with understanding second language acquisition, he could help his students to *add* English to their first language. The more Marco learned about literacy in contemporary times, the more he saw exciting opportunities to go beyond his own educational experiences. (Box 1.1 provides definitions of relevant terminology.) Marco's language arts education course provided him with learning opportunities that expanded his literacy options, allowing him to see literacy as comprising more than reading and writing, and it expanded his identity options by providing him opportunities to forge a sense of self premised in his multilingual literacy knowledge and his strengths as a communicator. ☐

In *Constructing Meaning*, you too will be given the opportunity to find your strengths and confidence as a language and literacy educator. Our goal is to help you be an educator who understands the importance of expansive literacy and identity options for learners and knows how to achieve these goals. To get started, we present some questions that Marco's story raises:

- What does it mean to be literate?
- What are the big ideas that form the foundation of the language and literacy pedagogy we espouse in this text?
- What are the implications of all of these things for educators?

BOX 1.1

TERMINOLOGY

There are many terms related to learners who speak languages other than English when they are in classrooms where English is the medium of instruction. What term to use and when is dependent upon time and place, and terms continue to evolve, taking on new connotations and denotations. Our preferred term is *culturally and linguistically diverse (CLD)* as it highlights the "assets" (Heydon & Iannacci, 2008), or knowledge that learners hold even when they "do not come to school already proficient in the language of the instruction" (Prasad, 2009, pp. 8–9). More common terms include **English language learner (ELL) and English as a second language (ESL)**, which are often used by governments or school districts to designate learners whose first language is not English or programs developed for them. Throughout *Constructing Meaning*, we use the term that relates best to the specific circumstance under discussion; for instance, if we are talking about a learner who has an official designation, then we use *ESL*.

Source: R. Heydon & K. Hibbert. "'Relocating the Personal' to engender critically reflective practice in pre-service literacy teachers." *Teaching and Teacher Education*, Vol. 26, Issue 4, May 2010, pp. 796–804.

* R. Heydon & K. Hibbert. "'Relocating the Personal' to engender critically reflective practice in pre-service literacy teachers." *Teaching and Teacher Education*, Vol. 26, Issue 4, May 2010, pp. 796–804.

These questions correspond to the sections of this chapter, which begins with an invitation to think about your responses to the questions and contemplate a few others: About what aspects of the above questions do you feel most confident? Where do you have the most learning to do? Think now about your past experiences as a student and how they compare to what is seen in today's classrooms. What are some of the questions you have already generated from your observations and experiences?

LITERACY IN CONTEMPORARY TIMES
The Dimensions of Language and Literacy

In this section we explore how the term *literacy* is defined in contemporary times, but to provide an overview and context for this conversation, we first talk about of the general *dimensions* of language and literacy, of which there are six (see Table 1.1).

The first four dimensions (the top two lines of the table) have been included in language and literacy programs for many years; hence, they are familiar. The last two, however, might need explaining. In general, *representing* refers to the practice of making a visual text to communicate an idea (e.g., drawing, map-making, or creating a computer graphic). *Viewing* refers to the practice of making meaning from a visual text (e.g., interpreting a map). Educators have long encouraged representing and viewing practices. For instance, a common sight in primary classrooms is children busily drawing, painting, and working with blocks.

Gunther Kress (1997) provided a rationale for educators to set up opportunities for learners to engage in these practices; he argued, for instance, that they support the learning of writing. With older learners, representing and viewing have not been as well supported in the classroom, though the sights of learners constructing models, diagrams, and maps in, for example, science and social studies lessons will be familiar to many. Even more, however, recent explosions in young people's involvement in instant messaging, photo sharing, gaming, and other digitally mediated literacy forms have made educators take notice. Learners' interest in new **media** is representative of the massive shifts in communication that are occurring globally. Therefore, representing, viewing, and media literacy have appeared more recently in curriculum documents, and a somewhat more expansive idea of language and literacy has resulted. All of this raises a question: What does literacy in this new era mean?

TABLE 1.1 **DIMENSIONS OF LANGUAGE AND LITERACY**

Expressive Dimensions	Receptive Dimensions
Speaking	Listening
Writing	Reading
Representing	Viewing

Defining Literacy

Decades ago literacy experts like Andrea Butler (1993) noticed that what Western societies took as being literate had changed over the years. In the 1700s, people who could sign their names were considered literate. One hundred years later, people had to be able to sign their names and read a prepared passage (usually from the Bible). The year 1915 saw the advent of the literacy test. Possibly one of the first such tests, created by the United States army, consisted of a short reading passage and then a list of literal comprehension questions. Gradually, new demands were placed on people's literacy skills just so that they could get by in their day-to-day lives (e.g., reading appliance and workplace manuals and completing income tax forms). Currently, the literacy demands made on people are greater than ever and require *all* the dimensions just discussed. A major innovation in language and literacy theory and pedagogy, called *multiliteracies*, can be useful for making sense of these shifts.

Multiliteracies

Communication technology is changing at an unprecedented pace. Blogging, gaming, social networking: the children and youth of today are communicating and living a life different from just a generation ago.

The term *multiliteracies* originated from the New London Group (NLG), a clutch of academics from Australia, North America, and Europe who gathered in New London, Connecticut. Since their first publication, in 1996, of *A Pedagogy of Multiliteracies: Designing Social Futures*, the NLG have studied literacy in everyday life and documented how literacy expands "beyond the linear text-based reading and writing of western schooling" (Cummins, 2006, p. 4). Literacy "means more than just literacy in English" (Cummins, 2006, p. 4). Indeed, the definition of literacy depends on where a person is standing. This is what the Language and Literacy Researchers of Canada meant when they said that literacy is "situational" (2008), and what is meant when others have said that being literate is not about owning a single "set of skills" (Pahl & Rowsell, 2006, p. 1) that are "autonomous" (Street, 1984). Instead, literacy is "ideological" (Street, 1984): "grounded in how it is used, and how it relates to power structures within society" (Pahl & Rowsell, 2005, p. 14).

One key notion of multiliteracies is **multimodal literacy.** Kress, a member of the NLG, and his colleague Carey Jewitt (Jewitt & Kress, 2003), foundational researchers in multimodal literacy, saw that the idea of literacy as related only to print text (reading and writing) was limiting. They observed that changes in communication have broadened the range of **modes** through which people express themselves and from which they read (or construct meaning from) the expressions of others. Modes are a set of resources people in a given culture can use to communicate—for example, print, image, music, and speech. All modes relate to at least one dimension of language and literacy.

To be recognized as modes, resources need to be regularized and organized in some way within a given **domain**. This means that when, for example, we use the mode of print in writing this book, we are following the rules, or **grammar**, of the mode as they are used in education

Rachel Heydon

Children making meaning with a digital tool

writing. We do this to increase the likelihood that our readers can make meaning from what we are trying to communicate. Grammar is what makes a text "comprehensible to members of the culture in which it is produced and received" (Bearne, 2009b, p. 157). People do not make up all the rules every time they try to express themselves, though grammars should not be thought of as hard and fast and true for all times and places. Instead, grammars evolve and are created as people use them and seek to communicate in new and more effective ways (Kress & van Leeuwen, 1996a).

In all communication, regardless of the mode one uses, people make decisions related to what they want to communicate and how they will communicate it (Kress & Jewitt, 2003). The question of how is mediated by

- people's access to various modes, media and literacy tools (e.g., pencils, computers)
- people's facility with a given mode, that is, what they know about the mode and how well they can use it
- people's understanding of what a specific situation demands (e.g., the audience's expectations)
- domain expectations
- people's interests

Learners' interests come from their "knowledge and experiences" (Albers, 2007, p. 6) and are tied up with their identities. The texts learners create contain evidence of their interests and senses of self (Pahl & Rowsell, 2005). Thus interests are important for educators to attend to.

Modes are rarely if ever used in isolation: hence, *multi*modal literacy. A web page, for example, generally includes image and print. It might also include sound effects. Similarly, even a lecture is multimodal in that it will usually involve speech and gesture, and maybe print and image, as on a PowerPoint slide. Also remarkable is that changes in one mode or medium can affect changes in different modes or media. For instance, since the advent of the Internet, increasingly, print materials, such as magazines and information books, are laid out to look like web pages: they might have little factoid boxes and text built around images. In turn, readers have developed strategies for dealing with this kind of nonlinear presentation, and some readers have even come to expect that this is how texts should be laid out.

Literacy, then, usually necessitates the ability to use and make meaning from a variety of modes. In Marco's case, when he needed to build web pages for his parenting magazine, being literate meant being able to call on his knowledge of representing and writing so that he could take advantage of the digital environment in which he was working. When Marco was writing his social foundations of education exam, being literate meant being able to read questions and answer them in traditional essay format.

Some modes are not just more useful to the communicator than others within a given situation, but may be valued differently depending on the situation (including domain). Kress (2003), for instance, claimed that print is "the preferred mode of the political and cultural elites" (p. 1). Witness that, although all six dimensions are included in curriculum documents across Canada, some educational policies and procedures communicate a valuing of print modes over others. For example, a pan-Canadian study of large-scale **assessment** in the middle years (Peterson & McClay, 2010) found that despite the changes that have taken place in the way people compose (e.g., through digital means like word processing), writing assessment is still largely structured in linear paper-and-pencil tests. Furthermore, several provinces insist on high-stakes, standardized literacy assessments that almost exclusively involve specific forms of reading and writing. In Ontario and New Brunswick these assessments are high stakes because without passing them, a student cannot gain a secondary-school diploma.

In *Constructing Meaning,* we work from a broad definition of literacy that comprises the six dimensions, includes new media, and recognizes that certain modes can be supportive of the acquisition of other modes; for instance, visual representational modes, such as drawing, are foundational to the development of reading (e.g., Albers, 2007) and writing (Kress, 1997). Given the importance of **print literacy** in Canadian society, however, we do place it at the forefront of our pedagogical focus. Print literacy is

> the reading and writing of some form of print for communicative purposes inherent in people's lives. Thus, it involves decoding and encoding of a linguistically based symbol system and is driven by social processes that rely upon communication and meaning. Because it is social, its practice reflects sociocultural patterns and purposes as well as power relationships and political forces. (Purcell-Gates, Jacobson, & Degener, 2004, p. 26)

This definition highlights literacy as a social, meaning-making activity and demonstrates the importance of the critical aspects of multiliteracies and the related **critical literacy** approach that we discuss later in the chapter.

Implications for Language and Literacy Education

How has language and literacy education responded to the literacy changes just mentioned? Until about 30 years ago, such education was dominated by a well-established field called "reading" (Lankshear & Knobel, 2003, p. 3). In their historical study of literacy, Gillen and Hall (2003) explained that this field saw reading as "primarily a perceptual activity centred on sound/symbol relationships" (p. 4). Educators were expected to follow a step-by-step approach to instructing learners how to decode and sometimes encode print text. Reading instruction was characterized by an inflexible, sequenced, hierarchical presentation of isolated parts of language whose mastery was thought to be necessary *before* learners could make meaning from text. There was an absolute distinction between "being a reader and not being a reader" (p. 4). Connected to this was the idea that children did not begin to learn to read until they came to school. There was little appreciation for **early literacy** practices or knowledge that might have come from the home (more about this in Chapter 4).

Related pedagogies looked like lots of direct **phonics** lessons with repetitive, fill-in-the-blank sheets, **basal readers** that had to be read in chronological order, literal comprehension questions, and occasional writing. Four basic assumptions about children and literacy underlined this approach:

- children's agency, that is their desires, needs and actions, was insignificant
- children could learn nothing for themselves
- children were objects to be manipulated by teachers
- reading and writing were [autonomous] acts involving sets of discrete perceptual skills. (Gillen & Hall, 2003, p. 4)

In contrast, multiliteracies has led to educators developing the ideas that reading should be conceptualized within a broader notion of litera*cies* and the acquisition of these literacies is not just a set of cognitive skills that can be transferred from educator to learner. Instead, literacies are developed within particular socio-cultural contexts.

Another foundational influence is the work of Russian psychologist Lev Vygotsky (1978) and his development of the **social constructivist model of learning**. Vygotsky theorized that people's learning occurs within social interactions and this includes their learning of language. According to Vygotsky, children are active in making their own meaning of the world, but other people in their immediate social worlds also play important roles. When people work collaboratively, they negotiate and develop shared meanings within their communication. In this way, literacy is about communicating, and the expressive and receptive dimensions of literacy are about constructing meaning that is socially and culturally situated—this is why we have titled this book *Constructing Meaning*. Some of the implications of this for how we view literacy and learners entail the following readjustment of assumptions of the reading field:

- Young people's agency is significant and will affect what they do (or do not) learn.
- Young people learn among themselves and with the support of more knowledgeable others.
- Young people must be provided opportunities to exercise their rights as citizens and thus be seen as full human beings with whom teachers need to negotiate (Heydon & Iannacci, 2005).
- Literacy is both a cognitive and a socio-cultural undertaking (Purcell-Gates, Jacobson, & Degener, 2004).

Some of the innovations in understandings of literacy have resulted in curricular changes; for example, all language curricula in Canada officially recognize some aspect of what might be termed *media education* (Media Awareness Network, 2010). The Ontario Ministry of Education, for example, has added a media literacy strand to its language (2006) and kindergarten (2010–2011) documents; hence, four- and five-year-olds are expected to "respond critically to animated works such as cartoons in which animals talk" (p. 91). In the British Columbia language arts documents, reading is grouped with viewing. Grade 6 learners, for instance, are expected to "demonstrate comprehension of visual texts with specialized features (e.g., visual components of media such as magazines, newspapers, web sites, comic books, broadcast media, videos, advertising, and promotional materials" (B.C. Ministry of Education, 2010a, p.16).

Also, curricular supports have been created to help educators with these changes. These include websites, such as Kathy Hibbert's (n.d.) *Salty Chip* website, which acts like a social networking site for educators, children, and youth to "share and build upon their work as they develop their use of multiliteracies" (n.p.); as well as edited collections, such as *Assessing New Literacies* (Burke & Hammett, 2009), which offers advice from prominent Canadian literacy researchers on assessing students' literacy work in new media (including social networking sites).

Despite the examples of how multiliteracies have been taken up in education, there is some indication that schools may have a way to go. For instance, in an **evaluation** of Canadian schools and multiliteracies, Jim Cummins (2006) noted that "only a relatively small fraction of students use computers regularly at school for meaningful or substantive academic work" due to difficulties with access and a gap in policy, which results in problematic curriculum and pedagogy.

He also pointed out that a "policy vacuum" exists in relation to linguistic diversity, resulting in at least three "problematic assumptions":

- Provision of instructional support for ELLs is the job of the ESL teacher;
- "Literacy" refers only to English literacy;
- The cultural knowledge and home language proficiency that ELL students bring to school have little instructional relevance. (p. 5)

Further, we have observed that being literate, according to most curriculum documents in Canada, means working in one of the official languages of Canada (English or French). This exclusion of other languages, which relates to Cummins's second assumption, jeopardizes expansive literacy learning opportunities and identity options. The issue of literacy being situational again arises. When Marco was at home and interacting with his family, being a proficient communicator meant using and drawing on knowledge of multiple languages (Spanish, Italian, and English). At school, however, he was challenged to use only the dominant language of the region (e.g., Spanish in Uruguay, English in central Canada) and was discouraged from drawing on his knowledge of multiple languages.

Later in the chapter we address some of the reasons why the above assumptions are flawed and suggest what educators might do to support CLD learners; however, we have included these observations here to make the point that multiliteracies, in particular, have helped many educators recognize that issues of power, equity, and social justice are tied up with how literacy is defined, used, and taught. (Nonetheless, for a great teaching **strategy** to support multiliteracies, particularly as it relates to supporting multilingual literacies, check out librarian Linda Ludke's list of dual language books featured in Box 1.2.)

BOX 1.2

DUAL LANGUAGE BOOKS

Children's public librarian Linda Ludke is one of our favourite resources. Here, she has recommended titles for books that are written in more than one language. Linda has run an Arabic/English storytime held over the school lunch hour so that children from the neighbouring school could participate. Linda reads the story in English, and an Arabic speaker she partners with reads the Arabic. Linda has also offered bilingual books for families to take home. With these books, children can read the English and their parents the first language, or vice versa, or they can all read together.

Bilingual Literature Recommended by Linda Ludke

Argueta, J. (2010). *Arroz con leche/ Rice pudding* [Text in English and Spanish]. Toronto, ON: Groundwood Books.

Brown, M. W. (2007). *Goodnight Moon 1 2 3: A counting book/Buenas noches, luna 1 2 3: Un libro para contar* [Text in English and Spanish]. New York, NY: Rayo.

(continued)

Carle, E., & Iwamura, K. (2003). *Where are you going? To see my friend: A story of friendship in two languages* [Text in English and Japanese]. New York, NY: Orchard Books.

Flett, J. (2013). *Wild berries* [Text in English and Cree]. Vancouver, ON: Simply Read Books.

Harter, D. (2003). *Walking through the jungle* [Text in English and Arabic]. London, UK: Mantra Lingua.

Isadora, R. (2010). Say hello! New York, NY: G. P. Putnam's Sons.

Jocelyn, M. (2005). *ABC x 3: English, Español, Français.* Toronto, ON: Tundra Books.

Shapiro, N., & Adelson-Goldstein, J. (2009). *The Oxford picture dictionary: English–Arabic.* New York, NY: Oxford University Press.

Critical Reflection

When literacy is complex, its education is complex and calls for critical reflection. This is why some researchers say that the requirements for "professional" literacy teaching are "psychological strength" (Duffy, 2002, p. 335), professional knowledge, creativity, resourcefulness, and "passion" (p. 334). Moreover, professional literacy educators are thought to be those who have (at least) the following forms of knowledge:

- "declarative" (knowing what to teach)
- "procedural" (knowing how to teach)
- "situational" (where educators "use their understanding of large conceptual purposes for literacy to rethink ideas and practices, to transform knowledge to fit situations, and to change what they are doing when, in their judgment, there is a need to do so") (Duffy, Webb, & Davis, 2009, p. 192)

Situational knowledge, with its emphasis on transformation, is suggestive of critical reflection, which educators can use to monitor and improve their teaching. Critical reflection is a way of seeing how a teaching and learning circumstance is constructed, then evaluating whether it promotes equity and social justice. In considering how an educator might "do" critical reflection, we draw on a related concept: critical literacy. Critical literacy has been defined in many ways by literacy educators and theorists.

Lewison, Flint, and Van Sluys (2002) reviewed definitions of critical literacy that have been forwarded over the past 30 years and synthesized them into four actions. We have adapted them to provide an example of how an educator could be critically reflective:

One: Disrupting the commonplace: Educators look at a situation and try to determine what is taken for granted within it. For instance, educators might look at particular curriculum documents and notice that they do not promote multilingual literacies. The documents might not say that they do not promote multilingual literacies, but then they might not also explicitly promote the use of more than one language in the classroom. As such, the documents take for granted that English is the only language that should be used or that counts.

Two: Interrogating multiple viewpoints: Educators consider the ways in which a teaching and learning situation might be approached; for instance, in contrast to a monolingual literacy approach, some other curricula do make explicit mention of multilingualism. The *Common Curriculum Framework for English Language Arts in Western Canada* (Western Canadian Protocol for Collaboration in Basic Education, 1998), for example, talks about the importance of using international literature, as it shows respect for diverse languages. The Quebec curriculum also makes an overt statement on the topic:

> Knowing several languages allows us to both enrich our knowledge of our mother tongue and to gain a better perspective on our cultural heritage. Moreover, learning a second or third language is one of the most important tools for advancing personal development in a pluralistic society that is open to other cultural realities. (Gouvernement du Québec Ministère de l'Éducation, 2001, p. 70)

Looking at multiple approaches to a teaching and learning situation can provide educators with new perspectives and help them identify what is taken for granted.

Three: Focusing on socio-political issues: Educators can consider the larger context that is informing the teaching and learning situation they are considering. Again in relation to language and curricula, consider how English is the language of the cultural elite and of commerce. As such, it often has more power than other languages, something that has implications for questions about the relationship between literacy and people's participation in the world as well as their identities.

Four: Taking action and promoting social justice: When educators can identify how power is manifest in teaching and learning situations, they can act in ways that seek to redistribute some of this power. They can, for example, create opportunities for multilingual literacies by encouraging learners to use their home languages in class (through, for example, librarian Linda Ludke's dual language books). Such a strategy can help support CLD learners' English language acquisition and can introduce diverse languages to all learners.

As educators, we might recognize the importance of dominant definitions of literacy and help learners to meet them, but we must do so in a way that acknowledges learners' **funds of knowledge**, that is, the various "resources" they bring with them to school (Gonzalez et al., 1993, n.p.). These resources can be cultural, intellectual, physical, and the like. Recognizing funds of knowledge can help to ensure that instead of seeing learners in deficit terms, or in terms of what they do not know or are not, we see all learners as "at-promise" (Swadener & Lubeck, 1995), as capable people with knowledge to share and develop. Learners, in turn, can be encouraged to be critically reflective on their own literacies through critical literacy.

Critical Literacy

Critical literacy is a key component of multiliteracies and can, for instance, help learners to interrogate all texts, whether in the form of books or digital sources, so that their understandings reflect the social, political, and power relations embedded in those texts and their readings of them. Only from this perspective are learners able to gain control over printed texts, media, and other technologies, and make use of their understandings of texts for personal and social transformation. The purpose of critical literacy, then, is to empower educators and learners to actively participate in a democracy and move literacy beyond text to social action (Cadiero-Kaplan, 2002).

Critical literacy approaches textual meaning as a process of *construction*. One constructs meaning, "imbuing a text with meaning rather than extracting meaning from it" (Cervetti, Pardales, & Damico, 2001, p. 5). Textual meaning is understood in the context of social, historic, and power relations. Literacy practices entail coming to know *the world* as well as *the word*, and can be a means to social change. The ultimate goal of social action is the creation of a more equitable and just society for all people regardless of race, culture, class, gender, sexual orientation, family structure, and the like.

Critical literacy has been defined in several different ways by literacy educators and theorists. The framework with the four actions established by Lewison et al. (2002), which we have just shared, is one of the most helpful we have seen for educators. When this framework is applied specifically to literacy, it asks readers to consider the four actions in relation to the texts they are working with. Although these actions are not sequential, Lewison et al. found that educators generally focus on the first two or three actions in their teaching than on the last one. To be critical, a consideration of action toward equity and social justice is a must. Note, however, that action can mean a change in attitude or the development of a new understanding.

Another helpful model for thinking about critical literacy and its place in language and literacy education is Luke and Freebody's (1997) Four Resources Model. Luke and Freebody put forward that readers (from which we might extrapolate similar roles for viewing and other receptive dimensions) can take up four roles: code breaker, text participant, text user, and text analyst. They maintained that successful reading means being able to accomplish all four of these roles simultaneously.

- Being a *code breaker* involves understanding the sound–symbol relationship and the alphabetic principle.

- Being a *text participant* means developing the resources to engage the meaning systems of **discourse**, that is, the processes of comprehension, drawing inferences, connecting textual elements and background knowledge, and so on.

- Being a *text user* means knowing how to use a variety of texts in real social contexts throughout daily life. In other words, it means knowing how to read and access different forms of text in given social contexts (e.g., newspapers, poetry, website content, and blogs).

- Being a *text analyst* means reading critically or having "conscious awareness of the language and idea systems that are brought into play when a text is used" (p. 13). A text analyst is able to recognize the ideological perspective of a text and to stand outside that perspective and critique it.

Throughout *Constructing Meaning* we outline some of the pedagogies that may help learners to practise the literacies in critical ways. Literacy practices and pedagogies, critical or otherwise, also connect to learners' identities—the topic of the next section.

Literacy and Identity

All of what we have discussed thus far has been leading to the connection between literacy and identity. Basing one's teaching on learners' funds of knowledge, which include their knowledge and skill in different modes, media, and languages; seeing learners as at-promise; and asking them to critically read texts can all offer learners a wide array of "identity options" where they are not limited by narrow expectations or visions of themselves. This can help students to learn and grow *and* help educators. As Cummins and his colleagues (2005) stated, "When we talk about the *whole child*, let us not forget the *whole teacher*. The process of identity negotiation is reciprocal. As teachers open up identity options for students, they also define their own identities" (p. 42). Literacy is thus connected to learners' and educators' senses of who they are in the world.

An important part of learners' attitudes and expectations in regard to becoming literate involves the purposes they see in literacy and the pleasures they derive from it. Children can experience pleasure from meaning making from an early age. Pleasure in meaning making means interest, passion, engagement, satisfaction, and caring, and those elements are also pivotal in learning and teaching the dimensions of language and literacy in schools (Murphy, 2010). Meaning making is one of the delights of childhood (and also of adulthood), and learners' engagements with literacies must, above all things, bring them satisfaction and pleasure.

No matter what approach is taken toward the teaching of literacy, *what is being communicated* is central, and meaning making takes precedence. Enjoyment and achievement go together, and educators need to experience pleasure in literacy if learners are to enjoy it too. Children (and their educators) need to see themselves as capable literate individuals—what Frank Smith (1988) referred to as being members of the *literacy club*. Educators need to ask themselves if they are creating opportunities for pleasure in their classrooms and if they are supporting learners to become and stay engaged with literacy of all types.

In further thinking about engagement with literacy and what it means to an individual to be literate, consider how Marco's experiences with literacy had an impact on his confidence and sense of self. Before his strengths and knowledge were recognized, he felt that he did not have much to offer. Once Marco felt his knowledge was valued, he became engaged in language and literacy and began to work hard at it. How others evaluate our language and literacy achievements, and also the degree to which we can use modes to express ourselves and construct meaning, affects our sense of identity and our engagement with the world.

To show the potential of language and literacy, here's a story from Rachel's teaching practice.

Rachel was working as a special education resource teacher in a school with a high population of CLD students. When she started to work at the school she met Arta, an 11-year-old girl who had been in Canada for about two years. Arta was from overseas, where she had fled war with her family. She had recently been diagnosed with a hearing impairment.

When Rachel met Arta, the girl was shy, said little, and clung to her cousin, who was in a neighbouring classroom. Arta preferred to spend her time in the shelter of the ESL resource room, but most of her day had to be spent in the regular classroom because of the structure of ESL programs in the school district. Arta needed opportunities to communicate in a safe way. This realization presented the team with a teaching puzzle: *How could Arta use expressive language when she had little English and was in an English dominant environment?*

Rather than focus on what Arta could not do, the team reframed the teaching puzzle to focus on her funds of knowledge: *How could the educators structure the environment so that Arta could use the communication skills she already had to further build her language and literacy skills?*

The team set up opportunities for Arta and her bilingual cousin to conduct short interviews with members of the school community about current events in the building. These interviews got written up and became part of a community bulletin board in the front hallway of the school. Initially, Arta's cousin did most of the speaking and writing. Arta's job? Digital photographer. Arta smiled and walked proudly through the halls with the camera around her neck. Through image, Arta was able to engage with the people around her and express her view of the world. As Arta began to increasingly connect with the people around her and take more risks, the school team paired her up with other peers and Arta took over more responsibility for the writing.

Family members of CLD learners should not usually be called upon to act as translators for educators. In this situation, however, Arta's cousin was not acting as a translator for educators but rather, engaging in learning opportunities that were appropriate and meaningful to her. The project set up a situation between Arta and her cousin where each was a contributing and important part of the whole. In this way there was a symmetrical relationship between them.

In assessing Arta's progress, the team used research into second language acquisition to gauge their expectations. For example, Cummins (1979) taught that **basic interpersonal communication skills (BICS)** (context-specific social language, such as what happens in the lunchroom or the playground) tend to develop more quickly than **cognitive academic language proficiency (CALP)** (academic language that students need to understand content lessons). The first can develop in two years, while the second may need five to seven years to be acquired in the "typical" case of an "immigrant" child "learning a second language" (Cummins, 2000, p. 61). The team saw that by the end of the year (and thanks to a new hearing aid), Arta was using all forms of expressive language (which included her photography as part of her representing) and had made significant gains in her English BICS. Given this progress, the team understood that with continued work and patience, Arta could be expected to improve in all areas of her communication. Thus, with her family all around her, Arta was honoured with a special award at the June assembly to recognize her growth.

What do Arta's and Marco's stories have in common and what can they teach?

First, they provide a lesson related to identity and literacy: they suggest how, when one's funds of knowledge are recognized, a sense of being a proficient language and literacy user and producer can help an individual feel like and be a member of a community. In Arta's story, she began to act like part of the school when the school welcomed and supported her communication. In Marco's case, he expressing beginning to feel like and be a professional educator.

Second, the stories suggest something about the nature of literacy: that literacy *is* as literacy *does*. The goal of literacy is not just to be good at literacy skills (or to score highly on some sort of evaluation); it is to fulfill some authentic purpose. Marco's and Arta's literacy goals were multiple and connected to what they wanted to accomplish: Arta, to communicate with peers and to express her observations; Marco, to understand the range of ways that people communicate and to share this understanding with his students.

Last, the stories begin to illustrate the interrelated decisions required in communication (Kress & Jewitt, 2003) and how educators can support learners in them, for instance:

1. Communicators decide what they want to communicate—this is the content of the message. In Arta's case, she attempted to communicate current events happening in the school.

2. Communicators decide on an "apt signifier" or the relationship between the "thing meant" and the "thing meaning it" (p. 11). We provided Arta with opportunities to

develop facility with new modes and media (e.g., digital photography) so that she could have a wider range of options for communicating.

3. Proficient communicators take into account the situation in which they are communicating to ensure they have selected the best mode and media for their purposes. Arta was supported, for example, to learn how to interact with her peers, thus giving her a better understanding of the context in which she was expressing herself.

FACTORS THAT MEDIATE TEACHERS' LANGUAGE AND LITERACY PLANNING
What to Teach?

This section discusses some of the considerations educators may negotiate when planning their language and literacy program.

If there is not one static definition of literacy, educators might ask, "What do I teach?" This is a fundamental curricular question. Common wisdom says that curriculum is a document that tells educators what to teach. As one teacher candidate, feeling overwhelmed by her provincial curriculum document, said, "What I teach is not up to me!" Yet educator Regie Routman (2000) counselled that curriculum is a "dialogue," not a "document" (p. xxxviii). When educators think of curriculum as a document, they are inclined to start their planning there. When educators think of curriculum as a dialogue, they are inclined to start their planning from the learners, thus asking, Who are the learners in front of us? What funds of knowledge do they bring with them to school? How do the responses to these questions compare to what the document says, what the field currently knows about language and literacy education, and my own values and beliefs?

The next section addresses these questions. It begins with a look at curriculum documents and extends from there.

What Do the Documents Say? Language and Literacy Learning in Canadian Classrooms

While being responsive to learners is essential, the context in which educators are teaching should also be a participant in the curriculum dialogue. We thus explore some of the major trends in language and literacy curricula across the country.

Although education is a provincial and territorial responsibility, there is considerable similarity across Canada in how language learning is viewed. In all parts of the country, language is seen as central to thinking and learning, as reflected in the following statements taken from provincial and regional documents:

- "Language is the basis of all communication and the primary instrument of thought.… Thinking, learning, and language are interrelated. From Kindergarten to Grade 12, students use language to make sense of and to bring order to their world. They use language to examine new experiences and knowledge in relation to their prior knowledge, experiences, and beliefs" (*The Common Curriculum Framework for English Language Arts: Kindergarten to Grade 12*, Western Canadian Protocol for Collaboration in Basic Education, 1998, pp. 1–2).

• "Language Learning is central to every learning project, for language is a vital aspect of communication and represents a vehicle for learning used in all subjects.… Since it provides access to knowledge, it is an essential tool for creating, analysing, exercising critical judgment and describing or expressing ideas, perceptions and feelings" (*English Language Arts Program of Study*, Quebec Ministry of Education, 2001, p. 70).

• "Language is central to students' intellectual, social, and emotional growth, and must be seen as a key element of the curriculum. When students learn to use language in the elementary grades, they do more than master the basic skills … they come to appreciate language both as an important medium for communicating ideas and information and as a source of enjoyment" (*The Ontario Curriculum, Grades 1–8: Language*, Ontario Ministry of Education, 2006, p. 3).

• "Language is the primary instrument of thought and the most powerful tool students have for developing ideas and insights, for giving significance to their experiences, and for making sense of both their world and their possibilities in it" (*Atlantic Canada English Language Arts Curriculum: Grades 4–6*, New Brunswick Department of Education and Culture, 1998, p. 8).

Table 1.2 presents website addresses for provincial and regional language and literacy curricula and selected support documents available on the Internet.

There is also similarity across Canada in the dimensions of language and literacy included in curriculum documents. Although these dimensions are called *strands* in Ontario and Saskatchewan, *processes* in the Atlantic provinces, *communication forms* in British Columbia, and *language arts* in Alberta and Manitoba, all six dimensions are included in all the documents.

TABLE 1.2 **PROVINCIAL AND REGIONAL CURRICULUM DOCUMENTS**

Atlantic Canada
Foundation for the Atlantic Canada English Language Arts Curriculum, 1996 *Available: http://www.ednet.ns.ca/pdfdocs/curriculum/camet/foundations-ela.pdf*

Specific Provincial Documents	
Prince Edward Island	*English Language Arts Grades E–3, 1996* http://www.gov.pe.ca/photos/original/eecd_ela_e3curr.pdf *English Language Arts Grades 4–6, 1996* http://www.gov.pe.ca/eecd/index.php3?number=1026534&lang=E
Nova Scotia	*Teaching in Action, Grades Primary–3: A Teaching Resource, 2006* *Teaching in Action, Grades 4–6: A Teaching Resource, 2007* *English Language Arts, Grades 4–6, 1997* *Active Young Readers, Grades Primary–3, Assessment Resource: A Teaching Resource, 2012* *Active Young Readers, Grades 4–6, Assessment Resource: A Teaching Resource, 2003* *Active Readers, Grades 7–9, Assessment Resource: Young Adolescents, 2005* https://sapps.ednet.ns.ca/Cart/description.php?ll=188&U ID=20070130113936129.100.42.210

TABLE 1.2 **PROVINCIAL AND REGIONAL CURRICULUM DOCUMENTS *(CONTINUED)***

New Brunswick	*Atlantic Canada English Language Arts Curriculum: Elementary K–3*, 1998 *Atlantic Canada English Language Arts Curriculum: Elementary 4–6*, 1998 *Reading and Writing Achievement Standards*, 2008 http://www.gnb.ca/0000/anglophone-e.asp#cd
Newfoundland and Labrador	*English Language Arts Curriculum Guide Kindergarten*, 2014 *English Language Arts Curriculum Guide Primary*, 1999 *Each grade has its own language arts document listed separately at English Language Arts Curriculum Guide Grades 4–9*, 2010–2014 http://www.ed.gov.nl.ca/edu/k12/curriculum/guides/english/index.html
Quebec	*Québec Education Program: Preschool Education, Elementary Education*, 2001 http://www1.mels.gouv.qc.ca/sections/programmeFormation/primaire/index_en.asp
Ontario	*The Full-Day Early Learning–Kindergarten Program (Draft Version)*, 2010–2011 http://www.edu.gov.on.ca/eng/curriculum/elementary/kindergarten_english_june3.pdf *The Ontario Curriculum, Grades 1–8: Language*, 2006 http://www.edu.gov.on.ca/eng/curriculum/elementary/language.html Supporting Documents for Ontario Curricula *Early Reading Strategy: The Report of the Expert Panel on Early Reading in Ontario*, 2003 *Literacy for Learning: The Report of the Expert Panel on Literacy in Grades 4 to 6 in Ontario*, 2004 *Many Roots, Many Voices: Supporting English Language Learners in Every Classroom*, 2005 *Supporting English Language Learners: A Practical Guide for Ontario Educators Grades 1 to 8*, 2008 *Supporting English Language Learners with Limited Prior Schooling: A Practical Guide for Ontario Educators (Grades 3 to 12)*, 2008 http://www.edu.gov.on.ca/eng/curriculum/elementary/language.html *Supporting English Language Learners in Kindergarten: A Practical Guide for Ontario Educators*, 2007 http://www.edu.gov.on.ca/eng/document/kindergarten/index.html
Western Canada	
The Common Curriculum Framework for English Language Arts, Kindergarten to Grade 12, 1998 http://www.wncp.ca/english/subjectarea/english-language-arts/ccf.aspx	
Specific Provincial Documents	
British Columbia	*English Language Arts Kindergarten to Grade 7: Integrated Resource Package*, 2006 http://www.bced.gov.bc.ca/irp/pdfs/english_language_arts/2006ela_k7.pdf
Alberta	*English Language Arts K–9*, 2000 *Illustrative Examples for English Language Arts, K–9*, 2000 http://education.alberta.ca/teachers/program/english/programs.aspx Resource Documents for Alberta Curricula *Supporting the Literacy Learner: Promising Literacy Strategies in Alberta*, 2008 http://education.alberta.ca/media/6450566/supporting_the_literacy_learner_promising_practices_from_aisi_2008.pdf *Supporting the Literacy Learner II: Promising Literacy Strategies in Alberta*, 2010 http://education.alberta.ca/media/6450570/supporting_the_literacy_learner_promising_practices_from_aisi_2010.pdf

(continued)

TABLE 1.2 **PROVINCIAL AND REGIONAL CURRICULUM DOCUMENTS** *(CONTINUED)*

Manitoba	*Manitoba Curriculum Framework of Outcomes and Standards* *A Foundation for Implementation* http://www.edu.gov.mb.ca/k12/cur/ela/curdoc.html Supporting Documents for Manitoba Curricula *Reading and Writing in Action*, 2006 http://www.edu.gov.mb.ca/k12/docs/support/read_write/ *Listening and Speaking: First Steps into Literacy. A Support Document for* *Kindergarten Teachers and Speech-Language Pathologists*, 2008 http://www.edu.gov.mb.ca/k12/cur/ela/list_speak/index.html
Saskatchewan	Saskatchewan Curriculum *English Language Arts: Grades K–9, 2008–2010* *Each grade has its own language arts document listed separately on the* *Saskatchewan Curriculum website with grade-specific resources and support* *materials.* http://curriculum.gov.sk.ca/index.jsp *Early Literacy: A Resource for Teachers*, 2000 https://www.edonline.sk.ca/bbcswebdav/library/Curriculum%20Website/ English%20Language%20Arts/Resources/Core/Early%20Literacy%20A%20 Strategic%20Resource%20for%20Teachers%202002.pdf
Northwest Territories and Nunavut	*Northwest Territories English Language Arts Curriculum K–6, 2011* http://www.ece.gov.nt.ca/early-childhood-and-school-services/school-services/ curriculum-k-12/english-language-arts/ela-k-6 *Northwest Territories English Language Arts Curriculum K-6 Support* *Documents, 2011* http://www.ece.gov.nt.ca/early-childhood-and-school-services/school-services/ curriculum-k-12/english-language-arts/ela-k-6-0

Integrating the Six Dimensions

All provincial curriculum documents indicate that the six dimensions of language and literacy are interrelated and interdependent, and stress the importance of teaching them in an integrated manner. There are at least three different levels of integration in kindergarten to grade 8 classrooms.

One level of integration involves the integration of the dimensions themselves. It capitalizes on reading–writing connections, speaking–writing connections, viewing–representing connections, and so on. For example, knowledge about how stories are organized helps learners to construct meaning when both reading and writing. Knowledge about the relationship between letters and sounds helps learners to both spell and identify words. Teaching language and literacy in an integrated way helps learners transfer strategies and knowledge developed in one context to another.

A second level of integration involves language across the curriculum, a movement founded in the United Kingdom in the 1960s by James Britton and his colleagues at the London Institute for Education. There are no aspects of the school curriculum where language does not play a major part. Music, health, mathematics, science, social studies, art, and physical education all have subject-specific language—a vocabulary and a way of speaking about that subject that must be learned.

The third level of integration goes beyond the curriculum, when learners bring their funds of knowledge into the classroom and take what they learn in the classroom to their home and community contexts. Many of the examples of practice found throughout *Constructing Meaning* demonstrate how this might look.

Who Are the Learners in Front of Us?

This section describes some of the social and cultural considerations that are salient in contemporary Canadian classrooms. Specifically, we address cultural and linguistic diversity, socio-economic status, and gender.

If, within *Constructing Meaning*, we see literacy as constructing meaning, and if we understand that to teach well we must begin with learners' funds of knowledge, then who the learners are before us is of critical concern. Within our curricular dialogue, we must consider how learners are socially situated in terms of race, socio-economic status, gender, language, and the like. Within this consideration, if we are to reject a deficit view of learners, we must remember to use the discourse of learners-at-promise rather than learners-at-risk. Thus, rather than trying to change learners to fit the school, we aim to create the best possible climate and curriculum to foster positive growth and wellness.

Betsy Reilly, an elementary school teacher and Teacher Hall of Fame inductee, knows this, and advice from her is presented in the Inside Classrooms box that follows. After this, we offer an overview of some major considerations for Canadian educators.

INSIDE CLASSROOMS

BETSY REILLY

What have you found to be the greatest joy of teaching language and literacy?

Story has been the most compelling part of my teaching. In the months leading up to my retirement, I found myself doing a kind of countdown and assessment of the things I would be doing for the last time. There was a kind of emotional barometer that intuitively registered the parts of teaching that mattered the most to me. While it is a cliché, it is first of all the children and their families. Teaching is a deeply intimate profession in which lives overlap and touch each other and where we carry the important narratives of children and their families. I loved being hip-deep in their stories and lives, and having them hip-deep in my daily school story and life.

As well, I loved sharing **children's literature** with my students, reading aloud a classic book, recommending a book to a child that was rich in story and language, and getting them

(continued)

excited about literature. While I continue to read a great deal of children's literature, I find it is far more powerful when literature is shared with children. I am reminded of the invitation in Kate DiCamillo's (2003) *The Tale of Despereaux*—

The world is dark, and light is precious.

Come closer, dear reader.

You must trust me.

I am telling you a story. (p. 7)

Perhaps teaching is more about composing a "living story" than anything else, establishing the trust and helping the learners be an active part of the story of their own learning.

What have you found to be the greatest challenge?

As testing has put more focus on curriculum rather than on the learner, I worry about the loss bit by bit, piece by piece, of our humanity as teachers and learners. The pressures to go faster, pack more curriculum in, move those learners along can cause the teacher to spin and the learner to spin with her. We lose their stories and our own, the ones about what matters most.

What does it mean to you to be a reflective practitioner?

Eve Merriman (1999) says it best in a poem about bustling adults: "It takes a lot of slow to grow" (p. 10). To reflect means stepping back and slowing down enough to really see the learners and what is important in learning. As teachers, we are so often doers that we don't slow down long enough to see critically what we are doing and to question both the purpose and the process of learning.

Cultural and Linguistic Diversity

It is not just communication modes that have changed in recent decades—the makeup of classrooms in Canada has changed too. Globalization has created unprecedented mobility, and Canada is at the forefront of these enormous shifts in demographics. In 2012 alone, Canada accepted an additional 257 887 permanent residents into the country (Statistics Canada, 2013b). Canada now has some of the most culturally and linguistically diverse cities in the world. Forty-six percent of the population in the Greater Toronto Area, for instance, is foreign-born residents (Statistics Canada, 2013b), and 40 percent of Vancouver's population is foreign-born (Statistics Canada, 2013b). This influx has added to Canada's already multilingual and multicultural heritage. For instance, 1.4 million people in Canada identify themselves as Aboriginal (Statistics Canada, 2013a). Consequently, 42 percent of Canadians claim their first language is a language other than English (e.g., Cree, Mandarin, Arabic, or French) (Statistics Canada, 2012) and 76.2 percent of foreign-born Canadians claim their first language is a language other than English (Statistics Canada, 2013b). What are these languages? Statistics Canada (2013b) explained,

Among the immigrants whose mother tongue was other than English or French, Chinese languages were most common mother tongues.… In total, Chinese languages were reported by 13.0% of the foreign-born population with single mother tongue. The Chinese languages were followed by Tagalog, a language of the Philippines, reported by almost 320,100 people; Spanish, reported by 306,700; and Punjabi, by 305,400. Completing the top 10 were Arabic, Italian, German, Portuguese, Persian (Farsi) and Polish. (pp. 18–19)

Many literacy researchers have noted that there can be a mismatch between the funds of knowledge (including literacy knowledge) and expectations of CLD learners' homes and school (e.g., Delpit, 2006). Diversity necessitates that educators be culturally responsive; the literacy education framework that we describe later in this chapter, and that structures the entire book, takes responsive teaching as one of its key foundations.

Socio-Economic Status

Regarding a potential relationship between socio-economic status and literacy achievement in school, researchers have identified low socio-economic status as a predictor of risk for literacy failure (Snow, Burns, & Griffin, 1998), and others have identified an achievement gap between learners who live in poverty and their more economically privileged peers (Pogrow, 2006). Learners who are living in poverty do not have the same access to capital as those with higher economic status. They may not have experience with the tools that form the basis of literacy learning at school, such as books, paints, and museum visits. Learners might also be hungry or suffer from poor nutrition. All of these differences in terms of life experience can affect their learning and literacy achievement, and demand responsive teaching that is sensitive to their needs.

Child poverty is too prevalent in Canada. In 2006, 17 percent of children were found to be living in poverty, and four in ten Aboriginal children lives in poverty (Macdonald & Wilson, 2013). Economic and educational policy analyst Richard Rothstein (2004) claimed that educators alone cannot even out the playing field for poor children at school. He argued that educators can play only one part in a solution that must include broad economic and social changes to improve children's living conditions.

So, what *can* educators do?

While Rothstein is accurate in arguing that child poverty must be attacked head-on and that it is not only an educational problem, we as educators do have responsibilities.

First, we can understand that we can and do make a difference in learners' lives. It has been found, for instance, that high-quality educators who have strong teaching skills and high expectations for all their students have positively affected the academic achievement of children who live in poverty (Holland, 2007).

Second, we can ensure that our teaching is culturally sensitive. In her research into literacy and white children who are poor and working-class, for instance, Deborah Hicks (2002) found that there can be a mismatch between children's out-of-school literacies and the middle-class literacies that are promoted in school. Hicks asserted that this situation is seldom recognized for what it is. She said that in North America, "white poor and working-class children are viewed negatively but without cultural sensitivity" (p. 4). The learners in Hicks's studies, for example, were viewed as deficient by their teachers. Hicks argued that educators should be on the lookout for the various forms of literacy knowledge that their students bring with them to school so they may build bridges between these and school literacy.

Complementing Hicks's findings are those of Canadian researcher Marianne McTavish (2007). While it may be true that there can be a mismatch between learners' home and school literacies, McTavish argued that socio-economic status "does not determine a child's literacy background and that great variation exists" (p. 476). She cautioned that educators should not jump to conclusions such as "working-class families don't 'do literacy' and the children in these families experience few [print] literacy events within the home" (p. 476). Instead, she counselled educators to "look carefully at what individual families do, either intentionally or unintentionally, to promote literacy in their children" (p. 483). Thus, while being sensitive to the challenges that many learners face, educators should also be alert to learners' differences and funds of knowledge.

Doing these things requires that educators confront their own biases, as research has demonstrated that teacher bias can affect their assessment. Researchers at the Canadian Research Institute for Social Policy, for instance, found that a significant number of teachers assessed their students' literacy level on the basis of their perceptions of how well educated the students' mothers were (Beswick, Willms, & Sloat, 2005).

Gender

Great attention has been paid to the ways gender can affect learners' literacy achievement. Evidence has shown for many years that girls outperform boys in assessments of reading leading up to secondary school. The most recent results of the Progress in International Reading Literacy Study (PIRLS) 2011 in 49 countries revealed that girls in grade 4 had significantly higher reading achievement than boys in all countries except Colombia, Italy, France, Spain, and Israel (Mullis, Martin, Foy, & Drucker, 2012). The latest reading assessment results of the Pan-Canadian Assessment Program of 13-year-olds also suggested a "persistent literacy gap" between boys and girls (Canadian Council on Learning, 2009, p. 1).

Not all research paints such an asymmetrical picture, although differences do exist between the achievement of girls and boys on standardized assessments. Other research, for example, has found evidence of boys' improved achievement and narrowed gender gaps. The most updated results of National Assessment of Educational Progress (NAEP)—that is, the Nation's Report Card—demonstrated that from 1992 to 2013, the gender gap in grade 8 reading in the United States narrowed (National Center for Education Statistics, n.d.). Large-scale writing examinations in Canada, the United Kingdom, and the United States, however, showed that girls scored consistently higher than boys on writing (Peterson, 2001; Salahu-Din, Persky, & Miller, 2008). These results have led to controversy about the relationship between gender and literacy: Why do girls seem to be doing better than boys in school, and what needs to be done?

To explain girls' apparent higher achievement, some researchers have focused on school practices that may favour girls. For instance, Kathy Sanford (2005/2006) indicated that educators tend to expect girls to be better readers than boys when they arrive at school. As literacy educator Brian Cambourne (1988) claimed that high expectations are a condition for literacy learning, this may help girls to perform better than boys. These expectations might also affect the way that educators perceive boys' and girls' literacy achievement. Others have identified the feminization of elementary school teaching as the reason for the achievement gap. They argue that since most teachers of kindergarten to grade 8 classes are female, boys have few male role models (Spence, 2006). Male teachers have been seen as better equipped to relate to boys, address their learning needs, and enhance their literacy achievement (e.g., Rowan, Knobel, Bigum, & Lankshear, 2002). Still others suggest that there is incongruity between supposed masculine behaviour, which has been described as "active, aggressive and independent" (Gambell & Hunter, 2000, p. 696), and classrooms that have traditionally valued passive, recipient learners (Mead, 2006). Finally, some researchers have pointed to the types of books that tend to be highly accessible and valued in K to 8 schooling (e.g., narrative-type texts, including storybooks and novels) (Doiron, 2003b); they suggest that these resources are out of sync with the kinds of texts that boys typically select (e.g., comic books and baseball cards) (Sullivan, 2004).

In trying to improve boys' literacy scores, many measures have been suggested. The education minister in the United Kingdom urged schools to spend more time having children read nonfiction texts rather than fiction (Canadian Council on Learning, 2009). Others have recommended that teachers use books with strong masculine themes so that boys' experiences are represented, and they become engaged with reading (Young & Brozo, 2001). In addition to text selection, recommendations pertaining to boys and literacy break down into general areas identified by the Ontario Ministry of Education (2004):

- Provide frequent opportunities for reading and writing.
- Address boys' learning styles.
- Use the arts in literacy.
- Focus on social interaction to engage boys.
- Use male role models.
- Use critical literacy.
- Make literacy relevant to boys' lives.
- Employ technology.
- Make use of appropriate assessment tools.
- Change the role that teachers take on.
- Partner with families.
- Take a school-wide focus to literacy.

The issue of gender and literacy, however, is not so easy to define or address. In reference to the cry to simply offer boys texts that they are assumed to like—for example, information texts—Moss (2000) found that boys' apparent preferences for nonfiction were more related to their attempts to escape judgments by their peers than a desire to read that type of material. Nonfiction texts were not as obviously graded as fiction. "Steering round these texts via the pictures, and ignoring the verbal text, weaker readers could nevertheless stake out territory as 'experts,' on a level with peers who read more competently" (p. 103). As for the suggestion to use more "masculine" texts, Josephine Peyton Young (Young & Brozo, 2001) has argued, as many others do, that this approach serves only to reinforce gender stereotypes and biases. Furthermore, a Canadian research study found that both girls *and* boys select fiction when they are given the chance; where there is a gender gap is in the low number of information texts that *girls* select (Doiron, 2003a).

As for the question of whether there are girl books and boy books, Doiron (2003a) concluded, "I guess I would have to say, yes, there are 'boy books' and 'girl books.' There are books targeted especially for stereotypical views of boys and girls…. As educators, we are definitely working with some stereotypical views ourselves" (p. 16).

So, is there really a "boy problem," and if yes, what is it? Some educators suggest that the problem is one of definition and values, that is, it is a problem of how schools and large-scale assessments define literacy and what they value as literacy. In reporting on a Canadian study of boys and literacy, Sanford and Blair (2004) suggested that "the reading gender gap may simply be a sign that girls are better at writing tests, and not necessarily one that boys don't read well" (p. A.18). Others have also identified a gender bias in reading tests (e.g., Lietz, 2006) such that Blair and Sanford's (2003) caution to educators not to see boys from a deficit perspective seems warranted. They find that quantitative data about boys' reading, such as large-scale test scores, can be misleading. To flesh out this information and to find out what is going on in boys' literate lives, they conducted extensive qualitative studies of boys' literacy practices. Through closely observing boys in and out of school, Blair and Sanford (2004) discovered that "boys can read, but are selective in what they read" (p. 459). Moreover, boys "are finding many literacy activities … that engage them and sustain long-term interest" (Sanford & Madill, 2006, p. 287). These activities generally, however, fall within the viewing and representing dimensions of language and literacy, dimensions that are often not sufficiently recognized in schools or included on tests. Blair and Sanford's (2004) data suggest that boys are taking the reading strategies they learn in school and "morphing" them "to make sense of new literacies that appeal to them" (p. 459).

What are educators to make of this? First, they can be careful not to see boys or girls in stereotypical ways or as being all the same. Even the Ontario Ministry of Education (2004), in its own guide to boys and literacy, admitted

> the differences among boys and among girls are greater than the differences between boys and girls. Consequently, educators must be careful not to focus on the gender differences between students, but rather to recognize that the effectiveness of certain approaches to literacy instruction may be tied to gender. With this understanding, teachers will be better able to provide appropriate and equitable opportunities for both boys and girls. (p. 7)

Educators can be sensitive to the needs of all learners and be aware of Sanford's (2005/2006) concern that in the race to improve boys' literacy scores, educators might be missing something crucial. She said, "And while the literacy of boys is of great concern to me as an educator, I am struck by the ease and speed with which girls are again made invisible in concerns of education, ignored in the general call for improved literacy skills" (p. 302). Thus, rather than gearing curriculum and assessment to approaches thought to favour boys, several researchers (e.g., Barrs, 2000; Moss, 2000; Young in Young & Brozo, 2002) recommend that educators create classrooms that nurture *all* students as literacy learners. In her research, Moss (2000) found that the most effective practice to increase boys' literacy involved building and sustaining a reading culture that encompassed the full range of interests in the class and also substantially expanded them. Brozo (2010) indicated that educators should take advantage of boys' multimodal literacy texts and practices outside of school to engage them in school literacy. Finally, in all their work, Sanford and Blair (n.d.) have called for educators to adopt an expanded, multimodal view of literacy that can benefit all learners by recognizing the full range of their literacy practices, interests, and funds of knowledge.

The classroom diversity created by learners' different languages, cultures, socio-economic statuses, and genders all help to make teaching and learning potentially fuller and richer experiences. They can also, however, be challenging. The first step in dealing with diversity is becoming aware both of the knowledge and abilities learners bring with them to school and of our own biases and preconceptions about the learning abilities of different learners. Only with this awareness can educators provide a learning environment that is equitable.

EDUCATORS' HISTORIES AS STUDENTS AND BELIEFS

Reflection in teaching often comes first by educators becoming aware of their beliefs, which are largely artifacts of their histories as students. To develop language and literacy programs that are responsive to learners, we must examine the beliefs that we take with us into the classroom. This task is not easy, as these beliefs are usually not conscious and are constructed from our prior experiences as students. Marco's case is an indication of this, and his story is connected to a larger one, which research into beginning teaching has uncovered.

Beginning teachers are influenced by their experiences as students. For example, in a study of learning to teach, Deborah Britzman (2003) found that especially in times of stress, beginning teachers tended to fall back on the practices they had experienced as students. Another study into how beginning teachers chose to teach writing discovered that teachers tended to teach writing in ways that corresponded with the identity they had of themselves as writers (Frager, 1994). This identity was forged through beginning teachers' experiences with writing when they were students in school.

Dixie Massey (2002) studied teacher candidates in language arts pre-service courses and found that new knowledge was hardest for candidates to assimilate in areas where they believed they already had knowledge. Learning, instead, tended to happen most easily in areas where candidates believed they had the least knowledge. As candidates could read and write, they felt they had little to learn in language arts methods courses.

Our last example of research comes from Lara Handsfield (2006), who studied how **monolingualism** was promoted in an elementary classroom because of the teacher's ingrained beliefs (many of which were unconscious). These beliefs were, in part, the product of the teacher's own history of schooling as a CLD student herself.

In your own practice, you will not want to simply fall back on the way you were taught. While some of these strategies might have worked in an era in which classrooms were largely homogeneous and notions of literacy were fairly simplistic, you will need to consider how your teaching addresses the current demographics and definitions of literacy that we explore in this chapter. Happily, the critical reflection that we discuss in this chapter can help each of us to make conscious, equitable choices within our classrooms. This attention to reflection with its cycle of questioning is at the heart of our approach to teaching language and literacy, which we next explore.

INTRODUCTION TO TEACHING LANGUAGE AND LITERACY

With the context of language and literacy teaching and learning now introduced, we turn to an overview of pedagogies that can support a diversity of learners in this new communication landscape. Then, in Chapter 2, we focus on some of the more nuts-and-bolts aspects of language and literacy pedagogy through the major considerations that educators must make when planning and organizing for language and literacy learning.

MULTILITERACIES PEDAGOGIES

We have called the collection of suggestions for teaching that we advocate in *Constructing Meaning* "multiliteracies pedagogies." In the NLG's (2000) classic work on the topic, their *pedagogy of multiliteracies* contained four components, which were later expanded upon by Cope and Kalantzis (2009). We offer an interpretation of these components in Box 1.3, where we follow each component with Cope and Kalantzis's corresponding "knowledge process." The NLG (2000) explained that "each [component] may occur simultaneously, while at different times one of the other will predominate, and all of them are repeatedly revisited at different times" (p. 32).

The multiliteracies pedagogies we advocate draw on these components and highlight fundamentals of the theory we described earlier in the chapter. We have, however, pluralized *pedagogy* to suggest that many pedagogies can be in the service of the ideals of multiliteracies, can be informed by other theories, and are always in development.

The pedagogies are designed to help enact the theories and understandings about literacy we describe earlier in the chapter. They are also intended to help support educators in becoming critically reflective professionals who can create language and literacy learning opportunities that may

BOX 1.3

AN INTERPRETATION OF THE FOUR COMPONENTS OF THE NEW LONDON GROUP'S PEDAGOGY OF MULTILITERACIES

1. *Situated Practice (Experiencing)*

   ▷ Educators should help to immerse learners in literacy practices that are meaningful and authentic to them and that help learners to navigate "between school learning and the practical out-of-school experiences of learners" (Cope & Kalantzis, 2009, p. 185).

   ▷ Learning opportunities are heightened when learners feel safe and liked, part of a community, and consider that what they are learning is in their "interest" (NLG, 2000, p. 33).

   ▷ Learners should be encouraged to play multiple and different roles in their learning community based on their "backgrounds and experiences" (p. 33).

   ▷ The community must contain "experts" or "people who have mastered" the literacy practices the learners are expected to develop (p. 33).

   ▷ Educators must carefully consider learners' "affective and sociocultural needs and identities" (p. 33).

▷ Two kinds of experiences should characterize this component: drawing on what learners know, which includes creating opportunities for learners to dwell with "familiar forms of expression and ways of representing the world" (Cope & Kalantzis, 2009, p. 185), as well as exposing them to the new through, for instance, unfamiliar text forms.

▷ **Evaluation** should be used to guide learners, not to make harsh judgments.

2. *Overt Instruction (Conceptualizing)*

▷ Learners require a degree of explicit or "active interventions" to **scaffold** learning activities" (p. NLG, 2000, 33).

▷ Overt instruction is not to be confused with "direct transmission, drills, and rote memorisation" (p. 33).

▷ Overt instruction should build on learners' funds of knowledge and help to direct them to the most important thing for them to learn within an experience.

▷ During this time, learners work on a task that they could not otherwise accomplish alone.

▷ Learners should be given support to "come to conscious awareness" of and control over their learning.

▷ These supports are to help mentor learners into the practices developed by "expert communities of practice" (Cope & Kalantzis, 2009, p. 185) and can be in the form of conceptual tools such as theories or frameworks or the sharing of information regarding resources for constructing meaning.

3. *Critical Framing (Analyzing)*

▷ Being critical in this component involves two things: *functional analysis*, with learners being supported to apply analytical strategies like deduction, and *critical analysis*, which involves learners drawing inferences and/or conclusions. In both forms of analyses, educators help learners to contextualize the learning and practices from situated practice and overt instruction so that they can see the relations of power that exist within and among them.

4. *Transformed Practice (Applying)*

▷ Educators support learners to apply and test out their knowledge and skill in "real-world" types of situations. Learners are then encouraged to go beyond doing something in a "predictable" way by applying knowledge and skill in "innovative" and "creative" ways. This type of "intervention in the world" is an opportunity for learners to apply their funds of knowledge in new settings (Cope & Kalantzis, 2009, p. 186).

▷ Educators should help learners to demonstrate how to carry out their new literacy practices in ways that are in keeping with the learners' "own goals and values" (NLG, 2000, p. 33).

▷ Educators here must also assess their own pedagogies and work to design and practise them in ways that are critically reflective.

Source: New London Group, (2000). "A pedagogy of multiliteracies: Designing social futures." In B. Cope & M. Kalantzis, *Multiliteracies: Literacy Learning and the Design of Social Futures.* NY: Routledge, reproduced by permission of Taylor & Francis Books UK.

lead to the expansion of learners' literacy and identity options. The pedagogies are built on the idea that literacy is a social undertaking, and all learners should be viewed as at-promise rather than as at-risk. Literacy pedagogy must be responsive to the funds of knowledge of both learners *and* educators. We recognize that literacy teaching needs to take on different faces at different grade levels and with different learners; it also calls upon educators to be *flexible* and *responsive* in their pedagogies.

We believe that educators, the people who spend every day with learners, are in the best positions to develop critically reflective decisions about how to teach; therefore, prepackaged programs and how-to guides have limited use. At the same time we recognize that learning to teach well is a process that takes time, and educators can be challenged at all stages of their careers depending on the demands of the circumstances. This thought is reminiscent of Betsy Reilly's "slow to grow" advice, which is corroborated by Britzman (1998), who found that educators need to be patient with learning—their students' *and* their own. In particular, beginning educators often require extra support (Hibbert & Heydon, 2010). All the suggestions we make, along with the instructional components of the multiliteracies pedagogies we advocate (see Figure 1.1), are therefore meant to offer educators enough structure to be helpful, but also enough flexibility that they can be responsive to their learners and contexts. In the end, the aim is to support and nurture the development of flexible literacy repertoires in both students and educators.

In sum, our notion of multiliteracies pedagogies involves educators in

- designing and using pedagogies that help learners understand the big and more focused pictures of literacy, or what Purcell-Gates and Waterman (2000) referred to as whole-part-whole instruction

- designing and using pedagogies that follow a gradual release of responsibility model, where learners move from having a particular practice modelled to them to being able to practise the model independently

- ensuring that all dimensions of language and literacy receive context-appropriate emphasis within literacy programs (thus ensuring instruction in multiple modes and **media**)

- knowing and basing their teaching on the funds of knowledge of their students

- understanding that to teach well requires ongoing professional learning informed by a range of up-to-date research

- considering their context and discriminating among a variety of resources and teaching strategies, rather than relying on prepackaged programs or commercial products to manage their teaching

- consciously negotiating and considering the range of socio-cultural and political factors that affect their classroom actions and student achievement (e.g., curricula and school district policy) (Heydon & Hibbert, 2010)

Next, we discuss the specific literacy teaching aspects of our multiliteracies pedagogies. First, we detail Brian Cambourne's conditions for learning as they apply to literacy learning (see Figure 1.1). This model, we believe, provides a helpful and important orientation toward literacy pedagogy, and much of it aligns with the situated practice aspect of multiliteracies pedagogies. We then introduce further key components of the multiliteracies pedagogies framework that we expand upon throughout this book.

FIGURE 1.1

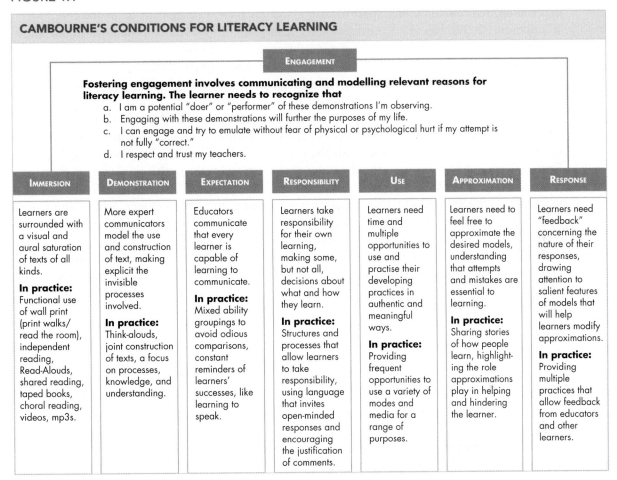

CAMBOURNE'S CONDITIONS FOR LITERACY LEARNING

ENGAGEMENT

Fostering engagement involves communicating and modelling relevant reasons for literacy learning. The learner needs to recognize that
a. I am a potential "doer" or "performer" of these demonstrations I'm observing.
b. Engaging with these demonstrations will further the purposes of my life.
c. I can engage and try to emulate without fear of physical or psychological hurt if my attempt is not fully "correct."
d. I respect and trust my teachers.

IMMERSION	DEMONSTRATION	EXPECTATION	RESPONSIBILITY	USE	APPROXIMATION	RESPONSE
Learners are surrounded with a visual and aural saturation of texts of all kinds. **In practice:** Functional use of wall print (print walks/ read the room), independent reading, Read-Alouds, shared reading, taped books, choral reading, videos, mp3s.	More expert communicators model the use and construction of text, making explicit the invisible processes involved. **In practice:** Think-alouds, joint construction of texts, a focus on processes, knowledge, and understanding.	Educators communicate that every learner is capable of learning to communicate. **In practice:** Mixed ability groupings to avoid odious comparisons, constant reminders of learners' successes, like learning to speak.	Learners take responsibility for their own learning, making some, but not all, decisions about what and how they learn. **In practice:** Structures and processes that allow learners to take responsibility, using language that invites open-minded responses and encouraging the justification of comments.	Learners need time and multiple opportunities to use and practise their developing practices in authentic and meaningful ways. **In practice:** Providing frequent opportunities to use a variety of modes and media for a range of purposes.	Learners need to feel free to approximate the desired models, understanding that attempts and mistakes are essential to learning. **In practice:** Sharing stories of how people learn, highlighting the role approximations play in helping and hindering the learner.	Learners need "feedback" concerning the nature of their responses, drawing attention to salient features of models that will help learners modify approximations. **In practice:** Providing multiple practices that allow feedback from educators and other learners.

Cambourne's Conditions for Learning: A Starting Point for Language and Literacy Teaching

Cambourne developed the conditions for learning through a study of young children as they learned to speak within their "natural" environments. After years of working with children and observing their learning in and out of classrooms, Cambourne continues to find these conditions to hold true (Cambourne, 2009). Since the advent of his model, many educators and researchers have found the conditions powerful guides for practice and for understanding what can facilitate literacy learning. For instance, one study of intermediate students' learning found that when the conditions were applied fluidly throughout an educator's literacy pedagogy, they helped learners to take ownership of their work and persevere when learning something difficult (Saccomano, 2006). Additionally, the conditions are understood to be useful within a variety of learning contexts, including reading in a second language (Kong & Pearson, 2003). Cambourne (2002) has studied the conditions cross-culturally and found them equally compelling.

In Cambourne's model there are seven main conditions: immersion, demonstration, expectation, responsibility, use, approximation, and response. Engagement is "at the core" (Cambourne, 2009). Figure 1.1 provides a brief description of the conditions, followed by an example of how the conditions can be put into practice in classrooms.

To explain how the conditions operate, witness this example of how a child might learn to speak. First, "Mina" is *immersed* in language. From the time she is born, she is spoken to and surrounded by the sounds of English. This immersion forms the basis of a *demonstration* of how English is spoken. In particular, her mother leans close to Mina when she is feeding her and says things like "Apple? Would Mina like an apple?" Mina's mother then follows up the verbal with the concrete by handing Mina a piece of apple. Everyone around Mina *expects* that she is going to learn to speak. In this way, there is the promise of speech. Mina is given *responsibility* for her speaking. She chooses when she verbalizes, to whom, and in which contexts. For instance, another day when Mina wants a snack, she might exclaim, "Apo!" In this way she *approximates* the demonstration. No one is alarmed that Mina does not pronounce "apple" in a standard way. It is expected that she will develop toward the demonstration. Mina's mother, in *response* to "apo," might say, "Yes, here's some apple!" In so doing, she provides feedback that can eventually help Mina pronounce the word in a standard way, and through her actions she tells Mina that her communication has worked. Gradually and then repeatedly, Mina *uses* her new word in similar and new contexts. And throughout this process, Mina has *engaged* with learning to speak. She has seen that speaking can get her what she needs and wants, that she can communicate without fear, and that she is in a relationship with her mother from whom she learns to speak.

Of course, not all the dimensions are learned in the way that speaking and listening are. Print literacy almost always requires far more explicit instruction than what is identified in the vignette above. What is important, however, is to think about how Cambourne's model might provide an overarching frame for classroom language and literacy programming. As a teacher, you can then fill in the form of instruction that you insert within the frame. For instance, an educator's demonstrations can be quite systematic and explicit (or overt), as in Read-Aloud. Conversely, a demonstration might entail an educator showing that she values reading by herself reading during Independent Reading time.

Throughout *Constructing Meaning* we point out ways that educators can address Cambourne's conditions. The conditions are not an add-on to our understanding of literacy pedagogy, but rather an integral part. Thus, when next we share the instructional components of our multiliteracies pedagogies, we highlight when there are explicit connections to the conditions.

INSTRUCTIONAL COMPONENTS OF MULTILITERACIES PEDAGOGIES

In our notion of multiliteracies pedagogies, we are aware that educators need to negotiate their responses to a number of fine-grained pedagogical questions such as these:

- Where should I begin my teaching? Should I start with the "parts" of language or "whole" pieces of language? For instance, when I'm teaching reading, do I focus on phonics first and then go on to reading a whole book for meaning?

- Upon which of the dimensions should I focus?
- There's so much research out there and it doesn't all say the same thing. Whom do I believe?
- How do I decide when and how to group students for instruction?
- There are many commercial programs available. Do I use them and how?
- How much teaching from the front of the class or explicit instruction should I do compared to centre time or implicit instruction?

Our multiliteracies pedagogies involve educators knowing and beginning with individual learners and considering the contexts in which they are teaching. To do this well, educators need to feel at ease selecting among a variety of instructional components to create learning opportunities that fit the situation at hand. Here is an overview of several important instructional components that are part of the framework we advocate (see Figure 1.2). We take up these components in great detail in upcoming chapters of the book:

- *Interactive Language Experiences.* These are the foundational ways that educators create language and literacy learning opportunities. Educators immerse learners in texts of all kinds by employing instructional strategies such as establishing daily routines (e.g., calendar and/ or daily news). They also capitalize on the environment for learning by setting up classroom libraries, spaces for multimedia use (e.g., tablet stations), literacy play centres, and drama centres. Furthermore, they provide ongoing opportunities for multimodal responses to popular culture and/or other content that builds on learners' funds of knowledge.

- *Interactive Read-Aloud.* Educators demonstrate proficient reading, provide learners with access to ideas from texts that they might otherwise be unable to read on their own, and expose learners to a number of **genres** of text by reading aloud to them. Educators carefully select texts to engage learners with high-quality literature and important concepts. Educators and learners transact with texts together, holding conversations about these texts throughout their reading.

- *Shared Reading.* Educators read texts together with learners (e.g., through the use of big books or interactive whiteboards). They scaffold learners' reading by demonstrating and providing strategies for word recognition and comprehension. Shared Reading is a prime time for learners to explore genres that are new or challenging to them.

- *Guided Reading.* Educators carefully match learners with texts that are at their **instructional reading levels**. Educators work with small temporary groups of learners to develop their reading and comprehension strategies. Learners are encouraged to read a variety of increasingly challenging texts.

- *Independent Reading.* Educators provide sufficient in-class reading time for learners to become engaged with self-selected material. They focus learners' attention on specific aspects of texts. Learners are provided with time to use what they have learned independently, and because they are given time for reading, educators are creating the opportunity for learners to see that the practice is valuable.

- *Reader Response Activities.* The purpose of these activities is to engage learners in the ideas of the texts they are reading, to promote understanding and appreciation of texts, to extend the content of the texts, and also to link reading with the other dimensions of language and

FIGURE 1.2

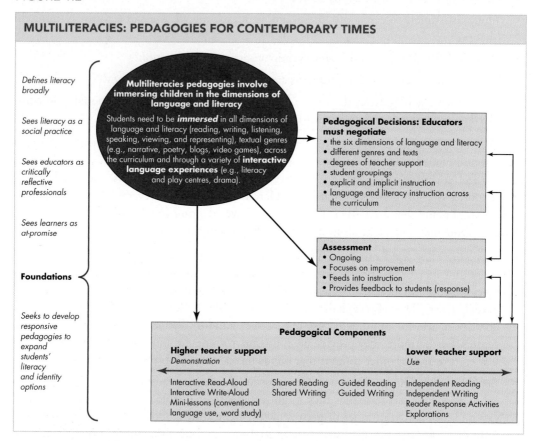

literacy. Response activities can be used with any combination of instructional components for reading.

- *Sound Study and Word Study.* These lessons and activities focus specifically on the parts of language that can help with reading and writing. For instance, there may be word walls, word building, and **phonological awareness** activities. They can be embedded within or remain distinct from the other instructional components of the literacy pedagogy framework.

- *Interactive Write-Aloud.* Educators demonstrate proficient writing, model various writing strategies and thinking processes, and expose learners to a variety of text genres by writing and thinking aloud in front of them.

- *Shared Writing.* Learners and educators work together to compose messages, stories, and texts from other genres. Educators can scribe learners' ideas and words and when appropriate, learners and educators can "share the pen."

- *Guided Writing.* Educators instruct small temporary groups of learners on the craft of writing in a variety of genres. As learners write, educators act as guides and use this time to reinforce strategies and skills, including those taught in Shared Writing.

- *Independent Writing.* Learners engage in the writing process: drafting, revising, editing, and sharing (publishing) their writing. Throughout the writing process, learners are provided with feedback and support from educators and their peers, some of it through conferencing.

- *Conventional Use of Written-Language Activities.* These lessons and activities can be embedded within or remain distinct from the other instructional components of the literacy pedagogy framework and focus specifically on the conventions of written language (e.g., spelling, handwriting, and punctuation).

- *Literacy Across the Curriculum Activities and Lessons.* Educators help learners to access and create texts within specific content areas (e.g., science and social studies).

- *Explorations.* This term refers to multiliteracies projects designed to extend students' understandings of concepts within and across content areas. Chapter 13, for instance, provides illustrations of multiliteracies explorations.

Instructional Component Considerations

There are many considerations relative to the pedagogical components we have included here:

Consideration 1. As both Cambourne and the NLG would say, one of the most important learning opportunities educators can create for learners is to *immerse* them in a language- and text-rich environment at all levels of schooling. Doing so means paying attention to the setup of the classroom, the resources within it, and the experiences in which educators invite learners to engage (e.g., discussion, play, and exploration). Many of the components in the framework contribute to immersion; however, we have included interactive language experiences as components to highlight the importance of the environment and routines educators create for learners and to provide an umbrella for a variety of rich literacy teaching strategies.

Consideration 2. Although some of the components focus on a particular language and literacy dimension (e.g., reading or writing), insofar as possible all the dimensions should be taught closely together. Doing this is perhaps easier than one might first think. For example, when educators conduct Read-Alouds of **picture books** (across all the grades), they are doing more than just exposing learners to reading. By discussing the book with learners, they are creating learning opportunities in listening and speaking; by drawing attention to the images in the book, they are inviting viewing. Moreover, writing components often include representing components, where educators and learners expand, augment, or clarify the print text they generate; they might perhaps include graphs, drawings, or 3-D models. Explorations, reader response activities, and literacy across the curriculum activities and lessons can capitalize on multimodality, in particular.

Consideration 3. All of the components should invite learning opportunities within a variety of genres and across the curriculum. Thus, Shared Reading, Guided Reading, and the like can be conducted using **narrative** texts of all kinds (e.g., novels, **graphic novels**, and picture books) or information-type texts (e.g., a science textbook or **hypertext** article online). The components can therefore be integrated in instructional strategies throughout the school day. Similarly, we have focused the components on print literacy given its **capital**. Reading and writing, however, can be viewed as dynamic and occurring in a variety of environments, including electronic. Thus pedagogies for the acquisition of reading and writing can also be dynamic and practised with a variety of media (from pencil and paper to keyboard).

Consideration 4. The components offer varying degrees of educator support—from higher to lower—and these degrees follow the trajectory of Cambourne's conditions, from demonstration to use. Educators, for example, might demonstrate a strategy in a Write-Aloud and then invite learners first to approximate this in Guided Writing and later to independently use the strategy in Independent Writing. Similarly, learners are supported in the four components of the New London Group's pedagogy of multiliteracies: through immersion, overt instruction, critical framing, and use of the literacy practice in (it is hoped) transformative ways.

Consideration 5. The conventions or mechanics of literacy can be taught through any of the instructional components. Educators must negotiate how much attention to direct toward these *parts of language* and when and how they do so. We have, however, included the components conventional use of written-language activities and sound study and word study to indicate that *parts of language* is a necessary component of a literacy pedagogy.

Consideration 6. As in consideration 5, we have included reader response activities to highlight the crucial nature of learners actively constructing meaning from text and having ample space in which to critically reflect on these meanings. Specifically, we advise educators to create abundant opportunities for learners to respond to a variety of texts in ways that can deepen their understanding and appreciation of them. All of the components invite response, but the focus and degree of the response will differ. For instance, in a Guided Reading lesson of a poem, educators might choose to emphasize a particular reading strategy rather than focus on the reader's impression of the imagery in the text. So the reader response activities component is included to alert educators to provide, where appropriate, opportunities for engaged response to text.

Consideration 7. In all of the components, educators have opportunities for assessment—collecting information about learners' funds of knowledge and progress through formal and informal means. Such assessment should be ongoing, focused on improving learning through informed planning of what and how next to teach, and geared to providing feedback so learners have a record of their practices, understand what they are doing well, and know what they need to do next.

Consideration 8. We believe that critical literacy, with its focus on what people *do* with text and what this text *does* in the world, is a vital part of multiliteracies pedagogies.

SUMMARY

This chapter lays the groundwork for all others in the book. Literacy is a multifaceted and complex concept that includes more than the ability to read and write. In our discussion, we provided information regarding changing demographics and curricular requirements and in so doing identified the need for a coherent framework for literacy teaching that can offer all learners optimum learning opportunities and identity options. We then offered a version of multiliteracies pedagogies in conjunction with critical literacy and Cambourne's conditions for learning. In Chapter 2 we visit Paul's classroom to discuss some finer-grained considerations when planning and organizing for language and literacy learning, and all subsequent chapters elaborate on the components of the pedagogies we introduced in this chapter.

SELECTED PROFESSIONAL RESOURCES

The Rethinking Schools Website: http://www.rethinkingschools.org/index.shtml

A non-profit organization made by teachers who are "firmly committed to equity and to the vision that public education is central to the creation of a humane, caring, multiracial democracy," Rethinking Schools publishes a variety of books and journals that forward the above critical goals. A couple of terrific journal issues to check out are those for Summer 2010, an issue on the power of poetry, and Fall 2008, titled *Language, Race, and Power* and including such articles as "Putting Out the Linguistic Welcome Mat," which suggests ways of "honoring students' home languages" to build "inclusive" classrooms.

Pahl, K., & Rowsell, J. (2012). Literacy and education: *Understanding the new literacy studies in the classroom* (2nd ed.). London, UK: Paul Chapman.

This little updated book takes what could be confusing or difficult literacy-related concepts, defines them clearly, and then shows how they work within real classrooms. Here is literacy for the 21st century presented in an accessible and comfortable way.

Sanford, K., & Blair, H. (n.d.). *Boys and literacy*. http://www2.education.ualberta.ca/boysandliteracy/

Want to learn more about gender and literacy from a Canadian perspective? Check out the Canadian Adolescent Boys and Literacy website. It includes all kinds of research on the topic as well as helpful links for classroom practice.

CHAPTER TWO

Planning for Language and Literacy Teaching

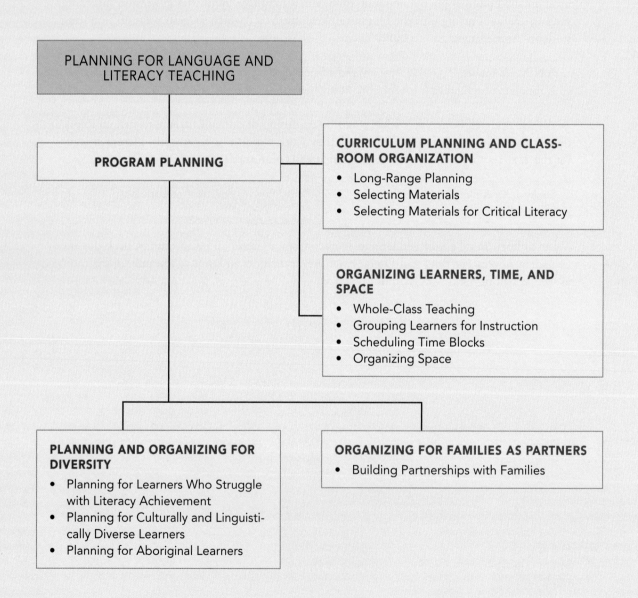

PLANNING FOR LANGUAGE AND LITERACY TEACHING

PROGRAM PLANNING

CURRICULUM PLANNING AND CLASS-ROOM ORGANIZATION
- Long-Range Planning
- Selecting Materials
- Selecting Materials for Critical Literacy

ORGANIZING LEARNERS, TIME, AND SPACE
- Whole-Class Teaching
- Grouping Learners for Instruction
- Scheduling Time Blocks
- Organizing Space

PLANNING AND ORGANIZING FOR DIVERSITY
- Planning for Learners Who Struggle with Literacy Achievement
- Planning for Culturally and Linguistically Diverse Learners
- Planning for Aboriginal Learners

ORGANIZING FOR FAMILIES AS PARTNERS
- Building Partnerships with Families

Every day when learners enter David Paul's grade 2 classroom, they are greeted with a letter he has written to them on the whiteboard. In the letter, David tells about novel class activities they will do that day or comments on class events from the day before. Today, the learners read the letter and David helps them use words on the classroom word wall as a resource when identifying unfamiliar words. On other days, David presents the letter as a minimal-cues message, where the message has words or parts of words missing and students must try to make sense of the communication.

David then draws the learners together on the floor in a group and reads them a poem about a dragon to set the content for the group composition they will write later. As he reads, he stops at the end of some lines to give learners an opportunity to predict meaningful words. Next, David tells the learners that together they are going to write a composition about an imaginary pet dragon. He planned this instructional activity because he noticed that many learners in the class were having difficulty generating and organizing ideas in their compositions; he selected dragons, because after observing his students, he learned of their interest in the *How to Train Your Dragon* books (Cowell, 2010) and movies (Arnold, DeBlois, & Sanders, 2010) and the *Dragon City* simulation game. As the learners in the class brainstorm ideas, David writes them on the board. Then, with the assistance of his questions, the learners organize the ideas into groups. As they do so, David uses specific colours to circle ideas in each group—for example, how the pet dragon looks, what it does, and what it eats. The children discuss what they want to write and then dictate ideas while David records the ideas. The completed text is read as a whole, and some suggestions are made for revisions. The revised text, revision marks and all, is transferred to the writing centre.

While the group is still intact, David and the learners discuss how to use their remaining time. He provides them with a sign-up chart to control the number of learners who choose to work at each centre, as well as to keep a record of what activities each learner completes during the week. Some learners indicate they are going to return to a composition from their writing files and renew writing. Others are working on a graphic text related to the dragon theme. Others decide to read independently or write a journal response to a book they are reading. One group of learners chooses to play a dragon game David has developed to reinforce a problematic spelling pattern. Another group works on a puppet play based on a story they had read in class. Yet another group checks their blog online for the update of the dragon toy they have sent across the world.

While the learners are working independently or in small groups, David asks six learners to join him at a small table in the corner of the room where he conducts a directed reading–thinking activity (see Chapter 7) as part of a Guided Reading lesson. He has noticed that these learners are making limited use of their prior knowledge when they read. Their responses to what they read tend to focus on story details rather than on linking story events or characters to their own lives, other texts, or their knowledge of the world. He will provide Guided Reading for another small group tomorrow, but will continue to work with this group in subsequent lessons until members are able to make more effective use of both print- and knowledge-based information.

With five minutes left before recess, David asks the class to come back together to share what they learned that morning. One learner talks about a book she is reading, another reads aloud a piece of writing, and another discusses the images she is making on the computer to create a graphic text. The learners working on the puppet play say they have completed their puppets and are ready to share their play with the class the next day, and the learners who checked the blog report that the classroom dragon has just made it to Italy!

PROGRAM PLANNING

As the vignette of David Paul suggests, in addition to the myriad pedagogical questions educators have that we raised in Chapter 1, they also have planning and organizing decisions to make. Questions to consider include these:

Lori McKee

- How do educators like David **differentiate** expectations, materials, lessons, and activities to meet the literacy needs of all learners?

- When do educators provide assistance to **scaffold** learners' skills and understandings, and when do they have learners work independently?

- How do educators negotiate their attempts to control students' learning with opportunities for them to control their own learning?

- How do educators decide when learners should work alone or with other learners?

The responses to such questions, as we demonstrate throughout *Constructing Meaning*, begin with the words "It depends." Several factors may affect the decisions you make as educators. Some of these include the needs of individual and groups of learners, the places students have reached in their learning, the resources available in your school, the program of studies mandated by government, your theoretical orientation to language and literacy teaching and learning, and the philosophy of your school and school district. No one response will be appropriate for all learners at any one time or for any one learner all the time. The planning process is a "dialogue" (Routman, 2000, p. xxxviii) based in learners' **funds of knowledge** and educators' appraisals of what is known about language and literacy education and the specific contexts in which they are working.

Another crucial guide to planning is the relevant provincial or territorial curriculum documents for language and literacy education that we introduced in the previous chapter. One of your tasks in planning is to determine your learners' funds of knowledge, skills, interests, and values and to juxtapose them against curriculum document objectives. This comparison will shed light on which objectives each learner has already achieved and what learning opportunities you need to provide next. Other tasks involve selecting appropriate materials, scheduling language and literacy time, organizing the physical space in the classroom to facilitate children's learning, and planning whole-class, small-group, and individual instruction and activities.

In Box 2.1 we have listed some questions you might ask yourself when you are considering the extent to which your classroom language and literacy program may offer learners expanded literacy and identity options. We recognize that depending on the circumstances of your teaching, you may have more or less negotiation room in your program. Knowing what you would like to work toward achieving, however, is a start. At this moment you might have little idea of how to respond to the questions, but as you go through the text and reflect on your teaching, you can return to them to gauge your professional growth.

BOX 2.1

QUESTIONS TO EVALUATE YOUR MULTILITERACIES PEDAGOGIES

1. In what ways are communication and the construction and sharing of meaning at the centre of my program?

2. In what ways does my program expand or limit my students' literacy and identity options?

3. In what ways does my program treat all my students as at-promise?

4. In what ways is my program based on my students' funds of knowledge, including the languages they speak and their interests?

5. In what ways does my program address all the dimensions of language and literacy, including a variety of **modes** and **media**, and recognize that different dimensions might need to be emphasized at different times depending on what my learners require?

6. In what ways might my program reflect the most crucial aspects of situated practice, overt instruction, critical framing, and transformed practice?

7. In what ways in my program have I considered and planned for all of Cambourne's conditions for learning?

8. In what ways do I recognize that my program is a work in progress? Am I pursuing the kinds of professional learning experiences that are required to support my teaching—talking with a mentor, reading a range of professional and research articles, taking courses, and so on?

9. In what ways is my program patient with learning (both my own and that of the learners)?

CURRICULUM PLANNING AND CLASSROOM ORGANIZATION

Different classrooms reflect different views of literacy learning. When classrooms are organized with desks in rows and learners facing the front, the focus is generally on the educator's talk, with the educator making most decisions about what learners do and when they do it. When learners are organized so that they are able to face one another, their talk is encouraged and some of the conditions for cooperative learning are created. Other decisions you will make about the use of space include

- where to place your work area (e.g., a desk)
- where to place reading and writing centres
- where to place the classroom library
- where to place students' computers and other equipment*

Space is just one variable teachers consider as they plan and organize their classrooms to facilitate learning.

---

* Source: New London Group, (2000). "A pedagogy of multiliteracies: Designing social futures." In B. Cope & M. Kalantzis, *Multiliteracies: Literacy Learning and the Design of Social Futures*. NY: Routledge, reproduced by permission of Taylor & Francis Books UK.

Time is also a crucial variable. Some jurisdictions recommend that a minimum amount of time be scheduled for language and literacy instruction at each grade level. However, educators have flexibility within this time allocation to decide whether to organize instruction in one or two large time blocks or to devote small time blocks to specific skills or activities.

A third variable is materials and equipment. Provincial and territorial governments have lists that recommend some types of materials that might be used in language and literacy teaching at each grade level. (A list of these materials is available from the Curriculum Service Canada website at http://www.curriculum.org/content/resource-library).

Educators must make decisions such as the following:

- how much diversity, as in range of difficulties, **genres**, authors, and topics covered, will be represented by the textual materials in classrooms

- when texts are selected by various parties (e.g., learners, educators, or both)

- how materials can be organized

Finally, the most critical variable is the learners themselves. How can learners inform the curriculum so that their funds of knowledge, interests, and investments are central to the learning opportunities in the classroom? Educators make daily decisions about when, why, and how to organize whole-class, small-group, and individual activities.

In the next sections, we describe ways educators can plan and organize materials, learners, time, and space to create expansive literacy and identity options for learners. Often in doing so we reflect back on David Paul's classroom from the opening vignette and foreshadow the book's content to come.

Long-Range Planning

Educators plan moment by moment, day by day, week by week, and also through long-range plans. Long-range plans provide an overview of the year and help establish a direction for educators and learners. As with all areas of the curriculum, even though these plans are written down before the school year begins, they should be seen as a guide that evolves and can be negotiated in light of educators' growing knowledge about their students.

The following Inside Classrooms box presents a discussion about planning. It engages teachers Linda Levely and Joelle Nagle to authentically highlight these important points as they relate to teaching learners of different ages:

- Curricular planning is an ongoing cycle of designing, implementing, assessing, evaluating, and revising.

- Planning can work well when it is long range and moment by moment.

- Planning is an individual and a collective activity.

- Getting to know your students, the resources in your school and community, and curricular mandates is fundamental.

- Planning is not just in the service of learners but is also a fundamental part of your own professional learning.

- Curriculum, insofar as possible, should be a meaningful dialogue between fine-grained features of literacy and big ideas; or, otherwise put, between the whole and the part.

INSIDE CLASSROOMS

EARLY YEARS AND INTERMEDIATE EDUCATORS DISCUSS PLANNING

In your first year, Linda, you taught junior kindergarten, and Joelle, you taught a split grade 7/8. Tell us how you planned. Did you make long-range plans?

Linda: I definitely did. The long-range plans that showed an overview of what I was going to do in the year weren't as formal as for the senior kindergarten. They were more guidelines for junior kindergarten, but you definitely needed to have a defined direction of where you were going.

Linda Levely

Linda Levely

Joelle: I found it was extremely important to have a general outline to guide my planning; it was important to outline the goals I needed my students to reach by the end of each reporting period. Especially with a split grade, I wanted to plan so the topics aligned with both grades, and there could be combined units of study as much as possible. The plans were just a guide though and were constantly changing. It was not until I started to let go of how I experienced school as a student (not a good place to start since the students you teach reflect a very different time and culture than when you were a student), and let go of the ideas I had for the students (based on my interests) and started to know my students better: their interests, et cetera so I could make more detailed plans and could tailor to their needs. It took a lot of planning and replanning.

Joelle Nagle

Elma Renders

Tell us about the experience of drawing up those long-range plans for the first time.

Linda: The first time you do it, it's more just trial and error. You're putting together your own map, and it's going to be changing continually, because when you draw up the plans, you don't know the children: you don't know their social skills; you don't know their academic background, what kinds of experiences they've had at home, and so on. So you can have your long-range plans all laid out, but honestly, after that first week of school, you may be back at home rewriting your whole set of long-range plans if the students are either going beyond where you thought they would be or if you're having to really slow down and spending way more time on certain areas.

Joelle: I was given a matrix from the school district that outlined general topics of study for each subject (corresponding with the curriculum document) to plan our year. Though it was easy to plan ahead for subjects such as science and history which have specific topics, language

(continued)

arts was more difficult to outline (in the matrix the topics were extremely general, for example, for term 2 it was listed as Novel Study only). Starting with the curriculum document is necessary to understand the skills set the students are expected to have, but understanding my students was important when planning how to engage the students in the curriculum. My plans were never definite and were constantly changing. Especially if an opportunity to go on a field trip or have some experience arose—like a play or presentation on bullying. I needed to make adjustments in my plans to capitalize on the learning and activities that were provided by the event. For example, writing a play review, learning how to view live theatre, creating a play; or creating a multimedia unit to address the social impacts of bullying.

Linda and Joelle, you're now no longer first-year teachers, and you've had the opportunity to teach the same grade for many years. Tell us about the planning process when you've had the same grade for a good amount of time.

Linda: Ah! It's fabulous! Not only do you have the background, but also when you've been in a school for a few years you know the students coming up. Now, I try to build a relationship and get to know the children that are in grade 1 so that at the beginning of the next year, I don't have such a brand-new "getting to know you time." There's a foundation.

Working on my long-range plans has also gotten easier. I write my long-range plans and put them in a binder. Then, as I'm teaching through the year, I'll just jot down little notes on the plans. When you're teaching, you're looking at the children, seeing what works, what didn't work. Did you provide all the learning experiences you could? If not, how can you juggle opportunities around and what can you combine to get two things addressed at once? I've also been lucky enough to team-teach with another grade 2 teacher, and we've done most of our planning together.

Joelle: After five years of teaching, it definitely gets a lot easier! I understand that planning is a dynamic process. I am better able to make adjustments and be flexible to who my students are. I realize just how important the needs and interests of my students are, and that they are an invaluable resource to draw upon. Also, it's important to call upon your colleagues as resources, instead of working in isolation. Now I have a better vision of the year ahead, starting to plan for the next year before the year is over.

What are the timelines for when you're planning for September?

Linda: Usually in May of the previous school year, we start meeting as a division. We start looking at the children, figuring out who they are and just start playing around without anything written in stone. We look at which groupings we want together, and ask: Are there students that work well together? We also look at teaching styles: there are some teachers who are much more into centres and group work and students have more freedom in their activities, and then there are teachers who are very structured, and you need to look at the children who will benefit from which teaching style. You need to see who will bring out the best in a child.

Then, we look at our long-range plans, which we build largely around the provincial curriculum. We just tear the curriculum apart and pick and choose what seems appropriate for which term. Of course, with language arts we have the different areas which we break into smaller chunks. A lot of the chunks we visit each term, but within each chunk we'll break it down, so that in term 1 it's very general. In term 2, we do more review and a lot of the building of the new skills. In term 3, we'll review those new skills and start to develop a little bit further. At the same time, we also look at classroom resources and school resources.

Joelle: At the end of the school year, each division meets with the principal and special education teacher to make decisions about student groupings. This is an important process. It prepares me for the dynamics of my classroom. Then I can start to gather resources needed to accommodate my students. (There could be students with learning, physical, or developmental disabilities, and they may need an educational assistant, they may have an Independent Education Plan, and there may also be **English language learners**). Having a general idea of your classroom dynamics can help decide what novels to study, what field trips to plan, what to begin with. Again, it's important for me to know who my students are. Regarding the curriculum, there may be new changes that need to be addressed, new mandates et cetera.

Toward the beginning of the school year, I have to plan that first little bit of time when I unfortunately don't have the advantage of knowing the students and the class dynamics yet. So I start with a lot of activities to get to know my students, and for my students to get to know one another (even though they might have been together for many years).

Does integrating curricular areas enter your planning?

Linda: Yes! For example, we just did a big science unit on animals, but we also wanted to work on our writing. We've worked in riddle writing, where we have the kids forming questions and doing research skills and mind mapping. So, we're covering their language aspect as well as reviewing what they've learned in science.

Joelle: You have to! There is too much curriculum that we are responsible for; you can't get it all done isolating subjects. Language and literacy involves every subject—by creating integrative projects, it makes the learning more holistic.

Is it a challenge integrating curriculum?

Linda: It's definitely a challenge in some areas. The unit we just finished on animals was very easy to do because the children were interested in it. Also, there are tons of books in our libraries that our kids can read independently. Also, there are other resources where the children can see the different setup of information books, such as table of contents, index, and glossary, and they can become more familiar with that.

Joelle: It can be challenging trying to integrate topics that capture students' interests—I find that more of the challenge. If you can't captivate your audience and make it meaningful to them, it doesn't matter how excellent or thorough your plan is.

(continued)

Is there a reflective practice component to your development of long-range plans?

Linda: When I'm planning, I also try to pick a focus on anything I want to improve on within my own teaching.

As a teacher, I like to pick one area to improve on. You can't focus on all the areas and you're not going to forget about the other areas, but something I've learned is that you take one step at a time. In my first classroom, I was trying to be perfect in all the areas, and it did take a bit to realize that no one can be perfect in all the areas.

Joelle: There is always reflective practice: whether I write it down afterward, make small notes in my day plan, or make mental notes while I'm delivering my lessons, it's crucial to be reflective.

Selecting Materials

There are different materials that educators commonly use in language and literacy programs. Each comes with its own considerations. Traditionally, language and literacy materials have been print materials in book form; increasingly though, language and literacy programs may be built around **new media** resources such as digital texts. That said, even textbooks are multimodal, containing visual material such as graphs, reflecting the notion that modes are rarely used in isolation (Jewitt & Kress, 2003). Consequently, if the materials educators use are not clearly identifiable as part of a **New Literacies** vein (Knobel & Lankshear, 2007), the way educators *use* them and *teach* learners how to access them to their fullest should be new.

Trade Books

Just like David Paul in the opening vignette, educators who want to expose their to a breadth of materials and provide them with a wide choice of reading selections base their language and literacy programs in trade books. The use of **children's literature** and **young adult (YA)** novels as the core of language and literacy programs is so fundamental that Chapter 11 is devoted to describing such literature. In addition, a list of recommended books is presented by grade level in the Appendix. However, simply including literature in classrooms may not provide expansive literacy and identity options for learners. It also depends on how educators use the material.

Some educators may be tempted to draw on teaching strategies that were developed to be used with the stories from old-fashioned **basal reading series**. In novel studies, for example, they might assign a chapter to be read and 10 questions to be answered, develop fill-in-the-blank worksheet exercises about the stories, or ask learners to define words on a list from the story and use each of them in a sentence. Such practices are problematic for many reasons. Not least of these is that they confuse *remembering* with *comprehending*; most of these activities ask readers to supply facts that they remember from reading a text rather than asking them to use their higher-order thinking skills and critical reading skills to construct meaning from text (Allington, 2006). Throughout the book, we demonstrate ways of working with and responding to literature that honours the importance of constructing meaning.

Nonbook Resources

Sometimes as educators we can imply to learners through what we do and say that books are the only legitimate literacy materials. Yet, if we consider all the items we read each day, books are only one of many reading sources. Some of the other texts learners read in an average day might include blogs, the text in video games, trading cards, magazines, brochures, advertisements, signs, labels, instant messages, and websites. Given the nature of this list, we indeed must provide learners with opportunities to expand their viewing and representing knowledge and skills. If learners are to be literate and communicate widely for both information and pleasure, they must engage with a wide variety of materials in school.

In terms of print resources, as we discuss in Chapter 4 most young children are aware of print in their environment before they go to school. They know the signs for fast-food restaurants, and they can identify their favourite cereal by looking at the box. When they begin school, they encounter print in their classrooms, including their names, the names of their classmates, the days of the week and months of the year on the calendar, labels on computers and other equipment in work centres, and words on charts. By making this print the focus of instruction, educators build on learners' experiences with printed language and help them make use of it.

For learners beyond an early level of literacy, nonbook literacy materials can include such items as

- pamphlets and brochures from a variety of sources (e.g., flyers and advertisements)
- instruction manuals (e.g., for video games)
- comic books
- trading cards and game cards like Pokémon
- online materials like gaming chat areas, **fan fiction**, and the like.

There are also newspapers and magazines designed specifically for young people—available online and off-line. Some of those available are listed in Chapter 11. These materials can be used for several instructional activities, particularly in relation to content-area reading. Also, it bears mentioning that gaming programs are increasingly important sources of instructional material (Gee, 2013).

As we suggest throughout the book, educators might expand learners' literacy options by making a wide range of materials available in their classroom. By including materials that cover various degrees of difficulty, genres, topics, interests, and the like, you will create opportunities for all learners to engage with both challenging and independent material every day. Also, materials to foster **print literacy** need not be the only literacy materials that educators offer to learners. Learners need access to a variety of modes and media such as art and modelling supplies.

From the available materials, we recommend that learners be provided as much choice as possible. When all materials are selected by someone else, learners may be less likely to gain a sense of ownership or control over their own literacy practices. They may feel that they are communicating for someone else rather than for themselves. Note that David Paul provides learners with controlled choices that allow them to take responsibility.

Further, in a multiliteracies vein, with its insistence on critical framing, any discussion of texts and what to do with them requires the addition of critical literacy as a talking point.

Selecting Materials for Critical Literacy

The types of texts we invite into our classrooms is a fruitful place to begin to promote critical literacy. Although most narrative materials can be used for critical literacy lessons, some educators have identified specific texts that are particularly appropriate for this use. Wason-Ellam (2002) called these *critically conscious stories*; Lewison, Flint, and Van Sluys (2002) referred to them as *social issues books*; and Leland, Harste, Ociepka, Lewison, and Vasquez (1999) used the term *critical books*.

Leland et al. (1999) developed the following criteria to identify critical books:

- They don't make difference invisible, but rather explore which differences *make a difference*.

- They enrich our understanding of history and life by giving voice to those who traditionally have been silenced or marginalized.

- They show how people can begin to take action on important social issues.

- They explore dominant systems of meaning that operate in our society to position people and groups of people.

- They don't provide "happily ever after" endings for complex social problems.*

Educator Pam Malins, who researches literacy curriculum and the promotion of diverse gender identities and family structures, assisted us in updating a list of critical books (see Box 2.2) written for use with children in K to 8 classrooms. Many of these books are Canadian in origin. Educators might also want to consult the Canadian Literature for Social Justice website (http://canlitsocialjustice.wordpress.com/), developed by a Canadian funded research team, which contains annotated lists of Canadian books for readers from elementary to secondary school selected by teachers for promoting issues of social justice.

After text selection, educators can guide readers to consider texts and their reading of them critically. Box 2.3 highlights some questions educators can use themselves or with students to help promote critical selections. These questions are designed to invite learners to interrogate the assumptions embedded in texts and their own beliefs about the world. The questions can help learners to identify issues of equity and social justice in the materials they encounter and can be amended to accommodate specific genres and modes of text.

---

* Leland, C., Harste, J., Ociepka, A., Lewison, M., and Vasquez, V. "Exploring critical literacy: You can hear a pin drop." *Language Arts*. Issue 77(1), pp. 70–77. 1999.

BOX 2.2

CRITICAL BOOKS TO PROMOTE CRITICAL LITERACY

Badoe, A. (2002). *Nana's cold days.* Toronto, ON: Groundwood Books.

Bannatyne-Cugnet, J. (2000). *From far and wide: A citizenship scrapbook.* (S. N. Zhang, Illus.). Toronto, ON: Tundra Books.

Browne, A. (1998). *Voices in the park.* New York, NY: DK Publishing.

Bunting, E. (1991). *Fly away home.* (R. Himler, Illus.). New York, NY: Clarion Books.

Butler, G. (1998). *The Hangashore.* Toronto, ON: Tundra Books.

Campbell, N. I. (2005). *Shi-shi-etko.* (K. LaFave, Illus.). Toronto, ON: Groundwood Books.

Cowen-Fletcher, J. (1994). *It takes a village.* New York, NY: Scholastic.

Cheng, A. (2000). *Grandfather counts.* (A. Zheng, Illus.). New York, NY: Lee & Low Books.

Davis, A. (2003). *Bagels from Benny.* (D. Petricic, Illus.). Toronto, ON: Kids Can Press.

Fletcher, R. (1998). *Flying solo.* New York, NY: Clarion Books.

Hesse, K. (1998). *Just juice.* New York, NY: Scholastic.

Highway, T. (2001). *Caribou song.* (J. Rombough, Illus.). Toronto, ON: HarperCollins.

Isadora, R. (1991). *At the crossroads.* New York, NY: Greenwillow Books.

Kaplan, W., & Tanaka, S. (1998). *One more border: The true story of one family's escape from war-torn Europe.* (S. Taylor, Illus.). Toronto, ON: Groundwood Books.

King, T. (1992). *A coyote Columbus story.* (K. Monkman, Illus.). Toronto, ON: Groundwood Books.

Littlechild, G. (1993). *This land is my land.* Emeryville, CA: Children's Book Press.

Loyie, L., & Brissenden, C. (2005). *The gathering tree.* (H. Holmlund, Illus.). Penticton, BC: Theytus Books.

Maclear, K. (2010). *Spork.* (I. Arsenault, Illus.). Toronto, ON: Kids Can Press.

McKee, D. (1987). *Tusk tusk.* London, UK: Beaver Books.

Myers, C. (2000). *Wings.* New York, NY: Scholastic.

Setterington, K. (2004). *Mom and Mum are getting married!* (A. Priestley, Illus.). Toronto, ON: Second Story Press.

Smith, D. (2011). *This child, every child: A book about the world's children.* (S. Armstrong, Illus.). Toronto, ON: Kids Can Press.

Spalding, A. (1999). *Me and Mr. Mah.* (J. Wilson, Illus.). Victoria, BC: Orca.

Yee, P. (1996). *Ghost train.* (H. Chan, Illus.). Toronto, ON: Groundwood Books.

BOX 2.3

QUESTIONS TO INTERROGATE TEXTS

▷ Who wrote/designed this text?

▷ Why did the author create this text?

▷ What is the author's experience and expertise on this topic?

(continued)

▷ What does the author have to gain from composing this text?

▷ What evidence supports what the author composed?

▷ What do other authors say about this topic?

▷ Who benefits from this text?

▷ What voices are being heard?

▷ Whose voices are left out?

▷ Is there another point of view?

▷ How are the [girls, boys, women, men, mothers, fathers, grandmothers, grandfathers] portrayed in this text?

▷ What is this text saying about [boys and girls, men and women, the elderly, people from different cultures, people with a disability, people living in poverty]? Is this true for all members of this group?

▷ What difference would it have made if the main character were a [boy, girl, man, woman, person from a different culture, person with a disability]?

▷ What is the world like for people in the text?

▷ Which people have power in this text?

▷ Is it fair that they have power?

▷ What is the author's/designer's underlying message?

▷ If violence was used to deal with a problem in this text, in what other ways could the problem have been solved?

▷ How has the author/designer used language or other textual elements (e.g., images) to position the reader?

ORGANIZING LEARNERS, TIME, AND SPACE

The classroom of Kathy Gillies

The decisions educators make about how to organize learners, time, and space for language and literacy instruction reflect the goals and philosophy of their programs.

When organizing learners, you might keep the following in mind:

• There is a range of experience, knowledge, and skills among any group of learners.

• Learners have their own unique funds of knowledge, skills, and interests.

• People learn at different rates.

For these reasons, we recommend that learners be organized in different ways throughout the school day and that time and space be organized to facilitate whole-class, small-group, and individual instruction and practice. This idea is in keeping with *Constructing Meaning*'s literacy teaching framework components. When considering these components, note how some may be more conducive to a whole-group situation (e.g., Read-Alouds and Write-Alouds), others more conducive to independent work (e.g., Independent Reading and Independent Writing), and still others more conducive to being conducted in a small group (e.g., Guided Reading and Guided Writing). Every form of grouping has its own considerations. The next sections highlight some of these.

Whole-Class Teaching

There are several advantages to whole-class teaching. Talking and working together as a whole class can help to develop a community in which learners support, collaborate, and respect one another. Students can learn a great deal from one another, and this learning may be enhanced when they are provided with the opportunity to interact with others of differing strengths. Whole-class teaching is also an efficient use of educator time. When introducing learners to something new, it is more efficient to work with the whole class at the same time than to teach the same thing to each learner individually. David Paul used a minimal-cues message to teach strategies for identifying words to his whole class. He also read a poem to the class and invited learners to brainstorm ideas for a writing project. The time spent on large-group teaching varies with the day and needs of the learners.

Furthermore, sharing time in a whole-class situation near the end of a language and literacy time block gives learners an opportunity to talk about what they have accomplished and to evaluate their learning. They may discuss books they have read, read aloud what they have written, or talk about what they have learned. When learners talk about their language processes, they can learn about themselves as language users and develop their **metacognition** (Taberski, 2000). In turn, learners and educators gain an opportunity to evaluate the effectiveness of the learning opportunities created in the classroom and a basis for planning the next day's objectives and activities.

Despite its benefits, whole-class teaching needs to be supplemented with other ways of organizing learners so that educators can be responsive to learners' individual differences.

Grouping Learners for Instruction

Ability Grouping

The major purpose of ability grouping is to produce a more homogeneous group, making it easier for educators to plan and implement lessons. Despite the long history of ability grouping, research has produced few conclusive findings to either support or refute its impact on achievement. Thus, many educators are today questioning the value of this grouping practice (McCoach, O'Connell, & Levitt, 2006). Ability grouping may offer some advantage to academically gifted students (Huss, 2006) and students who attend privileged educational settings such as private schools (Nomi, 2010), but study results are far from clear even for this group and questionable for average- and low-ability groups (Lleras & Rangel, 2009) or children in schools where there are many students who are CLD and low socio-economic status (SES) (Nomi, 2010).

In terms of reading instruction specifically, researchers have investigated whether learners are taught reading differently in high-ability as compared with low-ability groups. The findings are somewhat inconsistent, although there does seem to be cause for concern. Even when educators are careful in the names they select for different groups, children know which group is high and which is low. This awareness can have negative implications for the self-esteem of children in the low group (Lleras, 2008; Rubin, 2006). Some studies indicate that learners who are placed in the lower ability groups do not engage in as many instructional activities as their higher group peers, are less likely to be asked critical comprehension questions, and receive fewer opportunities to select their own reading material (Chorzempa & Graham, 2006). The instructional components of our literacy teaching framework thus take a more diverse approach to grouping where varied, flexible groupings based on a variety of factors, not just ability or achievement, are used every day.

Other Ways to Group Learners

David Paul organized the learners in his classroom into interest groups, research groups, next-step groups, and pairs. All these groupings are far less permanent than ability groups. Interest groups in his classroom are sometimes set up for one day, when, for example, learners come together to play a game. Other groups, such as the one working on the puppet play, stay together for several days.

- *Interest groups* are generally made up of learners at different levels of achievement who share an interest. They tend to exist for a relatively short time, disbanding when their purpose has been achieved.

- *Research groups* are similar to interest groups in that they are temporary. Educators are generally instrumental in a research group's formation. The focus of the research group is on a topic that the learners research rather than on completing an activity. Often, the educators and learners together set specific goals, and a written or oral presentation is made at the end. Like interest groups, these groups are frequently composed of learners at varying levels of achievement.

- *Next-step groups* are set up for different reasons than interest or research groups. Through careful classroom observation, educators identify the next step that learners may need to take in a dimension of language and literacy. For instance, David identified several learners who needed to make greater use of their own knowledge as they read. He brought these learners together into a small group for a few lessons to help them understand the importance of their knowledge and develop strategies for using it as they read. Once the objectives for special-needs instruction have been met, these groups are disbanded.

- In *collaborative pairs*, learners work together on a common activity, helping one another at points of difficulty. David organized his learners into collaborative pairs for part of the language and literacy time. Each pair found a space and shared books. While one learner read, the other listened. Each learner gained more reading practice than is the case when

Collaborative group work

learners read orally in groups or as the whole class. Because the learners chose the books, the books most likely interested them and were at an appropriate level. Collaborative pairs, also easily used for writing activities, have been found to help learners make connections between oral and print language (Wilkinson & Silliman, 2000). They have also been used to assist learners in their development of web literacy skills, with results showing knowledge gains (Kuiper, Volman, & Terwel, 2009).

- A more common way of organizing learners into pairs involves *peer tutoring*, either with same-age or cross-age dyads. Generally, a more proficient reader or writer is paired with one who is less proficient, and they complete a specific activity designed to facilitate skill development. This type of pairing can also be used when learners need to access information from a common text in social studies or science. The learner who has developed sufficient skills and strategies to construct meaning from the text reads it to the learner who has yet to reach this level of reading proficiency. Another type of activity that is appropriate for peer tutoring is paired reading. As with most types of groupings, research has yielded conflicting results on peer tutoring, but it seems that both the tutored and the tutor benefit from the experience (Monaghan, 2006; Pugh, 2005), and it appears to work best when programs are structured (Chipman & Roy, 2006), short in duration (Indrisano & Paratore, 1991), and focused on specific skills (Gordon, 2005). Educators might also consider using web-based interfaces in peer tutoring, which have been found to provide opportunities for digital problem solving, for effectively tracking learners' achievement and feeding this back into pedagogical activities, and for connecting learners (Evans & Moore, 2013).

Cooperative Learning

Many of the groupings described above lend themselves well to cooperative learning. Cooperative learning is an approach where "students work on learning activities in small groups and receive rewards or recognition based on their group's performance" (Slavin, 1980, p. 315). There are many ways in which cooperative groups can work in language and literacy pedagogy.

- In one scenario, two learners work together to complete a writing task, discussing what they will say and how they will say it. When they finish writing, they submit one text with both names on it.

- In another scenario, a group of learners attempts to make sense of a poem. They first jot down questions about the poem and then discuss and share different interpretations. The understanding the learners come to as a group is different and often deeper than most learners could have constructed individually.

- Still another example involves learners completing different parts of the same project and meeting regularly to discuss what they are doing. Such projects can be especially engaging and provide great learning opportunities when the modes of communication within them are open-ended. For instance, in one Canadian study of the resources that upper elementary learners drew on in a free-choice project on Confederation and how these communicated students' interests, Nagle (2009) found that learners used a rich array of modes and media (e.g., a doll skit, electronic slide show, and magazine) and were well engaged in communication practices and learning. One project is handed in as a result of such work (Golub, 1994).

Cooperative learning challenges the traditional authority structure of classrooms by placing more control in the hands of learners. Another major difference is that, instead of each learner being evaluated individually, learners work together and are evaluated as a group. They are thereby encouraged to work cooperatively rather than competitively (which happens when educators organize learners into groups but still base rewards on individual achievement). Some additional benefits claimed for cooperative learning groups include the following:

- is appropriate for learners of all ages (Bowman-Perrott et al., 2013)
- increases the exchange of ideas (Gillies & Boyle, 2006)
- develops social skills (Gillies & Boyle, 2006)
- develops cognitive skills (Stevens, 2007)
- increases self-esteem in learners (Miller, Topping, & Thurston, 2010)
- "encourages" learners to try to solve "problems they would otherwise abandon" (Evans & Moore, 2013, p. 154)
- assists learners to "confirm/deepen own understanding" (Evans & Moore, 2013, p. 154)
- fosters wider acceptance and respect for other learners (Gillies & Boyle, 2006)
- increases academic achievement (Baines, Blatchford, & Kutnick, 2007; King, 2007)
- increases motivation (Stevens, 2007)
- encourages development of a sense of group (Gillies & Boyle, 2006)
- is effective for learners with disabilities, and has been found to be particularly suitable for learners who ordinarily demonstrate problem behaviours (Bowman-Perrott et al., 2013)

Individual Activities

Learners need classroom time to independently use literacies to become more proficient language users; they learn to read *by reading*. Inviting learners to select a book for reading or to write something of their own choice after they complete their other work is not enough. Similarly, suggesting that they read and write at home is not enough. Independent time to practise one's literacies must be scheduled into each school day. The added bonus to independent work is that it is inherently multilevel, with each learner working at an appropriate level of difficulty.

Scheduling Time Blocks

In allocating time, educators are faced with two main choices. They must decide whether to divide language and literacy activities into a series of separate time periods devoted to different dimensions, or to designate large time blocks for language and literacy activities (or a cross-curricular unit) and organize a range of activities within these blocks.

Short and Long Time Blocks

A major advantage of short time blocks is accountability: it is relatively easy to account for how much time has been spent on each aspect of the language and literacy curriculum. For example, if families are concerned about writing, educators can assure them that a certain number of minutes are devoted exclusively to writing instruction every week. This way of allocating time also provides predictability for learners; they know what they will be doing at each point during the school day.

There are, however, several disadvantages to organizing different aspects of the language and literacy curriculum into separate time slots. First, it does little to foster links between or even within the dimensions or curricular aims. For example, when **grammar** is taught in a separate 10-minute block each day, some learners may not see its relevance for writing. Second, separate time blocks make it difficult for educators to pursue learners' interests as they arise in the classroom; for example, instead of teaching learners a reading **strategy** when they need it, the teaching is put on hold until the appropriate time in the school day. In addition, just when learners get interested in a topic they are discussing, it is often time to switch to another subject area. Third, short time blocks necessitate many changes in activity during the day, and time may be lost during transitions between activities.

An alternative to short time blocks is to organize one or two larger daily time blocks for language and literacy and to include language learning opportunities in other subject areas as well. With this structure there is more flexibility to be responsive to learners'. Furthermore, activities are neither cut off while learners are still engaged in meaningful learning, nor prolonged to fill a predetermined time slot when learners are no longer interested or learning.

Time Guidelines

Each educator's daily timetable will depend on many factors, including the requirements of the school system; the philosophy of the school; times allocated for recess, lunch break, gym, and library; the grade level involved; and learners' interests and learning needs. As professionals who are responsive to their students, educators must assess where learners are, what the context demands, and plan accordingly. You, therefore, decide on how much time you should spend with your class and individual learners on each of the instructional components we list in this and other chapters. Conscious that some educators need more explicit advice at some times than at others, we have, however, provided some general guidelines for allocating time:

1. Cunningham and Allington (2011) suggested the following:
   - ❑ *Every day.* Educators read books and other types of materials (e.g., newspapers, magazines) aloud to learners, learners read something they choose, and learners do a word wall activity or some form of word study.
   - ❑ *Two or three times a week.* Learners take part in a Guided Reading activity and a focused writing lesson, the educator models writing, learners write on a topic of their own choosing, and learners work with words.

❏ *Once a week.* Learners share something they have written and something that they have read, read to or with a younger learner, and do research related to a topic. One-third of the class revises, edits, and publishes a piece of writing.*

2. Every day learners are given opportunities to express themselves and make meaning from the communication of others through multiple modes and media, both digital and otherwise (e.g., visual art, drama, dance, and the like).

3. The language and literacy dimensions can be integrated within all the suggested instructional components. Reading can, for instance, involve reading hypertext, and writing can involve writing hypertext. These activities also promote learning opportunities for the development of viewing and representing.

4. Older learners often need longer time blocks to practise their literacies.

5. When timetabling, remember that language and literacy are involved in all areas of the curriculum. This is especially important to consider with older learners for whom content-area subjects can become quite demanding.

INSIDE CLASSROOMS

LINDA LEVELY AND JOELLE NAGLE ON TIMETABLING

Tell us about your timetabling and how you fit the various components of literacy instruction into your timetable.

Linda: We're always doing a Shared Reading story and that goes in everywhere. It doesn't matter what the subject is. I schedule literacy centres, which provide an opportunity to do Guided Reading lessons. Not every day, and some weeks it doesn't even happen! Instead, we go through cycles where we are often doing Guided Reading. Right now, as I'm team-teaching, we've created a great schedule to try to fit in Guided Reading. What we do is pair up our classes for a whole-group morning activity. One teacher does this with the majority of students, while the other does Guided Reading with a small group. Then we alternate. This large-group time is also used for other things. It just allows my partner and me time to work independently with a child or a small group, and we're able to do Shared Reading, Shared Writing during that time, and to get on top of our reading **assessment**.

Joelle: Language and literacy is part of every subject, so we do a lot of reading (either independent, guided, or shared) in other subject areas—also writing for different subjects (e.g., informational, expository). Teaching language and literacy across the curriculum allows us to focus on specific knowledge and skills, such as paragraph writing, in our longer language blocks. During these blocks students can work independently or in small

---

* Cunningham, P. M., and Allington, R. L. *Classrooms that work: They can all read and write* , *5th.* (New York, NY: Longman), 2011.

groups. I can sit in on groups to help facilitate, and regroup as a whole class when necessary for explicit instruction.

How does your timetabling change throughout the year? For instance, is it possible that at the beginning of the year you don't do as much independent work?

Linda: Right. Once the children get on to a routine and are used to working in different groups or doing the different activities, then everything runs much smoother. It doesn't take long to build the children up to that level. But it definitely takes some time to build their confidence and to give them strategies and the resources in the classroom to be able to work independently.

Joelle: Again, I have to know my students before I can let them work independently. It's important to give them a lot of guidance in the beginning of the year (especially the grade 7 students who in our province are starting in a new division with different expectations). Starting a new division can be daunting for many students, and I need to allow for that transition. Short, whole-class instruction followed by small groups, then reconnecting as a whole class is a good place to start. By the end of the year, my expectation is that most students work well independently.

Just as Linda and Joelle suggest in their discussions of timetabling in the Inside Classrooms box, we recommend that time schedules be flexible, extending the time for activities when learners are obviously learning and discontinuing activities when they are not. The goal is to consistently provide optimum learning opportunities without becoming beholden to the time schedule.

Organizing Space

When Rachel arrived to her first classroom one August where she was slated to start teaching in just a few short days, she discovered it was being used as a supply closet and was full of potato chips! While this situation is extreme, educators generally have little control over the amount of space or type of equipment or furniture in their classrooms. They do, however, usually have control over how that space and furniture are arranged. The physical arrangement of the classroom reflects the goals and philosophy of educators' language and literacy programs.

Creating Spaces for Whole-Class, Small-Group, and Individual Learning Opportunities

The learners' desks in David Paul's classroom are organized with pairs sitting in rows. He uses this arrangement at the beginning of the day for large-group instruction when learners discuss the minimal-cues message on the chalkboard. On the day we described, he then asked the learners to push aside the desks in the middle of the room to create a space for them to sit on the floor while he read them the poem. He preferred this arrangement so the learners would be closer to the book and to one another. Old tennis balls rescued from the trash bin split and put on the bottom of chairs (as in the photo of Kathy Gillies's room) can facilitate the movement of furniture and reduce noise.

In some classrooms, a rug in one corner provides a place for learners to come together for whole-class discussions, to listen to the educator read, and to share what they have accomplished. This setup can be used beyond the primary years. Learners can also be organized for whole-class activities by having their desks placed together in groups, so that everyone can view the board and screen. Tables can easily replace groups of desks in this arrangement.

In David's classroom, learners work together in groups in different locations:

- They play learning games at a table placed at the perimeter of the room.
- They sit together in pairs on the floor or at adjacent desks to read books to one another.
- On the day recounted, a small group joined David at a table for a lesson using the directed reading–thinking activity.

Learning Centres

Educators may choose to set up learning centres to provide opportunities for learners to work together in groups. Some centres, such as the reading and writing centres, can be permanent. Reading centres generally include a classroom library; comfortable rugs, chairs, or cushions; and often a listening centre. When you are setting up literacy centres, you might want to consider this classic advice:

- Select materials that draw on a range of learners' funds of knowledge and interests.
- Ensure that materials are at a range of level of difficulty.
- Introduce new materials regularly to ensure continued interest.
- Involve learners in planning and managing the centres, developing rules for their use, naming them, and keeping them neat (Morrow, 1989).

Writing centres, be it for younger or older learners, can include a display area for their writing and materials for writing, including computers or tablets. Create centres that include materials for making books, magazines, **graphic novels**, comics, and the like, and be sure to place texts made by learners in a reading centre to share with others. E-texts can also be distributed and viewed electronically. Other temporary centres can be set up to correspond with learners' interests and related topics in social studies, science, and other subject areas. To maximize the literacy and cooperative learning opportunities afforded by centres, educators are advised to integrate them into the curriculum rather than being add-ons. Educators might also consider the multimodal nature of the centres. Add, for instance, art supplies and, insofar as it is possible, digital tools (e.g., tablets, computers). Often schools will allow classrooms to borrow this kind of equipment from a central bank. On the topic of where to procure resources for the classroom, see the Inside Classrooms box, where Linda and Joelle talk about setting up their first and subsequent classrooms.

INSIDE CLASSROOMS

LINDA LEVELY AND JOELLE NAGLE ON CLASSROOM SETUP

Tell us about when you first found out that you had a teaching job. What was the first thing you did with your new classroom?

Linda: I was very excited, very overwhelmed, but the overwhelmed part doesn't start sinking in until you're actually in the classroom and see what's there. My first classroom was a junior kindergarten classroom and JK had just been brought in to the province, so when I walked into the classroom there was pretty much nothing. This would have been in August, so at that point I just had to start talking to my principal and finding out what resources I had to draw on to find the basics—even furniture!

The first thing I wanted to do was create centres. I really wanted to have some definite kitchen areas and craft area, definite reading area for the kids to use, and other centres depending on where I could find the furniture to go back there. We pulled that together and I quickly learned that in your first year of teaching, you will spend a lot of your own money. I went out and bought lots of stuff that I knew I could use. That has definitely changed, which is a nice part of many years of teaching.

Joelle: I first found out I had a job the Wednesday before the school year began (and I had to move three hours away for the job). It was exciting, but a bit terrifying. Immediately I got into the room and started setting up, desk positioning, decorating, etc. As I started with 36 students in grades 7/8, there was not a lot of room for setting up centres or even a reading corner—my room was too small. It made for a lot of creative positioning of desks during specific lessons, when I wanted students in small groups.

How do you now collect resources and supplies for your classroom?

Linda: I now have accumulated a lot of supplies, and I've learned that you don't have to always put out your own money. Today I scrounge around and talk to the principal and other teachers to see what funding and money is available to buy what I need. And I've also learned that I can make a lot of things and that it does not all have to be commercial products. The students can make things. For instance, when I first started teaching I used a lot of posters and press-outs directly from books, whereas now, I make my own posters with my students to really customize them. For example, instead of buying a signal-type chart for the kids to know when I want them to look at me and to listen, I've made my own for "freeze threes": it simply says, "Freeze three. Stop, look, and listen." I've learned that when you're setting up the classroom, instead of having everything set up, I like to leave an area now for the kids to personalize and make their own, during that first week of school. So that's taken a lot of pressure off getting ready for September.

Joelle: First are the resources that I need to use as a teacher to hone my pedagogy. I get this through lots of reading; the Internet is an excellent resource, colleagues, and most

(continued)

importantly, knowing about and registering for Board professional development workshops, a chance to connect with colleagues from different areas of the Board. Supplies, depending on the school, can be limited—so I've had to gather lots on my own ... books from used bookstores to establish a library, lots of recycled paper, containers, and the like for activities, and making trips to the dollar store for other basics.

How do the students contribute to the classroom setup?

Linda: They make the border to go around the bulletin board. They bring in pictures of themselves, their drawings of themselves, work that they have done in the past, and as the year goes on, we put up work that they have just done. It's a general area for them hang up work, not a specific subject area but just for them to have as their own area. We do have our usual artwork bulletin board we change with their work. It can be seasonal or just things that we're talking about, like a science area where we will have key words, pictures, and mind maps.

Joelle: When I first started teaching, I made myself responsible for "decorating" the classroom. But, not only is this expensive, but I found it to be "flat." I'm no longer a fan of precut, prepackaged art. Now my students are responsible for their classroom. It's fairly bare in the beginning, but the walls soon are covered with student work—examples for all subjects and artwork. Also, we create student expectations lists together, rubrics as a class that are displayed, and vocabulary from all subjects are visible around the room. My hope is that it would be evident to a guest, what we are currently studying, what we have accomplished, and what my students' interests are when looking around my classroom.

Finally, further to the question of how educators create spaces for learning, teacher Alison Ogilvie has this advice, developed with grade 7 and 8 students in mind yet equally applicable across the grades:

1. Learners should know that they have entered a place where they can take risks and where they can trust their teacher to acknowledge what they know and who they are as well as appreciate their effort.

2. The educator's support should be evident, manifested in timelines, word walls, subject charts, wall text that prompts, a class code of student and teacher rights and responsibilities, and supportive quotations.

3. Areas should be available to display work and to allow learners to personalize and "manage" areas themselves.

4. The space needs to be organized so the "choreography" of the classroom can occur for both effective teaching and support.

Alison Ogilvie

5. Educators might consider including an educator–learner area that lists strategies and has exemplars, educator-made and learner-made models, and frameworks that are very much related to the learning and that can be built on throughout the year, not commercially produced.

6. Supplies need to be obvious, central, and available so the learning "flows."

7. Educators should display their passion for literacy with in-your-face choices of literature and ways of responding, strong encouragement of questioning and opinions, and many Read-Alouds.

8. Educators might consider how to make connections to the learners' lives and the larger issues around them evident in their choice of books, posters, music, technology, and creative use of space.

9. Desks should be easy to move into various configurations and learners should be taught in the first days of school to help make these moves quickly. (There's the call for those old tennis balls again!)

10. Planning needs to include reciprocal teaching and lots of opportunity for the development of metacognition.

PLANNING AND ORGANIZING FOR DIVERSITY

There is no one way to organize classrooms so that all learners' funds of knowledge are reflected and their needs and interests are met all the time. The key to effective classroom organization is flexibility in organizing materials, time, space, and learners. The challenge of organizing an effective language and literacy program becomes even greater when we consider, as discussed in Chapter 1, the diversity of learning needs and funds of knowledge in today's classrooms.

The goal of educators should be to capitalize on the learning of *all* the individuals in their classrooms (including themselves!). We have designed this book and its literacy learning framework to support educators in this endeavour. Moreover, we have maintained throughout that when learners have been evaluated as having difficulties with their literacy achievement or when learners do not fit the idea of the standard student, educators should critically appraise the context in which this **evaluation** is taking place and question whose standard is being used, why, and with what effects.

What we might always fight against is seeing literacy achievement difficulties or differences as a within-child pathology. Consider the case of **culturally and linguistically diverse (CLD)** learners. Rather than viewing struggling learners as somehow deficient and in need of a cure, we should see them as "at-promise" (Swadener & Lubeck, 1995) and recognize that our pedagogies, while not the only variable that affects learners' literacy achievement, can and do make a difference.

Though the whole of *Constructing Meaning* has been created for all learners, we would here like to highlight some considerations for learners who are particularly vulnerable in schools, learners who seem to struggle frequently with their overall literacy achievement, particularly their *reading achievement*—CLD learners and Aboriginal learners. Accordingly, below we have collated and highlighted significant considerations when you're planning for these learners. Please note that our recommendations for such learners are not exhaustive; rather, they are a starting point when considered in conjunction with the recommendations made throughout the text.

Planning for Learners Who Struggle with Literacy Achievement

While it is tempting and sometimes helpful to refer to learners in ways that characterize them overall, for example, as a "good reader" or as a "struggling writer," Flurkey's (2008) work on reading suggested educators might be further ahead by concentrating on the specific literacy practice and the context in which it is taking place. Thus an educator would say, "John is having trouble writing his reports in science class" rather than "John is a struggling writer." The former recognizes that the learner has funds of knowledge and can communicate, although specific literacy practices within specific contexts may be difficult. This approach gives educators places to go with the learner rather than dismissing the learner as wholly struggling.

1. *Start at the classroom level.* The first, and perhaps best, line of support for all learners is an effective classroom literacy program. Regardless of any label they might carry, all learners require strong pedagogical support for literacy development. Allington (2009b) reported that only about 5 to 10 percent of learners who struggle require intensive, individualized tutorial interventions. McKenna and Stahl (2009) also noted that "though research in the field of neuropsychology continues to identify possible neurological causes for reading problems … this work has not produced definitive results, nor does it show promise of 'remediating' children with reading problems in the near future" (p. 2). Finally, we concur with Dudley-Marling and Paugh (2004), who revolutionized the way educators think about struggling readers when they suggested that we reframe our questions about children: "The question for us is not, what's wrong with Jeremy? But rather, what does Jeremy need to learn in order to continue his development as a reader and what can we do to support his reading development?" (p. vi). And their reply? "The key … is careful, routine assessment that seeks to identify what struggling readers know about language and literacy as the foundation on which reading instruction will build" (p. vi).

2. *Offer instruction in multiple modes and media.* Learners benefit from the opportunity to express themselves and to allow the various dimensions of language and literacy to support each other's development. As such, create opportunities for learners to expand their language and literacy resources through exposure to and instruction in a wide range of modes and media (Heydon, 2007). Using the Language Experience Approach is one example of a practical way to do this (see Chapter 4).

3. *Provide increased reading and writing time.* In terms of print literacy, whether in the classroom or in an interventionist setting, learners need plenty of time to read and write. When learners struggle with their literacy, they can spend more time completing activities related to parts of language than reading or writing authentic materials (Heydon & Iannacci, 2008). It is through extensive reading and writing of connected texts (not isolated words or letters) that learners consolidate reading and writing strategies (Allington, 2012). As such, educators should be cautioned about the utility of worksheets (Allington & Gabriel, 2012). In planning these reading and writing opportunities, educators might also be reminded of the reciprocal nature of reading and writing with each supporting the other (Flippo, 2012).

4. *Match materials, instructional context, and learners.* In terms of reading, be sure that learners have ample opportunity to be matched with texts that they can read independently and that match the instructional context (Allington, 2012). Recall too that reading means the

ability to construct meaning; thus learners need to be able to understand what they are reading. Spending much time with texts well beyond their independent reading level likely exacerbates the difficulties of many older struggling readers (Allington, 2009b). That said, all learners can benefit from reading something of their own choosing (Allington & Gabriel, 2012). Such opportunities can easily fit into the continuum of reading support that makes up part of the multiliteracies pedagogies framework we introduced in Chapter 1.

5. *Increase time for literacy instruction.* Educators need to devote more time to explicit instruction for learners who have difficulty with their literacy achievement. Rather than providing instruction in short time blocks once or twice per week, effective instruction involves consistent, daily, targeted reading instruction (Allington, 2009b).

6. *Ensure quality instruction.* Instructional time alone is not sufficient. For instruction or intervention to be most effective, the quality of the educator is also important. Indeed, "knowledgeable teachers are what matter most for students' literacy achievement" (Donnelly et al., 2005, p. 336). Being knowledgeable means engaging in and developing an "awareness of the complexities of educational practice and an understanding of and commitment to a socially just, democratic notion of schooling" (Kincheloe, 2004, p. 50). This requires that educators be "knowledge producers" and "knowledge workers who pursue their own intellectual development" within a "community of practice" (p. 51). In other words, educators need to work together and pursue ongoing professional learning (Hibbert, Heydon, & Rich, 2008).

7. Take appropriate measures when special intervention is needed.

   a. *Intervene early.* Most educators agree that when intervention for literacy difficulties is needed, it should occur early. Learners who are behind their peers can fall further and further behind. Prolonged failure can have negative consequences for children's self-concepts, which, in turn, can negatively affect their learning. That said, no time is too late for helping learners. Older readers who struggle (e.g., grade 4 students and beyond) do, however, often require at least a "full extra hour of intensive and expert reading intervention every day" to make the gains necessary (Allington, 2009b, p. 18).

   b. *Provide individual or small-group instruction.* The most effective interventions involve instruction for individuals or small groups (no more than four or five learners) (Allington, 2009b).

   c. *Provide expert instruction.* Many learners who struggle spend their explicit literacy learning time with para-professionals. Allington (2009b) suggested that learners with the greatest needs are the ones who most need to be instructed by the most highly qualified educators available. These are most likely classroom educators. In a study of what makes the difference for readers who struggle, Frey, Allington, and Fisher (2010) found teachers taking responsibility for their own students to outperform interventions from experts outside the classroom. Ensuring expert intervention, however, also means providing "high-quality professional development to teachers of lowest-performing students" (p. 19).

   d. *Coordinate with excellent classroom instruction.* If intervention is needed, it is more effective when the learner's total program is taken into consideration. For maximum impact, learners need to receive excellent and coordinated instruction both in their classroom and in intervention programs (Allington & Baker, 2007).

e. *Evaluate interventions.* Finally, Allington (2009b) offered an evaluation rubric for educators to consider the interventions that schools offer to learners who struggle with their literacy. Based on this, some of the main questions that educators might ask of interventions are these: To what extent is the intervention small group or one-to-one? To what extent are texts matched to learners rather than standard, allow learner choice in text selection, and offer interesting choices? To what extent does the intervention increase the reading volume—with triple being optimal? To what extent does the intervention focus on meaning and metacognition development as opposed to isolated skills development? To what extent is the intervention coordinated with classroom curriculum? To what extent is the learner assessed in ways that are "frequent and full" (p. 176)?

Planning for Culturally and Linguistically Diverse Learners

1. *Create opportunities for immersion, use, and feedback.* Culture and communication are closely linked, so learning a new language also involves learning a new culture (Palmer, Chen, Chang, & Leclere, 2006). Educators must thus ensure that CLD learners have abundant exposure to expert language users within context, opportunities to use the language, and feedback as to how well they are approximating the model (Black, 2005). The multiliteracies pedagogies described throughout *Constructing Meaning* are a way of achieving these ends, particularly if educators are alert to the importance of explicit "modelling of skills, strategies, and new content" (Aceves & Orosco, 2014) within these pedagogies.

2. *Organize your teaching to be culturally sensitive.* In keeping with the responsive, asset-oriented pedagogical frame in *Constructing Meaning*, which is rationalized through a recognition of the inextricable link between language, literacy, culture, and identity, educators should plan for *culturally responsive teaching*. Gay (2010) defined this type of teaching as "using the cultural knowledge, prior experiences, frames of reference, and performance styles" of CLD learners "to make learning encounters more relevant to and affective for them" (p. 31). Such teaching is a way of "improving achievement by teaching diverse students through their own cultural filters" (pp. 49–50). Accessing and building upon funds of knowledge and children's interests is a mainstay of *Constructing Meaning* and key to culturally responsive teaching.

3. *Be sensitive to language exposure and put language in context.* Classic research suggests that acquisition of a new language may be the result of **comprehensible input**, that is, exposure to the new language that is only slightly above where the learner already is (Krashen, 1982). As this is not always possible for an educator in a classroom, educators must strive to present materials in different ways and provide different opportunities to encourage language acquisition (Brown, 2007). The use of play, drama, poetry, visual art, and music within the classroom can offer educators diverse ways in helping CLD learners increase their linguistic competence, cultural understanding, and analytical thinking skills. Play is

especially important as it helps CLD learners "establish bonds of friendship" (Silver, 1999, p. 66); exhibit a sense of confidence that might not be "otherwise evident" (p. 68); develop a sense of autonomy (Little, 2007); and develop expressive and receptive communication (Burke, 2010). Note that even grade 8 students can engage in literacy learning through play (Nagle, 2009).

4. *Create a sense of safety.* Educators must remember that CLD learners might be dealing with a host of stresses that can affect their learning. For instance, many learners, if they have just moved to a new country, may be feeling fear, confusion, and alienation, including grieving for a lost homeland and culture (Gonzalez-Ramos & Sanchez-Nester, 2001). Consequently, educators need to be patient with learners and allow them to participate in their own time and through structured choice in classroom activities (Rowsell, 2006). Educators might give learners the chance to prepare or rehearse contributions before they perform them in a whole-class setting and offer them choice over activities and texts. In this way, learners may have fewer unknowns and be able to better connect with, for instance, texts, and have a degree of control over the topic (Alford, 2001). Educators might also be attuned to the fine balance between sheltering CLD learners when they need some extra support but not underestimating their content-area knowledge and potential (Gichuru, 2013). This last point speaks to the importance of having appropriate expectations of learners (Cambourne, 2000/2001) and seeing all learners as at-promise.

5. *Respect and build on CLD learners' funds of knowledge, including first languages.* CLD learners are not working from a deficit. They come to school with a knowledge and skills that can facilitate their English language acquisition and contribute to the classroom community. A strong first language better ensures an easier acquisition of a second language (e.g., Cummins, 2001). Educators can build on learners' first languages by encouraging them to use their first language and compare it to the new language, and by using multilingual bulletin boards and texts. As there is considerable overlap or interdependence across languages (Cummins, 2000), it can be helpful for learners to have access to texts in their first language within the classroom. It is sometimes beneficial for learners to be able to read the text in that language prior to reading the English text; at other times, it is useful for them to be able to read the text in their first language as a follow-up activity to review the information from the English text. Encouraging families to continue supporting their children in literacies in their first language is also an excellent idea. Educators too might try to understand the wide range of literacies that learners may practise in the home and capitalize on these (Gregory, 2008). They need not worry that using more than one language at a time will confuse learners. If a "program is effective in continuing to develop students' academic skills in both languages, no cognitive confusion or handicap will result; in fact, students may benefit in subtle ways from access to two linguistic systems" (Cummins, 2000, p. 39). Baker (2006) also contended that "bilingualism is more likely to lead to cognitive advantages than disadvantages" (p. 205).

6. *Adjust assessment to reflect the unique language and literacy acquisition of CLD learners.* Different dimensions of language and literacy can develop at different times in learners. CLD learners, it is not uncommon for print literacy to develop before oral language (Watts-Taffe & Truscott, 2000). Many CLD learners go through a normal period of silence where they are taking in what is going on around them. Burke (2010) recommended respecting

this silence "as a time when the students are practising listening skills and gaining confidence in learning about language" (p. 99). Some educators wrongly assume that this silent period is a problem (Iannacci, 2008b), and CLD learners are at a high risk of being misdiagnosed and overrepresented when they are referred for evaluation of possible disability (Spinelli, 2006; Venn, 2007). Educators, therefore, need to have an excellent grasp of second language acquisition before jumping to the conclusion that something is wrong with a learner or to consult experts in second language acquisition if they are unsure of a learner's development. Most schools have ESL teachers or consultants through the school district.

7. *Recognize the different language demands a situation places on learners.* As we described in Chapter 1, context-specific social language (e.g., what happens on the playground and at the water fountain) is usually acquired more quickly than academic language (e.g., what learners need to understand content lessons). The first can develop in two years; the second may need five to seven years to develop (e.g., Cummins, 2000). The **basic interpersonal communication skills (BICS)** and **cognitive academic language proficiency (CALP)** distinction here should be used by educators as a rough guide in their consideration of the language demands a situation is placing on a learner. It should not, however, be thought of as a "universal" or "complete theory" that is used in absolute terms to determine when a particular form of language and literacy should be taught (Baker, 2006, p. 175). Educators may do well to consider BICS/CALP as a reminder to be patient with learning and provide necessary scaffolding for learners' content-area literacy. Connecting learners' background knowledge and experiences with new content can also assist with this (Ruiz, Vargas, & Beltran, 2002).

Planning for Aboriginal Learners

The literacy education framework of *Constructing Meaning* has equally been created with the needs of Aboriginal learners in mind. We here use the term *Aboriginal* to refer to these learners, do so knowing that it is not an unproblematic term. We choose it, however, as *Aboriginal* is a commonly used term that is likely to be well-understood by readers of *Constructing Meaning*. Readers should know that it is a legal term that the Government of Canada defines this way: "Aboriginal peoples" is a collective name for the original peoples of North America and their descendants. The Canadian constitution recognizes three groups of Aboriginal people: First Nations, Métis, and Inuit. These are three distinct peoples with unique histories, languages, cultural practices, and spiritual beliefs (Aboriginal Affairs and Northern Development Canada, 2013).

This definition highlights the diversity of peoples who are subsumed beneath one signifier, and this is a diversity that we urge educators to recognize. In using the term, we also attempt to be aware of what it cannot convey. In expressing their preference for the term *Indigenous*, Donald and Krahn (2014), for example, said,

> The term Indigenous … is a better expression of the deep-rooted connectivity of the people to their home territories than other possible names (e.g., Aboriginal, status Indian) derived more directly from colonial impositions and associated identity politics. In using the term with these understandings, we intend to bring emphasis to the point that Indigenous peoples in Canada have unique relationships with their lands and the various entities that comprise them due to

the fact that they are indigenous to those territories; they have not come from another place. Their understandings of who they are as distinct peoples are derived from creation stories set in the lands that they call home. (p. 125)

We use the term *Aboriginal* with an eye to the situated nature of people's languages and literacies; their connection to history, culture, time, and place; and implications for identity. Next, we suggest some considerations that educators might add to the multiliteracies pedagogies we detail in the pages of *Constructing Meaning*.

The literacy education needs of Aboriginal learners are an essential part of an urgent conversation, given that these learners, even in situations where they are in the numeric majority in schools, may not have their funds of knowledge recognized and can thus be "minoritized" (Shields, Bishop, & Mazawi, 2005). For this reason and others, such learners can be vulnerable in schools.

For instance, most Aboriginal youth do not graduate from high school (Chiefs Assembly on Education, 2012). Many reasons have been offered in the education literature and mainstream media. Undoubtedly, poverty is a key issue (e.g., Walker-Dalhouse & Risko, 2008), but so is the legacy of the residential school system (e.g., Castellano, Archibald, & DeGagné, 2008), the effects of colonization (e.g., Widdowson & Howard, 2013), the potential mismatch between dominant definitions and forms of literacy and Aboriginal ways of communicating (e.g., Antone, 2003), and ineffective pedagogies (Rose, 2015). The relationship between English and Aboriginal languages must also be considered. The residential school system created almost perfect conditions for English to become a "killer language" (Skutnabb-Kangas, 2000), that is, a language that replaces other languages. Thus there may be tension between Aboriginal and English languages.

Educators must remember that Aboriginal languages are critical to "developing and consolidating culturally cohesive identity with links to the land, to traditional knowledge and to Elders" (Ball, 2007, p. 13). This is so much the case that a report from a task force on Aboriginal language and cultures in Canada summarized its consultations with Aboriginal people in this way: "Many stated that the ability to speak one's own language helps people to understand who they are in relation to themselves, their families, and their communities, and to Creation itself" (Canadian Heritage, cited in Ball, 2007, p. 13). Efforts for language revitalization are well under way in many Aboriginal communities across Canada (e.g., Government of the Northwest Territories, n.d.), yet many students learn their Aboriginal language as a second rather than as a first language (Ball, 2007) and we are living in an era of Indigenous language devastation in Canada (Ball & McIvor, 2013). Educators of Aboriginal learners in schools where English is the medium of instruction must be mindful to help learners add English to their linguistic repertoire rather than trading one language for another (Cummins, 1994).

While there is no research-based consensus "about the effects of promotion, prevention and early intervention strategies to improve Aboriginal children's language and literacy development" (Ball, 2007, p. 29), there have been attempts to redress the situation just described. Elders and educators from a variety of Canadian provinces and territories, for instance, produced a curriculum to promote "Aboriginal" perspectives (Western Canadian Protocol for Collaboration in Basic Education, 2001). The heterogeneity of Aboriginal peoples in Canada precludes an Aboriginal perspective, yet the perspective produced in this protocol reflects a shared principle that survival is dependent upon respectful and spiritual relationships with oneself, other people, and the natural world. Educators can draw on documents such as this one, as well as the principles of other documents developed expressly by and for educators of Aboriginal learners, to help them with their planning.

The First Nations and Métis Education branch of Saskatchewan Learning has a website with resources such as *Aboriginal Languages: A Curriculum Guide for Kindergarten to Grade 12* (1994). The principles of this document refer to the acquisition of Aboriginal languages, and are also helpful to our consideration of language and literacy acquisition in general:

• Second language acquisition must occur as holistically as possible.

• Language is used for meaningful purposes.

• The tenets of language acquisition are represented in the communicative approach and thematic base.

• The curriculum is resource based.

• Language acquisition and communicative competence is supported by an anxiety-free environment.

• The teacher's role is one of observer, adapter, coordinator, facilitator, and motivator.

• Assessment and evaluation strategies and techniques take into account the gradual and on-going nature of language acquisition: communicative competence and linguistic competence.*

Canadian researcher Jessica Ball (2007) echoed the need for holism, culturally appropriate practices, and collaborative research and practice in language and literacy education. She maintained that perhaps multiliteracies pedagogy could be useful in conceptualizing the literacy practices of and education for Aboriginal children. Highlighting the multiple modes and media through which people can communicate and the social nature of literacy can account for Aboriginal literacy practices that may be missed by more narrow definitions of literacy. Furthermore, pedagogies to support multiliteracies may be particularly important with reference to supporting Aboriginal parents' and Elders' goals for children's development, which often encompass learning to "read" the signs and symbols on the land in order to subsist on the land, to regulate community life according to changes of seasons, and so on.

Individual educators may not be able to solve large socio-political problems such as the underfunding of Aboriginal education or language loss, but there is evidence that educators can empower or disempower specific learners, and it is possible for educators to create language and literacy learning opportunities and identity options in their classrooms (e.g., Cummins, 2005). Thus apart from the recommendations just made, educators who do not share the same cultural and/or linguistic background as their Aboriginal students might also consider acting on these ideas:

• Recall that Aboriginal peoples are made up of distinct cultural groups with their own languages, practices, and worldviews; thus, generalizations should not be made.

• Learn about the history and current reality of Aboriginal communities and schools (Kavanagh, 2006).

---

* Saskatchewan Education. *Aboriginal Languages: A Curriculum Guide for Kindergarten to Grade 12.* (Regina, SK: Saskatchewan Education, Training and Employment), 1994, pp. 3–4.

- Insofar as possible, gain an understanding of the specific history and culture of the Aboriginal learners one is working with.

- "Reach out to parents [and families] as much as you can" (Kavanagh, 2006, p. 9).

- Demonstrate your "commitment to incorporating the language and culture into [your] classrooms" but do so "sensitively" as "each community has its own protocols for appropriately and respectfully using the language and culture, and there are specific rules regarding who can share the community's traditional knowledge" (Kavanagh, 2006, p. 27).

- Question what one takes to be fact (Starnes, 2006).

- Create teaching materials that are culturally appropriate.

- Be prepared for measured success.

- "Push" for professional learning opportunities (Starnes, 2006, p. 390).

- Draw on local knowledge wherever possible (Castagno & McKinley, 2012).

- If working in an Aboriginal community, "ask to be introduced to the community staff, including the Band receptionist, Band manager, accounting staff, social development, and health staff. Show an interest in the community outside of the school" (Kavanagh, 2006, p. 8) and "recognize and be proactive in addressing potential challenges. For example, avoid feeling isolated" or feeling like you must do everything on your own. Contact school district experts or attend Aboriginal education group–sponsored conferences and workshops to build a network of colleagues. "Also, try to build relationships with neighbouring public school staff to share ideas and resources" (Kavanagh, 2006, p. 27) and find mentors (Starnes, 2006).

ORGANIZING FOR FAMILIES AS PARTNERS

As we have been emphasizing, learners of all ages come to school with particular funds of knowledge, interests, and values already in place, and the intersections between in- and out-of-school literacies are where rich learning opportunities and identity options might reside. To underscore the importance, therefore, of home-community-school connections, we have here included a section on organizing for families as partners in learning.

The International Reading Association recommends that educators implement effective strategies to include parents as partners in the literacy development of their children (Armbruster & Osborn, 2002). By so doing, it recognizes that school success begins at home and that families are the first and most important people in the education of their children. Research shows that family involvement of almost any kind is positively related to school achievement in general and that there is a strong relationship between a child's home environment and success in learning to read and write at school (e.g., Purcell-Gates et al., 2004).

We would like to expand the notion of parents as partners to include family members as partners. We use the term *family* instead of *parent* to indicate that children are raised by a diversity of people, not just by a mother, a father, or two parents. In fact, children's literacy development can be positively affected by a range of people in the community (Gregory, Long, & Volk, 2004). What seems to make an individual's influence particularly significant is if the child values that individual (Hicks, 2002).

Home–family partnerships can be tricky as traditionally information flows from educator and school to families with the goal of the communication being to change the family (e.g., educators telling families that they need to read at home to their children). Joan Wink (2011) referred to this as the "'doin'-it-to-'em" model for parental involvement. Alternatively, educators can attempt to construct school–family partnerships that follow an alternative "doin'-it-with-'em" structure where all parties share in responsibilities and information, and work toward optimum opportunities for learners.

Next, we offer some general principles and practices that might assist in the building of partnerships.

Building Partnerships with Families

One way to promote family involvement is by supporting families to engage in literacy activities at home that complement school literacy (and vice versa). Educators should think of this as more than mere homework. Be careful that any language and literacy work that you ask a learner and/or family to complete is meaningful and authentic; it must truly complement the literacy learning goals of the learner. Homework should never be done just for its own sake, and educators must be vigilant that homework not place undue expectations or stress on the home and learners. When thinking about how to support families and learners at home, educators can, for instance, do the following:

- Encourage families to read to and with their children and to talk about texts being read. Educators can accomplish this by informing families of the importance of independent and shared reading and by encouraging them to help their children get a library card and use their local public library. Library use, however, might not "just happen"; thus, schools can introduce learners first to public libraries and teach them how to use their services. This initiative might be equally important for older and younger learners. It would be a mistake to take for granted that older learners have the means (including the knowledge) for using public literacy resources such as libraries. Reaching out to families and providing them with the resources to do what schools ask of them is crucial.

- Provide materials and methods for families to use with learners. Book bags for home are one way of doing this (Christie, Enz, & Vukelich, 2003). With younger children each bag can contain three or four books and informal, interactive activities for extending children's language and literacy abilities. Each bag may also contain two response journals (one for the child and one for the family). With older learners this might look like a single book or alternative shorter text such as a magazine or newspaper article and journal. For families that speak a language other than English, educators might include a book on tape to accompany the print text and a tape recorder. Each bag includes an inventory so families and learners can ensure that they return everything in the bag. A word of caution: In her own teaching, Rachel learned that some families can find the book bag stressful, as they worry that if something is lost they will not be able to pay to replace it. Educators need to expect a certain amount of loss and can help to defray some of the inconvenience and cost of this by working with school administration to budget for extra books, procuring multiple copies of books, using used books, and sending home paper *take-home books* that are educator, child, or publisher made.

- Build bridges between home and school literacy by including books in the bag from the family's culture, by having learners interview older relatives in families with a strong oral tradition, and by inviting family members to the classroom to share their literacy traditions (Armbruster & Osborn, 2002).

- Set up a homework club or see whether there are homework clubs in the community to provide support to learners when families may be unable to help with homework because of academic challenges, shift work, and so on.

- Where resources allow, consider sending home cameras or other technologies to allow learners to document what is of import to them, return it to school, and allow this to inform the literacy curriculum (e.g., Heydon & Rowsell, in press).

- Ensure that when needed you call upon translation services. Most school districts provide this service as they understand its critical importance.

Another way educators can encourage involvement of families is by communicating with them about language and literacy instruction in their classroom. Family–teacher conferences and open houses are common ways to do this, but it is better to use the following strategies to keep families informed throughout the year:

- Invite families into the classroom as observers, guest speakers, and volunteers.

- Send home letters, newsletters, and students' work. Along with samples of work, educators send an explanation of the nature of the assignment and what it tells about the learner's school progress. Some educators enjoy sending home a summer letter to the learners who will be entering their classrooms in the fall. Doing this welcomes the learners and defrays some beginning-of-school jitters.

- Call or visit families. It is most effective to do this if, at least some of the time, the educator plans to talk about what the learner does well at school (Armbruster & Osborn, 2002).

- Educators also need to see families as curricular informants—that is, as people who have some input into the curriculum. Making communication and resource sharing reciprocal is one way to accumulate the information necessary to accomplish this.

SUMMARY

No single organizational or pedagogical structure is best for all classrooms. Instead, when considering how to organize learners, time, space, and materials, educators must use their professional discernment honed through a survey of the research, a strong theoretical grounding, and practical wisdom (e.g., Kinsella & Pitman, 2012) to take into account the situated nature of their teaching so that they can plan from their learners' funds of knowledge, interests, and the like. Such discernment is cultivated over a career, and *Constructing Meaning*'s multiliteracies pedagogies are offered as support for educators to achieve the goals of offering all learners expanded literacy learning and identity options.

continued

SELECTED PROFESSIONAL RESOURCES

Allington, R. L., & MGill-Franzen, A. (Eds.). (2013). *Summer reading: Closing the rich/ poor reading achievement gap.* New York, NY, & Newark, DE: Teachers College Press & International Reading Association.

Saying goodbye to learners in the summer is not only difficult for educators, but it can put some children's reading achievement in jeopardy. Based on research that suggests 80 percent of the rich/ poor reading achievement gap in the United States occurs through summer reading loss, this little, highly readable book highlights real-world interventions to close the achievement gap.

Comber, B., & Kamler, B. (Eds.). (2005). *Turn-around pedagogies: Literacy interventions for at-risk students.* Newton, Australia: Primary English Teaching Association.

While it is getting a little long in the tooth, this friendly book remains highly relevant and feels like peeking into your next-door neighbour's classroom. It is written by teachers for teachers, and describes in the first person a special literacy-related professional learning program where newer and more established teachers paired up to see what they could learn together about creating programs that could support the students they found hard to reach.

Ontario Ministry of Education and Training. (n.d.). *Many roots, many voices: Supporting English language learners in every classroom. A practical guide for Ontario educators.* Toronto, ON: Author. Retrieved from http://www.edu.gov.on.ca/eng/document/manyroots/ manyroots.pdf

Ontario Ministry of Education and Training. (2007). *English language learners ESL and ELD programs and services: Policies and procedures for Ontario elementary and secondary schools, kindergarten to Grade 12.* Toronto, ON: Queen's Printer for Ontario. Retrieved from http://www.edu.gov.on.ca/eng/document/esleldprograms/esleldprograms.pdf

Both of these guides offer important information to help teachers assess, plan for, and understand English language learners. These are excellent companions for any curriculum document.

CHAPTER THREE

Language Development and Oracy

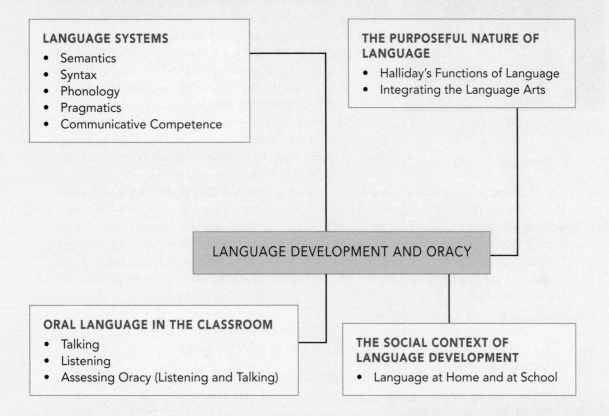

LANGUAGE SYSTEMS

- Semantics
- Syntax
- Phonology
- Pragmatics
- Communicative Competence

THE PURPOSEFUL NATURE OF LANGUAGE

- Halliday's Functions of Language
- Integrating the Language Arts

LANGUAGE DEVELOPMENT AND ORACY

ORAL LANGUAGE IN THE CLASSROOM

- Talking
- Listening
- Assessing Oracy (Listening and Talking)

THE SOCIAL CONTEXT OF LANGUAGE DEVELOPMENT

- Language at Home and at School

Julie Gellner

Julie Gellner and Anne Gordon teach in elementary schools in Alberta. Both are highly experienced educators and are deeply committed to actively engaging their students in language and literacy experiences. Both educators are aware that oral language lays the foundation for literacy learning. Julie teaches grade 4 and provides an environment where students learn through investigation, observation, and discussion. Learners are guided to develop interests in real-world topics. Anne teaches grade 2 and aims to provide learning experiences that are "memorable," not just "memorized." Learners often work cooperatively on open-ended tasks. Both Julie and Anne value talk in their classrooms and understand the role oral language plays in thinking and learning.

As they strive to help learners express themselves clearly and in appropriate language, Anne and Julie, like many educators, find themselves asking questions about language and also about how children learn and develop their oral language competencies throughout their years of schooling.

This chapter describes the basic elements of language and how children learn to construct meaning through language. Educators model appropriate language in their interactions with learners, and they understand that, in school, learners do two major things in their language development: they continue to learn and refine their language abilities, both written and spoken, and they learn how to use language in order to learn. These are two of the key things educators like Anne and Julie keep in mind when developing learning activities for their students. □

LANGUAGE SYSTEMS

As adults, we generally don't remember the elements of language we learned as children, but we teach language to our own children without having any training in how to do it, and usually without a conscious awareness that we're teaching it. We talk to children, listen to them, play with them, read and tell stories to them, and they seem to learn language without much effort or direct teaching. What is it that children learn and that adults take for granted?

Linguists describe language in terms of four systems: **semantics**, **syntax**, **phonology**, and **pragmatics** (often referred to as **cuing systems** when we are teaching reading). Together, these four systems make communication possible as we read, write, listen, and talk. In various chapters of this book, we address the phonological system

Anne Gordon

because children apply phonemic and phonics skills in order to decode and encode print when learning to read and write. In other chapters we include sections on affixes, inflectional endings, compound words, grammar, punctuation, capitalization, and sentence structure, which are all aspects of the syntactic system. Semantics, the meaning system of the language, permeates all of the language arts activities we describe in this book; reading, writing, listening, speaking, viewing, and representing are all essentially about communicating and constructing meaning.

The ability to manipulate the basic language elements of semantics, syntax, phonology, and pragmatics with relative ease and fluency can be called "native-like" speech. It is part of what enables speakers to understand the difference between "That mom is awesome" and "That, Mom, is awesome." It's what helps to create the humour in children's books such as *Eats, Shoots and Leaves: Why, Commas Really Do Make a Difference!* by Lynne Truss. Numerous cultural, social, and contextual factors influence language ability. Although all of the language systems are interrelated, for clarity we discuss them independently here.

Semantics

Semantics (from the Greek word *semantikos*, which means "giving signs," or "signifying") refers to the meanings that are expressed in a language or code (see Table 3.1). The meaning component of language consists mainly of vocabulary. From birth to age six, children learn an average of 21 new words a day, reaching a grand total of 6000 to 7000 root word meanings by the end of grade 2. From that time on, they learn about 1000 word meanings a year during the elementary grades (Biemiller, 2006). The first words children speak are usually labels for items in their environment and are items the child acts on, such as *cookie, milk, kitty, ball, sock,* and *daddy*. Through the years, children learn new words from talking with their caregivers and from listening to the world around them: conversations, stories, books, television, and,

TABLE 3.1 **SEMANTICS**

Language System: Semantics	Related Examples	Classroom Application
• the meaning component of language • synonyms (s) • antonyms (a) • homonyms (h) • metaphors (m) and similes (s)	chips (British)/fries (North American) happy/contented (s) happy/unhappy (a) so/sew (h), saw (viewed)/saw (cutting implement) (h) a glaring error (m) as brave as a lion (s)	All activities that develop children's vocabulary • word walls • words from different subject areas such as mathematics, science, social studies, music, art, and technology • word games • activities that encourage the use of a dictionary or thesaurus • connections made to words and their meanings in reading and writing

of course, their peers. In school they learn new words in social studies, physical education, mathematics, technology, and many other areas. As children get older, vocabulary development depends increasingly on their reading (McKeown & Curtis, 1987).

Everyone has both a receptive and an expressive vocabulary. The receptive vocabulary is generally much larger than the expressive vocabulary—we can understand many more words than we use in speaking and writing. New vocabulary items generally enter our expressive vocabularies slowly, for we need to feel confident about the meaning and context of new words before we use them with ease in our oral or written language. Once a word is comfortably fixed in our speaking vocabulary, we're more likely to use it in writing, where it becomes more permanent.

Educators are aware that vocabulary develops most effectively when learners are engaged in activities that stretch them to say new things in new ways. Reflective practitioners such as Julie Gellner and Anne Gordon know that vocabulary cannot be taught effectively through word lists and definitions because new words are best learned through their meaningful use. Thus, educators play an important role in vocabulary development through classroom talk and through drawing their students' attention to new words. They also help learners by showing them how to use a dictionary to check the meanings of words and to cross-check the meanings against the context in which the words are used. A recommended resource for teachers is the book *Creating Robust Vocabulary*, by Beck, McKeown, and Kucan (2008).

Word meanings are dynamic rather than static formations and they change over time. We've seen this especially in computer technology, where words such as *mouse* and *virus* have taken on new connotations. Similarly, children and young adults have their own language (or slang) in which certain words attain powerful meanings before becoming outdated.

Semantics is, however, more than simply the words and phrases we learn and use. Children quickly learn that words can have more than one meaning. They learn that it is not appropriate to use some words in certain contexts, and using the right word in the right context is critical. So, how do we know the meaning of a word? How do we know which word to use?

The meaning of a word is dependent on who is using it and the context in which the word is used. It's not so much that a word has a specific meaning, but that people *give* meaning to words. We also learn that, over time, words change their meanings. Take the many meanings and uses of *hit*. The word can be used to denote a person striking an object, such as in hitting a ball with a bat. It can also be used to denote the target of a crime, as in making a hit. We talk about the number of hits received by a website. There are hit movies and music. A person can be hit by a terrible illness, can hit the right tone in a speech, or can hit the bottle. A drug injection can be termed a hit, and one can be involved in a hit-and-run. One can hit back, hit up, hit below the belt, hit for six, hit the headlines, hit the hay, hit it off, be hit-or-miss, hit the roof, hit home, or be a hit man (and presumably a hit woman).

Learners must quickly become sophisticated in their use of words and in their understandings of both the denotative meanings of words and the connotative meanings (the literal and the figurative). They learn about words that sound alike and words that have similar meanings. They learn about idioms, metaphors, similes, root words, and affixes (see Classroom Activity 3.1). Learning words (and learning language in general) is a lifelong task. We continue to learn language because new language forms appear in our culture around us on a regular basis. Popular culture and social media play a huge role in our changing language, so educators, in particular, must be "tuned in."

CLASSROOM ACTIVITY 3.1

When teachers teach mini-lessons on vocabulary, homonyms, synonyms, antonyms, metaphors, and similes, they are teaching the semantic system of language. These features of language are most effectively taught in the context of the six language arts.

A whole-class mini-lesson during the "writing block" might invite learners to consider alternatives to the word *said* when writing dialogue. Learners can browse through a novel or picture book to find out how authors use synonyms for the word *said* in order to make the story more engaging. After the reading event, they can brainstorm a list of these words, while the teacher lists them on chart paper or a SMART Board. Learners can then revisit their writing and begin to change repetitive words they have used in their written dialogue, focusing particularly on *said*.

Syntax

The syntactic system is the way language is organized, the way words are strung together to create meaning (see Table 3.2). The basic unit in syntax is the sentence. Every language has its own syntax. In English, syntax and word order are almost synonymous: a change in the word order of a sentence almost always has an effect on meaning—sometimes minimally, sometimes drastically. Often a similar meaning is conveyed by two sentences that have different structures, as in "The child collected the books" and "The books were collected by the child." Rarely,

TABLE 3.2 **SYNTAX**

Language System: Syntax	Related Examples	Classroom Application
• The basic unit in syntax is the sentence.	"The dog bit the man."	• Encouraging children to use simple, compound, and complex sentences in their writing
• The way words are strung together to make meaning.	"The dog bit the man" is not the same as "The man bit the dog."	• Activities that promote an exploration of affixes.
• The basic element of morphology. (*Morphemes* are the building blocks of meaning and the smallest meaning units of language.)	Free morphemes (e.g., "ball," "girl," "play") Bound morphemes: *suffixes* (e.g., -ed, -er); *prefixes* (e.g., *anti-* as in "antiseptic")	• Activities that engage children in sentence combining and sentence building. There are many ways to combine these four kernel sentences: "The puppy is black."
• Compound words.	"housefly" (house + fly)	"The puppy barked at the rabbit."
• English syntax is mainly about word order.	"The I saw kitten the only garden in" is meaningless.	"The puppy belongs to Janet." "Janet lives on Third Street." Example: "The puppy belonging to Janet, who lives on Third Street, barked at the rabbit."

however, do changes in syntax have *no* effect on meaning. To illustrate the role of syntax, take the sentence "I saw the kitten in the garden" and insert the word *only* at various points throughout to see the major shifts in meaning. Because changes in syntax affect meaning, the rules for ordering words in English are extremely important. In K to 8 classrooms, syntax is usually taught under the heading of **grammar**. Here we refer to the rules that govern how words are combined to form sentences, not analyzing parts of speech.

As learners mature, they have a growing capacity to embed more and more meaning into each sentence they speak or write by using clauses and phrases, making sentences more compact and yet richer in meaning. The result is a more fluent language style as well as a more economical way of expressing meaning—in short, a more mature form of syntax. Classroom Activity 3.2 shows examples of sentence combining.

A basic element of the meaning system of language is its **morphology**. *Morphemes*, the building blocks of meaning, are the smallest meaning units of language. Helping to create meaning within words and sentences, they consist of bases (root words), suffixes, and prefixes. The morphology of our language is extremely complex, yet individuals learn this aspect of language at the same time as they learn the other systems that make up language.

Much of the meaning of a language has to be learned in the context of its use. For example, native-like speakers learn compound words (e.g., *fireworks*), two separate words that together create a new, single meaning. They know they can say that a plate broke or a briefcase handle broke, but they would not say that a sweater or a newspaper broke. These are examples of the colloquial restrictions that native-like speakers learn. All of it is part of our syntactic knowledge.

Although the words grammar and syntax are frequently used interchangeably, they do have different definitions. *Syntax* is a term linguists use to describe how human beings organize their language structures. *Grammar* is a term educators have traditionally used to define a prescriptive set of rules. Syntax and grammar are both derived from the spoken language, but when grammar is taught in school, it usually pertains to writing. Learners need to know the

CLASSROOM ACTIVITY 3.2

Sentence-combining and sentence-building activities are often helpful to learners because they demonstrate how language can be manipulated, and they provide options in constructing sentences. They are also frequently enjoyable and playful activities with no right or wrong answers—just many alternatives.

A whole-class mini-lesson on sentence building might start with just three words: *bears, eat,* and *berries*. From these three words, what sentence can learners build? If they add one more word, what might it be? Add one more word, and so on. Learners especially enjoy seeing the sentence variations written on the board and the ever-lengthening sentences they create. Playing with language in this way encourages learners to be creative in their use of language, and it demonstrates how generative the English language is. Learners might create "Black bears eat juicy red berries early in the morning." Or, "Could one black bear eat all the berries I have in my pail?"

difference between what is acceptable or appropriate and what is considered poor grammar. Unacceptable grammar in spoken language is reflected in such commonly used sentences as "I seen the girl go in the store" and "I should of went earlier." The labels describing parts of speech (such as nouns, adjectives, and adverbs) are also helpful to learners because they enable educators and learners to talk about language and how we use it, especially in the context of writing workshops. Grammar is rarely studied as a set of rules in isolation today, however. We are far more interested in people being able to use these rules in their speech and writing rather than in identifying them. This aspect of language teaching and learning is dealt with in later chapters, notably in Chapter 10.

Phonology

The phonology of a language is its sound system (see Table 3.3). Every language has a set of sounds that enables its users to communicate meaning. The smallest units of sound in a language are *phonemes*. The English language has between 45 and 52 different phonemes (depending on the classification system and dialect). When the phonology of a language is transcribed into symbols, it is referred to as the **graphophonic** system. In English, these sounds are represented by the 26 letters of the alphabet. Understanding the sound–symbol relationship is one key learning children accomplish in their literacy development. The manipulation of the graphophonic system forms the basis for children's reading and writing development in the primary years. It is important to note that the phonological system (sound system) and the orthographic system (written system) are two distinct systems of language, each with its own conventions. To complicate the situation even more, English is a morphophonemic language, and English words do not always reflect their sounds in writing: they often reflect their morphological structure instead (Bowers & Cooke, 2012). This is just one reason why learning to read and write in English is a complex undertaking, especially where spelling is concerned.

Literacy educators pay special attention to phonics, phonetics, phonemes, phonemic awareness, and phonological awareness. These are critical elements in the teaching of reading. Each term is described in more detail in Chapter 4.

TABLE 3.3 **PHONOLOGY**

Language System: Phonology	Related Examples	Classroom Application
• The sound system of language. • The smallest unit of sound is known as a *phoneme*. • The graphophonic system refers to the written symbols that represent the phonology of a language.	The English language has between 45 and 52 phonemes—for example, short /o/ as in "cot." The 26 letters of the alphabet.	• Developing students' phonemic awareness to help them understand that speech is composed of individual sounds. • Teaching the decoding of words. • Teaching syllabication. • Teaching spelling rules.

Pragmatics

Pragmatics (see Table 3.4) deals with the social aspects of language use in context. The way we write or speak varies according to our purpose and audience, and it also varies across social classes, ethnic groups, and geographic regions, giving rise to what we know as **dialects**. Pragmatics is a systematic way of explaining this language use. It's about the factors that govern our choices of language in social interaction, and the effects of those choices on other people. It's really about the implied meaning behind the words, and how people can understand those meanings without ambiguity. For example, when a person says, "The phone is ringing," it is often a request for someone else to answer it, not simply a statement of fact. The speaker's intent is at issue. Speech act theory, within the field of pragmatics, explains some of those processes. For example, when we speak or write, we can make things happen; we can ask, invite, promise, declare, order, threaten, humiliate, or amuse. These are speech acts.

TABLE 3.4 **PRAGMATICS**

The Language System: Pragmatics	Related Examples	Social Context of Examples	Classroom Application
• Explores the ways in which speakers use language in context. • Addresses the fact that language is always used in a social context. • Refers to a range of registers and styles that help people function appropriately in a wide range of situations.	"That needs to go here." (Gestures are used and speaker looks at conversational partner.) "Wanna go for a coffee?" "You are invited to attend a banquet in honour of ..." "I sentence you to three years ..." "Please, please, Mom, I really want that one." "Ms. Shariff, we really need to talk about Bobbi's progress in math." "Ladies and gentlemen, it's truly a pleasure to ..." "Oilers Burned by Flames"	In the office when directing furniture movers to place a new filing cabinet. Meeting a friend in the street on the weekend. Receiving a written invitation to a formal celebratory event. Formal words uttered in a court of law. Child to parent while shopping. Teacher speaking to parent. Formal speech made at a graduation celebration. Headline in newspaper.	• Activities that address the functional nature of language—the purpose for using the language. • Activities that address the range of written and oral language registers needed to meet the various purposes for writing and speaking. • Activities helping children to reflect on the use of dialogue in reading materials • Using dialogue in writing. • Developing an oral presentation (book talk, sharing time, science project, dramatization). • Creating titles for pieces of writing.

Most of the time, we don't consciously think about how we use language but we're generally aware of the audience around us. Among friends, we're likely to be informal and say or write things in a way that might be discourteous to strangers. In an email to a close friend we might use shorthand and slang, whereas in a business or professional email we would likely use more standard English. In conversation, we might say, "My feet are killing me," almost speaking to ourselves, or "Do you have any cash on you?" meaning that we don't have any money and we'd like to borrow some. Generally, in conversations and in our writing we know we should be polite, relevant, clear, truthful, and as informative as necessary. These are the maxims that pragmatics explores and explains.

When two or more people talk together, it takes a lot of coordination to keep a conversation flowing smoothly. Although we're not normally aware of it, the various speakers are careful not to talk at the same time or to interrupt each other, or to fail to answer a question when a question is asked. Pragmatics tries to explain these common understandings of the "rules" of language use.

Children don't learn language in isolation. The sounds, meanings, and grammatical principles they learn are embedded in the social-interactive framework of the child's world. This phenomenon comes under the pragmatics of language. As they become effective communicators, individuals learn to take the roles and perspectives of both writers/speakers and readers/listeners into account at the same time. In conversation, young children learn how to initiate an exchange, contribute to the topic, request clarification, create smooth changes in topic, provide both verbal and nonverbal feedback to keep the conversation going, monitor timing and pauses in the dialogue, and conclude the interaction appropriately.

Pragmatics also involves knowing how to establish rapport, get to the point, ask questions, check for understanding, be relevant, not talk overly long, supply all necessary information, and be truthful, clear, and comprehensible. If any of these elements is missing from a conversation, and a distortion in communication occurs, the conversational partner can ask relevant questions, focus the speaker, paraphrase, or say, "I'm not sure what you mean by that. Are you saying that …?" Naturally, we try to be as tactful as possible in a conversation to keep it focused and flowing.

Language use also varies according to the social norm, an aspect of language known as *register*. People learn a range of registers and styles that help them to function appropriately in situations ranging from formal (making a speech at high-school graduation) to informal or nonstandard (playing in the park with friends, reading a comic book). Learners who come from socio-cultural settings where nonstandard English is used are usually able to read textbooks and listen to television newscasts in standard English. They seldom have problems with comprehension. Competent speakers learn to control a range of registers that allow them to function in diverse situations in society. People who have strong pragmatics abilities are usually considered to be socially competent and confident. These skills, together with linguistic competence, form what is known as "communicative competence."

Communicative Competence

Communicative competence is the ability to appropriately combine and use all aspects of language, including nonverbal communication. It's not simply linguistic competence, in which a speaker knows the language and the rules of that language; it's the ability to make sense of the world through language, and to use language in diverse ways and situations to accomplish specific purposes.

The British Columbia Ministry of Education (1988) developed a "teacher's resource package," *Enhancing and Evaluating Oral Communication in the Primary Grades*, to assist educators in developing and assessing children's oral communication skills. Although this comprehensive document was published many years ago, it serves as a central source of information for educators. Listed in the document are seven areas of communicative competence:

1. *Affective behaviours:* revealing attitudes and values through their behaviours. For example, do children participate in an activity willingly and enthusiastically? Can they articulate their responses in a diverse range of media (writing, drawing, mime, puppetry, artwork, dance)?

2. *Language awareness:* demonstrating knowledge about their own language use and learning. For example, can they talk about how they performed a certain math activity? Do they feel it was easy for them? Can they say what they think was the most important thing they learned?

3. *Listening comprehension:* constructing meaning from what they hear. For example, did they meet the requirements of the task? Did they follow directions appropriately and accomplish the task? How much support did they need from the teacher or from peers?

4. *Speech communication:* accomplishing the objectives of their speech. How much support do they need in order to attain their goals? Do they attempt to expand their repertoire of speaking strategies by experimenting with new forms?

5. *Critical/evaluative behaviour:* developing abilities to monitor their own speech and the messages they receive from others. Are they aware of whether or not their message has been understood? Are they able to question and clarify messages received from others?

6. *Interpersonal strategies:* creating relationships with others through their play and work in school. Interpersonal strategies include conversing, solving problems, sharing stories, and engaging in drama *activities.*

7. *Oral language codes:* communicating effectively with different people in different situations both in and out of school. Are they aware of their audience, the content to be communicated, and the most appropriate ways to communicate their thoughts and feelings?*

Learners develop communicative competence when they are using language to achieve their own specific purposes. Purpose is what drives them to learn and to participate in language events as equal and demanding partners. The more learners spend time with others, with an agenda of their own and the freedom to explore their world, the more they will become competent communicators. Classrooms where there is a diversity of background experiences, family lifestyles, and cultural mixes provide a rich opportunity for developing communicative competence. Individuals learn to narrate, to explain and inform, and to express their personal ideas and opinions. They also learn to adapt their communication to the situation, to the age and status of the conversational partner, to whether this is a family member or not, to their familiarity with their partner, and to the physical location of the communication.

---

* British Columbia Ministry of Education. (1988). *Enhancing and evaluating oral communication in the primary grades: Teacher's resource package.* Victoria: British Columbia Ministry of Education, 2:5 & 2:9. Copyright © Province of British Columbia. All Rights Reserved. Reproduced with permission of the Province of British Columbia. www.ipp.gov.bc.ca

In short, learners speak differently on the playground than in the classroom, in the doctor's office, or at church or temple. The development of these competencies *at school* is the focus of the remainder of this book.

Classroom Diversity and the Pragmatics of Language

In Canadian classrooms today, learners from a wide range of cultural backgrounds come together to learn language arts and become literate. These individuals may have learned differing pragmatic systems for their use of language. Here we present a few examples of the difference pragmatics can make in communication. Pragmatics in spoken language includes such things as timing and pausing. When people from different ethnic groups communicate, there are differences in their expectations that can cause misunderstandings (Scollon & Scollon, 1983). For example, when two people, one Athabaskan (e.g., with Dene as a first language) and one native English speaker, meet to converse, the native English speaker will likely speak first. The native English speaker feels that talking is the best way to *establish* a relationship (and frequently asking a question will do that); the Athabaskan, however, feels it is important to know the relationship between the two people *before* speaking. Since the person who initiates a conversation usually also controls the topic, the Athabaskan might feel ignored or consider native English speakers egocentric and focused only on their own ideas. The native English speaker may misconstrue the Athabaskan individual as not having ideas to share.

Pausing between turns is yet another example of the differences that occur in interethnic conversation. Speakers of Dene Soun'line (a member of the Athabaskan language family) in Fort Chipewyan, Alberta, allow a slightly longer pause between sentences than English speakers. Where English speakers generally allow one second before beginning another sentence or entering a conversation, Dene Soun'line speakers allow one-and-a-half seconds. That half-second is long enough for native English speakers to innocently jump in and dominate a conversation, not allowing Athabaskan speakers enough time to continue their flow of ideas. Such subtle differences in **discourse** patterns can result in strong stereotypical responses to the other ethnic group.

When individuals do not understand differences in discourse patterns across cultures and languages, misunderstandings and frustrations occur. Aboriginal people, for example, do not necessarily maintain eye contact with other speakers, as lack of eye contact is considered a sign of respect. Non-Aboriginal educators, however, often feel uncomfortable by what they consider disrespectful behaviour (Cleary & Peacock, 1998). What the non-Aboriginal educator perceives as a lack of "assertiveness" in their Aboriginal learners' softer and slower communication style contrasts starkly with the Aboriginal learners' perceptions of the unfamiliar loudness and speed with which their non-Aboriginal educators speak (Delpit, 1995). Aboriginal learners can be left puzzled and annoyed that their comments and explanations are seemingly inadequate. Non-Aboriginal educators can feel frustrated that their Aboriginal learners appear to be disengaged with the verbal landscape of the classroom. A classroom environment that promotes positive communication for Aboriginal English-speaking individuals (as well as for all learners from minority groups) can be created when educators are sensitive to their own discourse patterns and to the discourse patterns of the individuals in their classrooms.

Differences in language use were the focus of Heath's (1983) highly influential study of learners from three communities in the Carolina Piedmont region of the United States.

The learners attended school together following desegregation in the 1970s. The teachers and parents wanted to find out why learners and educators frequently could not understand one another. Specifically, they wondered why youngsters who never stopped chattering at home rarely talked in class, and why learners who could explain a rule for a ball game on the playground were unable to answer simple questions in the classroom. Heath found that the children from the three communities had experienced different ways of learning and using language at home. The experiences of some learners matched the ways language was learned and used in school better than did the experiences of other learners:

- In "Maintown," a middle-class, school-oriented community, the focus of literacy-related activities was on labelling, explaining, and learning how to display knowledge.
- Families in "Roadville," a white working-class community, also focused on labelling and explanations, preparing learners for literal comprehension tasks in the classroom. However, the learners were unprepared for reading activities that involved reasoning or affective responses.
- In "Trackton," a black working-class community, the children were not taught labels or asked for explanations in their homes; instead, they were considered to be legitimate conversational partners, providing opinions and responses to events.

When learners from all three communities arrived at school, they had different ways of using language, including the ways in which they responded to questions asked by their teachers. If the teacher asked learners from Trackton, "What colour is the horse in this picture?" they thought the answers were obvious and didn't respond. However, when educators used large photographs of the town and its buildings, learners participated much more readily. Educators asked questions such as "Can you climb to the top of that building?" or "What's going on here?" These questions were similar to those the children were asked at home. Eventually they learned to respond to these and to more school-based questions as well.

THE PURPOSEFUL NATURE OF LANGUAGE

In this section, we draw heavily on the work of Michael Halliday, one of the most influential researchers and writers on language learning in the 1960s and 1970s. His work continues to shape practice in K to 8 language and literacy teaching today.

Halliday asked the question "What is language?" He maintained that children know what language is because they know what language can do for them. Children learn language because there is something they need to *do*, and in order to do it they need to communicate their intentions to another person (see Box 3.1). There is almost no limit to what children (or adults) can do with language. From birth onward, children develop the ability to communicate their intentions, and they develop that ability long before they develop language. In the early months, their gestures direct the behaviour of the adults around them: they hold up their arms to be lifted up, and they point when they drop a favourite toy. At other times they play, gurgling and repeating the sounds and rhythms they have learned, evoking playful responses from their caregivers. From these early intentions children begin to develop language.

BOX 3.1

LEARNING HOW TO MEAN

Michael Halliday maintained that children know what language is because they know what language does. In other words, children learn about language through using it. It was Halliday (1975) who coined the phrase "learning how to mean." Halliday explained:

▷ Children learn language to express meanings to others and to construct meaning for themselves. Most thinking is done through language. Although we sometimes think in feelings and images, we construct our most abstract thoughts through the vehicle of language.

▷ Children learn language in real situations where something is being accomplished; for example, the singing of a song at bedtime, the talk mothers engage in while changing a child's clothing, the conversation that goes on around the dinner table, the choice of a television program, or the completion of a job in the yard.

▷ Children are included in conversations even when they are not yet capable of speaking in complete sentences—an example is when older siblings ask infants what toys or books they would like to play with.

▷ Children come to understand language from their own experiences of language in use. For example, children do not learn explicitly what a noun is, but they do learn to label. They do not understand what grammar is, yet they learn how to string words together into sentences that make sense to them and to the people with whom they intend to communicate.

▷ The discourse that contributes most to the growth of children's language learning is the discourse that actively involves the child. Interaction, particularly with significant adults or more mature language users, is necessary for language development to occur.

▷ Watching television and being talked at are no substitutes for involvement. Genuine involvement and purposeful talk with children are the most important conditions upon which language development rests.

Source: Based on M.A.K. Halliday, "Relevant models of language," *Educational Review*, Issue 22(1), 1969, pp. 26–37.

Halliday's Functions of Language

Michael Halliday identified seven "functions" of language (Box 3.2), which are summarized here. In everyday life we encounter *instrumental language* every time we ask another person to help us. When we order a meal in a restaurant, we are using the instrumental function of language. Closely related to this is the *regulatory function*. Sometimes it is difficult to tell these two functions apart, since when we regulate someone else's behaviour, it is often in order to meet our own needs. A No Smoking sign, a handbook on how to make a kite, the requirements for an assignment for a university class—all are examples of the regulatory function. *Interactional language* is the language we use to maintain and establish relationships (or to have an argument, which is another way of maintaining a relationship). It is the social chat we engage in over coffee, and the conversations we have with friends and colleagues. *Personal language* is used when we tell about ourselves—our feelings, thoughts, and beliefs. Our personal

BOX 3.2

THE SEVEN FUNCTIONS OF LANGUAGE

On the basis of his observations of young children's language development in the early years, Halliday (1969) proposed a model that categorized language use according to seven functions.

Function

1. Instrumental (language as a means of getting things, satisfying material needs)
2. Regulatory (controlling the behaviour, feelings, or attitudes of others)
3. Interactional (getting along with others, establishing relative status and separateness)
4. Personal (expressing individuality, awareness of self, pride)
5. Heuristic (seeking and testing knowledge)
6. Imaginative (creating new worlds, making up stories, poems)
7. Representational (communicating information, descriptions, expressing propositions)

Example

1. "I want."
2. "Do as I tell you."
3. "Me and you" and "Me against you"
4. "Here I come."
5. "Tell me why."
6. "Let's pretend."
7. "I've got something to tell you."

Source: Based on M.A.K. Halliday, "Relevant models of language," *Educational Review*, Issue 22(1), 1969, pp. 26–37.

language reveals part of our unique identity. *Heuristic language* is used when we explore and question and when we wonder and hypothesize. We hear it when a child says, "I wonder what would happen if ..." The *imaginative* function of language comes into full play when we write stories or poetry, or when we daydream, make a wish list, or engage in play with a child. Jokes, riddles, and cartoons are part of this realm. *Representational language* is the language of reports, lectures, documentary programs on television, and textbooks. As educators and learners, we become very familiar with this type of language, because it predominates in classroom discourse.

Of importance to educators is Halliday's observation that the most useful functions of language in a classroom are heuristic and personal. However, he showed that the most common functions used in classrooms are representative and regulatory. Educators such as Julie and Anne, whom we introduced at the beginning of this chapter, are aware that all language use has a purpose behind it. They provide a wide range of experiences so that children have opportunities to use language for different functions across the school day. In Box 3.3, presented later in this chapter, we list some activities that Julie incorporated into her Remembrance Day project. Each activity is described in relation to one of Halliday's functions of language to help you see what these functions might look like in an elementary classroom.

Halliday's work suggests that children do not develop language in a haphazard or purposeless way. On the contrary, children develop language because they have needs that must be fulfilled, and they quickly see that language enables them to make sense of and, to some extent, control their world. Through language, children and adults can have their needs met, live in the world of the imagination, inquire, tell about who they are, tell what they know, and develop relationships. As children interact with others in classrooms, playgrounds, stores, and other public places, they use language with amazing proficiency. When children enter kindergarten classrooms, their language reflects an implicit knowledge of the rules of grammar and appropriate language usage. In their five years of life, they have mastered the most complex learning task they will likely ever have to accomplish—the learning of language—and they can use that language to do a multiplicity of tasks. Most of this language is learned in a two-year period, between the ages of two and four. At this age, children have often been called linguistic geniuses. By the time children are in school, they take language completely for granted.

Integrating the Language Arts

As an example of how educators can design purposeful and meaningful language and literacy projects, we turn to the learners in Julie Gellner's grade 4 class, who were invited to prepare a Remembrance Day assembly for the whole school. In developing the assembly, Julie wanted to open up a safe, supportive, and nonthreatening space for learners to consider some of the "big ideas" surrounding war, especially the Second World War. She decided to do this through the book *Hana's Suitcase* (Levine, *2002*). The book balances the deeply moving and tragic story of Hana, a Jewish girl who ultimately lost her life in the gas chambers of Auschwitz, with a story of hope and healing. Julie knew that the learners in her classroom would need to voice their feelings, fears, hopes, questions, and opinions about war, and she wanted them to be able to do it in a variety of ways—through their drawings, drama, movement, poetry, reflections, and research. As Julie's students read, discussed, and responded to the story, they embarked on a deeply meaningful journey.

The Process

- *Daily readings from the book with free-ranging discussions.* During whole-class interactive Read-Alouds of *Hana's Suitcase*, the learners in Julie's classroom took part in lively, heartfelt discussions. They shared the fears raised by Hana's predicament, as well as stories of family or friends who were touched by the Second World War.

- *Responding to particular passages in constructions or art.* Julie recalled Hana Volavkova's book … *I never saw another butterfly* … first published in 1993. It displays the artwork and poems of children from the Terezin Concentration Camp, where Hana was interned. Julie shared this book with her students. The ensuing discussion raised an important question: What would life be like if they were no longer allowed to attend school, or if

Charcoal sketch based on Hana's Suitcase

they had no materials to work and play with? The students spontaneously began to create artworks such as collages from assorted items they found in the recycling bin. Based on photographs in the book, they drew charcoal sketches depicting Terezin. The artwork was created carefully on retrieved paper (paper that had once been used for some other purpose). Julie's students wanted to do the kinds of things that Hana had done at Terezin.

- *Using prompts such as photographs, objects, and poetry to generate writing.* Julie brought in a poster of a 1950s photograph by Diane Arbus depicting a young boy standing in a park. With a hand grenade in one hand, his face displays a strange and almost grotesque expression. The discussion evoked by this poster was profound. Based on their developing knowledge of the Holocaust, and after listening to poems from … *I never saw another butterfly …*, learners responded by writing poems about fear.

  ❏ *Hana's Suitcase* also caused the students to think about what it would be like if they were forced to leave their homes. Julie provided them with the written prompt: "Before you go far, far away you must pack a bag, not only to survive, but to keep your heart warm. This is my survival kit.…" The students responded by writing about what they would pack.

  ❏ At about the same time, learners embarked on a research project and talked with family members, neighbours, and friends about the Second World War. They probed family history and their grandparents' memories, and they wrote in their journals. Some brought artifacts to school to share with their classmates.

- *Learner-generated projects.* Julie encouraged learners to consider a variety of ways to represent their ideas and understandings about war. Poems and other pieces of writing were eventually published in a book titled *The Hana Project.* Some learners wrote a list of items they loved and would hate to lose, and placed it in a bottle. Others worked on a play based on a poem that Julie had read in class. One group decided to collect pennies; one for each life lost during the Holocaust. They called their project "Save a Life for the Lives

That Were Lost," connecting the Hana project with an endangered animals project they had been working on. They used the money they collected to adopt two families of polar bears, eventually collecting $500. The students stored the pennies in a suitcase and rolled them during storytime and "free time" before taking them to the bank.

- *The assembly.* The Remembrance Day assembly was a place where learners could share their poems, their pictures, their play, and their ever-growing understanding about Hana's life and what they had learned about war. What the students learned during this project made a huge impact on them, and they returned to the ideas and concepts many times during the following months. In fact, the project continued in some form throughout the school year. For example, their book—*The Hana Project*—was published well after the assembly, and the money raised through "Save a Life for the Lives That Were Lost" was collected over a period of months.

Educators like Julie have learned to have confidence in their students as co-planners and thinkers in any teaching and learning endeavour. However, Julie understands that once learners begin to find a path into a project, her responsibility is to find ways to maintain their interest and to generate further enthusiasm about the topic. Julie is confident that the six language arts are naturally integrated in this type of classroom activity, as learners listen, speak, read, write, view, and represent their learning to one another and their parents, as well as to the broader community of the school. Undoubtedly, the talk generated in this project was at the heart of learners' successful reading, writing, and learning.

BOX 3.3

THE HANA PROJECT: FUNCTIONS OF LANGUAGE

In preparation for the Remembrance Day assembly, Julie and the learners in her classroom read *Hana's Suitcase* by Karen Levine and completed the following activities (among others). Many of these activities were created by learners. The activities are described here in relation to Halliday's functions of language.

1. Instrumental

Oral. "Save a Life for the Lives That Were Lost: We Want Your Pennies." The students aimed to collect one penny for every life that was lost in the Holocaust, with the money to be contributed to a charity that protected endangered animals. This was their way of memorializing Hana's life and making a contribution to life on Earth today. At the school assembly, learners announced the project, explained what they were doing and why, and then asked others throughout the school to collect pennies and bring them to the grade 4 classroom.

Written. Learners made posters advertising "Save a Life for the Lives That Were Lost: We Want Your Pennies." They also wrote notes to parents and friends inviting them to save and donate their pennies.

2. Regulatory

Oral. In small groups, learners generated lists of rules that Hana and her brother George had to follow in order to survive the Terezin Concentration Camp: whom they could talk with; where

(continued)

they could go; what materials/food they could save and share; how they could tell and write stories and poems; how they could create art; how they could protect their secret life at "school." The whole class then discussed the rules and what it would be like to have to live by those rules.

Written. The children in the Terezin Concentration Camp played a board game they called "Smelina." The game was similar to Monopoly but all the places on the board were inside the Terezin Concentration Camp. Learners in the grade 4 classroom created their own version of the game and decided how to play it. They created the board, which contained places such as the guards' barracks as well as an attic hideaway. The aim of the game was to avoid the prison guards and acquire a safe place to live. Students wrote out the rules for the game and posted them on the bulletin board.

3. Interactional

Oral. In organizing the school assembly, learners divided themselves into small groups and decided what each group would be responsible for. They talked about what would be included in the assembly, who would present different parts of the program, and how they would rehearse the play they planned to perform.

Written. As learners came up with ideas for the assembly and worked on the program, they exchanged e-mails with one another in the evenings and on weekends. They tested ideas out with one another and made suggestions about what they could do.

4. Personal

Oral. In small groups, learners responded to this prompt: "Before you go far, far away you must pack a bag, not only to survive, but to keep your heart warm. This is my survival list." They talked together about what precious possessions they would select for their suitcases and why they would select those items. They talked about which items were the most meaningful to them, as well as most necessary for survival.

Written. Journal writing was familiar to learners in this grade 4 class. They wrote about their hopes for Hana and George, and they wrote about their hopes for themselves and their own families.

5. Heuristic

Oral. Learners interviewed elderly family members and neighbours to discover whether they'd had any experiences of war, especially the Second World War. They brought their findings back to class to share with their peers.

Written. Learners wanted to know more about Nove Mesto, the town in Czechoslovakia where Hana lived before the war. They searched the Internet and reference books in the library for information, and they gathered their findings into a folder. They then wrote about the similarities and differences between Canada and Czechoslovakia.

6. Imaginative

Oral. Learners created a drama based on one poem from the collection, "But I Never Saw Another Butterfly," written and illustrated by children in the Terezin Concentration Camp. They performed the play at the Remembrance Day Assembly.

Written. Learners wrote poems about fear and being afraid. They placed their poems in a bottle, which Julie hid secretly so that no one would ever find it, just like Hana and George had done in the book. Some of the poems were later reproduced in the class book, *The Hana Project: Writings Inspired by the Novel "Hana's Suitcase."*

7. Representational

Oral. At the Remembrance Day Assembly, learners told the school about the entire Hana project. They spoke about the Holocaust and described the book they had read. They shared artwork, poems, a drama, and their announcement of the "Save a Life for the Lives That Were Lost" project.

Written. Learners collaborated on a letter to George Brady, Hana's brother now living in Toronto, telling him about the project and sending him a copy of their class-published book, *The Hana Project.*

It is important to note that many of the above activities fulfill more than one language function.

For more information, please read H. Volavkova & J. Weil, *… I never saw another butterfly …: Children's Drawings and Poems from Terezin Concentration Camp, 1942–1944*, 2nd ed. (New York, NY: Schocken, 1993).

THE SOCIAL CONTEXT OF LANGUAGE DEVELOPMENT

The next section of this chapter addresses the continuing development of language abilities from preschool through grade 8. In particular, attention is paid to the social context of language development and to the factors that influence the development of any individual's language.

Language at Home and at School

From birth onward, children creatively develop language in social situations. They use forms of language they have never encountered before, and actively figure out how language creates meaning by observing what it does. They attend to language selectively, however, using whatever is relevant to them. They speak and take note of how others respond, they notice how other people express meanings, they ask questions and imitate what other people say (and how they say it), and they use some general principles for figuring out how language works.

The primary social context for children's language learning is, of course, the home. Here, children first learn language in interaction with their caregivers. Slowly, a child's world gets larger. Children visit other homes, the daycare centre, stores, the playground, the doctor's office, and so on. When they enter school, children encounter a whole new social context, where adults' use of language is often different from what they have encountered in their homes (note Heath's study mentioned earlier in this chapter). Generally, there is far less personal interaction in school than there is at home.

Language in Preschool Settings

Over the years, some remarkable studies have explored the language environments of both home and school. Tizard and Hughes (1984) examined the language at home and at school of four-year-old children in nursery schools in the United Kingdom. Their finding was surprising—children did *not* encounter a richer language at school than at home (contrary to popular belief). Educators have little time to devote to individual children, and are busy with the organizational aspects of teaching. They speak *to* children but generally not *with* them. At home, most language interactions occur while adults are doing things with children, such as making dinner or watching television.

One of the most extensive studies of language development in the social contexts of children's lives was Wells's (1986) U.K. project that followed 32 children from the ages of two to nine years. The children were fitted with radio microphones and were audio-recorded during a number of 15-minute segments every day. Data were collected at various times and in a variety of contexts. The segments were analyzed for grammatical complexity and for the functions of language used. The study showed that children from homes of low socio-economic status used language that was much the same as the children of high socio-economic status. However, Wells also found that the language of all 32 children was *suppressed* at school. He stated, "For no child was the language experience of the classroom richer than that of the home—not even for those believed to be 'linguistically deprived'" (1986, p. 87). Wells discovered that teachers dominated conversations in school and that much of the talk children engaged in at school lacked the purpose and spontaneity of real talk.

Dickinson and Tabors (2001, 2002) reported on a longitudinal study that examined U.S. parents' and teachers' support of language skills in 74 young children from families with low incomes. The study tracked children from preschool to grade 7 and showed that the more parents used new and interesting words at home, the better were the children's emergent literacy skills in kindergarten. In addition, the language and literacy skills acquired by the end of kindergarten provided a strong basis for the acquisition of literacy and vocabulary skills in later elementary school years. The researchers discovered that when preschool teachers intentionally focused on language development, used interesting and new words with learners, and talked less during free play (i.e., they listened more and responded thoughtfully to the children's utterances), the children did better on language and literacy assessments. Dickinson and Tabors drew attention to the importance of encouraging children to put their own ideas into words.

These collected findings indicate that educators must explore possibilities for expanding children's **oracy** in school. They must fine-tune a balance between talking and listening to children and focus on their interactions with learners. As Dickinson and Tabors stressed, oral language is the foundation of literacy.

Language Development in Kindergarten to Grade 8

When children enter school at the age of five or six, they have mastered the complexities of the four language systems. They understand syntax and phonology, and they can create a multitude of meanings from what they say and hear around them. They are aware of the print symbols they see in their environment and can recognize print on cereal boxes, in grocery stores, and in fast-food restaurants. Most children know how to handle books by this age and take delight in being read to by a caregiver. They take pleasure in playing with language, and are beginning to understand the subtleties of language that underlie the creation of humour.

Throughout the school years, learners continue to develop and refine their language abilities in all areas, especially in language use and metalinguistic awareness. Metalinguistic awareness is part of an individual's thinking, the growing ability to use language to talk about language as a formal code. Young children's thinking is embedded; they make sense of language in the context of their everyday lives and experiences. In other words, they relate what they learn to what they know, and make sense of new experiences only in the context of what is familiar. A six-year-old child, hearing that the family was going to Seattle, said, "I don't want to go to see Attle because I don't even know who Attle is anyway." Children make sense of the tasks they are asked to do in school in similar ways. If children are introduced to new concepts by working with concrete objects in the context of a familiar situation (e.g., learning about fractions through cutting pizza or apples), they are more likely to understand the concept than if they are taught without concrete objects and in an unfamiliar context (e.g., learning about fractions through manipulating numbers on a whiteboard). As children get older they are able to understand language and thinking without embedding it in their everyday experiences. By the age of 11 learners are usually able to consider language outside the context of their own experiences. They can reflect on language as an entity separate from themselves, and hence manipulate it and learn about it with a new awareness.

Learners develop language abilities most effectively when they use language in school for the same purposes for which they use language out of school. Just as Julie's students did in *The Hana Project,* they write real letters to real people for real purposes, share their stories with people who are interested in hearing and responding to them, read books and magazines for pleasure and information, and generally engage in real-world language events, including listening and speaking.

Educators are deeply aware of the benefits that come to individuals of all ages through talking, working, and playing with others, sharing their lives and interests. On Vancouver Island, British Columbia, an intergenerational arts-based project has been hugely successful in enabling classes of kindergarten children, along with local artists, to visit the Berwick Comox Valley retirement community one morning each week for the duration of the school year.* The children and seniors develop personal and meaningful relationships as they engage in art and literacy activities together, taking risks and conversing about their endeavours. Activities range from drumming and art making to

Nolan and Barbara discussing their book

---

* The project was funded in part by a grant from the Artists in the Classroom program (ArtStarts in Schools, Vancouver), and facilitated by Jackie Holt, general manager of the Berwick, and by teachers Debra Fullerton and Karen Reimer, Comox Valley SD #71.

sharing toys, reading, and telling stories. The nurturing environment and the one-to-one relationships facilitate oral language interaction, as the children and seniors become friends (like Nolan and Barbara), support each other's efforts, and work collaboratively to explore new activities. Oral language flourishes in an authentic context of mutual interest and shared pleasure. Local language arts consultant Carol Walters reminds everyone that "reading and writing float on a sea of talk" (paraphrased from James Britton, 1972).

In Box 3.4 Anne Gordon relates the experiences she and her grade 2 learners had when they created "heart maps." Their talking, writing, listening, viewing, representing, and reading led to new discoveries and achievements for these young learners. Learning in school should provide numerous opportunities for learners to use language to solve problems and interact with the world, calling into play all of their linguistic knowledge and skills. Britton (1970) used the phrase "dummy runs" to describe many of the language experiences learners are required to engage in at school. He maintained that individuals must *practise* language in the sense that a doctor practises medicine and a lawyer practises law, and *not* in the sense that a juggler practises a new trick before performing it. When doctors practise medicine, they are totally engaged in problem solving with their patients in a professional capacity that calls upon all their knowledge and skills. When jugglers practise tricks, they repeat the same moves over and over as a rehearsal for the time when they will finally perform in front of an audience.

BOX 3.4

ANNE'S HEART MAPS—GRADE 2

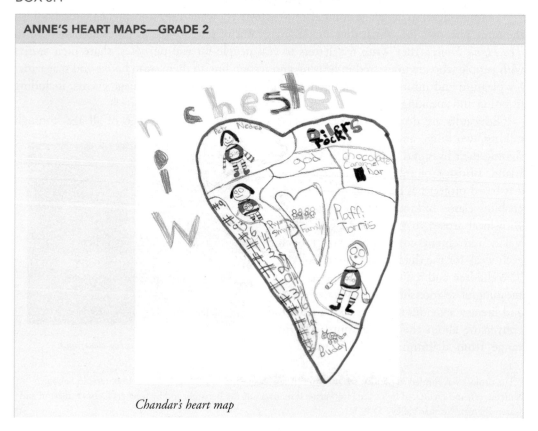

Chandar's heart map

Anne Gordon writes:

> I wondered how I could get my students to move away from rhyming when they were writing poems. I wanted to make them aware that poems are deeply meaningful and the language in a poem is sophisticated. Words are chosen with great care. Poems are not simply about words that rhyme. In order to show this to my grade 2 learners, I began to read a variety of poetry in different forms.
>
> As part of this exploration, I introduced *My Map Book* by Sara Fanelli, a collection of maps from the author's childhood, including a map of where she grew up and a map of her heart. The students were enthralled with the book as it provided information in a form unlike any other book they had seen, and it introduced a different perspective on how words and images represent memories, emotions, and feelings. During an interactive Read-Aloud of *My Map Book*, the students' discussion of the various symbolic maps was animated. The ideas and illustrations in the book provided food for thought as they considered mapping their own hearts.
>
> I provided the students with a short period of time to reflect on what might go into a map of their own hearts before they discussed their ideas with the rest of the class. I recorded their ideas on chart paper. We looked at our chart and compared the items we had listed to the items included in Fanelli's heart map. A discussion of the placement of items inside or around the heart was ongoing.
>
> After I modelled creating a heart map, the students drew their own maps. Halfway through the drawing/working time, the students and I toured the classroom and looked at the maps in progress. We talked to one another about what we saw. We asked one another questions, and then went back to our own heart maps and continued to work on them. At the end of the class, students shared their heart maps with each other. All of the maps were displayed in the classroom.
>
> The students connected with this lesson in a way I had not foreseen. Chandar's heart was full of family and the Edmonton Oilers. Emily's heart contained friends, pets, and her grandparents.
>
> One of my students, a struggling writer, demonstrated the power of the lesson both academically and emotionally. As our time for working on the maps was drawing to an end, I noticed Edward still working. As I drew closer, I shuddered. The top corner of his paper contained a number of large, prominent, black X's. I stepped forward, with a forced smile on my face.
>
> "Edward, you've got a lot of black X's at the top of your paper."
>
> "Mmmm-hmmm." No eye contact. An eyebrow was raised, but his focus was still on his paper. "Mmm-hmmm."
>
> "Can you tell me about these marks?"
>
> "Oh ... Mrs. Gordon, those are my numbers! I thought I had 10 things in my heart. There." His marker smudged finger pointed to an X, which upon closer inspection, covered the number 10. "But I had 20 things!" ... another X. "Mrs. Gordon, I have *62 things in my heart*!"
>
> Edward beamed. This active engagement in speaking, drawing, and writing had taken him on a new journey of self-expression and achievement.

For more information, please read: Sara Fanelli, *My Map Book* (Hong Kong: HarperCollins, 1995); Georgia Heard, *Awakening the Heart: Exploring Poetry in Elementary and Middle School* (Portsmouth, NH: Heinemann, 1999).

Children and young adults do not need to rehearse language in school for a time when they will have to use it in the "real world." When learners in Julie's classroom worked on the Hana project, and learners in Anne's classroom created their heart maps, they were engaged in activities that crossed the curriculum. As they used language in the classroom, they were encouraged to solve problems, make inferences, and express their own thoughts, values, opinions, and ideas. In this context, the learners did not need rehearsals. They were practising language in pursuit of their own goals and purposes.

ORAL LANGUAGE IN THE CLASSROOM

During the K to 8 years, learners continue to refine and extend all the language competencies that allow them to be full conversational partners in all walks of life, with many people, in many contexts. Students learn these competencies most effectively when educators talk *with* them on topics that are of interest to them, and in a manner that enables them to participate as *legitimate conversational partners*.

The term *oracy* was coined to refer to auditory and spoken language. Oral language skills form the foundation for literacy development. Learners come to Canadian classrooms from a range of ethnic, racial, political, and social backgrounds and they bring with them a similar range of oral language abilities. Many learners eagerly ask questions, tell about themselves, engage in play, listen to and read stories, and know how to interact with educators and others in diverse situations. Other learners may be shy or withdrawn, unwilling to participate, and unable to read. Many years ago, James Britton said, "A child's learning has its own organic structure. Hence … the importance of individual work in small groups, and of the sea of talk on which all our school work should be floated" (Britton, 1972, p. 58).

Maintaining a vital oral language curriculum means that classrooms cannot be quiet places. Educators distinguish between the busy chat and movement of actively engaged learners and the noise created by off-topic talking and irrelevant behaviour. Educators like Julie Gellner, Anne Gordon, and Carol Walters capitalize on activities such as collaborative projects, reader response groups, and drama activities in an effort to enhance their students' abilities to articulate their thoughts and feelings clearly and with confidence.

The next part of this chapter focuses on how language helps individuals to learn, or how language influences cognition. Everyone has a theory of how the world works, a worldview, and we develop that theory through our experiences of the world. Language plays a large role in this process as we put our ideas into words, listen to and read other people's opinions, and clarify our own thinking, thus adding to our learning. We relate new experiences to old ones and continue to make sense of them all through language. Language allows us to shape our thoughts, to ask questions, to explore, to clarify, and to create meaning. Words allow us to put meanings together and to create new understandings. In both children and adults, we can see the same processes taking place.

In this chapter we address talking and listening separately so that we can provide a clear explanation of how each can be facilitated in the classroom. In the life of the classroom, as in any social context, talking and listening always function together.

Talking

David Booth (2013) wrote,

> Talk is not a subject; rather, it is a condition of learning in all subjects. It has many functions: it leads students to understand new concepts; it enables them to communicate clearly as active learners with others; it lets them consider a diversity of viewpoints; it helps them develop a critical tolerance of others. When we are dealing with new ideas or coming to new understandings, talk helps us to make sense of both our thoughts and our feelings. If we can put our knowledge into words, then we will be able to reflect on that knowledge, to act on it, and to change it. (p. 12)

For most people, talking is the primary means of communication. Through oral language and nonverbal gestures, we communicate most of our needs, fears, and hopes to the people we encounter in our day-to-day lives. Through oral language we frequently work out our ideas, "bounce" ideas off colleagues and friends, and communicate the most prosaic, yet necessary, messages to those closest to us. It is therefore of utmost importance that learners' oral language abilities be fostered throughout K to 8 schooling.

Many individuals are self-conscious about their spoken English, whether they are English language learners or native-like speakers. Sometimes a person's accent or dialect is belittled, or his or her pronunciation is derided. These kinds of experiences silence learners. Oral language is part of our familial and cultural heritage and an important part of who we are as human beings. The language learners bring with them to school is to be built upon so that individuals can refine their knowledge and skills and become more articulate and confident speakers in a range of social situations. Effective educators like Anne, Julie, and Carol ensure that learners engage in small-group work that enhances their oral language abilities.

Many learners talk with ease on the playground, but have difficulty expressing themselves adequately in the classroom. Some feel comfortable moving from one language register to another and speak easily to different people in different contexts. While learners can usually use basic oral communication to get their needs met or to regulate the actions of others, they may not be as comfortable or as adept in using language in the academic context of the classroom or in using language to persuade, give directions, or make inquiries. These functions of language can be taught through everyday classroom interactions among students and teachers, helping learners to become more articulate, precise, and confident in their spoken language.

Boys working and talking

Exploratory Talk

When learners reflect on their learning through talk and conversation, ask questions, problem-solve, or hypothesize, they are using exploratory language. Exploratory talk is often spontaneous, and it helps individuals to discover what they think. In addition, it helps them to establish and maintain relationships. "Students use exploratory language when analyzing, evaluating and responding to texts, and when deciding how to use language more effectively. They use conversation to collaborate on projects and to develop a classroom community" (Alberta Learning, 2000a, p. 7).

Information is not processed in isolation, but is shared, built on with peers, and discussed as it relates to real people and real contexts. This aspect of learning is one of the strongest reasons for having learners engage in group projects, where they can study and work together, pooling information and helping one another to clarify and test out specific learnings. Through group interaction and exploratory talk, students make meanings more precise and reinterpret past experience (which is why a personal story is often told to make a point).

Educator Janet McConaghy holds "talking and thinking together" sessions with small groups of grade 6 learners on topics across the curriculum. In social studies, one topic was the consensus model of decision making within the Iroquois Confederacy. The brief excerpt below is taken from a fairly lengthy discussion about the characteristics and basic principles of the consensus model of decision making (McConaghy, 2014).*

LUKE:	Everyone would live in harmony because there wouldn't be any war, like fighting, there would be decision making—they also followed our same rules like our "speaking" rules.
JANET:	Does this mean in order to make a decision everyone would have to agree?
NICOLE:	Yeah, … they want everybody to agree on what they're doing. They don't just say okay because almost everyone agrees. It has to be that everyone is agreeing—it can't just be almost everybody.
LUKE:	But vice versa if that happened, say Joshua wanted lacrosse and I wanted hockey—you guys could also want hockey with me but it could be vice versa. You could want basketball next time and I want say baseball, right? It would have to be vice versa and I would have to agree with them and they would have to agree with me.
NICOLE:	Okay, this time we'll go with what you say, but next time we'll go with what I say—sort of a compromise.
JANET:	And sometimes in certain situations you do have to compromise.
NICOLE:	And someone might get really upset and say you guys never listen to what I say and I'm always the one that gets thrown out.
JOSHUA:	Maybe if one group doesn't always agree there could be a war.
NICOLE:	They don't do a war because of the Iroquois Confederacy but it might be like a little fight or something but not like a war.
LUKE:	Didn't they say they had a fighting sport?
JOSHUA:	No, because they put all the weapons … (Luke interrupted)
LUKE:	No, fighting sports, not like weapons. Because I know they had that in Athenian Democracy.

---

* Janet McConaghy. PhD dissertation, "The Centrality of Exploratory Talk in Dialogic Teaching and Learning," University of Alberta, 2014.

JANET:	Has anyone mentioned what some of the advantages are?
AMBER:	I did, that everyone gets a say in it. They don't exclude somebody, they bring everything together and make a decision together.
NICOLE:	Disadvantage is that it takes a very long time.
LUKE:	Yeah, because you have to go through so many processes and if everyone doesn't agree you have to do it again. It could take months maybe even years.

This interaction illustrates the collaborative effort and joint reasoning that took place as learners moved toward a better understanding of the issues surrounding a consensus model of decision making. They were clarifying ideas and building on one another's words. Through this kind of collaboration, social skills and interpersonal relationships of trust and respect were strengthened. Using exploratory talk, learners presented different viewpoints on the topic and supported their reasons by referring to what they had already learned at school as well as what they had experienced in their personal lives.

Interaction becomes crucially important as learners stretch their limits and move into areas that are uncertain, going beyond personal experience and specific situations. The following section of dialogue from a literature circle discussion in Denise Barrett's grade 8 classroom demonstrates exploratory talk. The students had all read at least as far as page 28 in *Tangerine* by Edward Bloor. Here, they try to make sense of a puzzling situation:

JORDAN:	But I don't get what's wrong with Paul's eyes. He has coke-bottle glasses and he wears them all the time, but then he says he can see.
RAJ:	It's the eclipse thing. You know, when he was just a kid. Maybe he thinks he can see better than he really can 'cos he doesn't want other kids calling him names and stuff. I mean, he even put his glasses on when he woke up in the night …
PETRA:	Yeah, well, he must need glasses or his mother wouldn't agree to an IEP at school—when she met with the principal. You know, she seems kinda fussy about stuff.
JORDAN:	Yeah, but it's weird that he doesn't remember what happened to his eyes. And there's this freaky Erik. He freaks me out. I think he had something to do with it.
PETRA:	You know, right at the beginning of the book there's this little section, even before the title page, like an introduction or something, "Out of Focus." And it says the big kids called him Eclipse Boy right from the beginning of kindergarten, so something must have happened…. Maybe the shock of what happened …
JORDAN:	I think his brother had something to do with it. Do you think they made him look at the sun on purpose, just as a joke or something?
RAJ:	I don't know, but right at the beginning, when they're leaving the old house, look, it says Erik told him not to look at the sun through his glasses….

The students here don't come to any specific conclusion about Paul and his glasses, but they do try out various scenarios as they put together the "evidence" they have gathered from their reading. They will carry this conversation with them as they read further into the novel.

The critical role of language in the learning process has caused educators to focus on processes such as collaboration, cooperation, group work, and the value of oral language in the classroom. Box 3.5 demonstrates how Julie helped learners to sustain conversations when they were engaged in grand conversations about literature.

BOX 3.5

ORAL RESPONSES TO READING

How can educators provide and prepare learners for successful talk opportunities during

▷ interactive Read-Alouds?

▷ literature circles?

▷ grand conversations?

(See Chapter 12 for descriptions of these activities.)
Children need mini-lessons on conversation routines, such as

▷ how to make a comment

▷ how to take turns

▷ how to encourage others to participate

▷ how to redirect the conversation

▷ how to stick to the topic

▷ how to be polite and supportive of their classmates

▷ how to share ideas

▷ how to build on classmates' comments

▷ how to sustain conversation

Mini-lesson on Sustaining a Conversation

Julie has found that sometimes during grand conversations, learners are not good at sustaining dialogue. She gathers learners together to listen to one group's conversation. She prepares the group ahead of time to model some "good things" and some "bad things" during their conversation. Learners watch carefully as four individuals engage in a grand conversation about the book they are currently reading. The students in the group take turns but do not extend or expand the conversation. They also behave in other ways that Julie hopes the class will notice.

After the grand conversation, Julie directs learners' attention to a chart that has two columns: "Strengths" and "Challenges." The students brainstorm the strengths of the grand conversation, and Julie writes them on the chart. The students then brainstorm the challenges.

Julie next indicates that during grand conversations in the coming weeks she will be watching for these behaviours:

▷ talking about the story and making connections between the text and the students' own lives

▷ showing politeness to one another

▷ paying attention and looking at the person who is speaking

▷ addressing one another by name

▷ responding to what other people have said

After two weeks, Julie will provide learners with a self-assessment list, and they will decide which of the items they have done well and which they need to work on in future grand conversations.

Listening

Of all the modes of language used in K to 8 classrooms, listening is undoubtedly the most prevalent and the most important. Learners make sense of oral language through attending, anticipating, predicting, focusing, visualizing, making connections, generalizing, and evaluating. Their success in school depends largely on their listening abilities. An educator's success in telling stories, providing instructions, organizing learners and activities, and teaching concepts all depend on the abilities of individuals to listen and to understand. It is important to recognize that learners are mainly required to listen to *directions* in the classroom rather than to information. Learners in kindergarten to grade 8 can easily be confused if they do not hear directions or do not understand an educator's instructions. Being able to listen attentively and respond appropriately accounts for a large part of a child's success in a primary classroom. Even in the upper elementary and junior high grades, listening remains vitally important for successful schooling.

Listening is probably the most used of the language modes from birth onward. Infants listen in order to learn language, to communicate with others, and to construct meaning in their world. The need to listen continues in school and through adulthood. Many educators today comment on what seems to be the short attention span of some learners in their classrooms. These learners, educators say, have difficulty in listening and paying attention to what is happening in class. However, research (e.g., Cazden, 1988) has also demonstrated that many educators have poor communication skills: they talk too much, explain too much, and do not actively listen to their students. By modelling appropriate listening behaviours (among other strategies), it would seem that educators can help learners to listen effectively throughout the entire curriculum.

Listeners understand speech at about double the rate a speaker can produce it, and so the mind tends to wander away from the topic of conversation and onto something else. The average length of time a listener can attend to one specific thing is only about 20 seconds. To lengthen that attention span, most people learn how to listen actively by nodding, agreeing with the speaker, making notes on paper, focusing on key words, formulating questions, and generally engaging in the stages noted above. When helping learners to become active listeners, educators can help them to establish specific purposes for listening. They can also provide them with lots of purposeful opportunities for listening and responding in the context of meaningful oral language experiences (Cox, 1999).

The purpose of listening to a message, as with any other language act, drives the way in which the listening takes place. If learners understand why they are to listen to a message, a story, a poem, or a list of instructions, they are more likely to listen effectively and focus on the appropriate element of the communication. Only three major purposes usually apply to classrooms: efferent, critical, and aesthetic. When educators state reasons or purposes for listening, and focus learners' thinking on ways they can accomplish the task, students' listening skills will be enhanced.

As in any other area of the language arts, students learn best when they are provided with opportunities to listen in the context of their learning. They do not generally need exercises and drills on listening. Educators can show learners how to vary their listening according to the specific purpose for listening, and can help them develop specific listening strategies. Some learners have only one strategy for listening no matter what the purpose—to listen hard and remember everything. Learners can be helped to understand that once a purpose is established for listening, they can vary *how* they listen and hence be more effective listeners.

Listening for pleasure to a story such as Michael Kusugak's *Baseball Bats for Christmas* allows students to enter the world of the imagination; to create images of the setting, characters, and events; and to respond emotionally and intellectually to the narrative. This is aesthetic listening. Learners can be encouraged to create pictures in their minds as they listen to the story.

Listening later on to an educator talk about author Michael Kusugak requires a different kind of listening—efferent listening. Here, learners attempt to make sense of information about Kusugak, including his childhood in Repulse Bay, where he now lives and works, how he began writing for young people, why he enjoyed listening to his grandmother's stories, and how he first learned English. Understanding this information adds richness to the story Kusugak wrote.

Yet another kind of listening is required when students and educators talk together about how Kusugak went by plane, at age six, to a school far away from his home, returning only in the summers: critical listening. At school, Kusugak had to learn to speak and read English and was forbidden to use his own language. As learners ponder the dilemma of having young children stay at home versus providing them with a formal education, and forcing them to speak English rather than their own language, they are required to listen critically, assess what they have heard, make judgments about situations, and perhaps attempt to understand two sides of a debate.

Learners can be encouraged to engage in active listening when they participate in writing conferences with their peers, engage in group projects, take part in drama activities, and read to each other in Shared Reading experiences. Further language arts strategies that enhance effective listening are listed in Classroom Activities 3.3 and 3.4.

CLASSROOM ACTIVITY 3.3

How to Engage Learners in Active Listening

Use interactive daily Read-Alouds. (See Julie's lesson earlier in this chapter.)

Select a book and preview it. Practise reading it for pauses where learners can be actively engaged with the text. Read the book aloud, modelling fluent and expressive reading. Stop periodically to ask questions about the text. Learners can discuss what has been read and participate in other types of response activities (see Chapter 12).

Play fortunately … unfortunately.

Here learners consider the flip side of a situation. You might say, "Fortunately, I found my mother's engagement ring." You can then invite the class to provide statements that begin with "Unfortunately," for example, "Unfortunately, the diamond was missing." Learners can take turns, but must ensure that their response is appropriate to the opening statement. They cannot repeat what has already been said by other participants.

Engage in participation stories.

Learners listen for specific words in a story and then, on cue from the educator, add in their own sounds or phrases. They can also chime in on sequential or recurring refrains or patterns in the text, as in *The Doorbell Rang* by Pat Hutchins. Young children will chime in with the recurring sentence, "'No-one makes cookies like grandma,' said Ma, as the doorbell rang." Learners could also add the sound "ding dong" at the end of the sentence.

CLASSROOM ACTIVITY 3.4

Mini-lesson: Directed Listening–Thinking Activity (DLTA)

DLTA is effective in both narrative and content-area listening. It helps learners to use their own thinking and prior knowledge, and it encourages creative and divergent thinking.

Select a story with a clear plot and distinct episodes. Before reading it to the class, plan where you can make two to four stops. All must be before important events are introduced into the story. At each stop

▷ elicit summaries of what happened

▷ encourage learners to make "wonder" statements between and beyond the lines of the text

▷ ask learners to justify their "wonder" statements

▷ read the next section, review the "wonder" statements, revise the statements, and continue

At the end of the reading, invite learners to reflect on how the DLTA focused their listening. For example, ask, "Did your predictions help you to listen more closely?"

Listening is made easier for learners if the following suggestions are put in place before and during classroom activities:

- Ensure that all learners have a clear view of the teacher and the main teaching area.
- If necessary, increase the distance between learners' desks.
- Consider the seating plan and seat learners where they will be able to focus most attentively.
- Seat learners who experience difficulty in listening attentively at the front and toward one side of the classroom.
- Do not seat learners close to high-traffic areas such as the pencil sharpener, cubbies, and the door.
- Ensure that recess snacks, lunches, and coats are not brought to the learners' work areas.
- Ensure that desktops are completely clear.
- Set regular times for activities to occur.
- Develop a language in the classroom that signals learners to listen (e.g., say, "I need to see eyes listening, ears listening, and feet listening," which indicates that hands need to be still, eyes need to be on the speaker, and feet need to be forward).
- Give instructions as simply and briefly as possible.
- Ensure that the language used is appropriate for the learners' developmental levels.
- Emphasize critical words such as "first, then, afterwards."
- Display an agenda and directly encourage learners to follow along with the lesson.

- Model good attending behaviours, and reinforce those learners who are doing the same.
- Be consistent in the wording of routine instructions.
- Complement oral instructions with written instructions.
- Ensure that your voice is interesting and not monotonous when presenting information.
- Have materials and visuals in clear sight of learners.

To facilitate talk, classrooms can be organized so that learners are able to talk to one another easily without having to move from their desks or speak in loud voices. Grouping desks together or seating learners around small tables works effectively. It is also important to consider the purpose of the grouping and to group learners differently at different times. Most of the time, heterogeneous grouping is most effective, as it facilitates learners' engagement in conversations, expressing what they know and asking questions of one another. Grouping of this kind enables learners to help one another and to develop expertise independently from the teacher.

Assessing Oracy (Listening and Talking)

Listening and talking usually occur together in any social or school situation. It is difficult to assess either one in isolation from the other. When educators *observe* learners' listening strategies and abilities, it is likely to be in the context of group work they are engaged in: a reader response group, a drama activity, a writing conference, a conversation with another student, a science activity, a parent–student conference, interactions on the playground, and physical education or art classes. Those are the same contexts in which educators will also collect information about learners' speaking abilities, through *listening* to what they say. Much of the information educators collect about learners' oral language proficiencies is anecdotal—it occurs in everyday contexts and is noted as it occurs. Educators keep notebooks about their students' progress in all areas of the curriculum. These notes complement learners' portfolios of writing, artwork, and so on. The notes can help educators make pedagogical decisions that affect their students' learning. If a learner is experiencing difficulty in participating in a literature circle, for example, educators will want to observe the interactions more closely and decide how the individual can be helped to participate more fully.

Box 3.6 displays a sample list of attributes related to listening. Educators could turn this list into a checklist that could be augmented with comments on the oral language behaviours of each individual learner. The assessment of oral communication abilities relies heavily on educators *listening* to learners—not only listening to *what* they have to say and responding appropriately, but also listening to *how* they create and communicate meaning. A list like that in Box 3.6 can be helpful in tracking learners' abilities and growth in this important area.

When using checklists and rubrics, it is helpful if educators are familiar with the learning outcomes for both a grade lower and a grade higher than the one at which they are teaching. In any one classroom there will be a wide range of oral communication competencies. Familiarity with a broad range of grade-level abilities helps educators to understand their own students' oral language development more clearly.

BOX 3.6

LISTENING CHECKLIST

We emphasize the importance of talking with and listening to learners, and of involving them in drama; listening to songs, poems, and stories; choral reading; sharing time; cooperative writing; group activities; Readers' theatre; improvisation; cooperative "cloze" activities (discussed in Chapter 7); storytelling; role-playing; group discussions; cross-age tutoring; and reporting.

At grade 4, educators can consider the following attributes when assessing a learner's use of oral language:

▷ tells personal anecdotes, in a relevant way

▷ recounts a story or repeats a song spontaneously

▷ retells scenes from a movie or play

▷ offers predictions about what will come next

▷ recites poems

▷ asks questions in conversation

▷ has a second try at saying something to make it more precise, and arouses and maintains audience interest during formal presentations (e.g., book talk, announcements)

▷ uses a range of vocabulary related to a particular topic

▷ maintains a receptive body stance in conversation

▷ speaks in a way that conveys feelings (while keeping emotions under control)

Source: *English Profiles Handbook*, Department of School Education, Melbourne, Victoria, Australia, 1991.

SUMMARY

Educators make every effort to understand how individuals learn language, and to understand language itself. Language is without doubt the most complex and sophisticated of all human behaviours—many researchers maintain that it is the use of language that sets human beings apart from other animals. Language consists of four major elements: semantics, syntax, phonology, and pragmatics. Semantics refers to the meaning element of language; syntax, to the organization of language; phonology, to the sound system of language; and pragmatics, to the ways in which language is used to communicate.

The social context of language is now known to be particularly important. Longitudinal research studies have demonstrated that learners' language can often be suppressed in school. More than ever, schools today need to take into consideration the cultural and social diversity of learners and provide a rich interactive language environment for all.

continued

Language and learning cannot be separated. Much of what students learn, both in and out of school, takes place through the vehicle of language—both written and oral. The processing of thoughts cannot be separated from the use of language. How would we think if we didn't have language? Educators understand that learners, to learn effectively, need the opportunity to work purposefully in groups, sharing ideas, questions, suggestions, and problem-solving strategies. As we talk through ideas, we think about them further, clarify them, refine them, and enhance our knowledge and understandings.

The oral language competencies of young children are directly related to their reading and writing abilities. Children entering school with strong oral language competencies are more likely to experience success in their literacy endeavours. Although the focus of K to 8 language arts is generally on reading and writing development, a great deal of classroom communication occurs orally. Learners can be helped to expand their listening and speaking skills so that they can maximize their learning opportunities. It is therefore important that oral language be nurtured and supported in classrooms so that learners become effective listeners and speakers wherever they are. It is also important that learners' oracy be assessed on an ongoing basis through informal observations and anecdotal records. Learners need to know how to strengthen their oral language abilities to improve their overall learning.

SELECTED PROFESSIONAL RESOURCES

Beck, I., McKeown, M., & Kucan, L. (2008). Creating robust vocabulary: Frequently asked questions. New York, NY: The Guildford Press.

Focusing on the meanings of words, and matching a written word with a meaning, the authors present suggestions and guidelines for teaching vocabulary from K to 12. They believe that instruction must be deep and rich, and must encourage learners to think about what they are learning. The book is full of teaching examples, explanations of which words to teach, when and how to teach them, and how to adapt vocabulary instruction for English language learners.

Booth, D. (2013). I've got something to say! How student voices inform our teaching. Markham, ON: Pembroke.

Drawing on his many years of teaching and research, David Booth here presents numerous teaching strategies for implementing student "choice and voice" in classrooms. He pursues talk as a medium for learning and for creating democratic classrooms. The 10 chapters cover topics from "why talk matters" to storytelling and story making, drama, writing, and multimedia.

Booth, D., & Thornley-Hall, C. (Eds.). (1991). The talk curriculum. Markham, ON: Pembroke.

This classic text, along with its companion volume Classroom Talk (Booth & Thornley-Hall, 1991), demonstrates how talk in classrooms is a vital aspect of the learning curriculum. The authors show how "language allows us to symbolize, structure, regulate, and give meaning to experience" (p. 7). Chapters include ideas for talking with children, observing children, assessing children's oral language, and engaging children in storytelling, drama, and literature.

Mercer, N., & Hodgkinson, S. (Eds.). (2008). *Exploring talk in schools: Inspired by the work of Douglas Barnes*. London, UK: Sage.

Bringing together the work of leading international researchers and drawing on the pioneering work of Douglas Barnes in the United Kingdom, this book suggests practical ways of improving classroom talk. The chapters address classroom communication and managing social relations; talk in science classrooms; using critical conversations in studying literature; exploratory talk and thinking skills; talking to learn and learning to talk in the mathematics classroom; and the "emerging pedagogy" of the spoken word.

4

Early Literacy

EARLY LITERACY
- What Literacy Knowledge Do Young Children Need?
- Phonological Awareness, Phonemic Awareness, and Phonics

ASSESSING EARLY LITERACY
- Informal Assessment
- Running Records
- Miscue Analysis

EARLY LITERACY

MULTILITERACIES PEDAGOGIES: EXPERIENCES THAT CREATE EARLY LITERACY LEARNING OPPORTUNITIES
- Creating a Rich Literacy Environment
- Read-Alouds
- Shared Reading
- Structuring Sustained Learning Opportunities through Literature
- Shared Writing: The Language Experience Approach

Early childhood educators Jennifer Miller and Andrea Dewhurst's early years classroom is a prime example of how opportunities can be enacted for the expansion of children's literacy and identity options, all in keeping with the principles of the multiliteracies pedagogies we have described thus far. Take a peek and see for yourself:

It's time for the daily morning meeting, and Jennifer and Andrea are inviting the children to form their circle. Morning meeting is an important ritual in the classroom, which is part of an early learning centre based in a Reggio Emilia–inspired early learning organization. The organization helps to support educators to enact emergent curriculum, a form of curriculum that is in large part generated from children's interests, funds of knowledge, and multimodal potential. All of this requires carefully listening to children, which morning meeting is designed to accomplish.

Jennifer and Andrea describe morning meeting as a "safe place" for the classroom community to "come together … and reflect, revisit, and plan our learning experiences each day." The educators take turns leading the meeting while the other documents what goes on. Documentation can take the form of notes, photographs, recordings, collection of artifacts, and other ways in which the classroom community records and reflects on what the children are doing, thinking, and feeling so that the educators, in concert with the children, can design where to go next with the curriculum. The classroom curriculum is proudly displayed as a map on a sharing board for all to experience. Here, information is added daily through texts such as the educators' documentation notes and children's writing, drawing, and photos. The photo of the curriculum map suggests how morning meeting fits in with other key components of the classroom curriculum, most notably novel study.

Morning meeting has a predictable rhythm, and multiple modes are used for communication. The meeting opens with a gathering song, which is expressed orally and through American Sign Language (ASL), a language that is used at the centre beginning with the infants to help them to expand their communication options. Today, Jennifer asks the group, "How are you feeling?" The children take turns answering, using oral language and ASL as they wish. The children also have the option to pass the question on to another person, using ASL to signal the individual's name. Next, the children are invited to revisit events from the day before and they plan for their day. The educators use prompts to elicit the children's input, such as, "What do you think of this?" Morning meeting is also used for collectively solving problems. For instance, on a day close

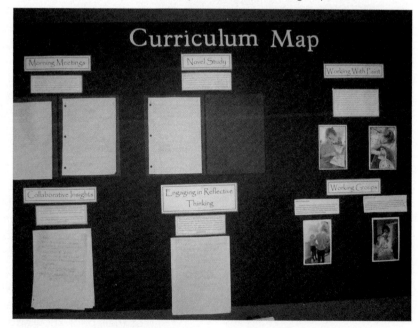

Curriculum map sharing board

to Mother's Day, the children had been working on developing special colours as a gift for their mothers. One of the boys in the class had a problem: How could he make a colour lighter? When he had encountered the problem the previous day, one of the educators asked him, "Would you like to see what your friends think of this?" Thus the next day, the class talked through the colour problem, finding a solution that all the children could put to use.

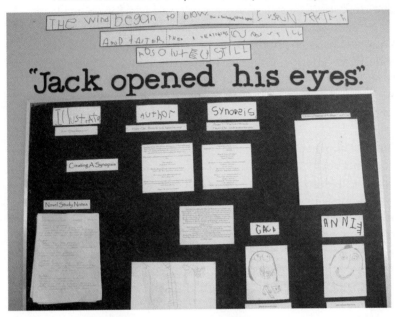

Novel study sharing board

A cornerstone of the program is novel study, and morning meeting is also a place where the class can explore ideas and language that arise there. The class has been reading the Magic Tree House series (e.g., Osborne, 2011), a popular children's book series where siblings Jack and Annie are transported by their magic tree house to exciting places and times. In the books, Jack and Annie meet major historical figures (e.g., Leonardo DaVinci and Mozart) and solve problems. Jennifer and Andrea chose the series because it provides content-rich learning opportunities in what they call "relatable" and "interesting" ways.

Novel study happens daily right after lunch. Like every other pedagogical feature in the classroom, it has its predictable rhythm and is well orchestrated between the educators. One educator leads discussion and reads the novel aloud to the children. The other documents, focusing on the children's engagement and understanding of the key concepts and vocabulary. Each novel study session begins with questions to activate prior knowledge and trigger anticipation (e.g., "Where did we leave off? "What do you think is going to happen today?"). During the reading, the educators pause to discuss key ideas through novel-specific vocabulary. Jennifer and Andrea decide on the places to linger by assessing what the children are ready to discuss (e.g., in terms of their prior knowledge and what else might be going on in the classroom). They also might choose

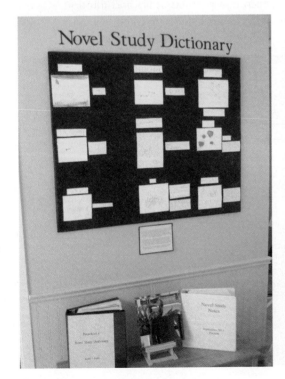

Novel study dictionary sharing board

to gloss over some ideas/words that might open up "risky stories" (i.e., ideas the children are perhaps not ready or equipped to deal with, such as the word *gory*).

Documentation from novel study goes up on the curriculum map sharing board, which is located near the children's cubbies. In this prime position, families can see what has been going on during novel study, allowing the conversations to continue outside the classroom. The notes stay up for two days before new notes are put up. The old notes go into a novel study binder located near the novel study bulletin board.

Documentation might also be brought back to morning meeting for discussion if there is something pertinent (e.g., "Michael, yesterday you said *valuable* meant really breakable...." If Michael then says something that could add to this definition, the educator might say, "Has your thinking changed?"). Additionally, the classroom includes a living novel study dictionary sharing board where the children draw and write their understandings of key vocabulary. New vocabulary is added all the time, and when it's time to take down featured words, they go into a novel study dictionary binder located on the table below the board.

The teaching of the vocabulary is always purposeful, as it serves the goals of expressing the big ideas in the novel and connecting to new understandings that arise in other contexts in the classroom. The educators explain that the vocabulary teaching "always has intention behind it"; for example, the word *valuable* is connected back to the children when someone brings in a toy from home: "This is valuable." Thus the teaching is woven throughout the children's days. Other events in daily classroom life also raise ideas from the novel. Once when Jennifer and Andrea were on a trail walk with the children, a cat followed them. The children remembered how animals follow Annie and Jack in the novels and wondered if they were being sent a challenge. The educators picked up this idea, and it became a game.

The classroom also provides ample opportunities for drawing and writing connected to novel study. When they recognize that an idea might need further consideration or could be better visible to others, Jennifer and Andrea invite a child to draw. They might, for example, say at a morning meeting, "I'd like to invite you to draw that and we can meet to discuss it." Sometimes the educators use drawing to facilitate interest, saying, for example, "I really liked your idea and want to understand it better...." Children might also initiate using another mode (other than drawing) to represent their thinking (e.g., blocks, clay, drama). Opportunities for writing are always connected to these opportunities; for instance, with the vocabulary study, the children are invited to print the word, draw it, and write what the word means.

Educators facilitate the children's drawing and writing acquisition right from the beginning of the year with a self-portrait strategy: they invite the children to draw a self-portrait facilitated by the use of a mirror. The educators ask the children to look into a mirror and direct their observation by giving them the language of the mode they are using (e.g., "Pay attention to detail").

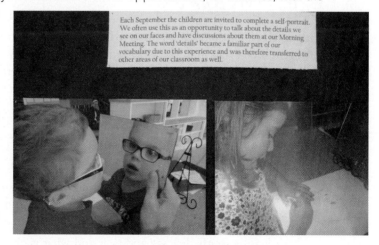

Portrait strategy

Learning to attend to the details: Kola's self-portrait

The portrait strategy photo shows elements of a sharing board that includes photos of the children engaging in the literacy event, descriptions of what is happening, and products. The educators then walk the children step by step through the drawing of the self-portrait, and next, invite them to create a portrait of a friend. This provides opportunities to solidify relationships through the literacy event. As with all elements of the curriculum in the classroom, the self-portraits become part of a sharing board, which the class and families revisit regularly through additions, viewings, readings, and sharing. For example, through their repeated drawings, the children are encouraged to continue to add detail, acquiring ever-stronger drawing, observation, and communication skills, and these strengths are noted on the board, as illustrated in the photo of learner Kola's self-portrait.

Our vignette of the classroom above raises questions about early literacy, among them the following:

- What is **early literacy**?
- How can educators of young children best create opportunities for constructing meaning, including through print literacy?
- Of what importance are other **modes** in the early years?
- How might educators create expansive literacy learning and identity options for all young children?

This chapter addresses just these questions. In getting at the roots of supporting young children's literacy practices, we hope to provide a foundation for educators of young children and older elementary learners. ☐

EARLY LITERACY

Early literacy is a theoretical approach to understanding young children's literacies. It owes a debt to **emergent literacy** and psychologist Marie Clay. Clay observed that most children come to school with some knowledge about print literacy. This discovery overthrew the prevailing understanding of the day, which was that children learn print literacy from scratch during their time at school. Clay recognized that young children sort out what print is for and how it works as they engage in a range of activities and experiences involving printed language. For instance,

- When read to by their loved ones, children experience the pleasures of a good story, and construct a **schema** for what stories are like and what book language sounds like.
- When they see their care providers making lists to take to the grocery store and refer to these lists as they shop, children begin to understand that print carries ideas across time and space.
- In the morning as they eat breakfast, children become aware that there is a relationship between the words they say and hear and what is on the cereal box.

Early literacy includes all the dimensions of language and literacy and is based on **social constructivism**, which sees that knowledge is tied to the context in which one is situated rather than being individually generated. Early literacy research has thus focused on the specific contexts (including **domains**) in which children practise their literacies, with an eye, as Kendrick (2003, p. 41) put it, to how "learning occurs through social participation in, and adoption of a community's practices for using and interpreting" literacy. As a child's context is seen as affecting his or her literacy practices and acquisition, early literacy does not find that there are universal developmental stages of literacy. It does regard children's literacy practices as just as important or meaningful as adult literacy practices. Julia Gillen and Nigel Hall (2003) explained that early literacy

> allows early childhood to be seen as a state in which people use literacy as it is appropriate, meaningful and useful to them, rather than a stage on a path to some future literate state. It is not about emergence or becoming literate, it is about *being literate* [emphasis added]; and it allows the literacy practices and products of early childhood to be acknowledged as valid in their own right. (p. 10)

The importance of context means that rather than change the child to fit school, the goal is to change schools and literacy instruction to better respond to children's **funds of knowledge**.

What Literacy Knowledge Do Young Children Need?

Though all children may not take the same literacy path, certain early understandings about print can help them along their way. Box 4.1 highlights some of the major categories of these understandings, and we describe each in turn below while suggesting some of the ways that these understandings can be developed early in a child's life. Following this, we offer suggestions for further promoting early literacy within the classroom.

Cultural Views and Functions of Written Language

Before explicit instruction of print can be valuable to children, they need to develop what Purcell-Gates (1996) called the "big picture" of literacy or general understanding of written language (David et al., 2000). For instance, we can try to teach children to write, but they may have difficulty with this if they do not first understand that writing is meant to convey a message and that the practice of writing a message is purposeful.

Children's views about the value and functions of written language are a reflection of their experiences within their homes and wider social contexts. In some homes, children are read to from birth and print literacy is a part of the fabric of home life. Although young children in these homes may not recognize letters and words as such, many do understand that what they see written on screens, in books, or written by parents as lists, memos, notes, and cards, contains meaning. From the age of about two onward, they often become involved in representing and expressing meaning, using a variety of modes. As adults read books to them, children come to expect pleasure and that books will make sense. In turn, they try to make meaning as they interact with texts independently.

This immersion in and interactions around text has much to teach. Classic research into young children's understanding of the formal aspects of the graphic system has shown, for

BOX 4.1

COMPONENTS OF EARLY LITERACY KNOWLEDGE

Cultural Views and Functions of Written Language

▷ expecting meaning from written language

▷ expecting purpose from written language

Nature and Forms of Written Language

▷ understanding that oral and written language are related

▷ matching words heard with those in print (eye–voice matching)

▷ internalizing the language of books

Oral Language–Print Relationship

▷ differentiating between pictures and print

▷ understanding how print works (conventions of print)

▷ matching sounds and letters in words (alphabetic principle)

▷ understanding terms related to books, reading, and writing

Source: Purcell-Gates, V. "Growing successful readers: Homes, communities, and schools" in J. Osborn & F. Lehr (Eds.), *Literacy for all: Issues in teaching and learning* (New York, NY: Guilford Press), 1998, p. 54.

example, that children can determine by the number of characters in a textual phrase and the variation in these characters whether the phrase is something that can be read (Ferreiro & Teberosky, 1993).

Early in their lives, children may see their families using reading and writing for a range of purposes. Family members may read manuals or directions to assemble new toys, furniture, and tools. They may read items on the Internet for information and entertainment, and write emails for different purposes. Children may also see literacy enacted in a variety of ways by their siblings, grandparents, and peers, and in their communities (e.g., readings of the Bible or the Qur'an) (Gregory et al., 2004). By talking to their families and other important people in their lives about what they are doing, imitating or taking a reader/writer role alongside them, and playing with literacy, children learn why people read and write: for the fun of it, to find out something, to learn how to do something, or to communicate with someone. Much of this learning is structured in the way Cambourne (1988) described in his conditions of learning (outlined in Chapter 1), and the learning is particularly powerful because it is coming from people whom children value (Hicks, 2002).

Not all children's out-of-school literacy practices, however, are in sync with those of the school. There is a heavy weighting toward print in school, yet many children's out-of-school literacy practices are more multimodal.

Another consideration is that many children in schools are **culturally and linguistically diverse (CLD)**. Schools must thus provide for a wide range of individual differences when planning language and literacy instruction. We also advocate always basing instruction on children's funds of knowledge and keeping open their identity options.

Nature and Forms of Written Language

Another understanding of print literacy that children need to develop involves the relationship or connection between oral and written language. Children need to know, for example,

> that the talk that is inspired by a text is not a free-form commentary on the pictures, nor a story that changes a little with each telling, but rather a sort of frozen discourse that must come out just so every time the text is read. (Temple & Gillet, 1989, p. 113)

Most children come to this understanding by constructing the big picture of written language. One clue children can give us that they understand that the story is a "frozen discourse" is when they show intolerance if every word in a text is not read exactly as the time before during a Shared Reading or Read-Aloud. They also demonstrate an understanding that spoken messages can be written down in their early writing when they make marks or print letters, and ask that these be read back to them.

But children need to go beyond this general understanding of the relationship between oral and written language to a more specific understanding that each written word is related to one word they hear or say. Repeated readings of a familiar text are one way that children are able to begin matching words on the page with words in memory. They are engaged in what is frequently referred to as "eye–voice pointing" or "speech-to-print matching." The child looks at each word at the same time as he or she is saying it (Pinnell & Scharer, 2003). Such repeated readings are a familiar practice in many households, where children ask to be read the same story again and again.

Not only experiences with books in homes contribute to awareness of the relationship between oral and written words. Children can also acquire this knowledge through interaction with literacy in their surroundings, such as seeing demonstrations of email, writing in cartoons, video games, and exposure to environmental print, that is, writing and any corresponding symbols (e.g., the golden arches that go with the word *McDonalds*) that children may encounter in their day-to-day environments (Mayer, 2007). In the supermarket, for example, young children see products being named as they are selected. Pop-up ads, household products, and signs attract attention to print and help children become aware that every word they hear is linked directly to a word in written language. This awareness allows children to focus attention on the appropriate units of print as they try to read.

When they are exposed to different forms of print, children also become aware that there are differences between the language in, for example, storybooks, and the spoken language of their daily lives. We rarely talk like the giant in "Jack in the Beanstalk" ("Fe, fi, fo, fum!"). This is known as learning the language of books (Doake, 1988) and "talking like a book" (Clay, 1972, p. 28). Children who come to school with little exposure to books will need to acquire this new **discourse** (Gummersall & Strong, 1999). As educators, we must also remember that book language is not a single discourse, as content-area texts such as information books have their own structures that must also be acquired (Moje, Ciechanowski, & Kramer, 2004). Thus young children should also receive learning opportunities related to various **genres** of text (Anderson, Moffat, & Shapiro, 2006).

Oral Language–Print Relationship

Perhaps the most basic knowledge children need to construct about print is that there is a difference between it and pictures. Like our discussion in Chapter 1 about how modes generally are not used in isolation, young children often employ writing, drawing, and talk together to express themselves (Baghban, 2007). Very young children may not initially differentiate their drawing from writing, but in relatively little time they do (Mayer, 2007). One way we can tell that children understand the difference between pictures and print is when they point to print rather than pictures when reading a book from memory.

Early writing begins from children's attempts to express themselves. This expressive communication can be manifest through many modes, including art and model making. Two studies in particular are helpful in thinking about children's literacy practices where they attempt to make a concept or idea concrete: First is Kress's (1997) documentation of how young children's meaning making through drawings, collages, cut-outs, and the like leads to and enhances their writing practices. Next is Pahl's (1999) study of what she calls "transformations" in preschool settings. A transformation is when a person moves an idea from one mode or **medium** to another. An example of this in a classroom would be when children orally tell a story, then draw, and then write the story. Transformations have been found to create spaces for learning, creativity, and concept development (e.g., Stein, 2008). Pahl (1999) has also observed that children can "express complex ideas in a material form, without the need for access to written modes of expression" (p. 23). What these and other studies show is how providing young children with multiple modes and media for expression can aid in their development of print literacy.

Regarding writing, children often play and experiment with making marks with large, rounded gestures or scratchy straight lines. These marks evolve in form toward more standard print, with letters and familiar shapes emerging that children repeat as they perceive a likeness to models in their own world. This early writing plays a significant role in developing children's knowledge about how print works (Clay, 1975). Children come to understand that the same letter can be written in various ways (Puranik, Lonigan, & Kim, 2011). We see this when a child fills a piece of paper with different versions of the letter *A*, for example. We might see a tall, thin *A*, wide, fat ones, ones that are upside-down, and ones with no stroke across the middle.

Children also learn about **directionality** as they engage in early writing. They learn that in the English language

- print begins at the top of a page and continues to the bottom
- people read and write from left to right on the page
- the front of a book opens on the right
- directionality is important to the identity of letters: for instance, *b* and *d* are "distinguished by the direction in which they face" (Cook & Bassetti, 2005, p. 10)

Educators need to be aware of the language systems that CLD learners are familiar with. For CLD learners whose first language has a writing system similar to English (e.g., Spanish), concepts about directionality usually transfer well between first and second languages. In the case where two languages differ in terms of these concepts (e.g., English and Hebrew), educators need to be explicit in addressing the specific difference among the writing systems. Knowledge of these systems is paramount as the directionality of writing can affect many aspects of learners' representations, not just print. It can, for instance,

> even affect how people represent time. English speakers who want to advertise a washing powder will show a pile of dirty laundry on the left, followed by the washing powder in the middle, and then a pile of clean laundry on the right. Hebrew speakers, whose writing system runs right-to-left, show the same events in the opposite direction. (Bassetti, n.d., sec. 3.4)

To support learners, educators "need to learn about the writing systems their students use and the extent to which they are literate in them" (Peregoy & Boyle, 2000, p. 242).

In terms of concepts of print, some express concern when young children write their names backward or confuse the letters *b* and *d*. However, such reversals are common in the early days of print literacy (Ritchey, 2006). Until children encounter written language, they have an implicit understanding that directional orientation does not affect the identity of an object. For example, a cup is still a cup, whether the handle is turned toward the left or the right. Directionality has not been used to differentiate objects in the child's environment, but with letters and numbers, all that changes. Nines and sixes are different numbers, *b*'s and *d*'s are different letters, and *on* and *no* are different words.

Although it is largely an artifact of reading instruction, children also learn the terms we use to talk about reading and writing. They come to understand what educators mean when they say, "Find the *word* cat," "What *sound* do you hear at the *beginning* of the word cat?" and "Read the first *sentence*" (Mason, 1984). Terms about reading and writing, such as *word*, *letter*, *sentence*, and *sound*, make up part of what is known as **metalinguistic awareness**, and young children frequently have quite different concepts from adults about terms (McGee & Richgels, 1996). Other conventions they learn involve the use of punctuation and the associated terminology, as well as words to describe books (e.g., *front*, *back*, *author*, *cover*).

Phonological Awareness, Phonemic Awareness, and Phonics

Regarding print literacy, children need to make the connection between letters and sounds: **phonics**. This understanding is related to **phonological awareness** and its subcomponent, **phonemic awareness**.

Phonological awareness, along with letter knowledge, has been used as a key predictor of reading achievement in grade 1 (Hill & Nichols, 2006). It operates at the level of sound, and it includes the awareness of "basic sound units" such as the ability to

- recognize "that words represent a sound unit"
- detect "that words are made up of different parts" (i.e., syllables)
- recognize that "words are made up of individual sounds" (**phonemes**) (Opitz, 2000, p. 6)

Every day in early literacy classrooms, educators ask children to use their phonological awareness, though they may not even be aware that this is what they are doing. For instance, when an educator asks learners to sound out a word that they are trying to spell, they must know what a word is and be able to isolate its sounds (e.g., identifying beginning, middle, and final sounds). Not necessarily an easy feat!

What is challenging about beginning sounds is not the sound but its location. Understanding place or location is important in learning to read. Children cannot pay attention to the beginning sound if they do not know where the beginning is (Invernizzi, 2003).

Middle sounds in particular are difficult for children to isolate. Moreover, as we explored in Chapter 3, except on rare occasions, oral language is the basis for print literacy learning. When children do not have a firm command of oral English because they speak a different first language, many phonological awareness tasks can be difficult. For instance, "natural speech is a continuous blend of words; so, word boundaries are not clearly identifiable. The pauses one hears between words are not really present in the acoustic signal" (Carlo, 2007, p. 107). Children are able to hear these pauses when they can draw on other cues, such as pragmatic and semantic cues.

How can children develop phonological awareness? In this and other chapters, we look at instructional strategies to help children in this regard. What is crucial to recognize now, however, is that "much of the research in this area highlights the idea that phonological awareness, rather than a precursor to reading and writing, may be reciprocally involved in early literacy acquisition" (Hill & Nichols, 2006, p. 161). This means that children do not master phonological awareness *before* they engage in other early literacy practices; other literacy practices, such as those that make up multiliteracies pedagogies, *help* children to develop phonological awareness. This goes for all children, including those who are CLD. As Opitz (2000) said,

> If children are exposed to a rich language environment in which they enjoy Read-Alouds, songs, nursery rhymes, poems, and other forms of language play, most acquire some aspects of phonological awareness with relative ease at a very young age. In fact, some acquire all levels of phonological awareness before they even start school. (p. 8)

The area of phonological awareness that is classically accepted, however, to be a key area of difficulty for many children who struggle with their print literacy is phonemic awareness (Juel, 1988).

The three aspects of phonological awareness that we list above could be seen as moving from simpler to more complex understandings of language. The third aspect, to recognize that "words are made up of individual sounds" (Opitz, 2000, p. 6), constitutes what is known as phonemic awareness. Phonemic awareness involves the understanding that "every word can be conceived as a sequence of phonemes" (Adams, 2002, p. 76). It includes the "ability to hear, identify, and manipulate the individual sounds (phonemes) in spoken words" (Ontario Ministry of Education, 2003a, p. 77). Some key phonemic awareness skills are as follows:

- recognizing rhymes
- recognizing when words begin with or contain the same sound
- generating words that begin with or contain the same sound
- generating words by blending sounds together
- segmenting sounds within words
- playing with the sounds in words by substituting, adding, or deleting sounds to create new words (Opitz, 2000)

Phonemic awareness is thought by some to be an "essential" component of reading (Rothenberg & Fisher, 2007, p. 142) and "one of the best predictors of success in learning to read" (Cunningham, 2007, p. 160). Just as in the case of phonological awareness in general, however, phonemic awareness is "only *one* part of a beginning literacy program" (p. 160), and most children develop it through rich literacy activities such as Read-Alouds, rhyme saying, wordplay, and the other instructional components of multiliteracies pedagogies. Simply "drilling and skilling" learners in phonemic awareness will not contribute to their literacy acquisition (International Reading Association, 1998), including reading comprehension (Cummins, 2007). Accordingly, some educators have shown that explicit phonemic awareness instruction should account for *no more* than 10 to 15 minutes per day of a teacher's reading instruction time (University of Oregon, n.d.).

Phonics refers to readers connecting "the sounds they hear with the print they see on the page in order to make meaning" (Ontario Ministry of Education, 2003a, p. 17). To make this connection, children draw on their phonemic awareness and "learn the symbols that represent … sounds" (Peregoy & Boyle, 2004, p. 108). Consequently, children need to develop a "comfortable familiarity" with the letters of the alphabet—to be able to sing them, say the letter names, write them, and recognize them (Adams, 1998). Writing one's own name is also seen as an important milestone in developing this familiarity (Puranik et al., 2011). Children can then move into how letters and combinations of letters represent various sounds. Whereas phonemic awareness is based at the level of sound, phonics is print based and draws on auditory and visual information. As mentioned, many children come to school with phonemic awareness already in place. Similarly, through interactions with print in the environment and activities at home such as playing with letters (e.g., magnetic letters on the refrigerator) and book reading with parents, many children also have a sense of the alphabet and have started to construct sound–symbol relationships.

Likewise to the development of concepts of print (e.g., directionality), the accessibility of the alphabetic principle for CLD learners is premised to a great extent on the compatibility of their first language and English. Consider that

> transfer of literacy ability from one language to another depends on the similarities and differences between their writing systems, including the unit of speech symbolized by each character. For example, alphabetic writing systems, such as the three different ones used for English, Greek, and Russian, represent speech sounds of phonemes with letters or letter sequences. In contrast, in logographic writing systems, such as Chinese, each written character represents a meaning unit or morpheme; while in syllabic writing systems, such as kana in Japanese and Sequoyah's Cherokee syllabary, each written symbol represents a syllable. (Peregoy & Boyle, 2004, pp. 109–110)

In all situations, ensuring that children have the big picture of literacy in place and providing a program that builds from their funds of knowledge will help them to develop these important literacy basics. In the next section, we discuss where to start with instruction: specifically, the role of **assessment** in determining the basis for what to teach, when to teach it, and how to teach it.

ASSESSING EARLY LITERACY

As an educator, you need to know what understandings your students have constructed about literacy in order to provide appropriate learning opportunities. What are learners able to do? What are their funds of knowledge? What do they value? The collection of information to answer questions such as these constitutes assessment. We agree with Mary Renck Jalongo (2007) that assessment in general should be as follows:

- *Responsive*, to capture individual differences and be culturally fair so that assessment is child centered, rather than planned around administrative convenience

- *Interactive*, to emphasize the interactive nature of learning and to show what children learn through working with adults, other children, and materials

- *Relevant*, so that connections between and among teaching, learning, and assessment are made explicit to all stakeholders—students, teachers, parents, administrators, and policymakers

- *Comprehensive*, to provide evidence of children's learning in all areas of development (physical, emotional, social, cognitive)

- *Integrative*, to highlight and reveal the complex processes of language learning, thereby enabling students to set goals and teachers to make better instructional decisions
- *Communicative*, to demonstrate to others the advantages of learning activities and materials that are concrete and meaningful to young children
- *Supportive*, to promote teachers' efforts in counteracting a test-driven curriculum by establishing a system for organizing and recording observations (p. 330, emphases ours)*

In this chapter we present assessment strategies that are in keeping with the above criteria to highlight how assessment might be used with young children and to make evident the assessment and instruction cycle. These strategies, however, need not only be used with young children, and other assessment strategies can also be used in the early years. Thus the following strategies should be considered in tangent with the other assessment information throughout the book (e.g., reading assessment information in Chapter 5 and writing assessment information in Chapter 10). In the end, educators can use their own best judgment to decide which assessments are appropriate to use with which learners at which times.

Informal Assessment

Informal assessment provides a basis for daily lesson planning and responsive instruction. Through it, educators can discover what children know about literacy and what they can do with this knowledge. The literature describes four major types of informal assessment. The first three—observation, interviews, and samples of children's work—involve informal assessment by the educator, and provide the focus of the next section. The last involves student self-assessment. Note that all the information from these forms of assessment should be considered *in tangent* and *in context*.

Observing Children

As educators, we collect information every time we interact with learners. However, even though these observations are often not recorded, they might still influence our pedagogical decisions. Some educators keep anecdotal records, jotting down key observations of learners' literacy practices during or at the end of the day. Others work in teams, as in the case of Andrea and Jennifer in the opening vignette, to carefully document in situ. To aid the process of documentation when they are alone in a classroom, some educators keep all the materials they need to record observations of children at various stations in the classroom (rather than lugging around binders). Near a literacy play centre, in the library corner, or at the guided reading table, educators, for example, can keep clipboards stocked with sheets of printer labels. Educators can then record observations of children on the labels and later affix them to the child's file. Other educators prefer to use mobile devices like phones that can be at one's side for documentation. Educators can use these informal notes to track individual growth, ascertain the effectiveness of their instruction, and plan future class and small-group activities.

Goodman's notion of "kidwatching" refers to the ongoing observation by educators of children in classrooms. She suggests that kidwatching needs to be done consciously if teachers are to "gain the greatest insights from it" (1991, p. 58).

---

* Jalongo, Mary R., *Early Childhood Language Arts, 4th Edition*, © 2007, p. 350. Reprinted by permission of Pearson Education, Inc., New York, New York.

Beginning educators, in particular, can benefit from supports such as the Early Literacy Checklist in Table 4.1 to help them know what to watch for and when. As mentioned, it may be preferable for educators to organize their observations according to the contexts in which children are practising their literacies. In this way, they can better understand the circumstances that give rise to particular kinds of literacy practices. The Early Literacy Checklist is therefore structured around the literacy events or pedagogical components that we describe in this chapter. Many of the components of the multiliteracies pedagogies we introduced in Chapter 1 are involved. Also, earlier in this chapter we presented components of early literacy, indicating the understandings that young children construct in the early stages of learning to read and write. The Early Literacy Checklist is organized around attitudes and understandings related to literacy. For each attitude or understanding, the checklist identifies behaviours that indicate a child has developed an attitude or understanding in specific learning contexts. Educators can document if a child is *C*, consistently demonstrating the behaviour; *B*, beginning to demonstrate the behaviour; or *N*, not yet demonstrating the behaviour.

TABLE 4.1 **EARLY LITERACY CHECKLIST**

Attitudes and Understandings	Learning Contexts	Behaviours	Comments and Examples
Has a positive attitude to books and print	Read-Aloud Shared Reading Independent Reading Language Experience Approach (LEA) Writing Functional interactions with print	___ Displays enjoyment and interest in reading and being read to ___ Chooses books as centre activity ___ Rereads shared stories in centre time ___ Chooses to write during centre time ___ Shows interest in print around the classroom, school, community	
Recognizes written language as meaningful	Read-Aloud Shared Reading Shared Writing Independent writing Functional interactions with print	___ Makes comments or asks questions during reading ___ Predicts meaningful words when words are covered or missing ___ When rereading, can communicate the meaning of the text ___ Contributes ideas for writing ___ Produces meaningful messages when reading what has been written ___ Responds meaningfully to labels, calendar, charts in classroom	
Understands that message stays the same in written text	Read-Aloud Shared Reading LEA Functional interactions with print	___ Chimes in during reading ___ Knows when teacher or another child makes a miscue during rereading ___ Responds to labels/words the same way every time	

(continued)

TABLE 4.1 **EARLY LITERACY CHECKLIST (CONTINUED)**

Attitudes and Understandings	Learning Contexts	Behaviours	Comments and Examples
Knows how written language sounds	Shared Reading LEA Independent writing	___ Memorizes favourite books ___ "Talks like a book" when rereading ___ "Talks like a book" when dictating/writing stories	
Has story sense	Read-Aloud Shared Reading LEA Independent writing	___ Predicts what will happen in a story ___ Retells beginning, middle, and end of stories ___ Is able to draw or dramatize stories ___ Includes beginning, middle, and end in stories (and/or uses a logical organization)	
Recognizes importance of print	Shared Reading LEA Independent writing Functional interactions with print	___ Points to print during reading/rereading ___ Makes letters or letter-like forms when writing ___ Points to print in classroom, school, and community	
Knows directional aspects of print	Shared Reading LEA Independent writing	___ Begins reading at top of page ___ Points from left to right when tracking print ___ Reads left page before right page ___ Writes from top to bottom of page ___ Writes left to right across page	
Makes speech-to-print match	Shared Reading LEA	___ Points to each word while saying it during reading/rereading	
Understands terms and concepts of print	Shared Reading LEA Independent writing	___ Uses print literacy terms (e.g., *letters* and *words*) while reading (e.g., "What's this word?") ___ Leaves a space between words ___ Uses print literacy terms (e.g., *letters* and *words*) while writing (e.g., "How do you spell the word 'on'?") ___ Uses literacy terms such as *author, page, sentence* while reading and writing	
Has decoding/ encoding strategies	Shared Reading LEA Independent writing Functional interactions with print	___ Identifies same word in different contexts ___ Uses initial letter sound to help identify words ___ Verbalizes letter sounds while writing ___ Bases spelling on letter names or sounds	

The checklist can be used either as a general guide for unrecorded observations or in a more systematic way to record information on some or all of the children in a class. When used at regular intervals, the checklist provides an indication of a child's progress and is a useful component in the portfolios of children who are not yet reading independently. The right-hand column in the checklist is a space to record specific comments and examples. For instance, if an educator has checked "Chooses books as free-time activity," this column might include information on what types of books the child chooses (e.g., big books, animal books, familiar books), how frequently this happens (every day, once a week), and whether the child reads alone or with another child. Consider the following examples of how information collected on this checklist might be interpreted:

- Children who are beginning to point globally at print as they read or reread books are showing that they understand the importance of print (as compared with pictures) in reading.
- When they point to words as the educator reads, or they read a familiar book or shared story as the teacher points, children demonstrate that they are ready for speech-to-print matching activities.
- Children who have acquired the speech-to-print match when rereading familiar books or language experience stories show that they are ready for instruction that involves identifying specific words, first in familiar books and language experience stories, and later in less familiar materials.

Interviews

If educators take seriously the notion that learners' funds of knowledge are significant for new learning, then families have a great deal of information that can serve as a basis for instructional planning. How educators can collect such information in a way that can foster home and school partnerships is a tricky question, in part, because traditional parent–educator interviews typically see information flowing from educator to parent with the goal of the communication being to change the parent. Patricia Edwards (2004), who has worked extensively in the area of home and family communication, suggests that educators might conduct interviews in a different way. She has found that many families respond well to the invitation to tell stories about their home practices.

For years now, Edwards has been eliciting stories from families by using story starters, such as the ones we present in Box 4.2. Within, for example, a conference setting, educators can encourage children to share with their families the work that they have been doing in class, educators share their own stories of what goes on in the classroom, and the story starters are used to involve families in the sharing. Edwards's notion of story sharing creates an environment of reciprocity, where all participants are invited to share information for the benefit of the child's learning. This is more in keeping with Wink's (2011) doin'-it-with-'em model, in which all parties learn and change.

Edwards (2004) found that through families sharing stories, educators can gather information about home literacy practices that can aid in their planning. For instance, if educators want to construct literacy play centres that build on children's knowledge, they might build

BOX 4.2

DISCUSSION STARTERS WITH FAMILIES

▷ What do you and your child enjoy doing together?

▷ All children have potential. Did you notice that ___ had some particular talent or "gift" early on? If so, what was it? What did your child do to make you think that s/he had this potential? Were there specific things you did as a parent to strengthen this talent?

▷ Is there something about your child that might not be obvious to the teacher, but might positively or negatively affect his/her performance in school if the teacher knew? If so, what would that something be?

▷ What activities/hobbies do you participate in as a family?

▷ Can you describe "something" about your home learning environment that you would like the school to build upon because you feel that this "something" would enhance your child's learning potential at school?

Source: Edwards, Patricia A., *Children's Literacy Development: Making it Happen through School, Family and Community Involvement*, 1st edition, © 2004, p. 145. Reprinted by permission of Pearson Education, Inc., New York, New York.

on the finding that the families of children in their classrooms work in restaurants and thus construct a play restaurant. Children might then be invited to read menus, write out orders, follow recipes, and carry through on a number of literacy-related activities, all within their play. Similarly, educators could ensure that the kitchen in the house centre, for example, contains artifacts (e.g., boxes and cans of food) that are consistent with children's ethnic backgrounds. There could also be an opportunity to include print in different languages.

Educators can also use information from the story sharing protocol to build into preexisting curricular themes. For example, if educators knew that many of the families in their classrooms took the bus, they could start with buses in an inquiry on transportation. Educators can also solicit specific information at specific times from families to build curriculum. In one cross-cultural teaching situation, educators sent home newsletters that both informed families of important information and invited the sharing of information. Here is a sample from that newsletter:

Beginning the week of February 18, we will be studying transportation. Here are some of the books we will read:

- *Freight Train* by Donald Crews
- *Firefighters A to Z* by Chris L. Demarest
- *Little Toot* by Hardi Gramatky
- *Tina's Taxi* by Betsy Franco
- *City Sounds* by Rebecca Emberley

We have copies of all of these books in the library. Borrow one to share with your child at home.
We want to learn from you. What transportation-related experiences have your children had? Please write to us and tell us about them. (Paratore, Melzi, & Krol-Sinclair, 2003, p. 110)

The response to the newsletter was crucial to the educators for their planning. Here is some of what one teacher learned about her students' transportation experiences:

- T train [subway] from East Boston to downtown very often—Rāmon
- Bus from Chelsea to East Boston to see relatives every week—Dimas
- Bus from Chelsea to Haymarket and then took T train to Medical Center—Jeimy
- Boat in El Salvador to sightsee—Encarnacion
- Boat to see Boston Harbor Islands—Dina
- Plane from Germany to Boston—Senija
- Car from Bosnia to Germany—Sevida
- Car from Everett to Chelsea every day—Maria (p. 112)

In a sharing protocol such as this the flow of information goes back and forth: resources are made available to families so that they can assist their children at home (e.g., specific content-area texts are made accessible), and educators are provided with information that can help them plan.

Educators can also augment family interview information by working with children directly. A whole-class, interactive interview, not dissimilar to a morning meeting, is one way of doing this. Educators can work with children to identify the types of literacy experiences that they have in the various domains they inhabit in their daily lives. Adapted from Riley (2006), educators can also work with children in various groupings (e.g., small group or whole class) to map the places where they spend time, then fill in on sticky notes the kinds of litera-cies they practise there before affixing them to the map. For instance, next to Home, children might list the kinds of literacies practised by themselves and family members such as reading "recipes," filling out "forms," and playing videos. To prepare for this type of interview, children and families can be invited to keep a Literacy Log, in which they track their literacy practices. Educators can choose for the logs to focus on just print-based or broader literacy practices.

When the circumstances call for it, educators can also use a more direct form of individual interview to, for example, learn about children's home reading habits. Box 4.3 shows such an interview protocol.

BOX 4.3

CHILD INTERVIEW QUESTIONS

Family Reading and Writing Habits

1. Who reads at home?
2. What kinds of things does X [mother, father, sibling, other person] read?
3. Why do you think X [repeat for each person named in point 2] reads these things?
4. Who writes at home?
5. What kinds of things does X write?
6. Why do you think X writes these things?

(continued)

Child's Home Reading Experiences

1. Who reads to you at home?

2. Do you enjoy reading? What do you like most about reading?

3. How often does *X* read to you?

4. Tell me the names of some of your favourite books.

5. Do you read to yourself at home? If so, how often? What do you read? What do you do when you read?

6. Do you write at home? If so, how often? What do you write? What do you do when you write?

Despite the information educators can gain about children's concepts and knowledge of literacy by observing and interviewing them, there are times when further information, particularly in relation to reading, is needed. Several educators have developed interview schedules for this purpose. The one in Table 4.2 incorporates questions and concepts from book-handling interviews suggested by classic sources Doake (1981), Alberta Education (1993), and Clay (1993a).

TABLE 4.2 **BOOK-HANDLING INTERVIEW**

Questions	Literacy Concepts and Knowledge	Comments
1. How books work • Can you show me the front of the book? • Where is the title? What does it tell you? • Open the book so we can start reading at the beginning of the book.	___ Identifies front of book ___ Identifies title ___ Identifies first page of text	
2. Importance of print • Show me with your finger where to start reading.	___ Identifies print	
3. Directional aspects of print • Show me the top/bottom of this page. • Show me which page to read first. • Show me with your finger which way I go as I read this page.	___ Identifies top/bottom of page ___ Reads left page before right ___ Points left to right across line of print	
4. Speech-to-print match • Point to the words as I read.	___ Partial matching ___ Exact matching	
5. Terms and concepts of print • Point to one letter/word. • Point to the first/last letter in a word. • Point to an upper/lowercase letter.	___ One letter ___ One word ___ First letter ___ Last letter ___ Uppercase letter ___ Lowercase letter	

TABLE 4.2 **BOOK-HANDLING INTERVIEW** *(CONTINUED)*

Questions	Literacy Concepts and Knowledge	Comments
6. Letter/word identification • Point to the letter ___. (Name two letters on the page.) • Point to the word ___. (Name two high-frequency words on the page.)	___ Letter names ___ Words	
7. Meaning in written language • Retell what happens in this book.	___ Retells by naming pictures ___ Retells part of text ___ Retells all of the text and uses the text's organization to do so (e.g., beginning, middle, end)	

Samples of Children's Work

Early Writing Educators can gain information about children's literacy development by collecting samples of their work over time. It is easier to gather the artifacts of children's writing than of their reading. As we discuss in Chapter 10, educators can collect writing samples throughout the school year and keep them in a folder or portfolio. They can select samples on their own and also help children to select samples that represent something special that they would like to document. Linda Levely, from Chapter 2, makes it part of her routine to collect a specific writing sample from each student every month. Learners complete, as part of their journal, a page called "This is me in [fill in the month]" (see Figures 4.1 and 4.2 for Evan's samples), where they write about what has been happening with them lately. Children then share this work with each other in the classroom Author's Chair. Linda analyzes the samples to understand the children's literacies and gain more general knowledge about their interests, experiences, emotional state, and the like. The samples also make wonderful story starters during family interview times.

In terms of analyzing children's writing, educators can use the components of early literacy knowledge we highlighted earlier in this chapter in Box 4.1. Consider, for example, Evan's samples against the components that might apply to the writing context: Which has Evan mastered? Where might he still need room to grow? What is Evan telling his teacher about his knowledge? This kind

FIGURE 4.1

EVAN'S DRAWING

This is me in February

What's new? in February I like playing vitYOO GamSe I Play X Box aS and

FIGURE 4.2

EVAN'S WRITING SAMPLE

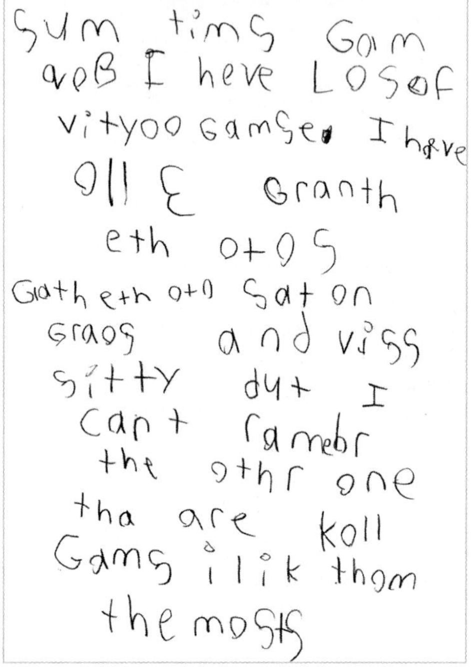

Sum tims Gam
aoß I heve LoSof
vityoo gamses I have
oll E Granth
eth otos
Gath eth oto Sat on
Graos   and viss
sitty   dyt   I
Cant   ramebr
the othr one
tha are koll
Gams ilik thom
the mosts

of analysis is more appropriate than comparing samples against lists of developmental stages (e.g., first, children do this; then, they do this). While children do move toward writing in standard ways (e.g., standard spelling and formatting of letters) when the conditions for learning are right, they do not progress in a lockstep manner with every child developing in the same way (Prince Edward Island Department of Education and Early Childhood Development, 2008). Also, in an early literacy vein, we believe that children's expressive communication is meaningful and purposeful and should thus be analyzed in its own right and contexts. In *Before Writing*, Kress (1997) also alerted us to the need to consider young children's writing in relation to other dimensions of language and literacy, including reading. In the section of his book that dealt specifically with print, Kress offered samples of young children's writing to show their attention to and interest in different aspects of writing. These ranged from recognizing writing as a block of print to expressing an understanding of how genre operates (e.g., newspapers). As he stated,

> In the multiple readings which children perform [including reading their own writing], the different "takes" they have, looking at print now this way now that, now as "block of print," now as "letter," now as "sequence of letters," now as "newspaper as object," now as "newspaper as message," now as "text as genre," children gradually develop a sense of what this "stuff" is. (p. 79)

In each of these examples, Kress explained, children see "print as a different object" and "what we as adults take (too naively) as simply print or writing … is an enormously complex phenomenon." Children recognize this complexity and uncover it "bit by bit" (p. 79). To guide our pedagogies, as educators we must use assessment to understand which bit children are interested in and help them develop it further toward increased writing proficiency.

Educators can also analyze children's understandings of the purposes of writing. When children are seemingly "scribbling" (we prefer the term *mark making*), they are indicating that they realize writing and drawing are different. When they begin to use letter or letter-like forms, they show an awareness that writers use symbols when they write. They start to talk about what they have written (or ask someone to tell them what they have written), indicating that they are aware that written language holds meaning. As they continue to grow, children produce **invented spellings** and are aware that a message is encoded in the words they write.

Again, writing development is not necessarily linear nor universal. Many children, even until mid- or late grade 1, move between forms and understandings of writing (Sulzby, 1991). Whereas children may write a short sentence using invented spellings and be able to read it accurately on request, they might use markings other than letters on a more difficult task such as writing a whole book. This movement between more and less sophisticated writing is to be expected. Thus we recommend that educators collect many samples in a variety of contexts rather than a single sample, to provide a more comprehensive picture of a child's literacy than might otherwise result.

We now offer a couple of samples of children's writing to think about what they can teach regarding assessment and writing.

Learning about Children's Literacy Knowledge from Samples of Their Writing: Children's Samples

Consider the samples of writing of two six-year-olds, Rachel (Figure 4.3) and Jillian (Figure 4.4). Rachel was at home with her sister, Xian, and was invited by her mother to write about a topic that was of interest to her. She chose the Power Puff Girls. Jillian was invited within the context of her classroom to write a story. By looking at the samples, what can you tell about the children's understanding of print literacy?

In analyzing the samples from Rachel and Jillian, you do not have the benefit of the observation information that we have. Still, consider whether what you see in the samples corresponds with what we feel we learned about the children's literacy knowledge.

Rachel's writing says: "These are Power Puff Girls. They are main characters. They keep their town safe from crimes. They put them in jail. Rachel." The writing is accompanied by a very detailed drawing of two Power Puff characters. Of the context of the writing, Rachel's mother, Linda, explained that Rachel and Xian had been drawing Power Puff Girls after they found DVD copies of this 1980s cartoon at the library. Rachel and Xian had been inventing some new characters and discussing if it was acceptable to "copy." Linda said she and the girls had recently had a discussion about copyright and the Internet.

When writing, Rachel asked Linda how to spell "Power Puff." She indicated that she knew she could find it on the video box label, but following Linda's suggestion to give the

FIGURE 4.3

RACHEL'S WRITING IN GRADE 1

FIGURE 4.4

JILLIAN'S WRITING IN GRADE 1

To Ashley From

Ashley

Ashley
From
Mom
Dad
Yello
red
To
Kritsa
c to

spelling a try on her own, she did. Linda also offered that, as of late, Rachel had tended not to speak out the words as she wrote. The sample and details of the context illustrate Rachel's knowledge of writing and other elements of literacy. For example, her writing is an elaboration of her drawings, showing that she knows how the modes can complement each other. She was working multimodally, pulling on her interests and reading of the DVDs to redesign the characters. Her writing suggests that she was aware of the importance of directionality to letter identity and that she used letter sounds for spelling. Her inclination to use the video box to help her spell also shows she is aware of spelling resources and the reading and writing connections. The sample suggests that Rachel has some knowledge that writing is organized in sentences or at least that periods are used as some type of sign in writing. That Rachel was silent as she wrote and that this is somewhat new indicates that she knows that writing is the encoding of a message in print and that she no longer needs the support of speaking as she writes.

Rachel's writing reflects a greater understanding of the nature of written language than Jillian's. When asked to write a story, Jillian produced a labelled drawing for her friend Ashley. When asked to write all the words she could, Jillian produced the list at the bottom of her page. Many of the words are the names of important people in her life, including her parents, friend, and sister. This list, however, is rather restricted. In relation to components of early literacy, Jillian showed that she was developing an understanding of how people use print to relate to other people. She also knew that words are used in writing. She too worked multimodally, using a picture to convey most of the message and to compensate for the writing that she could not yet do. In this sample Jillian demonstrated a beginning understanding of the alphabetic principle.

Early Reading   When children read orally or silently, no permanent record remains of their reading. While some educators audiotape learners reading, there are drawbacks to this as an assessment tool: It is not easy to use these recordings to assess growth, it takes a great deal of time to listen to them, and it is difficult to remember what the child did on one recording when listening to the next. A practical solution to this challenge is for educators to make a written record of children's reading.

Running Records

Running records are a means for assessing learners' reading levels and their growth as readers. Originally developed by Clay to literally document learners' reading behaviours on the run, this strategy can be used by educators throughout the primary grades and sometimes beyond. It is ideally used with readers who are early in their reading practice. In this section, we offer a glimpse of teacher Lori McKee's use of running records in her classroom practice. We then suggest how to take a running record.

INSIDE CLASSROOMS

LORI MCKEE: RUNNING RECORDS

Why do I use running records?

Running records provide a structure that allows me to connect with learners on a one-to-one basis to discuss their reading. They give me a lot of information about learners' interests as well as the cues and strategies they are using and/ or neglecting while reading. This information allows me to provide focused instruction that reflects the interests and strengths of learners.

Running records also help me become more reflective and critical in my teaching. Clay (2002) explained that "when we become neutral observers and watch children at work in systematic and repeatable ways we begin to uncover some of our own assumptions and notice how wrong these can sometimes be" (p. 9). Running records help me to analyze children's reading with greater objectivity, so that I am better equipped to guide instruction.

How do I use running records in my classroom?

I use running records with several learners each day. I conduct running records whenever I need more information about an individual child's reading. Since running records only offer a "window" (Ontario Ministry of Education, 2003b, p. 12.44) into what learners are attending to while reading a particular text, and because the ways learners interact with

(continued)

texts rapidly changes as they grow as readers and writers, I take running records frequently with a variety of texts (e.g., fiction and nonfiction, texts that are familiar and unseen, and texts selected by me or the learners).

I often take running records while the rest of the class is reading independently. The running record happens within the context of a conversation that I have with learners about their reading (affectionately called a "Book Talk" by my students).

I document the running records on a blank page within a notebook that learners keep in their desks. This notebook holds my running record documentation and the child's responses to their reading (spontaneous and prompted). Over time, the notebook becomes a co-constructed portrait of learners' reading and writing acquisition as they and I contribute to the notebook collaboratively through the Book Talk conversations and individually as I document learners' reading through running records and other notes, and learners document their own responses to texts through pictures and/or words.

What does it look like when I take running records?

Before I conduct running records

▷ I quickly look back at the learners' previous running records to see the genre of books they have been reading, the level of books, the accuracy rates, and the teaching prompts that I have given to them. I also look at their entries in the notebook to see what they have recorded (through pictures and/or words) about what they are enjoying in reading, or how they are connecting to the texts they are reading.

▷ I engage learners in a short conversation about their reading. I might ask, "What have you read lately that you like? What has been hard?" Over time, I encourage the children to take the lead in these conversations. Near the end of the conversation, I might say something like, "Last time, we were working on [name the strategy]. Is this something that you are still working on?" We select a book to read. Most often, I encourage learners to select the book.

▷ At the top of the page in the notebook, I note the date, the title of the book, the genre of text, who selected the text (i.e., teacher or learner), whether the book was familiar or unseen, and if there was a particular reason that the children/teacher selected the text (e.g., a child wants to learn more about hamsters). I might also document part of our conversation.

During the running record

▷ I listen to learners read and record them using the conventions for running records. I usually listen to the child read about 100 words.

▷ I record observations about rate and fluency (e.g., Is the reading too fast or slow? Does the reading sound smooth or choppy?).

▷ I listen for and record when learners have applied a strategy, or followed through on something that we have been working on. I also record where they have almost applied a strategy, or not applied the strategy.

After the running record

▷ While sitting at a learner's desk, I analyze the running record, looking for the strategies and sources of information that the child has used and/or neglected (e.g., meaning, structure, and visual information).

▷ I praise learners for applying the strategy that we have been working on, or *almost applying* the strategy we have been working on (i.e., I applaud responses that are partially correct).

▷ I prompt learners to attend to information or strategies neglected (e.g., if learners say "I runned" instead of "I ran," I might prompt them by saying, "You are right, the picture shows the person running and it starts with the letter *r*, but does that *sound* right?" This prompt may encourage learners to use meaning, structure, and visual sources of information when reading).

▷ I record what I have praised and prompted at the bottom of the running record. We often discuss this information the next time we do a running record.

▷ At times, I will conduct a second running record immediately with learners when this might support them in applying a new strategy. Following the running record, I also may ask learners questions about their reading comprehension or ask them to retell.

Taking Running Records

Simple running records require nothing more than a pencil and blank sheet of lined paper; however, sometimes educators like to have a copy of the reading text to mark up as learners read. To create a reading record, educators work with learners individually and invite them to read a text orally. Educators use a standard notation system to record what the readers do with the text. While learners read aloud, educators listen carefully, noting when learners read a word correctly (marked by a check mark), omit a word (marked by a dash), self-correct (marked by the abbreviation *SC*), substitute a word (marked by writing the substituted word above the text word), insert words (marked by recording the insertion above a dash to show that there was no corresponding word in the text), repeat parts of the text (by marking an *R* and using an arrow to show what part of the text they've repeated), and when learners rely on educators' prompts to read a word (by recording a *T* for *tell*). Educators can invite learners to read familiar or unfamiliar texts, bearing in mind that they will garner different kinds of information from each. To make early readers more comfortable, educators might select a book that learners have some familiarity with. However, it can also be informative to choose an unfamiliar book, to see how learners approach new texts, or to use levelled texts to get a sense of learners' progress as readers.

For an e-workshop that allows you to practise taking and analyzing a running record, visit the Ontario Ministry of Education and TFO website workshop.on.ca (http://www.eworkshop .on.ca/edu/core.cfm?L=1). Select Literacy Modules, then Grades K to 3, and then Running Records.

Interpreting Running Records

Running records can help educators match books to readers and provide useful data concerning how a child approaches the task of reading, including reading a particular text. The qualitative information educators can derive from the records can be telling in this regard. Educators can also use the records to glean quantitative information about a reading by doing the following:

- Multiply the number of words learners read correctly by 100 and then divide the answer by the number of words in the text. For example, if a learner read 75 words correctly in a text that had 121 words, then the learner would have read 62 percent of the words correctly ($75 \times 100 = 7500 \div 121 = 62\%$). Please note that self-corrections are counted as correct words in this kind of tally.

- Generally, if learners are able to read 95 to 100 percent of the words in a text, the text is considered to be at readers' *independent* level, meaning that learners most likely will not need support to make meaning of the text. This is likely to be a good choice for Independent Reading time.

- If learners can read only 90 to 94 percent of the words in the text correctly, then the text may be considered to be at learners' *instructional* level. In this case, the text provides some challenges, but not so many that learners will become frustrated if some support is provided. This text is ideal for helping learners grow as readers as it is in learners' **zone of proximal development**. It is a good choice for Guided Reading.

- If learners can read less than 90 percent of the words in a text correctly, the text may be considered to be at learners' *frustration* level and might be best kept for situations such as Read-Alouds and Shared Reading.

There are some caveats here.

Correct word reading does not necessarily equate with being able to construct meaning from text. Educators will want to pair up the information from running records with information they have collected through other assessments (including retell). In this way, educators acknowledge that reading is about more than just being able to *word call*. They are also recognizing that reading aloud is different from silent reading. Smith (2007), for example, said, "Reading aloud is more difficult [than reading silently].... Reading aloud—especially if someone else is listening—involves an extra step: putting a sound to the meaning" (p. 9). Also, "reading aloud makes many people, of all ages, nervous. Unfortunately, teachers often want to hear children read aloud to assess how well they are doing, a situation that can give limited and unreliable information but arouse maximum anxiety" (p. 9).

Another caveat is that when matching books to learners, educators will want to consider in what circumstance the book will be read. They can ask of the situation, for instance, how much support there will be for the learner. Educators additionally will consider learners' interest in a text, their background knowledge in the text's topic and genre, and the purposes of their reading. These factors can sometimes call for the reading of a book first judged too hard or too easy to be a good choice.

To make the most of running records, educators will need to combine them with another assessment strategy: **miscue analysis**.

Miscue Analysis

Developed by Goodman (1969), a miscue analysis can help to make the invisible process of constructing meaning somewhat visible. Here, educators pay careful attention to readers' deviations from text and the types of information they use to produce these deviations. The term **miscues** is used to refer to these deviations rather than *errors* to remove value judgment as Goodman contended that miscues need not be seen as negative; rather, they are a normal part of reading practice. As people read, they may use picture, print, and **context cues** to predict words, and their miscues provide insight into which cues they are (or are not) using. For classroom purposes, we recommend a simplified system for analyzing miscues, although it might be necessary for educators to use a more sophisticated system for readers who have significant difficulty reading.

Conducting a Miscue Analysis

To conduct a miscue analysis, educators note any miscues that a reader makes. A running record, for instance, would contain this information. Educators then code and analyze these miscues to determine if there is a pattern in the types of meaning-making strategies readers do or do not use (see Box 4.4 for a synopsis of the coding system). For example, if a reader says "dad" when "father" is the word in the printed text in front of her, we could surmise that the reader is paying attention to the meaning (**semantics**) of what she is reading ("father" is a logical substitution and would make equally good sense in the sentence). However, with this kind of substitution, we may wonder about her attention to printed letters: it is difficult to visually mistake an *f* for a *d*, or *ather* for *ad*. Alternatively, if a learner reads "shop" for "sharp," we could guess that he is paying some attention to the letters on the page, but not paying attention to the meaning of the sentence: there would be few sentences where "shop" could be substituted for "sharp" without significantly changing sentence meaning.

BOX 4.4

MISCUE ANALYSIS CODING SYSTEM

Meaning (M) (refers to semantic cuing system): Does the word make logical sense in the context of the passage or sentence? Does the reader seem to understand the text as he or she reads?

Structure (S) (refers to syntactic cuing system): Does the word sound like language that follows a grammatical form? Does it sound the way the reader speaks?

Visual (V) (refers to graphophonic cuing system): Does the word have a graphic similarity or sound similar to the word in the text? Does the reader attempt to sound out beginning, middle, or endings of words?

Self-Correction (SC): Does the reader self-correct? If so, what cues does the reader use to do so?

In conducting a miscue analysis, educators try to isolate the source of readers' miscues by asking questions of the miscues, then recording the cuing system(s) they believe readers were drawing on:

1. Did the reader substitute a word that made logical sense in the context of the passage or sentence? This question concerns Meaning (M), or the semantic cuing system.

2. Did the reading sound like language that follows a grammatical form? Did the reader follow the structure of the text? Either of these questions concerns Structure (S), or the syntactic cuing system. Note, however, that when asking questions about structure, educators must determine if readers might be following a **dialect** structure in their reading. Could readers be expecting the text to read a certain way because that is the grammatical structure they are most familiar with? To figure this out, educators can ask themselves this question: Does the miscue sound the way this person talks?

3. If the reader substituted a word while reading, was the substitution a word that had graphic similarity or sound similarity to the word in the text? This question concerns the Visual (V), or the graphophonic, cuing system and can help educators recognize when learners are using their knowledge of letter–sound relationships. If a reader substituted a word that had no visual or sound similarity to the word on the page, the educator would want to investigate the child's use of visual cues.

4. What self-corrections has the reader made? Educators should examine the kinds of self-corrections a reader makes to gather additional information about the reader's practice. Self-corrections provide clues to which cuing system (meaning, structure, visual) a reader appears to be drawing on.

BOX 4.5

CODING OF MISCUES ON A PREDICTABLE BOOK

T

"Whistle, Mary, Whistle, and you shall have a trout."

MS

fell

"I can't whistle, Mother, because my tooth is out."

"Whistle, Mary, Whistle, and you shall have a rabbit."

MS   MS MS

I   my tooth

"I can't whistle, Mother, because I've lost the habit."

V

dandy

"Whistle, Mary, Whistle, and you shall have a daisy."

T

"I can't whistle, Mother, because it looks so crazy."

Note: *T* means teacher prompt.

Understanding what children can do, know, and value is the first step in meeting the challenge of providing the right learning opportunities for them to have expansive communication and identity options. The rest of this chapter is designed to help you construct pedagogies to meet this challenge.

MULTILITERACIES PEDAGOGIES: EXPERIENCES THAT CREATE EARLY LITERACY LEARNING OPPORTUNITIES

All the principles and teaching components we introduced in Chapters 1 and 2 apply equally in the case of working with children in the early years. Particular components, however, can be structured to address the unique needs of young learners. In this section we highlight the following instructional components:

- creating a rich literacy environment with opportunities for functional interactions with print
- Read-Aloud
- Shared Reading
- structuring learning opportunities through literature
- phonological awareness, phonemic awareness, and phonics learning opportunities
- Shared Writing: Language Experience Approach

Creating a Rich Literacy Environment

Educators can create learning opportunities by trying to ensure that all of Cambourne's (1988) conditions for learning are accounted for in the classroom. The vignette at the beginning of this chapter has already shown how, with the right setup, the classroom environment can meet many conditions, most notably those of immersion, use, responsibility, and engagement. Environmental print (e.g., signs, labels, calendars, charts, and lists that can be used to organize the classroom) can be a great teacher when it is functional in nature. Putting labels and signs up in the classroom is not, by itself, sufficient. Children need to interact with print in meaningful ways to maximize their learning. Examples of opportunities for authentic experiences with environmental print include the following:

- Educators *and* children make labels to identify children's cubbyholes and show where things belong.
- Educators and children use calendars to keep track of the days of the week and of special days like birthdays. These calendars can be created by the educators and children using traditional media such as laminated paper (so that one calendar can be created, erased, and re-created for the next month), or they can be made like those in Lynn Hill's

kindergarten classroom using **new media**. Specifically, Lynn creates an electronic calendar with input from her students, adding in weblinks to sites such as the weather network, then using the interactive whiteboard for presentation. As the class views the calendar and works through that day's activities together, the children can simply touch an icon on the board to check on and then record the day's weather. Children enjoy returning to the board during centre time to further explore the calendar and its links.

- Educators can use attendance charts to help children learn to read one another's names. Lynn uses the interactive whiteboard to create a functional interactive attendance activity where children sign in to class and see the names of their classmates to learn who is present.

- In Jennifer and Andrea's classroom in the opening of the chapter, the rhythm and roles of mealtime are posted on a bulletin board near the tables. Under a heading entitled "Sharing a meal is a way to connect to nourish our minds, our bodies, our relationships," children have drawn and written captions to accompany photographs of themselves performing mealtime rituals.

- Field trips provide vital opportunities for children to use written language for functional purposes. They might consult printed material when making plans for the trip, use environmental print to find their way around during the trip, and write thank-you letters upon return.

- Play centres can also support literacy. For example, a play restaurant can draw on literacy-related props like menus, order pads, and signage. Other ideas include a cooking centre, store, and doctor's office. Educators, as mentioned earlier, can connect these centres to larger inquiries and to the kinds of experiences that are familiar to children and that correspond with their funds of knowledge. For more on the importance of play to literacy learning, see the Inside Classrooms box featuring educator Wambui Gichuru.

INSIDE CLASSROOMS

WAMBUI GICHURU: THE IMPORTANCE OF PLAY IN LITERACY LEARNING

Wambui Gichuru has taught in a variety of settings, including in kindergartens internationally (e.g., Kenya) and a Waldorf school in Canada. We corresponded by email to get a glimpse of how she understands the role of play in literacy learning and how she has used play in her practice. Here is how she responded.

What can play provide young children, particularly in relation to their literacy learning?

My experience and knowledge of the research on play (e.g., Christie & Roskos, 2009; Kendrick, 2003; Welsch, 2008) tells me that play in the early years can provide young children with an engaging and meaningful context for acquiring essential early literacy knowledge and practices. Play provides children with awareness and understanding of their world. As a process

Wambui Gichuru

of inquiry, play consists of exploration, testing, imitation, and construction (Burke, 2010). Play is an enjoyable vehicle for children to create imaginary situations and infuse their own meanings into objects and actions and provides an opportunity to try out the literacy tools, routines, and scripts that flow through daily life (Chakraborty & Stone, 2009; Kendrick, 2003). Also, I understand that play provides opportunity for the representational abilities that children acquire in pretend transformations to transfer to other symbolic forms such as written language. The potential exists for a strong literacy and play connection as theoretically, play and literacy share higher order, cognitive processes, such as imaging, categorizing, and problem solving, particularly dramatic play (Christie & Roskos, 2009).

You mentioned dramatic play. What are the different kinds of play that educators can capitalize on in the classroom?

There are many different forms of play. Dramatic play is a process by which children represent themselves in imagined situations. For example, in dramatic play, children invent and act out a role, and may play many roles simultaneously. Children may use a variety of materials to act out everyday events, something that requires the use of reading and writing. Toys or props—for example, dolls, cars, and action figures—usually support this kind of play. Dramatic play situations represent children's life experiences and assist children in discovering and understanding the world (Saracho, 2001).

The social nature of dramatic play engages children in using new words that are tied to meaning and experience (Stone, 1993). In this play, symbolic transformations are precursors to print literacy as they support children's development of representation and abstract thought (Chakraborty & Stone, 2009). Children learn to represent their world in play. For example, children may use a block for a phone or a car. The use of various modes and media to convey meaning increases in range and scope, and by the preschool years, these modes may include oral language, gestures and body movement, visual arts (drawing, painting, and sculpting), construction, dramatic play, and writing. The children's effort to represent their ideas and concepts in different modes enhances knowledge (NAEYC, 2009).

Social pretend play, also referred to as "symbolic play," is when children take on social roles and invent increasingly complex narrative scripts, which they enact with friends in small groups. Play of this type helps children to practise and consolidate broad cognitive skills, such as symbolic representation, and emerging literacy skills, such as print awareness (Christie & Roskos, 2009).

(continued)

Pretend play as a context for learning enhances comprehension and contributes to growth in mental capacity and social competence. There are three basic activities of pretend play (Welsch, 2008):

▷ playing with objects

▷ playing at being like someone or something

▷ making up people, places, and things

How can educators create the conditions that foster the kind of play that produces literacy learning opportunities for children?

There are definitely lots of ways that educators can create and enrich play environments to enhance young children's literacy experiences. Literacy-enriched play centres are stocked with theme-related reading and writing materials (Chakraborty & Stone, 2009; Saracho, 2001; Tsao, 2008). Literacy-enriched environments have been shown to result in at least short-term–gain knowledge about functions of writing, ability to recognize play-related print, and use of comprehension strategies such as self-checking and self-correction.

Here are some things for educators to remember about materials and environments:

▷ Selecting and defining materials for pretend play is critical (Chakraborty & Stone, 2009). It is rare to have a centre or activity that is enjoyed by every child—a broad appeal is needed. You need to get to know your learners and to build centres for and with them (rather than for a generic learner).

▷ Because children's play worlds reflect their understanding of their social worlds (Kendrick, 2003), centres equally need to reflect who they are and where they come from. With increased diversity in today's classrooms, centres need to reflect this diversity by providing a range of familiar materials for children to choose from. For example, include foods that children can relate to—for example, pizza, samosas, and empanadas. With appropriate materials and supportive adults, young children can construct knowledge about print and gradually become more literate (Tsao, 2008).

This last point raises the question of the role of the adult in play. What can that be?

Because literacy is a social and constructive process, children develop literacy concepts and skills through everyday experiences with others (Christie & Roskos, 2009), including peers. Vygotskian theory focuses on the role of adults and peers in the acquisition of social literacy practices during play. It emphasizes that language and literacy learning happen when children play with more expert users of the language. For example, educator scaffolding increases the amount of literacy activity during play as educators provide props, model for children how to use the props, and encourage peer interaction (Christie & Roskos, 2009; Tsao, 2008). Therefore, educators might want to do the following:

▷ Educators may provide opportunities, time, and materials for play to unfold, and guide children to take charge (Wassermann, 1992).

▷ Educators might provide children with props for pretend play and include materials that would require imagination. What does that mean they should do?

▷ Select materials that encourage play.

▷ Vary prop types.

▷ Provide repeated exposure.

▷ Support connections.

▷ Allow for self-direction.

▷ Observe children at play (Welsch, 2008).

▷ At various times educators may choose to help engage children to play in a world of their making rather than our own (Kendrick, 2003).

▷ Recall that during their play children negotiate with and coach each other, which helps them learn about literacy during play (Saracho, 2001; Tsao, 2008). Yet, educators' scaffolding of children's play can increase the amount of literacy practices that occur during play (Christie & Roskos, 2009). This means that at times, educators may want to take a more active role in the play than as just an observer or person who sets up the play environment. For example, educator use of appropriate forms of scaffolding can encourage children to integrate literacy props into their play (Tsao, 2008).

▷ Educators can structure play by making direct connections between literacy-enriched play centres and the academic parts of the curriculum, rather than having play experiences as stand-alone activities (Christie & Roskos, 2009; Saracho, 2001).

Play should be pleasurable, voluntary, imaginative, and social. I have been a lucky witness to the learning that happens through and because of play. Just as importantly, I have seen the learners in my classroom play in joy!

Read-Alouds
What Learning Opportunities Do Read-Alouds Create?

In Jennifer and Andrea's classroom, novel study hinges on Read-Aloud. "The single most important activity for building the knowledge and skills eventually required for reading appears to be reading aloud to children" (Adams, 1990, p. 46). Reading aloud to children creates opportunities for them to acquire

- positive attitudes toward books and reading
- the understanding that written language is meaningful
- the language of various genres of text
- an understanding of the structures of various genres of text
- an understanding of what fluid, proficient reading sounds like and looks like
- knowledge of the content of the texts that they might not be able to access on their own if the text is beyond their independent level

Also, Jennifer and Andrea placed Read-Aloud in the afternoon following lunch when they noticed that the children could benefit from a quiet retreat from an otherwise busy day. Reading a section of a novel every day refreshed the class.

Conducting a Read-Aloud

To optimize learning opportunities for children during Read-Aloud, they need to be given the chance to express ideas they have constructed from books *before*, *during*, and *after* the reading. The nature of the interaction varies depending on the genre of text, but below, we offer some general guidelines.

Before Reading

The major understanding children are exposed to in this phase of the reading is that written language is meaningful. They may also develop understanding of different purposes for reading as they talk about what to expect in different types of books. It is often the development of an anticipatory set that enables readers to track the meanings that are being created during reading. This set provides readers with a valuable source of information for identifying new words and self-correcting miscues.

- When starting a new book, educators can draw children's attention to the picture on the cover and invite them to predict what they think the book is about. They can encourage children to talk about their own experiences related to the topic, and ask children to make predictions (e.g., will the book tell a story or tell about something).

- For information texts, educators may need to demonstrate key concepts in the book if it becomes clear that several children have limited knowledge to bring to the topic.

- In emergent classrooms, the books that are read together are selected based on what seems to be of interest to the children at the time. For instance, noticing that the children were fascinated with life cycles and the natural world, the educators in one study of kindergarten literacy curriculum (Heydon, Crocker, & Zheng, 2014) selected *Charlotte's Web* (White, 1952) for their next Read-Aloud. Interest presupposes a degree of knowledge about a topic; hence the children were already well positioned to construct meaning of the text.

During Reading

- While reading any book, educators can encourage learners to react to and comment on the story or ideas as they listen. Educators can also ask questions occasionally to monitor the meaning children are constructing. The educators in the research above structured these questions as "I wonder" statements. For instance, in their reading of *Charlotte's Web*, the educators focused on extending ideas, asking, "I wonder what would happen if …?"

- For information books, educators may need to give examples of difficult ideas. This teaching can be based on the children's responses, and educators can help by encouraging children to ask questions when they do not understand something.

- Educators can rephrase the text when it is clear the children do not understand something. They can ask the children periodically to evaluate their earlier predictions and formulate new ones. It is important for children to evaluate their own predictions rather than having the educator do it for them.

After Reading

- For all books, children can be asked to talk about what they have heard, relating the ideas to their own experiences.
- Educators can also do like Jennifer and Andrea, and invite the children to keep track of key events, vocabulary, concepts, and characters on sharing boards.

Shared Reading
What Learning Opportunities Does Shared Reading Create?

Children construct different understandings about written language from Shared Reading experiences depending on their literacy backgrounds. Children who come to school with experience with being read to will likely construct understandings about the forms of written language and the nature of the print–speech relationship. However, for children with more limited book experience, the goal of instruction might be developing positive attitudes toward books or helping children understand the functions and nature of written language. Depending on the form of Shared Reading—that is, the degree of interactivity—it can create many of the same learning opportunities as Read-Alouds, but also allow children to try out adding some words, repeating phrases, or approximating strategies. Shared Reading can additionally allow educators to more explicitly model reading strategies that children may use during independent or guided reading.

Conducting Shared Reading

There are three key differences between Read-Aloud and Shared Reading. In Read-Aloud, the text may be well beyond what a child can read independently. In Shared Reading, the text is more accessible than this for the children. This leads naturally to difference two: that in Read-Aloud, the educator reads, whereas in Shared Reading, the reading is shared between the educator and the children. Finally, with Read-Aloud, educators may use a book where children cannot see the print. In Shared Reading, educators use big books (oversized versions of books) or projections of books so that all children can follow along with the print. They can thereby read *with* rather than *to* children.

The guidelines presented above for Read-Aloud interactions before, during, and after reading are also appropriate for Shared Reading. During readings educators can point to words as they read, demonstrating one-to-one correspondence between oral and written words and emphasizing the left-to-right and top-to-bottom directional nature of print. They can also encourage learners to read along, sometimes stopping their reading at predictable places so that the children can fill in the text; encourage children to use context and letter cues to make and confirm their predictions; and talk about aspects of the text using terms children need to learn. (For example: "The first word in this *sentence* is …," "There is a *question mark* at the end of this sentence, so we need to sound as if we are asking a question when we read it.")

When selecting appropriate Shared Reading texts, educators might ask themselves questions like these:

- Does this text relate to an idea or concept that we are currently investigating in the class or that has been recently provoked?

- Is this text accessible for most of the children and is it something that builds on their funds of knowledge and that they will find engaging?
- Is this book rich enough in terms of, for example, content or artistry of language so that it can be a catalyst for new learning? (Kaufman, 2002)

Predictable books are particularly useful for Shared Reading in the early years, because the repetitive and rhythmic structure of the text supports early reading attempts. We provide a list of classic and newer predictable and big books for early years in Box 4.6.

BOX 4.6

PREDICTABLE BOOKS FOR THE EARLY YEARS

Adler, D. A. (2004). *Bones and the dog gone mystery.* New York, NY: Viking.

Arnold, T. (2006). *Hi! Fly Guy.* New York, NY: Scholastic.

Bailey, L. (2006). *The farm team.* (B. Slavin, Illus). Toronto, ON: Kids Can Press.

Bailey, L. (2007). *Goodnight, sweet pig.* (J. Masse, Illus.). Toronto, ON: Kids Can Press.

* Baker, K. (1990). *Who is the beast?* New York, NY: Harcourt Brace & Company.

Banks, K. (2006). *Max's words.* (B. Kulikov, Illus.). New York, NY: Farrar, Straus & Giroux.

Beaton, C. (2001). *There's a cow in the cabbage patch.* Bristol, UK: Barefoot Books.

Brown, K. (2001). *The scarecrow's hat.* London, UK: Andersen Press.

* Brown, R. (1981). *A dark, dark tale.* New York, NY: Scholastic.

Campbell, R. (2007). *Dear zoo.* New York, NY: Little Simon.

Campbell, S. (2008). *Wolfsnail: A backyard predator.* Honesdale, PA: Boyds Mill Press.

Carle, E. (1983). *The very hungry caterpillar.* New York, NY: Scholastic.

* Cowley, J. (1983). *The jigaree.* Auckland, NZ: Shortland Publications.

* Cowley, J. (1983). *Who will be my mother?* Auckland, NZ: Shortland Publications.

Cranstoun, M. (1967). *1, 2, buckle my shoe.* New York, NY: Holt, Rinehart & Winston.

Dann, P. (2000). *Five in the bed.* London, UK: Little Orchard Books.

Dragonwagon, C. (2012). *All the awake animals are almost asleep.* (D. McPhail, Illus.). New York, NY: Little Brown

Hoberman, M. A. (2001). *"It's simple," said Simon.* (M. So, Illus.). New York, NY: Alfred A. Knopf.

* Hutchins, P. (1986). *The doorbell rang.* New York, NY: Scholastic.

Keats, E. J. (1971). *Over in the meadow.* New York, NY: Scholastic.

Lipsey, J. (2007). *I love to draw cartoons!* New York, NY: Lark Books.

Lock, F. (2009). *Ponies and horses.* New York, NY: DK Publishing.

Martin, B., Jr. (1970). *The haunted house.* New York, NY: Holt, Rinehart & Winston.

* Martin, B., Jr. (1970). *Monday, Monday, I like Monday.* (D. Leder, Illus.). New York, NY: Holt, Rinehart & Winston.

* Martin, B., Jr. (1972). *Brown bear, brown bear, what do you see?* (E. Carle, Illus.). New York, NY: Holt, Rinehart & Winston.

Martin, B., Jr. (1991). *Polar bear, polar bear, what do you hear?* (E. Carle, Illus.). New York, NY: Henry Holt & Company.

Mayer, M. (1975). *Just for you.* New York, NY: Golden Press.

* Melser, J. (1980). *Lazy Mary.* Auckland, NZ: Shortland Publications.

* Melser, J. (1980). *Sing a song.* Auckland, NZ: Shortland Publications.

* Morris, W. B. (1970). *The longest journey in the world.* New York, NY: Holt, Rinehart & Winston.

Paye, W., & Lippert, M. H. (2002). *Head, body, legs: A story from Liberia.* (J. Paschkis, Illus.). New York, NY: Henry Holt & Co.

Pichon, L. (2008). *The three horrid little pigs.* Wilton: Tiger Tales.

Polacco, P. (2004). *Oh, look!* New York, NY: Philomel Books.

Root, P. (2001). *Rattletrap car.* (J. Barton, Illus.). Cambridge, MA: Candlewick Press.

Rylant, C. (2006). *Henry and Mudge and the great grandpas.* (S. Stevenson, Illus.). New York, NY: Aladdin Paperbacks.

Serafini, F. (2008). *Looking closely along the shore.* Toronto, ON: Kids Can Press.

Shea, S. (2012). *Do you know which ones will grow?* (T. Slaughter, Illus.). New York, NY: Roaring Brook Press.

Silverman, E. (2005). *Cowgirl Kate and Cocoa.* (B. Lewin, Illus.). Orlando, FL: Harcourt.

Tolstoy, A. (1968). *The great big enormous turnip.* (H. Oxenbury, Illus.). New York, NY: Franklin Watts.

Van Leeuwen, J. (2007). *Amanda pig and the really hot day.* (A. Schweninger, Illus.). New York, NY: Puffin Books.

Wetherford, C. B. (2008). *Before John was a jazz giant: A song by John Coltrane.* (S. Qualls, Illus.). New York, NY: Henry Holt.

* Williams, S. (1994). *I went walking.* (J. Vivas, Illus.). New York, NY: Harcourt Brace & Company.

Wise Brown, M. (1947). *Goodnight moon.* (C. Hurd, Illus.). New York, NY: HarperCollins.

* Wood, A. (1984). *The napping house.* (D. Wood, Illus.). New York, NY: Harcourt Brace & Company.

* Wood, A. (1992). *Silly Sally.* New York, NY: Harcourt Brace Jovanovich.

*Available in "big book" form.

Though Shared Reading is often conducted with the whole class, by its very nature it is a differentiated form of instruction. For example, while one child is developing an understanding of the alphabetic principle during a Shared Reading, another might be just beginning to internalize the language of books. A repetitive book is useful for both of these children, and they will both be able to predict words when educators stop reading at predictable points; however, only the first child will be able to respond to the educator's invitation to point to the words in a line of print while it is being read. Furthermore, the use of predictable books in Shared Reading is well suited to the needs of CLD learners and children who are just coming to print literacy. Children can join in reading the repetitive parts of the story before individual words have become meaningful to them. Additionally, children are supported to construct meaning from these texts because they know what to expect next with the language and structure of the text, and they can also refer to the text's illustrations or diagrams.

Structuring Sustained Learning Opportunities through Literature

Discovery

Literacy researcher Don Holdaway's (1979) notion of the shared book experience is in many ways the foundation for Read-Aloud and Shared Reading. Holdaway described three phases in his shared book experience format that could be used to structure sustained literacy learning opportunities using the literature introduced in Read-Aloud and Shared Reading: *Discovery* (the initial sharing of the book), *Exploration* (e.g., rereadings of the book in the group as a whole), and *Independent Experience* (individual and small-group rereadings and follow-up activities, such as some of the response activities offered in Chapter 12). Read-Aloud and Shared Reading can essentially account for the Discovery phase of this format.

Interpreting the story: What we know about Jack

Exploration

The next phase, Exploration, consists of a choice of various group activities that can provide further opportunities for children to investigate the book and its ideas. These include

- rereading
- investigating innovations on literary structures
- interpreting the story through multimodal means such as dramatization, art, and/or writing. (See, for example, the photograph of one aspect of the Magic Tree House novel sharing board in Jennifer and Andrea's classroom, where the children drew images of the main characters and contributed understandings of what the characters were like, which the educators collated and typed up.)

Children learn about the nature and forms of written language, and they begin to construct an understanding of the speech–print relationship through involvement in these activities.

Rereadings of predictable books are often done at the request of children. With this type of book, educators can encourage children to join in the reading as much as possible to learn the language of books, conduct a choral reading of the book, and read along with the children when they need support. By pointing to words as they read, educators help children to hear the words as separate units and to match them with printed words on the page. By rereading the book several times, children may internalize the oral language they need to establish eye–voice matching when later reading the book independently or in a small group. Rereadings are also great opportunities for phonological awareness, phonemic awareness, and phonics learning.

During rereadings, educators can invite children to innovate on literary structures to help them develop greater awareness of the language of books. For example, educators can use the structure of a predictable book such as Bill Martin Jr.'s *Brown Bear, Brown Bear, What Do You See?* to help children collectively make a new text that fits with a current theme. For instance, at Halloween, a class might create something like this:

White ghost, white ghost, what do you see?

I see a black cat looking at me.

Black cat, black cat, what do you see?

I see a green witch looking at me.

The educator can scribe the text on chart paper while the class comes up with the ideas, and later, the story can be used both for group and independent rereadings.

Kindergarten teacher Laura Barr also used the structure of *Brown Bear, Brown Bear, What Do You See?* to help her tie literacy to other areas of the curriculum. For instance, when she was focusing on colour words and shapes in mathematics, Laura invited the children to co-construct an interactive story on a pocket chart. As a class, children were invited to build the story using key words and shape cards that reinforced the words and concepts.

For the same unit, Laura again used the structure of the Bill Martin Jr. book to emphasize colour words in a class book (see the class book photograph). Laura gave each child a page that showed a picture of a different animal and that had written at the bottom, "___, ___, what do you see? I see a ___ snake looking at me." Children were invited to write their own name on the first two blanks. In the blank before the animal word (e.g., *snake, butterfly, pig*), Laura wrote in a colour word with a coloured marker. Children could then colour the picture of the animal that same colour. Educators might also leave the colour word blank and allow the children

Class book

Brown Bear centre

to select a colour and write it in. To offer support for this, educators can refer children to environmental print such a colour word bulletin board.

Independent Experience

Children can benefit from having time to independently interact with the texts from Read-Aloud and Shared Reading time, as well as the class books they have created. Independent time to interact with these texts gives children the opportunity to share responsibility for their learning by making some choices about what they read. It also allows them to approximate and use what they've been learning. Giving children the chance to read independently demonstrates that this activity is valuable (*What is balanced literacy?*, n.d.). Children can reread books alone or with a peer as often as they wish, relying on meaning and print cues to reconstruct the text. Educators can encourage them to point to words as they read to more fully establish eye–voice matching. Children who are early in their print literacy acquisition may find it helpful to retell the story in their own words as they look at picture cues.

To give children more control over the number of times they hear favourite stories, educators may create listening centres and judiciously select interactive digital book forms that provide children with opportunities to listen, read along, and/or interact with the text. Educators may also build centres where children interact with phrases and images from familiar texts. The photograph here shows a centre from Laura's classroom, where children can manipulate laminated images and words to retell or create their own version of *Brown Bear, Brown Bear, What Do You See?*

Shared Writing: The Language Experience Approach

What Learning Opportunities Does the Language Experience Approach Create?

To create texts for sharing, educators may draw on the Language Experience Approach (LEA). LEA builds on learners' experiences and oral language as a source of material to be used for reading instruction. Its design honours children's funds of knowledge, including their own vocabularies. Educator Sylvia Ashton-Warner (1986), who worked with Maori children in New Zealand, viewed LEA as a way to "build a bridge from the known to the unknown" (p. 28). Since then, LEA has been found to assist learners in their development of phonological awareness, phonemic awareness, and phonics knowledge (Invernizzi, 2003). It also creates opportunities for children to learn that written language is meaningful and that a relationship exists between oral and written language. Beyond that, children can become familiar with terms related to reading and writing and learn about the conventions of print.

Using the Language Experience Approach

Educators can use LEA with the whole class, small groups, and individuals. As with Shared Reading, children at varying points in their literacy acquisition can work effectively together on an LEA text, although the language learning will differ for each child. LEA essentially contains five components:

1. *Experience.* LEA begins with a shared experience. Trips, classroom events, wordless picture books, and films can all provide springboards for discussion. Grade 1 teacher Susan Bennett, for instance, used the experience of baby chicks in the classroom as her focal experience for LEA.

2. *Discussion.* Discussion provides children with opportunity to acquire the vocabulary and sentence structures that will eventually be recorded. Educators use questions and prompts such as "I'm interested—tell me more" to expand and clarify as well as to elevate the children's language beyond a listing of ideas. Susan had her students imagine they were chicks, show how they would peck their way out of shells, and talk about the first thing they might see.

3. *Recording.* To foreground some of the differences between oral and written language, as a group children select the ideas to be recorded and provide an oral composition. Then, as children dictate ideas, educators record them in large print on chart paper. As educators write each word, the children observe to help them establish the link between oral and written words. Educators may think aloud and request help during the writing (e.g., asking about where they should begin writing, in what direction the print goes, about the use of capital letters and punctuation marks, and about special visual features of certain words such as length and initial letter).

   If the children have some awareness of letter names and sounds, educators can invite them to suggest which letters to include in some of the words being written. For example, when the children in Susan's class dictated a sentence about the chicks pecking out of their shells, she asked, "What letters do we need to write the word *peck*?" One child said *p* and another *k*. Susan printed these letters and added the *e* and *c* herself, slowly articulating the sounds so the children would hear them as she wrote. She also commented on the *ck* at the end of the word. She knew the children did not have enough knowledge of letter sounds to supply these letters without help.

   A question that educators face when scribing in LEA is whether to write exactly what children say or to make changes. It is generally recommended that educators use standard English spellings regardless of dialect (e.g., *going to*, not *gonna*) and use standard punctuation. However, controversy surrounds the question of whether to scribe ungrammatical sentences such as "I don't got no pencil." The answer depends on whether you are working with a group or an individual child and your goals in using LEA. With individual children who are early in their understanding of literacy, educators generally recommend scribing children's vocabulary and **grammar** to help them develop an understanding of the one-to-one correspondence between oral and written words (e.g., British Columbia Ministry of Education, 2010b). For example, if the child dictates "Me and another chick saw a cow" and the teacher changes it to "Another chick and I saw a cow" the child may reread the first part of the sentence as "Me and another chick," associating the wrong spoken words with what is written.

Preserving what children have dictated is also important when working with CLD learners. The context, vocabulary, and language structures will be familiar to the children, and hence will support their initial reading experiences.

Educators will need to use their own best judgment about how and when to change nonstandard English into the standard form. This practice is particularly prevalent when most of the children in the group use the standard form. It is also appropriate with children who are already able to match spoken and written words (e.g., Ontario, 2003b). One purpose of making changes to the standard form is to help children understand that there are differences between oral and written language. Children need to learn what book language sounds like to help them predict words as they read.

4. *Reading.* Immediately upon completing the story, educators read it to the children, pointing to words as they do so. As a follow-up activity, educators may ask children if they want to make any changes, to engage them in revising what they have written. Educators can demonstrate revision by using carets and arrows, crossing out words, and writing in the margins. Once the children are satisfied with what they have dictated, the class reads it together to ensure that their first reading will be successful. During subsequent rereadings, the children can read more independently, with educators providing support as needed. Finally, when the children feel ready, individuals can read the story alone.

5. *Follow-up activities.* Follow-up activities can round out or extend LEA for groups and individuals. Here are some examples:
   - During rereading, educators can ask children questions about where to begin reading, in what direction to read, how to know to stop at the end of a sentence, and so on, to develop concepts about print conventions.
   - Educators can encourage individual children to read the story independently and point to the words as they read. Some educators type the LEA text and make copies for the children to keep and read individually.
   - Educators can invite children to find words containing a common letter (e.g., all the words that begin with the letter *m*). The class can talk about how all of these words begin with the same sound and the fact that some of the words begin with an uppercase M and others with a lowercase *m*.
   - Educators can cut apart the sentences in an LEA text and ask children to arrange the sentences in order, referring to the LEA chart if necessary. When the children are able to handle this task easily, individual sentences can be cut into words for them to put in order, again matching the words against an intact sentence strip if necessary.
   - Educators can cover selected words in the LEA text and ask the children to predict words that make sense and sound right in the space. They can then check their predictions by looking at the print.
   - Educators can create booklets out of the LEA text, invite children to illustrate them, and then use them for home reading or independent reading practice.

As may be obvious, LEA provides so many rich opportunities for print literacy acquisition that it need not be reserved only for young children. It is particularly helpful when teaching older learners who might have limited print literacy knowledge. It is often used in adult basic education as it creates texts whose content is appealing to readers at a level they can read.

SUMMARY

All children come to school with knowledge of their worlds and ways of expressing that knowledge. The primary goal of early years language and literacy programs should be to help young children expand their literacy and identity options. Educators can then help children build bridges between the known and unknown. This chapter has presented options for educators to do this. The first consideration in any pedagogical strategy is to understand what learners know, are able to do, and value. Informal assessment strategies can help in this regard. Key within these strategies is getting at children's funds of knowledge, including their home literacy practices. Educators can then take this information and build instruction that is responsive to the knowledges, interests, and needs in their classrooms by drawing on a range of pedagogical strategies.

We have highlighted some foundational strategies, including Read-Alouds, Shared Reading, the Language Experience Approach and the creation of environments where children can transact with and produce texts and ideas. Throughout all of these components, the interrelatedness of the six dimensions of language and literacy are highlighted. In particular, many aspects of this chapter echo Chapter 3, as early literacy builds from children' oral language. Significantly, the foundations of literacy acquisition and early literacy pedagogies can help educators at all levels to assess and plan for their learners.

SELECTED PROFESSIONAL RESOURCES

Burke, A. (2010). *Ready to learn: Using play to build literacy skills in young learners.* Markham, ON: Pembroke.

This gorgeous little Canadian book shows in very practical terms how to support young children's literacy acquisition through play. Written by a teacher turned educational researcher, this highly useful text is based in at-promise visions of children. It is powerfully rationalized.

continued

Hall, E. L., & Rudkin, J. K. (2011). *Seen and heard: Children's rights in early childhood education*. New York, NY: Teachers College Press.

At first glance this book that chronicles one school's approach to promoting human rights *with* children might not seem to be about literacy. But on second glance readers might then notice that everything the school does promotes literacy and identity options, and they can then see the flourishing of early literacy practices for *real* purposes.

Wholwend, K. E. (2013). *Literacy playshop: New literacies, popular media, and play in the early childhood classroom*. New York, NY: Teachers College Press.

Undergirded by first-rate research and sophisticated contemporary theorizing, this book illustrates in practical terms how educators can work with children to build classroom playshops where multiliteracies practices can flourish.

CHAPTER FIVE

The Nature and Assessment of Reading

PERSPECTIVES ON READING
- Bottom-Up Perspectives
- Top-Down Perspectives
- Interactive Perspectives
- Social Constructivist Perspectives
- Your View of Reading
- Our Approach to Reading: Implications for Practice

THE NATURE AND ASSESSMENT OF READING

READING ASSESSMENT
- Purposes of Assessment
- Considerations for Culturally and Linguistically Diverse Learners
- Assessment and Aboriginal Children
- Curriculum Documents: Part of the Assessment Dialogue
- High-Stakes Assessment

ASSESSMENT WITHIN MULTILITERACIES PEDAGOGIES
- Strategy One: Observation
- Strategy Two: Conferencing
- Strategy Three: Work Samples

THE VIEWS OF ERIN AND TAYLOR ON STANDARDIZED READING ASSESSMENT

Kathy Hibbert (2005), who contributed to this book, met with sisters Erin (grade 4) and Taylor (grade 6) to talk with them about their views on language and literacy learning opportunities at school. Their views on testing had particular relevance for this chapter.

Erin and Taylor

Erin on a Provincial Assessment

Kathy asked Erin to tell her about the Ontario provincial standardized test commonly known as EQAO (as the assessment comes from the Education Quality and Accountability Office). Students write the tests at the ends of grades 3 and 6. They contain items related to **literacy** and numeracy.

> **Erin:** Last year when I was in grade 3 we did something called EQAO. It's a lot of number of pages. We had to do one every day or something, and then there's a little magazine and you read a book, and it usually has two stories in it. There's math questions, like quarters, this person turned her radio up this much and then someone turned it down, and there's normal writing stuff, like there's this guy and his apple tree—oak tree—whatever, and a storm blew his tree down, and he was really sad, because he had planted the tree, but then in the end he could just use it as a reading stump. (*Pause*) After the teacher looks at it [the test], he sends it to the board [school district] or whatever and they mark it, and we also have to use a special pencil to write it out, and I never got it back, even though I'm in grade 4, and (*shrugs*) I don't know! (*Laughs*)

Taylor on a Standardized District-Wide Assessment

Kathy asked Taylor to tell her about the kinds of tests that she is asked to do in school. As the following demonstrates, Taylor chose to talk about participating in the Comprehension Attitude Strategies Interests Reading Assessment (CASI) (Doctorow, Bodiam, & McGowan, 2009), a standardized, commercial reading assessment.

> **Taylor:** This year I did one CASI, and I don't know (*shrugs*), I guess I didn't feel so well about it, because it was just the beginning of the year. I've been doing CASI now for four years, three each year, and when I first started out, in my first year, my marks weren't really too great, because I was just getting used to it, and I hadn't done much problem solving and all that stuff, then the last year I started to get my marks up higher, but then this year my marks started to go down, because I'm in a 6/7 [split-grade class] and it was a bit harder. The first [time] I [did well, the] CASI

[was] about figure skating and that was one of my highest marks just because it's active and I like those kinds of active stories—real-life stories—but then this year at the beginning, we did a basketball, Vince Carter, and that wasn't very much my favourite. I just don't really like basketball. It was a long story, so I didn't get as many marks as I should have.

Issues That Arise from the Interviews

A few key questions regarding the nature and **assessment** of reading arise from the interviews conducted with Erin and Taylor. For example,

- What might be the affordances and constraints of the kinds of testing that the girls participated in?
- In these types of tests what is the view of reading and its relationship to literacy in general?
- What might be alternative forms of assessment and **evaluation** that could create optimum learning opportunities for learners such as Erin and Taylor?

These questions, in turn, beget even more questions that have implications for us as educators. For example,

- How might your assessment experiences affect the kind of educator you want to be?
- What are the various ways that educators can assess students' reading?
- In what ways can reading assessment be used?
- How do the ways that educators choose to assess reading forward a particular understanding of what reading is?
- What *is* reading and how *do* people do it?

    We have designed this chapter to help you construct responses to these and other questions you may have about the nature and assessment of reading. We begin with a discussion of how different educators see reading, discuss the context in which educators are making decisions about reading assessment, and examine strategies for assessing learners' reading achievement and needs. ☐

PERSPECTIVES ON READING

Before being able to assess reading, educators have to have a clear notion of what they understand as reading. Much to the chagrin of some new (and not so new) educators, figuring out what constitutes reading is not an obvious thing. Because educators' beliefs and experiences with language and literacy can be powerful mediators of how they approach education, we begin by asking you to think about your own perspective on reading. To assist with this process, in Box 5.1 we have listed several statements about reading. We invite you to read each of the statements and rate it from 1 to 5, with 1 indicating that you strongly agree and 5 that you strongly disagree.

BOX 5.1

YOUR PERSPECTIVE ON READING

Rate each of the following statements about reading: 1 (strongly agree), 2 (agree), 3 (no opinion), 4 (disagree), or 5 (strongly disagree).

___ 1. Learners should master letter sounds before reading sentences and stories.

___ 2. When they come to a word they don't know, learners should be encouraged to guess what would make sense and go on.

___ 3. Learners should use both word knowledge and letter sounds to figure out unfamiliar words.

___ 4. Learners should talk about why different people construct different meanings for the same story.

___ 5. Flashcard drills with sight words are necessary for children to learn to read.

___ 6. It is not necessary to introduce new words before learners read them in stories.

___ 7. Learners should predict what stories will be about before they begin reading, and revise these predictions using information in the text.

___ 8. It is useful for learners to discuss texts in groups to negotiate meanings.

___ 9. Correcting a learner as soon as she or he makes a mistake when reading orally is a good practice.

___ 10. Educators should base the selection of reading material on quality of literature rather than on word or vocabulary difficulty.

___ 11. Learners need to develop strategies for both comprehension and the identification of words.

___ 12. Learners should relate what they read in stories to what they see and do in their lives outside the school.

Source: Some of these items are based on DeFord, 1985.

There is no unanimous perspective on what reading is and how people best learn to read, yet the field of literacy has been dominated by four influential perspectives on reading: bottom-up, top-down, interactive, and social constructivist (see Figure 5.1). As you read through these perspectives, think about which one might align with the responses you have given to the above statements. See where you might place yourself within these various perspectives.

Bottom-Up Perspectives

Natalie, a teacher candidate, described the reading instruction she received in elementary school this way:

> I remember spending an eternity on phonics. I became quite adept at reading sentences, such as "That fat cat sat." I could not wait to get my first reader so I could experience first hand the adventures of Dick, Jane and Spot, characters my older siblings often spoke of. My heart sank when finally

FIGURE 5.1

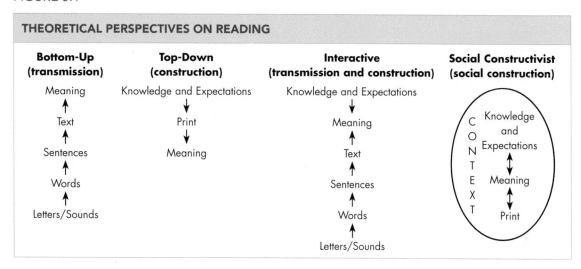

Sources: Cooper & Kiger, 2001; Jalongo, 2007; McCarrier, Pinnell, & Fountas, 2000; McLaughlin & Allen, 2002; Opitz & Ford, 2001.

my first reader was placed in front of me on my desk and Spot was nowhere to be found. My disap-
pointment quickly dissipated when I was introduced to the new reader's main character, Mr. Mugs.
We read out loud as a class, each student reading a single sentence. I followed along until my name
was called, then I prayed I would know all the words. (Hibbert & Heydon, 2010, p. 800)

Natalie's vignette sums up the major trend in reading instruction in the 1960s and 1970s. This
type of instruction was designed to teach a series of skills, often ordered hierarchically. For example,
a certain number of sight words were introduced before letter sounds, and consonants were usually
dealt with before work on vowel sounds. Comprehension was also broken down into component
skills, with literal comprehension tasks assumed to be easier than those involving inferential and
critical comprehension. Educators thought that reading could be taught by breaking it down into
component skills to be learned one at a time, often through drill and practice.

In Chapter 1, we provided a brief history of the definition of literacy, which began with a
view of literacy as reading only—this view is consistent with bottom-up perspectives. Here are
a few important points about how bottom-up perspectives see reading specifically:

- Reading is viewed as a "linear, hierarchical process" (Lipson & Wixson, 2003, p. 5).
- Reading is primarily a perceptual activity.
- Meaning resides in the text.
- Processing proceeds from parts to the whole.

Top-Down Perspectives

While letters and words have been the focus of bottom-up theorists, those who view
reading as top-down processing emphasize the key role that readers' knowledge plays in the

reading process. A metaphor for reading in this view might be a psycholinguistic guessing game (Goodman, 1970). To figure out what Ken Goodman might have been getting at with this metaphor, take a look at Box 5.2, and see whether you can make sense of the text by filling in the blanks.

Most likely, even if you cannot fill in the exact words in the "Porcupine Necktie" paragraph, you will be able to use most of the cuing systems described in Chapter 3 to make meaning from this short blurb. This is, in part, what Goodman meant by the psycholinguistic guessing game. He maintained that readers use their knowledge about language and the world to generate hypotheses about a text's meaning, which are then tested against the print. In top-down perspectives, readers are seen as problem solvers, and a complete analysis of print is not considered necessary, or even desirable, for the construction of meaning.

Before encountering text, readers have expectations about what they will read. As they read, they process text in relation to these expectations and use this information to formulate predictions about what will come next in the text. If the prediction sounds right and makes sense, readers continue reading, checking out the meaning as they read subsequent text. If the prediction does not sound right or make sense, readers reformulate their predictions and reread the text to check out these new predictions. Top-down processing can explain why many writers have so much difficulty proofreading their own writing; they have such clear expectations of what they will read that they do not notice on-the-page deviations from what they predict.

From top-down perspectives, what readers know is just as important as what they see. In top-down models of reading,

- reading is viewed as a language-thinking process
- meaning resides in the reader
- processing proceeds from whole to part

Interactive Perspectives

In the late 1970s, certain educators (e.g., Adams, Anderson, & Durkin, 1978; Rumelhart, 1977) began to question whether either top-down or bottom-up perspectives of the reading process were adequate. Bottom-up perspectives were critiqued for focusing on the minute analysis of words and for failing to account for either comprehension or the impact of meaning

BOX 5.2

> **PORCUPINE NECKTIE**
>
> When I ___ little, my uncle Pete had a necktie with a ___ painted on it. I thought that necktie was just about the neatest thing in the ___. Uncle ___ would stand patiently before me while I ran my ___ over the silky surface, half expecting to be stuck by ___ of the quills. Once, he let me wear ___. I kept looking for one of my own, but I could never ___ one.

Source: Jerry Spinelli, *Stargirl* (New York, NY: Knopf Books), 2006, p. 1.

on word identification. The major criticism of top-down perspectives was their vagueness in generating practical implications for teaching and their inability to account for research findings on the significant impact of word-level factors (such as **phonics**) on reading achievement. As a result of these critiques, many educators began to consider how the two positions could be combined to produce a more fulsome model of reading.

In Rumelhart's (1977) interactive model of reading, reading is viewed as neither top-down nor bottom-up, but rather as a process of synthesizing information from letters, words, sentences, and larger units of meaning. A major advantage of interactive models is that they help to account for different ways of processing information under different circumstances. For example, even people who could generally be characterized as good readers encounter material that is difficult to read (e.g., we may be baffled by engineering textbooks). When that happens, we adjust our reading to process the print information more carefully than we would when reading a novel or magazine article on a familiar topic. From interactive perspectives,

- reading is seen as a cognitive process
- meaning results from interaction between the reader and text
- processing proceeds from whole to part and part to whole

Social Constructivist Perspectives

At the beginning of this book we introduced **social constructivism**, including the ways in which educators need to consider learners in relation to their socio-cultural positioning (e.g., race, class, and gender) to understand how literacy is acquired and what meaning it might have for individuals and their contexts. At first glance, social constructivist perspectives and interactive perspectives might seem the same. Indeed they are similar in how they see the mechanics of reading. For instance, both perspectives find that

> the processing of text is a flexible interaction of the different information sources available to the reader and ... the information contained in "higher" stages of processing can influence, as well as be influenced by, the analysis that occurs at lower stages. (Lipson & Wixson, 2003, p. 6)

Yet a major difference is that interactive perspectives still see reading as a process where the reader attempts to find the meaning of a text that the author has put there: in such perspectives "the author [is seen] as originator of meaning, the text as symbolic or representative of meaning, and the reader as receiver of meaning" (Straw, 1990, p. 171). In contrast, social constructivist perspectives perceive reading as a practice that involves the active construction of meaning from a text. In addition to the text and the reader's knowledge, meaning is constructed on the basis of the social background of the reader and the social context of the practice of reading, both within and outside of the domain of school. Readers may therefore generate multiple meanings of a given text.

To illustrate, consider the case of Cara Garcia.

Education professor Cara Garcia (1998) grew up in a working-class section of Michigan during an era when "Dick and Jane" readers were everywhere in elementary schools. In these readers with controlled vocabulary, a "perfect" white suburban family was featured. In reflecting on the use of these texts in her own schooling, Garcia creates a somewhat comical picture, but one that speaks to why a social constructivist perspective on reading fills in some of the gaps left by interactive perspectives. As you read the following excerpt of Garcia's story, consider

- What is reading to the young Cara?
- What is reading to her teacher, Mrs. Swenson?
- What are the implications for understanding the reading process?

To respond to these questions, you will need to draw on your own background knowledge, including our discussion in Chapter 3 of **cuing systems**.

No Fun with Dick and Jane

Six of us are sitting in front of the big storybook called *More Fun with Dick and Jane* in Mrs. Swenson's first-grade classroom. She is pointing to our pages for today's lesson: the words Mother and Father. The picture shows a man in a brown suit and hat carrying a suitcase and standing in a doorway. On the facing page, there is a woman in a dress and apron and high heels standing in front of a stove.

Mrs. Swenson is saying, "And in this picture, who is coming in the door?"

"Father!" we all chime.

"And who is he saying hello to?"

"Mother!" we exclaim.

"And what do you think is happening?"

Silence. I look at the group to see if I'm the only one who is going to tell. The others are still staring at Father and Mother. I can see it's going to be up to me. I raise my hand slowly.

"Yes, Cara?"

"Well, he's coming to see if he can come back home. She had maybe put him out for drinking and now he's gotten sober and dressed up nice and he wants to come home. He has his dirty clothes in his suitcase." I point to what the illustrator meant as a briefcase, an item no first grader from the poor part of a rural Michigan town would ever have seen....

I see that the others are listening carefully as I lay out the story.

Mrs. Swenson is silent and cold. I know that I'm off somewhere. This is the look she gets when she stops someone in Show and Tell right when they're telling about a big fight at their house....

"Un-hunh, Cara. Well, maybe Father just is coming home from work in time for supper?"

Home from work? I look around the circle. Sharon Wiedermann is next to me. Our dads hang wallpaper together. Past her is Garth Fallows, whose Dad is an oiler on the Lower Lakes. Past Garth is Margie Spencer, whose Dad wears coveralls and a plaid shirt all the time. (1998, p. 606)*

This piece of Garcia's story highlights that reading is about constructing meaning from text and that readers try to make sense of text in relation to their own lived experience. Louise Rosenblatt's (1978) **transactional theory** helps to account for this phenomenon. Rosenblatt expressed that the reader and text have a reciprocal relationship, with each affecting the other. Readers actively construct meaning, relying on the text, their knowledge of language and the world, their background experiences, and their worldview.

Young Cara seems to understand that she is supposed to construct meaning when she reads, though obviously her use of pragmatic cues is off: she does not know how to "read"

---

* C. L. Garcia. "No Fun with Dick and Jane." *The Reading Teacher.* Issue 51 (7), pp. 606–607. 1998. Reproduced with permission of John Wiley & Sons, Inc.

a briefcase in the way that the dominant culture is asking her to. In contrast to Cara, Mrs. Swenson sees reading as the extraction of the correct interpretation from a text. If you read the rest of Garcia's story, you'd see that Mrs. Swenson is determined to transmit this one interpretation to the children. You would also see that Cara learns that she should try to acquire this dominant reading, as this is what would make her acceptable to her teacher. Cara, therefore, begins to learn that she needs to adjust her reading to fit the text and the circumstance.

The Reader, the Text, and the Circumstance

To what extent might a particular circumstance demand a particular type of reading? Rosenblatt (1978) taught that readers' responses are conditioned by their contexts, depending on their purpose for reading a particular text. How we as readers approach a text affects the degree to which we transact with it.

Furthermore, the type of text that we read affects transaction, as some texts are more "closed" than others (Eco, 1979). Rosenblatt, for example, pointed out that we read materials differently depending on our purpose for reading. With informational types of material, the primary purpose for reading is usually to take away information from what we read, whether it is following the directions for putting together a new desk or reading a science textbook. Rosenblatt referred to this as an **efferent** stance to reading. An efferent stance does not mean that each of us will construct identical meanings from the text, but it does suggest that our purpose in reading the material is to construct a meaning as similar to the author's as possible. Moreover, an instruction manual offers less room for a reader to negotiate meaning within it. It is therefore more of a closed text.

In contrast to an efferent stance and closed texts, Rosenblatt maintained that an **aesthetic** stance is more appropriate for narrative material. Readers enter into and live through stories rather than taking information away from them. The texts are more "open" (Eco, 1979): they have greater "gaps" within them where readers might insert themselves to make meaning (Iser, 1974). Rosenblatt also asserted that readers can change their stances during the reading of any one text and the two stances are not mutually exclusive.

There is one last lesson that we would like to highlight from Garcia's story that can help flesh out social constructivist perspectives of reading. The story shows the conflict that can occur when school is not in sync with children's **funds of knowledge**. Clearly, there is a clash of cultures in the story—the result of differences in class. Thus, the story illustrates that being able to read words on a page is not enough to be a reader (or to be literate). One must also be able to read the world. Educators working in a **critical literacy** vein would therefore see it as their responsibility to assist their students to read print and comprehend what it means across domains. Part of their role is to help learners to understand which readings of a word are dominant and which help to inform one's identity (e.g., the interpretation of a suitcase as a briefcase).

Thus to sum up, from social constructivist perspectives,

- reading is a socio-cultural practice
- reading is achieved through readers' use of higher- and lower-order information
- readers construct meaning as they transact with texts, educators, and peers within the classroom and in a broader social context
- there can be dominant and minority readings of a given text

As evidenced in multiliteracies and related theories, and in our discussion of how young children come to literacy in Chapter 4, it is also helpful to think of the practice of reading or learning to read as connected to other **modes** or dimensions of language and literacy.

Your View of Reading

Now that you have read about some different perspectives on reading, we invite you to revisit your own views by looking at your responses to the questionnaire in Box 5.1. Note that proponents of bottom-up perspectives would strongly agree with statements 1, 5, and 9, whereas proponents of top-down perspectives would strongly agree with statements 2, 6, and 10. Statements 3, 7, and 11 reflect interactive perspectives of reading, and statements 4, 8, and 12, social constructivist perspectives.

We realize the difficulty of clearly identifying your total perspective of reading through a questionnaire. However, readers who agreed or strongly agreed with all three statements in any of the four groupings delineated above may have a leaning toward the perspectives associated with those statements. If you have a leaning toward one perspective, consider what might be informing this view. Most likely, many teacher candidates and beginning educators are still developing coherent views of reading, which will be refined as they gain professional experience and delve further into the professional literature.

Our Approach to Reading: Implications for Practice

Focusing on what readers *do* as opposed to what reading *is* may be more productive than arguing about definitions. Smith (2007) agrees. When asked, "How do you define reading?" he answered, "I don't try. It's better to describe reading than to define it" (p. 5). Smith then went on to describe reading as "making sense of things" (p. 5). This response is in keeping with our notion of reading as constructing meaning from print text, be that text linear (e.g., a printed book) or not (e.g., reading on a website that involves hyperlinks).

Further to our description of reading is that we subscribe to a social constructivist perspective that is also based in multiliteracies theory. In keeping with our goal of educators as professionals, we do not ask that you construct a perspective on reading that is identical to the one we have shared; instead, we urge you to think about what you believe and why. Doing this will provide you with a framework for determining what you will be assessing when you assess reading. Our perspective leads us to a particular understanding of what reading is, and therefore we are able to operationalize a view of what a good reading usually entails. Specifically, we find that a good reading (usually) involves the following:

- establishing a purpose for reading
- concentrating more on constructing meaning from texts than on identifying all the words in a text correctly
- constantly monitoring comprehension, noticing when meaning has gone awry, and, when necessary, doing what is needed to restore meaningfulness

- consistently orchestrating semantic, syntactic, pragmatic, and graphophonic cues
- having at hand a variety of strategies for when a text gets rough and knowing which strategies to use depending on the situation
- drawing on **text structure** and **genre** to make meaning
- drawing on oral language from various contexts (including knowledge of one's first language if the reading is in a second language) to help make meaning
- being engaged and self-directed (Weaver, Gillmeister-Krause, & Vento-Zogby, 1996)
- constructing meaning from print in conjunction with the other modes that might be present within a given context (e.g., a reader makes meaning from **hypertext** and any accompanying sounds or images)

You may note that the above discusses a good *reading* and not a good *reader*. As mentioned in Chapter 2, educators have a tendency to refer to readers in ways that characterize them overall as readers (e.g., "a struggling reader"). Doing this, however, may be unhelpful, as it negates what the struggling reader is reading or the context in which he or she is reading. Alternatively, Flurkey (2008) asked that educators differentiate between the terms *reader* and *reading*. The reader is the person who engages in the practice; the reading is the practice itself, located in a specific context and concerning a specific text. Almost all "readers can be efficient readers of some texts" (no matter how few or simple). "Likewise, mature readers may struggle over texts with high concept loads, unfamiliar content, or complex syntax" (p. 284).

To evaluate and characterize a reading requires that educators consider not only what a reader does with a text but also what that text is and the context in which it is being read. For instance, Maggie, in grade 7, loves science fiction and has read much in the genre. When she meets a new science fiction text, she is not only interested and likely to be engaged and thus persevere with it, but she will also have much of the genre worked out, including its common vocabulary and plot structure. Her readings here will probably be quite efficient. However, when Maggie read a newspaper article about sailing, a topic she confessed to knowing nothing about, she read some of it with expression and at a reasonable pace, needing only infrequently to stop and problem-solve words or self-correct, but she read haltingly the parts of the article that concerned nautical vocabulary and concepts. In the end, she was unable to demonstrate that she had been able to construct a high degree of meaning from the reading. What the examples of these readings show is that the same reader's readings can change depending upon the circumstances of the readings.

Maggie's experience also illustrates an important point about a feature of reading that many people and organizations consider a marker of good or poor reading—fluency.

There are at least three ways in which the term *fluency* is used today:

- Fluency is reading aloud with accuracy, appropriate speed, and expression. This is the oldest … and most common definition.
- Fluency is reading accurately while also comprehending what is read.… This is also a historical definition.…
- Fluency is reading aloud fast and accurately. This is a recent definition … one at odds with both historical definitions because neither "expression" nor "comprehension" is typically evaluated in calculating a student's fluency performance. (Allington, 2009a, p. 2)

One of the reasons fluency is considered an important component of reading achievement is that reading is thought to be "laborious" rather than "meaningful" or "pleasurable" to those who read "in a flat monotone" and without expression (p. 5). There is also research to support a link between fluency and comprehension (National Reading Panel, 2000) and the notion that any assessment and subsequent teaching of fluency must be conducted within the context of reading comprehension (Pikulski & Chard, 2005). A helpful way to think about fluency is through Flurkey's (2008) notion of *flow*. Rather than labelling a reading fluent or disfluent, Flurkey used the metaphor of flowing water. When water runs through a stream, there are times when the movement is smooth and fast but also times when the water slows down or becomes choppier to navigate around the features of the stream. Readers too can have an easier or rougher time moving through the features of a text (as Maggie did). Needing to move back to self-correct or pause to problem-solve does not necessarily make for an unsuccessful reading if the reader is able to construct meaning from the text. By the same token, a fast, linear reading does not necessarily indicate a reading where meaning is being constructed. Thus we suggest that educators consider the reader, the demands of the text, and the supports available (or not) during the reading, and whether the goal of constructing meaning has been reached. We also need to highlight in this discussion Allington's (2009a) reminder of the importance of pleasure to reading flow. Thankfully, flow (and fluency) can be supported through many of the pedagogical strategies we set out in the book, especially the modelling of fluent reading through Read-Aloud and Shared Reading, repeated readings of favourite texts, independent reading of texts that are interesting and accessible to readers, and basically, just lots of good, old reading where the text fits the situation (Allington, 2009a).

Because our definition of reading is multifaceted, we must have an equally multifaceted assessment protocol. We present such a protocol in part of the upcoming section on assessment, but first we provide an overview of assessment options within a discussion of the purposes of reading assessment; then, to provide a glimpse of the context in which educators and children are learning and teaching, we move to an overview of the foundation for reading assessment provided in Canadian curriculum documents.

READING ASSESSMENT

The interviews with Taylor and Erin at the beginning of this chapter raise questions about the natures of reading and reading assessment. For instance, what are the purposes of assessment? How might different assessments serve different purposes? How might assessment serve the child, the educator, the school district, and the public? What options might educators have for reading assessment?

Purposes of Assessment

Jalongo (2007) argued that there is a continuum of assessment types ranging from those that are "formal" and highly structured to those that are more "informal" and less structured. Each type has its own "purpose" or goal; "basic assumption," which seems to relate to one or more of the orientations toward reading and/or literacy just discussed; "focus";

and type of information collected (p. 329). Each also allows educators greater or lesser control over the assessment; some, such as a norm-referenced achievement test, are highly prescriptive, while others, such as an educator observation, may be entirely created and implemented by the educator. To help orient you to assessment types and goals, we have adapted Jalongo's continuum (see Table 5.1). We invite you to consider this table and see how you respond to each of the assessment types. Further, as you read through this chapter and the assessment information in Chapter 4, you may want to picture where each type of assessment falls on the continuum.

A major purpose of reading assessment should be to obtain the information learners and educators need to optimize reading practices and learning. Learners find out how they are doing and what they should do next. Educators find out if what they are doing is working

TABLE 5.1 **LANGUAGE ASSESSMENT CONTINUUM**

Formal (more prescriptive) (less educator control) ←——————→ **Informal** (less prescriptive) (more educator control)

	Norm-Referenced	**Criterion-Referenced**	**Observation/ Documentation**
Purpose	To rank or compare one learner's performance on a set of test items with that of learners belonging to the same group on which the test was standardized	To assess the learners' performance on specific objectives or tasks	For an educator and a learner to understand a learner's overall performance over time and the learner's funds of knowledge
Basic assumption	The whole is the sum of its parts	The whole can be analyzed as components	The whole is more than the sum of its parts
Focus	Products or outcomes (e.g., reading comprehension)	Particular aspects of a literacy practice (e.g., reading) or product in accordance with the criteria guiding the assessment	Holistic language practices
Data	Generally quantitative (e.g., raw scores, percentages)	Qualitative and/or quantitative; limited contextualization	Descriptive, naturalistic, contextualized
Examples	Achievement tests; IQ tests	Large- and small-scale assessments that use rubrics (e.g., many provincial tests)	Anecdotal records; portfolios; self-assessments and inventories; observation inventories

Sources: Cooper & Kiger, 2001; Jalongo, 2007; McCarrier, Pinnell, & Fountas, 2000; McLaughlin & Allen, 2002; Opitz & Ford, 2001.

and what to do next. Toward these ends, the following checklist can help guide educators in their daily assessment decisions. Educators can consistently monitor what, whom, and how they assess by asking themselves these questions:

- Is this a valid and useful assessment:
  - ☐ For this student at this time?
  - ☐ For our curriculum and standards?
  - ☐ To inform my teaching?
  - ☐ To share with the student?

- How am I using this assessment:
  - ☐ To note and celebrate the student's strengths [and funds of knowledge]?
  - ☐ To build on those strengths [and funds of knowledge]?
  - ☐ To note weaknesses?
  - ☐ To inform and determine my instruction?
  - ☐ To help the student become more competent?
  - ☐ To teach what the student needs to know next?

- What goals am I setting:
  - ☐ For myself as teacher?
  - ☐ For the student?
  - ☐ With the student?

- Who else do I need to inform:
  - ☐ The principal?
  - ☐ [Family?]
  - ☐ Support personnel?
  - ☐ [Other teachers]? (Routman, 2003, p. 99)*

Considerations for Culturally and Linguistically Diverse Learners

As the checklist above suggests, the ultimate goal in assessing any learner's reading (and learning in general) is the improvement of instruction and hence, the learner's literacy practices. This effort must be made while keeping open learners' identity options and engagement with literacy learning. We believe that these goals of reading assessment can be achieved only if educators see and treat learners as at-promise. Unfortunately, there can be a tendency for assessments to be used in a deficit-oriented fashion, sometimes without educators even meaning to. Take, for example, the term *diagnostic assessment*. Some educators might use it in a familiar, off-handed way, but it is actually suggestive of a medical model where the educator, like a medical doctor, must "identify [a difficulty] and respond appropriately with instructional techniques designed to have a medicinal or therapeutic effect" (McKenna & Stahl, 2009, p. 2). In the case of reading, a problem with the medical model is that reading is

---

* From *Reading Essentials: The Specifics You Need to Teach Reading Well* by Regie Routman. Copyright 2003 by Regie Routman. Published by Heineman, Portsmouth NH. Reprinted by permission of the Publisher. All rights reserved.

a complex socio-cultural and cognitive practice, and difficulties in reading achievement within the context of school cannot be reduced to "a single remediable cause" (p. 2). Additionally, the medical model suggests that the reason for the difficulty in reading achievement is some kind of sickness that belongs to the learner. This focus on the learner as the site of pathology can shift the responsibility away from other factors that might be causing the difficulty (e.g., the assessment itself, the school's definition of literacy) (Heydon & Iannacci, 2008).

Pathologizing learners who struggle with their literacy happens too frequently with **culturally and linguistically diverse (CLD) learners**. Luigi Iannacci (Heydon & Iannacci, 2008) has some helpful guidelines for educators when they are assessing CLD learners.

First, educators should do what they can so that the learners can perform to the best of their abilities in an assessment situation. Drawing on research in the area (Swain, 1984, cited in Mendelsohn, 1989), Iannacci counsels that educators can do this by

- using "various resources to aid [learners] (e.g., picture dictionaries, charts, or other reference materials)"
- allowing "sufficient time" for learners to complete an assessment
- giving opportunities to learners to "review completed work relevant to the assessment"
- ensuring that learners have sufficient instructions and suggestions to begin an assessment task
- "offering suggestions" to learners regarding "how to set about the task"
- "cueing and prompting" learners during the assessment
- "going 'off-script' when using packaged assessments in order to make the material relevant to students' background knowledge or to fill in any gaps that may prevent them from demonstrating their assets" (Heydon & Iannacci, 2008, p. 139)

Before they begin assessing CLD learners, Iannacci also advises, educators should fully take into account learners' "experience with the language of instruction and the cultural factors that may impact their performance" (p. 139). This means that educators should add questions such as these to Routman's list: "Who are my students?" "What resources do they possess?" "Are these resources being accessed or ignored in [this assessment]?" (p. 139). These assessment strategies and questions make sense when we think of assessment within the context of the literacy framework we have been advocating: discern the students' knowledge, what they are able to do and value, then plan from there.

Assessment and Aboriginal Children

Most provinces recognize that Aboriginal children can bring different worldviews to schools and that these views need to be taken into account in assessment. It is difficult to generalize one Aboriginal view because there was never one nation in North America (Weber-Pillwax, 2001). That said, the literature does point to some considerations that might be pertinent when assessing Aboriginal children's language and literacy.

For some Aboriginal learners, English is not their first language, and these learners are "readily acknowledged as students learning English" (Peltier, 2009, p. 3). Yet educators must equally be sensitive to learners who speak First Nations English **dialects**. Sharla Peltier (2009), a First Nations speech-language pathologist, studied the importance and prevalence of First Nations dialects and their features. She found the following:

- The diversity of dialects that exist are "as diverse as the Aboriginal peoples of North America" (p. 1).

- Dialects are evident among peoples who speak their Aboriginal language and those who do not.

- Dialects can serve important purposes: "It can be said that First Nations English dialects are used purposely as an indicator of opposition to colonization and assimilation" (p. 1).

- Dialects may be particularly important to their speakers as in some communities these may be the only remaining connection to the Aboriginal language.

Peltier observed that there is limited research on the features of the dialects. Ball and Bernhardt (2008) agreed that research in this area is "urgently needed." Among the reasons are to help "educators … distinguish between language impairments and dialect differences and to develop culturally relevant assessment and intervention practices" (p. 570). Ball, Bernhardt, and Deby (2005) contended that typical language assessment tools and procedures (especially those that are standardized) are based on the standard English dialect, which can result in speakers of non-standard dialects being misdiagnosed as language impaired. Peltier (2009) argued that "misunderstandings" regarding dialects have led to an "epidemic" of "mislabelling of students as developmentally delayed and language deficient" (p. 4). This, in turn, has led to "widespread implementation of inappropriate language and literacy programming" and "Aboriginal language loss" (p. 4).

In the absence of solid research into dialects, educators might bear the following in mind when thinking about assessment and Aboriginal learners:

- All educators must be alert to the presence of Aboriginal children in their classrooms. In terms of First Nations young people, Peltier (2009) reminds us that most of them attend schools outside of First Nations territories.

- Learners who use English dialects are, like their acknowledged ESL counterparts, also "learning a new language—the Standard form of English" (p. 3).

- Assessment practices such as those described above for CLD learners in general might thus be considered.

Next, to flesh out the issues we have raised here, we call upon some classic studies that highlight cultural and linguistic differences between specific Aboriginal learners and mainstream cultures which could affect language and literacy assessment.

First, a foundational study by researchers Scollon and Scollon (1981) suggested some differences in the use of language by Athabaskan and mainstream English-speaking Canadians that have implications for children in schools, including assessment. At the time of the research, Athabaskan languages were spoken by Aboriginal people in the northern parts of Manitoba, Saskatchewan, Alberta, and British Columbia, as well as in the Northwest Territories. Scollon and Scollon found that the Athabaskan speakers in their study avoided conversation unless the point of view of all participants was well known, whereas English speakers felt that the main way to get to know the point of view of people was through conversation with them.

This difference could lead to English speakers feeling that Athabaskan speakers are taciturn or silent and to Athabaskan speakers feeling that English speakers talk too much. Scollon and Scollon also found that how much people talk was related to social relations of dominance. In schools, children are expected to show off their abilities to the teacher, who is in the spectator role. For the Athabaskan speakers in the study, though, expectations were different: in their culture adults were expected to display abilities for the child to learn. The adult was in the exhibitionist role while the child was in the spectator role. These differences have the potential to lead to misunderstanding.

Ball and Lewis's (2005) study showed the contrasting views of European-heritage parents and First Nations parents about talk. The study contended that European-heritage parents generally see themselves as effective parents if they encourage their children to be talkative and engaged in parent–child conversation. In contrast, First Nations parents reported, "First Nations children learn through listening, observing, doing and being included in family and community activities, more than by talking about their experiences and asking children a lot of questions" (p. 4). However, typical assessment and instruction in Canadian schools involve question-response modes that "appear to be much more common and familiar to European-heritage children than to many Aboriginal children" (p. 4).

Differences have also been documented in studies related to the ways different groups of people tell stories and in what they think are good stories. This finding was highlighted in a series of inquiries into sharing time in kindergarten classrooms (Cazden, 1988; Cazden, Michaels, & Tabor, 1985; Michaels, 1981; Michaels & Cazden, 1986). Sharing time, sometimes called "show and tell," is a common activity in primary classrooms when children are invited to share a story or personal experience about their lives outside of school. Michaels and Cazden (1986) found that teachers' reactions to children's stories revealed specific expectations about what the stories should be like. "Good" stories were those with a beginning, middle, and end, with all the ideas related to one topic. In one classroom, 96 percent of the stories told by white children met these criteria, but only 34 percent of those told by black children were topic centred. Instead, many black children provided chains of loosely related actions or events, often with the topic left unstated.

Teachers tended to negatively assess episodic stories, whereas they praised children who produced topic-centred stories. Michaels and Cazden subsequently presented a selection of both topic-centred and episodic stories to black and white teachers and asked them to assess how well formed the stories were. Teachers were also asked to predict the probable academic success of the child who told each story. White teachers frequently rated episodic stories as hard to follow and predicted the children would be low achieving, while black teachers rated both topic-centred and episodic stories positively. This study is important to understanding assessment and Aboriginal children, as episodic stories are also common in Aboriginal groups. It is not that children from these communities cannot tell stories; it is that the stories they tell may not match their teachers' expectations.

The above studies are not meant to essentialize Aboriginal cultures. Individual circumstances can and will vary—sometimes greatly. What the previous research signals, however, is the need for educators to be vigilant about noticing any mismatch between school practices and the learners in their classrooms and to question if assessments are culturally sensitive. Additional to scrutinizing the tools of assessment is questioning our own biases and viewpoints as educators and checking to see how they might be affecting assessment results and interpretations. After this awareness, educators can adjust assessments so that learners are able to show what they know, are able to do, and value.

Curriculum Documents: Part of the Assessment Dialogue

Complicating literacy assessment matters is that there can be competing goals of assessment (and instruction) between administrators, policy-makers, parents, and taxpayers. To deal with these tensions, we suggest that educators return to the notion of curriculum as a dialogue and consider how this dialogue includes assessment: what educators teach and assess and how educators teach and assess affect each other. To highlight a few of the voices in this dialogue, we now turn to a brief overview of regional curriculum documents and demonstrate how they may relate to assessment.

With an increased focus on accountability in education in the 1990s, many Canadian provinces and regions began to redevelop their curriculum documents to explicitly include "clear learning outcomes and high learning standards" (Alberta Learning, 2000a, p. 1). Most documents across the country (see Chapter 1 for a list of websites containing these documents) include outcomes, standards, expectations, and/or objectives for elementary children, nearly always organized by grade levels. For example, the British Columbia Ministry of Education (2006) specifies three broad categories of curriculum organizers: Oral Language (speaking and listening), Reading and Viewing, and Writing and Representing. These categories are further subdivided into purposes, strategies, thinking, and features. These documents become part of the assessment (and curriculum) conversation through two main pathways: provincial or territorial achievement tests and teachers' reporting procedures.

Most provinces and territories have developed achievement tests based on the outcomes stated in curriculum documents, and often administration of these achievement tests is mandatory. The most frequent scheduling of provincial and territorial achievement testing in reading for elementary students is at the ends of grades 3 and 6, although scheduling is different in some provinces (e.g., in British Columbia elementary students are assessed at the end of grades 4 and 7 and New Brunswick assesses Anglophone learners in grades 2, 4, 7, and 9).

Provincial and territorial reading achievement tests are similar across the country (see Erin's description of her EQAO reading test at the beginning of this chapter): students read passages and answer multiple-choice or sometimes short-answer questions to determine whether they have met the expectations/outcomes specified in curriculum documents. Tests generally include both narrative and informational passages and sometimes also poetry. Manitoba's Middle Years Assessment is "a unique assessment program in Canada" where the engagement of grade 7 learners in school is assessed followed by reading comprehension and **expository writing** assessments in grade 8. Interestingly, these assessments are classroom based and **formative**, that is, the assessments happen along the way, not just at the end of a unit or year (Klinger, DeLuca, & Miller, 2008, p. 12).

Most provinces and territories identify a standard or expected level of student performance in their curriculum documents. This standard is used to mark the achievement tests.

The Ontario Ministry of Education (2006), for example, has set out four levels of achievement that are related to expectations in four areas of knowledge and skills: Knowledge and Understanding—"Subject-specific content acquired in each grade (knowledge), and the comprehension of its meaning and significance (understanding)"; Thinking—"The use of critical and creative thinking skills and/or processes"; Communication—"The conveying of meaning through various forms"; and Application—"The use of knowledge and skills to make connections within and between various contexts" (pp. 20–21). Level 3 is the provincial standard, representing the expected level of achievement at each grade level. Level 1 represents achievement below the standard; Level 2, achievement approaching the standard; and Level 4, achievement surpassing the standard. In addition to the evaluation of the achievement test being conducted and communicated in these ways, the Ontario government mandates a provincial report card that is correlated with these achievement levels.

Results on provincial and territorial achievement tests are widely distributed and generally broken down by school district and sometimes by school. Many school districts also administer reading tests at the end of each grade, providing even more data on reading achievement levels of children in specific schools. Taylor's experience with CASI is such an example. The data collected can significantly affect the viability of some school programs when financing is provided on a per-student basis. The next section examines high-stakes assessment and its potential to help and to hinder the reading achievement of children in schools.

High-Stakes Assessment

Competing goals of assessment can also affect the types of assessments that are privileged in educational settings. How many readers recall year-end reading tests when they were in school? Were you ever aware of what these tests were for or what happened with the results? Sometimes the results may have been simply placed in your file and not much else happened. Other times, the results may have been used by your teacher to determine a mark on your report card. In a small number of instances, the results may have been used as a basis for grade repetition or placement in a special class.

The stakes were much higher in the last than in the first instance; hence the term *high-stakes assessment*. Much depends on one test, just as a gambler might have a lot of money riding on one hand of blackjack. In North America, as we have mentioned, one assessment is often used to make important and complex decisions involving such things as promotion or retention in grades, graduation, entrance into an educational institution, teacher salary, or a school district's autonomy.

The most common high-stakes tests are standardized norm-referenced and criterion-referenced tests.

Nature of Standardized Tests

Standardized tests have been used in North American schools for many decades as one way to gather information about students' reading. Such tests are "administered, scored, and interpreted in a standard manner" and, as mentioned, may be norm or criterion referenced

(Council of Chief State School Officers, n.d., n.p.). Standardized, criterion-referenced tests are those in which learners are given the same set of questions or tasks in the same way and their performance is judged against a standards-based set of criteria, such as curricular outcomes or expectations. Standardized, norm-referenced tests are also tests that are implemented in a standard way, but they go a step further in that they are scored against a *norm*. Such tests are developed by selecting items at a range of difficulty levels and administering them to children at various grade and age levels. Tables of norms are then developed, providing educators with percentiles, grade equivalents, and/or standard scores corresponding to the number of items a learner completes correctly. When a standardized, norm-referenced test is administered, it determines how well the learners in the class perform on the test in relation to the learners in the standardization sample.

The primary reason school systems and provincial governments administer both kinds of standardized tests is accountability—to show that the programs provided in the school system are producing the desired results. Administrators compare the scores of one class, school, or system with those of the standardization sample (in the case of norm-referenced tests) and/or of other classes, schools, and systems. Sometimes scores are compared across provinces, states, and even nations.

At this point you might have many questions regarding the potential benefits and limitations of such assessment. As educators working within a social constructivist perspective who understand literacy as a broad and complex set of situated practices, we have many concerns with standardized tests and high-stakes assessment.

Some Problems with High-Stakes Testing

High-stakes testing has come under considerable criticism in recent years (e.g., Kohn, 2002). One common criticism involves the extent to which a single assessment, as well as a standardized assessment, can be consistent with the language and literacy programs being implemented. Because curriculum is a dialogue, one test cannot "represent the curriculum and instructional diversity among teachers" (Paris & Hoffman, 2004, p. 205). As Erin's description of the reading passage in her EQAO test shows, such tests also fail to address the multifaceted, rich types of texts that we promote in *Constructing Meaning*. Often, the passages used to assess comprehension are short and contrived rather than high-quality **children's literature**, and even when a reasonably well-written text is used, because the tests are standardized, learners must read the same materials—there is no accounting for the role of funds of knowledge or engagement in the reading process. Witness Taylor's situation with the CASI. In the year when she read about figure skating, something she knew about and enjoyed, she did well. In the year where she had to read about basketball, she found the text long and hard going. The roles of background knowledge and engagement affected her scores on these tests. As such, a single, standardized assessment cannot "capture the variety of skills and developmental levels," not to mention funds of knowledge of "children in most … classes" (p. 205).

Another feature of many standardized, high-stakes tests is their frequent reliance on multiple-choice items. Multiple-choice items fail to measure what really counts in reading when reading is considered to be a meaning-making process (e.g., critical thinking, construction of meaning, and collaborative learning); they tend to reinforce the notion of one right answer, which can be offputting for learners who have developed more robust notions of what reading is about. For instance, consider this quotation about one of her students from an educator in a study about the effects of high-stakes testing:

> He sat down to take the test and tears were coming down his face and he looked up at me and he said—I was teaching third grade—and he said, "*I thought I could read.*" And I thought, from that minute on, that's never going to happen to me again. My kids are all going to feel comfortable. No one is going to look at this test and start crying. (Valli & Chambliss, 2007, p. 57)

Aspects of high-stakes assessment have been hurtful to learners. Some high-stakes tests promote antiquated notions of literacy that do not account for the types of literacies that are demanded in contemporary times (e.g., Au & Valencia, 2010). High-stakes assessment tends to highlight learners' deficits, rather than their knowledge or strengths (Heydon & Iannacci, 2005). Indeed, this can be a feature of norm-referenced assessments.

In the construction of the norm, test items are deliberately selected "to produce failure among some and success among others" (Field, 1990, p. 108). How does this happen? When items are being selected for inclusion on a particular test, those items that all learners get right or all learners get wrong are eliminated because they do not help to differentiate among learners. In other words, unless a set percentage of learners fail an item, it is not included. And by linking scores on these tests to grade equivalents, it is predetermined that some learners will be at grade level, some will be above, and some will be below. In other words, when norm-referenced tests are used, half of the learners will succeed and half will fail.

This situation leads to a basic contradiction between the goals of schooling and the use of standardized, norm-referenced tests. On the one hand, most people believe that a goal of schooling should be to ensure that all learners are able to read at a level appropriate to their grade. On the other hand, the use of these tests means that this will *never be achieved*.

Another problem with the tests in question is that, through them, some learners are identified very early as functioning below expectations, the emphasis being on what they cannot do rather than what they can do. Many educators are, therefore, concerned about the potentially negative impact that test results can have on individual learners by marginalizing them and telling them that they are not good enough. Particularly problematic is that the learners who are most often marginalized by these types of tests, because of built-in bias in test items, are the poor and those from minority groups (Giambo, 2010). Problematizing the situation is that because the assessments are high stakes, test results are usually communicated publicly. This practice has been found to "undermin[e], even stigmatiz[e] the reputations of the local community, the school, the principal, the teachers, and the students" (Sloan, 2007, p. 29).

Some additional identified unanticipated negative outcomes of high-stakes testing have been narrowed curricular content (to be in line with the test), fragmented knowledge, and an increase in teacher-centred pedagogies (Au, 2007) described as "a focus on low-level knowledge and skills" delivered through "rote level, discrete, individual drill and skill practice" (p. 70) which not only affects what is learned and how, but also learners' engagement (Jones, 2007). This can result from what is commonly referred to as "teaching to the test." Teaching to the test has been seen to result in stilted teaching that oversimplifies literacy and leads learners to develop a form of literacy that is overly simple (Valli & Chambliss, 2007). Rather than the tests measuring what is taught, the opposite is often the case—what is taught is determined by what is tested. This is frequently the case in high-poverty schools that tend to have the lowest test scores. The use of high-stakes tests accelerates an emphasis on lower-level skills and drill-and-practice activities rather than higher-level thinking (Kohn, 2002). Additionally, there is now the concern that CLD learners

> may be put at greater risk of disengagement from school and from literacy development because of high-stakes testing programs. That finding is particularly ironic because many [governmental] content and performance standard programs were adopted to address gaps in the performance of students from diverse ethnicities. Self-determination theorists and researchers argue that reward- and punishment-oriented approaches that pressure students cannot succeed. (Unrau & Schlackman, 2006, p. 99)

Finally, we must include in this list of problems the time testing takes away from instruction. It is not only the time spent in testing, but also the time for preparation and recovery (Voke, 2002). In 1999 the International Reading Association argued that the "consequences of lost instructional time, particularly for low-performing students, are too great for information that can be gathered more efficiently" (p. 4). Just think, for instance, of all the instructional time that was lost for Taylor and Erin. Suggesting that the problem is persisting, in 2006, Zajda, Majhanovich, and Rust also lamented the lost instructional time, adding that standardized tests were also taking away from learning opportunities related specifically to music, art, and physical education.

Despite the above bad-news story, educators in Canada, unlike their colleagues in some countries, still have some flexibility to see high-stakes tests and other assessment issues just discussed as part of a dialogue, rather than as a wholesale takeover of their professional autonomy. So, what might a reading assessment that is compatible with multiliteracies pedagogies look like? This is the central concern of the rest of this chapter.

ASSESSMENT WITHIN MULTILITERACIES PEDAGOGIES

Just as there is no one right way to bring learners to literacy, there is no one best reading assessment. Educators need to have at their disposal a range of assessment tools and procedures. When they are selecting how and when to assess, educators may take into consideration the counsel of the Language and Literacy Researchers of Canada (2008) that literacy assessment should

- be part of the teaching and learning process
- incorporate multiple and varied sources of data
- when designed for one purpose, should not be used for another
- reflect the complexity of literacy processes
- be developmentally and culturally appropriate
- not use one measure in making decisions regarding certification or access to programs or resources
- encourage student and family participation (n.p.)

Just like the principles of assessment we defined in Chapter 4, we believe reading assessment should be multifaceted and "look at the different means of expression a [learner] might use to demonstrate reading ability" (Jalongo, 2007, p. 330), always consider the context in which the assessment is being conducted, be classroom based, and be largely characterized by **performance assessment** whereby learners are assessed on their *application* or use of language and literacy.

TABLE 5.2 **ASSESSMENT STRATEGIES**

Strategy One: Observation	
Contexts	Recording
• interactive Read-Aloud, Shared Reading, Guided Reading, Independent Reading, reader response activities, explorations • mini-lessons • oral reading/retelling • drama	• checklists • anecdotal records • reading logs • audiotapes • running records • videotapes
Strategy Two: Conferencing	
Contexts	Recording
• teacher–student conferencing • conferences with families (including student-led conferences)	• conference logs • anecdotal records • questionnaires • surveys • story collection
Strategy Three: Work Samples	
Contexts	Recording
• interactive Read-Aloud, Shared Reading, Guided Reading, Independent Reading, reader response activities, explorations, mini-lessons	• artifacts from contexts (e.g., Venn diagrams, character maps) • anecdotal records • portfolios

In the next section we lay out three major reading assessment strategies that can become part of an educator's repertoire (observation, work samples, and conferencing). Table 5.2 (adapted from Hibbert, 2005) is based on Kathy Hibbert's classroom practice and understanding of key pieces of assessment literature (e.g., Cooper & Kiger, 2005; Vacca, Vacca, & Begorary, 2005). The table lays out the strategies, the contexts in which they might be conducted, and the ways in which assessment information can be recorded. Educators can mix and match strategies, contexts, and ways of recording information to suit their needs. When interpreting assessment results, they can triangulate their data, that is, check to see how the information they have collected from various sources compares and whether it is consistent. When inconsistencies emerge (and they do!), educators may choose to collect more or different data in a variety of contexts until they have a clearer picture of what is happening with a learner.

Strategy One: Observation

Observation can be at the heart of assessment. It can provide contextualized information about reading achievement and process, including how well learners are reading, how they are reading, and what types of activities and texts engage them. The reading checklist in Table 5.3

TABLE 5.3 **READING CHECKLIST**

Aspects of Reading	Reading Strategy	Comments
Shows positive attitude to reading	— Is able to name favourite books and authors — Enjoys reading silently in class time — Engages in extensive independent reading	
Integrates background knowledge and information from text to construct meaning	— Is able to set a purpose for reading — Is able to predict what a story or text will be about from the title — Is able to predict what will happen next in a story — Uses both knowledge and text information to answer inference questions — Includes inferences as well as text information in retellings	
Uses knowledge of story structure to construct meaning	— Is able to answer questions about the setting, characters, events, and ending of stories — Includes information from setting, events, and ending in retellings of stories — Retells stories in sequence	
Uses knowledge of expository text structure to construct meaning	— Is able to answer questions involving main idea, sequence, cause and effect, and comparison/contrast relationships — Uses organizational patterns of informational texts (enumeration, cause and effect, sequence, comparison/contrast) in retellings	
Uses context cues to identify words	— Provides oral reading miscues that make sense and sound right in relation to prior text — Gives real-word rather than nonsense-word responses when reading — Corrects miscues that do not make sense	
Uses graphophonic cues to identify words	— Makes oral reading miscues that look and sound like the words in the text — Represents most sounds in inventive spellings — Identifies words by processing letter groups, syllables, or words within other words — Corrects miscues that do not "look right"	
Integrates context and graphophonic cues to identify words	— Mainly uses miscues that both make sense and look right — Corrects most miscues that change the author's meaning	

is designed to help educators observe and interpret learners' reading behaviours during daily classroom reading instruction.

The headings in the left-hand column reflect those aspects of reading that are used to organize the pedagogical strategies discussed in Chapter 7. So, if a learner does not display reading behaviours associated with a particular aspect of reading, educators can go directly to the appropriate section in Chapter 7 to discern the strategies to use with that learner. For example, a learner who is not yet able to include information from the setting, events, and endings of stories in **retellings** may benefit from work on narrative text structure. A learner who is not yet representing most letters in inventive spellings and whose **miscues** bear little resemblance to words he or she is reading may benefit from work on **phonemic awareness** and phonics.

Strategy Two: Conferencing

Conferencing can provide educators with information about learners' interests, attitudes to reading, and the strategies they use and know about. It can also be a means of engaging learners in their own goal setting and self-assessment. Interests, attitudes, and engagement are all critical areas of concern for assessment. Cambourne (1988), of course, instructed that engagement is a necessary condition of learning, and researchers such as Richard Allington (2012) and Kelly Gallagher (2009) have taught that unfortunately, more learners *can* read than *do* read. (Gallagher coined the term *readicide* to refer to educational practices such as overzealous testing regimes that kill the joy of reading.) Reading volume, Allington has explained, is positively correlated with reading achievement, so the more educators can learn how to engage learners in reading (e.g., by finding out what books they would be interested in), the more effective instruction is likely to be. Given that good readings involve readers using strategies for dealing with text when it gets rough, it is also important to find out what learners do or do not know about strategies. Conferencing in the form of interviews is an excellent way of ascertaining learners' understanding of reading strategies, especially for older learners (McKenna & Stahl, 2009).

Conferencing can take many forms. During classroom interactions, educators can encourage learners to talk about what, why, and how they read. The interview schedule outlined in Table 5.4 can help educators collect specific information about a learner's reading interests, habits, and knowledge about reading and strategies. Educators can add the following survey items to target older learners' motivation to read:

As an adult, I will spend

- none of my time reading
- very little of my time reading
- some of my time reading
- a lot of my time reading

When I am in a group talking about what we are reading, I

- almost never talk about my ideas

- sometimes talk about my ideas
- almost always talk about my ideas
- always talk about my ideas

I would like my teachers to read out loud in my classes

- every day
- almost every day
- once in a while
- never

(Albright et al., 2004, cited in Gambrell & Gillis, 2007, p. 57)

TABLE 5.4 **READING INTERVIEW**

Area	Questions
Interests	• What kinds of things do you like to do in your spare time? • What is your favourite subject at school? Why? • What kinds of texts do you like to read? • What are two things you have read recently and enjoyed?
Attitudes	• If you could read a story or watch it on television, which would you choose? Why? • How much time do you spend reading each day at home? At school? • How many books do you own? Do you go to the library to get books? • How do you feel about reading?
Knowledge about reading Functions of reading	• What is reading? • Why do people read?
Reading strategies	• Think of a time that someone read a text well. How do you know the text was read well? What did the reader do? • How would you help someone who was having trouble reading? • What do you think about as you read? • What do you do when you are reading and come to a word you don't know? • What do you do when you are reading and something doesn't make sense? • What do you do to help you remember what you read (e.g., in social studies)? • Do you ever read something over again? Why? • Do you read some things faster than others? Why?
Self-appraisal	• How would you describe yourself as a reader? • When is reading the easiest? When is it the most difficult? • What kind of help do you think you need with your reading?

In all, educators must develop interview questions and other survey items that target the information they are looking for and that are crafted for their specific learners.

Despite the plethora of new publications on reading assessment, many reading assessment interviews continue to rely on tried-and-true interview protocols. We are no different in this regard. Hence, our interview schedule is made up of old favourites (Atwell, 1987; Goodman, Watson, & Burke, 1987; Lipson & Wixson, 1991).

Note that in the interview you will not likely ask any learner all of the questions in one sitting. Instead, educators will think about what they need to know about a learner and select the questions that might help elicit this information. For example, if a learner rarely chooses books to read independently, you might ask the questions about interests and attitudes. If a learner appears to have few strategies for making meaning, you might ask the last four questions in the reading strategies section.

Strategy Three: Work Samples

Just as we described in Chapter 4, educators can save samples of learners' reading throughout the school year to assess growth. Here are some forms that these samples can take:

- Reading logs provide information on what learners read and are commonly kept in their reading portfolios. In their logs, learners keep a list of books they have read during the year and make note of the amount, genre, and level of material read. Learners can include the date each book was selected and completed, along with comments about the book. These entries help educators and learners chart learners' growth in voluntary reading behaviour and track the types of texts that learners are reading.

- Response to literature is another way to sample learners' meaning making in reading (see Chapter 12 for a full discussion of response activities). Educators (and learners) can analyze these responses in numerous ways to add to assessment data. Responses may, for example, be analyzed in terms of learners' ability to *retell* (e.g., identify main ideas and story structure), *relate* (e.g., connect the text to other texts, the world, and themselves), and *reflect* (e.g., evaluate ideas, ask questions) (Schwartz & Bone, 1995). Learners' responses to texts illustrate how they transact with a given text rather than their specific use of reading strategies. Keep in mind when examining responses that they are often as much a reflection of expressive ability—writing, representing, and speaking—as reading comprehension.

- **Running records**, described in Chapter 4, can be used to collect samples of learners' oral reading, to determine what level of material is appropriate for instruction, and to examine learners' growth in using meaning and print cues to identify words. As with young children, running records can be kept of learners reading stories from basal texts, books, or passages specifically designed for this purpose. While it is more authentic to gather running records on materials being used in the classroom, educators may wish to use informal reading inventories (IRIs) with older students. Given the somewhat rigid nature of these inventories, however, we recommend that educators use them sparingly and only when the specific information they can provide is called for.

Informal Reading Inventories

Designed in the early to mid 20th century (Lipson & Wixson, 2009) and still frequently used, informal reading inventories usually consist of two components: a series of word lists and passages with comprehension questions at increasing levels of reading difficulty. The word lists included on the inventories are used to estimate the reading level at which to begin administering reading passages. That level is the one at which learners can identify all or most of the words. Establishing this base ensures that learners do not spend time reading passages that are much too easy or much too difficult for them.

Educators then invite learners to read passages orally and silently and answer questions about them. Learners continue to read passages of increasing difficulty until they are no longer able to identify 90 percent of the words or answer 70 percent of the questions correctly. As learners read orally, educators keep a running record of oral reading miscues and write down learners' answers to comprehension questions. The marking system used for taking a running record with early readers is also an appropriate means of recording miscues for more independent readers.

Educators may choose to use informal reading inventories because the passages and questions are all in one place and they do not have to search out a series of books at a range of reading levels and design tasks to assess comprehension of passages in these books. Such inventories are designed to be administered individually, so they are used primarily with learners when the educator is puzzled and needs more information to plan appropriate instruction. Inventories have also been found to be appropriate for use with CLD learners (Gandy, 2013). A wide range of inventories are available: these include the *Informal Reading Inventory* (Burns & Roe, 2007), *Classroom Assessment of Reading Processes* (Swearingen & Allen, 2000), and the *Qualitative Reading Inventory—4* (Leslie & Caldwell, 2011). The last two inventories include both narrative and expository passages. Even the Developmental Reading Assessment (DRA) (e.g., Beaver, 2006) is modelled in part from an informal reading inventory. Please note that when using "graded" or "levelled" passages, the grades and levels need to be taken with a grain of salt. This quantitative information can provide a ballpark idea of where learners are, but grades and levels are never absolute and vary from context to context.

Interpreting Informal Reading Inventories

Educators can glean two major types of information from an informal reading inventory: achievement and what is sometimes referred to as diagnostic information, which we prefer to consider as information about some of what readers do when they are reading. The learner's level of reading achievement is the highest level at which he or she meets the criteria set in the test for **instructional reading level**.

Although tests vary, as mentioned in relation to Running Records in Chapter 4, the instructional reading level is generally the level at which learners are able to identify 90 percent or more of the words accurately *and* answer 70 percent or more of the comprehension questions correctly. Learners are able to read material independently if word identification and comprehension are close to 100 percent. Material is probably too difficult for learners if they read with less than 90 percent accuracy *or* less than 60 percent comprehension. It is important to remember that informal reading inventories provide only a rough indication of the level of material learners can handle. Learners may be able to understand more difficult material if they know a great deal about the content or are very interested in it. The corollary of this is that if the topic in a narrative or informational passage is unfamiliar, learners may have difficulty with it even if the text is at their instructional reading level as determined on an informal reading inventory.

Many of these inventories include an activity for learners to do before they read each passage, to assess their background knowledge. On the *Qualitative Reading Inventory* (Leslie & Caldwell, 2011), for example, learners are asked to associate meanings with key concepts in passages to be read. On other inventories, they are asked to read the title and predict what passages will be about. Still others ask learners to rate their knowledge about the content of the passage after they have finished reading it. From a social constructivist perspective, a reader's background knowledge is a critical component in the reading process.

How the reader uses this knowledge along with print and text information is even more important. Note that because educators cannot get inside learners' heads to see reading as it occurs, they have to rely on indirect evidence to interpret what they are doing. Two major sources of data from informal reading inventories that provide this evidence are (1) oral reading miscues and (2) answers to questions.

Effective Readings and Miscues

In effective readings readers use cues both in context and within words as they read. An analysis of miscues, which we discussed previously, can help educators determine where to place the instructional focus at a given time. For example,

- If learners focus almost exclusively on print cues in material at their instructional level, they need less attention to cues within words for a while and a heavier focus on using context cues.

- If their miscues make sense but are not consistent with print cues, they need instruction on strategies for processing cues within words.

- Ultimately educators want to provide learning opportunities that support readers to use multiple sources of information to identify unfamiliar words and construct meaning from text.

Questioning

Educators can use question data to determine how a reader might be constructing meaning from text. If learners are successful in answering factual questions, they appear to be able to use text information to construct meaning. If they are successful in answering inferential questions, they appear to be able to integrate their world knowledge with text information to construct meaning as they read.

Learners who are able to answer factual but not inferential questions may think reading is a meaning-getting rather than a meaning-making enterprise, or they may not know how to use their knowledge along with text to construct meaning. They could then benefit from the teaching/learning strategies described in Chapter 7 in the section on integrating knowledge-based and text-based information.

Learners who are able to answer inferential questions better than factual ones may be relying too much on their background knowledge to construct meaning. Often, if they are asked to retell what they have read, they demonstrate limited processing of text information. They frequently benefit from teaching/learning strategies designed to help them use the structure of narrative and expository texts to construct meaning.

Classroom Reading Miscue Assessment

Another way that educators can collect information to understand readers' use of the cuing systems in their attempts to construct meaning and their basic comprehension of texts is through the classic *Classroom Reading Miscue Assessment* (CRMA) (Rhodes & Shanklin, 1993). The CRMA can be very useful as it

- provides information other than that from standardized tests about learners as readers
- can be integrated into classroom instruction on an ongoing basis because it does not take too much time
- supports educators in practising current pedagogies because it works from contemporary views of the reading process and instructional strategies

The CRMA asks learners to read a complete text passage, perhaps a whole story, chapter, or section of an information text that has a sense of "completeness" (p. 178) so that educators can ascertain the answers to four fundamental queries:

1. Of the sentences read, what percentage makes sense?
2. In what ways is the reader attempting to make meaning?
3. In what ways (if at all) is the reader arriving at nonsense?
4. How well is the reader able to retell what she or he has read?

The basic steps for completing the CRMA are outlined below, and we share a sample CRMA scoring sheet, which is composed of three sections, in Box 5.3.

1. Educators invite learners to read a complete passage. Passages should be slightly difficult for learners so that they will miscue, thereby providing educators with information about how learners attempt to construct meaning.
2. Educators inform learners that, after the reading, they will be asked to retell everything they recall about the passage.
3. Educators advise learners that if they come to a word they do not know, they should do what they would normally do when this happens when they are alone.

4. Educators prompt learners if they come to a word they don't know while reading, by saying something like, "Remember, do what you would do if you were by yourself" (p. 178).

5. If readers seem to be giving up, then educators can give assistance during readings. They can recommend that learners skip the word or phrase and go on. This approach helps to ensure that readers stay engaged with the reading and helps educators "discover the full repertoire of strategies" (p. 178) readers know and use.

6. In section I of the CRMA educators keep a tally of the number of sentences in the read passage and record if they are "semantically acceptable or unacceptable" (p. 179). In other words, they determine whether or not the sentences make sense in the context of the passage. If learners miscue but the miscue does not change the meaning of the sentence, then the miscue is semantically acceptable and recorded as such.

7. After the readings, educators calculate the percentage of sentences that are semantically acceptable to get an overall picture of how much meaning learners are making as they read.

8. In section II of the scoring sheet, educators are prompted to "make judgments about the sense-making strategies" (p. 180) learners employ during reading. They are invited to use their observational skills and professional discernment to consider these items. Educators may want to fill out this section in pencil before the retelling and then return to it later to see if the judgments still hold.

9. Next, in consideration of section III, educators invite learners to retell what they have read. They might say, "Please tell me everything you remember about what you have read." Once learners have responded, educators can provide wait time and then invite more: "This was such a long story that I'm going to give you a minute to think of any other things you remember" (p. 181). This process is called an *unaided retelling*.

10. Educators then ask learners carefully crafted, open-ended questions that do not provide learners with more information about the passage than they mentioned in the unaided retelling. The purpose is to gather data about aspects of the passage learners have left out. Box 5.4 provides examples of helpful sample questions. This activity is known as an *aided recall*.

11. Now educators can complete section III of the scoring sheet.

Two caveats: First, the CRMA may not be the best choice for really proficient readers who would likely read any text well orally. Instead, educators might want to invite such learners to read silently and then complete comprehension activities to check for understanding. Educators could then use the CRMA with those learners who do not appear to do well in these activities. Second, the aided recall is just that—a *recall*. It should not be confused with other higher-order types of comprehension (e.g., making connections and/or critically reflecting on a text).

BOX 5.3

CLASSROOM READING MISCUE ASSESSMENT

Reader's name _____   Date _____
Grade level _____   Teacher _____
Selection read _____

Classroom Reading Miscue Assessment

1. What percentage of the sentences read makes sense? Sentence-by-sentence tally   Total
   Number of semantically acceptable sentences: _____   _____
   Number of semantically unacceptable sentences: _____   _____
   % Comprehension score:

   $$\frac{\text{Number of semantically acceptable sentences}}{\text{Total number of sentences read:}} \quad \text{x} \quad 100 \quad = \quad \_\_\%$$

2. In what ways is the reader constructing meaning?	Seldom	Sometimes	Often	Usually	Always
A. Recognizes when miscues have disrupted meaning	1	2	3	4	5
B. Logically substitutes	1	2	3	4	5
C. Self-corrects errors that disrupt meaning	1	2	3	4	5
D. Uses pictures and/or other visual clues	1	2	3	4	5
In what ways is the reader disrupting meaning?					
A. Substitutes words that don't make sense	1	2	3	4	5
B. Makes omissions that disrupt meaning	1	2	3	4	5
C. Relies too heavily on graphophonic cues	1	2	3	4	5

3. If narrative text is used:	No		Partial		Yes
A. Character recall	1	2	3	4	5
B. Character development	1	2	3	4	5
C. Setting	1	2	3	4	5
D. Relationship of events	1	2	3	4	5
E. Plot	1	2	3	4	5
F. Theme	1	2	3	4	5
G. Overall retelling	1	2	3	4	5
If expository text is used:	No		Partial		Yes
A. Major concepts	1	2	3	4	5
B. Generalizations	1	2	3	4	5
C. Specific information	1	2	3	4	5
D. Logical structuring	1	2	3	4	5
E. Overall retelling	1	2	3	4	5

Source: Classroom Reading Miscue Assessment (CRMA) scoring sheet, Fig. 4.10, p. 177. In Lynn K. Rhodes & Nancy L. Shanklin, *Windows into literacy: Assessing learners K–8* (Portsmouth, NH: Heinemann), 1993.

BOX 5.4

AIDED RECALL PROMPTS

For Narrative Texts

Narration:	Who is telling this story? How would the story change if someone else in the book or an outside narrator told the story?
Character Recall and Development:	Who is in the story? What can you tell me about them?
	Why are they important to the story?
	Some characters may only play a small part in the story. Does this story have a character like this? Why is this character necessary for the story?
Setting:	Where did ... happen?
	When did ... happen?
	Tell me more about... place.
Events:	What else happened in the story?
	How did ... happen?
	Could you change the order of the main events or leave any of them out? Why or why not?
Event Sequence:	What happened before ...?
	What happened after ...?
	Were there any flashbacks, flashforwards, or time warps? How did they add to the story?
Plot:	What was X's main problem?
Theme:	What did you think *(the major character)* learned in the story?

For Expository Texts

Major Concept(s):	What was the main idea in the text?
Generalizations:	What other important information about ... was in the text?
Specific Information:	Is there any other information you remember from the text?
	What specific facts do you remember?
	What did you learn from the text that you didn't know before?
	What was the most surprising thing you learned from this text?
	After reading this text, what questions do you now have?
Logical Structuring:	How did the author go about presenting the information? (For example: comparison, examples, steps in a process.)

Source: Adapted from Rhodes & Shanklin, 1993, p. 181; Routman, 1991, pp. 118–119; Booth, 1996, p. 44.

Portfolios

Portfolios have been defined as "collections of artifacts of students' learning experiences assembled over time" (Valencia, Hiebert, & Afflerbach, 1994, p. 14). Reading portfolios provide information on learners' reading, including strategies that they use in a range of everyday reading activities. The process of developing and discussing the portfolio is also intended to help learners develop **metacognition** as they reflect on their reading (Wiener & Cohen, 1997).

While there are many different kinds of portfolios, two major types are the working portfolio and the showcase portfolio (Christie, Enz, & Vukelich, 2003). The items in the working portfolio represent a learner's typical, everyday performance. From the working portfolio, the learner and educator can select pieces to include in the showcase portfolio, which contains the learner's best work.

Portfolios can also take different physical forms, from the digital, where materials are created digitally or digitized, to the material, where papers and such are literally assembled in some container. Among the many imaginative containers from which to select, we have seen educators choose everything from unused pizza boxes to binders, to tag-board folders. The key is to select a format that is easy for educators and learners to use and is accessible.

We now invite you to take a moment to consider the interview we conducted with John Guiney Yallop, an experienced teacher, poet, and educational researcher, about his use of portfolios (see the next Inside Classrooms box). When you read John's responses, think about the following:

- What goes in the portfolio?
- Who decides what goes in?
- By what process are artifacts put into the portfolio?
- What are the various ways that the portfolio is used?
- How might portfolios be directly linked to assessment and to student improvement?

INSIDE CLASSROOMS

JOHN GUINEY YALLOP

What do you see as the benefits of portfolios?

The main benefit, I think, is that they give students ownership of their learning and the assessment of that learning as well. They take responsibility. They can look back on their work and see their journey as a learner. That, for me, is the most exciting. Students are able to say, I read this book or I read this chapter, or I read this section aloud in class and here is how I feel about my reading now and here's how I felt about my reading before.

What do you notice about your students' ability to self-assess?

Sometimes students feel uncomfortable even giving themselves a pat on the back, and maybe from having come from a more formal environment where they have been evaluated, they got used to the idea that the teacher tells me if I'm good or not. The teacher tells me if I can read or not. So my goal is to get them to a point of being able to say, I make decisions about how well I'm reading. I'm noticing my progress. I'm reading better this month than I did last month, because here's what I'm noticing I can do now that I didn't do before.

Do you require the students to reflect on their journey as a component of the portfolio?

Yeah. For every piece that goes in, they write a reflection. Over the years, I've borrowed some reflection sheets and other times I develop them to tailor them to my students' needs. The sheets ask students to answer a couple of questions: What is this piece? What growth is it showing? What subject area? I also have them answer these questions: Why am I putting this in my portfolio? What do I like about this piece?

I often saw on the borrowed forms the question "What can I improve?" And I grew to dislike that question because it always gave the message that this work is never good enough. So I tended to drop that question, and instead I ask them, "If you were showing this work to another student or someone else, what would you like to draw their attention to?" What I try to do with this question is to make the students aware or help them to talk about what particularly is attractive to them about this piece of work or something that they wanted to build on in a future piece of work. I also sometimes just want students to stop and celebrate a success.

What sorts of things do the students include?

We talk about the idea of a showcase portfolio, where you have these final pieces. That tends not to be the kind of portfolio that I do. The students have the option, of course. Final pieces are included there as well, but sometimes pieces along the way showing the journey are included. The idea is to show progress and growth.

How are the items in the portfolio organized?

One way is to organize by the subject area of the report card. Another option is to organize the items chronologically. And the form of the portfolio I use has evolved over time as well. I started basically with shoeboxes, and just about everything went in there. Then I noticed that having folders would be helpful, so I went to hanging folders as portfolios in a filing cabinet. That's probably the one that I find most useful, because it is easier to organize in terms of classroom space.

How do you use the portfolios?

I use them by sitting with students and talking to them about their work and their learning journey. Usually the last day of the week in a six-day cycle I have a period or two where we say this is our portfolio time. It is important to put it in the timetable, because if I don't put it in the timetable, the message would be given that it's not valued. During this time the students select a piece and reflect on it and then put it in the portfolio. I confer with students who are having some difficulty finding a piece of work. I help them to find it, or if they aren't sure what to write about the piece, I chat with them to help them find a way to reflect on the piece.

I also use portfolios when it comes time for report cards. I sit with the portfolios, just one at a time. It gives the feeling of being with a student's body of work. It allows me to be

(continued)

able to go back and forth and make connections in the comments that I make about their work.

The other way I use them that is probably one of the most effective is in student, parent, teacher conferences. I introduce the process by saying: "Your child is going to show you some of their work and talk about it, and then I'll make a few comments about what I've noticed and what I may have said in the report card already. What's most important, if you have some comments about the work, you can direct those to your child, or, if you have some questions for me, I can answer those, as well." What is really powerful is when children share their work with their parents. Often parents are getting the work going home, but they're unaware about how much their children accomplish during the day; often the students themselves are unaware of how much they accomplish during the day as well. Because sometimes if a project is unfinished it feels like we're not making any progress. But you need to go back and look at your journey.

The other way we use portfolios is for portfolio parties. I try to do them once a term, but sometimes it ends up being twice a year, where we basically put the desks in a circle around the room, with the fronts of the desk facing into the circle, and have some spaces there for people to enter. Students are behind their desks—and this is where they select pieces because this is a very public showing of their portfolios. So it isn't the whole portfolio that is on display, although some choose to do that, but I explain to them that you could leave in whatever you want to leave in and take out anything you don't want to show. We invite other classes. Teachers come in with their students and circulate around the room and look at the portfolios, and the students are there showing their work. I invite parents to the showing day as well. The administration and anyone who had been involved in our learning that term are invited. For example, if we did a unit on cities or if it was an election year and we had had a politician in, they would be invited back. I found those portfolio parties really festive times: the students were celebrating and others were celebrating their work as well. So they were really proud.

What else do you notice about how your students use portfolios?

I don't do this every year, but I sometimes have students do their own report card—before I do one. I tell them: "Sit with your portfolio and just get a sense of yourself, so now you're reporting on your progress. Create a report card using the model we have to use. You make the decisions about what you think you've learned, how you learned, and how you've grown."

Content of Portfolios The content of reading portfolios reflects the reading theories of educators, the reading programs in classrooms, the type of portfolio, and learners' interests, goals, and strategies. Hence, there is considerable diversity in the nature of portfolios across learners and classrooms. In addition to information obtained from observations, interviews, and reading samples as outlined above, portfolios often include

- anecdotal notes
- learning logs

- reading response artifacts
- family information
- the results on standardized reading tests

In short, portfolios can contain the range of data that we have described in this chapter.

When trying to determine what to include in a portfolio, educators should reflect on the purpose of the portfolio they are building. One strength of **portfolio assessment** is that it can be used to promote educators' (and learners') reflections on learners' understandings, attitudes, and reading achievement and abilities (Serafini, 2001). When we take seriously a social constructivist approach to reading, we find that learners must be included in the assessment process. Doing this involves much more than a change in how assessment is done. It suggests a fundamental alteration in the power relationships between educators and learners. Learners participate in decisions about what goes into portfolios and what counts as a good reading.

Educators may ask learners to select at least some of the reading samples included in their portfolios. They sit down with learners periodically to consider and discuss the reading growth shown in their portfolio samples. Learners share their portfolios with their families when they visit the school. When teaching a new reading **strategy** in the classroom, teachers invite learners to comment on whether the strategy works for them and why or why not. These and other comments are included in learning logs in portfolios.

Learning logs are used by learners to keep a record of their learning in the classroom. Learning logs generally focus on what students have learned, what they did not understand, and what they did or did not like. Educators use this information to modify plans for subsequent lessons. Educators can also invite learners to complete their own learning and goal charts for inclusion in the portfolio. For instance, educators can make a table in which they list in the first column the areas of reading that they are addressing in their teaching (e.g., vocabulary). This list can come from conferencing with learners, curriculum guidelines, and assessment data. Next to this, learners can complete a "Things I Can Do" column in which they list what they can do (e.g., "I can read chapter books") and indicate where there is evidence to demonstrate this ability (e.g., reading response journal). The next column is titled "Things I Am Working On" (e.g., "I am working on reading informational text"), and the final column is titled "Goals" (e.g., "I want to be better at understanding what I read in informational books"). In this last column students can also provide a plan for how they will accomplish this goal (e.g., "What I will do: Look at important words and find out what they mean") (Barone & Taylor, 2007, p. 134).

In addition to learning logs, learners or educators can complete short forms that they attach to each piece chosen for the portfolio. On this form the person making the submission can indicate why the entry was selected, what it shows, the date, and any other pertinent information that could provide a context and rationale for its inclusion as assessment data. Portfolios can then be used to guide educator–learner conferences and conferences with families (which can be led by the learners themselves).

SUMMARY

Before educators can teach others to read they must first assess what learners know, are able to do, and value. Before educators can assess, they must have a clear understanding of what is meant by reading. We have invited you to think about how you would describe reading and juxtapose it against some of the key definitions in the field (top-down, bottom-up, interactive, and social constructivist perspectives). Recognizing the importance of social interactions and social contexts in learning underlies social constructivist theories of reading. Acknowledging the interconnectedness of modes within a wide frame of communication and the fact that reading may be done through a variety of **media** (e.g., hypertext) are part of multiliteracies and accompanying theories that can account for literacy practices in contemporary times. In all, we describe the practice of reading as the active construction of meaning from cues in texts (of all kinds) and from the reader's background knowledge within a social context.

Educators need different information to serve as a basis for daily planning, and performance assessment is widely employed for this purpose. This type of assessment focuses on what readers do as they read. Checklists and interviews can be used to assess how learners use print-based and knowledge-based cues to construct meaning as they read, as well as to assess learners' interests. Reading logs are records of what learners have read, and response journals provide an indication of how learners interpret and react to literature. Samples of readers' oral and silent reading can be collected using informal reading inventories and miscue analysis protocols; results will provide an indication of students' instructional reading level and their use of print-based and knowledge-based cues as they read.

Portfolios are collections of artifacts documenting learners' reading growth and development over time. Some of these artifacts include checklists, interview data, anecdotal notes, reading and learning logs, written responses to literature, running records, completed projects, and sometimes results on standardized tests. Portfolio assessment can either be completed within a procedural framework, where the focus is on the collecting and scoring of information, or within a process framework, where the focus is on reflection concerning learners' understandings, attitudes, and reading abilities.

Reading assessment is part of an educator's curricular dialogue. It must always be multi-faceted, reflect the complexity of one's definition of reading, and be focused on benefits for the learners. Educators must be careful to select assessment measures that can provide as full a picture as possible of learners' reading practices and to see learners as at-promise.

SELECTED PROFESSIONAL RESOURCES

Au, W., & Tempel, M. B. (2012). *Pencils down: Rethinking high-stakes testing and accountability in public schools*. Milwaukee, WI: Rethinking Schools.

A potent, scholarly, and fascinating collection of chapters, this volume takes readers through the nuts-and-bolts of standardized tests (e.g., see the chapter called "Common Questions about Standardized Tests") to implications of standardized assessments for learners and their educators from kindergarten (e.g., see the chapter called "Testing Kindergarten: You May Not Believe How Many Tests Kindergartners Take—and What They Are Missing as a Result") on up (e.g., see the chapter on teacher testing that's making news in the United States).

Barone, D., & Taylor, J. M. (2007). *The practical guide to classroom literacy assessment*. Thousand Oaks, CA: Corwin Press.

As the title suggests, this is a practical guide to conducting a variety of reading assessment protocols. It is important to note that the book looks at reading within the totality of all the dimensions of language and literacy. Written in an accessible and friendly tone.

Stooke, R. (2010). *Achieving the best for London's children, youth and families: Supporting literacy in community settings*. London, ON: Child Youth Network of the City of London. Retrieved from http://londoncyn.ca/wp-content/uploads/2012/07/Literature-Review-Report-June-28-2010.pdf

Chapter 1 of this report is a comprehensive literature review of the nature of literacy in contemporary times and an in-depth account of the various ways that researchers and practitioners conceptualize literacy. What makes this report brilliant is how it takes difficult concepts and distills them into the most straightforward and easy-to-understand terms.

CHAPTER SIX

Reading Instruction: Major Components

PERSPECTIVES ON READING AND READING INSTRUCTION

PEDAGOGIES TO SUPPORT READING PRACTICES: CONSIDERATIONS

- Phonics and Meaning
- Explicit and Implicit Instruction
- Incidental and Systematic Instruction
- Dimensions of Language and Literacy
- Fostering a Love of Reading

READING INSTRUCTION: MAJOR COMPONENTS

READING INSTRUCTION COMPONENTS

- Read-Aloud Beyond the Early Years
- Shared Reading
- Guided Reading
- Independent Reading
- Scheduling the Components

LEARNERS' VIEWS OF READING AND READING INSTRUCTION

Learner engaged with book

Long-time teacher Sharon Taberski (1996) has some older but terrific videos that document her language and literacy program. The end of the last video shows her students talking about reading and how she has helped them with it. Whenever we listen to learners read and talk about their reading, we are offered a "window" into their literacy (Rhodes & Shanklin, 1993) and into some of the experiences that may have brought about their learning. We have transcribed some of Taberski's students' comments below. As you read these comments, consider: What are the learners illustrating that they know, are able to do, and value about reading?

Sharon Taberski's Learners on Reading

GIRL 1:   Sometimes when I have [reading] conferences with Sharon, she helps me so much. It's like she gives me really good books to read.

BOY 1:   I think I'm reading better, because I'm not just staying on one book. I'm going on to different levels, and trying my best.

BOY 2:   Sharon helps me by like, giving me a hint, or she helps me by telling me to skip the word, or look at the period and stuff. That really makes it go clearer to me, and I understand the book more.

BOY 1:   Sometimes when a book is too hard, Sharon reads it first, it's like better for me, because she's read it.

GIRL 2:   I like the second reading we have, because you can read more in that time; it's a longer period of reading. [Note that Taberski's classroom has two Independent Reading periods, one short and the other long. We'll show you more about Independent Reading later in this chapter.]

BOY 3:   It's very important to practise reading, because you're supposed to learn, because when you're learning, you're actually teaching yourself to read, and when you're reading, you're actually learning, learning a lot, a lot, a lot.

BOY 4:   My favourite thing about reading is that I really like mysteries a lot, and when I read the mysteries I have clues to do, so it helps me read more mysteries easier.

BOY 3:   Sometimes skipping a word helps you. Sometimes phonics helps you, but sometimes they both help you.

BOY 2:   When you read, you're reading writing, and when you're writing, you're reading.

GIRL 2:   Well, my favourite part about reading is *reading*!

Implications of the Transcripts

If you review the list in Chapter 5 of what a good reading (usually) entails, you will find that Taberski's learners are expressing much of this knowledge about reading, exhibiting many of these values, and displaying an awareness of these skills and strategies. We define a strategy as an overall, conscious plan for performing the task that readers can apply across contexts, while skills may be unconscious, are more context bound, and are used in the service of a strategy. Examples of strategies include summarizing and monitoring comprehension. In terms of knowledge, values, skills, and strategies, in the transcript Taberski's learners show

- an appreciation of reading and literature
- the ability to self-assess and see one's reading progress
- the ability to read progressively more challenging material
- an engagement with reading
- a knowledge of a variety of reading strategies and the use of a variety of **cuing systems**
- an emphasis on comprehension
- the ability to use oral language (in this case, listening) to help support reading
- the ability to engage in sustained periods of reading
- the recognition that reading is purposeful and that we learn when we read
- the ability to use the conventions of a genre for comprehension
- a recognition of the important relationship between reading and writing

Some of the major questions that arise from this list are these: What clues does the transcript offer about what Taberski did with the learners that helped them to develop these understandings? Furthermore, what could you do with your own students to help them achieve these ends? This chapter is designed to introduce you to several components of reading instruction that are compatible with multiliteracies pedagogies and to expand on some of the components already introduced. It begins with a look at perspectives on reading and reading instruction and then explores the instructional strategies of Read-Aloud, Shared Reading, Guided Reading, and Independent Reading. □

PERSPECTIVES ON READING AND READING INSTRUCTION

In the last chapter we discussed various perspectives on the nature of reading. How you conceptualize learning to read will affect how you decide to teach reading. We invite you now to consider how you would finish this sentence: Learning to read is like … (e.g., building a tower, riding a bike, baking a cake, or dancing) (Weaver et al., 1996).

When Rachel became a teacher candidate, she assumed that reading instruction would be a sequential process that probably focused on phonics and built up to focus on reading comprehension. The metaphor that best fit her conceptualization of learning to read was building a big tower, where one part of the tower was put on top of the other and each learner's tower was built in the same way. Her own early reading instruction had been from a bottom-up perspective, and she anticipated this familiar course of instruction. Ironically, Rachel did not learn to read through this form of instruction.

Rachel still has a dog-eared copy of one of her kindergarten report cards. The report consists of a list of criteria next to which the teacher wrote either a "yes" (yes, the criterion had been achieved), a dash (to indicate that the criterion had not been achieved), or an "OK" (which we take to mean progressing toward a "yes"). We have listed some of the highlights from this report below. Rachel's teacher indicated that Rachel

- recognized at least half the alphabet
- could write her first name from memory
- had an "OK" expression of ideas
- had no phonetic understanding of letters
- could not rhyme
- had listening ability and could follow directions
- was "OK" in terms of courtesy
- was "OK" in terms of self-control

Like all report cards, the structure of this report, partly by what it included and excluded, reflects the then-dominant views of important predictors of reading achievement. It also reflects the expectations of what a learner of this age could do. What the report never asked—and, therefore, could not convey—was whether Rachel was reading. At the time it was written, Rachel was reading whole books independently—something she had learned to do at home through means that looked very much like Cambourne's (1988) conditions for learning. In fact, Rachel's nickname at home was "Rachel Books" as she could always be found with a book tucked under her nose. Rachel is not sure whether her kindergarten teacher ever recognized that she could read books. She, like all others in her classroom, received the same instruction regardless of her **funds of knowledge**. So, instead of being given books to read during class time, Rachel was given phonics sheets, which she found tedious (which might explain her struggle with courtesy and self-control!).

This story indicates some of the limitations of the *tower* model of teaching reading and one of its features, which is that every learner is treated the same. When she was a teacher candidate and then progressively as she began to teach and to think like an educator, Rachel came to conceptualize learning to read not as building a tower, but instead akin to learning to swim. The metaphor of swimming is apt given that reading and swimming are both processes where the whole is accomplished by different component parts working synergistically. To illustrate, consider Victoria Purcell-Gates's (2001) take on the metaphor:

> While moving one's arms in designated ways (termed *swimming strokes*), kicking one's legs in designated ways, and breathing out of the water in designated ways are all component processes of swimming, not one of them alone can be termed *swimming*. Nor can swimming be learned and mastered by practicing and mastering any one of these parts alone [or] by mastering all of these parts separately and then putting them together. Swimming must be learned by actually swimming, all the while coordinating the processing of the component processes so that swimming—and not sinking—is achieved.

Reading and writing are also processes . . . while they are for the most part mental processes . . . they still require the synergistic coordination of component processes to achieve the goal processes of reading and writing.… So while the component processes (or skills) of reading—like eye movements, letter and word perception and recognition, decoding, comprehension, and so forth—can be isolated and practiced, they must be used in process for the synergistic workings of each to result in *reading*, defined as comprehension of print. Since the workings of each part of a process look and act differently in process, the individual processes involved in reading and writing must be, and are, learned in process. (pp. 121–122)

Pedagogies to support reading acquisition, then, are systematic, but unlike a universal lock-step approach, must involve learners having numerous, context-specific opportunities to engage in with reading, and when the situation demands, having opportunities to engage in "side-of-the pool" (p. 123) learning, where learners are provided with explicit instruction in skills. In the case of swimming, side-of-the-pool learning might involve improving one's kicks. In reading, it might involve phonics, comprehension strategies, and the like.

Unlike swimming, however, reading is not just a process: it is also a socio-cultural *practice*. Subsequently, educators must consider the context in which learners are learning to read; their funds of knowledge, including the extent to which they have developed the *big picture* of **literacy** (Purcell-Gates, 1996); and reading engagement. The suggestions for reading instruction that we offer are designed to address this view of learning to read. Note that these suggestions must be considered within the larger definition of literacy and the multiliteracies pedagogies framework that we offer in *Constructing Meaning*.

PEDAGOGIES TO SUPPORT READING PRACTICES: CONSIDERATIONS

Learning to read is one of the most important outcomes of schooling, and as educators we hold a vital role in learners achieving this outcome. Unfortunately, where reading is concerned, there is "no quick fix" (Allington & Walmsley, 1995), and any program or model claiming otherwise is just selling "snake oil" (Larson, 2001). Instead, experts such as the International Reading Association (2002; since renamed the International Literacy Association) continue to promote the view that there is no one right way to teach reading, and one of the best opportunities to learn to read is to have knowledgeable educators who can responsively draw on a variety of methods:

> We believe that there is no single method or single combination of methods that can successfully teach all children to read. As a result, teachers must be familiar with a wide range of instructional methods and have strong knowledge of the children in their classrooms in order to provide the most appropriate instruction for all learners.
>
> Numerous large-scale research studies support the position that children can learn to read from a variety of materials and methods. Though focused studies show that various methods "work," no one of these methods is necessarily better than others.
>
> Controversy about the "best" way to teach reading cannot be resolved by prescribing a single method. Because there is no clearly documented best way to teach beginning reading, educators who are familiar with a wide range of methodologies and who are closest to children must be the ones to make decisions about what instructional methods to use. And further, these professionals must have the flexibility to modify those methods when they determine that particular children are not learning. (International Literacy Association, n.d., n.p.)

Though there may not be one best way to teach reading to all children, educators have identified some essential methods to have in one's reading instruction toolkit, and there are key considerations for educators to negotiate with the help of research. Thus we offer next some issues to consider in the teaching of reading, followed by foundational instructional components from which educators can choose as the situation demands. The components are outlined in Figure 6.1, and in this chapter we focus on Read-Aloud, Shared Reading, Guided Reading, and Independent Reading.

There are numerous factors that educators need to consider in their programming (see Table 6.1).

In her study of teacher candidates, Deborah Britzman (2003) identified "cultural myths of teaching." One of these myths is that educators must control students' behaviour or no learning can happen. It is, therefore, not uncommon for classrooms to be set up so that the major role of learners is to listen and the major role of educators is to tell. For instance, in Chapter 5 teacher John Guiney Yallop talked about how his learners found it difficult at first to gauge their own reading progress, because they were used to someone else telling them if they could read, and teacher candidate Natalie discussed her experience of being told exactly what she would read in class when she was an elementary student. **Social constructivists** understand, however, that learners' identities, funds of knowledge, and interests are all key factors in learning. Cambourne's (1988) conditions also suggest the importance of learners being able to take "responsibility" for their learning. They need some measure of choice to do so.

What is the role of an educator engaged in reading instruction in keeping with a multiliteracies pedagogies framework? It is multifaceted, including at least the following dimensions, all of which correspond with Cambourne's conditions:

- Educators are *providers* of reading resources and *organizers* of space and time so that learners have the opportunities and materials they need for learning (Lindfors, 1987).

- As *demonstrators* (Cambourne, 1988), educators show how reading is done (e.g., through a think-aloud in Shared Reading).

- For reading to be a lifelong activity, it is important for learners to see educators' own enthusiasm, processes, and questioning as readers. Thus again in the role of *demonstrator*, educators need to share their reading lives with their students (Routman, 2003).

FIGURE 6.1

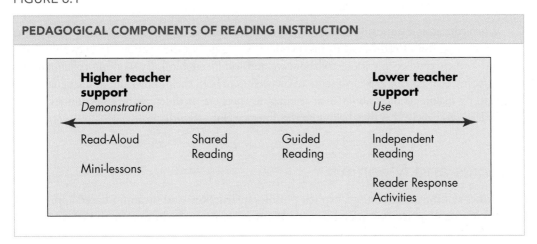

PEDAGOGICAL COMPONENTS OF READING INSTRUCTION

Higher teacher support
Demonstration

Lower teacher support
Use

Read-Aloud	Shared Reading	Guided Reading	Independent Reading
Mini-lessons			Reader Response Activities

TABLE 6.1 **CONSIDERATIONS IN READING INSTRUCTION**

Ownership and Control	
Hierarchical relationships	Collaborative relationships
Teacher ownership	Learner ownership
Competition	Cooperation
Phonics and Meaning	
Focus on words	Focus on meaning
Teaching from parts to wholes	Teaching from wholes to parts
Teaching and Use of Language	
Explicit instruction	Implicit opportunities for learning
Systematic	Incidental
Approach to Dimensions of Language and Literacy	
Focus on reading	Integration of dimensions of language and literacy
Level of Difficulty	
Common expectations	Differentiated expectations
Relatively easy tasks for automaticity	Challenging tasks for new strategies
Independent learning	Scaffolding

- Educators are *responders*. When reading something new, exciting, or confusing, it is helpful to share it with another. This person can respond to questions, question further, support learning, and provide information on how the reading is going. That is not the same as judging a person's performance. Response is productive and occurs as educators actively follow what learners are trying to do and strive to further that learning. This is why **assessment** should be a constant in reading instruction.

- In the role of *observer* or "kidwatcher" (Owicki & Goodman, 2002), educators gain insight into learners' reading practices and come to understand what learners know, can do, and value.

- In observing, educators can also learn how to be *catalysts* for engagement (Cambourne, 1988), leading learners to want to read and to feel that reading is accessible to them and can be undertaken without risk.

When educators assume roles like these, learners can take increasing responsibility for their own reading, moving from Read-Aloud to Independent Reading, and the relationship between educators and learners can become more collaborative and less hierarchical. By working collaboratively in classrooms, learners can develop a sense of ownership of both their knowledge and language and literacies. By making choices about their reading, learners are provided with opportunities to feel like readers—to believe that they belong to the "literacy club" (Smith, 1988).

Phonics and Meaning

Sometimes skills instruction (e.g., explicit phonics instruction) and meaning-based approaches to teaching reading are positioned as a dichotomy—you must do one or the other. In the version of reading pedagogy that we espouse, however, we take constructing meaning as the centre of reading and at the same time recognize the importance of strategies, such as those related to using the cuing systems. In other chapters we discuss cuing systems and demonstrate how the graphophonic system is a primary tool for reading. Educators must help learners acquire *all* cuing systems and use them in tangent with one another. In fact, most educators now recognize that part of what learners need in reading instruction is a context-specific "balance" between a focus on words and a focus on meaning (e.g., Cunningham & Allington, 2007; Gambrell, Malloy, & Mazzoni, 2007).

Balance does not mean equal parts but involves educators considering the context and what the learner needs to make meaning. Otherwise put, Purcell-Gates (2001) advocated that educators consider teaching through a "whole-part-whole" structure. Learners are provided with a context (the focus on meaning). From that educators can demonstrate how a part of language (e.g., a letter's sound) operates or how a specific reading skill (e.g., using knowledge of a letter's sound) can help one create meaning. They then demonstrate how the part/skill relates to the whole. For example, in an application of the swimming metaphor, learners swim—that is, they engage with the "whole" practice; the instructor or swimmer identifies the skill swimmers need to strengthen (e.g., kicks), swimmers go to the side of the pool to strengthen their kicks (the "part"), and they then return to swimming to implement the improved kicks—they re-engage with the "whole."

Whenever possible, explicit teaching of parts of language should be taught within a meaningful whole. Thus when educators teach skills, they do so, for example, within the context of a whole text (e.g., book, story, or poem). Box 6.1 shows a sample early literacy lesson plan, adapted from Invernizzi (2003) and Doiron (2002), that demonstrates this whole-to-part structure, builds on learners' knowledge of a predictable book, and promotes a variety of knowledge and skills, including aspects of **phonological awareness**. Following this, in Box 6.2, is a lesson for older readers shared by long-time teacher and principal Wendy Crocker. This lesson also follows a whole-part-whole format, focusing on mapping a **narrative** text.

BOX 6.1

EARLY LITERACY LESSON PLAN

Learning Opportunities

Oral Communication

▷ Listen and respond orally to language patterns in stories and poems.

▷ Demonstrate awareness of individual sounds and sound patterns in language.

Reading

▷ Demonstrate awareness of some conventions of written materials.

▷ Demonstrate understanding that letters represent sounds and that written words convey meanings.

(continued)

Resource Materials

▷ Carle, E. (1997). *From head to toe.* New York, NY: HarperCollins. (This predictable picture book shows animals making gestures and asks the boy in the book, "Can you do it?")

▷ sentence strips

▷ tape or pocket chart

Set: Getting the Learners Ready

▷ Invite the learners to stand up.

▷ Invite them to look at the cover of the book and tell them the title.

▷ Generate some guesses on what the book is about.

▷ Pose as the gorilla, and tell them the book is about some things humans and animals can both do.

▷ Tell the learners there is movement in this book and they have to listen closely so that they'll know what to do. When you say, "Can you do it?" they can respond with the appropriate movement.

▷ Demonstrate actions throughout and encourage learners to recite the book's refrains.

Instruction

Input. Tell learners that letters form words that form sentences to make our story make sense.

Model. Ahead of time, take the refrains from the book and have them cut up as sentences, words, and letters. Model how to sort these sentences, words, and letters into groups, taking care to read and discuss the form and function of each example before placing it in the proper group. (Do this on a board, pocket chart, or carpet.)

Check understanding. Do another example as a group, but invite the learners to come up and place the sentence, word, or letter in the appropriate space.

Guided practice. Learners practise the new learning with the educator.

Activity. Take another sentence from the book and read it while showing the text to the learners (can be done on the board or, if big book, can be done in the book—cover any other sentences up with sticky notes to avoid distraction). Have each word from the sentence written on a different large card. Give each word card to a learner and name the learner by the word (e.g., "Kaleigh, you are the word *giraffe.*"). Learners work together to arrange themselves into the sentence. Another student can read the sentence to check for direction and order. Each "word" can step forward as it is read.

Closure. The goal is for students to make the connection between the learning and the activity from guided practice, and to do a final check for understanding. Repeat the activity using another sentence. Invite learners to discuss which sentence is longer by counting the number of learners or words in the lineups. You can also discuss which word is the longest by inviting learners to count the number of letters.

Independent practice. Give learners envelopes with cut-up sentence strips, words, and letters to sort out and paste into sentence, word, and letter groups on their own. (Vary the difficulty of the activity according to learner achievement.) You will be able to check that students' practice is consistent with the outcomes identified in the lesson plan.

BOX 6.2

LATE ELEMENTARY LESSON PLAN: MAPPING A NARRATIVE TEXT

Learning Opportunities

Reflecting on Oral Communication

▷ Identify strategies that are most helpful to a reader before, during, and after listening and speaking in response to text and identify steps to improve oral communication.

Reading

▷ Analyze increasingly complex texts to identify organizational patterns used in them and explain how the patterns help to communicate meaning.

Educator Wendy Crocker

Resource Materials

▷ selected text for Read-Aloud and follow-up by learners individually, in pairs, or in groups: Muth, J. (2002). *The Three Questions*. New York, NY: Scholastic Press.

▷ narrative map related to the text structure or the organization of the narrative text

▷ enlarged copy of narrative map for use on SMART Board or overhead

Set: Getting the Learners Ready

▷ Remind learners that a strategy to improve the reading of a challenging text relates to the structure or form of the text, and the vocabulary that relates to that form. (For example, invite the learners to review in pairs the structure of a description and the word choices of this type of text.)

Instruction

Input. Share with the learners that together you will investigate the text structure of narrative. Remind them of their responsibility to their partner or group to assist in the completion of the graphic organizer—in this case, the narrative map. One group member will be selected to present their work to the class or another group. Invite the learners to brainstorm different types of narratives—for example, lyrical, fable, myth, and fairy tale—and key features of that type of story.

Model. Demonstrate the expectations of the class related to the text structure using a think-aloud and a sample of the map. Show an enlarged sample of the text and invite the class to read aloud with you. At preselected points, stop and ask reflective questions such as these: "What words indicate that this is narrative text? How is punctuation used? How does the illustration support the text?"

Check understanding. Using another section of the story, invite the learners to work in pairs or groups to map the next page from *The Three Questions*. Confirm by adding to the enlarged

(continued)

version on the interactive whiteboard or overhead (done by the educator or by members of the class).

Activity: Assign each pair of learners additional pages in the text that highlight key features of this structure. Learners map their assigned pages of text. They are given sufficient time for the activity and for checking their response, but 10 minutes are left before the end of the class for closure.

Closure. In Numbered Heads learners number themselves from 1 to 4. All of the 1s move to another group on a given signal to share with the new group how they completed the organizer and their thinking related to the key features of the text structure. At another signal, they return to their original group and compare the work that they completed with the work from the visiting student. Together, the class addresses any questions or apparent disconnects that people may have.

Independent practice. Learners read the entire text and complete an individual narrative map along with key words or phrases related to the narrative structure. The copies created by the groups may be used as a reference for the completion of individual copies.

FIGURE 6.2

NARRATIVE TEXT MAP BASED ON *THE THREE QUESTIONS* (JON MUTH)

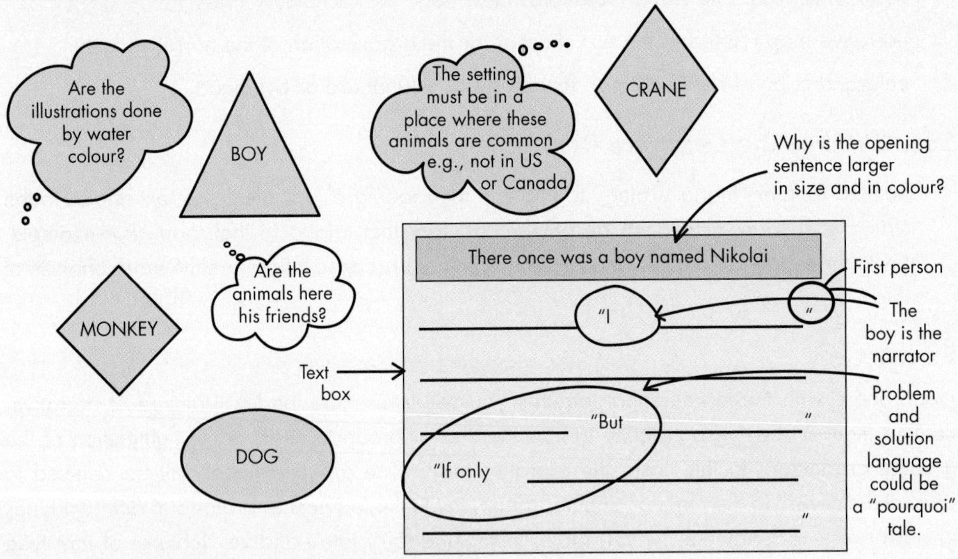

Source: First Steps, 1997; McLaughlin & Allen, 2002.

Explicit and Implicit Instruction

Educators also need to be flexible with respect to explicit and implicit teaching. Explicit instruction involves educators explicitly teaching knowledge and/or skills and then inviting learners to use them in new situations (e.g., moving from Shared Reading to Independent Reading). Classroom Activity 6.1 shows how explicit instruction can work when applied to strategy instruction. In addition to explicit instruction, educators need to create the

CLASSROOM ACTIVITY 6.1

Example of Explicit Instruction as Applied to Strategy Instruction

1. Educators identify what a specific strategy is, explain why the learners are learning the strategy and when and where they should use it, and model the strategy to make the mental processes visible to the learners. This modelling can be done in Shared Reading or Read-Aloud.

2. Educators involve learners in guided practice (e.g., during Guided Reading), during which educators provide support, but require learners to take more and more responsibility for the strategy.

3. Educators provide learners with opportunities for independent practice and application, monitoring their performance and reinstating support if necessary (e.g., in Independent Reading time).

Source: Armbruster, B. B., & Osborn, J. H. *Reading instruction and assessment: Understanding the IRA standards.* (Boston, MA: Allyn and Bacon), 2002, p. 70.

conditions within their classrooms in which learners can learn inductively or can learn the rules or big ideas about reading by experiencing reading in use and then building generalizations. Cambourne's (1988) conditions apply here as well, in particular, his condition of immersion.

Ultimately, educators should negotiate explicit and implicit instruction according to their assessment of what the situation at hand demands. Moreover, educators should never assume that learners will just know how to do something unless they have created the conditions in which they can learn it. Some learners, particularly **culturally and linguistically diverse (CLD)** learners, may require more explicit instruction so that all expectations are clear (Delpit, 2006). We know too that learners need time to explore, experiment, and learn alongside educators, and even when educators decide to use explicit instruction, they should expect that no two learners may develop exactly the same understanding of what is being taught.

Incidental and Systematic Instruction

Another question faced by educators is the degree to which reading skills and strategy instruction should be provided incidentally in mini-lessons or sequentially in a systematic set of planned lessons. Should practice be provided on an occasional basis or on a continuous basis? The answer will depend, as it did for implicit and explicit teaching, on the educator's appraisal of the learners and the context.

Sometimes incidental instruction or occasional practice will be sufficient, but usually it is not. Many times it is possible to teach skills *as* learners read, but again, this is not always the case. Once more, professional discernment is needed. By carefully observing learners in the classroom, educators decide when and how to provide instruction at any point. They also decide how much practice learners need in order to generalize skills and strategies to other reading and writing contexts.

Dimensions of Language and Literacy

Each dimension of language and literacy can help to support the acquisition of the others: Reading is no exception. In a study of researchers who had divergent views of how to teach reading, one point they could agree on was that, insofar as possible, educators should "use every opportunity to bring reading/writing/talking/listening together so that each feeds off and feeds into the other" (Flippo, 2012, p. 16). You may note that representing and viewing are missing here, but the research literature demonstrates how representing and viewing also help to support the development of print literacy (McKee & Heydon, 2014), students' engagement in literacy practices (Malloy & Gambrell, 2006), and comprehension of what they read (Albers, 2007). Within their curricular dialogue, educators must decide what is important to emphasize and when.

Learning opportunities need to be at an appropriate level of difficulty. Many learners experience daily frustration in the classroom and are unable to engage in reading learning opportunities because they cannot complete tasks that are too challenging for them. Others are not sufficiently challenged to maximize their learning. Only when learning opportunities are at an appropriate level of difficulty for the situation will learners experience success *and* grow. There are three major ways educators can achieve this:

- by adjusting their expectations for performance during the initial stages of learning something new
- by setting different expectations for different learners on the same learning task
- by providing different levels of materials and tasks for different learners

Each of the reading pedagogies components that we present in this chapter attempts to provide differing levels of educator support—ranging from the greatest (Read-Aloud) to the least amount (Independent Reading). Most components also allow for a degree of **differentiation**—that is, a lesson or activity can allow for learners to perform differently on the same learning task. For example, in a kindergarten class, the educator might have very different expectations for what learners will be able to do with a predictable book once it is read to them.

- Some learners will be able to identify words in the book as they reread it.
- Other learners may point to the words as another learner reads them, developing an understanding of the one-to-one relationship between words in oral and written language.
- Still other learners may listen to the book and chime in, developing an understanding of how written language sounds.

Differentiation can occur in a similar way with older learners. Wendy Crocker, for instance, has had these types of expectations for grade 7 and 8 students after a Read-Aloud:

- Some learners will need to flag unfamiliar vocabulary using sticky notes to mask (cover) the word or noting the word for later dictionary work.
- Some learners will skim and scan—grouping words as they read into meaningful chunks—to highlight the key idea of the paragraph.
- Still others may connect what they are reading to their own related experiences to deepen understanding and assist with predictions of unfamiliar words.
- Some learners will need to buddy-read with a peer. By slowing the pace of the reading and using the illustrations for support, the learner reads alternate pages and then listens as the buddy takes a turn.

- Learners will also need to think critically about the text being read, the facts being presented, or specific terminology.

- Learners can also engage in a story circle or book club with peers who have all read the same text. They can discuss the text to deepen their understanding of it and ask questions to improve their meaning making, make use of vocabulary, or view the text from a different perspective.

In other words, different learners do different things with the same book in order to achieve different objectives.

Sometimes, however, educators need to adjust the materials and tasks for different learners and different situations. For example, a goal for some learners may be to improve the flow of their reading. At least some of the time they need to be working in their **zone of proximal development** (Vygotsky, 1978), that is, a level that is just beyond where they can work independently. Such texts are perfect to use in Guided Reading. This type of support is frequently referred to as **scaffolding**. It is much like the interaction between young children and their mothers, in which the mothers support their children "in achieving an intended outcome" (Bruner, 1975, p. 12). The children decide to do something and the mothers provide the assistance (such as a helping hand, gesture, or word) that allows the children to do it. In schools, educators use scaffolds as temporary supports to help learners extend their skills and knowledge to a higher level of competence (Dorn & Soffos, 2001).

We encourage you to think about the reading instruction components in Figure 6.1 on page 195 as a gradual "handover of responsibility," as Routman (2003, p. 44) put it, from educator to learner. Read-Aloud offers the highest degree of educator support and is consistent with Cambourne's (1988) immersion and demonstration. Shared Reading is a "shared demonstration" (Routman, 2003, p. 44). It allows learners to "approximate" the demonstration and to receive important "response" on their attempts (Cambourne, 1988). Guided Reading marks a shift to a greater amount of responsibility for learners, which transitions into Independent Reading, in which there is the least amount of educator support and the greatest opportunity for readers to "use" (Cambourne, 1988) or "practice" (Routman, 2003, p. 44) what they have been observing and approximating. Thinking about the components in this way can help educators plan and develop targeted learning opportunities for their students.

Fostering a Love of Reading

In addition to all the considerations already discussed is the awareness that if learners are to read and keep on reading, they must feel that the practice is forwarding the purposes of their lives (Cambourne, 1988). Cambourne's notion of engagement expresses the importance of pleasure, and as educators we must remember this principle in our pedagogies. We agree

> Children must indeed acquire accurate and automatic word-recognition skills in order to progress in reading acquisition.... But their engagement with text and their interest in reading also push forward their decoding skills.... Children become "hooked" not on phonics, but on stories, books, and ideas. (Gangi, 2004, p. 6)

Box 6.3 offers a glance at some of the ways educators can promote a love of reading. This list also includes in parentheses the conditions from Cambourne (1988) that the various strategies can fulfill.

BOX 6.3

HOW EDUCATORS CAN FOSTER OR RENEW A LOVE OF READING IN LEARNERS

▷ Find texts that you love and let learners see you reading (demonstration) (Routman, 1991).

▷ Make a high volume of texts accessible to readers (immersion) (Allington, 2006), especially texts that are "high-interest" (engagement) (Gallagher, 2009). Books authored by learners themselves, such as those created during a Language Experience Approach, are excellent engagers, especially when older learners need a reading level that might be relatively low, but content that is age appropriate.

▷ Give readers ample time to read (use) (Allington, 2001), including reading for recreation and fun (Gallagher, 2009).

▷ Give readers chances to share what they are reading and to respond to their reading (response) (Daniels, 2002).

▷ Provide readers with high-quality choices that suit them and the situation (e.g., difficult texts for Read-Aloud and Shared Reading, slightly challenging-level texts for Guided Reading, and easier texts for Independent Reading). To facilitate this, become familiar with children's and young adult literature (responsibility and engagement). (Educators can begin this amazing journey by getting acquainted with Chapter 11 and the Appendix of this resource.)

▷ Kelly Gallagher (2009), who coined the term *readicide* to refer to the ways in which some schools can foster a dislike of reading and discourage the practice, suggested how educators can renew learners' engagement in reading:

  ▷ Remember that the "highest priority" in teaching reading is to support learners to "become lifelong readers" (not just good test-takers).

  ▷ Refuse to allow "test preparation" to be "justification for killing time to really read and to read for pleasure."

  ▷ Acknowledge the importance of "academic reading" but also the vital necessity of "recreational reading."

  ▷ Resist "chopping up recreational books with worksheets and quizzes" and insisting that all reading be evaluated.

  ▷ Recognize that recreational reading is "actually test preparation" as learners "are building valuable knowledge capital that will help them in future reading." (p. 117)

READING INSTRUCTION COMPONENTS
Read-Aloud Beyond the Early Years

In Chapter 4 we discussed Read-Aloud within the context of early literacy. We now build on that information to demonstrate how Read-Aloud can be used even past grade 8. All the reasons for conducting Read-Alouds that we listed in Chapter 4 remain for learners through the higher grades. In fact, research shows that readers of all levels and ages can benefit in a variety of ways from participating in Read-Alouds (Blessing, 2005; Lesesne, 2006). Even beyond educators modelling for students *how* to read and exposing them to new texts and content they might not otherwise choose or be able to read independently, Read-Alouds can demonstrate that we as educators love to read. This sharing of our "reading lives" with others can help to bond us to learners (Routman, 2003). It also illustrates our "expectation," as Cambourne (1988) put it, that reading is a lifelong endeavour offering pleasure and enrichment.

To illustrate the importance of Read-Aloud, consider the case of David and Jacquie, two grade 7 students whom Betsy Reilly (from Chapter 1) taught in grade 1. We asked these learners about some of their views on reading instruction and learning (see Box 6.4). In grade 1, the students had different reading profiles, yet they expressed similar views about the kinds of experiences that helped them become avid readers. As you read through the interviews, we encourage you to think about what kind of foundation Betsy must have established for her class, and notice what David and Jacquie draw our attention to through what they decide to include (and exclude) in their responses. From this, you might want to think about the implications for your own teaching of reading.

BOX 6.4

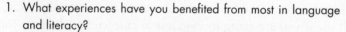

LEARNERS' PERCEPTIONS OF READING EXPERIENCES

In Chapter 1 we introduced teacher Betsy Reilly. When they entered seventh grade, we asked two of her former first-grade students, David and Jacquie, to talk about their reading experiences. Here is some of what they shared with us. Note that while we have listed their responses together, David and Jacquie were not together when they responded to these questions—suggesting the strength of the impression of Read-Aloud.

David

1. What experiences have you benefited from most in language and literacy?

   David: Our teachers reading aloud—if they are good readers.... Ms. Reilly read [The] *Secret Garden* to us, and I loved that.

   Jacquie: Read-Aloud. I have benefited the most from the books that were read to me.

2. What is one pet peeve you have about what teachers do (that teachers should avoid)?

   David: When you read a book to the class, make it interesting: it should be a good book and the teacher should be a good reader to bring the characters to life.

Jacquie

3. What started you on your literacy journey or were you always interested in reading?

   David: My mom started me. I loved when stories were read aloud to me, and I wasn't so interested in reading myself at first. I listened to stories on CD at night and still like to do that. For example, I listened to *Lemony Snicket*.

   Jacquie: Really wanting to be able to read "little books" at home by myself, and I will remember grade 1 and [being read] *The Secret Garden* and *The Trumpet of the Swan*.

Conducting Read-Alouds

Out of all the experiences that David and Jacquie have had around reading, they both identi-fied being read to as significant, and of all the educators who have taught them and texts they have been exposed to, it is Betsy and her Read-Alouds that they remember and share. So, what might it be about how Betsy conducted Read-Aloud that stayed with David and Jacquie, and how can educators conduct Read-Aloud to similarly entice their learners?

Read-Alouds can be conducted from primary beyond in the ways that we suggested in Chapter 4. Additionally, they can be used to highlight one or a combination of the following:

- to introduce learners to a new unit or topic (Lesesne, 2006)
- to introduce learners to a new author, series, or **genre**
- to highlight the aesthetic quality of a text
- to provide pleasure (Lesesne, 2006)
- to model specific skills and strategies (e.g., context clues, word attack skills, or main idea) (Lesesne, 2006)
- to demonstrate a proficient reader's thinking as she or he reads (Routman, 2003)
- to create an effect in learners, such as to settle them after recess or get them excited for a new lesson or activity

While Read-Alouds are usually done with a whole group, they can be conducted with a small group. They can also take the form of learners listening to a book (e.g., on MP3) (Lesesne, 2006).

Here are a few more tips on how to conduct Read-Aloud:

- Always read a text that you intend to read for Read-Aloud ahead of time, and be sure to plan out how you will read it. For example, determine what you want to emphasize, what kind of voice you will use if you are going to switch into character, and where you will leave off so that you finish with your students wanting more (Reid, 2007).
- Practise how you will show any illustrations (Braxton, 2007).
- When reading to older learners, you will likely need to talk with them about why you are reading aloud to them, as this practice might be unfamiliar for them (Blessing, 2005).
- Consider allowing learners to get physically comfortable for the reading. Younger learners may appreciate being able to cuddle up with a stuffed toy. Many learners, even those after the early elementary years, might also like to get together on the carpet for the reading. Even though she teaches upper grades, Kathy Gillies, for instance, keeps a specific space for Read-Aloud in her classroom—it is carpeted and contains a rocking chair.
- Signal in some way to your learners that it is time for Read-Aloud. Doing so can help them focus and know what kinds of behaviours are expected (e.g., listening). You can do this in a variety of creative ways, perhaps lighting a candle or lamp, putting on a costume or piece of clothing like a hat, sounding a chime or playing some music, or pulling out a prop that goes with the story. Some learners are better listeners when they are invited to doodle. If students are doodling, you can encourage them to draw what they are hearing (Blessing, 2005).

- Some learners may need the accommodation of having the text in front of them. Be ready to allow this (Reid, 2007).

- If this is the first time in a long while that your learners have been read aloud to, begin with something short, such as a short story, magazine article, or poem (Blessing, 2005).

- While you are reading, monitor your learners' reactions so that you can adjust your reading if you are not getting the response you had hoped for (Blessing, 2005).

- Watch the tempo of your reading. Learners will be able to better follow if you read more slowly than you normally speak.

- Use every opportunity to allow learners to interact with the text during the Read-Aloud. Identify if there is a line or phrase that they might repeat; pause when and if appropriate and encourage learners to predict what might come next; think aloud about your own predictions and indicate what clues are leading you to think in this way. Be sure, however, not to interrupt the text too often or this could ruin the flow of the reading (one seven-year-old told us she prefers Read-Aloud at home to Read-Aloud at school for this reason).

Instruments for Donna Schulz's Read-Alouds

- Feel free to substitute words or skip pages if it makes the text more accessible to your listeners.

- Enjoy the reading yourself, and do not worry too much about a word perfect reading. You can use any miscue as an opportunity to demonstrate your own process as a reader.

- Consider multimodal, creative ways of engaging learners such as in teacher-librarian Donna Schulz's practice. Donna uses instruments like rain makers, maracas, and drums—one for each person—to use at various points in her Read-Aloud: to make the sound of the weather; follow the rhythm of the language and/or story; help sing song-based picture books, which have been found to be a potent tool for literacy learning (e.g., Montgomery & Smith, 2014); and to accompany books like *When I Get Older: The Story Behind "Wavin' Flag"* (K'naan & Guy, 2012), which tells the story and contains the lyrics for the powerful song "Wavin' Flag" (CBS Interactive, n.d.).

Selecting Materials

When selecting materials for Read-Aloud, educators have many options and their situation can help guide their choices. First is the need for educators to select high-quality texts that represent a variety of genres "with which students can identify" (Routman, 2003, p. 20). Think about your learners' background knowledge. Pay attention to what texts can "expand this knowledge" (p. 20), while also allowing opportunities for some degree of accessibility so that learners can understand what is being read to them. As you survey a selection, question what kinds of learning opportunities or experiences the text might create. Then ask yourself, Is the text's content and language appropriate? How might the text relate to the demographics and funds of knowledge of my group? For example, "Is this protagonist likely to appeal to most of the group?" (Blessing, 2005, p. 44). Consider whether you can engage with the text; if you cannot, chances are you will not be a very engaging reader for your audience. You will also want to select your texts on the basis of the grade.

Many early elementary learners enjoy "rhyme and repetition" and "themes of families, friends, pets, animals, toys, and teddies" (Braxton, 2007, p. 52). When selecting theme-based texts, consider what kinds of issues your learners are experiencing and draw on texts with these themes. Note that many fiction texts for learners of this age will anthropomorphize animals and have these characters play out the concerns of young children. Think, for instance, of books such as *The Bike Lesson*, part of the classic Berenstain Bears series. Riding a two-wheeler is certainly a topic that will be on the minds of much of the class! (For more on the Berenstain Bears, see their official website at http://www.berenstainbears.com.) Recall too Betsy Reilly's lesson that young children can benefit from Read-Alouds of **chapter books**. These books can provide opportunities for the building of children's vocabulary, consideration of big ideas, and linking with content area knowledge (Heydon et al., 2014). When selecting these longer books, consider which have natural breaks or good places to pause between one reading session and another.

Another consideration when selecting materials for learners is the quality of the illustrations or other visual information to accompany the print. Inexperienced and/or CLD learners, for instance, can be offered support for comprehension when the picture matches the oral story. Strong visuals can "orient" (Braxton, 2007, p. 52) readers and provide a concrete reference point for what might be an unfamiliar concept.

Students in grades 4, 5, and 6 can benefit from slightly more sophisticated material than their younger counterparts. Braxton has found that these learners still like animals, but their interest in them has shifted. Instead of stories where animals are anthropomorphized, these learners tend to prefer to learn *about* animals. This is where nonfiction texts can find a natural place. Adventures and mysteries can be favourites, provided their plots are not too complicated. Horror and **fantasy** can also be favourites, but these learners might tend to prefer to "identify with the characters or visualize themselves in the story" in such a way that "the underlying theme is one of a vicarious empowerment that readers do not have yet in real life" (p. 52).

Slightly older learners (e.g., grades 7 and up), like people of all ages, can benefit from Read-Alouds of texts of all genres. Conducting such Read-Alouds, however, can be slightly more challenging, as Routman (2003) has discovered that older learners may have come to "believe that if it's not a chapter book, it's not acceptable" (p. 21). Braxton (2007) has also noted that finding a text for a whole class at this age is difficult, because most learners' tastes are now fairly well established. Nonetheless, Routman (2003) includes picture and poetry books in her repertoire, but she selects them carefully. One of her favourites to read aloud is *My Name Is Jorge: On Both Sides of the River* by Jane Medina, which she describes as "a touching book of poems in English and Spanish that deals with respect for one's culture" (Routman, 2003, p. 21). In general, Braxton (2007) has found that educators conducting a Read-Aloud with older learners are likely to find success with texts that deal with time travel (both forward and back) and **historical fiction** that can tie in with other areas of the curriculum. Humour can also be a popular choice (Reid, 2006).

Braxton (2007) also points out that many learners in grades 7 and 8 are quite aware of world issues (both current and historical) and might find texts that are issues oriented appealing. Accounts of the Holocaust, for example, would fall into this category. These kinds of texts can be very important for educators to expose their learners to, as

> What is at stake in these texts is not just the provision of information and the humanization of impersonal historical accounts and statistics.… Our hope is that stories of persecution and suffering will become part of a remembrance that will have some progressive, moral force. This hope is based on the familiar assumption that literature has the power to facilitate an ethical sense which enhances a concern for others, responsibility to the values of diversity and human rights, and a sense of hope that, while developing the capacity to look life in the face, maintains a vigilance against injustice. (Simon & Armitage-Simon, 1995, p. 27)

At the same time, educators must remember that many of these texts are "risky" (Simon & Armitage-Simon, 1995), in that they deal with difficult and sensitive subjects (e.g., violence) that can be traumatic to witness and easily misconstrued. When considering the use of risky material, educators should use their own **critical literacy** skills to ask questions about the text, the readers, and the context in which they are going to be conducting the Read-Aloud. We advise them, for instance, to

- consider the maturity and background knowledge and experience of the readers
- select texts that are historically accurate
- select texts that avoid vivid descriptions of violence and cruelty
- select texts that focus on the strength of the human spirit and people's incredible efforts to preserve human dignity and life (Simon & Armitage-Simon, 1995)

Here are two classic examples of fiction that meet these criteria:

- *The Diary of a Young Girl: Anne Frank.* First published in 1952, this book confronts the reader with "individual death and suffering," yet "there are no scenes directly dealing with the Nazi practices of systematic degradation and genocide.… The focus is on Anne's sensitivity, intelligence, and hopeful outlook, without any direct confrontation with the realities of genocide that lead to her death" (Simon & Armitage-Simon, 1995, p. 28).
- *Sadako and the Thousand Paper Cranes* by Eleanor Coerr is about a child who develops leukemia as part of the aftermath of the A-bomb being dropped on Hiroshima. This "is a story through which children can celebrate human courage and optimism while keeping the realities of mass destruction contained in the abstractions of 'war' or 'the bomb'" (Simon & Armitage-Simon, 1995, p. 29).

Other examples are included in the books for social justice section of Chapter 11, such as the notable Canadian text *Fatty Legs: A True Story* (Jordan-Fenton & Pokiak-Fenton, 2010).

Text selection is, of course, only one part of the equation when dealing with risky texts. The context you set as an educator will also guide their appropriate use. For that reason, consider the following when you are thinking about using a risky text within any reading instruction component:

- Use the book when the class feels like a community, when members have gotten to know one another and feel safe.
- Use the book when you have time to really deal with the issues.
- Prepare learners by providing a context for the content of the text (e.g., embedded within a unit of study).

- Be ready for the fact that risky texts may disrupt the practices of school that learners normally experience (Simon & Armitage-Simon, 1995).
- Structure opportunities for readers to respond to the text.
- Structure response activities to allow responses at a variety of levels.
- Anticipate the kinds of questions that learners may ask.
- Take the time to debrief the response activities.
- Help your learners to read critically, that is, with an eye to putting the text and its reading in context and questioning how equity and social justice operate within these.
- Think about the kinds of experiences that learners are likely to have had in the past (e.g., experiences with war) or the present (e.g., experiences with violence in the home). Might these make certain texts or issues particularly risky for them? Consider whether you are able to offer the degree of support that might be necessary to deal with their needs.

Shared Reading

As we discussed in Chapter 4, Shared Reading is similar to Read-Aloud. Both are usually conducted with a text that would be at a frustration level if the learner were to attempt to read it alone (Rog, 2003). However, Shared Reading involves the educator reading *with* rather than *to* students. During Shared Reading, learners may read aloud with the educator, follow along silently, or chime in at appropriate points, for example, filling in gaps when the educator conducts an oral cloze and pauses (Routman, 2003). Shared Reading requires that everyone can see the text. Early grades typically use big books or charts for this reading. Older grades normally use overheads or an interactive whiteboard (though, of course, these too are appropriate for use with younger students). If learners have their own copies of the text, educators might still use a master copy that everyone can see so that when appropriate, they can draw their attention to specific features of the text. Educators might, for example, want to use a compound word from the text to talk about strategies for decoding unknown words, or show how different levels of headings work in an information text.

The goals of Shared Reading are for educators to support learners in reading the text and to model what readers can do when they are reading and the going gets a bit tough. For example, they might address the question "What do I do when I come to a word I don't know?" Shared Reading is therefore an opportunity to share with students how to use reading strategies in the construction of meaning. Taberski (1996, 2000) uses Read-Aloud and Shared Reading to work with the whole class before she meets in guided reading groups, where learners have the chance to practise using these strategies in smaller, targeted groups. We suggest that educators think of how to demonstrate what they would like learners to do, then move into giving them the chance to do this with a gradual handover of responsibility.

Guided Reading

Guided Reading is a reading instruction component for intensively working with learners on reading strategies for making meaning. Drawing on the work of educators such as Marie Clay (1993b), Irene Fountas and Gay Su Pinnell (1996) developed Guided Reading to help learners become strategic, independent, and self-extending readers. At the same time, other educators have developed their own ways of conducting Guided Reading. Figure 6.3, for instance, shows our interpretation of how Taberski (1996) uses Guided Reading within her reading program and how these components relate to some of Cambourne's (1988) conditions.

Regardless of the exact form Guided Reading may take, its goals remain the same:

- to reinforce skills and strategies
- to engage learners in questioning and discussion
- to allow educators to be guides (e.g., by selecting texts and strategies to target)
- to allow learners to do the reading with the educator as supporter
- to build independence in reading that can cross over into Independent Reading time (*What is balanced literacy?*, n.d.).
- The main questions you will need to answer to determine how to conduct Guided Reading within your own teaching situation include the following:
- How can guided reading sessions be run? (For example, what procedures can I use?)
- How may groups be formed?
- How may texts be selected?

FIGURE 6.3

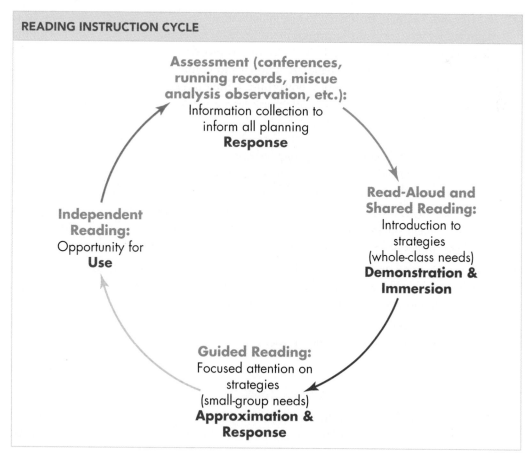

READING INSTRUCTION CYCLE

Assessment (conferences, running records, miscue analysis observation, etc.): Information collection to inform all planning **Response**

Read-Aloud and Shared Reading: Introduction to strategies (whole-class needs) **Demonstration & Immersion**

Guided Reading: Focused attention on strategies (small-group needs) **Approximation & Response**

Independent Reading: Opportunity for **Use**

Running Guided Reading Sessions

At all grade levels, Guided Reading usually involves intensive work with a small group of learners using materials at a moderate degree of difficulty. By assessing learners' reading, educators identify what they should be working on (e.g., reading strategy). Then educators can follow steps like these:

- *Introduce the text to learners.* The introduction is intended to create interest, raise questions, prompt expectations, and highlight or foreshadow information, concepts, and strategies. Introductions might include

  - ❏ "cover and publication information"
  - ❏ a short "summary" statement about the text
  - ❏ initial connections to what is known already about the text (e.g., "This book takes place in medieval times which connects to our social studies unit.")
  - ❏ the setting of a "purpose for reading" (e.g., the educator says, "I wonder …" or "Let's read this section of the book and see whether we can find …")
  - ❏ inviting "predictions," which the group will revisit later (e.g., "What do you think will happen when …?")
  - ❏ a preview of the book, that is, showing some or all of the pictures in the text without the words (Rog, 2003, pp. 50–51)

- *Read the text.* Learners are invited to read quietly or silently. While learners read, educators might confer with individual learners, inviting them, for example, to read aloud, with the educator observing and noting how the learner is processing text, occasionally providing guidance in use of reading strategies. As Pinnell and Fountas (2009, p. 9) put it, this "on-the-spot assessment may prompt a powerful teaching interaction" between educator and learner. In older grades, educators might ask learners to make notes on their reading in lieu of individual conferences. Alternatively, educators might allow for reading pairs (Rog, 2003), where readers confer over "predictions, connections, questions, and responses" (p. 49). Further, during the whole-group sharing time, learners can be invited to "tell the group what their *partner* said," hence encouraging active and purposeful listening. Use of reading pairs might allow for more active participation than might otherwise be the case.

- *Discuss and revisit the text.* After the reading of the text, learners discuss what they read and the problem-solving strategies they used. They might reread a portion of the text to provide examples of their observations, processes, and practices.

- *Teach for processing strategies* (optional). The educator might here decide to do some more explicit teaching. The educator selects a strategy that the learners need further help with, and explains and demonstrates the strategy by revisiting the text.

- *Extend understanding* (optional). Educators might create opportunities for learners to extend their understanding through reader response activities (see Chapter 12).

Forming Guided Reading Groups

Some educators conduct a reading assessment such as a DRA with their learners and then place them into guided reading groups this way. Educators might also use less-formal assessment measures such as **running records** (with or without miscue analysis). Educators like Taberski (1996) combine running records, information from reading conferences, and their observations of learners during all the reading instruction components in their literacy programs to decide which learners might need to work on similar strategies. When grouping learners this way, educators are able to put them together not just according to a level from a test, but also by analyzing qualitative data about what learners are (or are not) doing in their reading and what they might need to work on next. Accordingly, you might decide that five learners should go together because they all need help using text features to improve their comprehension of reading information texts. These learners might, however, all score differently on a standardized assessment (e.g., DRA or CASI). If educators do group learners in ways that are not just about levels, during the reading portion of the Guided Reading session they can do as Taberski (1996) has, having some learners read independently and reading along with others to support them.

No matter how readers are put together, Guided Reading groups are not like the old "round robin" reading groups of yesteryear. Groups today should be flexible and short term, and always capitalize on learners' funds of knowledge and interests. In other words, all the learners who are having difficulties should not always be lumped together.

Selecting Texts

Educators should select texts that go hand-in-hand with the types of strategies that they want learners to work on. For instance, Taberski (1996) selects series books and mysteries to help learners understand how using the structure of various genres can boost comprehension. When selecting texts for guided reading, educators may want to ask themselves these questions:

- Is the text within the learners' zone of proximal development?
- Is the text something the learners would find engaging?
- Does the text tie in with what is being studied in other parts of the curriculum?
- Do the learners have the background knowledge to access the text?
- What genre is the text?
- How long is the text?
- What is the text's layout?
- Does the text contain supportive visuals?
- Is the text's use of language (e.g., vocabulary) appropriate?

Additional Considerations

During a professional development day with elementary teachers from variety of school districts, Rachel asked the teachers to identify what they felt they did well in their literacy program. Many of the teachers said they had come to feel confident about Guided Reading. Yet, when the teachers started to talk about what they did with Guided Reading, a heated discussion ensued, with teachers disagreeing about what they felt really counted as such. One group expressed that Guided Reading had to be done with **levelled** texts; another said no, it could be done with any literature that addressed the group's specific needs. So, who was right? In our estimation, both were. Effective Guided Reading instruction depends less on doing Guided Reading the one right way and more on reflecting on the purposes of the instruction, most particularly which strategies you feel your learners need to work on. We recommend that educators critically appraise all instructional components in relation to both the needs of the learners in their classrooms and the curriculum guidelines for their jurisdictions. Educators need to communicate to learners before, during, and after Guided Reading what the goals of the instruction are. Educators and learners will have more success if they understand what a strategy involves as well as why, how, and when to use it. Strategy instruction will not reach its potential of developing active, strategic readers unless it is taught in a thoughtful, responsive way (Villaume & Brabham, 2001).

Independent Reading

In Independent Reading learners select their own texts and read on their own. They have opportunities to "use" (Cambourne, 1988) what they have been learning in the other components of their reading program. This time for practice is critical to learners' achievement, as Allington (2012), in his analysis of studies of reading volume and achievement, has found that time spent reading is positively correlated with reading achievement. Allowing time for learners to read also indicates to them that reading is valuable (*What is balanced literacy?*, n.d.). It helps to provide for reading practice of particular kinds of texts that learners might not otherwise get outside of school.

Independent Reading might also help foster learners' engagement with reading and, in turn, with school in general (Clausen-Grace & Kelley, 2007). Engagement is of prime concern as learners progress through elementary school because the "proportion of students who are not engaged or motivated by their school experiences grows at every grade level and reaches epidemic proportions in high school" (Biancarosa & Snow, 2004, p. 9).

Concerns over reading, however, might be tempered if we broaden our conception of what counts as reading. Studies are finding that reading happens, but it is not with traditional texts; for instance, in one study of the reading practices of Australian youth outside of school, researchers found that all participants were reading quite a bit; however, their reading choices were often non-traditional (e.g., texts on cell phones, email, and magazines). Readers who were engaged by reading read traditional types of texts (e.g., novels) *in addition to* digitally oriented and popular media (Rennie & Patterson, 2010). It was also found that "interest and pleasure clearly informed this reading" (p. 216). The three-part takeaway message is

- reading begets reading
- multiple forms of reading, including digital, must be recognized by educators
- the licence to follow one's interests and to pursue pleasure (i.e., be engaged) can help to grow readers and their reading practices

As such, the texts that we as educators invite learners to read are paramount to their reading success (or failure).

Materials for Independent Reading

One of the first considerations for setting up Independent Reading is ensuring that there are ample texts available from which learners may select. Choice helps readers to engage by taking responsibility (Cambourne, 1988). Generally, learners should be encouraged to read texts that they can handle independently, that is, read with about 96 to 100 percent accuracy (Rog, 2003). However, there may be times when it is appropriate for learners to select texts that might seem to us to be more advanced than we initially think they can handle. These times include when learners are intensely interested in a subject, know the content or genre well, or are supported through other **modes** (e.g., visuals). What is crucial is that learners have guided choice and that a large variety of texts are accessible to them (Allington, 2012). When educators are building their classroom library of texts, they might think of including

- multilevel texts
- texts from a variety of genres (e.g., information and fictional texts)
- series books
- books that draw on a variety of modes (e.g., graphic novels and **hypertexts** that can be read on the computer)
- reference material (e.g., dictionaries, thesauruses, and online encyclopedias)
- student publications (e.g., Language Experience Approach stories, class books, newsletters, fan fiction, blogs)
- magazines (print and online)
- comics
- graphic novels
- texts associated with games (e.g., Minecraft reference books and online supports)
- gaming texts (e.g., Pokémon cards)

Accessibility can mean that there are texts at arm's length, titles and covers are clearly visible and inviting, the texts are well organized so that learners can find what they want, there are ample opportunities to browse and borrow texts, there is a high volume of texts, and generally, texts are embedded in the entire structure of the classroom.

To further make texts and text selection accessible, here are some ideas:

- Store texts in tubs or on shelves, and have them organized by theme, authors, series, favourite characters, or some other organizational structure that makes sense to you and the class.
- Showcase a selection of texts with their covers showing by placing them in plastic rain gutters that are affixed to the wall. Running the gutters under the chalkboard can work well. (For installation directions, see Cunningham, Hall, & Gambrell, 2002, p. 36.)
- Create text baskets that can rotate through groups of desks or learners. These can contain a selection of material that goes with a theme and/or topic. The crates or baskets can literally be kept at arm's length to the learners.

Classroom library

• Create a classroom library that is well stocked and contains space for browsing and relaxed reading. The photograph here shows the classroom library that Kathy Gillies has built over the years.

In Chapter 2 we also provided some tips for building your own library, which can be an exciting task when you are starting out.

To match books to readers, some educators first conduct an assessment such as a DRA (Beaver, 2001); they then invite learners to pick from a selection of books that come with a level from the publishers or that have been levelled by the educator using a guide such as Fountas and Pinnell's (2006). While we have mentioned that it is important for learners to have time every day to read books at their independent reading level, we do not advise text selection that is solely or even primarily based on level because of factors related to the nature of reading and what is required for children to be proficient, independent readers. Readers' funds of knowledge, culture, identity, language, interests, and the like all have an effect on how easy or difficult it is for them to access specific texts. Readers' profiles, however, are not part of levelling.

Levelling occurs in a variety of fashions, but is most commonly related to readability levels, calculated through "a formula that measures sentence difficulty and word difficulty"; levelling can also be the result of applying "multiple criteria related to language predictability, text formatting, and content" (Dzaldov & Peterson, 2005, p. 222). Either of these forms of levelling seems to be premised on and promotes the belief that "the diversity of students' social, cultural, and experiential backgrounds can be whitewashed when matching readers to books" (p. 222).

Also problematic with levelling is the observed phenomenon of "levelling mania," in which levels are placed on "every text that students encounter during their school day" (Dzaldov & Peterson, 2005, p. 222), including library materials (Hedrick, 2006). This practice reduces learners' exposure to the variety of texts that are necessary for a full, rich language and literacy program, and it can lead some learners to resist reading because they are embarrassed to be reading within "their" level only. Levelling can restrict the amount of high-quality literature and authentic texts that make it into the hands of readers, even though we know that such texts attract and sustain readers (Bowen, 2006). Students can also construct their identity in terms of their reading level and be constrained from reading texts that interest them because they don't correspond to that level (Heydon, 2013). Furthermore, by restricting or even eradicating readers' choices in text selection, readers are not helped in learning how to make good text decisions, and Cambourne's (1988) condition of responsibility is unlikely to be fulfilled.

So, what are educators to do?

First, we acknowledge that levelling texts can be a useful practice, but it is how educators use these texts that can make the difference. Educators, for instance, can combine levelling with interest inventories to help capitalize on readers' background knowledge and interests when facilitating text selections (Clausen-Grace & Kelley, 2007).

Next, educators can reserve levelled texts that are combined with interest inventories for only some parts of their program. Guided Reading might be the most appropriate component for these types of texts (Dzaldov & Peterson, 2005).

Perhaps most important, educators can implement a variety of strategies to help readers select appropriate texts during Independent Reading time. Box 6.5 shows two versions of similar strategies for text selection to share with your students. The first requires that readers spend some time with a book before deciding on its suitability. The second provides more of a quick scan of the book for suitability.

BOX 6.5

STRATEGIES FOR TEXT SELECTION

Routman's (2003) Goldilocks Strategy Easy Books

Easy Books

Ask yourself these questions. If you answer yes, this book is probably an easy book for you. EASY books help you to read more smoothly and are fun to read aloud and silently.

▷ Is it a favourite book you have read before?

▷ Do you understand the story (text) well?

▷ Do you know (can you understand and read) just about every word?

▷ Can you read it easily and smoothly?

Just-Right Books

Ask yourself these questions. If you answer yes, this book is probably a "JUST-RIGHT" book for you. "Just-right" books help you learn the most, because you can figure out most of the words and you understand what's going on in the text.

▷ Is this an interesting book that you want to read?

▷ Are you familiar with the content, author, series, genre?

▷ Can you tell another person what is happening in the story and/or what you're learning?

▷ Do you sometimes need to reread a part to understand it?

▷ Are there just a few words per page you don't know?

▷ When you read are most places smooth and some choppy?

Hard Books

Ask yourself these questions. If you answer yes, this book is probably a HARD book for you. Spend a little time with it now and learn what you can. Perhaps someone can read the book to you. Give it another try on your own later (perhaps in several months).

▷ Are you interested in reading this book?

▷ Are you confused about what is happening in most of this book?

(continued)

▷ Is it hard to understand even when you reread?

▷ Do you need lots of help to read this book?

Selecting a Book While Browsing: The Five Finger Test

▷ Take a look at the books on display.

▷ Pull out a few that attract you.

▷ While you're considering whether the books are interesting to you, examine text features such as the title, illustrations, genre, and size of the type, as well as the length of each book.

▷ Now, pick a book and read the first page, if it's a novel, or the first couple of pages, if it's a picture book.

▷ Put up a finger for each word you don't know or that you really struggle with.

▷ If you get to the end of the section and have five or fewer fingers up, then this is likely a book that you can read independently.

▷ If you have more than five fingers raised, consider coming back to this book another time.

Source: From *Reading Essentials: The Specifics You Need to Teach Reading Well* by Regie Routman. Copyright 2003 by Regie Routman. Published by Heinemann, Portsmouth NH. Reprinted by permission of the Publisher. All rights reserved.

Running Independent Reading Time

There are many ways to run Independent Reading time. Educators can make this time more or less structured depending on their goals. Essentially, Independent Reading is an opportunity for readers to put into practice the strategies they have been taught in other parts of the reading program and to engage with texts in meaningful ways. What we mean by *meaningful* is that the reading is not done simply to practise a skill, but that readers have their own purposes for reading, such as pleasure, to learn more about a topic, or to find out how to do something—these purposes relate to the importance of ensuring that learners can make quality choices of their reading material. When running this component of your program, consider the following:

• Select a predictable, daily reading time.

• If learners are not used to Independent Reading, educators might have to start with a short amount of time and gradually work up to a longer period.

• This time can be a prime opportunity to run Guided Reading groups, conduct reading conferences, and/or assess readers.

• Readers usually need to debrief or at least reflect on what they are reading to help with comprehension. You can do this through reader response activities (see Chapter 12).

• Allow learners to get physically comfortable when they read.

- To cut down on learners who spend all of Independent Reading time browsing for books they never read, consider having them put together their own close-at-hand reading material made up of the following:

  1. *My now text.* The text I'm reading right now.

  2. *My next text(s).* The text(s) I want to read next.

  3. *My quick-and-easy reads.* Some things that are good, quick, easy reading—such as a book of poetry, or magazines with short articles (*Highlights, Guinness Book of World Records*, etc.). (Cunningham et al., 2002, pp. 68–69)

- Having these materials at the ready means that students do not need to be wandering around the classroom or visiting the library when they could be reading.

- Consider using reader response journals or logs for learners to document their reading.

Scheduling the Components

A foundational principle of *Constructing Meaning* is that educators, as professionals, must be responsive to the needs of their learners. We do not recommend, therefore, a prescribed schedule for the pedagogical components that we present in this book. We instead recommend that educators assess where learners are and what the context demands, and plan accordingly. You, therefore, decide, in concert with your students, how much time to spend on each of the reading instruction components that we list in this and other chapters. There are, however, some guidelines that might be helpful:

- Richard Allington (2012) concludes that one of the keys to reading achievement is that learners need lots of time to actually read. Allington explains that every learner is different, but the more time we can create for learners to read, the better. He, for example, reports that learners in the 90th percentile for reading achievement read 40.4 minutes per day compared with learners in the 10th percentile for reading achievement, who read for only 1.6 minutes per day. Thus, regardless of what instructional strategies you select, it is wise to include as much reading time as possible. Allington recommends a full 90 minutes a day of in-school reading time. This amount might seem unrealistic, but remember that reading can and should happen across the curriculum.

- Many educators advocate that Read-Aloud and Shared Reading happen daily (Brown & Fisher, 2006). Routman (2003) has found that educators can often combine these two instructional strategies when called for. While she considers about 20 to 30 minutes daily optimum for Read-Aloud, librarian (2005) finds that learners can get restless after about 15 to 20 minutes, hence the need for you to judge your learners and the circumstance.

- Beginning readers may need more Guided Reading than more experienced ones. Guided Reading can be scheduled at the same time as Independent Reading, with educators meeting with a few groups a day for about 15 minutes per group (Routman, 2003, p. 158).

SUMMARY

This chapter has highlighted some of the major components of a responsive and flexible reading program: Read-Aloud, Shared Reading, Guided Reading, and Independent Reading. Each component offers learners differing levels of educator support, with the ultimate goal of creating independent readers who have purposes for reading, and who have a variety of strategies at their disposal to make sense of a diversity of texts. Within our discussion of the components, we have offered information to help educators make decisions regarding critical instructional issues such as the amount of time to spend on each component, the grouping of learners, the selection of texts, and the running of the components.

This chapter must be combined with the other chapters in this book to help teachers put together a comprehensive reading program. Chapter 7 is a particularly important companion to Chapter 6, as it offers specific ways to teach strategic reading within the context of the major reading instruction components.

SELECTED PROFESSIONAL RESOURCES

The International Children's Digital Library Foundation. (n.d.). *The International Children's Digital Library: A library for the world's children.* Available at http://www.childrenslibrary.org

The International Children's Digital Library is an online resource whose mission is to excite and inspire the world's children to become members of the global community—children who understand the value of tolerance and respect for diverse cultures, languages, and ideas—by making the best in children's literature available online. Use this site to augment your classroom resources and to engage learners with a diverse range of texts. One wonderful thing about this site is that readers can access texts in a number of different languages.

Pinnell, G. S., & Fountas, I. C. (2010). *Research base for guided reading as an instructional approach.* Retrieved from http://teacher.scholastic.com/products/guidedreading/pdf/2.0_InYourClassroom/GR_Research_Paper_2010.pdf

This freely accessible and readable paper is useful for understanding the research base for Guided Reading (i.e., the *why* behind the *how*).

Miller Burkins, J. (n.d.). *Using guided reading to develop student reading independence.* Newark, DE: International Literacy Association. Retrieved from http://www.readwritethink.org/professional-development/strategy-guides/using-guided-reading-develop-30816.html

A perfect companion to the research, this website from the International Reading Association provides a plethora of downloadable and other resources to help educators to implement and enrich guided reading sessions.

CHAPTER SEVEN

Pedagogies to Foster Strategic Reading

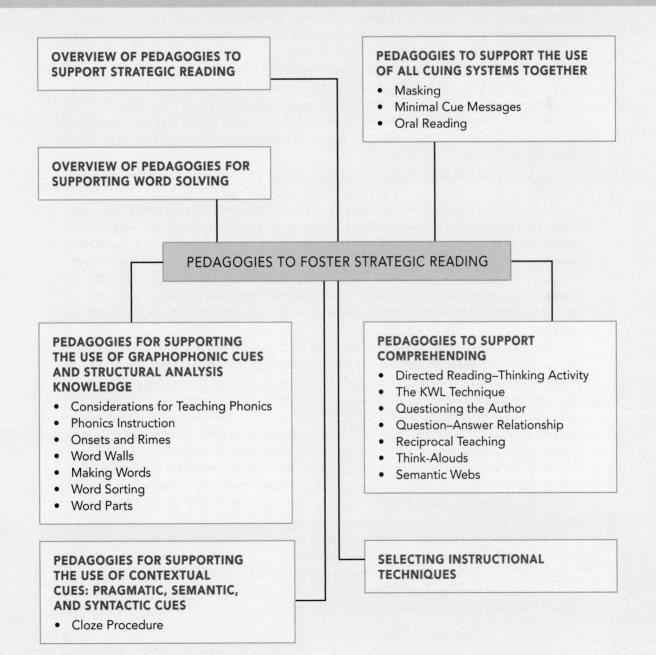

OVERVIEW OF PEDAGOGIES TO SUPPORT STRATEGIC READING

PEDAGOGIES TO SUPPORT THE USE OF ALL CUING SYSTEMS TOGETHER
- Masking
- Minimal Cue Messages
- Oral Reading

OVERVIEW OF PEDAGOGIES FOR SUPPORTING WORD SOLVING

PEDAGOGIES TO FOSTER STRATEGIC READING

PEDAGOGIES FOR SUPPORTING THE USE OF GRAPHOPHONIC CUES AND STRUCTURAL ANALYSIS KNOWLEDGE
- Considerations for Teaching Phonics
- Phonics Instruction
- Onsets and Rimes
- Word Walls
- Making Words
- Word Sorting
- Word Parts

PEDAGOGIES TO SUPPORT COMPREHENDING
- Directed Reading–Thinking Activity
- The KWL Technique
- Questioning the Author
- Question–Answer Relationship
- Reciprocal Teaching
- Think-Alouds
- Semantic Webs

PEDAGOGIES FOR SUPPORTING THE USE OF CONTEXTUAL CUES: PRAGMATIC, SEMANTIC, AND SYNTACTIC CUES
- Cloze Procedure

SELECTING INSTRUCTIONAL TECHNIQUES

STRATEGY INSTRUCTION FOR CONSTRUCTING MEANING WHEN READING: WENDY CROCKER

This chapter is a companion to Chapter 6, which presented the large instructional components that educators can use to construct a reading program (Read-Aloud, Shared Reading, Guided Reading, and Independent Reading). Now we focus on the smaller instructional strategies that can fit within these components or occasionally be used on their own to help learners acquire, in Victoria Purcell-Gates's (2001) terms, the *parts* of reading. In this chapter the goal is to help educators develop an instructional repertoire to support pleasurable, strategic reading that makes sense to readers.

In Chapter 6 we introduced Wendy Crocker, who has decades of experience as an educator. We talked with Wendy about her reading strategies pedagogy, learning that the ultimate goal of her pedagogy is to help readers construct meaning from text. Rather than an end in itself, the teaching of strategies is one way of helping to achieve this goal. Strategies create optimum opportunities for readers to become independent meaning constructors, as strategies, unlike skills, which are the ability to do something within a particular context, are a conscious plan for doing something that might be helpful when used across contexts.

To begin, here is how Wendy says she structures her teaching to support strategic reading:

"I have found that to plan effectively for my learners so that they may have the strategies to make meaning from a variety of texts, I must know where they are, what knowledge and skills they have, and where they need support. I use a variety of **formative assessments** in my classroom, including informal reading inventories, **running records**, audiotapes, and self-assessments. These I collect in files that both the learners and I can access. They provide an ongoing look at each learner's progress and are a terrific tool at family conferences to illustrate what their child has mastered and where he/she needs to go next.

"In addition to a personal look at what each learner knows, is able to do, and values, ongoing **assessment** informs my planning for the entire class. If I recognize that the majority of the class needs to learn a particular reading **strategy** (e.g., using key words when reading to enhance comprehension of informal texts), then I can address this need during a whole-group Shared Reading. To do this, I select a piece of text and enlarge it for everyone to see readily. Then, as a think-aloud where I pretend that I am reading to myself, I narrate what I am doing as a reader when I am using the strategy. I draw attention to where I am using the strategy and why as well as how I would use it. I find that when I demonstrate and talk it through, it demystifies the act of reading so that students feel 'Ah, so that's what she meant!' and can begin to use the tool on their own.

"But you can't stop here! Just because I have demonstrated the strategy doesn't mean that it is firmly within the learners' repertoire. It is important that I follow up with small groups of readers using the same text, so that they can try the strategy, and I can provide support and feedback. I then offer the learners a new piece of text for them to try out the strategy on their own or in pairs. I continue to monitor their use of the strategy and invite them to give me feedback and include this feedback as self-assessment in their portfolio. After monitoring the use of the new strategy, if there are still learners who require additional practice and guidance, I group them together during Guided Reading. Using another piece of unseen text, this small group of learners has an opportunity to practise the strategy in a supportive environment that provides focused attention and lots of feedback.

"Finally, I expect and give my students opportunities to use the strategy on their own during Independent Reading. As I conference with learners, review their portfolio, or observe them during class, I can continue to check in on their progress. Often, I will ask learners in a different context—for example, in science—to use a strategy that was taught in the language block to illustrate that reading crosses over subjects and that the same strategies that we learned while reading together in the morning can be put to use in a content area later in the day.

"If I observe that learners struggle with taking a strategy from one context to another, I may specifically reference it when setting the task in another subject. For example in science, I may suggest that reading for key words would be a good introduction to the reading of a new chapter. I could also follow up and pull a group of learners together for a few minutes to remind them of what the strategy is and how to use it with this new text.

"If I observe that only some of the learners require the specific strategy, then I introduce it during a small-group Guided Reading session designed for that purpose. Why do a large-group lesson when it is only useful for a small group? However, even though it may be a handful of learners, I always demonstrate the strategy and narrate what I am doing as the first step to introducing learners to something new." ☐

OVERVIEW OF PEDAGOGIES TO SUPPORT STRATEGIC READING

Wendy's pedagogy is similar to the reading instruction cycle in Figure 6.3 (that is, moving the teaching of a strategy through from Read-Aloud, Shared Reading, and Guided Reading to Independent Reading while assessing) and follows Cambourne's (1988) conditions for learning. Next, we unpack the pedagogy and indicate through italics how it relates to the conditions.

First, Wendy bases her teaching in assessment, where she collects multiple forms of information over time to learn what her learners know, are able to do, and value. This information informs responsive planning. If, through this assessment, Wendy recognizes that most of the class needs to learn a particular reading strategy, then she will first teach this during Read-Aloud and later through Shared Reading. Here, Wendy *demonstrates* the strategy, thinking aloud and drawing the learners' explicit attention to what she is doing and why.

Wendy then follows up the use of this strategy and tailors it to specific small-group needs during Guided Reading. Guided Reading allows the learners to *approximate* or try out the strategy in a supportive environment that provides focused attention and lots of feedback or *response*.

Next, Wendy *expects* her learners to *use* the strategy during the course of Independent Reading. She structures her teaching so that learners take *responsibility* for deciding when and where the strategy can best promote meaning making.

If Wendy judges that only some learners require the specific strategy, then she introduces it during Guided Reading and forms a group for that purpose. Wendy still, however, models the strategy in a little mini Read-Aloud or Shared Reading type of situation at the beginning of the Guided Reading session. Just like when a strategy is taught to the whole class, the learners in the Guided Reading group are expected to follow through on strategy use during Independent Reading.

Finally, Wendy's use of conferencing allows her to check on the learners' progress and feed this information back into the cycle. The remainder of this chapter is designed to help you develop a repertoire of strategies to engender strategic reading in your learners.

There is no shortage of advice for educators about the strategies they can teach learners to use when reading in the content areas (e.g., Frank, Grossi, & Stanfield, 2006), for reading comprehension more generally (e.g., McNamara, 2007), with learners who have been identified with specific learning difficulties (e.g., Bender & Larkin, 2003), with **culturally and linguistically diverse (CLD)** learners (Farrell, 2009), and most generally with learners across the elementary grades (e.g., McCormack & Pasquarelli, 2010). There are numerous reading and instructional strategies, but any reader or educator is unlikely to need them all. Thus we offer in this chapter a sampling of different types of strategies organized according to those that address reading at the level of the word and those that can help readers make sense of a text at more macro-levels. Because the wholes and parts of reading are inextricable, note that our division between reading words and comprehending text is an oversimplification adopted to provide some focus to the discussion.

OVERVIEW OF PEDAGOGIES FOR SUPPORTING WORD SOLVING

As our earlier discussions of miscue analysis and comprehension demonstrate, word-perfect reading is not always necessary for constructing meaning from text and is not always an indication that readers have made sense of text. Purcell-Gates (2001), however, discussed the importance of the part within the whole, which is where the section on word identification comes in. Coming to a word they do not know is an occasion when readers need to draw on strategies so that meaning does not break down. Educators such as Reggie Routman (2000) advocate for educators to sit down with readers and generate lists of strategies they can employ when they come to an unknown word (see, for example, Box 7.1). Inviting learners to generate their own list with educator support in large or small groups or individually provides the responsibility necessary for learners to take ownership of the strategies and to see reading as a problem-solving practice. If the list is short to begin with, then educators will know where to go next with their teaching, and new strategies can be added so that the list is a living record of what readers know and are able to do.

BOX 7.1

WHAT I CAN DO WHEN I COME TO A WORD I DON'T KNOW

▷ Look at the picture.

▷ Get my mouth ready to say it.

▷ Look at how the word begins.

▷ Ask myself, "Does that make sense?"

▷ Ask myself, "Does that look right?"

▷ Ask myself, "Does that sound right?"

▷ Put in a word that makes sense.

▷ Skip the word and then come back.

▷ Think of the story or what this text is about.

▷ Compare the unknown word with a word I know (e.g., "fright" is unknown, but "night" is known).

▷ See if there's a part of the word I do know.

▷ Break the word apart.

▷ Look back at what I've read to see whether I recognize the word from somewhere else.

▷ Decide whether this word is important to know (e.g., knowing how to say a character's name might not interfere with my understanding of the story).

Sources: Routman, 2000; Scanlon, Anderson, & Sweeney, 2010; Taberski, 2000.

All the strategies outlined in Box 7.1 draw on one or more of the **cuing systems**. Of course, to read requires the use of all the cuing systems, introduced in Chapter 3. The following, adapted from Saskatchewan Education (2000), explains how the systems can help readers problem-solve unknown words to construct meaning.

Syntactic Knowledge. When readers are "familiar with the patterns of word order or grammar that determine meaning in sentences, they can use this knowledge to predict unfamiliar words" (n.p.). Readers "with good oral language have internalized a rule of word order" (n.p.). Having this helps them to know that the blank word in the following sentence is a noun (even if they do not know how to define a noun): "Bobby threw a ___." Educators can support readers to draw on this knowledge by asking them to focus on making sense and differentiating between something that "sounds right and something that does not" (n.p.).

Semantic Knowledge. When readers' **funds of knowledge** are a good match for a text (e.g., they have a personal experience related to the topic of the text), they are able to make use of this knowledge to "predict what an unfamiliar word or phrase might be" (n.p.). For instance, a reader who knows about skateboarding is more likely to predict than those who are not that *coping* is the unfamiliar word in this sentence: The skater did a grind on the ___ of the bowl. In this example, the reader would also be drawing on syntactic knowledge and could check out a prediction with graphophonic knowledge. Educators can promote the use of semantic cues by prompting learners with questions like these: "What would make sense there?" "Did that make sense?" They can also help readers combine cues by asking questions along the lines of "Did that sound right?" (n.p.).

Pragmatic Knowledge. Readers draw on pragmatic knowledge when they "understand that people use language differently in different contexts" (n.p.). Learners may notice, for example, that "adults talk differently to a baby than to another adult," and those who speak an English **dialect** different from that of the dominant dialect of the school may notice that "the language spoken by teachers at school is different than the language spoken by members of their family even though they both are speaking English" (n.p.).

Helping readers pay attention to the context in which a text is written and read, and elements such as where a story is supposed to be taking place, can all assist readers to problem-solve through unknown words. For example, consider this sentence: *Tony Hawk was totally stoked that he pulled off the trick.* Educators can support readers to figure out the unknown words and make meaning from the sentence by drawing their attention to the fact that the text concerns skateboarding and they should think of how skateboarders use language.

Graphophonic Knowledge. Readers can use their understanding of letter–sound relationships to "predict what an unfamiliar word might be" (n.p.). For example, readers who knew the letter–sound relationship for *c* could use it to support the prediction of *coping* as opposed to *bottom* in one of the earlier examples. Combining graphophonic with semantic and syntactic knowledge would also provide readers with more highly predictive guesses as to what the word might be (e.g., knowing that a grind cannot be done on the bottom of a bowl would tell readers this guess was wrong).

In strategic reading it is useful to be able to use as many cuing systems as the situation demands to deal with unknown words and to teach reading with whole, connected texts. That said, a key question of many of the educators we have met concerns how to help readers develop **graphophonic** knowledge. We thus begin there, then move into structural analysis of words, which often involves identifying words by larger and more meaningful units such as prefixes and suffixes, discuss pedagogical techniques for focused work on semantic and syntactic cues, and finish with pedagogical strategies for helping readers integrate multiple types of cues. Table 7.1 gives you an overview of these strategies.

TABLE 7.1 PEDAGOGIES FOR WORD SOLVING

Pedagogy	Cuing System(s) Emphasized	Helps Readers Develop Strategies To
Names and other concrete words	Graphophonic	• Hear sounds at the beginning of words • Hear rhyming words • Relate sounds with letters • Differentiate upper- and lowercase letters
Hearing sounds in words	Graphophonic	• Hear sounds in all word positions • Relate letters with sounds

TABLE 7.1 **PEDAGOGIES FOR WORD SOLVING (*CONTINUED*)**

Pedagogy	Cuing System(s) Emphasized	Helps Readers Develop Strategies To
Word walls	Graphophonic (also can call on structural analysis knowledge)	• Identify common words as sight words • Hear rhyming words • Relate sounds with letters • Use knowledge of letter sounds to identify words • Use knowledge of word patterns and parts, including prefixes and suffixes, to identify words
Onsets and rimes	Graphophonic (also can call on structural analysis knowledge)	• Relate sounds with letters • Identify new words through analogy to familiar words
Making words	Graphophonic (also can call on structural analysis knowledge)	• Relate sounds with letters • Use knowledge of letter sounds to identify words • Use knowledge of word patterns and parts, including prefixes and suffixes, to identify words
Word sorting	Graphophonic (also can call on structural analysis knowledge), Semantic	• Form generalizations about the sound and visual features of words • Consider the meanings of the words within a given context to identify words
Word parts	Structural analysis knowledge	• Use roots, affixes, and syllabication to identify words
Predictable books	Semantic, Syntactic	• Use meaning and language cues to predict words
Cloze procedure	Semantic, Syntactic	• Use meaning and language cues to predict words • Use meaning and language cues to monitor predictions
Masking	Graphophonic, Semantic, Syntactic	• Use context cues to identify words • Use letter sounds to identify words • Use word parts to identify words
Minimal cue messages	Graphophonic, Semantic, Syntactic	• Use context cues to identify words • Use knowledge of letter sounds and word parts to spell and identify words
Oral reading	Graphophonic, Semantic, Syntactic	• Use context and print cues to identify words • Use context and print cues to correct miscues

PEDAGOGIES FOR SUPPORTING THE USE OF GRAPHOPHONIC CUES AND STRUCTURAL ANALYSIS KNOWLEDGE

In this section we describe pedagogies for helping readers use the letter–sound relationship and their knowledge of the structure of words to predict words as they read. First, however, we discuss of some of the considerations educators may face when planning their teaching of **phonics**.

Considerations for Teaching Phonics

When Rachel was in her first year of teaching, she used a commercial phonics program with her students who were all Cree–first language. The program included worksheets that moved learners in a sequential fashion through various letters and letter combinations and their corresponding sounds. The sheets mainly consisted of pictures with accompanying parts of words, where learners were asked to fill in the missing letters (e.g., a picture of a cat labelled with the word _at). Rachel used this program because she had understood that a structured, sequenced program such as this one was fundamental to learning to read.

Rachel will never forget the day, however, when she watched a frustrated learner try to make sense of why a picture of what he interpreted as a donkey was on the worksheet for the [*m*] sound. Though the intent of the picture was to convey a mule, not a donkey, Rachel realized that her student's interpretation of donkey made sense: she herself first saw a donkey too. It was only because she knew how such sheets worked and not because of her reading proficiency that Rachel was able to figure out the donkey/mule situation. Thus, in her witnessing of this scene, Rachel understood that these sheets, with their decontextualized images and shaky connection to reading as constructing meaning, made no sense to most of her students. They represented a one-size-fits-few approach to creating learning opportunities about graphophonic cues. Moreover, Rachel saw that using mules in the sub-Arctic to teach reading was probably not the most culturally appropriate way to go!

The question that's important to consider is not *whether* to teach phonics, but *how* to teach phonics, in particular, how to teach phonics in a way that allows readers to use their graphophonic knowledge in a strategic way that helps them in their construction of meaning.

Terminology

How important is it for educators to use the technical language of phonics with learners? Box 7.2 presents definitions of some of the more common terms in phonics programs. Rather than inundating learners with all these terms, you might prefer to think about what is key for your learners to know and be able to do with their phonics knowledge. These terms serve primarily to facilitate communication between and among learners and educators when talking about letters and sounds in words. Also, researchers have posited that perhaps "an understanding of the explicit definitions of phonics terminology is a different type of knowledge than being able to identify examples of phonics terms within sample words" (Binks-Cantrell, Joshi, & Washburn, 2012, p. 162). It might therefore be more helpful to invite readers to learn the possible sounds that are associated with a letter (e.g., for the letter *a*, the possibilities are the sounds in *can*, *cane*, *car*, and *call*) rather than learn that these sounds are called "short, long, *r*-controlled, and *l*-controlled."

Phonics Rules

Should an educator teach phonics by teaching rules like "When two vowels go walking, the first one does the talking"? In the 1960s, Clymer (1963) showed that many phonics rules do not work very often. For example, in Clymer's study, the "two vowels go walking" rule worked only 45 percent of the time for words in four primary **basal reading series**. There are many exceptions to the rule, including all the vowel diphthongs (e.g., *join*, *about*). Consider as well the final *e* rule. Clymer found that this rule worked only 63 percent of the time. Many common words, such as *give, love, some,*

BOX 7.2

PHONICS TERMINOLOGY

▷ *Consonants* refers to all the letters of the alphabet except the vowels. There is one sound for most consonants, with the exceptions of *c* and *g*, which have both hard and soft sounds (e.g., *car* and *city*; *go* and *gem*).

▷ *Consonant blends* consist of a combination of two or three consonants in which the sound of each of the consonants is retained and blended (e.g., *blue, free, smoke, street*).

▷ *Consonant digraphs* refers to combinations of two or more consonants that produce a new sound (e.g., *shoe, this, chick, phone*).

▷ *Vowels* are the letters *a, e, i, o, u* and sometimes *y* (when it is not the initial letter of a word, as in *my*) and *w* (when it follows a vowel, as in *how*).

▷ *Long vowel sounds* are the letter names of vowels (e.g., *made, bead, kite, mope, flute*).

▷ *Short vowel sounds* are other sounds associated with single vowels (e.g., *had, bed, hit, mop, cup*).

▷ *Vowel digraphs* refers to combinations of two vowels that have one sound (e.g., *coat, meat, wait*).

▷ *Vowel diphthongs* consist of combinations of two vowels in which the sound of each of the vowels is retained and blended (e.g., *join, boy, how, out*).

▷ *Controlled vowels* are those vowels that are followed by the letters *r* and *l* and which alter the sound of the vowel (e.g., vowels influenced by *r* as in *far, her, fir, for, purr*; and *a* influenced by *l* as in *fall*).

▷ *Onset* is the initial consonant or consonants in a syllable (e.g., *b-* in *bat*; *br-* as in *brake*).

▷ *Rime* (also known as *phonogram* or *word family*) consists of the vowel and remaining consonants in a syllable following the onset (e.g., *-at* in *bat*; *-ake* as in *brake*).

▷ *Syllable* refers to a group of letters that forms a unit and has only one vowel sound.

▷ *Closed syllable* is a unit in which one vowel appears between consonants (e.g., *cat, shop, back*). The vowel sound is usually short.

▷ *Open syllable* is a unit with a vowel at the end of it (e.g., *go, she, try*; *to-* in *total*). The vowel sound is usually long.

come, and *live*, do not follow the rule. The most reliable rules are those involving consonants, for example, that *c* and *g* are soft following the vowels *e* and *i*.

Another complication with phonics rules is that readers are often able to recite them but are unable to use them to identify unfamiliar words. For example, a reader may be able to describe in detail how the *e* at the end of the word jumps over the letter in front of it and kicks the vowel to make it say its own name, but that same reader then identifies the word *mate* as *mat*. We do not recommend rule memorization as an effective way to help readers learn to map sounds onto letters.

But readers could still be taught the common sounds associated with vowels. In a reconsideration of the utility of phonic generalizations, Johnston's (2001) still popular study found that some vowel pairs are more consistent with the "two vowels go walking" generalization than others. For example, the most reliable pair is *ay* at 96.4 percent. Also highly regular vowel pairs where the first vowel does the talking are *ai, ay, oa, ee,* and *ey.* Vowel pairs that are highly regular but do not have long vowel sounds are *aw, oy, oi,* and *au.* Other vowel pairs have two or more sounds (e.g., *boot, book; snow, how; seat, head*) and cannot be taught so easily. Johnston indicates that learners need a flexible strategy with these pairs: they need to try more than one sound and check the results with their oral language and context. We suggest that if phonics is taught within a whole-part-whole structure, readers can read for meaning and use context to help them discern the right sound.

Synthetic or Analytic Phonics

Another consideration in the teaching of phonics concerns whether instruction should be synthetic, in which readers are taught letter sounds and then how to blend them to pronounce a word, or analytic, in which readers examine known words to discover patterns and regularities to use when identifying unknown words.

An advantage of synthetic phonics is that readers can use letter sounds to try to predict new words even when these words are visually dissimilar to words they know. However, it is important to recall (as we indicated in Chapter 4) that isolating sounds for letters without distortion is difficult. Another problem involves using this approach with words of more than one syllable. It is not uncommon to hear readers who have been encouraged to emphasize graphophonic cues trying to identify words such as *hammer* by saying, "huh, a, muh, muh, eh, er," and then having no idea what the word is. In addition to the helpful information that could be supplied by context and the use of other cuing systems, these learners might benefit from learning how to organize words into syllables in order to use their knowledge of letter sounds.

In analytic phonics, educators can invite learners to identify words by mapping sounds to larger chunks of letters. The chunks, generally labelled phonograms or rimes, consist of a vowel sound plus a consonant sound (e.g., *-ack, -ake, -eat*). These phonograms are used to create word families, such as *back, pack, quack,* and *sack* belonging to the *-ack* family. There are several advantages to this approach. Learners find it easier to identify words using phonograms than rules, phonograms are fairly consistent, and a relatively small number of phonograms are found in many of the words in primary reading material (Vacca, Vacca, & Gove, 2006). Still, learners may come across words in which they do not recognize a phonogram and therefore could benefit from being able to map sounds onto smaller units of words. The question is how this might be taught.

The National Reading Panel (2000) did not find that one approach to teaching phonics was better than another. As in any other aspect of reading instruction, one size does not fit all. The National Reading Panel advises educators to be flexible in the phonics instruction they provide in order to adapt it to individual needs.

The Ontario Ministry of Education (2003a) provides direction too. Whenever teaching phonics, educators should ensure that skills are used in "authentic contexts" and that reading materials are "engaging and meaningful" for readers (p. 23).

Separate or Integrated Instruction

Another consideration in the teaching of phonics is the extent to which it should be taught as a separate entity. Sometimes educators schedule phonics instruction in its own time slot and it is taught in virtual isolation from the rest of the language and literacy program. The concern with this way of teaching phonics is that learners may be able to associate sounds with isolated consonants and vowels and to recite phonics rules, but they may have difficulty using this knowledge when they read. The National Reading Panel (2000) cautions that "programs that focus too much on the teaching of letter–sound relations and not enough on putting them to use are unlikely to be very effective" (p. 10). Instead, the panel recommends integration of phonics instruction into "complete and balanced programs of reading instruction" (p. 11). Because of researchers such as Tse and Nicholson (2014), who have found that phonics instruction within the context of Big Book reading is more effective than either phonics instruction or Big Book reading alone, we recommend pedagogies that focus on helping learners use their knowledge of letter sounds to identify words in the context of real reading: just as Purcell-Gates (2001) recommends with her whole-part-whole structure.

Incidental or Systematic Instruction

A related consideration is whether phonics should be taught through explicit instruction in systematic lessons or incidentally when learners experience difficulty as they are reading or writing. During the 1980s and early 1990s, phonics was frequently taught in mini-lessons as educators identified specific needs while learners were reading or writing. There has long been support for systematic teaching of phonics (e.g., National Reading Panel, 2000) such that reading researchers like Washburn and Mulcahy (2014) continue to advocate for it. It may be that the power of systematic phonics instruction lies in organizing lessons such that they logically reveal the nature of the alphabetic system, so instruction moves from less to more complex understandings (Adams, 2002).

Like Strickland ("Strickland Discusses," 2011), we interpret the literature to suggest that all aspects of phonics instruction, including the question of incidental or systematic instruction, needs to be differentiated as "not all children progress in the same way or at the same rate" (p. 6). Readers develop phonics knowledge two ways: through instruction and from experiences with print (Johnston, 2001). Some people are better at implicit learning than others, and some aspects of phonics knowledge are easier to learn than others. Thus,

> a little phonics instruction may go a long way with some children, while others may need long-term systematic instruction to become independent readers. Teachers will need to carefully observe their students as they read and as they write to determine who needs what. (Johnston, 2001, p. 141)

And even if systematic phonics is called for, educators will need to determine a way to teach it that is meaningful to learners (just as the donkey/mule story suggests is needed) and "in the context of helping children think with text" so that instruction is "intellectually engaging" ("Strickland Discusses," 2011 p. 6) and is focused on constructing meaning.

Phonics Instruction

Related to the need for educators to make decisions about the best ways to teach grapho-phonic knowledge, as we discussed in Chapter 4, educators must also make decisions about the teaching of **phonemic awareness**. In a survey of the literature regarding the relationship between phonemic awareness and identifying words, Beck (2006) found that educators generally hold one of three main positions:

1. Phonemic awareness is a prerequisite for instruction in decoding (such as phonics).
2. Decoding instruction can result in phonemic awareness even if phonemic awareness is not explicitly taught.
3. There is a reciprocal relationship between phonemic awareness and decoding.

In general, Beck suggests that phonics instruction may be taught at the same time as phonemic awareness, particularly once learners are beyond preschool. Some researchers advocate that phonemic awareness instruction is more effective when letters are included (National Reading Panel, 2000; Rycik & Rycik, 2007), or at the very least instruction should move "quickly" from "awareness of a particular sound to an association of that sound with a letter symbol" (Perez, 2008, p. vi). As such, we next provide two sample instructional strategies that create phonemic awareness and phonics learning opportunities within meaningful wholes: (1) names and other concrete words and (2) Elkonin boxes. Both strategies involve looking at written letters as well as listening for sounds.

Sample Instructional Strategy 1: Names and Other Concrete Words

When we asked educator Tara-Lynn Scheffel to share one of her favourite instructional strategies for this section, she told us that it was the names and other concrete words strategy adapted from Cunningham and Allington (2011). Tara-Lynn likes this strategy because it begins not with arbitrary words and sounds that are so often the focus of commercial phonics programs, but rather with the meaningful whole or context of children's names and words that they can easily identify with concrete objects. Here is how the strategy works:

Tara-Lynn writes the learners' first names on sentence strips and cuts the names apart, with long names on long strips and short ones on short strips. Every day she draws a name, and the learner selected becomes "king" or "queen" for the day. His or her name becomes the focus of several language and literacy activities.

Tara-Lynn Scheffel

- The learners interview the king or queen, finding out what he or she likes to eat, play, and do after school, as well as other personal information the learner would like to share (e.g., how many brothers, sisters, dogs, and cats the child has). Tara-Lynn writes this information using a modelled or shared writing format on a chart, which later becomes part of a class book.

- Tara-Lynn focuses the learners' attention on the name of the featured child (e.g., *David*), pointing out that this word is David's name. She indicates that it takes many letters to write the word *David*, and the children count the letters. Tara-Lynn then says the letter names, *D-a-v-i-d* and has the children say them with her. Tara-Lynn notes that, in this case, the word begins and ends with the same letter and helps the children label one uppercase and the other lowercase.

- Tara-Lynn writes the child's name on another strip as the learners watch and chant the spelling of letters with her. Tara-Lynn then cuts the letters apart, mixes them up, and has children come up and arrange the letters in the right order to spell the child's name, using the original sentence strip as a model.

- Tara-Lynn distributes large sheets of drawing paper to the class, who write David's name on one side and draw a picture of him on the other side. The featured child takes these drawings home.

- As a new child's name becomes the focus, the children compare the names, talking about which are longer or shorter and whether the names contain any of the same letters. When two names begin with the same letter, Tara-Lynn helps the children hear that they also begin with the same sound (e.g., *Luke* and *Linda*).

- When a single-syllable name such as *Sam* is selected, Tara-Lynn has the children listen for rhyming words. For example, Tara-Lynn says pairs of words (Sam—ham, Sam—big), and the children indicate whether the two words rhyme.

- When two names that begin with the same letter but different sounds are selected (e.g., *Caroline* and *Cynthia*), Tara-Lynn uses the opportunity to help children understand that some letters have more than one sound. Tara-Lynn writes the two names on the board and prompts the children to say the two words several times, drawing out the first sound. She then says several words beginning with the letter *c* but having different sounds (e.g., *cat, celery, candy, cookies, city, cereal, cut*). For each word, the children point to either *Caroline* or *Cynthia* to show which sound they hear, and the teacher writes the word under the name on the board.

Cunningham and Allington (2011) recommended using a similar technique with other concrete words, such as the names of colours or animals. The major focus is on hearing sounds at the beginning of words and associating these sounds with letters. The following instructional strategy can help learners hear sounds in all word positions.

Sample Instructional Strategy 2: The Modified Elkonin Technique

To help learners hear sounds in words and make the connection between letters and sounds, Tara-Lynn also likes to use Marie Clay's (1993b) modified "Elkonin technique" (Elkonin, 1973). To use this technique, Tara-Lynn decides which words she wants to work with. For early-years learners, you might use their names or concrete words associated with the sound you want to emphasize and connect this strategy to the one above; with younger or older learners, you might also use this strategy with a word that learners generate within the context of writing (including shared and independent writing); or, as in the example, you could select words from a shared reading text. After selecting words, Tara-Lynn follows the pattern we present in Box 7.3. Note that this technique can also be used in any or all parts of the reading instruction cycle.

BOX 7.3

THE ELKONIN TECHNIQUE

1. In a whole-class, small-group, or individual setting, Tara-Lynn Scheffel prepares and shares cards on which squares are drawn for each sound unit in words of two, three, and four sounds. The words are drawn from whole texts that the learners have experienced (e.g., stories, rhymes, student writing). For example:

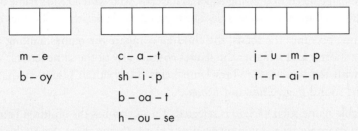

m – e	c – a – t	j – u – m – p
b – oy	sh – i - p	t – r – ai – n
	b – oa – t	
	h – ou – se	

2. Tara-Lynn provides a selection of counters for the learners.

3. Tara-Lynn articulates a word slowly. The learners watch her lips and copy her.

4. The learners articulate the word slowly. (A mirror can be used if it helps learners become more aware of what their lips are doing.)

5. Tara-Lynn articulates the word slowly, putting one counter in each box, sound by sound.

6. The learners put the counters in the boxes as Tara-Lynn says the word slowly, or she puts the counters in boxes as the learners say the word.

7. The learners put counters into boxes as they say the word.

8. Once the learners are able to hear sounds in words, this strategy is applied to spelling words as the learners write (within the context of, for example, guided or independent writing).

   a. Tara-Lynn encourages the learners to slowly articulate the word they want to spell.

   b. Tara-Lynn draws a box for each sound segment and asks: "What can you hear? How would you write it? Where will you put it?"

   c. Initially the learners write the letters they are able to associate with sounds heard and Tara-Lynn, the others. For example:

B	i	ll

b	oa	t

t	r	u	ck

9. After the learners are able to hear and record most consonants and some vowels correctly, Tara-Lynn draws them a box for each letter. Clay suggests using broken lines initially when two letters do not represent distinct sounds. For example:

h	a	m	m	e	r

Source: Adapted from M.M. Clay, *Reading Recovery: A Guidebook for Teachers in Training*, (Portsmouth, NH: Heinemann), 1993, pp. 32–35.

Onsets and Rimes

As we have mentioned, there are several advantages to teaching learners how to use word families (variously called *phonograms* or *rimes*) to identify words, particularly at the primary level. Perhaps one of the greatest advantages to this strategy is that students learn how to connect a known word and its pattern (e.g., *ball*) to an unknown word that has the same pattern (e.g., *tall*). In this way, learners figure out unknown words through analogy, and they build their decoding from what they already know.

Instruction in word families begins with onsets, which are the consonants that precede vowels in syllables. The sounds associated with onsets are fairly consistent, and traditional phonics instruction for onsets works well (Rasinski & Padak, 2001). There is research to support that pedagogies for manipulating words through their onsets and rimes through word families can help readers to develop more fluent (or, as we like to call it, fluid) reading (Hudson, Isakson, Richman, Lane, & Arriaza-Allen, 2011), which can aid in comprehension (Kuhn, Rasinski, & Zimmerman, 2014) and can be useful to CLD learners' understanding of the parts of language (Laufer, 2013). Rather than isolating letters and sounds, educators can teach beginning consonant sounds by associating them with concrete words that begin with these letters. They may invite learners to listen to words that begin with the sound (e.g., *bicycle* and *ball* start with *b*), ask them to brainstorm other words that begin with the sound, read words beginning with the letter, and read texts in which many of the words begin with the targeted letter.

Educators can also teach rimes and help learners to use knowledge of onsets and rimes to identify words. Almost 500 primary grade words can be made from just 37 rimes! These rimes are as follows: *-ack, -ail, -ain, -ake, -ale, -ame, -an, -ank, -ap, -ash, -at, -ate, -aw, -y, -eat, -ell, -est, -ice, -ick, -ide, -ight, -ill, -in, -ine, -ing, -ink, -ip, -ir, -ock, -oke, -op, -or, -ore, -uck, -ug, -ump, -unk* (Starrett, 2007).

Here is one way that Tara-Lynn and other educators have structured teaching rimes. This method has been adapted from Rasinski and Padak (2001):

- Identify a rime (e.g., *-at*) from a shared piece of text, such as a poem.
- Print the rime on the board and say the sound it represents several times, asking the learners to do the same.
- Brainstorm a list of words that contain the *-at* rime and print them on chart paper.
- Read the words with the learners and invite them to read the words in groups and individually.
- Invite learners to respond to riddles for which the answer is two or more words containing the rime.
- Revisit the shared poem, read the poem to the learners pointing to the words as you read, and invite the learners to join in. Read the poem chorally, in small groups, and then invite the learners to read it individually throughout the day. Once the poem has been read many times, invite learners to find individual words and word parts in the poem. The poems can be selected from collections and anthologies (see Chapter 11 for poetry resources) or written by the educator.
- Share with learners a sheet of words containing the rime as well as the poems used for the rime. Learners can take these resources home to practise reading and be invited to write a poem of their own, using words containing the rime.

- Later, perhaps the next day, invite the learners to share their poems, read one another's poems, read the poems from the previous day, and identify individual words in the poems. You might consider introducing two rimes each week, with a review at the end of the week. You might also invite learners to read and write books containing the rimes, use words containing the rimes for word sorts, complete cloze passages with words containing the targeted rimes, and use words containing the rimes in their daily writing. Educators can also place some of the words on a word wall for further activities.

Word Walls

Through Cambourne (1988), we have seen the importance of immersing readers in print. Word walls are one way of doing this and provide learners with a reference for reading and writing. A word wall is a systematically organized collection of words displayed in large letters on a wall; the word wall is interactive, as it is a tool and not a display (Pinnell & Fountas, 1998). Word walls can be the core of phonics and spelling programs and used to document what has been taught (Brabham & Villaume, 2001). When "doing a word wall," Cunningham and Allington (2011) recommended that educators

- be selective about the words on the wall, including only the most common words in their learners' reading and writing
- add words gradually—normally no more than five each week
- make the word wall accessible to everyone, writing words in large, clear letters
- invite learners to practise words by chanting or writing them
- provide a variety of review activities so that learners are able to identify and write words automatically
- encourage learners to spell word-wall words correctly in their writing*

Cunningham and Allington (2011) also suggested that educators arrange the words alphabetically on the word wall, giving learners an immediately accessible dictionary for the most troublesome words when they are reading or writing. Learners can also complete several activities with words on the wall. For example,

- Learners can find words on the wall that rhyme with a word given by the educator. ("Find a word that begins with *r* and rhymes with *sock*.")
- The educator writes a letter on the board and then says a sentence, leaving out a word that begins with that letter. ("Write the word that begins with an *f* and fits into the sentence *Sandro wants to catch ___*.")
- The educator thinks of a word on the wall and gives five clues, some related to visual features ("It has four letters"), some to sounds ("It begins with the sound /*r*/"), and others to meaning ("It fits into the sentence 'I want to climb that big ___'"). The learners write the word they think the educator has selected after each clue.

---

* Cunningham, P. M., & Allington, R. L. *Classrooms that work: They can all read and write, 5th ed.* (New York, NY: Longman). 2011.

In addition to the ABC word wall described above, educators can also create word walls containing

- theme words that change as units of study are completed
- words that are examples of the different sounds each letter can represent
- commonly misspelled words
- high-frequency words that lack predictable patterns
- words organized by the common spelling patterns of vowels (Brabham & Villaume, 2001)

Some of the most powerful instruction occurs during conversations that come up as learners are reading and writing (Brabham & Villaume, 2001). For example, when a learner asks how to spell the word *feet*, the educator can point to *meet* on the word wall and ask how it can help. In this way, educators scaffold the acquisition of strategies.

Making Words

Making words (Cunningham & Allington, 2011) is an instructional strategy where educators and learners use letters on cards to problem-solve to make words. During a period of about 15 minutes, learners can make 12 to 15 words, beginning with two-letter words and working up to longer words until they make a target word. Educators (or learners) prepare a set of small letter cards for each learner and one set of large cards to be used in a pocket chart or on the ledge of the board. Each card has the lowercase letter on one side and the uppercase letter on the other. Educators begin planning a lesson with a target word that ties in with some aspect of a shared text and contains letter–sound patterns the learners need to learn. Educators then generate a list of shorter words that can be made with the letters in the word. In the case of *winter*, shorter words include *in, tin, ten, net, wet, win, twin, went, rent, tire, wire, twine*. Educators write these words on index cards and order the cards from shortest to longest and according to patterns. Once these materials are prepared, educators may follow the steps outlined in Classroom Activity 7.1. Making words is a terrific activity for older learners too. Educators might want to consult *Making Big Words* (Cunningham, Hall, & Heggie, 2001) to increase the challenge for these learners or consult the Cunningham and Hall (e.g., 2007, 2008) series on making words, which differentiates words from kindergarten to fifth grade. Note, however, that as with levelled texts, the notion of grade must be tempered by educators' best judgment regarding what is right for their own learners.

Word Sorting

As learners become more knowledgeable about letters and words, word sorting can be used as part of the making-words technique or separately for older learners. This technique is designed to focus learners' attention on particular cues in words. Learners compare, contrast, and sort words according to specific print or sound features. Word sorts can help learners form generalizations about properties of words, and also help them link new words to ones they already know how to identify and spell. Educators and/or learners can begin by developing a word bank of known words for word sorting. These words can come from specific shared texts.

CLASSROOM ACTIVITY 7.1

Steps in a Making-Words Activity

1. In a large or small group and following the reading of a shared or common text, the educator places the large letter cards in a pocket chart or on the board ledge.

2. Each learner has corresponding small letter cards. The educator holds up the large letter cards, names each, and invites learners to hold up their matching cards.

3. The educator writes the number 2 or 3 on the board and says a word with this number of letters in a sentence. He or she invites the learners to make the word using the small letter cards (e.g., "Take two letters and make the word *in*"). The learners all say the word *in*.

4. A learner who has made the word correctly using the small letter cards forms the word using the large cards in the pocket chart or on the ledge, and the other learners check their word.

5. This process continues for other words, with the educator giving cues such as the following: "Add a letter to make the three-letter word *tin*. Many cans are made of tin." "Now change one letter and the word *tin* becomes *ten*." "Move the letters around in the word *ten* and make the word *net*." Before telling them the last word, the educator asks if anyone has figured out what word can be made with all the letters. If they don't know, the educator tells them the word, and they make it. This mystery word should tie in with the shared or common text in some way, perhaps in terms of theme.

6. Once all the words have been made, the educator places the word cards one at a time in the pocket chart or on the board ledge, and the learners say and spell them. The educator then chooses a word and invites the learners to find other words with the same pattern.

7. To maximize learning, the children use the patterns they have found to identify new words written by the teacher and to spell new words dictated by the teacher.

Source: Cunningham, P. M., & Allington, R. L. *Classrooms that work: They can all read and write, 5th ed.* (New York, NY: Longman). 2011.

There are two types of word-sorting activities. In a *closed sort*, the educator specifies the feature the learners are to use to find words (e.g., all words with the same vowel sound, all words with two syllables, all words with a soft *g*). In an *open sort*, the educator does not specify how words are to be grouped—instead, the educator invites the learners to group words so that they are all the same in some way. In both types of sorts, it is important that learners talk about words as they sort them; doing this helps them better understand generalizations. It is also important that the educator model the process several times so that learners understand what to do and why they are doing it.

Here are some basic approaches to sorting words:

- *Sort words by how they sound.* Learners begin with initial sounds and move to ending and middle sounds.

- *Sort words by how they look.* Learners sort words that have double letters, double vowels, double consonants, and other common patterns.

- *Sort words by connections between meaning units.* Learners sort words in relation to root words, inflected endings, prefixes, suffixes, compound words, synonyms, antonyms, and so on. (Pinnell & Fountas, 1998)

Word sorts can be done before or after reading. They are likely to be more helpful for learners in constructing meaning if the words have a semantic connection, that is, if they come from a shared text of some kind. Word sorts can also be a pre- or post-reading activity where the educator provides readers with words that have something in common semanti-cally. Readers can group the words to try to predict what a story might be about (pre-reading) or group according to themes the educator provides or the learners generate (post-reading). These types of word sorts can provide an excellent way for learners to activate prior knowledge about a topic and organize and demonstrate the knowledge they may have for a text. They are also a fantastic point of departure for conversations about many facets of words within the meaningful context of a text.

Word Parts

Structural analysis is the term used to refer to the identification of words using larger, more meaningful units than letters. It generally includes compounds, roots, affixes (e.g., *-ly*), and syllabication.

One way educators can help readers learn to use structural units to identify words is by demonstrating how they can organize difficult polysyllabic words into units. The educator selects a word from a shared text, writes the word in parts on the board (e.g., *but ter fly*), pronounces each part, blends the parts, and checks to ensure that the word makes sense in its context. The educator then encourages learners to employ a similar strategy when they encounter other unknown words while reading. For many learners, this is sufficient to help them develop an understanding of how structural analysis works and intuitive strategies for organizing unfamiliar words into parts. Precise syllabication is generally not necessary, since context is available to check possible pronunciations.

For those learners who require more explicit instruction, we recommend instructional strategies such as the following.

Compound Words

A common starting point to help learners who have difficulty analyzing units larger than letters is compound words. Analyzing these words into two known real words is a concrete task. It also takes advantage of words that learners already know how to identify. After a brief discussion of compound words, the educator gives learners a passage containing several compound words, with the compounds underlined. Learners are invited to read the passage silently and to prepare to talk about what they have read. When learners encounter difficult compound words, they or the educator can write them in units on the board and discuss them.

Syllabication

The goal of this instructional strategy is to invite learners to identify syllables by hearing and seeing places in words where structural breaks occur. This is a means toward identifying longer unknown words independently. Exact division in accordance with the dictionary is unnecessary until learners reach the point where they begin to hyphenate words at the end of lines in their writing. Classic advice for educators to give to readers is "Break the word down to the point where you can see how to say it, say it and move on" (Gallant, 1970, p. 93). Classroom Activity 7.2 presents steps for teaching syllabication.

Affixes and Inflectional Endings

We recommend focusing on specific inflectional endings (e.g., *-ed*, *-es*) or affixes (e.g., *pre-*, *-ness*, *-tion*) when they cause difficulty in reading and writing: systematically working through all affixes or inflectional endings is unnecessary. A resource for affixes and inflectional endings is the Nifty-Thrifty-Fifty list (Cunningham & Allington, 2007)—a list of 50 words that contain examples for all the common prefixes and suffixes as well as common spelling changes. The Nifty-Thrifty-Fifty list can be found online at http://teachers.net/4blocks/frazierNiftyThriftyFifty.pdf.

This section has focused on helping learners develop strategies for using cues within words to identify them. It is important that learners know why they are learning these strategies. Phonics instruction is particularly useful when employed in conjunction with other word identification strategies when readings are constructing meaning. The next section focuses on helping learners develop strategies for using cues beyond individual words.

CLASSROOM ACTIVITY 7.2

Steps for Teaching Syllabication

1. The educator begins by helping learners develop a concept of what syllables are in the words they hear. The educator pronounces a polysyllabic word taken from a shared text, accentuating the syllable breaks (*in for ma tion*). The educator and learners repeat the word together in syllables. Learners who have difficulty hearing syllables in words often benefit from
   ▷ clapping every time they hear or pronounce a syllable or
   ▷ putting their hand under their chin and feeling it move down for each syllable

The learners then repeat the words in syllables without the educator's aid. It is not important for the learners to show how many syllables are in a word; rather, they need to be able to pronounce words in syllables.

2. To relate the concept of oral syllable to written language, the educator presents familiar polysyllabic words to the learners with syllable boundaries shown (e.g., *re port; fun ny*). Since the learners already know how to identify these words, the focus is on syllables and how spoken syllables relate to the visual units. The learners then learn the following visual clues that can be used to analyze words into syllables:

   ▷ Prefixes and suffixes form separate syllables.

   ▷ Double consonants or two consonants together are divided, except in the case of blends and digraphs.

   ▷ A single consonant between two vowels often goes with the second vowel.

   ▷ The consonant before *le* usually goes with it.

   The educator selects one or two words to provide a visual reminder of each clue as it is introduced. He or she prints these words on a chart (with syllable divisions shown) and places them where learners can refer to them when a difficult word occurs in context. Eventually the learners have models for all four visual clues.

3. The educator invites the learners to silently read texts containing polysyllabic words, reminding them to organize words into syllables if they have difficulty identifying them. They might lightly underline words that cause them difficulty, and these can be discussed after they finish reading. The educator or learners write selected words on the board in syllables for identification and discussion.

4. Finally, learners use this strategy to identify polysyllabic words when reading independently. It is important that flexibility be stressed. If the word identified does not make sense, learners are encouraged to try it another way until they get a meaningful word.

PEDAGOGIES FOR SUPPORTING THE USE OF CONTEXTUAL CUES: PRAGMATIC, SEMANTIC, AND SYNTACTIC CUES

Context cues are one of several sources of information learners have available to deal with unfamiliar words when reading for meaning. This section provides examples of pedagogical strategies to help educators create learning opportunities for readers to develop their use of context cues so that they will be able to use them along with print-based information.

Cloze Procedure

In the cloze procedure, words are deleted from a written passage and readers fill in the blanks using their knowledge of language and the world, along with clues available from the context.

Readers identifying words in context during a family reading session at school

Material at a range of reading levels, including both **narrative** and informational texts, can be used to make cloze passages. For early readers or those experiencing difficulty, the educator initially deletes only a few words, selecting those that are highly predictable from the context. As readers begin to make more effective use of meaning and language cues to predict words, the educator deletes more words, including those that are less predictable. An easy way to make cloze activities is to cut up pieces of self-adhesive notes to cover selected words in texts. An example of a cloze passage created from a story in the magazine *Ranger Rick* is shown in Box 7.4. Using cloze passages is an instructional strategy that easily fits into the reading instruction cycle that moves from Read-Aloud to Independent Reading.

When introducing cloze activities, you might begin with a whole-class activity focused on material that everyone can see (e.g., a projected text or big book). The educator models the process by reading through the entire passage with the learners before they try to fill in the blanks. Once all learners have read through the passage, either of two basic approaches is taken. A learner volunteer reads the first sentence and supplies the missing word and other learners who responded differently read the sentence and provide their responses, or, the educator can organize the solving of the missing word through a think-pair-share, where learners work on their own, then share with the person beside them before finally sharing with the whole class. Educators can focus class discussion on questions such as these:

- Why did you choose this word?
- What do you know about the topic in this passage that helped you predict this word?
- What in the passage helped you to make this prediction?
- Is there a difference in the meaning when we choose your word rather than X's?
- Why did different people predict different words?

BOX 7.4

SAMPLE CLOZE PASSAGE

The first paragraph (not shown here) is left intact so learners will already have begun to make meaning by the time they get to the first blank. In that paragraph, Scarlett Fox and Ranger Rick Raccoon are in a picnic area near the ocean when they see a white shapeless form in the fog.

"Look, it's coming back!" Rick whispered in horror as the Thing came right toward them. Suddenly it ___ over their picnic basket and fell in a heap. Now Rick and Scarlett could see that the white thing was a ___ and out from under it crawled their friend Boomer Badger. He laughed gleefully between gulps of ___ as he tried to catch his breath.

Source: Reading passage excerpted from N. Steiner Mealy, "Adventures of Ranger Rick," *Ranger Rick*, Oct. 1994, p. 40.

Later, the educator shares cloze passages with learners to complete individually, and invites learners to explain, in small-group discussions, why they used particular words, again focusing on knowledge and text cues. The small-group discussions might then lead to large-group discussion of some of the more interesting or controversial items.

In cloze activities learners do not have to predict the author's exact words. As long as the predictions make sense and sound right in relation to the rest of the passage, they are acceptable. If the educator were to insist on exact replacements, the message sent would be that word-perfect reading is more important than constructing meaning; the task would be reduced to a guess-what-word-the author-used activity.

Again, it is important that learners understand the purpose of the cloze activities. Otherwise, they may not realize that they should use similar strategies to predict words when they come to unfamiliar words in other texts.

PEDAGOGIES TO SUPPORT THE USE OF ALL CUING SYSTEMS TOGETHER

Making meaning from text requires all the cuing systems. This section begins with a description of how one teacher provides instruction that helps readers use multiple cuing systems within the context of Shared Reading.

Masking

Masking can be used by educators to help children use semantic, syntactic, graphophonic, and pragmatic cues as well as structural units to problem-solve through unknown words in reading (Holdaway, 1979). Working with a text that everyone can see, the educator uses a strip of paper to mask text lines and slides it aside to gradually expose parts of words, complete words, and phrases. Learners read to the point where the next word is covered and predict what will come next. Then the educator uncovers the word so the learners can use print cues to check their predictions. The class discussion focuses on how predictions are made and where cues come from.

Minimal Cue Messages

A modification of the cloze procedure, minimal cue messages are set up to encourage integration of print and meaning cues and to aid spelling and word identification. Educators can develop minimal cue messages to focus on specific types of print cues (e.g., endings, vowel digraphs) when they identify this need.

The educator writes a message to the learners with some of the letters missing. Dashes are generally used to show how many letters are required. For example:

Tod_ _ is a _ery sp_cial d_ _. W_ are go_ _ _ to th_ m_seu_.

These messages work best when they are relevant to the learners and the language is natural and predictable. It is important that educators discuss with learners what cues they used in unlocking the minimal cue message. Discussion focuses on both meaning and print cues, for example, "I knew the word had to be *museum* because you told us yesterday that we were going to the museum today. I also saw that the word began with the letter *m*."

Initially the educator fills in the learners' predictions, but gradually the learners take over the writing. Learners who have been exposed to this technique often begin to write minimal cue messages to other learners or the educator.

Oral Reading

When learners are reading orally, the way the educator responds to their reading communicates a great deal about what cues and strategies the educator thinks are important. If an educator constantly says, "Sound it out" when the reader has difficulty, the reader may come to believe that reading equals sounding out. We recommend the following guidelines:

- If a reader pauses during reading, give readers ample wait time to use multiple cues to identify the word. Encourage the reader to predict a word that makes sense, sounds right, and checks out.

- If a reader makes a substitution while reading that makes sense, ignore the **miscue**. Research shows that even good readers do not read with 100 percent accuracy; instead, they make some meaningful slips because of the constructive nature of reading. Ignoring such miscues communicates to readers that making meaning is the essence of reading.

- If a reader self-corrects, reinforce this by commenting on the appropriateness of the correction, rather than focusing on the miscue.

- If a reader makes miscues that do not make sense, leave time for self-correction. If the reader does not self-correct, ask whether what he or she read sounded right and made sense. Focus discussion on the meaning the learner constructed from the reading.

- Creating and using a list of what readers can do when they come to unknown words can help readers problem-solve and grow as readers within the context of reading. See the list in Box 7.1.

For each instructional technique included in this chapter, we recommend having readers talk about the strategies they use. Through discussion, they develop both metacognitive awareness of strategies and control of their reading.

Next, we turn from a focus on what is on the page to the practice of constructing meaning from a more macro-perspective.

PEDAGOGIES TO SUPPORT COMPREHENDING

As we discuss throughout this text, we understand reading to be a transactional process (Rosenblatt, 1978) whereby readers construct meaning from text. Thus in relation to the question of how to help readers comprehend text, we, like Flurkey (2008), differentiate between *comprehension* and *comprehending*. The first, a noun, suggests something that has an end point, while the second, a verb, suggests a practice that is dynamic and ongoing—where when the context and reader change, so too might the meaning that is constructed. In the remainder of this chapter, we focus on helping readers develop strategies for comprehending by using what they know with what is on the page. We present an overview of the strategies and specific objectives for each strategy in Table 7.2.

Note two recommendations about the reading strategies we describe in this chapter. First, we advise that these strategies be applied across the curriculum as well as during language and literacy instruction time proper. Second, educators must discern when they need to teach strategies and when they might provide opportunities for readers to delve deeply into the big ideas generated from a transaction with texts and readers' responses to such readings (as per Chapter 12).

TABLE 7.2 **PEDAGOGICAL STRATEGIES FOR INTEGRATING KNOWLEDGE-BASED AND TEXT-BASED INFORMATION**

Pedagogy	Type of Text	Helps Readers
Directed reading–thinking activity	Narrative texts with strong plot lines	• Set purposes for reading narrative texts • Make and evaluate predictions during reading
KWL	Informational texts	• Set purposes for reading informational texts • Ask and answer questions during reading
Questioning the author	Narrative and informational texts	• Construct meaning during reading • Monitor meaning during reading • Understand character and plot • Fill in gaps in text • Summarize text information
Question–answer relationship	Narrative and informational texts	• Determine which information sources are required to answer specific questions • Answer text-based and knowledge-based questions
Reciprocal teaching	Informational texts	• Summarize text information • Ask questions • Clarify parts of texts that are confusing • Make predictions
Think-aloud	Narrative and informational texts	• Make predictions • Form visual images as they read • Link prior knowledge with text information • Monitor ongoing comprehension • Correct comprehension confusions
Semantic webs	Narrative and informational texts	• Activate knowledge before reading • Construct relationships among ideas • Relate text information to prior knowledge

Directed Reading–Thinking Activity

The directed reading–thinking activity (or DRTA) (Stauffer, 1975) is a long-standing pedagogical strategy for use with narrative or expository material and for helping readers develop critical thinking (Fischer, Brozo, Frey, & Ivey, 2007). Readers first predict what they will read and then check their predictions through subsequent reading. The technique helps readers actively seek information from the material they read. The educator acts as a catalyst to thought by asking such questions as these:

• What do you think?

• Why do you think so?

• How can you support it?

As readers predict what they will read, they rely on their knowledge, and as they check their predictions, they use cues in the text.

The DRTA is most appropriate for narrative material with a clearly defined plot that can easily be read in one sitting. Short mystery stories are ideal for this activity. The basic steps in the technique are outlined here and summarized in Figure 7.1.

1. On the basis of the title and illustration or first paragraph of a story, the educator invites learners to predict what will happen by asking questions:
   ❑ What do you think this story will be about?
   ❑ What do you think will happen in this story?
   ❑ Why do you think so?

   This last question is particularly important, because it gives readers an opportunity to refer to both their knowledge and the cues in the title, picture, or first paragraph.

   During the prediction process, the educator's role is not to evaluate predictions, but rather to activate thought by asking readers to defend their hypotheses. Educators can invite readers to whisper their predictions to a partner to ensure that all are engaging in the predicting process. The readers then share their predictions in the group context, and the educator writes them on the board for later reference. Once readers are able to read and write independently, they can fill in prediction charts and share them with partners.

FIGURE 7.1

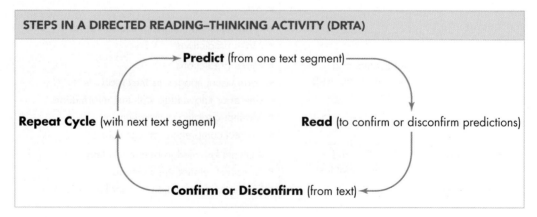

STEPS IN A DIRECTED READING–THINKING ACTIVITY (DRTA)

Predict (from one text segment)

Read (to confirm or disconfirm predictions)

Confirm or Disconfirm (from text)

Repeat Cycle (with next text segment)

2. Learners are invited to read silently to a certain point in the material to confirm or disprove their hypotheses. It is particularly effective to ask readers to pause at suspenseful points in the story.

3. After the readers have read to the designated point, they discuss which of their hypotheses were confirmed. The educator asks for what in the text provoked this prediction to support the plausibility and accuracy of the hypotheses.

   ❑ What do you think now?
   ❑ Find the part in the text to confirm or not confirm your prediction, that is, show why you think what you do and use information from the text to help explain that.

   Readers might read aloud a sentence or paragraph to provide this evidence. Again, this helps to focus attention on both text-based and knowledge-based information.

4. After readers have completed the three-step process of predict, read, and rationalize with one segment of the material, they go on to the next segment. The process continues until they have read the entire text. Throughout, the educator serves as a mentor to refine and deepen the reading–thinking process, but takes care not to evaluate the predictions. It is also useful to emphasize the importance of evaluating and finding proof in the text rather than deciding who is right or wrong.

It may be best to make no more than five stops in one reading in one sitting so as not to interrupt the readers' reading too frequently (Gillet & Temple, 1994). The DRTA is particularly helpful for readers who take a passive approach to reading and who appear to believe that the message is in the text. However, the technique will help these readers become active, purposeful readers only if they know why they are doing it and how they can use a similar strategy when they read independently. Indeed, recent research regarding reading comprehension and motivation and engagement (Guthrie & Klauda, 2014) suggests that the version of the DRTA we recommend must also include support for learners to feel competent (or what in Cambourne's terms involves learners sensing that a task is *doable*). The DRTA must also include opportunities for learners to make choices (fulfilling Cambourne's condition of *responsibility*) and promote the message that the reading is meaningful or purposeful (a prerequisite of Cambourne's *engagement*). The literature suggests the importance of collaboration in the DRTA as well as the need for learners to be scaffolded to make meaning of the text, by moving from demonstration through the independent use of meaning-making strategies as we suggest in Figure 7.1.

The KWL Technique

The KWL technique supports readers to deepen reading comprehension and encourage active learning when reading expository texts (Gammill, 2006). Based on the active thinking required to read for information (Ogle, 1986), the technique involves readers in following three basic steps:

1. They access what they *know*.
2. They decide what they *want* to learn.
3. They recall what they *learned* as a result of reading.

The readers use a group or individual chart to guide them through these steps. Box 7.5 shows the beginning of such a chart.

BOX 7.5

A KWL CHART		
Topic		
K	W	L
What I *Know*	What I *Want* to Find Out	What I *Learned*

Source: Adapted from D.M. Ogle, "KWL: A teaching model that develops active reading of expository text," *Reading Teacher, Issue 39* (6), 1986, p. 565.

1. *K: What I know.* The readers brainstorm information they know about the topic or a key concept in the material (e.g., wolves). The educator records what the learners brainstorm in a way that allows all to see. The goal of this brainstorming is to activate whatever knowledge the readers have that will help them construct meaning as they read. Ogle (1986) suggested deepening students' thinking by asking:
   ❑ Where did you learn that?
   ❑ Why do you think that?

   To avoid implying a transmission model of knowledge, educators can invite learners to differentiate between ideas they are sure about (everyone agrees) and those they are not so sure about (some agree).

   Educators may also invite learners to complete a second, optional part of this step—thinking about what general categories of information they are likely to encounter when they read. The readers consider the information they have brainstormed and group it into more general categories (e.g., what wolves eat, where they live).

2. *W: What I want to learn.* As the readers think about what they know on a topic and what categories of information might be included in what they read, questions emerge. After the group discussion, each reader records his or her own questions in the W column to focus attention during reading. The readers then read the material.

3. *L: What I learned.* After the readers finish reading, they write down in the L column what they learned from reading. The role of the educator is to invite readers to explain and rationalize their findings by the information in the text they used to complete this column.

If not all of the readers' questions are answered in the material, readers can generate a list of "Questions I Would Like Answered," and the educator can suggest further reading on the topic. Doing this ensures that the readers' desire to learn takes precedence over what the author has chosen to include.

Sometimes learners include information that is incorrect in the K component of the technique. To deal with this, Sampson (2002) extended the KWL technique by adding a confirmation component. Educators, for instance, can change the heading of the "K" column to "What We *Think* We Know." This heading provides support for brainstorming without giving the impression that the items listed are all accurate.

After the learners brainstorm what they think they know and what they want to know, they search for sources to either confirm information in the "What We Think We Know" column or answer questions in the "What We Want to Know" column. Columns labelled "Source" are inserted beside both the "What We Think We Know" and the "What We Learned" column, and sources (books, Internet addresses, magazines, electronic media) related to each item or question are listed as students locate them. A check mark is put beside a brainstormed item in the "What We Think We Know" column when students are able to confirm it with a minimum of two sources. Sampson's extension is appropriate to help upper elementary students learn to do research, check resources, and evaluate accuracy of information.

Questioning the Author

The Questioning the Author, or QtA, strategy can help more mature readers in particular construct meaning during reading of both expository and narrative texts. The strategy brings the author to the foreground, and readers learn to question the author with a "reviser's eye" (Beck, McKeown, Hamilton, & Kucan, 1997). The strategy also allows opportunities for constructive conversation, where readers can negotiate meaning with one another and with the text (Nichols, 2006).

Educators can begin planning a QtA by conducting a careful reading of the text they are asking the learners to read. As they read, educators identify the major ideas and potential challenges learners are likely to encounter. They then segment the text so they can ask learners to stop reading where the major ideas or challenges are located. Finally, educators develop queries, which are different from questions in that they are not used to assess comprehension after reading but rather to help students construct meaning *during* reading.

There are three types of queries: initiating, follow-up, and narrative.

1. *Initiating queries.* Such queries draw attention to major ideas and the fact that ideas come from the author and are communicated through a text.
   - ❑ What does it seem the author is trying to say here?
   - ❑ How does it seem the author is trying to say it?

2. *Follow-up queries.* Their role is to help learners construct meaning from the text, connect ideas previously learned with the text, and determine the effect of the author including certain information.
   - ❑ From what the author has said, what meaning do you make of the text here?
   - ❑ Does the author explain this clearly?
   - ❑ Does this make sense with what the author told us before?
   - ❑ Why do you think the author tells us this now?

3. *Narrative queries.* These queries deal with characters and plot.
   - ❑ From what the author has told us, what do you think this character is up to?
   - ❑ How does the author let you know that something has changed?

To implement QtA, educators can follow these steps:

1. *Introduction of QtA.* It is ideal that the classroom be arranged to facilitate discussion (e.g., a U shape), and the first time QtA is used, that educators tell learners they will be discussing a text in a new way. The educator talks about author fallibility, indicating that

sometimes ideas are not as clear as they might be. The job of the learners is to discern by the way the author has constructed the text what the author might have been trying to convey. The educator then demonstrates through a think-aloud the kind of thinking involved in constructing meaning from a text and that characterizes a QtA discussion. After the demonstration, learners are allowed to ask questions about what the educator was doing. They can discuss the meaning that each constructed from the text.

2. *QtA process.*
   - [ ] As learners read a text, the educator asks them to stop at the end of predetermined segments and poses queries to initiate discussion.
   - [ ] The learners contribute ideas that can be refined, challenged, or developed by other learners and the educator. The learners and educator work collaboratively to grapple with ideas and construct understanding.
   - [ ] The educator serves as an initiator, facilitator, guide, and responder. In addition to querying, the educator uses the first three "moves" listed below to make ideas students have offered in the discussion more productive and the next three to bring themselves into the interaction with learners more directly:
     - ◆ *marking:* paraphrasing or explicitly acknowledging an idea's importance
     - ◆ *turning back:* turning learners' attention back to the text or turning responsibility back to the learners for figuring out ideas
     - ◆ *revoicing:* rephrasing ideas learners are struggling with
     - ◆ *modelling:* demonstrating strategic processes learners can use to grapple with text
     - ◆ *annotating:* providing information to fill in gaps or add information
     - ◆ *recapping:* pulling information together or summarizing the major ideas learners have constructed to that point in the discussion. (Over time, learners assume greater responsibility for recapping.)

Question–Answer Relationship

The question–answer relationship (or QAR) was developed for enhancing readers' ability to answer questions when reading (Raphael, 1986). Research on the strategy has found that it is particularly helpful for reading expository text (Jones & Leahy, 2006) and when reading online where information might be available not just in one text, but "across multiple sources of information and web sites" (Raphael, George, Weber, & Nies, 2009, p. 461). The explicit teaching of how to respond to questions is also thought to be helpful in supporting CLD readers' practice of higher-order thinking and critical thinking (e.g., Fairbanks, Cooper, Masterson, & Webb, 2009). The technique is based on a taxonomy of questions:

- textually explicit (answer in the text)
- textually implicit (answer involves use of both the reader's knowledge and text)
- scriptally implicit (answer is in the reader's knowledge) (Pearson & Johnson, 1978)

This taxonomy reflects the notion we discussed earlier in the book, that certain types of texts can be more *open* or *closed.* Different types invite readers to have more or less leeway in constructing their own meaning of the text (Eco, 1979). Information texts, for example, are more closed than open. They tend to require readers to pay strict attention to the information on the page. As Rosenblatt (1978) put it, they invite more "efferent" types of readings. By contrast, narrative texts invite types of readings that are more "aesthetic" (Rosenblatt, 1978); they are therefore more open and tend to require readers to draw more heavily on their prior knowledge.

Educators can use this strategy within the reading cycle, first demonstrating the types of questions readers might ask themselves in looking to respond to questions when reading and leading to readers independently employing the strategies, perhaps with the use of a strategy reference card that lists the questions (Bender & Larkin, 2003). A QAR focuses on two major categories of information used for answering questions:

- *in the book* (text-based information)
- *in my head* (knowledge-based information)

Each of these categories is subdivided into two question types, as shown in Table 7.3.

When using the QAR strategy, educators first introduce learners to the two major categories—*in the book* and *in my head*—before having them deal with the four question types shown in Table 7.3. In the initial stages of instruction, the learners' answers to questions are less important than their being able to indicate which source of information is required. You might find the following suggested steps in teaching QARs helpful:

1. The educator begins by explaining to the learners that they are going to talk about questions and the best way to answer them. Some questions ask for information that the learners can easily find in the book. Other times, they won't find it there and will need to use what they know to answer the questions. Each question can be answered by figuring out where to get the information needed for the answer.

2. The educator asks specific questions, and discussion focuses on where the learners get information to answer each question.

3. The educator gives the learners short passages and questions for which both answers and QARs are provided for further discussion.

TABLE 7.3 **QUESTION–ANSWER RELATIONSHIPS**

In the Book	In My Head
Right There	Author and Me
The words in the question and in the answer are "right there" in the text in one place. I can find the words used to make up the question and look at the other words in that sentence to find the answer.	The answer is not in the text alone. I need to think about what I know and what the author tells me and fit it together.
Think and Search (Putting It Together)	On My Own
The answer is in the text, but I need to find it in more than one sentence or paragraph. The answer comes from more than one part of the text.	The answer is not in the text. I need to use what I already know about the topic.

Source: Adapted from T. Raphael, "Teaching question-answer relationships," *Reading Teacher*, Issue 39 (6) (1986), p. 519; W.N. Bender & M.J. Larkin, *Reading strategies for elementary students with learning difficulties*. Thousand Oaks, CA: Corwin. 2003.

4. The educator gives the learners short passages with questions and answers, and the learners indicate which QAR each belongs to.

5. The educator gives the learners passages and questions, and they identify both the QARs and the answers to the questions.

6. The learners then move to the two questions for in-the-book and in-my-head categories and eventually to longer passages.

7. The educator provides regular review and extends the use of QARs to content-area texts. (Raphael, 1986)

Note that the terms *in the book* and *in my head* can be confusing for some young readers. Some educators have found that substituting the terms *on the page* and *off the page* helps young readers gain a better understanding of the QARs involved in this instructional strategy.

Reciprocal Teaching

Reciprocal teaching, an idea developed by Palincsar (1986), is a dialogue between an educator and learners to jointly construct meaning as they read. Reciprocal teaching is usually reserved for more mature learners. It is designed to promote four comprehension strategies:

- summarizing a passage in a sentence
- asking one or two good questions about the passage
- clarifying parts that are confusing
- predicting what the next part will be about

The educator models these strategies using expository passages, and then the learners assume the role of educator, using segments of the text. There are four critical foundations necessary for capitalizing on this technique: **scaffolding**, thinking aloud, **metacognition**, and learning cooperatively (Oczkus, 2003). Here are some steps in using the technique:

1. *Demonstrating the strategy.* The educator demonstrates the four comprehension strategies while reading a paragraph from a content-area text. Each learner has a copy of the text.
   a. The educator summarizes the paragraph, and the learners decide whether the summary is accurate.
   b. The educator asks questions about the paragraph, and the learners tell whether the questions involve important information in the passage and then answer the questions.
   c. The educator identifies parts of the paragraph that could be confusing and, with the learners' help, clarifies these parts.
   d. The educator predicts what the next passage will be about, and the learners judge whether the prediction is logical.

2. *Learners assume role of teacher.* After the educator has demonstrated the strategy with several segments of text, he or she asks a learner to be the teacher. As the learner-teacher summarizes, asks questions, identifies confusing parts, and predicts what will come next, the adult educator provides feedback and coaches the learner through the strategies. The other learners are asked to judge the adequacy of the summary, importance of the

questions, and logic of the predictions, as well as to help clarify points and support the learner who is acting as educator. The following steps indicate how reciprocal teaching is used when learners assume the role of the educator:

a. The educator presents the learners with the title of the material they will be reading and asks them to use any background knowledge they have about the topic to predict what they will learn in the material. A learner-educator is then appointed for the first part of the material, and the group reads it.

b. The learner-educator asks a question that the other learners answer and then summarizes what has been read. The learners judge the accuracy of the summary and the importance of the questions.

c. There is a discussion about clarifications that the learner-educator and other learners made while reading, or about points that they think still need to be made.

d. The learner-educator and other learners make predictions about the next segment of the material, and a new learner-educator is appointed.

Throughout the period where the learner assumes the role of the educator, the adult educator provides the learners with feedback and instruction on how to use the four strategies more effectively. For example, the educator might help the learners to produce shorter summaries or to ask questions about main ideas as well as details.

At the end of a reciprocal teaching session (which can last half an hour), the educator may share a passage that learners have not read before and invite them to summarize it or answer a few substantial questions about it.

Think-Alouds

Think-alouds, as we describe them here, are used to help readers clarify their views of reading and their use of strategies. For all learners, but particularly for CLD learners, participating in think-alouds can let educators in on how the learners make meaning from text (Farrell, 2009). Making this invisible process visible can help educators assess what learners know and are able to do. At the same time, think-alouds allow the readers to become more aware of the strategies they are using and could be using (Israel & Massey, 2005). The strategy has also been found to promote self-efficacy, engagement, and comprehension in reading (Walker, 2005). You might consider structuring your think-alouds by using the following four steps (Davey, 1983)*:

1. *Provide an educator demonstration.* Verbalize your thoughts while reading orally to provide a demonstration. Select a short passage that contains points of difficulty, contradictions, ambiguity, or unknown words. As you read the passage aloud, learners follow silently, listening to how you think through the reading. The following are examples of points that can be made during reading to help learners acquire metacognitive awareness and control:

   ❑ *Make predictions.* Demonstrate to learners how to make predictions during reading. For example, you might say, "From the title, I predict that this story will be about

---

* B. Davey. "Think aloud—modeling the cognitive processes of reading comprehension." *Journal of Reading, Vol. 27*(1), 1983, pp. 44–47.

a boy who wanted to fly. In this next part, I think we'll find out why the boys got into a fight."

❏ *Describe the picture you're forming in your head from the information.* Demonstrate how to develop images during reading. For example, you might say, "I have a picture of this scene in my mind. The boy is walking through a dark alley and there are no other people around."

❏ *Share an analogy.* Link prior knowledge with new information in the text. In other words, you would take a "like a …" approach—"This is like a time we went to West Edmonton Mall and Sean got lost."

❏ *Verbalize a confusing point.* Demonstrate to learners how to monitor their ongoing comprehension. A typical comment might be "This just doesn't make sense" or "This is not what I thought would happen."

❏ *Demonstrate fix-up strategies.* Demonstrate to learners how to correct their comprehension confusions. You might say, "I'd better reread," "Maybe I'll read ahead to see if it gets clearer," "I'd better change my picture of the story," or "This is a new word to me—I'd better check context to figure it out."

2. *Enable practice with partners.* After several modelling experiences, learners work together with partners to practise think-alouds. The partners take turns reading and thinking aloud with short passages.

3. *Institute independent use.* Learners practise independently with the use of checklists such as the one in Box 7.6.

4. *Use in other subject areas.* Both model and provide opportunities for learners to try out and use think-alouds with content-area materials. Doing so helps readers learn when and why they should use certain strategies.

BOX 7.6

CHECKLISTS FOR THINK-ALOUDS				
	Not Very Much	A Little Bit	Much of the Time	All of the Time
Predicting				
Picturing				
"Like a …"				
Identifying problems				
Using fix-ups				

Source: B. Davey. "Think aloud—Modeling the cognitive processes of reading comprehension." *Journal of Reading, Vol. 27*(1), 1983, p. 46.

Semantic Webs

A **semantic web** is a visual representation of relationships among ideas. These graphic arrangements (sometimes also referred to as **semantic maps**) show the major ideas and relationships in texts (Sinatra, Stahl-Gemake, & Berg, 1984) or among word meanings. A web consists of nodes containing key words, with connecting lines between nodes. Webs can also help to create a visual representation of a reader's prior knowledge and the knowledge that is generated from transacting with a text (Irvin, Buehl, & Radcliffe, 2007). The theory that underlies this strategy is that "new knowledge is gained from finding new relationships in old knowledge and from relating new information to old information" (Schirmer, 2010, p. 120).

Educator Joyce Bodell uses prior- and post-knowledge webs to achieve a number of significant purposes. Before beginning a new unit or theme, Joyce writes the name of the topic or idea on the board and reads it aloud. She then invites the learners to take a minute or two to think of everything that they know about it and to record their ideas in a web on a piece of paper.

Joyce invites the learners to complete this activity individually for two reasons:

- First, she wants to know what level of understanding each learner is bringing to the unit of study. This informs her teaching and enables her to plan for content and lessons that will build on the learners' funds of knowledge most effectively.

- Second, the activity enables learners to recognize for themselves how much they already know and to raise questions about particular ideas, facts, or aspects that they are not sure about.

After the webs are finished, Joyce collects and reads them, and then stores them away until the learners have finished their unit. Joyce then does a whole-class brainstorming activity and records it on chart paper. She leaves this written record of the learners' combined knowledge posted in the classroom. The learners may refer back to it during whole-class lessons and discussions when they learn something that validates (or invalidates) what they thought they knew, or when they find an answer to a question that someone raised.

At the end of the unit, Joyce returns the webs to the learners and asks them to use a coloured pencil to add their new knowledge to their webs and to cross out ideas that didn't really belong. The result is a two-colour web that provides the learners with a powerful visual representation of all the learning they accomplished. Learners may ask for a second, larger piece of paper so that they can fit in all their new ideas. They glue the original web in the centre and branch out onto the larger sheet. If a whole-class web was done, Joyce revisits this with the entire group, and together they build on their combined prior knowledge, adding all the new information and understandings that they acquired. In the semantic web shown in Figure 7.2, the ideas within thick lines indicate the learners' prior knowledge about Canada. The rest of the ideas indicate what they learned.

Roz Stooke retelling a story with a flannel board

FIGURE 7.2

A SEMANTIC WEB OF CANADA

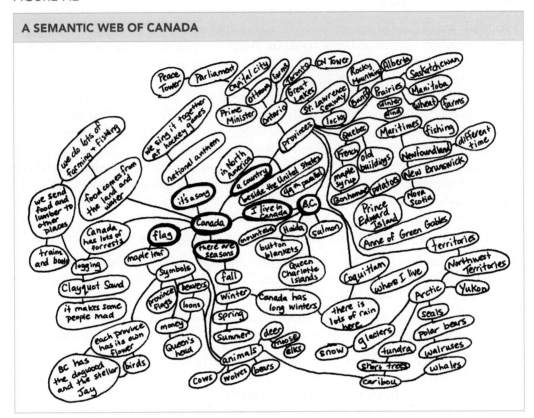

Source: Joyce Bodell Jackman. Reprinted with permission.

This second round of webbing offers the educator a valuable assessment/evaluation tool. It demonstrates the breadth and depth of understanding that each learner acquired. It can also be used to note what has not been learned, either by individuals or by most of the class. For example, if an important concept seems to be missing from most of the post-knowledge webs, it might indicate to the teacher that some additional instruction time needs to be spent on that area before the unit is drawn to a close.

There are many ways in which educators can help readers view and represent ideas from text. Particularly germane for younger children is using a classic flannel board. To illustrate, we have included a photograph of educator Roz Stooke using a flannel board with flannel pieces she has created to retell a story. Besides making it a whole- or small-group activity, Roz also likes to set up the flannel boards in centres and have the students re-create and expand upon the stories they have learned. Educators might also employ digital technology to view and represent what they and their learners have read. Interactive whiteboards, for instance, can be used for constructing, manipulating, and viewing semantic webs.

All the instructional strategies included in this section have the potential to help readers develop awareness and control over their reading. This potential is likely best achieved when educators demonstrate strategy use and the learners have opportunities to approximate and use strategies in large and small groups and individually, discuss what they are doing, and receive feedback. We also recommend inviting learners to evaluate which strategies work best for them in different contexts and for different purposes.

SELECTING INSTRUCTIONAL TECHNIQUES

The major focus of this chapter has been on pedagogies to foster the development of effective reading strategies. You may choose to teach these strategies within the context of the reading instruction cycle. Your professional discernment, which begins with you assessing your students, will guide you as to which strategies, at what time, and in what way should be taught. It is important to note that the strategies are appropriate for readers at all levels of reading proficiency. Table 7.4 summarizes common patterns of reading processing and identifies pedagogies that are appropriate to use with readers who display each pattern.

TABLE 7.4 **MATCHING READING PATTERNS AND PEDAGOGIES**

Type of Pattern	Recommended Pedagogies
• Reader word calls and needs to make more effective use of background knowledge along with text to construct meaning.	• Select pedagogical strategies to support comprehending.
• Reader relies too heavily on phonics knowledge to decode words and produces nonsense words when reading orally.	• Begin with strategies to support the use of contextual cues and move quickly to those for supporting the use of all cuing systems.
• Reader has few strategies for using cues within words and constructs a different meaning from text information or little meaning at all.	• Begin with strategies to support the use of graphophonic cues, and as soon as the reader demonstrates some of these strategies, move to those for the use of all cuing systems.
• Reader can decode short words but has difficulty with longer ones.	• Select word sorting or word parts strategies.
• Reader uses strategies for processing cues within words but constructs meaning that is not rationalized in text information.	• Select strategies for supporting comprehending with an emphasis on text-based information initially, and from strategies for the use of all cuing systems.
• Reader appears to think the meaning is in the text and can deal only with factual questions.	• Select strategies for supporting comprehending.

SUMMARY

Reading acquisition arises from a complex interaction of factors within the reader, the immediate circumstance, the school, and the broader community. The job of educators is therefore equally complex. Educators must exercise their professional decision making to learn about their students, what research has to say about learning to read and larger language processes, the context(s) in which they are teaching, and the various forms of instruction that fit their own teaching styles.

The instructional framework for reading we present in Chapters 6 and 7 is designed to align with the greater multiliteracies pedagogies framework that we introduced in Chapter 1. The purpose of the reading framework is to help learners produce readings that are in line with the characteristics of good readings. As listed in Chapter 5, aspects of good readings are establishing a purpose for reading; concentrating more on constructing meaning from texts than on identifying all the words in a text correctly; consistently orchestrating semantic, syntactic, pragmatic, and graphophonic cues; and having at hand a variety of strategies for when the text gets rough and knowing which strategies to use, depending on the situation. Chapter 7 examines focused pedagogical strategies to foster strategy development and implementation related to the cuing systems, structural analysis knowledge, and comprehending, with the goal being the construction of meaning.

SELECTED PROFESSIONAL RESOURCES

Algozzine, B., O'Shea, D. J., & Obiakor, F. E. (Eds.). (2009). *Culturally responsive literacy instruction*. Thousand Oaks, CA: Corwin Press.

Literature-based reading instruction, drawing on multimodal resources and using many of the pedagogical strategies discussed in this chapter, *Culturally Responsive Literacy Instruction* brings compatible sensibilities to *Constructing Meaning* to bear while specifically targeting CLD learners. A clear and handy resource.

Caldwell, J. S., & Leslie, L. (2013). *Intervention strategies to follow informal reading inventory assessment: So what do I do now?* (3rd ed.). Boston, MA: Pearson.

The subtitle of this book addresses the big question on educators' minds: I've assessed my students and now need to match my teaching to the results. How do I do that? As with all the resources offered in this section, *Intervention Strategies to Follow Informal Reading Inventory Assessment: So What Do I Do Now?* focuses on similar strategies to those presented in this chapter, which are designed to help learners understand the parts of language so as to help them to better make meaning of print.

Tovani, C. (Writer), & Hartman, L. (Producer & Director). (c. 2004). *Comprehending content: Reading across the curriculum, grades 6–12* [Videorecording]. Portland, ME : Stenhouse.

This suite of videos by Chris Tovani, educator and author of books like *I Read It, But I Don't Get It: Comprehension Strategies for Adolescent Readers* (2000), focuses on the teaching of reading comprehension. From the vantage of the classroom, the videos can illustrate a range of pedagogical strategies, from supporting readers to draw inferences to reflective practice.

CHAPTER EIGHT

Literacy Across the Curriculum

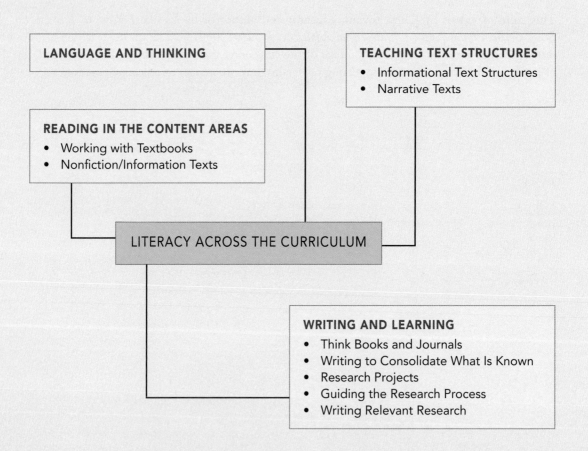

LANGUAGE AND THINKING

TEACHING TEXT STRUCTURES
- Informational Text Structures
- Narrative Texts

READING IN THE CONTENT AREAS
- Working with Textbooks
- Nonfiction/Information Texts

LITERACY ACROSS THE CURRICULUM

WRITING AND LEARNING
- Think Books and Journals
- Writing to Consolidate What Is Known
- Research Projects
- Guiding the Research Process
- Writing Relevant Research

JANET MCCONAGHY'S "LIFE-CYCLE" PROJECT

Grade 3 teacher and consultant Janet McConaghy has a wealth of experience in teaching literacy across the curriculum. She says, "Every teacher is a teacher of literacy across the curriculum and across modes. It's about knowing the language of the discipline in mathematics, science, social studies, and all the other elementary subject areas, as well as about how to use language and literacy to make sense of what we're learning. Literacy across the curriculum includes terms—that is, vocabulary—concepts, and content. It's about reading critically; thinking about what we are reading. It's knowing the difference between fact and opinion, and understanding how we are influenced by what we read, see, and hear, and how we make choices based on that information."

Janet McConaghy

Every spring in her grade 3 classroom Janet embarked on a science project on life cycles, in this case, metamorphosis. In Janet's words,

> The students each received one caterpillar in a small, lidded cup (also containing food). They were always excited by this project and they watched their caterpillars hour-by-hour, using every spare moment to check on them. They were intrigued by the changes that took place, and they took a very personal interest in their caterpillars' progress. They needed to know their caterpillar was safe and well cared for. Usually, one or two caterpillars didn't thrive so I kept a few "on reserve" so that no child was disappointed at the end of the project.
>
> The students watched in awe over a two-week period, as their caterpillar created a hook shape and attached itself to the lid of the container. By the next day the caterpillar was inside the chrysalis stage. It happened fast. At that point I transferred each chrysalis to a shoebox the learners had prepared. Leaves, grass, and twigs made a good home for their butterflies. I added a small cup of water and sugar mixture to the bottom of the box and then I covered the box securely in plastic wrap. After about seven or eight days the butterflies finally emerged. The whole process took about three weeks. We then released the butterflies into the bushes outside the school, but they would usually sit on the students' fingers before they flew away. It was a very special experience for those learners.
>
> The learners kept a journal and recorded the caterpillars' changes. They drew what the caterpillar and chrysalis looked like, their colouring and movement. They kept a time log, and they paid special attention to the sequence of events that took place. They also wrote expressively about the entire experience of metamorphosis from the perspective of their caterpillar. (One entry is shown in Box 8.1.) The learners spent a lot of time talking with me and with one another as they interpreted what was happening and checked the books I made available so they could hypothesize what would happen next. I had lots of books—both nonfiction and fiction. We read *Butterfly House* by Eve Bunting, and nonfiction books such as *Animal World: Butterflies* by Donna Bailey and *Butterflies* (Animal Ways series) by Gloria Schlaepfer. ☐

BOX 8.1

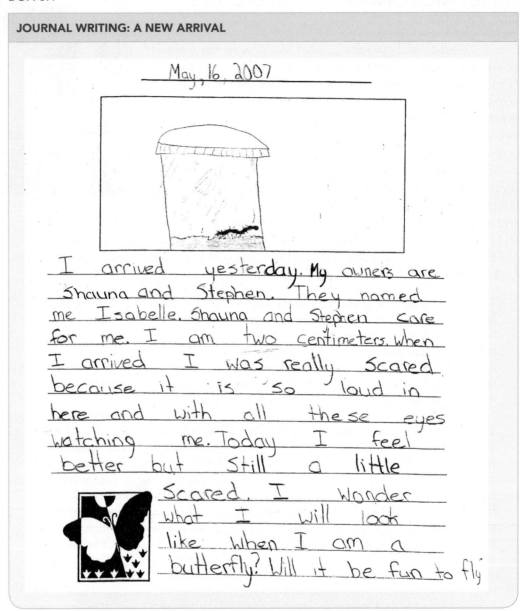

JOURNAL WRITING: A NEW ARRIVAL

May, 16, 2007

I arrived yesterday. My owners are Shauna and Stephen. They named me Isabelle. Shauna and Stephen care for me. I am two centimeters. When I arrived I was really scared because it is so loud in here and with all these eyes watching me. Today I feel better but still a little scared. I wonder what I will look like when I am a butterfly? Will it be fun to fly

LANGUAGE AND THINKING

Throughout this book we emphasize the important role language plays in learning and thinking. That is why we say that every teacher is a teacher of language and literacy, no matter the age of the learner or the content material taught. When learners write in a journal or talk with each other about what they have observed and learned, what they have read and what they know, they are reflecting upon their knowledge and understandings. Through this use of language, learners grapple with new ideas and often come to new realizations. We highlight the importance of learners working together, as they did in Janet's classroom, to collaboratively explore new knowledge, and to reinforce the importance of the individual expression of ideas and understandings in both written and spoken words.

Using Halliday's functions of language as a guide for developing language learning tasks (see Chapter 3 where we presented Julie Gellner's work with *Hana's Suitcase*), educators have been able to develop integrated, meaningful, purposeful, and cohesive learning experiences for learners. The guiding principles outlined in this chapter, as well as those presented in Chapters 3 and 13, can be applied to learning activities not only in language and literacy and in multiliteracies, but also in subject areas such as social studies, science, mathematics, music, and health.

Today, literacy is considered in a broad sense that includes text in many forms and media, such as fine arts, film, video, television, and digital media. Kress (2003) maintained that our use of language is increasingly governed by the screen, and learners need to understand language use within electronic media. Being literate no longer means being able to read printed texts that include incidental images, but instead consists of reading texts of all kinds with colour; in different fonts; on monitors, phones, and mobile computing devices; with sound, gesture, movement, and interactivity. This broad view of literacy makes it possible for learners to make meaning through a variety of representational modes.

Educators keep in mind the following tenets of language across the curriculum, or LAC as it is sometimes called:

- Language plays a central role in learning.
- Learners are actively engaged in meaning-making processes.
- Educators work as facilitators and guides.
- All six language arts strands are involved in active learning.
- Learners are encouraged to express and explore their understanding of concepts and the curriculum using their own language.

LAC requires teaching strategies that encourage active, constructivist meaning making. The heuristic (exploratory) function of language is especially important and should be used deliberately to investigate concepts and questions. The best way for individuals to learn language is to engage in its purposeful use where they are actively engaged in meaning making and are not expected to be passive recipients of another person's knowledge. Such learners predict, observe, discuss, read, problem-solve, and write about their learning.

Janet McConaghy maintains that the most important teaching strategy is modelling. Learners need to see how to do something and they need to be shown how. For example, the kinds of discussion educators engage in with learners set the tone and climate for the kind of learning that is expected in the classroom. To get learners thinking, Janet asks questions such as, "What surprised you in what we just read about [Peru]?"

Julie Gellner's Hana project (see Chapter 3), Janet McConaghy's Life-Cycles project, and Sandra Marianicz's grade 7 Historica project, which is presented later in this chapter, all provide examples of teaching that fit the criteria listed for LAC above. The learning activities that Julie, Janet, and Sandra designed were authentic and relevant to their learners' lives, and they met the objectives of the mandated curriculum. Later in this chapter we provide samples of student writing from a Restaurant project, which Julie's students initiated and which Julie supported and guided. It too is an example of an integrated, cross-curriculum project.

In a classroom that socially constructs literacy teaching, information is not simply processed in isolation, but is shared, built on with peers, and discussed as it relates to real people and real contexts, especially to learners' own lived worlds. This aspect of learning is one of the strongest reasons for individuals to engage in group projects, where they can study and work together, pooling information and helping one another to clarify and test out specific learnings. Through reading, writing, group interaction, and exploratory talk, learners question, make meanings more precise, and reinterpret past experience (which is why a personal story is often told to make a point). Interaction becomes crucially important as learners stretch their limits and move into areas in which they are uncertain, going beyond personal experience and specific situations. Recognizing the role of language in learning has caused educators to focus on processes such as collaboration, cooperation, and group work, and to value the many roles of language and literacy in the classroom.

Reading, writing, and representing can create new worlds for the learner, but it may be that writing, even more than speech, "not only reflects our knowing … but … also causes our knowing" (Dillon, 1985, p. 9). We usually write papers, reports, emails, blogs, tweets, and text messages for an intended external audience, and write poetry, stories, notes, diaries, logs, and so forth just for ourselves.

Journal writing is one way we attempt to recall and understand our experiences. Writing and then rereading our thoughts, pondering them, and revisiting them kindles personal and cognitive growth that we often cannot complete with other people. It is a task we have to accomplish alone. Writing encourages us to make our ideas separate from ourselves—putting our thoughts out there so we can examine them and hold on to them for future reference and ongoing reflection.

Language across the curriculum pertains to three levels of integration: the first is integrating the six language arts; the second is using language for learning; and the third is using learners' funds of knowledge to take learning from the classroom into the community and the broader world. In all three levels, learners and educators expand their knowledge and use of language at the same time as they use language in order to learn. In this chapter we provide examples of these three levels of integration, as well as present teaching scenarios that show how educators can include the community in their students' learning.

READING IN THE CONTENT AREAS

If we want learners to be critically aware, discuss ideas, and get excited about what they are learning, they need to read material that will both interest them and engage them in reading and writing for real-life purposes. Reading nonfiction or information texts can do just that. These texts connect language learning to content in specific subject areas, such as science, mathematics, physical education, and social studies, and they activate learners' interests and curiosity.

Readers bring a reservoir of both linguistic and life experiences to the reading event. They "transact" with the text (see Chapter 12) in order to make meaning and construct individual knowledge. In content-area reading, educators play an important role in helping learners to construct meaning: they carefully scaffold their background knowledge and language in order for learners to successfully access and navigate the text. The term **scaffolding** refers to the nature of the intervening role of the educator in assisting the learner to work through a problem or to complete a task. It is an enabling process. The emphasis is on social interaction, emphasizing the role of language as a mediating tool in constructing meaning.

Most of the reading we do in everyday life involves nonfiction or informational text. We read phone books, recipes, letters, bills, lists, directions, web pages, emails, blogs, and advertisements. Because many information books and grade-level textbooks can pose problems for young readers, it is even more important that educators provide and read aloud to their students many different forms of nonfiction text. They can thus help learners to become familiar with the structure of nonfiction writing and the textual features relevant to information text.

Working with Textbooks

Information texts are written in a number of forms, including biographies, brochures, directions, manuals, letters, newspapers, website content, and textbooks (see the section in Chapter 11 on information texts). One of the most commonly used information texts in schools is the grade-level, subject area textbook. A good textbook is written at the learners' reading level, but even a good textbook can be inappropriate for some of the learners in our culturally and linguistically diverse classrooms, where not all of them can read at the level presented in the text. Educators who use textbooks need to consider how the textbook supports individual learners' needs. We recommend that educators who use a textbook in a given subject area go through the book carefully with learners, reading some of the book to their learners and leaving parts for individuals to read themselves.

Here are some other pointers for educators working with a textbook:

- Always scaffold learners' reading so they know how to use the text.
- Talk with learners about what they have read in the book.
- Teach learners how to pick out the main idea and the details in any paragraph.
- Teach learners how to use the table of contents, the index, and the glossary.
- Engage learners in as many hands-on activities as possible, to make the contents of the textbook real to them.
- With younger students (grades 2 and 3), guide them to the appropriate page and paragraph when they are involved in a research project.
- Supplement a textbook with many other resources, including fiction and nonfiction trade books. For example, in early grades math, you could use *The Doorbell Rang* by Pat Hutchins.
- If there are questions in the book, take some time to work through what they mean with learners. Many math questions, for example, have more than one part, and young learners can find this confusing.
- Draw learners' attention to key words and phrases (e.g., *how many more, altogether, how many left*).

Nonfiction/Information Texts

There are many well-written and beautifully illustrated information books that address many topics, concepts, and practices in all subject areas. These texts are also written at many different levels and more readily meet the diverse needs of learners in today's classrooms. (See this book's Appendix for specific titles of information texts suitable for learners at each grade level.) During Independent Reading time, learners can be encouraged to choose information books if that is where their interests lie. Individual interest is a vital aspect of developing a reader's ability to comprehend text, especially nonfiction text.

Allington (2006) maintained that the diverse interests of readers can be met only if readers have a wide range of books to choose from. He recommended that every classroom have at least 500 books available, with these books split evenly between fiction and nonfiction. He did, however, state that no "specific quantity can serve all classrooms equally well" (p. 71). Some classrooms may need even more than 500 books. Educators can invite learners to talk about their inquiries and hobbies in order to cultivate their interest in reading nonfiction books.

Information texts can be used in K to 8 classrooms for a variety of purposes, including these:

- to provide a context out of which inquiry might grow (Julie Gellner's use of *Hana's Suitcase* in Chapter 3 is a good example of this.)
- to stimulate discussion (Anne Gordon's activity with "heart maps" in Chapter 3 demonstrates this.)
- to provide information (In Chapter 3, Julie Gellner's students used a nonfiction text to provide information about the Holocaust.)
- to provide examples of quality informational (expository) writing
- to teach young readers about the textual features of information books in general, for example, graphs, indexes, and diagrams (Janet McConaghy used information texts in her grade 3 Guided Reading sessions.)
- to teach specific strategies for reading information text, for example, cause and effect
- to retrieve information pertinent to their exploration, for example, clicking on hyperlinks and navigating the Internet, or skimming through headings in a book (as Sandra Marianicz's grade 7 students did in their Historica project, described later in this chapter)
- to increase readers' interest and appreciation of information texts, for example, Janet McConaghy's classroom collection of books on life cycles

TEACHING TEXT STRUCTURES

It is easier for learners to construct meaning when reading texts if they know how authors organize and relate ideas in various forms of text.

Informational Text Structures

Since parents generally don't select information texts to read aloud to their children, few learners come to school with an awareness of the structure of such texts. Informational **text structures** are the consistent features, such as subheadings and bold type that cue the reader during reading. Writers use these text structures so that readers can make meaning of a text more effectively. Educators know that if learners don't understand and make use of text structures, they will likely not be able to focus their reading, monitor their understandings, and effectively retrieve text for study purposes (Allen, 2004).

Two major types of text structures are "text organization" and "conventions of print." Text organization includes such things as titles, subheadings, paragraphs and sentences, diagrams, keys or legends, and photographs and illustrations. Conventions of print include bold type, italics, white space, and punctuation.

When educators introduce a new text structure to learners, they often point out the new feature. Sometimes, they will provide a chart in which learners can identify the specific structures used in the text (see Table 8.1). Learners are also asked to consider the writer's purpose in using these structures.

Janet McConaghy often taught informational text structures in grade 3 during her Guided Reading sessions. Working with a small group of four or five learners, she could introduce various aspects of text by talking about the cover, asking learners to predict the content, and posing a question for them to consider while they were reading. Janet sometimes asked her students to begin by reading together chorally; at other times they took turns. They then continued reading quietly to themselves. Janet sat next to one learner at a time and listened to that child read. She worked with learners individually, providing a follow-up task for each. Janet's students enjoyed reading aloud—and would vie for first spot. In Guided Reading, the texts are at the reader's instructional reading level and are therefore not too difficult for them. In addition, individuals feel safe with one another in the small group. They usually enjoy both the small-group environment and the interaction they have with their teacher.

The five most common types of organizational patterns for informational material are description, sequence, compare/contrast, cause–effect, and problem–solution. Description consists of a straightforward description of the item of focus, for example, a description of a building, a place, or a person's clothing. The sequence pattern, which presents information in chronological order, is commonly found in historical texts, recipes, directions for assembling furniture, and scientific experiments. Cause–effect and compare/contrast patterns appear in a wide range of content areas. We used the cause–effect pattern in Chapter 3 when we explained that an individual's language development can be suppressed in school if the child is not engaged in authentic conversations. We used the comparison/contrast pattern in Chapter 4 when we contrasted concepts of emergent literacy with early literacy. Problem–solution involves stating a problem or posing a question and then suggesting solutions or answers. An overview of these five organizational patterns for informational texts, including characteristics, signal words, and examples, is presented in Table 8.2.

TABLE 8.1 **INFORMATIONAL TEXT STRUCTURES**

Title of Book	
Heading	Example
Subheading	Example
Photograph	Page number
Boldfaced words	Example & page number
Italics	Example & page number
Caption	Page number
Diagram	Page number
Focus question	Page number
Glossary/Key words	Example

TABLE 8.2 **ORGANIZATIONAL PATTERNS FOR INFORMATIONAL TEXTS**

Pattern	Signal Words	Example Passage
Description		
Describes a topic by characteristics and features.	*consists of, characteristics are, for example,*	Canada is situated in the northern part of North America and is the world's second-largest country by total area. It consists of 9.98 million square kilometres and extends from the Atlantic to the Pacific and northward into the Arctic Ocean.
Sequence		
Lists events or items in order	*first, next, last, finally, then, how to, directions*	Here are the directions for making a peanut butter and jelly sandwich. First, take two pieces of bread. Then, put some peanut butter on one piece of bread. Next, spread some jelly on the other piece of bread. Finally, put the two pieces of bread together. Make sure you put the jelly next to the peanut butter!
Compare/Contrast		
Tells how people, places, things, and ideas are similar or different	*different, like, however, same, both, but*	Kate's runners are different from Jordan's. Kate's have a Velcro fastener and Jordan's have laces. However, both pairs of runners are the same colour.
Cause—Effect		
Links one or more causes with one or more effects	*because, why, so, reasons, therefore, as a result*	Because the water in Stoney River is highly acidic in the spring, most of the fish eggs will not hatch. As a result, the fish population in the river is declining. If acidity could be lowered, the fish might thrive again.
Problem–Solution/Question–Answer		
States a problem and suggests one or more solutions. Or asks a question and then answers it.	*problem is, difficulty, challenge, puzzle, dilemma, solution, answers*	Cold and snowy winters can pose problems for Canadians. One difficulty is the accumulation of plowed snow in "windrows" down the middle of the roads, creating poor visibility for drivers and pedestrians. The issue is often resolved by trucking away the piles of snow and dumping the snow in the countryside.

Narrative Texts

Learners often read nonfiction or information material for pure pleasure as well as to gain specific information. Many information books for readers today are especially appealing because they are written in the form of **narrative** (e.g., Laurence Anholt's *Stone Girl, Bone Girl: The Story of Mary Anning*). Through narrative nonfiction, readers are presented with information that is embedded into the story. Chapter 11 provides more information on narrative nonfiction, and the titles of many high-quality nonfiction materials appear in this book's Appendix.

As noted in Chapter 11, young children who have heard stories read or told to them on a regular basis learn what stories are like. It becomes relatively easy for them to construct meaning from narrative because it is the form with which they are most familiar. They learn to connect ideas as they read and to anticipate what comes next. Educators often find it helpful to create story maps collaboratively with their students. In the early grades, the maps might consist of a simple "Beginning," "Middle," and "End," with learners adding their own drawings to each of the three sections of the map. As we describe in Chapter 12, the map might literally be an invented map of where the story takes place or the route a character in the story may have travelled. More often, in a story map, learners, or learners and teacher together, plot the main events, the key points in the narrative. Students can draw scenes, objects, or characters from the story on their maps. A story map can serve as a useful summary of the story as well as a means of focusing attention on the main events—the turning points on which the story rests. A basic story map for W. D. Valgardson's short story "Garbage Creek" is shown in Box 8.2.

Story structures are attempts to delineate the basic elements of a well-formed story. Nearly all stories written in the Western tradition contain a plot, a setting, characters, a point of view,

BOX 8.2

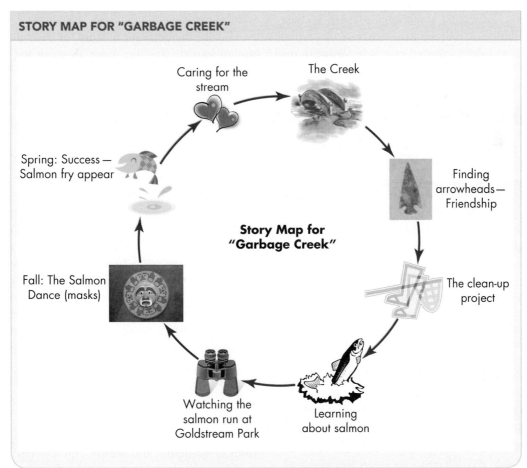

STORY MAP FOR "GARBAGE CREEK"

Caring for the stream

The Creek

Spring: Success — Salmon fry appear

Story Map for "Garbage Creek"

Finding arrowheads — Friendship

Fall: The Salmon Dance (masks)

The clean-up project

Watching the salmon run at Goldstream Park

Learning about salmon

and a theme. The *plot* is the sequence of events that characters go through in order to achieve a set of goals or resolve a problem. It is the tension or conflict in the plot that makes readers want to continue reading. The most basic plot structure is that of beginning, middle, and end (or introduction, development, and resolution). The *characters* are frequently the most important element of a story. Well-rounded, strong characters make the story come alive. The *setting* tells where and when the story takes place; it can vary from a general "once upon a time" backdrop to a specific location, time, and climate. *Points of view* are first-person (I), omniscient (seeing and knowing everything), limited omniscient (focused on the thoughts and view of one character, but told in the third person), and objective (confined to recounting events with no insight into any character's thoughts or actions). The *theme* is the underlying meaning of a story, such as friendship, acceptance of self, or overcoming fear.

Story structures and specific terms should never be taught for their own sake, but to help readers construct meaning. Rather than imposing this terminology on learners, it's more useful for them to generate their own terms, such as *who*, *where*, *what*, *why*, and *how*. The best way to build knowledge of story structure is to provide learners with experiences with stories on a regular basis. However, some explicit attention to story structure will benefit those learners with limited story experience and those who do not appear to reflect this knowledge in their storytelling or writing.

Educators sometimes prepare a chart or web, something like the one presented in Table 8.3, reflecting the structure of a typical story. Usually, the best type of story for charting is a problem-centred one. Educators can read a story to learners, and as a group they can analyze the story, completing a large copy of the chart. From there, the class can do activities, such as filling in a missing story element.

It is crucial that learners understand why they are being asked these questions and how the information they are asked to locate relates to the overall structure of the story. Unless learners are clear on the purpose for this activity, it will test their comprehension but not teach them how to construct meaning.

In narrative nonfiction, the specific setting, characters, and problem are usually essential to the presentation of information. In Anholt's biography *Stone Girl, Bone Girl: The Story of Mary Anning*, the characters and setting of the story in Lyme Regis, England, are crucial in presenting information about the first discovery of fossils. Criteria for evaluating the quality of nonfiction books are presented in Chapter 11.

In addition to accessing information books, students and adults increasingly search and retrieve information from the

TABLE 8.3 **STORY STRUCTURE CHART**

Setting
• Where did the story take place?
• When did the story take place?
• Who is the main character?
Events
Problem/Internal Conflict
• What is the problem faced by the main character?
• What does this character need?
• Why is this character in trouble?
• What conflict does the main character have?
• What does the character decide to do?
• How does the character feel about the problem?
Attempt(s) and Outcome(s)
• What did the character do about the problem?
• What happened to the character?
• What will the character do now?
Resolution/Reaction
• How did the character solve the problem?
• How did the character feel at the end?
• What would you do to solve the character's problem?

Internet and from other digital resources. Accessing and navigating these electronic resources successfully calls upon particular skills. In Chapter 13, which deals entirely with digital literacies, Kathy Hibbert addresses the use of multimodal forms of text in today's classrooms.

The next section of this chapter moves from reading in the content areas (across curriculum) to writing across the curriculum. Here, learners take field notes, write in learning logs or journals, make lists of the steps they must take in a project, diagram their observations and understandings, take photographs, and write about their thoughts and opinions on a wide range of topics. They do this to capture their thinking, to reflect on their learning, and to make new meaning from the material and ideas they are encountering in their lives.

WRITING AND LEARNING

In many classrooms, educators and learners write to explore topics, ideas, and subject-area content, as well as to demonstrate their understandings. Writing not only demonstrates what we have learned, but it also provides a powerful tool that can help us to make sense of our learning as we engage in it. When individuals write about new information and ideas—in addition to reading, talking, and listening—they usually learn and understand those ideas better, especially if those ideas are relevant to their own lives. When we write about things we are interested in, we can discover what we know and also what we don't know.

Educators are acutely aware of the importance of helping learners to make their thinking visible, to develop confidence in their ability to think, and to value their own thoughts. Thus, writing for learning is not restricted to particular forms or genres. Journals, notes, letters, diaries, scripts, commercials, brochures, invitations, reports, presentations, and posters all provide opportunities for learners to demonstrate the meanings that they have constructed. In addition, journals, think books, notebooks, and learning logs allow individuals to share their thinking with educators or with their peers in a supportive environment that encourages them to expand and explore their ideas further.

Young writers develop organizational skills *as they write*. They learn and organize their ideas through writing about the world they know. Once they are comfortable with doing that, they can begin to represent their understandings of the world more abstractly. What they need is opportunity.

Tanya's writing about seasons, Box 8.3, completed when she was in grade 1, was prompted by her winter vacation in the Caribbean. While on vacation, Tanya began to think about seasons across the world and the similarities and differences that exist between her own experiences in Canada and the experiences of people elsewhere. The piece suggests that although Tanya usually experiences winter as being very cold, she now understands that in some parts of the world even winter is warm. Thus educators encourage learners to record and examine their immediate experiential world before they move on to more formal and abstract writing.

As illustrated in the writing done for the Restaurant project in Julie Gellner's classroom (exhibited in Boxes 8.8 through 8.11), learners demonstrate their capacity for writing in a variety of genres to meet a range of purposes. Their writing demonstrates, in particular, their abilities to organize their thinking and record it on paper. Overall, it is clear that learners can write in many genres, and for many purposes, from the very beginning of schooling.

BOX 8.3

TANYA'S WRITING ABOUT SEASONS

About Seasons

It is almost spring. The weather changes to be warmer because
the season is changing to be spring.

After spring is summer which is very hot.

In some countries are even very hot during winter because they
are closer to the equator, especially Africa. Some of Africa is on
the equator. That's why giraffes live there.

After summer comes fall again. In the fall the leaves start to fall off
the trees and get ready for winter.

Winter has a lot of snowstorms and people wear a lot of clothes
because the weather is very cold and people think that if they
wear a little more clothing they will keep warmer.

Each season is different every year.

Think Books and Journals

We don't need to have fully formed ideas before we write. We often learn as we write. Writing to learn is an intrinsic part of the total learning process. It makes learning personally meaningful and creates what we might call "action knowledge" rather than "book knowledge" (Barnes, 1976). When learners of any age write in journals, they reflect, reshape, and redraft as they engage in learning; a cycle of learning we repeat throughout our lives.

The writing learners do as they learn—writing about emerging ideas, insights, thoughts, and reflections—represents part of their own picture of how the world works. Because that picture is constantly changing, the writing is not moving toward a finished product, but is part of the process of helping learners clarify their thinking and develop new understandings. Journal writing acts as a platform on which other ideas can be built. Learners can go back to the writing and re-examine the ideas captured there, reflect upon them, refine them, and build on them as they integrate new knowledge with the old.

Barnes (1976) wrote, "As pupils write they can—under certain circumstances—reshape their view of the world, and extend their ability to think rationally about it" (p. 76). James Britton (1982) referred to this same process as "shaping at the point of utterance." The advantage of learners writing about their ideas as they are processing them is that they are forced to focus on them to a far greater degree than when they simply talk about them. Talked-over ideas are often lost; we may be distracted and lose the thread of our thoughts. But writing provides a record of where we have journeyed in our thinking. It points to where we might travel next.

The writing in a journal is usually conversational in tone and it reads much like talk. Journal writers begin with what they know and build their understandings as they write. The journal entry in Box 8.4, written by Sarah in grade 3, provides an example of what is meant by writing to understand. Sarah clearly explains the concept of multiplication as repeated addition, demonstrating her learning by drawing six bookshelves each with seven shelves. Here, Sarah is actively making meaning from new learning.

In 2000, the U.S.-based National Council of Teachers of Mathematics published *Principles and Standards for School Mathematics*, in which "learning to communicate mathematically" was listed as a primary learning outcome for all students. This publication has strongly influenced Canadian provincial programs of study in mathematics. It suggests that instructional programs from pre-kindergarten through grade 12 should enable all learners to

- organize and consolidate their mathematical thinking through communication
- communicate their mathematical thinking coherently and clearly to peers, educators, and others
- use the language of mathematics to express mathematical ideas precisely

Communication and the exploration of ideas both orally and in writing have thus taken on a more prominent role in mathematics education: a significant move away from the transmission model of mathematics teaching prevalent for many years. Learners are urged to explore, problem-solve, and link learning to their own lives. They are increasingly challenged to validate their own mathematical ideas and abilities and to learn to communicate their mathematical thinking clearly, especially in writing.

BOX 8.4

SARAH'S MATH JOURNAL ENTRY

$6 \times 7 = 42$ feb 4, 200c

I did 6×7=42 I knew the awnser because I know how to count by 6's So you go. 6.12.18,24,30,36.42. You could count by 7's or 6's Ceunt how many digi'ts you wrote in the 6's or 7's if you did 6'S you needed to write by 6's like I did, Count how many digi'ts there are like if you did 7×6=42 you would take the second number and Plus it as many times as the first number, (how many shelfs all together?

I did 6 x 7 = 42. I knew the answer because I know how to count by 6's. So you go 6, 12, 18, 24, 30, 36, 42. You could count by 7's or 6's. Count how many digits you wrote in the 6's or 7's. If you did 6's you needed to write it like I did. Count how many digits there are. Like if you did 7 × 6 = 42, you would take the second number and plus it as many times as the first number. How many shelfs all together????

Many high-quality resource materials are available to help educators understand and implement writing in mathematics. *Math Is Language Too: Talking and Writing in the Mathematics Classroom* (Whitin & Whitin, 2000) is a U.S. joint publication of the National Council of Teachers of Mathematics and the National Council of Teachers of English. Marilyn Burns's publications are also highly recommended, including *Math and Literature (K–1), (Grades 2–3)* (2004a, 2004b). A further resource is *Classroom Discussions in Math: A Teacher's Guide for Using Talk Moves to Support the Common Core and More, Grades K–6* (Chapin, O'Connor, & Anderson, 2013). Online resources include *Think Literacy–Ontario* (2011), designed for learners in grades 7 to 9 (http://www.edu.gov.on.ca/eng/studentsuccess/thinkliteracy).

Journals can provide a safe and challenging environment for students to display what they know (as Sarah did in Box 8.4); and for them to come to terms with what they do *not* know. For example, learners can be encouraged to leave spaces in their journals so their teacher can provide feedback or answer a question. Learners can draw a line on which the teacher can respond. For example, in her grade 2 math journal, Julia wrote: "I get up at 7:30. What time do you come to school? ____." A further journal entry from grade 2 is shown in Box 8.5.

Through their journals, learners can make connections with their prior learning and consolidate it into a more holistic understanding of the world. For example, Billy noticed that words used in one context could be used in a completely different context. He related his new

BOX 8.5

GRADE 2 MATH JOURNAL PAGE

We learned about time. It was fun. We learned 60 minutes is 1 hour and 30 minutes is a half hour. 24 hours is 1 day. I like time very much. Math is fun. Did you know time is math?

knowledge of temperature and thermometers with prior knowledge in science, and observed a rule of capitalization:

> Today we learned about temperature and Celsius and Mr. Celsius. A thermometer is something that tells the temperature. Do you know what the grey stuff is in a thermometer? It is called mercury. There is a planet named Mercury. The grey stuff in a thermometer is spelled with a smaller m and the planet is spelled with a big M. Mr. Celsius is now dead. He was called Mr. Celsius! He invented the thermometer! He named the thermometer after him.

Through their **expressive writing** learners' communication skills improve, leading gradually to greater facility with **expository writing**. Learners need to feel their way through the concrete world of the known before they can begin to represent their understandings abstractly. Learning journals provide one vehicle through which they can do this.

Journals are not only beneficial learning experiences for learners, but are powerful vehicles that encourage educators to examine their teaching and knowledge base. As educators read their students' journals, they learn much about how they can improve their own practice. They might reflect on

- the complex and sophisticated questions learners ask
- their own knowledge and understandings of various subject areas and how these can be improved
- the need for extremely clear and explicit teaching
- the effectiveness of journals as informal assessment tools
- the clues learners' writing provides as to what they understand and what they do not understand
- how all this information can be used to adjust and adapt specific teaching content, methodology, and groupings of learners in the classroom

When educators use journals in their classrooms, they

- read the journals regularly to see how they might adapt their instruction and further facilitate individuals' learning
- teach learners what constitutes an appropriate entry
- model entries on the overhead projector to help learners become comfortable with a journal (not to tell them what to say, but to demonstrate a variety of ways in which they might write about their learning)

Sandra Marianicz

Writing to Consolidate What Is Known

Many forms of writing serve to consolidate what a person knows, including journal writing and writing in notebooks. As we drafted the manuscript for this book, we rethought our understandings, worked through difficult ideas, consolidated what we knew about teaching and learning in language arts, and raised more questions. The writing of this book is part of our own continuing search for understanding.

Writing that consolidates what a person knows meets the representational function of language that Halliday (1969) identified. It is a reflection of what the writer knows at the time of writing, and it acts as a kind of summary of the learning journey. Box 8.4 demonstrates Sarah's consolidated knowledge of multiplication.

Box 8.6 demonstrates Adam's consolidated knowledge of the Second World War and the role of Mona Parsons in the resistance movement. Teacher Sandra Marianicz understands that learning and knowledge can be represented in many forms. Adam's grade 7 Historica project is presented as a radio drama, a form suitable to both the historical time period and also to Adam's creative interests. Before reading and audio-recording the radio drama, Adam prepared the script well, marking it in red where it needed pause or emphasis. The result was a practised reading that intrigued and entertained his classmates.

BOX 8.6

EXCERPTS FROM A GRADE 7 RADIO DRAMA

The Rest of the Story with Adam Corvette

"This is *The Rest of the Story* with your host Adam Corvette. Good afternoon. Today we take a look at one of Canada's Heroes. WW II forced many ordinary Canadians to do many extraordinary things. Who would have suspected that a young woman who grew up in a peaceful little town on the coast of Nova Scotia would play a huge role in the resistance movement. Today's story is about courage, perseverance, determination to do the right thing and bravery. Today's story is about Mona Parsons! Mona was a nurse, an actress and *a resistance fighter*.

"Mona was born on February 17, 1901 in Middleton, Nova Scotia. She had an upbringing like most youngsters in the early 1900's. Her family worked hard and her dad was a business man who owned and ran a home furnishing business. He ensured that Mona was well educated and understood the family business. But Mona knew at a very young age that she did not want to take up the family business as she wanted to become an actress. This would later prove to be an essential skill for Mona's 'life'. She eventually convinced her father that she needed to move to New York to become the actress she always dreamed of being.

...

"When WW II broke out, Mona and her husband Willem were increasingly concerned with the treatment of their fellow citizens in Amsterdam. They knew they could not sit back and do nothing. This was not the way Mona was raised. Willem and Mona and a few close friends started a resistance group. Together they intended to help downed Allied Airmen, both British and Canadian at this time. Mona and Willem decided to build a small apartment in the attic of their home as a base for their operations. They understood that they were taking a huge risk to their own personal safety when they sheltered and helped these soldiers. As a resistance organization they were able to help dozens of British soldiers.

"Their resistance did not last long at all. The resistance had been infiltrated by a Nazi Informer. Knowing they were 'found out' Willem decided to go underground assuming that Mona would be protected because of her gender. Mona prepared for her visit by the Germans and offered them cigars and brandy. It was all no good and she ended up in jail! Mona was the only woman to be sentenced to jail by the German army! This is where her acting skills became a matter of life or death! …"

Understanding can be consolidated at key junctures in the learning process, not only as a final activity. Learners record what they have learned, with specific reference to content and processes (such as measuring or estimating in mathematics). After teaching a grade 6 unit on scale and its uses, one teacher asked her students to write a consolidating entry about scale in their math journals. Here is a selection of the class's entries:

Scale is used for maps, to tell you how far it is from one place to another. Scale tells you the distance and how many kilometres or miles it takes to get from one place to another.

Scale is anything that you can measure in linear instead of drawing the real size of whatever it is! You have to do this because if you don't it could take the rest of your life to draw it the real size!

I know scale a little better now because I know some questions I didn't know before like who does scaling? People who build houses and cartographers. Now I know that you can measure scale with anything. What do you measure money and time with?

The specialized vocabulary of any discipline becomes much more important and relevant to learners when they understand the concept embedded in the language. The talk that takes place when learners write in a journal, as well as the actual writing, provides a forum for sharing and clarifying ideas that leads to understanding the concept and to internalizing the specialized vocabulary. Box 8.7 presents a science notebook entry from Thomas in grade 1. Here, Thomas was consolidating his learning.

This kind of writing reveals the range of meanings learners create and the ways in which they are able to apply that knowledge to the world. The writing provides excellent feedback for educators and also enables learners to discover for themselves what they know and how well they know it.

Research Projects

In adult life, research reports are frequently written in engineering, law, medicine, social services, business, and academia, to name just a few professions. Reports in these contexts are always predicated on a question or line of inquiry. Researchers gather data to help answer questions.

BOX 8.7

THOMAS'S WRITING IN SCIENCE

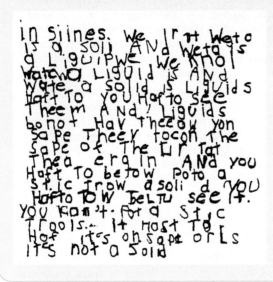

In science we learned what is a solid and what is a liquid. We know what a liquid is and what a solid is. Liquids have to, you have to see them and liquids do not have their own shape. They take on the shape of the jar that they are in and you have to be able to put a stick through. A solid you have to be able to see it. You can't put a stick through it. It has to have its own shape or it's not a solid.

Source: A. Ozdoba, "Writing to Learn: Science Journals in Year One," M.Ed thesis. (Edmonton, AB: University of Alberta) p. 100, 1992.

Research reports in school contexts should develop in a similar way. Learners need to be clear about the purpose of their research project, and the projects should be based on clear and thoughtful questions. The most interesting and most motivating questions are those developed by learners themselves. Ideally, learners and teachers work together to formulate the research questions, and this is usually the first step in any research endeavour. When learners conduct research in school, it is essential that they have a genuine interest in the topic, and be motivated to discover answers to their questions. Educators play a key role in establishing interest and motivation, in guiding learners to formulate their questions, and in helping them to learn relevant research strategies.

Teacher Julie Gellner supported learners in her grade 4/5 classroom as they designed a Restaurant project in Health Education. (In Chapter 4, we described how she supported her students' research into the Second World War and the Holocaust in preparation for a Remembrance Day assembly.) The Restaurant project grew out of learners' interest in media reports of unsanitary conditions in some city restaurants. The students conducted extensive research into restaurants and organized a "restaurant evening" at their school as a culminating experience—not all research must end with a formal written report. The total project lasted for about three months.

Julie strove to maintain an atmosphere in which learners' interests were piqued and their thinking and writing were challenged. She created a community of learners who supported one another in asking and answering questions, and who respected the ideas of both peers and teacher.

The artifacts gathered by the children constituted an audit trail that represented their thinking. These photographs, posters, newspaper cuttings, magazine advertisements, and printouts from the web were displayed in the classroom. The display of artifacts allowed the children to revisit their learning and to rethink their ideas over the course of the project.

As they conducted their research project, the students visited a number of restaurants and markets, and invited guest speakers, including a local health inspector, to their classroom. They made field notes about how the restaurants were run, wrote reviews of the restaurants they visited, and explored the jobs people hold in restaurants, and how restaurants plan and organize for their patrons. Box 8.8 shows how Kennedy organized his field notes after he visited a local organic market and café.

BOX 8.8

KENNEDY'S FIELD NOTES

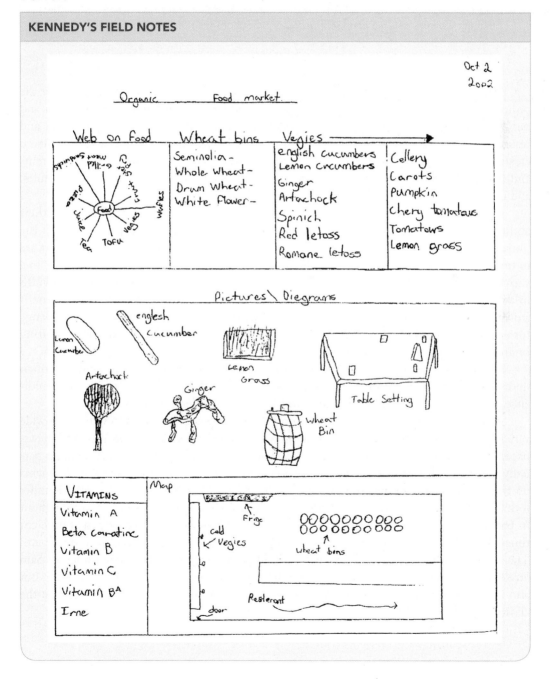

BOX 8.9

"WHAT CAN I GET YOU?": WILL'S JOB DESCRIPTION

A waitress is someone who serves people and asks for their orders. They use a notepad and a pen. Now the waitress brings their order to the kitchen. When they are done ordering the people have to wait for a little bit before they get their food. Finally, the waitress comes back with the food on the tray. She gives people their food. After the people are done eating the waitress takes the dirty dishes, and then goes and gets the bill. After that the waitress gets the change if necessary. So that's what the waitress does.

Each person in the class applied for a job in the restaurant. Will's job description for the position of waitress is presented in Box 8.9. The students created letters of application and personal résumés, which they sent to the manager (Julie). Allisa's letter of application and résumé are presented in Box 8.10. Learners determined which dishes would be on the menu, created and wrote menus for the evening (shown in Box 8.11), designed invitations for parents and friends, made placemats, and organized the various jobs, timetables, cooking schedules, and cleanup.

To write about their research in a school context, learners need to develop their abilities with expository writing. Children's early writing is usually expressive, as in the journal entries we presented earlier in this chapter, but as they pursue questions that are of interest and relevance to them, they learn to organize their ideas and begin to write in a variety of forms. This was evident in Tanya's piece, "About Seasons," in Box 8.3, and also in the writing completed during Julie's Restaurant project. However, learners still benefit from instruction in expository writing, as well as in the research process. The challenge for educators is to help learners make the transition from expressive to expository writing in an interesting and enjoyable way.

For many learners, the only audience for expository prose is an educator (and that often means the teacher as evaluator), but writing in school can be created for a much wider audience, both inside school and in the community, as Julie's students showed.

Sandra Marianicz also provides opportunities for her grade 7 learners to write for a wide variety of audiences. Box 8.12 presents an excerpt from the text of Jennifer's grade 7 newspaper "The Northern Gazette," which she created as part of a Historica project. Jennifer partially documents her experiences as a researcher in this newspaper article, and she comments on the experience of visiting a university archive or "special collection" in that role. Jennifer formatted the article in columns and added photographs and quotations in boxes throughout its pages. She also created some journal entries that Sam Steele might have written at different times throughout his career and put these, together with some photographs, in an album. The newspaper and album accompanied a trifold poster display on the same topic: Sir Sam Steele and his role in Canadian history. The intended audience was not only the teacher, but also Jennifer's peers in the classroom and the friends and family members who would visit the classroom to view the projects.

BOX 8.10

ALLISA'S LETTER OF APPLICATION AND RÉSUMÉ

Allisa Garden
306 Dalrymple Road
Winnipeg, MB
M9X 5P2
325-4709

Ms. Gellner, Manager
Trail End Café
Dalrymple Community School
Winnipeg, MB

Dear Ms. Gellner:

My name is Allisa Garden and I am a very talented chef. I always do my best and try really hard. So right now I am trying to get a job at the Trail End Café. I would love to be a dessert chef, a salad chef, or a bar tender.

I think I would be the best person for the dessert chef job, because I went to a mini-chef camp this summer for two weeks. There I made lots of good treats. My family and friends really enjoyed the pleasant treats that I made.

I hope you will consider me for the dessert chef position. I have lots of enthusiasm and you will not regret hiring me. I hope to meet you soon and I think it would be a great pleasure to work for you.

Sincerely yours,

Allisa Garden

Allisa Garden

Résumé

Allisa Garden
306 Dalrymple Road
Winnipeg, Manitoba
M9X 5P2
325-4709

Education

September 2014
Dalrymple Community School
Winnipeg, Manitoba
Grade 5

Experience and Extracurricular Activities

I cook with grandmother often
I help my mother make supper
I took a cooking camp at Maple College for two weeks this summer
I like swimming, rock climbing, dancing, and skiing

Special Skills

I have good people skills
I am very creative
I love to cook
I like to experiment with recipes
I wash my hands frequently

Name of References

Nora Garden
Mom
Phone: 325-4709 or 562-3798
Malcolm Garden
Dad
Phone: 325-4709 or 562-5103
Alison Sung
Best friend
Phone: 896-3568

Learners have a much greater chance of successfully completing a research project when educators provide specific guidance for them. Effective educators teach learners how to

- use library resources
- use the table of contents and index of a book
- locate information in books, encyclopedias, and magazines
- interpret information from pictures, charts, graphs, videotapes, and audiotapes
- use the Internet effectively
- paraphrase what they read, make notes, and put what they read into their own words
- translate information into visual form on charts, graphs, and diagrams
- conduct interviews
- search archives
- organize their findings into a report
- where appropriate, accurately record and reference the sources they have used

These strategies are best taught in the context of the research process, presenting the various strategies at times when learners need them. As learners move into grades 6 and 7, educators begin to teach referencing skills. The concept of "intellectual property" is important as learners begin to pull information together from different sources and paraphrase or synthesize material into their research reports. Learning how to reference sources and how to quote from material accessed in libraries or online is a skill learners will need throughout their formal education. Educators have a responsibility to teach learners how to track, record, and accurately reference the resources they use.

Educators may begin by helping students to develop a report or multimodal presentation collaboratively. Young children learn to conduct library research and write exposition

BOX 8.11

MENU FOR THE TRAIL END CAFÉ			

Trail End Café

Appealing appetizers		Delicious desserts	
Veggies and dip	$2.50	Variety of squares, cookies,	
Chips and salsa	$3.00	tarts, and cakes	$2.00
Hummus and pita bread	$3.00	**Desirable drinks**	
Scrumptious salads		Italian soda	$2.25
Caesar salad	$3.00	Shirley temple	$2.25
Tossed salad with vinaigrette		Fruit punch	$2.25
dressing	$3.00	Cherry cola	$2.25
Exotic entrée		**Complimentary**	
Veggie bagel melt	$4.00	Coffee and tea	

BOX 8.12

HISTORICA PROJECT: SAM STEELE

The Forrest Gump of Canadian History

Sir Sam Steele is an icon in the history of western Canada. He participated in many historical events that formed Canada. As a North West Mounted Policeman and military leader he participated in many of the influential events and crusades in the West, the far North, and abroad that assisted Canada and was a major factor in the military history of the British Empire. Steele was also a keen observer of his surroundings, making laws that were reasonable and just.

The Steele Collection contains a great number of primary sources for research that helps illuminate and enrich the Canadian historical background. In addition to uniforms, medals, and military accessories, the Collection includes thousands of pages of his letters, manuscript memoirs, pocket-diaries, standing order books, official reports, scrapbooks, printed papers, and photographs that document his career as a militiaman, Mounted Policeman, and soldier.

"Sam Steele was the Forrest Gump of Canadian History."
—Lynn McPherson

The University of Alberta Bruce Peel Special Collections Library houses the Sir Sam Steele Collection and on Friday February 11th, I was able to see the Collection with my own eyes.

Lynn McPherson is the amazing archivist that is in charge of the Collection held at the U of A. At 2:30pm we entered the Bruce Peel Library and met with her. When she showed some of the papers, letters, and photographs, I was truly astounded.

The Sam Steele Collection is a massive collection and surprisingly the entire collection was kept together by Sam and Marie's middle child, Gertrude. Gertrude was the only child of the Steele family to marry and she kept the total collection intact.

or develop presentations more effectively when educators and learners find information together, working as a class, than if they work independently. The more learners are shown *how* to do research and the more they are actively *involved* in doing it, the more effectively they will learn.

Guiding the Research Process

Many educators find the Research Quest model (British Columbia Teacher-Librarians' Association, 2001) a useful tool in guiding learners through the research process.

Historica Project: Sam Steele

Available online, this one-page guide encompasses five areas: focus (What is my research challenge/purpose?); find and filter (What are the most appropriate resources?); work with the information (read, view, listen); communicate (prepare and share findings:); and reflect (What did I learn?).

Educators in grades 1 to 4 sometimes provide learners with an outline, matrix, or web to help them organize information once they have located it. These devices help learners make decisions about what information is relevant and what is not. These outlines, matrices, or webs are graphic organizers that help learners make sense of their research. Graphic organizers provide a sense of direction for those who need some structure and guidance in putting together a report or presentation. An example of one graphic organizer—a data-collection chart—is shown in Figure 8.1. Another form of graphic organizer is that used at the beginning of each chapter in this textbook to help the reader see the "big picture" as well as see how the sections of the chapter relate to one another. Kennedy's graphic organizer (shown in Box 8.8) was self-designed as he sought to make sense of the field notes he made at the market.

In one grade 3 class, when focusing on the concept of adaptation in animals, the guiding question for the research was "How do animals survive?" A class case study was created around the polar bear. Learners located resources and found relevant information that helped them answer their question. Their reading was conducted from a specific perspective. Information was noted through words, phrases, charts, diagrams, and so forth as they collected their data. The following headings emerged as learners compiled their findings:

• physical appearance
• food

FIGURE 8.1

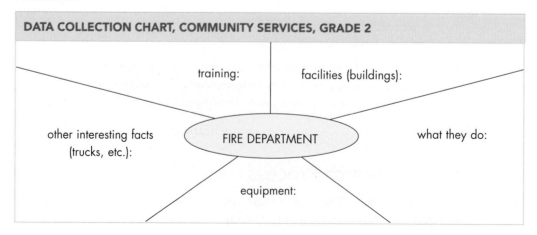

- enemies
- migratory patterns
- conclusions (how the research answered the question)

These headings were not meant to dictate how the research findings were to be presented, but instead provided structures that guided the learners' developing sense of organization.

Today, research reports often consist of interactive, visual, or imaginative multimodal presentations, as noted in Chapter 13. They provide opportunities for learners to represent their learning using a range of formats and media. Learners also develop new ideas for research reports from reading nonfiction books. Many nonfiction materials, such as *Starry Messenger* by Peter Sis, employ formats and strategies that are compelling and intriguing. Expository prose can be full of the enthusiasm and excitement we feel when we discover something new and want to share it with a wider audience, as was evident in Box 8.6, which features the excerpt from Adam's radio drama.

Writing Relevant Research

Before researchers begin the process of writing/creating a research report/presentation, they try to understand their subject as much as possible so that they can communicate their findings clearly and interestingly.

Jessie Haché, a grade 4 teacher in Lunenburg County, Nova Scotia, supported her learners in understanding "What makes this community unique?" In their data collection, learners interviewed citizens of the community and businesspeople, and searched the public archives in Halifax in order to answer their guiding question. Learners worked collaboratively as they interviewed, video-recorded, discussed, listened, made notes, read, and wrote as part of the project. Learners received guidance and structure, but at the same time they had opportunities to make individual contributions and pursue areas of research that were meaningful to them.

Once the research was completed, they wrote and presented their findings in books that were printed by a local company and sold by the school. Stories, drawings, biographies, history, lists, poems, recipes, directions for games, minutes from meetings, maps, and posters were all included. Every student had one piece of work included in the book. One excerpt from *History of Crousetown* is shown in Box 8.13.

The final stage of the project was an evening presentation in the community hall to which everyone in the community was invited. The students prepared an evening of entertainment based on the project (readings, drama, and an old-fashioned singsong) and then served food prepared by their parents. The importance of this celebration for the community, and for the students, was lasting and significant.

The purpose of the project was clear to the learners from the very beginning and through their involvement in this personally and socially relevant project, they developed their ability to write effective exposition. In addition, they learned to write for a much broader audience than their immediate families, teachers, and peers.

Contemporary learners are particularly visual in their learning. They watch television and movies, play video games, and use the Internet more than any young learners

BOX 8.13

STORES IN CROUSETOWN

The first store in Crousetown was owned by Beechum Crouse. It used to be attached to the house that Robert Crouse is living in today. Beechum Crouse's Store sold pipes, tobacco and many different things.

Robert Crouse's father (Merle Crouse) opened a store in 1936.

Later Arthur Bolivar ran Merle Crouse's store. Merle sold the business, but he wouldn't sell the building. Arthur Bolivar then retired from the store in the early 1970s.

Johnny Himmelman had a store and a post office in Crousetown at the same time as Merle Crouse's store. John Himmelman's store is still standing across from the Community Cemetery.

Source: Petite Riviere Elementary School, *History of Crousetown*, (Lunenburg County, NS: Petite Riviere Publishing), 1993, p. 24.

in the past. Frequently, integrated multimodal presentation formats are more appealing to them than more traditional research reports. Similarly, charts, graphs, maps, and diagrams often provide learners with opportunities to share their understandings more fully. The importance of creating reports and presentations lies in the thinking and organizing learners must do in order for the information to be clear and interesting to others, and to themselves.

SUMMARY

Integrating literacy across the curriculum provides an opportunity for learners to read and write as they are learning, and to think about their learning, making greater sense of what they know. It provides opportunities to question, hypothesize, predict, and consolidate knowledge. Reading and writing across the curriculum can be done from grade 1 onward, as shown by the samples of writing presented in this chapter. Reading and writing for learning is best taught when it is modelled by educators or developed in collaborative efforts with learners and educators working together.

In addition, research and study skills are taught with the aim of helping students to become independent learners who feel confident in locating and using library and online resources and in accessing primary sources through such means as interviews and archival searches. Many of the skills needed to conduct research involve organizing information. This important ability can be taught collaboratively in the early grades as learners use webs, grids, and charts to facilitate their learning.

Learners can have difficulty in reading textbooks and information books if educators have not specifically taught them how to attend to the organization of information material and how to use the features of an information text. The successful reading of information material calls on different skills than those required for reading narrative. Students must be shown how to read content materials through the use of such features as subheadings, glossary, index, and table of contents. It is important that educators model these skills for learners, for example, through an interactive whiteboard.

Being able to write thoughts on paper or screen is one way in which people remind themselves of what they know and think. It is also a way to communicate those thoughts to others. As learners develop their abilities to read and write for multiple purposes and for varied audiences, they take greater control of their own learning. The ability to reflect on their experiences and emerging understandings is a critical life skill. Beyond that, through the skills students develop as they write in journals, conduct research inquiries, and complete reports and presentations, they are developing a repertoire of powerful learning strategies. Through these strategies, they make personal sense of their learning and connect themselves and their learning to the world at large.

SELECTED PROFESSIONAL RESOURCES

Harvey, S., & Goudvis, A. (2000). *Strategies that work: Teaching comprehension to enhance understanding*. York, ME: Stenhouse.

This useful book is full of information and practical ideas that can help learners become more reflective, critical, and thoughtful readers. The section on inferential thinking is particularly helpful in teaching learners how to "read between the lines"—a powerful strategy for deepening their understanding of what they read.

continued

McLaughlin, M., & Allen, M. B. (2002). *Guided comprehension: A teaching model for grades 3–8*. Newark, DE: International Reading Association.

This book provides educators with helpful suggestions on how to effectively engage learners in comprehension strategies, with information on the multiple roles of assessment, and with many other teaching ideas. It includes material to use right across the curriculum.

University of Western Ontario, Education Library. (2003). *Lesson plans and additional resources*. Retrieved from http://www.lib.uwo.ca/education/lessonplans.shtml

This Canadian site connects educators (including non-UWO pre-service teachers) to a wide range of web-based resources for use across the curriculum. It includes lesson plans, library resources, drama ideas, science, social studies, art, and more—and most of it involves writing.

CHAPTER NINE

The Process of Writing

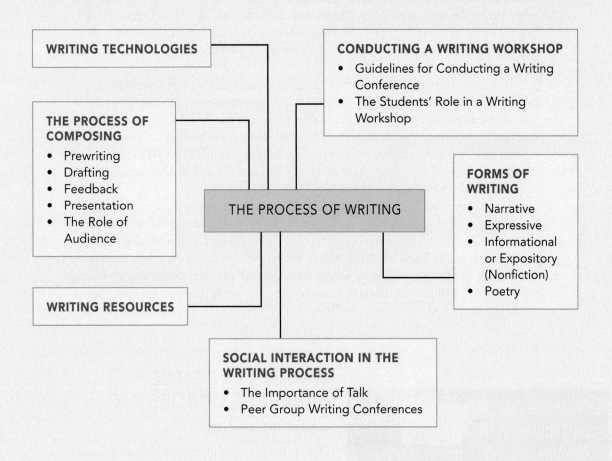

WRITING TECHNOLOGIES

CONDUCTING A WRITING WORKSHOP
- Guidelines for Conducting a Writing Conference
- The Students' Role in a Writing Workshop

THE PROCESS OF COMPOSING
- Prewriting
- Drafting
- Feedback
- Presentation
- The Role of Audience

THE PROCESS OF WRITING

FORMS OF WRITING
- Narrative
- Expressive
- Informational or Expository (Nonfiction)
- Poetry

WRITING RESOURCES

SOCIAL INTERACTION IN THE WRITING PROCESS
- The Importance of Talk
- Peer Group Writing Conferences

Here is an excerpt from "Iris and Kostos: A Creation Myth," written by Sondra in grade 7.

Iris, the most beautiful maiden in Greece, had a secret. Every day she would go to the edge of a cliff, which overlooked the blue sea, and whisper her secret away into the breeze. Her secret was, she was in love. She was in love with the youth named Kostos, who was handsome and kind. Almost every girl loved him with all her heart. She watched him everyday. When she called his name he barely gave a glance, but when he did look, she had always already turned away.

Like Iris, Kostos had a secret as well. He loved Iris but was afraid if he told her she would reject him. One day, Kostos was chosen to be part of a ship's crew. They would set sail to the small island just beyond the horizon. There, they brought offerings to the temple of Zeus. Kostos wanted to tell Iris all of this before he left, but he never got the chance. The time came for him to depart. The ship left at sunrise, before the sun was high, so they wouldn't be blinded by it. And so they went....

The next morning, at daybreak, instead of whispering her secret into the breeze, she whispered a prayer of safety for Kostos to Poseidon, the god of the sea, and trusted that Kostos would be safe. Little did she know that it was already too late.... In one of the storms, the ship that Kostos was sailing on sank, taking Kostos with it. Back on shore, Iris yearned for Kostos' return. Every day she walked along the edge of the water, searching the horizon for a ship that would never come, the ship that Kostos was on.

After many years, Poseidon took pity on Iris, for she was living a life no human should live, one of grief and sorrow. One morning as the sun rose, Iris was standing on the shore, the waves washing at her feet. She looked down to see her feet turning into roots. Soon enough, where Iris had been standing a few moments before was a graceful weeping willow tree. Just as Iris had been, the weeping willow stood, head bowed, silently weeping in the wind, forever standing as an enduring symbol of her unrequited love. ☐

Denise Barrett

WRITING IN DENISE BARRETT'S GRADES 7/8 CLASSROOM

Denise Barrett uses a writers' workshop model in her grades 7/8 classroom in St. Albert, Alberta. She urges her writers to "write what you know and write what you like." She maintains that if writers don't like what they're writing, readers won't like it either. She also tells her students that the first time she reads their writing should not be the last time. In other words, she needs to see their writing and provide feedback on it throughout the process, not only when she is providing a summative evaluation, which is usually in the form of a grade or mark. Denise does not mark all of her students' writing, though she does try to give feedback on it.

The cycle of Denise's teaching year usually begins with readers' workshop, and once learners have become familiar with that process, she introduces story writing. In grade 7 she often begins the year by focusing on one genre such as creation myths, and she uses examples such as Jon Stott's "Sedna," an Inuit myth, or versions of "Cupid and Psyche." The opening to this chapter presents a myth created by one of Denise's students. In grade 8 Denise might begin the year with mystery and wonder stories, the students having read such books as *Double Identity* by Margaret Peterson Haddix, *Tangerine* by Edward Bloor, or *Merchant of Death* by D. J. MacHale. The stories they write should be short enough to be read in one sitting, and so Denise urges her students to write no more than about 20 pages. This process usually takes about a month of in-class time, and the students do one major piece of writing per month throughout the school year.

Denise frequently shows a movie in class to stimulate discussion of ideas. For example, Disney's *Watcher in the Woods* provides excellent material for exploring character development and the art of creating suspense without the impact of visuals (and without overdoing it!). She encourages writers to think "what if …" They might take an ordinary situation and put a spin on it, as in Caroline B. Cooney's *The Face on the Milk Carton*, where a girl in the cafeteria looks at the milk carton she is drinking from and sees her own face on the "missing child" panel.

Denise's students usually write beginning ideas, brainstorming, and first drafts on paper. Once they have made a start they transfer to the computer. Writers share their work with each other and with Denise, and she makes sure that the writers are fully aware of the due date for the final edited draft. Denise sits with one student at a time to provide feedback, while the rest of the class is writing or meeting in pairs or small groups. If writers are stuck or get lost along the way, she tells them to "just write the ideas in your own words and polish it later." Sometimes she has a student use a digital voice recorder to get the work moving. Spelling and sentence structure are taught only in the context of the writing, with writers paying attention to Spell Check and using a dictionary frequently. She insists that students know the importance of using a word only if they are sure they know what it means—and she shares many humorous anecdotes with them to make her point.

When assessing writing, Denise uses her own tailored version of the Alberta Provincial Achievement Test rubric. She encourages writers to think of their audience and to consider their own responses to the books and short stories they read. "Know your characters," she tells them. "What sort of car do they drive? What's their favourite music? You won't write that into the story, but you must know those things if you are to write about them believably." Denise knows the details must flow and fit together if the story is to be successful.

WRITING TECHNOLOGIES

In many ways, the teaching of writing in K to 8 classrooms has remained largely unchanged over the last 15 to 20 years, but in terms of writing technologies, there have been dramatic changes. The touch screen and the keypad on a mobile computing device, for example, have made a significant difference in how we write and what we write. A good place for beginning teachers to start thinking about writing is to reflect on their own experiences as writers today, and to think about what learners need in order to develop their abilities to create and express their ideas in writing in many different forms and formats.

It is imperative that today's language and literacy educators attend to multiliteracies if they are to ensure that learners become "cognitively and socially literate with paper, live, and electronic texts" (Anstey & Bull, 2006, p. 23). Anstey and Bull reminded educators that with the increase in film, video, gaming, the Internet, and social media, and the increased visual content in books and magazines, a whole range of texts that are not print based has developed. Print knowledge is now seen as necessary but not sufficient in today's knowledge economy. With the advent of new technologies and new forms of media, print text is no longer the only basic.

Today's K to 8 learners are creating text that is mediated through popular culture. Many children come to kindergarten and grade 1 with sophisticated levels of technological literacy (Merchant, 2005). Digital media are now an entrenched part of the culture of childhood. When young writers are creating stories in school, they draw on their experiences with these media and expect to use new media in their classrooms (read more about this in Chapter 13).

Educators like Denise Barrett work alongside their students learning together about **new media** as they create and respond to **multimodal texts**. They learn how to talk about these new forms of texts (including still and moving images) and their meanings. Here, print information blends with visual, audio, spoken, nonverbal, and other forms of expression produced through a range of technologies. Visual literacy plays a more crucial role in literacy education than ever before. At the same time, educators still need to be aware of the role of text (of all kinds) in our lives and of the teaching approaches that can help them be effective teachers of both written and multimodal forms of text.

FORMS OF WRITING

Writing is always carried out with a specific purpose and for a distinct audience. We use different **voices**, styles, genres, formats, and media, depending on the purpose for our writing and the audience the writing is intended for. Different genres help us to achieve our communication goals: letters, memos, poems, reports, editorials, invitations, journal entries, blogs, diaries, essays, plays, film scripts, multimedia stories, textbooks, novels, short stories, lists, recipes, instruction manuals, and so on, are all intended to accomplish specific goals. As writers, we can never separate a piece of writing from its form, function, or audience. It is therefore important that learners encounter many different real-world purposes, situations, and genres in their classroom writing. The goal of writing instruction is for individuals to communicate and express their ideas, questions, knowledge, and opinions to others whom they may wish to influence or inform.

Narrative

Narrative writing links a series of events together either through a sequence in time or through cause and effect. The purpose of most narrative writing is to entertain. Much of the narrative writing completed by learners in K to 8 classrooms is fictional, but narrative can also be used for nonfiction texts. Narrative seems to be a significant way for human beings to make sense of the world. Barbara Hardy (1975) wrote that narrative is a "primary act of mind." We seem to think in narrative, retelling events to ourselves to see how the pieces fit together, or telling ourselves how something works as we try to figure out a problem.

A distinction must be noted between a *recount* and a narrative story. A *recount* is simply a retelling of events with no particular attention to setting, plot, problem, conflict resolution, or climax. When writers develop a *story*, however, they craft the narrative in a certain way. In Western cultures a story is usually structured around an introduction, a middle section with a problem or conflict (sometimes a series of conflicts), and then an ending, which achieves some resolution of the problem.

The writing of a recount or anecdote, however, can form the foundation for a highly descriptive verbal picture of a scene or event. Such writing invites the reader to participate in the experience through rich sensory detail. Careful crafting can make a descriptive recount particularly dramatic. Below is an excerpt from a recount written by a learner in grade 4.

The Living Room

There are many special places in my house but I think the one I like best is the living room. The living room is not that big, but it has hiding places and interesting books and even a little box with musical instruments. There is one window which looks out onto a forest and you can hear the birds in the trees. Late in the day we often sit on a cushion and find images in the flickering firelight. We close our eyes and try to guess the names of the birds who are singing. Once a year we each get one marshmallow to roast upon the fire. I always look forward to those happy days—in the living room.

—Skye

Applebee (1978) suggested that children have to learn to do two things simultaneously to successfully write or tell a story: chain events together and focus on a theme, problem, or character. Applebee's research demonstrated that children begin to form stories from the age of two onward, but they learn to apply these two essential elements over time, mastering the story form (or "story grammar," as it is sometimes called) over a period of years.

As young writers mature, their stories become more complex and cohesive. Learners become aware of an audience for their writing, and strive for clarity and an engaging text. An excerpt from a story written jointly by Sharon and Erica in grade 5 is shown in Box 9.1. Unfinished at the end of the school year, the story was put "on hold" by the girls because they were not sure what to do with it next and they had another piece of writing they wanted to start. This story will be referred to again later in the chapter, in the section about the importance of talking about writing; at that point, the girls' struggle with crafting and ending the piece becomes more apparent.

Expressive

Expressive writing, found in blogs, diaries, and journals, is the kind of personal writing we do informally as thoughts form in our mind. We rarely revise or craft expressive writing. Expressive writing is generally done for an audience who knows the writer, and sometimes

BOX 9.1

EXCERPT FROM "THE WELLINGTON STORY" (WRITTEN COOPERATIVELY BY SHARON AND ERICA, GRADE 5)

When the story begins, Mr. Wellington, a well-known artist, and his wife are hosting a dinner party.

After [the guests] arrived they all sat down for dinner. "Cheers to Mrs. Wellington for having this party," said Miss Murphy in a loud voice. Then they all lifted their glasses and clinked them together. "I'll go get my husband for dinner," said Mrs. Wellington and left. A few minutes later, Mrs. Wellington came back into the dining room. "My husband will be coming shortly," she said as Yvette started carving the turkey. After about ten minutes had passed Mrs. Wellington asked Yvette to go see where her husband was.

Yvette left the dining room and went to the paint house. There was a moment of silence and then Miss Murphy spoke. "The strangest thing happened to me yesterday," she said. "I I … Ahhhhhh." Miss Murphy was interrupted by a loud scream. Mrs. Wellington dropped her fork.

"It's coming from the paint house," said Mr. McGregor. They all rushed out to the paint house and saw Yvette shaking, with a knife in her hand. Mrs. Wellington gasped and walked into the paint house. She saw her husband lying dead on the floor. "Yvette," she screamed.

"How could you?" Mrs. Landenburg walked into the room, looked at the body and fainted. "Somebody call the police," said Mrs. Hunt. Mrs. Wellington started to cry. Mr. McGregor called the police. About 5 minutes later they arrived. "We were in the neighborhood," they said. "Now what happened?" Mrs. Wellington explained the whole thing. "Then we walked in and saw her," she said pointing to Yvette, "standing there with a knife in her hand. She did it officer, I know she did."

"Why don't you go into the house and rest while we look around and take the body away," said the police officer. Mrs. Wellington went into the lounge with the other guests. "It's all right Margaret. It had to happen sooner or later being a famous painter and all," said Miss Murphy. "He was such a kind husband to me," said Mrs. Wellington and then started to cry. Meanwhile in the paint house officer McCarther was searching around the floor when he spotted a loose floorboard.

He pulled back the floor board and saw a white dress with a red wine stain on it. "Hmm," he said. Then he put on a pair of rubber gloves, picked up the dress and placed it in a plastic bag. Then he took a second look, and saw the top of a broken wine bottle. He picked up the wine bottle and put it into a plastic bag. Then he walked over to where Mr. Wellington was lying and picked up the knife that Yvette dropped and went into the lounge. "I'll have to take finger prints," said officer McCarther and pulled out a stamp pad in front of Mrs. Wellington. "Are you accusing me of killing my own husband? Why would I kill him?" asked Mrs. Wellington. "You might kill him for his money and besides everyone in the room is a suspect," said officer McCarther. "Why didn't I wait until he dies?" asked Mrs. Wellington.

The girls ended the story with the following note to themselves:

tired of story change some parts

Stop story for now

want to start cat bylaw not doing a play

yet at least!

Source: C. Lewis. *Partnership writing: Ten-year-olds talking and writing together.* M.Ed. thesis. Edmonton: University of Alberta, 1989.

the audience is the self. Expressive writing is a means through which we present our ideas, thoughts, feelings, and interpretations of events. It may include responses to books we have read, movies we have seen, or events that have taken place. Expressive writing is essentially exploratory. In expressive writing, just as in expressive speech, we speculate, hypothesize, predict, and generally articulate our thoughts. Below is an excerpt from a piece of expressive writing by a learner in grade 4, written as she thought about the novel *On My Honor* by Marion Dane Bauer:

> Chapter eight confused me at the beginning. It didn't exactly say that Joel had gone home. When he was at home, I think I understood why and how he lied. Telling the truth in tough situations is very difficult. I would never lie at all, even in a problem like that. My friend's mom just moved here a little while ago and the apartment they lived in was allowed no children. Quite absurd! She only got to live there because she said she was a doctor. Stuff like that makes me very untrusting of the world. Taking a person by how much money they have etc. When I read that chapter I felt Joel's insecurity. He seems to be not acting normal with the problems he's having. A kid dealing with something like that is real scary!

In this piece, the writer was thinking through her feelings about lying. As she wrote about the character in the book, she reflected on her own experiences with telling the truth and how, at times, people are moved to lie in order to survive. The writer struggled with the ambivalence she felt, knowing that lying is wrong, but understanding a little of why at times even good people might be dishonest.

In the following excerpt, a grade 4 learner responded to a different passage in *On My Honor*. He wrote:

> I hate it when my friends try to convince me to do things they want to do. I think Tony is being quite mean to Joel. I think that Tony just wants Joel to do what he wants to do. I can swim but not too good. But even if I was a professional swimmer I'd never swim in a river. I think it's a bad idea because the water is pushing you. It would just suck you up. A few minutes later you'd be dead.

Both learners were making text-to-self connections as they read the novel and thought about how they or their friends would respond in similar situations. Both considered the difficult decisions people have to make at certain times in their lives, and the kinds of decisions they felt they would make in the same circumstances.

Informational or Expository (Nonfiction)

Intended to explain, persuade, or instruct, **expository writing** requires the writer to be well organized, clear, and coherent. This writing is not meant to convey feelings or to be primarily entertaining, but to pass on information to an audience. Reports, textbooks, memos, flyers, editorials, and the writing from Julie Gellner's Restaurant project presented in Chapter 7 are examples of expository writing. Lewis and Wray (1995) identified six nonfiction genres used regularly in our society: persuasion, recount, explanation, report, procedural, and discussion. They maintained that learners in kindergarten through grade 8 should be taught the basic elements of each of these genres and should have many opportunities for using them in the classroom. An excerpt from a piece of Xian's grade 6 expository writing, "Garbage, Garbage, Garbage," is shown below.

> Let's help the environment by reusing, reducing and recycling. To help the environment we need to use less packaged things, use more big bulk things and more reusable things. instead of getting a water bottle from the store that you can recycle instead get a reusable bottle that doesn't have to be recycled. It's not just recycling it's about not littering and keeping the world clean we have so many islands that are garbage islands. That means we have to do our part by throwing stuff in the garbage instead of putting stuff on the ground that gets squished. If you have a recyclable bottle that is from the store try to find a recycle bin. If you don't have a recycling bin, get one from the store. you can use a blue bag or a blue bin. What goes in the bag is papers. Instead of throwing your fruits and veggies in the garbage try using a compost. Then it will make more soil. If you have worms then you can put them in a worm bin and it will help make more soil. If you live near the ocean or near a lake, don't use the ocean as a garbage, because then it will get polluted. Eventually it will go in a big clump and then it will turn into a garbage island. So, to help reduce that we have to put things in the garbage and things that are recyclable are put in the recycling bin.

Persuasive writing is used more often in Western society than we realize. Advertising, editorials, political campaign literature, and religious tracts, as well as much of the unsolicited junk mail that arrives in mailboxes, consist of persuasive writing. Someone wants to persuade us to do something, buy something, or believe something. Learners use persuasive writing when they create a poster presentation about a book they have read or advertise an event that is to take place in their school. They write persuasively when they want something and have to convince an adult to allow them to have it. At school, for example, persuasive writing may take the form of a letter or petition to government agencies to request some kind of change. The writing might be part of a social studies or science project.

Box 9.2 presents an excerpt from a grade 2 letter to Santa, written in application for a job as a Christmas elf. Jaden is clearly trying to make a good case as to why Santa should hire her.

Explanatory writing is frequently required in social studies, science, and mathematics. Learners must think carefully and logically when writing an explanation, and educators need to scaffold such writing assignments so that students will be successful. Dr. Perry Klein at the Western University studied learners' writing of explanations in science. He found that, overall, students who were taught to write explanations were better able to use writing as a tool for learning about science. The grade 5 learners in his study participated in Guided Reading of several explanations with their teacher. They learned that the purpose of an explanation is to tell how or why something happens, that an explanation often includes several steps, and that it tells why each step happens. The students also learned that when writing an explanation, it is important to make good use of sources of information, whether these are science observations, written texts, or other kinds of media.

Learners were asked to complete a piece of explanatory writing with a partner. Their goal was to explain what had happened to the young fish that were missing from the Stony River. They received a small portfolio that contained a variety of documents: a newspaper clipping,

BOX 9.2

GRADE 2 PERSUASIVE WRITING

Elf Application Letter

Dec 18, 2014

Dear Santa

Santa I am looking for a job. I really want to be an elf. Please keep me in mind. I am an animal lover. I have three dogs. I know some Christmas carols. I have a beautiful singing voice. I could sing any song to keep the day going. I rush when I do work. I've swept the floor running pretending it was a fast horse. I like to decorate. Once my mom bought me a shirt and I decorated it. I can

paint. I like to take test drives. I could test the reindeer. Please please please take me into consideration. Will I get paid? I would really like to work for you. Elves are awsome. If I were an elf right now I'd be excited because Christmas is near. If you hire me you won't regret it.

Your Friend,

Jaden.

a map of the town, "Fast Facts" about acid (see below), a "backgrounder" on what causes acid rain and snow, a line graph of acidity in the river throughout the year, and a table on the effects of acidity on water animals. The documents did not tell what had happened to the missing fish, but they provided a host of clues.

Fast Facts: What Is Acid?

- An acid is a substance.
- Acids are usually found dissolved in water.
- Mild acids taste sour.
- Vinegar, lemon juice, and orange juice are mild acids.
- Strong acids rust metal and burn skin.
- Acidity is measured in "ph."
- Pure water has a ph of 7.0.
- *Lower* ph means *more* acidic.

Through oral discussion and writing, the partners worked together to interpret the documents and build an explanation. One example is provided in Box 9.3.

BOX 9.3

THE MYSTERY OF THE MISSING FISH

Missing Young Fish

We think that the young fish in Stoney River are missing because the water in stoney River is very acidic & most young fishies will not survive. Since there is high acidity in the spring & most fish lay there eggs then, the eggs may not hatch. If they do hatch, they have a very little chance of surviving. Since the water is frozen in the winter months, there is very little chance that acid would et into the water. When it melts in the spring all the acid that has gathered in the iec will melt & go staight into the river. Since the fish are usually babies during the spring months then their bodies cannot hold the acid. as well as adults, they will die if they stay in the acidic water for too long. If the fish had their babies in Juin-August then they will have a better chance of surviving.

So that is why we think that there are so many young fish missing from the stoney River!! Thank you for reading our paper!!

Poetry

Although poetry is a genre of writing rather than a specific form such as narrative, explanatory, or persuasive writing, we are including a section on writing poetry here because beginning teachers frequently ask for advice on how to teach poetry writing in K to 8 classrooms. Poetry is a genre that focuses on capturing feelings, events, places, and people in an aesthetically pleasing way. A few poetic words or phrases can convey a whole set of meanings in a particularly striking manner. Poetry is not defined by a rhyme scheme or rhythm; it is uniquely artistic, although sometimes disconcerting. K to 8 learners seem to find poetry a singularly appealing genre for their writing, and find the genre to be most effective for the meanings they want to convey. "My Brother," "Soccer" (p. 300), and "In My Mind" (p. 302) were written by learners in Diana Dixon's grade 5/6 class.

My Brother

My brother is like the weather
You have to prepare for him
If you don't, it will be a big mess
When crying, it's raining
When smiling, it's sunny
A tantrum is a tornado
I wish I knew the forecast better.

—Peter

Learners in kindergarten to grade 8 write much excellent poetry when they are encouraged to make each word do its "most effective job." We stress here that it is not helpful to provide students with a pattern for their poetry writing (such as haiku, cinquain, limerick, or diamante). When children are faced with fitting their words into an already established pattern, they frequently encounter difficulties because the constraints of the form are too limiting. Writing a good limerick or haiku, for example, is extremely difficult and takes a great deal of hard work, even for an experienced writer. Learners can end up with a poorly written poem that has been created simply to fit the assigned form. Teaching various forms of poetry is appropriate only insofar as learners are being introduced to the form and are aware of its structure and its name.

Educators can prepare their students for writing poetry by encouraging them to use strong and colourful verbs and specific nouns in all of their writing, rather than decorating their writing with adjectives and adverbs. In addition, learners can be encouraged to experiment with syntactical patterns to create particular effects. Poems can be changed radically if the last line becomes the first—do that with "Soccer," below, and note the impact—or if the poem is given a different, often more simple title. Sometimes, educators may challenge young writers to capture an event, scene, or idea by "saying the most with the fewest words possible."

Educator Diana Dixon reads at least one poem aloud to her grade 5 class every day, and she has books of poetry available for free reading in her classroom. Diana frequently talks about poetry with her students, and together they compile lists of their favourite poems. Similarly, Denise Barrett uses music and popular songs as a starting point for poetry writing in her grades 7 and 8 classes. She finds that songs evoke memory associations for her students, and learners seem to speak more fluidly about songs than they often do about poetry. Anne Gordon, in Chapter 3, explained that she engages and motivates her young writers by encouraging them to create "heart maps." Writing poetry helps the students in these three teachers' classrooms to focus their writing and to realize just how flexible and powerful written language can be.

Diana Dixon and reading group

Soccer

A soccer ball
Is like
An eraser
It erases away my thoughts.
When I kick it
I do not think.
My mind is lost
In the game.
The ball flies
Towards the net.
The ball bends
In mid air
The goalie jumps one way
The ball flies the other.
We win the game!

—Jarico

A number of "verse novels" suitable for grades 4 through 8 have fostered student interest in writing poetry. Sharon Creech has two verse novels: *Love That Dog* and *The Unfinished Angel. Love That Dog* is a series of "found poems" written by the protagonist, Jack, on the urging of his teacher. Although Jack doesn't consider himself a poet, he writes about the poems and the poets his teacher introduces to the class. His poems reveal his thoughts and feelings about himself as a writer and about what is most important to him. *The Crazy Man*, a Governor General's Award winner by Canadian writer Pamela Porter, is set in Saskatchewan in 1965. Here, Emaline comes to know Angus, a patient from the local psychiatric hospital. Although the small town's prejudice creates a cloud of suspicion around Angus that nearly results in tragedy, Angus inadvertently helps Emaline to overcome the effects of an injury and the loss of her father. Two Australian titles, *The Spangled Drongo* and *Tom Jones Saves the World,* both by Steven Herrick, recount the humorous and heartwarming adventures of two boys as they come to terms with the opposite sex and with their parents. These two books make superb Read-Alouds, and they demonstrate to learners how "saying the most with the fewest words possible" can create lasting images and tell intriguing stories.

INSIDE CLASSROOMS

DIANA DIXON AND *LOVE THAT DOG*

Diana Dixon so enjoyed Love That Dog *that she decided to introduce the book to her grade 5 students. She says,*

I didn't really know what to do with the book. I knew I didn't want to ruin it by "teaching" it, so I decided that we would just enjoy the book as a class. It took us just over a week to read. We read together, discussed, and responded to the book. At the beginning of the book the students were obsessed with the yellow cover and the blue print (interestingly, I didn't notice the blue print the first time that I read the book—yikes!). The students were comfortable saying that they didn't understand the poems or the storyline. As a teacher I have (finally!) stopped trying to explain everything to them. I underscored the idea that we don't all understand everything in the same way, or at the same time, and that's okay. So my students felt free to question and ponder. I was impressed that they did not hesitate to share their ideas.

In their written responses, students were given various options—they could write a response journal entry, write a detail/response chart, draw, cartoon, or respond in any way they desired. At the beginning of the book many students didn't know how to respond. They ended up copying print directly from the text, just as early readers copy environmental print from the classroom. I was shocked, as this class had never done anything like this before. However, as the book progressed, they started getting more comfortable with using different types of responses to get their ideas down.

One student said, "The pages are so short I can read this easily in a week." Another student said, halfway through the book, "I don't know why this is such a special book." But most students enjoyed the book and many responded in poetic form—they enjoyed creating shape poems but struggled if they tried to make a poem rhyme. At times they just shared their thoughts in free verse or drew in their notebooks. One student drew Walter Dean Myers and described him in this way: "a soft man and is not too old but has white hair already. He also has a peachy smile on his face."

One student asked, "Why does Jack take stuff from poems? I think I know the answer … but what is your opinion?" This same student also said at the end of the book, "I can't tell if *Love That Dog* is a book or a boy saying stuff like someone would in a diary. What is your opinion?"

Our final activity with the book was a group activity where the students listed the poetry lessons that Jack learned throughout the story. Here are a few of the things they came up with:

▷ Poems include repetition.
▷ Poems don't always rhyme.
▷ Writers get inspiration from other poems.
▷ Lines can be as long as you want.
▷ Both boys and girls can write poems.
▷ Write about what you know lots about.
▷ Start small.
▷ Don't be scared to let your ideas flow.
▷ Poems should be read over and over again.
▷ Any words can be poems.
▷ Any poem can be powerful.
▷ You don't have to understand poems to enjoy them.
▷ Don't be afraid to let poems out of your heart.
▷ Poetry is not just words put into sentences; it is feelings.
▷ Poems can be funny, sad, happy, exciting, serious, rhyming, or nonsense.

(continued)

▷ In some poems you make up words.

▷ Some poems relate to you and some don't.

▷ Poems have to sound and look good.

I enjoyed reading the book and I felt that it engaged many of my enthusiastic readers. My reluctant readers were happy with the length of the book, the time we took to read a whole book, and the Shared Reading that we used throughout. I know the book is still in my students' thoughts as a boy suggested yesterday, during oral recitation of a poem, "Well, girls are better at 'singing' poems than boys," and one of his classmates responded, "No, they aren't! Didn't you learn anything in *Love That Dog*?"

Learners can have a great deal of fun with *found poetry*. Found poems, like found art objects, are everyday items that are re-presented in an artistic way (advertising posters, notices). Found poems are created by separating phrases or words in a fresh way in order to create a new meaning, or to make the original meaning more impactful. Alternatively, words can be culled from newspapers, magazines, menus, advertisements, songs, and stories. These poems can be authored by individuals or by groups of students working together.

As a reader response activity, students may collect their favourite words and phrases from a story and reorganize them to express their responses to the book. Tasha created "In My Mind" after teacher Diana Dixon and her students looked at examples of found poetry on the Internet. Diana led a guided practice, and then the students went to the library, where they gathered 50 to 100 words from the titles on book spines. They then looked through their collection of words and "found" their poems.

In My Mind

At last
There they were
Standing in that
Creepy abandoned place
The dragon
The mummy
And the brave knight
As I walk towards them
They disappear
Into the darkness
My imagination.

—Tasha

THE PROCESS OF COMPOSING

Teachers like Denise Barrett and Diana Dixon take a workshop approach to the teaching of writing. Learners work with one another and their teachers, composing, drafting, revising, editing, and publishing their works. The grade 7 piece "Iris and Kostos: A Creation Myth" went through this process: a cycle of writing, reading, revising, rereading, and revising some more. With the use of word-processing programs, the revising and editing processes have become easier over the years. Young writers must be taught the importance of revision when creating any piece of writing, including expository writing, which needs just as much attention as **poetic writing**. An early draft is generally focused on getting the ideas into print. As writers reread their drafts, they make the piece more explicit, more interestingly worded. They add ideas and ensure the piece reads fluently. They check spelling, notice that words have been omitted (or repeated), and attend to punctuation.

Not every piece of writing will be shared with others. Much of our writing stays in a writing folder, with only a few pieces making it through to the "sharing with a public" stage. The process requires time and thought with the focus placed on the *process* of composing and on the *thinking* that goes into developing a successful piece of writing.

When teachers take a workshop approach, they often engage in writing themselves and so can demonstrate to learners what a writer goes through to create a composition, making it clear and conventionally appropriate for an audience. As writers go about the writing process, they receive feedback, and they revise, develop new ideas, begin new pieces, share old ones, and continue to develop their writing skills. As one aspect of thinking, writing both reflects and facilitates the exploration of ideas. The composition process is more spiral than linear, for writers do not stay "in the same place" for long when they write; their writing changes along with their thinking.

Prewriting

The first stage of composing is often called collecting or prewriting. Here, writers collect ideas, memories, and experiences that help them to decide on a topic. They decide on what should be included in the composition, and what memories and recollections they can use to develop it. Writers use mixtures of people they have known, places they have visited, and their own experiences, whether real or vicarious. We retain our memories and emotions, and these become the raw material of our writing. K to 8 learners are just as capable as adults of choosing a topic and working with their experiences, but they do need help and encouragement, and they need a sense of ownership of their writing as well. The more responsibility they assume for key decisions about topic choice, format, audience, and production timelines, and the more their topics interest them, the more they are likely to work at their writing and improve it. We learn to write by writing.

At this stage, writers think about the form or medium they will use for the composition. Sometimes a text generates visual images or sounds, and at other times an image or a song will generate a text. Will the piece of writing have artwork or illustrations along with it? Will still or moving images be incorporated? Will it include sound? Will it have a print form, or will it be entirely a digital presentation?

Drafting

Once a topic has been determined, the writer begins to draft a text, putting into print the intentions developed in the prewriting stage. The text may go through many drafts, and be modified and reworked. It is important to emphasize that expository writing needs just as much care in revision and editing as poetic forms of writing do. During the drafting stage, the writer becomes clearer about the ideas or information conveyed and what needs to be improved, deleted, or changed. The writer may play with the drafts, changing words here and there, changing images and sounds, or deleting parts that are not effective, and rewriting parts that simply don't work. During this stage the writer asks, "Am I meaning what I say and saying what I mean?"

Writers strive for clarity, but sometimes thoughts do not fall into place until the writer starts creating the text; the actual process of writing or of creating a digital presentation enables ideas to flow. In a sense, writing seems to slow down thinking. As writers write, they have time and opportunity to capture their thoughts, reflect on them, and connect them to previous thoughts in a generative process. Published writers go through dozens of drafts of a text before it's ready for an audience. Grades 2 to 6 learners might complete only three drafts of a text, especially if they are just beginning to work with the writing process. Grades 7 and 8 learners might do considerably more drafts.

Editing and revision skills can be taught in mini-lessons before or after Writers' Workshop, or in group and individual conferences like the ones Denise Barrett conducts with her students. When learners are writing on paper, they can prepare for revision by writing on one side of the paper only and on every other line. These practices enable them to cross out, write over top, use carets to insert text, and make other changes without having to copy a whole piece over. When writing with a word processor, drafting and editing are much easier, which is one reason why most educators today ensure that learners have easy access to a word processor.

The writing shown in Boxes 9.4 and 9.5 demonstrates the changes that Wendy, in Frieda Maaskant's grade 2 class, made to her report on whales as she worked through the writing process. The two pieces presented here are excerpts from the first draft and the final draft of the report. The learners in Frieda's classroom were accustomed to working through the writing process with both their poetic and expository writing.

One grade 6 teacher enlisted the support of a high-school class to help her young writers create digital stories in response to Gordon Korman's *Dive. Book One: The Discovery*. In addition to making several reading and writing responses, learners used a computer paint application to paint their favourite scenes from the book. The elementary and high-school students wrote a blog in which they negotiated the animated story that would be developed from each young writer's picture. The high-school students dissected the paintings and animated them. The "stories" lasted between 30 seconds and one minute. Sound effects, music, and narration were added. The grade 6 writers drafted the story and collaboratively planned the visuals, the sound effects, and the movement of the characters on the screen. At the end of the project, the students had a face-to-face meeting in which the animations were unveiled and screened to the combined classes. The grade 6 writers, their parents, and friends enjoyed the digital stories, which were eventually posted on the school website.

A distinct advantage of posting learners' work online is that relatives (especially grandparents) can participate in school life even if they are separated by geography. Although some educators express concern at posting school work on the web, school district technology consultants can assist in creating secure sites.

Many software tools are available to help youngsters with their writing and presentations. Google Docs is used for group-editing and group-writing activities. IntelliTools Classroom Suite, which contains templates for writing and also includes graphics and animation, is much

BOX 9.4

EXCERPT FROM FIRST DRAFT OF WENDY'S REPORT ON WHALES

Source: F. Maaskant. *Children's perceptions of writing in a grade one/two classroom.* Appendix, M.Ed. thesis. Edmonton, AB: University of Alberta, 1989.

BOX 9.5

EXCERPT FROM FINAL DRAFT OF WENDY'S REPORT ON WHALES

Whales

Whales have big large tails, they look like this but way bigger.

Whales will make a sound and it will go 100 miles Killer Whales have points on the top of their backs. Whales come out of the water every 20 minutes they let go of the air and get new clean air. the mouth is not hooked on to the lungs

Source: F. Maaskant. *Children's perceptions of writing in a grade one/two classroom.* Appendix, M.Ed. thesis. Edmonton, AB: University of Alberta, 1989.

appreciated and enjoyed by learners. The graphic novel applications such as Comic Creator (Marcopolo), Comic Book Creator (CNET), and Comic Life (Plasq) enable learners to make photo comics. The applications turn photos into comic artwork with a choice of fonts, templates, panels, balloons, captions, and lettering art, all available in one place. These and other software programs are either free or inexpensive. Photographs can be imported or clip art from the programs can be used to create a story or to write an imaginative report in science or other subject area. One group of learners used these programs to create comic books about various types of clouds; it provided an interesting and creative alternative to the research report. Other learners use the software to tell family or classroom stories, or to create their own comic book character and adventures. Xtranormal and Toontastic are other comic-based applications that are effective for experimenting with story arcs. There are many other online animation applications for creating multimedia stories, and some educators also use basic filmmaking applications, such as iMovie, as they work with learners on various projects, from stop-action animation to DIY filmmaking.

For screenwriting, as well as research reports and other forms of writing, many educators use Scrivener, a word-processing program that provides a management system for notes and documents, including text, images, PDF, audio, video, and web pages. After writing a piece of text, users may export it to a standard word processor for formatting.

Some grades 7 to 12 educators are using social-consciousness video gaming (so-called not-games) as contemporary text in their classrooms, focusing on the free-to-play games of Molleindustria and Tiltfactor Labs. The Tiltfactor Laboratory is a game research centre that focuses on critical play, an approach that uses games and play to investigate and explain ideas. The lab has produced video games, urban games, board games, and performances. Tiltfactor's games are aimed at promoting social change. They encourage learners to engage in new ways of thinking about important social issues through games and play.

Researcher Jason Wallin at the University of Alberta has been using social media to experiment with forms of writing, from Twitter poetry to role-played Facebook strands where students take on the vantage of literary characters in conversation with others.

Feedback

While creating a composition, young writers need feedback, both from peers and from educators. Peer conferences *and* group or one-on-one conferences with the teacher are necessary so that learners can obtain this feedback when they need it, and not when it's too late to make changes. During these conferences young writers have the best opportunity to learn about writing. This is where Denise Barrett does most of her teaching of writing. Some guidelines for conducting writing conferences are presented later in this chapter.

Presentation

The very last phase of the writing process is presentation, publication, or celebration. When a piece of writing or multimedia presentation is finished to an author's satisfaction, the piece can be shared with a wider audience. It might be sent home to family, read aloud to a whole class or group, displayed to the class on-screen, or posted on the school website or the class blog. It might be made into a book and placed in the classroom library, or shared with residents of a retirement home. This phase is a time for celebrating the accomplishments of the writer. The work is ready for a reading or viewing audience. Such was the case with Skye's prose piece "The Living Room," Peter's poem "My Brother," and Sondra's "Iris and Kostos: A Creation Myth," all presented earlier in this chapter.

The Role of Audience

Establishing an authentic audience for student writing makes a difference in how young writers go about the process of composition and revision. Awareness that a real audience is going to hear or see their created pieces makes all the difference in the world. When learners write together, talk about their writing, read their writing to each other, and listen to published authors talk about their work, they have a different purpose and motivation in learning to become good writers. Writing is not simply a functional skill to be learned in order to engage with social media, send text messages, or complete school assignments. It becomes an art that can entertain and delight, and it can produce great pride in young writers who see their writing valued and appreciated.

CONDUCTING A WRITING WORKSHOP

One teacher-researcher who significantly influenced the teaching of writing and the development of writing workshops is Nancie Atwell (1987, 1998). Atwell laid out expectations for writers' workshops and developed guidelines for student writing sessions. Although Atwell's suggestions were made largely with learners in grades 5 to 9 in mind, many of her ideas are modifiable for educators and learners in grades 2 to 4. Box 9.6 lists some of Atwell's suggestions for conducting writing workshops in the classroom.

Guidelines for Conducting a Writing Conference

Atwell (1998) pointed out that young writers want to be listened to and want honest responses to their work. Sharing a piece of writing with an informed audience can be a valuable means of obtaining feedback. Educators can teach or model feedback strategies that are productive and sensitive to the fact that every piece of writing is special to its author. Writing is deeply personal, and as such it must be respected by the audience. Learners in a classroom can be taught how to give constructive feedback and positive comments, and how to make suggestions for future drafts and new pieces of writing. Educators who model and promote a constructive and respectful process help to ensure that, when learners share their pieces of writing with a group, they will feel safe and will be able to accept the feedback.

In a writing conference, the writer usually reads the piece to an educator or to a group of peers. The listener(s) can thereby focus on the ideas, wording, and flow of the piece of writing. At the grades 3 to 8 level, a three-part response system works well:

1. provide a positive comment about the piece—what works well or sounds good

2. ask questions about anything that is not clear in the piece

3. make suggestions about what can be done to make the piece better

A conference might be very brief—just a few minutes of conversation with an educator—or it can be a more formal and lengthy affair with a small group of learners. In a conference, an educator's goal is to provide formative feedback designed to improve learners' writing. The conference is effective when an educator's responses provide strategic information that the writer can act on. Conferences can be conducted at a table in a quiet part of the room, or if the conference is one-on-one with educator and writer, it can be at the writer's desk.

BOX 9.6

CONDUCTING A WRITING WORKSHOP

1. A writing workshop has a predictable format: learners must know when it is to occur, what is expected of them, and what they can expect from the teacher and the situation. Time is provided for writers to write, as well as respond to each other's writing, and time is also provided for educators to respond to an individual's work. Educators also try to build into their schedules time for their own writing, so that learners can see them modelling the writing process.

2. A writers' workshop is something like an artist's studio. All the necessary resources are there: different colours and sizes of paper, felt pens, pencils, pens, staplers, rulers, whiteout, dictionaries, computers, printers, and software programs so they can create their own booklets or media presentations. Older writers need a thesaurus and reference books, and all learners need a safe way to save their work and some degree of privacy while they keyboard.

3. Writers' workshops can be noisy because writers need to talk about their writing; however, educators like Denise Barrett plan quiet times when all the participants are writing. These times are agreed upon by the writers. Many learners complain that they cannot do any real writing or reading at school because it is too noisy. Educators try to respect this need for quiet as well as the need for interaction. The quiet time is used for writing only, and any conversation must be in a whisper. There is also open time, when learners can write or meet together in a response group. In addition, some educators schedule group conferences where they interact with learners in a more traditional way.

4. A writing folder or large notebook is essential for each person in the classroom, including the teacher. Rather than have learners keep these folders or notebooks in their desks, it is usually easier if they are kept in a filing cabinet or bin that is accessible to all participants at all times. These folders can store some drafts printed from the computer as well as handwritten drafts.

5. All pieces of writing are dated and drafts are saved, usually with a draft number printed at the top. Writers save even those pieces that "don't work." Doing this allows them to see how their work is changing. Sometimes a writer will go back to an earlier draft of a piece because it is better than a later one.

6. A list of possible writing topics is placed at the front of the folder or notebook. Learners can add to it regularly as they discover new topics that will make good stories. Educators encourage learners to take a few minutes every few weeks to update their list of possibilities, and discuss topics they have chosen to put on their lists.

7. Writers are encouraged to put a line through changes and insert new material above rather than erase their work. Writing on every other line and on only one side of the paper facilitates this process. It also encourages learners to make changes and insertions without rewriting the whole piece. When writers compose on a word processor, they should label or number the drafts, and save them to a folder on the computer.

(continued)

8. Writing conferences might focus on the content of a piece, the topic, or the organization, clarifying the ideas and focusing the writing toward a more cohesive whole. A writing conference generally deals with only one of these elements at a time, because young writers cannot revise everything at once. The information given in a writing conference should be in small chunks so that the writer can think about it and act on it.

9. Lessons are taught as a result of specific points that arise in a writers' workshop, and may include many writing skills, such as capitalization, the use of commas and periods, particular spelling that is difficult, and clarification of ideas. The aim is always to improve the piece of writing, making it more interesting, effective, and enjoyable.

10. In writing conferences, educators invite the writer to read the work aloud. Educators are then free to listen and to encourage the writer to lead the conference as much as possible. The writer can thus remain in charge of the piece. The role of the educator and the other learners is to make suggestions and share responses as interested listeners and co-writers. The conventions of writing can be attended to later in the process, when the ideas and organization are firmly in place.

11. In order to be authentic and to model the writing process, educators write themselves, either with learners or at some other time if they are too busy during the writers' workshop. In addition, educators share their writing with their students. Learners need to see that even adults struggle with creating good writing.

Source: This material is based loosely on N. Atwell, *In the middle: Writing, reading, and learning with adolescents*, (Portsmouth, NH: Heinemann), 1987, pp. 83–84, 94.

Teacher with child engaged in a writing conference

One key element of a writing conference is response time. Most educators find "wait time" difficult and frequently jump in with a suggestion before the young writer has had a chance to think and respond thoughtfully. One of the greatest challenges facing educators in a writing conference is allowing the learner time to think, not rushing in with a ready-made solution. The writing belongs to the writer, and the educator's role is to help learners become better writers. Box 9.7 contains suggestions from Atwell (1998) for conducting writing conferences.

Writing conferences are not restricted to poetic writing. Expository writing also benefits from peer and educator responses. In fact, any piece of writing we wish to do well may require input from others along the way. Letters to a business or government agency, reports, and play scripts can all benefit from feedback from others. Writers may work on their ideas

BOX 9.7

GUIDELINES FOR CONDUCTING WRITING CONFERENCES

1. Keep an eye on the time, and do not spend too long with any one young writer.

2. Meet with as many writers as possible each day.

3. Circulate from one area of the room to another. Go to learners' desks whenever possible.

4. Make a conference personal. It is a conversation. Kneel or sit next to the writer.

5. Whisper and ask writers to whisper when they confer with you. Do not distract other writers.

6. Build on what writers know and have done rather than telling them what they have not done.

7. Avoid generalized praise and evaluation, such as saying "good." Attending to the writer in a serious manner is more effective than giving a few words of praise.

8. Focus on one aspect of the writing in the conference, and don't try to "fix" everything or clarify all the "fuzzy" thinking.

9. Focus on meaning, and ask the questions you genuinely want to know about.

10. At the end of the conference, ask the writer to summarize the points discussed.

11. Invite writers to note their intended actions.

12. Be prepared to take notes of your questions and observations.

13. Don't take over the piece of writing, making it your own. Ask for permission (e.g., "May I show you a way to do this?").

Source: Some of this material is based loosely on N. Atwell, *In the middle: Writing, reading, and learning with adolescents*, (Portsmouth, NH: Heinemann), 1987, pp. 94–95.

and original drafts alone, but at some point they require feedback to clarify and present those ideas to a reading public.

The Students' Role in a Writing Workshop

Atwell (1998), among others, provided guidelines to help learners in working through drafts of their writing, eventually leading to pieces they feel proud of sharing with an audience. These guidelines (see Box 9.8) are appropriate for writers engaged in both poetic and expository writing, where a finished draft is important. Writers who are engaged in journal writing or other forms of expressive writing may not need this structure. They do, however, need quiet time to write, assistance with the conventions of written language, and an opportunity to discuss their writing and their ideas with others.

BOX 9.8

GUIDELINES FOR STUDENTS IN A WRITING WORKSHOP

1. Save everything. You never know when you might want to refer to a piece of writing again.

2. Use a writing notebook or sketchbook instead of loose sheets of paper.

3. Date and label everything so you can keep track of what you have done. Be especially careful to do this when working on a word processor.

4. When a piece of writing is finished, clip all the drafts, notes, and brainstormings together with a copy of the final draft on the top.

5. Write on one side of the paper only, and always double-space (write on every other line only).

6. Format your writing as you go (in paragraphs, lines, or stanzas).

7. Try to attend to conventions as you write, but don't allow them to disrupt the flow of your ideas. Check spelling as soon as possible. Attend to punctuation as you write. Ask for help when you need it.

8. When working on a word processor, print every couple of days or every few pages of text. Read the piece through with pen in hand, so you can attend to the flow of the whole piece and not just chunks of the text as they appear on the screen.

9. Begin each writing session by reading over what you have already written. Doing this allows you to establish where you are in the piece and creates momentum for the day's writing.

10. Writing is thinking. Don't interrupt other writers while they are writing. Don't attempt to tell other people what to write.

11. If you need to talk to the teacher, speak in a whisper.

12. When you need to receive feedback from learners or educator, move to the conference area and write down the comments as they are made. This way you will have a record of suggestions to take back to your writing.

13. Edit your work in a different colour from the text.

14. Always write as well, and as much, as you can.

Source: Adapted from N. Atwell, *In the middle: New understandings about writing, reading, and learning*, 2nd ed. (Portsmouth, NH: Heinemann), 1998, pp. 115–116.

WRITING RESOURCES

Experienced educators such as Denise Barrett, Diana Dixon, and Julie Gellner have continued their professional education through taking university courses and workshops about teaching writing. They recommend that, in order to establish writing programs in their own classrooms, beginning teachers access some of the published writing resources noted below.

6 + 1 Trait Writing, developed by the Northwest Regional Educational Laboratory in the United States, is based on sound research and is probably the most widely used program or model in Canada. It is important to note that the producers of 6 + 1 Trait Writing maintain that the model is intended to *support*, not supplant, rich teaching and that it aims to help educators to prioritize, focus, and individualize writing instruction. It is intended to complement reading-writing workshops and writing across the curriculum, not to *dictate* a writing curriculum. The developers believe that the model creates a consistent vocabulary for the teaching of writing and facilitates educators' provision of feedback on writing and the assessment of that writing. 6 + 1 Trait Writing describes the qualities of writing (traits) as ideas, organization, voice, word choice, sentence fluency, conventions, and presentation. You will note that these traits are very similar to the criteria Canadian provincial ministries of education use to assess writing at various grade levels (see Chapter 10).

The 6 + 1 Trait model aims to make explicit the use of the traits in various genres of writing, the features of good writing, and some of the techniques writers can use to craft their writing for particular audiences and purposes (Culham, 2003). In this model,

- ideas make up the content of the message
- organization refers to the internal structure of the piece—the pattern of ideas
- voice is what makes the writer's style unique—the writer's feelings and beliefs come through the writing
- word choice is the specific selection of rich and appropriate words
- sentence fluency is the flow and "sound" of the language
- conventions are the accepted, or "correct," ways to use grammar, punctuation, capitalization, and so on
- presentation refers to the form and the layout of the piece—the visual aesthetics

In her book, Culham (2003) quotes and accesses the work of many leading educators in the field of writing instruction (e.g., Mem Fox, Donald Murray, and William Zinsser). She provides well-organized and well-researched suggestions for using the 6 + 1 Trait model, and she writes for the thoughtful teacher. Her ideas and suggestions fit perfectly into a writing process model and can only strengthen a classroom writing program.

We also highly recommend the use of *First Steps* (2nd ed.), a literacy program produced by the Department of Education and Training in Western Australia (2006a). *First Steps Writing Resource Book* (2006b) draws on contemporary research and developments and focuses on the explicit teaching of different forms of text and on writing processes, forms, and conventions. The program suggests a daily block of time for writing, which includes time for explicit instruction and time for learners to engage in independent writing and feedback. The recommended procedures for teaching writing are based on the gradual shift of responsibility for the writing from educator to learners. These procedures include

- modelled writing
- language experience
- shared and interactive writing

- guided writing
- independent writing
- author's chair

First Steps Writing Resource Book provides specific and detailed examples of each of these procedures and ideas for implementation. The program also contains a Writing Map of Development, which is designed to help educators record and monitor student progress. The map is organized according to seven phases of development: role play, experimental, early, transitional, conventional, proficient, and accomplished. The Writing Map of Development resource will be referred to in greater detail in Chapter 10. *First Steps* provides a strong foundation for a classroom- or school-based writing program, with excellent assessment procedures built in.

Gail Boushey and Joan Moser's book *The Daily Five: Fostering Literacy Independence in the Elementary Grades* (2nd ed.) is a management system for helping teachers organize and set expectations for their language and literacy block K to 6. It's important to note that this book provides a structure for a language and literacy program, not the content for it (what to teach). The authors aim to create routines and procedures that foster independent literacy behaviours that are ingrained to the point of being habit—an environment where reading, writing, and self-monitoring are closely tied together. Based on student choice (to increase motivation), as well as authentic reading and writing activities, the Daily Five is a workshop model. It consists of five activities that children engage in each day, which vary according to age and capability: Read to Self, Work on Writing, Read to Someone (especially for younger learners), Listen to Reading, and Word Work. While learners engage in these independent activities, educators work with small groups of children in writing conferences, Guided Reading, and so on. Uninterrupted time for reading and writing are key elements of this approach.

Units of Study for Teaching Writing, Grades 3–5 is a high-quality resource from Lucy Calkins. The series of books is based on many years of research and implementation in elementary classrooms. *Launching the Writing Workshop* contains information on establishing the writing workshop approach, recognizing qualities of good writing, holding writing conferences, choosing ideas for writing, drafting, revising, editing, ascertaining timelines for the process, and celebrating finished work. Other books in the series are *Raising the Quality of Narrative Writing*; *Breathing Life into Essays*; *Writing Fiction: Big Dreams, Tall Ambitions*; *Memoir: The Art of Writing Well*; *and Literary Essays: Writing About Reading* (particularly helpful in reader response). All the books contain numerous examples of student writing, teaching ideas, tips on assessment, and additional resources. We highly recommend this series for beginning teachers.

A helpful and popular resource teachers recommend is the series entitled *Empowering Writers* by Barbara Mariconda and Dea Paoletta Auray. The series includes guides to teaching expository (informational) writing in grades 3 to 8; narrative and personal experience writing in grades 2 to 7; kindergarten to grade 1 writing; opinion writing; and editing and revising writing.

SOCIAL INTERACTION IN THE WRITING PROCESS

Although educators have long realized that learning to talk is a social process, only recently have we acknowledged the importance of social interaction when writing. If, as Moffett

(1979) maintained, true writing occurs only when we revise inner speech, then learners need to become aware of what the revision of inner speech entails. Teachers such as Diana Dixon, Julie Gellner, and Denise Barrett encourage learners to make their inner speech explicit and to wrestle with the ideas they want to articulate. They encourage the notion of "writing in community," and their students learn from one another by talking about their writing and by sharing their writing with one another. Moffett wrote that teachers "have no choice but to work in the gap between thought and speech" (1979, p. 278). He also suggested that "writing cannot be realistically perceived and taught so long as we try to work from the outside in" (p. 279). In other words, true writing comes from within the writer, who must learn to articulate thought and put it into print. When learners work collaboratively in the writing process (and in creating multimedia projects), they have opportunities to explore the gap between thought and speech. When educators listen to them, they can find out how individuals negotiate meaning and how they come to understand the structural elements of writing. Through their talk, as Michael Halliday (1969) has said, students learn "how to mean."

The Importance of Talk

As learners talk together or with educators, continual scaffolding is evident. Through constant interaction, students become teachers and learners interchangeably. The following excerpt is a planning session where Erica and Sharon, in a grade 5 classroom, considered each other's opinions and incorporated them into a written discussion of the city bylaw on cats (Lewis, 1989).

SHARON: Want to do a debate?

ERICA: Yes, then we can each have our own opinion.

SHARON: What's yours about?

ERICA: My what?

SHARON: Your issue you want to debate. I want to do the cat bylaw. OK?

ERICA: OK. I'll just put "Cat Bylaw" at the top of the page.

SHARON: OK. If I was in charge of the world I'd change the cat bylaw.

ERICA: Do you want to do this one … together? I don't have a cat, you do, so it makes a difference, doesn't it?

SHARON: Cats should be able to walk around.

ERICA: And I'm going to write against that! Cats go to the bathroom everywhere and—

SHARON: Good, we disagree then we agree on that. (*Laughter*)

ERICA: And it smells! Write on the top of the page "Cat Bylaw" again.

SHARON: Why?

ERICA: Because we're going to do it together.… We'll put my opinions and your opinions so we know whose is what.

SHARON: I want to ask you a question. If you don't have a cat, would you still not like the rule as much? I still think it's dumb.

ERICA: Ya, but you wouldn't like it as much, like it wouldn't be.… Even if you had a cat, would you still hate it more?

SHARON:	No, exactly the same.
ERICA:	What! I'm writing against you, right?
SHARON:	Well, cats … I agree that cats do that, go to the bathroom, I mean.
ERICA:	I agree in a way. (*Writes this down slowly.*)
SHARON:	Don't write this next part down till I figure it out. (pp. 230–231)

In their continuing negotiation of meaning, the two girls found that they became very much aware of writing for an audience. They began to negotiate meaning and work out details, where each sentence, and at times each word, was important. Disagreements were common, and they questioned the logic of each other's ideas. The following excerpt, from a discussion Sharon and Erica held while co-writing "The Wellington Story," concerns the phrases "looked closer" and "looked again."

ERICA:	"He looked closer into the hole …"
SHARON:	"He looked again," sounds better.
ERICA:	Well, Sharon, if you looked closer, would you stick your head right into the hole?
SHARON:	It doesn't mean that.
ERICA:	Well, it does to me!
SHARON:	Closer isn't sticking your face into the hole, but "looked again" just sounds better.
ERICA:	Sharon, you don't listen!
SHARON:	So, we don't use "closer" or "again." We say "he looked into the hole and saw the top of the wine bottle."
ERICA:	No, "he looked closer." A bit closer. Know what I mean?
SHARON:	Why would he look closer to see the wine bottle?
ERICA:	'Cause the dress might have covered it up, you know. Then "he looked again" doesn't mean "he looked closer."
SHARON:	Yes, it does!
ERICA:	Sharon, I don't know. It's the way the sentence, the way …
SHARON:	The way you put it sounds dumb.
ERICA:	Well, where did he actually look?
SHARON:	Under the floorboards.
ERICA:	Well, I don't think he needs to get closer to see under the floorboards; that's what I really mean.
SHARON:	When you say "looked closer," it doesn't necessarily mean you looked closely right in the hole; it means you sort of took a second look.
ERICA:	Ya, that's it! He took a second look!
SHARON:	Oh, wow, we got it!
ERICA:	Phew! (pp. 70–71)

Peer Group Writing Conferences

The following group conference was initiated and conducted by four young writers who relied on strategies their classroom teacher had taught them. The transcript, taken from Lewis (1989), shows how the writers used these conferences to further their own writing development. Erica began by reading the unfinished "Wellington" story quoted in Box 9.1.

ERICA:	"'It's coming from the paint house,' said Mr. McGregor. They all rushed out to the paint house and saw Yvette shaking, with a knife in her hand."
SHARON:	That's as far as we've got.
CRAIG:	I have a question. Who's Yvette?
ERICA:	The maid.
CRAIG:	What's her husband's name?
ERICA:	The maid? She doesn't have one.
DANA:	No, Craig. Mr. and Mrs. Wellington.
CRAIG:	Oh, right.
DANA:	All of a sudden, you brought in that Mr. McGregor. Who's he supposed to be?
SHARON:	One of the guests. When it says, well, we didn't want to just list them all.
DANA:	You could say, "Mr. McGregor, one of the guests …"
ERICA:	Good idea.
DANA:	Where do you guys go from here?
SHARON:	Well, we're not sure. We have to have the loose floorboards so the police can find the …
ERICA:	We also think we want it to be a play, and we talked about highlighting the speaking parts, except Sharon wants to write it all out so …
DANA:	Hey, you guys, we forgot to say our favourite parts. The part about the paint house really catches my eye. Is this guy a painter, a famous one?
ERICA:	Ya, and that's why Yvette kills him because he painted a picture of her and she is afraid that Mrs. Wellington will find out.
DANA:	Wouldn't it just be easier to destroy the painting than to kill the guy?
SHARON:	Well, another idea we had is that it's not Yvette. It's the wife and she kills him for his money. We aren't exactly sure about that part yet.
CRAIG:	I like the part where they find her holding the bloody knife.
ERICA:	We didn't say it was bloody.
CRAIG:	Well, it would be, you know. (pp. 130–131)

Because of the importance of talk and the amount of learning that takes place in group conferences, it's important to encourage and facilitate this kind of dialogue as part of a writers' workshop. Through interaction, writers become more aware of their covert writing processes and of the conventions necessary for effective communication with an audience. Sharon said,

> I like to talk about all my ideas and I like to figure it all out with someone else. It got kind of hard, you know, because I get really excited and I yelled at Erica, she's so picky, though, you know. (*Smiles.*) (p. 156)

The following statements illustrate the learners' thoughts on writing conferences:

DANA: Some days it's easy—all goes well—and some days it's bad, it's really hard.

ERICA: Well … it's both actually easy and hard. Maybe at different times it's harder …

CRAIG: It helps me. I love talking to someone.

SHARON: She helps me about quotations and … other things, too. (p. 157)

The extensive use of expressive language enables learners to clarify and extend their thoughts as they write. Learners benefit from talking through their understanding at every stage of the process. Some days, there is more talk than writing, but through this talk young writers make explicit their understandings of what writing is and what writing can do. They also articulate their understandings of literary structures and what makes a piece of writing work. In "The Wellington Story" (see Box 9.1), Sharon and Erica demonstrated a command of the mystery story genre and of the conventions of story writing. Carefully crafted with an audience in mind, their story undoubtedly reflects some of their recreational reading.

SUMMARY

Writing is both an art and a skill, an activity that can give enormous pleasure to the writer as well as to the reader. In the process approach to the teaching of writing, educators help learners to develop both composition and presentation skills. Process writing stresses the purpose for writing, the audience for the writing, and the relationship of these to the form and the function of the writing itself.

As they compose, learners are encouraged to write for a variety of audiences and for particular purposes. Expressive writing is written either for the self or for an audience close to the writer. It records or captures personal thoughts, feelings, and intentions. Informational or expository writing is used when the writer wants to convey information to others in a formal report, list, essay, or textbook. Poetic writing is usually created for an audience other than the self. It contains aesthetic or literary elements and is the voice used in stories as well as poems. In a process approach, all genres of writing are taught so that learners can learn to write effectively for a range of audiences and purposes.

When composing and crafting a piece of writing or a multimedia project, young writers need a structure in the classroom that will allow them large chunks of quiet writing time, conferences that provide feedback from an interested and informed audience, and the opportunity to share finished pieces with "the public." Writing conferences help writers to draft and revise their thoughts until they are sure they are saying exactly what they want to say. It is in writing conferences that most of the teaching occurs. Working through the process of drafting, revising, editing, and sharing helps learners to become better writers.

Educators recognize the importance of talk in the development of writing. When learners are on-task and are engaged fully in a shared writing experience, they learn a great deal from one another through exchanging and negotiating ideas. The quest for clarity and appropriateness of language, the response of the readers, and the power of words to evoke images and feelings are the elements young writers learn about as they write together in classrooms.

SELECTED PROFESSIONAL RESOURCES

Atwell, N. (2002). *Lessons that change writers: A yearlong writing workshop curriculum.* Portsmouth, NH: Heinemann.

In this publication, Nancie Atwell presents more than 100 mini-lessons and samples of writing in order to focus educators on the mini-lesson as a vehicle for helping learners improve their writing. Although the intended audience is middle-years educators, this resource is extremely helpful in grades 4 and up. In loose-leaf binder format, the resource includes many samples of Nancie's own writing, and of writing done by students, which beginning teachers can easily use for mini-lessons. The binder includes numerous bibliographic references.

Booth, D., & Swartz, L. (2004). *Literacy techniques for building successful readers and writers* (2nd ed.). Markham, ON: Pembroke.

This book is virtually an encyclopedia of approaches to literacy. It can help beginning teachers to reflect on their teaching style and select the best approaches for meeting the needs of every learner in their classrooms. Full of checklists and guidelines, it is a useful tool for substitute teachers, parents, study buddies, and other volunteer partners.

Janeczko, P. (Comp.). (2002). *Seeing the blue between: Advice and inspiration for young poets.* Cambridge, MA: Candlewick Press.

Compiled by a children's poet, this book contains letters and poems from 32 internationally renowned poets. These writers provide words of wisdom and examples of their own work. Contributors include Kalli Dakos, Rob Farnsworth, Bobbi Katz, Naomi Shihab Nye,

continued

Jack Prelutsky, and Jane Yolen. The letters are personal, friendly, and supportive. The contributors encourage young writers to read and emphasize the importance of revision. There's lots of humour in the book, and the selected poems cover a wide range of styles, moods, and subjects.

Tompkins, G. (2004). *50 literacy strategies: Step by step.* Upper Saddle River, NJ: Pearson/ Merrill Prentice Hall.

Page by page, Tompkins describes literacy strategies for elementary classroom use, including author's chair; clusters, webs, and maps; learning logs; data charts; writing groups; gallery walks; and the "tea party," among many others. The resource is practical and easy to use, and it fits perfectly into the contemporary writing classroom.

CHAPTER TEN

Assessment and Conventions of Writing

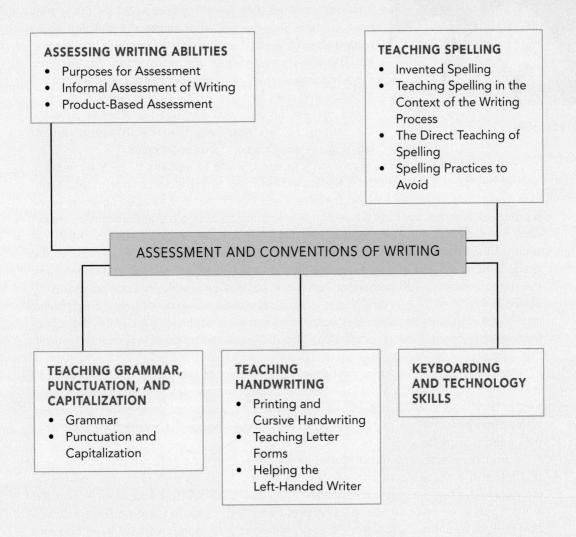

ASSESSING WRITING ABILITIES
- Purposes for Assessment
- Informal Assessment of Writing
- Product-Based Assessment

TEACHING SPELLING
- Invented Spelling
- Teaching Spelling in the Context of the Writing Process
- The Direct Teaching of Spelling
- Spelling Practices to Avoid

ASSESSMENT AND CONVENTIONS OF WRITING

TEACHING GRAMMAR, PUNCTUATION, AND CAPITALIZATION
- Grammar
- Punctuation and Capitalization

TEACHING HANDWRITING
- Printing and Cursive Handwriting
- Teaching Letter Forms
- Helping the Left-Handed Writer

KEYBOARDING AND TECHNOLOGY SKILLS

Eileen Loughlin

ASSESSING WRITING IN EILEEN LOUGHLIN'S GRADE 2 CLASSROOM

Eileen uses the writing process in her classroom, but her learners take only two narrative pieces each year through to the publishing stage. In grade 2, revision and redrafting is hard work, and many are still struggling with manuscript printing. Their spelling is often slow.

Eileen and her students keep writing notebooks and writing folders so it's easy to see what they have written, how many pieces they have finished, and how many they have started. She can tell what topics the children enjoy writing about the most and what they do their best writing on. The folders help Eileen with assessment *for* learning. From reading learners' writing, she can tell what she needs to teach, and she often gathers a group of learners for a particular mini-lesson on a skill they need to learn or develop. The writing folders also help Eileen with assessment *of* learning—when it's time to do report cards.

Eileen is not expected to give a mark or letter grade to learners for all the pieces of writing they do, but she does provide detailed feedback to them based upon criteria listed in a rubric collaboratively created by Eileen and her students. She uses numbers when scoring work for her own use when she is preparing to assign a standard on the report card. For example, she uses the numbers designated in the Provincial Achievement Test writing rubric to help her devise a standard for each learner's report card. She uses the grade 2 rubric developed by her school district to assess learners within grade level and the grade 3 Provincial Achievement Test rubric to provide criteria for learners achieving above grade level. In her school district, the standards are excellent, proficient, basic, insufficient, or unable to assess (perhaps used when a learner has just arrived in the school from another country). More information about Eileen's report cards is presented later in the chapter.

Assessing learners' writing abilities is a crucial part of the planning and instruction cycle. Ongoing, formative assessment in the classroom provides teachers with the information they need to make instructional decisions that will enhance their students' learning. It also provides learners with information so they can see how well they are doing and what they need to work on.

Summative assessment at the end of the school term or year provides the school district with a measure of the success of their programs and provides individual learners with a regular statement of their progress in school. To become well-rounded writers over their years in school, students need assistance in learning the transcription skills of spelling, punctuation, and grammar, as well as involvement in writing and reading workshops. This chapter addresses the areas of assessment of writing and the direct instruction of transcription skills, often referred to as the conventions, or tools, of writing. ☐

ASSESSING WRITING ABILITIES

Purposes for Assessment

There are ways in which the teaching of writing and the assessment of writing are so closely interconnected that teachers cannot do one without doing the other. Effective educators like Eileen conduct ongoing assessment in order to provide learners with appropriate feedback on their writing. This does not mean *grading* student work but *assessing* their work using appropriate criteria. One set of criteria is not sufficient for assessing all writing, although some general concerns such as "organization" or "quality of ideas" may be valid across genres. As learners of all ages write in a range of genres, educators need criteria appropriate to the genres, and they also need to *show* learners how they can improve their writing. Many educators find it helpful to develop assessment criteria and rubrics alongside learners. It becomes part of the teaching. If learners know what good writing looks like, and what constitutes good writing, they are more likely to be able to compose good pieces.

In their classroom practice, teachers use a variety of strategies for assessing writing depending on the purpose for the assessment. Writing assessment is always focused, in some way, on improving the writing abilities of the learners in our classrooms. Most often, assessment is conducted informally to guide a teacher's planning and instruction. The more information educators possess about learners, the more effectively they can understand and meet an individual's learning needs. A second purpose for assessment is to provide feedback to individuals so they know what they do well and what they can focus on in order to become better writers. A third purpose is to provide information to parents and caregivers about student progress. A fourth purpose is to provide information to school districts and provincial governments about the writing abilities of the learners in their schools. Successful educators strive to maintain a balanced approach to assessment, developing a broad picture of their students' learning. They do this through using a wide range of assessment techniques, including observation, anecdotal records, profiles, portfolios or writing folders, learner self-evaluation, writing conferences, analyses of samples of writing, and provincial or local district achievement tests.

In order to describe and assess students' writing effectively, educators attend not only to the surface features of the writing (transcription skills such as handwriting, spelling, and punctuation) but also to the content or message of what is written, which is, of course, the purpose for the writing. Rather than marking, correcting, or grading learners' writing, educators usually respond to the writing or provide feedback to the individual. Like Eileen, they offer comments, either orally or in writing, on the form of the writing (the extent to which the writing meets the purpose or genre) or on the content of the piece. Only later do they attend to transcription errors.

Knowledgeable educators look not only at samples of student writing but also observe learners at work, listening to the running commentaries they engage in as they write, listening to student conversations and conferences with peers, watching the way they form letters or attempt to spell unknown words. In their instruction and evaluation of writing, educators show respect for the idiosyncratic nature of the writing process and value both the written products and the writing processes of individual writers.

Educators and researchers know that it is not possible to objectively assess any single piece of writing. Every reading of a text is affected by the values and cultural expectations of the reader (most often the teacher). We also know there is no *one* way to evaluate a learner's writing, no way to generate one mark or grade that represents the student's level of development in writing as a whole. The primary focus of assessment is on helping learners to enhance their learning and on helping teachers to plan for instruction. As a result, a range of assessment strategies is necessary depending on the purpose for the assessment. Table 10.1 summarizes some of the methods educators find useful in assessing learner progress in writing in relation to the purpose for the assessment.

Informal Assessment of Writing

Teachers need to keep track of student progress in their classrooms every day. No other area of the curriculum is as complex to assess and monitor as that of writing, but educators have found a number of informal strategies valuable when they use them regularly. These are observations, anecdotal records, conferences, learner self-assessments, writing folders and portfolios, and profiles.

Observations

Focused observations (and keeping relevant notes) of learners as they write, participate in writing groups and conferences, revise and proofread their writing, and share their finished pieces with an audience can provide much useful information for educators. Learners' attitudes to writing, their writing strategies, how they interact with others, and how they seek out others for assistance or in sharing their writing can be revealed through observation. While making observations, educators can ask learners questions to clarify what they have observed, for example, "Would you like to share that with a partner?" "Do you have a title for this piece?" Tompkins (2007) suggested that, while making observations, the teacher sit next to, or across from the writer, and simply say, "I'm going to watch you as you write so I can help you become a better writer."

Anecdotal Records

Notes taken by educators informally in the classroom can be much more useful than a simple grade or mark recorded in a grade book. Anecdotal notes provide detailed information about a learner's writing and knowledge of written language. These notes describe specific events and observations *without evaluation or interpretation*. They can be collected in a binder, notebook, or set of cards, and they can be entered into a database on the computer. A collection of notes taken over a period of months can provide a powerful tool for ongoing literacy assessment. Teachers usually approach note-taking systematically, concentrating on a small number of learners each day (three or four). Time is set aside for reviewing the notes periodically, rereading them, analyzing them, identifying each learner's strengths and weaknesses, and making inferences about their writing development.

TABLE 10.1 **WRITING ASSESSMENT STRATEGIES**

Purpose	Informal/Formative	Product-Based/Summative
To inform instruction	• writing conferences (group and one-on-one) • observations of performance (including checking for spelling and other transcription skills) • anecdotal notes • journals/learning logs • student self-assessment • review of writing folders	• teacher-developed, whole-class tests (e.g., spelling, word usage) • whole-class writing tasks with teacher- or school-developed rubric • analytical reviews of writing samples • portfolio assessment • learner writing profiles
To inform learners	• writing conferences (group and one-on-one) • responses to journals/learning logs • responses to writing folders and portfolios • review of writing folders	• whole-class writing tasks • tests • parent-learner-teacher conferences • portfolio review
To inform parents	• portfolios of written work • learning logs/journals • learner self-assessment	• whole-class writing tasks • tests • parent-learner-teacher conferences • learner writing profiles
To inform school administration, school district, provincial department of education	• writing samples with analysis	• norm-referenced achievement tests (e.g., provincial achievement tests) • teacher-developed tests and writing scales

Conferences

One-on-one or small-group conferences (two or three individuals) might focus on a particular topic or principle, or they can be general in scope. These conferences provide opportunities for joint assessment of writing as educators and learners together discuss student progress. Unlike the instruction or process-oriented conferences listed in Chapter 9 (such as prewriting conferences, drafting conferences, and editing conferences), assessment conferences are usually held on completion of a composition. Educators invite learners to reflect on their piece of writing, their writing competencies, and their growth as writers. Educators also ask learners to set goals for future work. In a portfolio conference, teachers meet with learners individually, review the writing samples in the portfolio, and discuss the writing with the learner. Educators may also use this occasion to decide on a grade for the project in collaboration with the learner.

Learner Self-Assessment

It is generally agreed that effective assessment must begin with the learner. If students are to improve their writing, they must be able to see the need for that improvement—hence the need for learner self-assessment. In self-assessments, learners are asked to consider what they have learned and what has been important from their own perspectives. Opportunities for learners to assess their progress are provided when they select writing for a portfolio or when they are at the end of a unit or writing project. What learners may think is significant in their learning may not seem important to an educator or parent. Asking learners to assess their own work (and providing a rationale for the assessment) is important, therefore, because it gives them the opportunity to be responsible, confident, independent, and autonomous learners. Learners are required to be self-evaluative throughout the writing process when they decide on ideas for a piece of writing, make decisions about what to revise and redraft, and decide when a piece is finished or when it needs more work. These decisions and evaluations are made explicit in a learner's self-assessment. Educators often provide prompts or guidelines (questions) for learner self-assessments. Learners who are too young to write a self-assessment may provide an oral self-assessment to the teacher and the teacher makes notes.

Educators frequently use these self-assessment conferences as an opportunity to prepare for student-led conferences with parents. Individuals select the piece of writing they want to share, and they think about and write notes about why they want to share this particular piece with their parents and teacher. They might also be asked to select one piece of writing they plan to work on, and they explain why they want to work on it and what they might do. In other words, what can improve this piece of writing?

Writing Portfolios

Portfolios and **performance assessment** promote and assess the *application* of the language arts. Keeping a portfolio, and selecting artifacts to include in a portfolio, enables students to become active learners and allows them to take control of their own development as readers and writers.

Writing portfolios and writing folders are each used for quite different purposes. A writing folder is a "working file," containing work in progress, some finished work, and topics that might be the basis for future pieces, whereas a writing portfolio is a collection of one learner's completed work, carefully selected to demonstrate what that individual can do. As described in Chapter 9, a writing folder may contain stories, reports, poems, recipes, movie reviews, résumés, letters, and other informal material learners are working on (including notes for forthcoming pieces). Learners are encouraged to keep all their drafts and finished compositions dated and clipped together, and their self-assessments of finished work may be attached to the written pieces. If learners take a piece of writing home permanently, teachers usually photocopy it for the writing folder. From time to time, learners are invited to select their best pieces of writing for review, and these are placed in a portfolio. It's important that a range of genres be included in a portfolio, as the aim is to showcase the writer's abilities.

The portfolio itself might be a concertina folder that expands to accommodate objects other than sheets of paper. Small books and reports might go into the portfolio, as well as comments from peers who have read or heard pieces written by the individual. Learners usually create a list of contents to go at the front of the portfolio, and older students might add a letter stating why each piece of writing has been selected. Educators can use the portfolios to document and illustrate learners' writing progress, and the portfolios can be used productively during parent–teacher conferences. When reviewing portfolios, educators emphasize what learners know and can do, rather than what they are learning to do or cannot do. Many educators find it helpful to review portfolios with a colleague. The practice helps to inform teachers' assessment criteria and helps them develop a greater range of strategies for supporting an individual's learning.

Portfolio assessment is a form of process or performance evaluation. The aim is not to take one piece of writing in isolation, but to look at a collection of a person's writings in many genres and voices. A portfolio might include stories, poems, letters, journal entries, lists, semantic maps, responses to literature, book reviews, artwork associated with the language arts, and writing from across the curriculum. In this way, learners can see their writing as more than separate, isolated pieces. Portfolios also give learners the opportunity to self-evaluate their work in choosing what they wish to put into the portfolio.

Suggestions for developing and assessing portfolios include reviewing the volume of work in the portfolio, the interest and attitudes of the writers, and, of course, the development and growth of the writing (Farr & Tone, 1998). Educators can use portfolios to aid them in their instruction. Through discussion, writing, and reflection, portfolio assessment helps learners become better thinkers and communicators. Portfolio assessment is not something educators do *to* learners but rather *with* them. Portfolio assessment is a reflection of holistic, constructive language learning and teaching in action. A sample of one teacher's comments on learners' portfolios is presented in Box 10.1.

BOX 10.1

ASSESSING THE CONTENTS OF A PORTFOLIO

What the Teacher Notices in the Portfolio	What That Suggests
This fifth-grade boy reads one comic book after another and does not record all of them on his logs. Most are humorous types; many are about Garfield the cat.	The teacher should look for some humorous stories about cats for him to read—perhaps with a character as ornery as Garfield.
Anders has a note attached to two mysteries he has written, saying that they are his favourites. He also has indicated on his log that an adventure story he wrote is his best because "it is exciting." There is not a large amount of writing in the portfolio, however.	The teacher could develop more opportunities for Anders to write. The adventure is a good story. Perhaps if Anders shared it with some fellow students and saw how they enjoyed it, he would be encouraged to write more.
Tad doesn't write a lot, but he draws well and is considered the best artist in the class by his classmates. His journal, which is spotty, is mainly about sports heroes. He also seems to write kinds of reviews about scary movies he has seen somewhere.	The teacher might ask Tad to be the sports editor on the next issue of the class newspaper. He could also illustrate one of his friend Adam's stories and perhaps write a sequel to it. The teacher decides to see if Tad might like to read *Joe Montana and Jerry Rice* by Richard J. Brenner and the mystery *Is Anybody There?* by Eve Bunting. He could review the ones he reads for the paper and/or for the bulletin board and do illustrations for them.

(continued)

What the Teacher Notices in the Portfolio	What That Suggests
Heriyadi's story "A Pizzaman's Adventure" is a kind of string of things that happen to a delivery person. It is the same character name as the "Gary" in his story "The City Street." Both of these stories have stringy plots but are very rich in details that build and build until offering the reader a rather complete picture of the character.	There is keen evidence that Heriyadi is thinking about what he writes and its impact on his reader. It's as if he keeps wanting to ensure that the picture is really complete enough for his readers to see it as he does. He should be encouraged to write some detailed descriptive pieces.

Further examples and ideas for portfolios can be found in *Portfolios Matter: What, Where, When, Why and How to Use Them* by Easley and Mitchell (2003). This book is a quick reference for information about both portfolios and student-led conferencing.

Profiles

Once data have been collected through writing conferences, observations, checklists, samples collected in writing folders, written conversations, note-taking, published writing, and discussion with parents, educators can create writing profiles of the learners. One reliable and much-used resource for describing what children can do and how they can do it is the *First Steps Writing Map of Development* (2nd ed., 2006), developed by the Department of Education and Training in Western Australia. First Steps "acknowledges the importance of sociocultural perspectives to the teaching of writing" (p. 3) and takes a multidimensional view of writing instruction. The Map of Development is based on seven phases of development: role play, experimental, early, transitional, conventional, proficient, and accomplished. For each phase of writing development, a global statement summarizes the general characteristics of the phase and describes the types of texts learners in that phase might create. A list of key indicators is then presented for each phase, and major teaching emphases are suggested. The indicators listed are not meant to provide evaluative criteria; rather, "the purpose is to link assessment, teaching and learning in a way that best addresses the strengths and needs of all students" (p. 11). First Steps pays particular attention to learners who speak English as a second language. The Map of Development is a useful tool for deciding on teaching strategies for individual learners, for small groups, or for whole-class instruction. An overview of the first phase, role play, is presented in Box 10.2.

Product-Based Assessment

From time to time, educators must complete more formal assessments of learners' progress in writing. These assessments may be part of the ongoing formative or diagnostic assessments

BOX 10.2

In this phase, writers emulate adult writing by experimenting with marks to represent written language. Role-play writers are beginning to understand that writing is used to convey meaning or messages; however, as understandings about sound–symbol relationships are yet to be developed, their messages are not readable by others. Role-play writers rely heavily on topic knowledge to generate text.

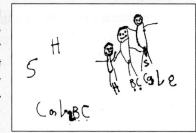

Key Indicators

Use of Texts

▷ Assigns a message to own written and drawn symbols.

▷ Demonstrates awareness that writing and drawing are different.

▷ Knows that print carries a message but may "read" writing differently each time.

Contextual Understanding

▷ States purposes or audience for own writing—for example, "This is a card for Dad."

▷ Identifies and talks about characters from literary texts.

▷ Identifies and talks about people and ideas in informational texts.

Conventions

▷ Begins to demonstrate an awareness of directionality—for example, points to where print begins.

▷ Uses known letters or approximations of letters to represent writing.

Processes and Strategies

▷ Relies upon personal experiences as a stimulus for writing.

Major Teaching Emphases

Environment and Attitude

▷ Create a supportive classroom environment that nurtures a community of writers.

▷ Foster students' enjoyment of writing.

▷ Encourage students to experiment with different facets of writing—for example, using known letters, composing messages.

▷ Encourage students to value writing as a social practice.

Use of Texts

▷ Expose students to a range of text forms pointing out purpose—for example, recipes tell how to make something.

(continued)

▷ Provide opportunities for students to "write" a range of texts for authentic purposes and audiences.

▷ Model the connection between oral and written language—for example, what is said can be written down.

▷ Demonstrate that written messages remain constant.

▷ Foster students' sense of "personal voice" and individual writing style.

▷ Teach students the metalanguage associated with writing, and encourage its use.

Contextual Understanding

▷ Discuss that writing has a purpose and an intended audience.

▷ Draw students' attention to decisions writers make when composing texts.

▷ Draw students' attention to the way characters are represented in literary texts.

▷ Draw students' attention to the way people and ideas are represented in informational texts.

Conventions

▷ Provide opportunities for students to develop and use new vocabulary.

▷ Begin to build the bank of words students can automatically spell and use—for example, personally significant words.

▷ Build phonological awareness and graphophonic knowledge, such as:
  ▷ recognizing, matching, and generating rhymes
  ▷ listening for sounds in words
  ▷ linking letter names with their sounds, focusing on the regular sound

▷ Teach students the conventions of print.

▷ Model one-to-one correspondence between written and spoken words.

▷ Model the composition of simple sentences, including the use of punctuation—for example, capital letters, full stops.

Processes and Strategies

▷ Build students' semantic, graphophonic, and syntactic knowledge—for example, topic knowledge, sound–symbol relationships.

▷ Teach strategies used throughout the writing process—for example, connecting.

▷ Teach spelling strategies—for example, sounding out.

▷ Model simple publishing alternatives—for example, text and illustration.

▷ Model how to find required information in texts.

▷ Model how to reflect on the writing process and products, and encourage students to do the same.

Source: Reprinted from: *First Steps, (2nd Edition): Writing Map of Development: Overview (2005)*. Copyright © Minister for Education, Western Australia. http://det.wa.edu.au/stepsresources/detcms/education/stepsresources/first-steps-literacy/writing-map-of-development.en?cat-id=13601995.

that contribute to effective classroom instruction, or they may be summative assessments used for report cards or end-of-year school district testing. This type of assessment is usually conducted through a review of written products rather than assessing the processes learners engage in when writing. Assessment of a portfolio or writing folder and the creation of writing profiles can also be useful summative assessment tools; however, it is frequently the finished product or the test score that parents, school administration, school districts, provincial departments of education, and employers use to judge writing abilities.

Unfortunately, the assessment requirements of some school districts and provincial governments are frequently at odds with the needs of learners and educators. Where learners want to know how they can improve their writing, and educators want to inform their planning in order to meet their students' learning requirements, school districts and provincial governments (and sometimes parents) want to know how learners' abilities compare with the abilities of those in other jurisdictions. They also want a measure of how much learners know and can do—and the more objective, the better. As a result, educators need a broad repertoire of assessment procedures, including formal ones that demonstrate accountability to the general public as well as informal procedures designed to provide feedback to individual learners and input to instructional planning.

Learner performance on product-based tasks cannot be "machine-scored," but must instead be judged according to well-defined criteria. The vehicle containing these criteria is commonly known as a *scoring rubric*—a fixed scale and a list of characteristics describing performance for each of the points on the scale. A rubric differs from a scoring key in that a scoring key does not contain descriptive characteristics, just a list of how points are to be assigned. Various provincial ministries of education and school districts in Canada have developed their own rubrics for the assessment of student writing. Samples of these are presented later in this chapter in Boxes 10.3, 10.4, 10.6, and 10.7. Teachers are trained to mark these writing tests as objectively as possible, minimizing reader bias and ensuring that scoring is consistent. Reliability checks are conducted regularly throughout the marking sessions.

Analysis of Writing Samples

When reading samples of learners' writing, educators are mindful that writing is not a single skill. Writing is a complex and sophisticated process that involves the effective utilization of syntax, organizational strategies, vocabulary, transcription tools, and ideas. Each of these varies according to the purpose and audience for the writing. The purpose and intended audience for a piece of writing shape the composition. Expressive writing is writer oriented: its purpose is to reveal feelings, attitudes, and perceptions. Expository writing is subject oriented: it is meant to explain or present information on a subject. Persuasive writing is audience oriented: the writer takes a position on a topic and tries to convince others to adopt it. The stimulus, or prompt, for a writing task also frames the piece of writing and influences the piece considerably. Therefore, when educators read and score writing samples, they take all of these factors into consideration, varying their reading of the piece according to the purpose for the writing and the stimulus provided.

Many teachers and language arts consultants develop rubrics and scoring guides for assessing and marking writing in their own classrooms. Frequently, these guides are developed in collaboration with learners. Teacher Eileen Loughlin reminds educators that the collaborative process facilitates three things:

1. As learners and teacher together develop the guide, they explore what constitutes a good piece of writing.
2. Learners become aware of the criteria on which they will be evaluated.
3. Learners remain in control of all aspects of their writing from outset to completion.

Eileen firmly believes that the collaborative nature of the process demonstrates her respect for her students and recognizes their contributions in the classroom.

Holistic Scoring

In **holistic scoring** learners are evaluated on what they do *well* rather than on what they fail to do. This method encourages educators to focus on the specifics they have in mind for rating essays and other pieces of writing before reading them. These specifics may include

- learners' attention to purpose and audience, and the ability to organize ideas according to the needs of communicating with that audience, whether through poetic, persuasive, expressive, or informative modes
- learners' attention to the visual and verbal cues of the assignment (e.g., "Give at least one reason …")
- learners' developmental capabilities, allowing for the general language characteristics of students of a similar age (e.g., the invented spelling of children in the primary grades)
- constraints of the evaluation situation—that is, the context or setting where the writing takes place (In many evaluative situations, for example, learners do not have time to revise, edit, or ask for peer or teacher assistance.)

A number of different methods for conducting holistic assessments have been established, and many rubrics have been developed over the years. The rubric displayed in Box 10.3 was developed by the Regina Board of Education. It's used for scoring writing at the grades 4, 8, and 10 levels.

An alternative method of holistic assessment, and probably the simplest, is *general impression marking*. The rater scores the paper by deciding where it fits in the range of papers produced for that assignment on that occasion. Although there is no analysis of specific features and no summary of scores, this method has high reliability because experienced raters use an implicit list of features in much the same way as classroom teachers. If teachers were to spread out in front of them a set of writing from all the students in their class, written on the same day and on the same topic, it would be fairly clear which were the "best" pieces of writing and which were the least well developed. The middle-ranked pieces would be more difficult to arrange in some kind of order, but eventually a teacher would be able to make the decision on the basis of an implicit or internalized set of criteria. The use of this method for scoring or assessing writing can be facilitated in a school setting by a second teacher working collaboratively on the assessment. On such occasions, the educators' implicit criteria are made explicit as problematic pieces of writing are discussed and a grade is decided upon.

BOX 10.3

HOLISTIC RUBRIC FOR WRITING ASSESSMENT

Upper-half papers are characterized by well-supported, original ideas, clear evidence of an organizational plan, and general mastery of the conventions of standard English, although even the strongest papers may contain some developmentally appropriate errors in spelling or sentence structure.

▷ The "6" paper contains original, sophisticated ideas, well supported by relevant details. Organization is clear and logical, with a strong lead and effective conclusion. Vivid and precise word choice, varied sentences, and a clear, well-developed writer's voice combine to create a coherent and original piece of writing. Any errors in conventions are usually the result of risk taking.

▷ The "5" paper contains original ideas with relevant and appropriate details. It is well organized and usually has a strong lead and adequate conclusion. Clear and descriptive word choice and a developing writer's voice are evident. There may be some variation in sentence length and complexity. Minor errors in conventions do not interfere with the meaning of the piece.

▷ The "4" paper is likely to have somewhat mundane, but adequate ideas that are somewhat supported by details. A hint of writer's voice may be apparent. There is evidence of a good organizational plan with an adequate lead, though the conclusion may be weak. Word choice is generally appropriate, though lacking in precision and originality, and sentences may lack variety. Some errors in conventions are common.

Lower-half papers lack originality or effective support for ideas. Vocabulary may be immature, and control of conventions of standard English is inadequate.

▷ The "3" paper is likely to contain unoriginal ideas with marginal support, or irrelevant details that do not support the main idea. The organization is limited, with a weak or missing conclusion. A writer's voice may not be evident. Word choice may be correct, but lacking maturity, and sentences tend to be simple in structure. Frequent errors in conventions are common, but the piece should be readable.

▷ The "2" paper contains trivial ideas without supporting details. It is characterized by an inadequate organizational plan, immature vocabulary, short, simple sentences, and frequent errors in conventions that may, at times, interfere with understanding of the piece.

▷ The "1" piece is characterized by such inadequate mastery of conventions of standard English that the piece may be barely comprehensible. Ideas are incomplete or confusing, organization appears haphazard, and vocabulary choice is very limited.

▷ An asterisk code (*) is used for papers that are blank, illegible, or written on a topic other than the one assigned.

Source: Based on the Regina Board of Education Scoring Guide. Originally adapted from the Northwest Educational Laboratories Six Traits Writing Program by Sandra Pace, Lori Rog, Trudy Loftsgard, Myra Froc, and Greg Smith.

Analytic Scales

Analytic scales break the writing performance down into component parts, such as organization, wording, and ideas. It takes longer to accomplish than holistic scoring, but provides more specific information and is usually regarded as being more objective. The list of features assessed may range from 4 to 12, with each feature described in some detail and with high, mid-, and low points identified and described along a scoring line for each feature.

Analytic assessment of writing is used by many school districts, including Edmonton Public Schools. Their Highest Level of Achievement Tests (HLATs) are administered in the spring of each school year and are intended to provide grade-level achievement and growth data at the learner, school, and district levels. Each learner's writing is assessed as excellent, proficient, adequate, or limited at each grade level. Box 10.4 presents the performance and achievement criteria, along with a writing sample, for writing judged to be of "excellent" quality at the grade 3 level. The task in 2010 was to write about the qualities and attributes that make an individual (or a group) a hero. The piece was considered to be expository writing. The criteria used in the HLATs have proven useful to teachers in developing a vocabulary for discussing and conducting formal writing assessments, and in developing an explicit sense of what constitutes good writing.

Most provinces use some form of analytic assessment of writing in their annual achievement tests. Ontario's Education Quality and Accountability Office website provides rubrics and sample student responses for grades 3, 6, and 9, along with annotations. They can be

BOX 10.4

CRITERIA FOR "EXCELLENT" WRITING AT GRADE 3

Performance Criteria: EXCELLENT

The writer **fulfils the task** and purposefully **crafts details** and language to shape the writing.

The paper shows **overall unity** and artistry of communication.

The writing sustains the reader's interest, and **engages the audience.**

The ideas are **focused** and **memorable**; topic development is **skilful.**

Vocabulary and usage are often clever, and **chosen intentionally** for the form and purpose.

The organization of the paper is **controlled,** and the style creates a sense of voice **unique to the writer.**

Spelling, grammar, capitalization, and punctuation applications are controlled to **enhance the impact** of the writing; errors are hardly noticeable.

Achievement Criteria: GRADE THREE

▷ Audience appeal
  ▷ choose words and language patterns to create desired effects
  ▷ hold the reader's interest in presentation of ideas

▷ Content and planning
  ▷ support the piece of writing with some specific details
  ▷ elaborate on ideas in plan and/or writing
▷ Vocabulary and usage
  ▷ choose words appropriate to the context of their writing
  ▷ use a variety of applicable words to add interest and detail
▷ Organization and clarity
  ▷ use sentence variety to link ideas
  ▷ order information in a connected sequence
  ▷ provide an introduction
  ▷ provide closure
▷ Style and voice
  ▷ express thoughts and ideas using an authentic personal voice
  ▷ choose words and language patterns to convey personal feelings
▷ Sentence structure and grammar
  ▷ vary sentence beginnings by using different words
  ▷ show general control of subject and verb agreement
  ▷ construct complete sentences correctly
▷ Mechanics: Spelling, capitalization, punctuation
  ▷ use conventional spelling for most common words
  ▷ use capitalization for sentence beginnings, proper names, I, acronyms, and titles
  ▷ use end punctuation correctly (. ? !)
▷ Editing and revising
  ▷ make changes in word choices and spelling
  ▷ Key:
    ▷ Sample shows evidence of this criteri[on].
    ▷ No evidence of this criteri[on] in sample.

A Sample of Student Work

Planning

(continued)

Writing

Once upon a time, there was a young girl she had a cat named Fluffy. Fluffy was a fun and energetic cat. He liked to climb things. The girl also had a mom and dad. They were very loving and caring to her. She thought they were real heroes. But what she didn't know was that when she went to school in the morning Fluffy got stuck in a tree!

Her mom and dad raced outside like a bolt of lightning until they got to one of the biggest trees in the whole city! Her parents got a huge ladder the size of a building and climbed and climbed and climbed until they got to Fluffy. The girl's mother ran inside and got a bowl of Fluffy's favorite food and a nice cozy blanket. "Meow Meow!" said Fluffy delightfully when his parents gave it to him … "I think he likes it," said the girl's dad. Just then the girls school bus arrived with a "honk honk"!!

The girl jumped off the school bus and waved to her bus driver. "That was sure nice of you". said, her mother. "I had a awesome day at school today". said, the girl. We made crafts and learned about dinosaurs. "That sounds very interesting". said her father. "Now let's go in for some fresh baked raisn cookies, lemonade and carrott sticks". said, her mother.

"Mmmm!" the little girl and her father said together hungrily. "A perfect snack for good heroes" said, her mom "because that's what we are!" "Meow" whimpered Fluffy "Okay, you can have a snack too". And happily the whole family walked together into the house to have there heroeic snacks.

Applying Criteria to the Sample "Fluffy in the Tree"

The sample "Fluffy in the Tree" was judged *Excellent* because the ideas are very focused. Word choice is selective and demonstrates a clear intention to engage a reading audience.

Evidence of graded criteria in "Fluffy in the Tree" includes the following:

Writer chooses words and language patterns to create desired effects (e.g., "… like a bolt of lightning").

Writer uses a variety of applicable words to add interest and detail (e.g., "… fresh baked raisn cookies, lemonade and carrott sticks").

Writer expresses thoughts and ideas using an authentic personal voice (e.g., "Mmmm!" the little girl and her father said hungrily. "A perfect snack for good heroes" said, her mom "because that's what we are!")

Next Steps

Students like this writer may be ready to work on more fully developing characters or people referred to in the writing. The teacher could ask the student to pick one character for elaboration.

Student Input

How does this piece of writing compare to other writing you have done this year?

It is fun and exciting and we have a very good subject.

What is something you did well in this piece of writing?

I think I described the characters well.

If you could work further on this piece of writing, what would you do?

I would add more about what the parents do and the girl also.

Source: Reproduced from Edmonton Public Schools, Resource Development Services, *Teacher Resource for Highest Level of Achievement: HLAT Writing, 2010 Edition* (Edmonton, AB: Edmonton Public Schools). 2010. Reproduced with permission.

found at http://www.eqao.com/pdf_e/14/3e-Lang1-Wtg-SC-2014.pdf. British Columbia's Foundation Skills Assessment (FSA) is conducted in grades 4 and 7. Learners write a long and a short piece for assessment. The rubrics and sample responses can be found at https://www.bced.gov.bc.ca/assessment/fsa/training.htm.

In Alberta, learners in grades 3, 6, and 9 are required to produce two writing samples: one a narrative piece prompted by a story starter, and the other a functional piece prompted by a stated specific purpose for a specific audience. The test provides for some choice of topic and includes time for planning and discussion with peers. The functional piece may be a business letter or a news article, for example, and is assessed according to "content" (development and organization, fulfillment of the purpose, tone of the piece, and awareness of audience) and "content management" (accuracy and effectiveness of words and expressions, control of sentence structure, usage, mechanics, and format).

Narrative writing is assessed in the Provincial Achievement Tests in Alberta according to five criteria: content (context, plausibility, details, and awareness of audience), organization (introduction, cohesion, and closure), sentence structure (type, length), vocabulary (specific, image-creating, accurate, and effective), and language conventions (capitalization, spelling, punctuation, format, usage, clarity, and flow).

Below are the grade 6 descriptors for a narrative text that meets the standard of excellent:

Content

- The context is clearly established and consistent.
- The ideas and/or events are creative and deliberately chosen for the context established.
- Supporting details are precise and consistently effective.
- The writing is confident and/or creative and holds the reader's interest.

Organization (or Development)

- The introduction is purposeful; interesting; effectively establishes events, characters, and/or setting; and provides direction for the writing.
- Events and/or details are developed in paragraphs in a purposeful and effective order, and coherence is maintained.
- Connections and/or relationships among events, actions, details, and/or characters are consistently maintained.
- The ending ties events and/or actions together.

Sentence Structure

- Sentence structure is effectively and consistently controlled.
- Sentence type and length are consistently effective and varied.
- Sentence beginnings are consistently varied.

Vocabulary

- Words and expressions are used accurately.
- Precise words and expressions are used to create vivid images and/or to enrich details.
- Words and expressions are used to enhance the student's voice.

Conventions

- The quality of the writing is enhanced because it is essentially error free.
- Errors, if present, do not reduce the clarity or interrupt the flow of the communication.

As a demonstration, Box 10.5 presents an excerpt from a composition, "Zulu," written by a grade 6 student, together with an evaluation of the piece based on the above criteria.

BOX 10.5

ZULU

They came over to me talking in soft mumbling sounds that I couldn't understand. I backed into the corner of the stall and watched as they brought out a small harness. The creature reached out a hand and stroked my neck.

"He's a big one Alana, are ya still sure you want 'im?" One asked, obviously refering to me.

"Yes, the bigger they are the higher they jump."

The first speaker stepped forward and held out the soft leather thing, which they called a halter, for me to smell. It had no scent but I drew my head back and turned away. I looked for my mother, she was watching, but did nothing. The one they called Alana took the halter and slipped it over my head. I shook my head, not liking this thing tight on my face. I ran around the stall and rubbed my face on the rough wood of the wall.

"He's a spirited one alright." Henry said (The first one)

"Yeah, I don't intend to break that." Alana commented

"What are you going to call him?"

"Well his sire is Zulu Royaal and then his mother is Gotoit, so his name is Go to it Zulu. A pretty good name I think."

Henry came over, took hold of the halter and rubbed my ears. His hands were strong and gentle, I now knew why my mother was kind to these creatures.

A week passed. I got used to the halter and lead rope. I saw Henry and Alana each day. I asked my mother about them. She told me that Alana was her master and mine too. She said that I was to do what Henry and Alana wished me do and never to kick or bite. They have big plans for you, she would say, you will become great one day, till then you must do as they say.

When they came into the stall I could tell that there was something different about them. Not as happy. Alana came over to me right away and rubbed my nose and ears. I sniffed at her pockets as I had seen my mother do. She patted my side and slipped the halter over my head. I had grown much stronger over the last few days and loved to play tug'a'war with the shank. I looked at my mother, who I still would not move far from, Henry had put a halter on her too. I knew something was different today.

Analysis

Content. The piece of writing demonstrates a strong voice. Written as a first-person narrative, its details and description create an immediate engagement with the central character, a horse.

The vivid description is enhanced by the use of dialogue. Rather than telling the reader that Zulu is a large horse, the writer demonstrates it in Henry's comment: *"He's a big one Alana, are ya still sure you want 'im?"* The reader is also forewarned of coming events through Alana's response: *"Yes, the bigger they are the higher they jump."* The entire excerpt from the story is focused on the events in the stall, the early breaking of the young horse and his introduction to the harness. There are no extraneous details, no irrelevant content. The reader's interest is captivated and sustained.

Organization. The introduction is interesting and clearly establishes a setting and a point of view. The events of the story are arranged in paragraphs in a coherent sequence and are clearly connected, creating a cohesive piece of writing. The unfolding of events reveals the horse's character and situation, and the ending ties events together, as well as foreshadowing the events of the next chapter.

Sentence structure. The sentence structure is effectively controlled, with a variety of sentence lengths and types from coordination (*"I backed into the corner of the stall and watched as they brought out a small harness"*) to subordination (*"The first speaker stepped forward and held out the soft leather thing, which they called a halter, for me to smell"*). There are no sentence fragments or run-on sentences. The sentence beginnings are varied (*"When they came into the stall, …"*

Vocabulary. Words and expressions such as *halter, shank,* and *lead rope* are used accurately. The vocabulary is varied and colourful. Words such as *mumbling, creative, scent,* and *spirited* create vivid images and add to the rich detail presented in the piece.

Conventions. The conventions of written language are of a high standard and the piece is enhanced because it is virtually error free. Quotation marks are used appropriately, as are question marks and periods. Paragraphs are well formed, and the indentation of paragraphs and direct speech is formatted correctly. Occasionally dialect is used, and appropriate punctuation is used to mark this (as in *'im*). There are numerous commas where periods or semicolons would have been more appropriate, but this does not reduce the clarity or break up the flow of the text (*"I looked for my mother, she was watching, but did nothing"*). This usage is likely connected to the reading the student has done. The writer's favourite book was *Black Beauty* by Anna Sewell, originally published in 1877. *Black Beauty* uses a more old-fashioned style, with the frequent use of commas to break up the text, rather than periods or semicolons.

The reporting category of content for the grade 6 narrative writing task (2014–2015) is shown in Box 10.6. Box 10.7 presents the descriptors for content for the grade 9 narrative writing task. Each category is scored from poor to excellent on a scale from 1 to 5.

Assessing Learners' Progress for Report Cards

Each school district has its own method of reporting learners' progress to parents through report cards, and sometimes there are differences in report cards from one school to another within a district. However, there are similarities among them. Few districts ask for percentages or numeric marks.

BOX 10.6

ALBERTA EDUCATION GRADE 6 DESCRIPTORS FOR CONTENT (NARRATIVE WRITING)

Focus	
When marking **Content** appropriate for grade 6 narrative writing, the marker should consider how effectively the writer • establishes a context • uses ideas and/or events that are appropriate for the established context • uses specific details (of characters, settings, actions, events, etc.) • demonstrates an awareness of audience	
Excellent **E**	• The context is clearly established and consistent. • The ideas and/or events are creative and deliberately chosen for the context established. • Supporting details are precise and consistently effective. • The writing is confident and/or creative and holds the reader's interest.
Proficient **PF**	• The context is clearly established and appropriate. • The ideas and/or events are intentionally chosen for the context established. • Supporting details are specific and generally effective. • The writing is purposeful and draws the reader's interest.
Satisfactory **S**	• The context is established and generally appropriate. • The ideas and/or events are adequate for the context established. • Supporting details are general and may be predictable. • The writing is straightforward and generally holds the reader's interest.
Limited **L**	• The context is vaguely established and/or may not be appropriate. • The ideas and/or events are vague given the context established. • Supporting details are few and/or may be repetitive. • The writing is superficial and does not hold the reader's interest.
Poor **P**	• The context may be unclear and/or inappropriate. • The ideas and/or events are undeveloped and/or unrelated to any context established. • Supporting details are scant. • The writing is confusing and/or frustrating for the reader.
Insufficient **INS**	• The marker can discern no evidence of an attempt to fulfill the assignment, or the student has written so little that it is not possible to assess **Content**.

Note: Content and Organization are weighted to be worth twice as much as each of the other categories.

Source: Alberta Education. *Alberta Provincial Achievement Testing Subject Bulletin, 2014-2015 English Language Arts Grade 6.* Found at: http://education.alberta.ca/media/6738131/08_ela6_bulletin_2014-15.pdf. Reproduced with permission of the Minister of Education, Province of Alberta, Canada, 2015.

BOX 10.7

ALBERTA EDUCATION GRADE 9 DESCRIPTORS FOR CONTENT (NARRATIVE/ESSAY WRITING ASSIGNMENT)	
Focus	
When marking **Content** appropriate for the Grade 9 Narrative/Essay Writing Assignment, the marker should consider how effectively the student • explores the topic • supports the response • establishes a purpose • considers the reader • presents ideas	
Excellent **E**	• The student's exploration of the topic is insightful and/or imaginative. • The student's purpose, whether stated or implied, is deliberate. • The ideas presented by the student are perceptive and/or carefully chosen. • Supporting details are precise and/or original. • The writing is confident and/or creative and holds the reader's interest.
Proficient **PF**	• The student's exploration of the topic is adept and/or plausible. • The student's purpose, whether stated or implied, is intentional. • The ideas presented by the student are thoughtful and/or sound. • Supporting details are specific and/or apt. • The writing is considered and/or elaborated and draws the reader's interest.
Satisfactory **S**	• The student's exploration of the topic is clear and/or logical. • The student's purpose, whether stated or implied, is evident. • The ideas presented by the student are appropriate and/or predictable. • Supporting details are relevant and/or generic. • The writing is straightforward and/or generalized and occasionally appeals to the reader's interest.
Limited **L**	• The student's exploration of the topic is tenuous and/or simplistic. • The student's purpose, whether stated or implied, is vague. • The ideas presented by the student are superficial and/or ambiguous. • Supporting details are imprecise and/or abbreviated. • The writing is uncertain and/or incomplete and does not appeal to the reader's interest.
Poor **P**	• The student's exploration of the topic is minimal and/or tangential. • The student's purpose, whether stated or implied, is insubstantial. • The ideas presented by the student are overgeneralized and/or underdeveloped. • Supporting details are irrelevant and/or scant. • The writing is confusing and/or lacks validity and does not interest the reader.
Insufficient **INS**	• The marker can discern no evidence of an attempt to address the task presented in the assignment, or the student has written so little that it is not possible to assess **Content**.

Note: Content and Organization are weighted to be worth twice as much as the other categories.

Student work must address the task presented in the assignment. Responses that are completely unrelated to the topic and/or prompts will be awarded a score of **Insufficient**.

Source: Alberta Education. *Alberta Provincial Achievement Testing Subject Bulletin, 2014-2015 English Language Arts Grade 9.* Found at: http://education.alberta.ca/media/6738135/06_ela9_bulletin_2014-15.pdf. Reproduced with permission of the Minister of Education, Province of Alberta, Canada, 2015.

Some districts require a letter grade, but most districts today require descriptors to be used instead. These descriptors are generally tied to the criteria set out in the provincial or school district writing assessments. Some school districts use the learner outcomes listed in the provincial language arts program of studies when developing their assessment criteria. Since there are hundreds of learner outcomes, consultants carefully reduce the list to a manageable number. Eileen Loughlin's district uses a total of 60 outcomes, and each teacher can select 10 to 12 outcomes per term as a focus for teaching and assessment during the term. These are the criteria then listed on the report card for that term, and teachers assess each learner according to one of the following standards: excellent, proficient, basic, insufficient, and unable to assess. Box 10.8 contains a sample of report card remarks Eileen has put together to demonstrate what her report cards look like. The attention to detail included in the comments is a reflection of the time Eileen has taken over the years to familiarize herself with the provincial program of studies and the school district's assessment practices.

BOX 10.8

SAMPLE REPORT CARD COMMENTS, GRADE 2

Key learner outcomes for writing for this period were as follows:
- ▷ generates and organizes ideas during prewriting
- ▷ writes and illustrates original texts based on formats explored in class
- ▷ revises written and illustrated work to clarify and enhance the text message
- ▷ edits for missing words, spelling, capitals, and end punctuation

Constantin

One focus this term has been upon narrative writing. Constantin is an imaginative author, creating delightful stories that express his developing style. His story beginnings are well developed, with clear characters and settings. This clarity of organization is not as evident throughout the middle and end of his stories. Although not yet consistent, his use of lively verbs and phrases when a character is experiencing a strong emotion adds energy and creates visual images in the reader's mind. Once Constantin is finished a story, he must take more time to revise the middle and end of his stories to be sure that the events written on the page clearly describe those in his imagination. More careful editing of punctuation and legibility will also assist in this area. Constantin needs to take more care with his manuscript printing.

Paisley

One focus this term has been upon narrative writing. Paisley is able to write delightful stories that draw the reader into the plot. Her beginnings are well developed, clearly introducing the character, events, and setting; however, middles and ends do not consistently maintain organization, causing the reader to pause and reread for clarification. Paisley uses vocabulary to create a picture in the reader's mind, with phrases like "the sweet green pine tree smell" and "her hands shot up like fireworks." Well done! Paisley must take more responsibility for editing all of her work, in all subjects. Her lack of attention to this area, despite direct instruction and assistance, impedes her written communication. Paisley has a wealth of wonderful ideas that need to be shared in a manner that more closely reflects her ability.

Eileen is a master teacher, and beginning teachers can learn much from working with colleagues like Eileen once they begin teaching. Eileen recommends that beginning teachers examine provincial and local scoring rubrics so they have a standard to work with. They need to see what students across the grades can do, not just those at the grade level they teach. This will provide them with a broader view of learners' competencies and the ways in which students grow across the grades.

The assessment strategies we have discussed in this chapter provide educators with information about all major aspects of student writing. The strategies are designed to meet the many purposes for which teachers are required to make assessments. In classrooms such as Eileen Loughlin's, instructional decisions are based primarily on the learners' needs. Information about those needs is gained through appropriate assessment strategies. Whether assessments are informal or formal, completed through observation, anecdotal records, profiles, portfolios or writing folders, learner self-evaluation, writing conferences, analyses of samples of writing, or provincial or local district achievement tests, the aim is always to effectively teach to the learners' needs.

TEACHING SPELLING

In the 1970s, researchers began to explore how learners develop the ability to spell correctly and the factors that affect their development. Is correct spelling tied to reading ability? Do word lists and frequent spelling tests help learners become better spellers? Do students learn correct spelling as they read and write?

Invented Spelling

Children's very early writing attempts demonstrate what is known as **invented spelling**. It is part of the developmental progression children make as they journey toward mastering orthodox spelling, and it occurs as a result of them listening acutely to the spoken language they hear around them and attending to the meaning of words. Young children are particularly sensitive to the sounds of words, and as they attempt to encode words into print, they try to put the sounds they hear into symbol form. Learners' early spellings can be thought of as approximations or experimentations with the sounds, patterns, and meanings of words.

There are three layers to the orthographic structure of spelling (Bear, Invernizzi, Templeton, & Johnston, 2004). The *alphabet layer* represents the relationship between letters and sounds in English. In a left-to-right sequence, the word "can" is represented by three different letters for the three different sounds heard in the word. Sometimes two letters represent one sound, like the *sh* in "push." The *pattern layer* overlays the alphabet layer. English has evolved over time and is an amalgam of many languages. One letter does not represent only one sound. Instead, in English there are patterns of spelling to guide us through groupings of letters. These patterns give rise to some of the rules of spelling—even though they are inconsistent. Consider the silent *e* that makes a vowel long, as in "cake." The third layer is the *meaning layer*, where prefixes and suffixes, root words, and words borrowed from other languages come in. If we know the root word, we can build the correct spelling of other forms of the word from it—for example, *connect, reconnect, disconnect,* and *connection.*

During the process of acquiring orthodox spelling abilities, learners generally move through five or six major stages of invented spelling (depending on which researcher's work you use). The process can last from age 3 or 4 through to age 11 or 12 (the grade 6 or 7 level). Before the age of 3, most children draw and make letter shapes. Their attempts are not usually referred to as spelling, though it is recognized that these young learners are "writing." Children generally develop through the stages with some overlap across stages. A few stages may be evident in any one piece of writing.

These are the five stages of invented spelling we find most useful to know:

1. *Prereading or emergent spelling.* This stage of invented spelling consists of the random orderings of whatever letters children can draw. There is no awareness of sound–symbol relationship, and so strings of letters such as Phoenix's writing (in Box 10.9) of *xxmHORP HepBnen* might appear on the page. Children may have their own "meaning" to go along with the letters, and may tell a coherent story to accompany them. An adult might transcribe this story onto the same page as the child's print. In Phoenix's case, his grandmother provided this transcription: "I did my homework today." At this stage, Phoenix has no knowledge that specific configurations of letters and words are needed to create meaningful print. However, he does have a firm grasp of the message concept—that what is written on a page signifies a particular meaning.

2. *Prephonetic or semiphonetic spelling.* In this stage, learners have a primitive concept of the alphabet and of letter names, and so letter names are used as clues in spelling. Learners in this stage might write *NHR* for "nature," or represent a whole word with one letter, usually an initial consonant. Rarely are vowels used; a learner's spelling in this stage consists almost entirely of consonants. Ian's writing, shown in Box 10.10, is moving into the phonetic stage, but much of his spelling still reflects semiphonetic elements, as in his spelling of *GRL* for "girl" and *JWP* for "jump."

BOX 10.9

PHOENIX'S PREREADING SPELLING

BOX 10.10

IAN'S PREPHONETIC SPELLING

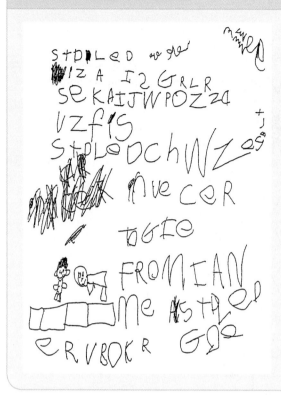

Stella is a nice girl
She can jump over the fence
Stella chewed the seatbelt in the car
To Granny
From Ian
Me and Stella go around the block

3. *Phonetic spelling.* This is the stage most commonly seen in learners from kindergarten through grade 3. These learners have an understanding of sound–symbol correspondence, but they represent the features of words according to how they hear and articulate the words. This often leads to the omission of preconsonant nasals, such as the *M* in *NUBERS* or the *N* in *SWIMIG.* Box 10.11 illustrates Kara's spelling during this stage. She spells some words correctly, but in many words she listens intently in order to represent the sounds she hears; for example in "Vaicogr" and "sieais."

4. *Transitional spelling.* In grades 2 through 4, writers generally include a vowel in every syllable and use familiar spelling patterns, though they are frequently used incorrectly. The word "make" may be spelled as *maek,* or "was" as *whas.* Rules are overgeneralized, and the aspects of spelling an individual is currently learning become obvious through error patterns in the writing. In Box 10.12, Zak spells "came" as *caem,* and "family" as *famle.* In Box 10.13 Michael spells "watched" as *watht.* These learners are exploring the nature of spelling conventions such as the use of *ch,* the *ed* suffix, and silent vowels. They are also developing a core vocabulary of standard spellings (*I, of, the, out*).

BOX 10.11

KARA'S PHONETIC SPELLING

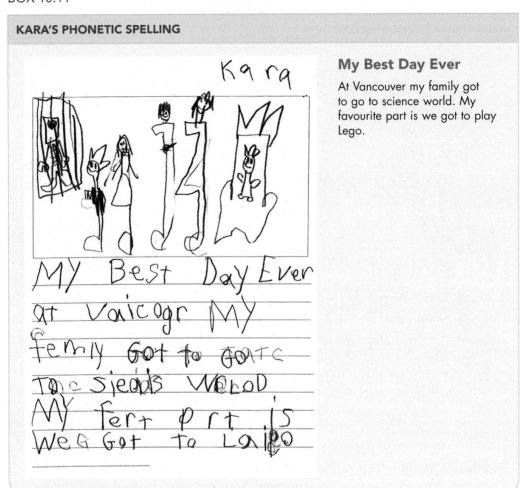

My Best Day Ever

At Vancouver my family got to go to science world. My favourite part is we got to play Lego.

BOX 10.12

ZAK'S TRANSITIONAL SPELLING

When pig blew up and the family came out of pig's stomach.

BOX 10.13

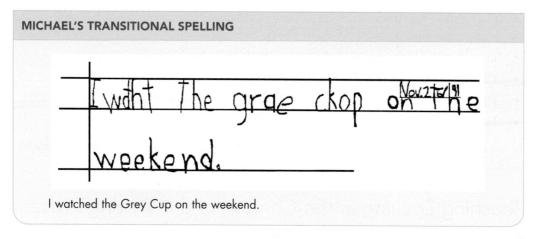

MICHAEL'S TRANSITIONAL SPELLING

I watched the Grey Cup on the weekend.

As we have mentioned, learners also use the meanings of words to help them spell. One writer wrote a note to his mother who was attending university at the time: "I hope you have a good time at youknowvursdy." There is no doubt that he understood that university is a place where people come "to know."

5. *Standard spelling.* Generally, at about grade 5 or later, learners demonstrate a more sophisticated understanding of spelling. They understand the constraints of syntax and morphology on their spelling—that is, the conventions of spelling—and they use dictionaries to assist in correct spelling. Students at this age have learned that correct spelling is a courtesy to the reader, as well as necessary for expressing meaning clearly to an audience.

Although these stages appear to be a natural progression for most young writers, the question remains as to how and when conventional spelling should be encouraged or required in classrooms. The answer is that spelling always counts, and conventional spelling can always be encouraged—but learners must first of all be helped to compose their own texts before they are *required* to adhere to the conventions of written language. In addition, it is important that educators and caregivers focus on the words learners use in their writing most frequently—words such as *I, was, and,* and *but.*

Much standard spelling can be taught during editing conferences, but some young writers need a more structured approach to learning conventional spelling. When adults write in journals or write letters to friends, even their spelling may not be 100 percent correct. What is important in these cases is that they make an effort to spell correctly so they can communicate with themselves (through a journal or lists) or friends (through emails or letters). When focusing on spelling in student writing, it is helpful for educators and parents to keep in mind the audience and the purpose for the writing. There are many occasions when the message to be conveyed is more important than correct spelling, especially if the piece is to be read by a limited audience.

Educators and parents can, however, help learners to become better spellers by being mindful of the things that *good* spellers do, emphasizing these behaviours with young writers. Most of the time good spellers do the following:

- They recall spelling patterns and generalizations they have learned through their reading and writing.

- They learn about words and how to use them.
- They build a repertoire of spelling strategies to choose from and do not rely only on one or two strategies.
- They choose which strategy is the best to apply in a given situation.
- They do not rely on sounding out words, as this is an unreliable practice.
- They do not rely on spelling "rules" because these are too unreliable.
- They use visual memory in conjunction with other strategies.

In summary, good spellers *think* about their spelling and do not rely on rote memorization.

Teaching Spelling in the Context of the Writing Process

Many learners develop competency in standard spelling entirely through reading, writing, and sharing their writing with an interested audience. However, standard spelling usually requires effort to master, as it is a skill used only in writing. An awareness of the need for correct spelling can be taught from grade 2 onward. It's easy for any writer to become lazy about spelling, but it is essential for a committed writer to adhere to conventional forms. Habits formed in childhood often persist into adulthood, though usually adults have only one or two major error patterns in their spelling. For some, the error pattern will be confusion over double consonants (words such as *embarrass*); for others it will be problems with reversing letters, or omitting letters in a word (e.g., *contain* spelled as *contian* or *cotain*). Once adult writers become aware of the nature of their error patterns, they can make efforts to learn the specific words they have difficulty with.

Educators can help their students learn conventional spelling by conducting regular brief lessons using a SMART Board, focusing attention on common misspellings, and encouraging learners to watch for these specific words in their spelling that particular week. More idiosyncratic misspellings can be addressed in writing conferences, but usually not until a piece is ready for a final draft, unless the word is an unusual one for the learner to write (e.g., *cornucopia* and *satellite*).

Use of brief lessons also applies to errors in capitalization, punctuation, and grammar. In elementary schools, teachers rarely focus lengthy language arts lessons on these aspects of writing, nor do they provide worksheet exercises for learners to complete. The skills are more likely to be addressed in the context of their students' current writing, and through the mini-lessons interspersed with other activities.

Lessons that are 10 minutes long are usually more effective than drills and worksheet pages of exercises. It is the context of the usage and the relevance to the individual that make an impact on their learning. Skills learned out of context are rarely transferred to writing completed in workshops or to writing done across curricular areas. If a number of learners in the class have problems in one specific area, a group can be formed so the teacher can give direct instruction to those who need it. There is no point in teaching to a whole class if only a few learners really need to learn that skill. Through reading students' writing, and through listening to the talk they engage in while they write, educators can gain much useful knowledge about who needs to be taught certain skills and who has already mastered them.

INSIDE CLASSROOMS

WAYNE MCNAMARA

Generally, Wayne McNamara teaches the conventions of writing in the context of the revising and editing processes. Learners in his classroom write on every other line of their paper so they can make revisions to their work without having to rewrite the entire piece. Grade 4 writers' editing skills are not strong, so he tries to encourage editing whenever he can without turning writing into an onerous task. Interestingly, Wayne finds that when he teaches learners to use a thesaurus, they thoroughly enjoy it and make use of one regularly—though on occasions he has had to negotiate with some writers about just how many "thesaurus words" they should use in one sentence!

Wayne focuses on a few writing criteria at a time, depending on what he is teaching in mini-lessons and what he sees in learners' writing. Sometimes he may focus on organization or content (ideas), and at other times on sentence structure, word usage, or voice. Wayne tracks learners' spelling growth in two ways: through weekly spelling lists with a test and through their everyday writing.

In Wayne's school district, learners move from manuscript printing to cursive hand-writing in grade 4. Many of them are eager and excited to learn (and some have already been developing their cursive handwriting on their own). But some learners are anxious and nervous, and they begin to hold their pencils too tightly, or they labour over every letter in an attempt to create perfect copy. Wayne, first of all, teaches how to form each letter correctly, and later he talks to learners about developing a personal style. Legibility is the criterion that matters the most, closely followed by size and spacing. Wayne has found that learners are very critical of their peers' handwriting if they cannot read the words on a spelling test, for example. At a certain point in the year, learners are required to do all their writing in cursive hand rather than in manuscript printing.

The school district uses a keyboarding program called "All the Right Type," which is on all the computers in the labs across the district. Wayne believes the sooner learners can keyboard the better because it is a crucial skill for everyone.

The presence of *spell-check tools* on word-processing programs provides both advantages and disadvantages for learners. Before working with the tools, writers need guidance in using them effectively and appropriately. Learners can be encouraged to use the tool as a first step in eliminating typographical errors and in identifying misspelled words. Following this, writers must check for homonyms and homophones. Which word did they intend to use? The computer does not make distinctions of this nature and will not catch such misspellings. Here, the spell-check tool provides an interesting focus for instruction, teaching writers an awareness of homonyms and homophones as spelling items *and* teaching young writers not to rely on computer spell-checkers completely. The program will also not make up for the misspelling of an intended word that is another, different word, such as "fog" instead of "frog." It's up to the writer to proofread the piece for these kinds of errors. Many spell-check tools have an "auto-correct" feature that individuals (or the class as a collaborative whole) might want to program with their own frequent misspellings. Again, this process provides a vehicle for instruction as learners identify their common misspellings and focus their attention on them.

Following are some specific strategies for aiding learners in their spelling development:

- Ask learners to write on every other line of a paper so they can make changes without rewriting or erasing.

- Encourage writers to leave blank spaces for words they do not know how to spell. It is important that thoughts continue to flow; omitted words can be inserted later. Learners can be encouraged to write the first few letters of the omitted word so they will have a greater chance of remembering which word they had intended to use.

- Note spelling errors by putting an asterisk in the margin of the writing. Ask learners to find the errors themselves. Learners can frequently recognize incorrect spelling, and in doing so they are reminded of the words they have difficulty in spelling.

- Encourage writers to have paper at their desks so that words they are unsure of can be written down for them.

- Refrain from providing only an oral spelling of a word; always accompany it with a written model. Spelling is essentially a visual memory activity that is conducted only in writing. It is therefore important that learners *see* the word they need help in spelling.

- Teach young writers how to use a dictionary, thesaurus, and other word books effectively, and encourage their use. A spelling dictionary is usually more effective for elementary school learners than a conventional dictionary. A writer who needs to spell *rein* will usually look under *ra* in a conventional dictionary, thus meeting with little success.

- Alphabet games help young writers to understand how dictionaries and encyclopedias are organized. Activities such as lining up in alphabetical order according to last name or first name also help learners understand how to use telephone books and other reference aids.

The Direct Teaching of Spelling

Spelling competence is relatively easy to test. A word list can be dictated to learners, and an examiner can check to see whether the words are spelled correctly. However, words spelled correctly on a word list will not necessarily be spelled correctly in a piece of writing created in a different context such as a shopping list, journal entry, greeting card, letter, or essay. Words usually have to be internalized and become part of the stored knowledge a writer possesses before correct spelling becomes automatic.

Adding to the problem in schools is that activities in spelling textbooks generally do not present the teaching of spelling in ways that are consistent with research findings about learning to spell. Many of the activities in those books are repetitious and rarely help poor spellers become strong spellers. Even the most recent spelling textbooks do not focus on *teaching* spelling, but focus instead on word games.

Research has shown many times that the only real way to become an effective speller is to do lots of writing for audiences other than oneself, read widely, and check spelling in a dictionary or word book whenever there is doubt.

Good resources available to assist teachers in helping learners become strong and independent spellers include *The Spelling Teacher's Handbook* by Jo Phenix (2001), and *Words Their Way* (3rd ed.) by Bear et al. (2004).

Learners are more likely to become effective spellers if their motives for using correct spelling stem from communicative needs rather than a desire to please the teacher. If writers have something important to say, and they have an audience they wish to address, correct spelling will help them convey their message clearly to the reader. Correct spelling is a courtesy to the reader and is also important in transmitting a clear message.

Correct spelling adds to a writer's credibility, something that is especially important for educators, who are generally perceived as role models. Teachers are expected to spell every word correctly. (If a word is spelled incorrectly on a wall chart or on the chalkboard, one can almost guarantee that a visiting educators or parent will notice it!) Educators should not send to parents or the public any of their writing that has not been carefully checked for correct spelling.

A Word List Approach

When employing a word list approach in the direct teaching of spelling, educators ensure that they use

- a reliable word list created from either the words learners in the classroom have difficulty spelling or from a reliable resource book such as Thomas (1979)
- a self-corrected pretest of 10 to 12 words
- a study procedure to ensure that learners learn effective strategies for memorizing words
- "check tests" with a buddy throughout the week
- a mastery test of the entire list of words originally provided on day one
- a record of spelling achievement (on a chart at the back of the spelling scribbler)

Word Lists

When a teacher has observed learners' writing and has identified those individuals needing direct spelling instruction (which would rarely be more than half the class), a word list approach is usually effective. The word list compiled by Ves Thomas (1979) remains one of the most reliable and thorough resources for educators today. Those word lists are based on the frequency of usage of words in learners' writing in Canada, so that the most frequently used words are on the word list for the youngest students (grade 2), and so on up through the grades. It is suggested that word lists and study procedures *not* be used with learners before grade 2.

If teachers choose to create their own word lists, they may base them on the spelling errors they notice in the writing in their classroom. The use of either a pre-existing list or a teacher-compiled list should provide an effective vehicle for learners to study the correct spelling of words. It is suggested that learners do *not* use lists of words compiled from current units of study across the curriculum. Words on such lists are not usually the most frequently used words in the learners' writing in general. The most important factors in creating a word list are that the words be relevant to students' lives and be used regularly in their writing.

It has been found that the most common 100 words used in their writing by learners in grades 2 to 6 make up about 60 percent of all the words they write. The most common 500 words make up 70 percent of all words written, and the most common 2000 words make up 83 percent of all words written (Simpson, 1980). The average grade 2 to 6 program teaches between 3500 and 4500 words over a five-year period. It is therefore essential that the words taught on those lists form part of a learner's *core* spelling vocabulary.

The remainder of the words grades 2 to 6 learners (and all other writers) use in their writing have to be learned by memory from the experience of writing them and checking for correct spelling in dictionaries and other word books. It's not possible to teach all these words by memory through an elementary school spelling program. Table 10.2 displays one well-known list of the 100 words most frequently written by learners in elementary school (Carroll, Davies, & Richman, 1971).

TABLE 10.2 THE 100 MOST FREQUENTLY USED WORDS IN GRADES 2 TO 6 WRITING

a	find	like	over	up
about	first	little	people	use
after	for	long	said	very
all	from	made	see	was
an	has	make	she	water
and	have	many	so	way
are	he	may	some	we
as	her	more	than	were
at	him	most	that	what
be	his	my	the	when
been	how	no	their	where
but	I	not	them	which
by	if	now	then	who
called	in	of	there	why
can	into	on	they	will
could	is	one	this	with
did	it	only	through	words
do	its	or	time	would
down	just	other	to	you
each	know	out	two	your

Source: Copyright © 1971 by Houghton Mifflin Harcourt Publishing Company. Adapted and reproduced by permission from *The American Heritage Word Frequency Book.*

Self-Corrected Pretest

A word list is most effectively used when it is preceded by a self-corrected pretest. All the learners in a spelling group are given a test *before* the words are presented to them in list form for study. This procedure allows learners to identify which words they have difficulty spelling correctly. As learners self-correct the pretest, they become aware of the spelling errors they have made, and this feature alone allows most learners to correctly spell the word the next time they use it. The self-corrected pretest is probably the single most effective strategy for improving spelling ability. It provides each learner with an individualized list of words that need to be studied, because the words spelled correctly can be put aside until the end of the week. At that time, a mastery test that includes all the words on the original list will be given.

It's very important that learners correct their own pretest, for much learning occurs while they check their spelling. Sometimes only two or three words might be incorrectly spelled, and at other times there may be as many as five or six. If an individual is presented with more than five or six words to study in one week, it is usually too many to be learned effectively. Learners who experience difficulty in spelling need to work with small amounts of material and short lists of manageable words. In the early grades, a pretest of 10 words is usually sufficient. In upper elementary school, the list may include from 10 to 12 words.

Study Procedure

Words spelled incorrectly on the pretest are written out correctly and are used as a model for the study procedure (see Classroom Activity 10.1). On the day after completion of the study procedure, learners can work in pairs, giving each other buddy tests of their own personal spelling words. All can benefit from learning a study procedure for spelling. There are many variations of study procedures, and if learners do not have success with one version, they can

CLASSROOM ACTIVITY 10.1

Spelling Study Procedure

1. Look at the word, pronounce it, and say the letters (auditory and visual stimulation).

2. Listen to the sounds and notice how they are represented (sound–symbol relationship).

3. Close your eyes and try to see the word as you pronounce it (recall–visualization).

4. Keep your eyes closed and say the letters in order.

5. Open your eyes and check.

6. Write the word without looking at the model. Check writing (kinesthetic recall).

7. Write the word a second time and check it.

8. Write the word a third time. If it's correct, consider it learned.

try a modified version. Spelling is a visual memory task, and a good study procedure provides weak spellers with a concrete structure for their learning.

A sound study procedure focuses energies on the direct learning of specific words that an individual finds difficult. There are likely to be occasions in the classroom when other methods of teaching spelling are necessary. For example, learners with special needs may require alternative strategies that more specifically meet their learning requirements.

Mastery Test

A final mastery test given at the end of the week consists of the complete pretest list originally provided to learners at the beginning of the week. Spelling scores can be recorded on a chart at the back of a spelling scribbler so that learners can track their own progress.

Spelling Practices to Avoid

Over the years, educators have become aware that some teaching strategies have not proven helpful in assisting young writers with improving their spelling:

- Pointing out the "hard spots" in words may be helpful only to a small number of learners, and the hard spots are likely to be different from one person to another.

- Teaching spelling rules is not effective since few spelling rules can be applied regularly. Sayings such as "*i* before *e* except after *c*" may be very useful to most writers, but if they are taught as rules, then words that do not follow the rules must also be pointed out (such as *weigh* and *neighbour*). It is more effective to teach how to add suffixes (e.g., *baby* becomes *babies*) than it is to teach specific spelling rules. Most rules have almost as many exceptions as adherents.

- Avoid having learners copy spelling lists as a punishment as this establishes a negative attitude toward spelling that is not helpful to learners' feelings about writing in general. Educators try not to detract from the joys of writing by making writing, or any other school activity, abhorrent to children.

TEACHING GRAMMAR, PUNCTUATION, AND CAPITALIZATION

Grammar

As discussed in Chapter 3, educators often use the terms *grammar* and *syntax* interchangeably. *Syntax* is the term linguists use to describe the organization of language structures. *Grammar* is a term teachers usually use to define a prescriptive set of rules to be followed. Syntax is derived from the spoken language, but when it is taught in schools, it usually pertains to writing and is labelled "grammar." Educators and researchers have long believed that grammar should not be taught in kindergarten through grade 8 in a formal manner. However, learners need to know the difference between what is acceptable or appropriate and what is considered poor grammar. They also need a vocabulary to be able to talk about language if they are to engage in writing conferences and develop an awareness of the writing techniques good writers use. Three basic perspectives on grammar are presented in Box 10.14.

Grammar is not taught in schools as an end in itself, but as one of the tools to be used in the process of writing. Knowledge and control of grammar enables writers to strengthen their writing and clarify meaning, facilitating effective and precise communication. Correct and appropriate grammar also enables people to speak in a manner approaching "standard English," the form of English that conforms to established educated usage and is generally considered correct.

Studies in language development have shown that many concerns voiced by educators about "grammar" are mostly concerns about usage, and usage depends on the dialect learned when people are young. A person's dialect can change when he or she moves from one area to another, or works among people speaking a closer approximation of standard English.

BOX 10.14

THREE PERSPECTIVES ON GRAMMAR

Linguists describe the structure of language in three ways, and all three ways influence the way grammar is taught.

1. The best known is *traditional* or *prescriptive* grammar, which provides rules for socially correct usage. This perspective dates back to the Middle Ages and has its roots in the study of Latin. The major contribution of traditional grammar is in the terminology it provides for learners and teachers to talk about language. Because this form of grammar is based on Latin, it is not entirely appropriate for use with the English language, as it cannot adequately explain how language works. However, the three elements of grammar continue to be taught and prove useful to writers as they work their craft—types of sentences (declarative, interrogative, imperative, exclamatory); parts of sentences (simple, compound, complex, compound–complex); and parts of speech (nouns, pronouns, verbs, adverbs, adjectives, prepositions, conjunctions, and interjections).

2. *Structural grammar* attempts to describe how language is used. It is not prescriptive, but descriptive, and it highlights the differences between written and spoken language patterns. The study of structural linguistics has provided detailed information about language in use, but it focuses on form and does not attempt to relate meaning to usage. Seven basic sentence patterns are identified, and the variations and combinations of these seven patterns make up all the sentences people speak or write.

3. *Transformational grammar* is the most recent approach to the study of grammar. Transformational linguists attempt to describe both the way language works *and* the cognitive processes used to produce language. They refer to two levels or structures of language (the surface structure and the deep structure) to describe how meaning in the brain is transformed into the sentences people speak.

A thorough exploration of grammar and its teaching can be found in Constance Weaver's *Teaching Grammar in Context* (Portsmouth, NH: Boynton/Cook, 1996).

However, the basic rules of grammar learned in childhood usually persist throughout life, and the majority of those rules are correct. By the age of six, when most children enter school, they have already mastered most of the grammar of the language.

It is agreed that grammar needs to be taught in schools so that individuals can become effective writers, while they also retain the opportunity to move between dialect and standard English in their speech.

Teaching grammar in isolation from writing is generally ineffective. Creating teaching units and providing worksheets on grammar have little effect on a person's writing and speaking. The most effective learning occurs when grammar is taught as part of the editing process of composition, and in mini-lessons when necessary. Learners can sometimes detect grammatical errors in their compositions, especially if the flow of the language or the meaning is disturbed by the error. However, much of the time, learners cannot detect their own grammatical errors because the writing makes sense to them.

As members of language communities, we accept certain phrases and incorrect usage as the norm, and it is difficult to teach learners to change that usage. This is where a direct lesson is useful, because the whole group can focus on that particular item of usage and there is more likelihood that learners will retain an awareness of it. Learners can be taught that when with friends, it may be acceptable to say "I should've went," but when they are in school their writing and oral language are expected to more closely adhere to standard English, and "I should've gone" is correct and appropriate. Likewise, learners need to know that writing "should of" instead of "should have" is neither acceptable nor correct. One caution: learners should at no time be embarrassed by their language usage. Learners in K to 8 classrooms (as well as adults) feel belittled if their language is criticized or faulted. Effective educators handle this issue sensitively, aware that one dialect is not better than another, but different.

A lesson on the differences in usage between *taught* and *learned, lent* and *borrowed*, or *seed* and *saw* might, for example, be necessary in some classrooms. A lesson on misplaced modifiers can be fun for learners in the elementary years, as they can see the humour in sentences such as "I saw the lady walking down the hill with purple hair," and they enjoy figuring out why the sentence is ambiguous as well as how to fix it. It is through meaning that grammar can be taught most effectively, not through parsing sentences or learning definitions of parts of speech.

Knowledge of labels and definitions of parts of speech allows writers and speakers to talk about the language they are using. In writing conferences and during the editing process, labels such as noun, adverb, and clause can be used. A 10-minute presentation, using examples on the board and involving learners in discussion, can be effective in reminding learners about grammar and usage and in introducing certain concepts for the first time. Lengthy lessons with exercises on worksheets are generally not necessary. It *is* necessary, though, for learners to know these labels and their meanings so they can talk about their writing and hence improve it.

Punctuation and Capitalization

Punctuation and capitalization are the "mechanics" of written language. Again, writing conferences and short lessons are the most effective and appropriate vehicles for teaching the skills of punctuation and capitalization. (See Classroom Activity 10.2 below.) Worksheets of drill-and-skill exercises are not effective. Novels provide a quick reference for checking how direct speech, paragraphing, and the capitalization of names and places are addressed. Learners often remember rules of capitalization and punctuation for a short time after they have been taught, but then forget to use them when they are composing and focusing on ideas. Lessons are enhanced when teachers make them directly relevant to situations that affect learners—for example, through questions individuals have raised themselves.

TEACHING HANDWRITING

Today, the focus of instruction has shifted from penmanship to composition, and the use of the keyboard has changed the amount of handwriting we do. However, for adults as well as young writers, notes, jottings, journal entries, memos, and greeting cards are usually hand-written. The need to teach handwriting in school still exists so that learners can produce legible script with a minimum of *time*, *effort*, and *concentration*. Learners need to be able to read their own handwriting, and we all need to be able to read the handwriting of others.

Some points for teachers to remember:

- Learners are greatly helped if they are taught to write in a way that is fluent, easy, routine, and comfortable.

- The true test of handwriting is in situations where it is used on a day-to-day basis, doing such regular jobs as making lists, writing notes, leaving messages, and writing letters.

- In handwriting instruction, good teaching and modelling are essential, not just in the early grades but throughout schooling.

- A teacher's handwriting on the board, on wall charts, and on student work is a model for learners of how letters are formed and what good writing looks like.

CLASSROOM ACTIVITY 10.2

Quotation Marks

Farha is writing a story and wants to use dialogue for two of the characters. She stops in her writing at "Who's going to run for help and who's going to stay here she asked." Farha doesn't know where to place the quotation marks. Her teacher could make an overhead transparency of a comic strip to demonstrate how quotation marks are used. Whenever the words spoken by a character are shown in a comic strip, they are inside a "balloon." In a story, quotation marks are used instead of a balloon. Only the words spoken belong inside the quotation marks. The teacher can demonstrate this with an overhead transparency of a section of a familiar story that includes dialogue.

Reviewing Farha's original piece of writing, the class can work with the teacher, putting in the quotation marks where they belong. As in many other learning situations, a collaborative approach is helpful, since learners can engage with the problem as a group rather than in isolation. Lessons can be repeated, using different examples, whenever appropriate.

Printing and Cursive Handwriting

Two styles of handwriting are taught in elementary school: **manuscript printing** (also called manuscript writing) and **cursive writing**, which now receives much less attention than in the past. Learners generally begin with printing, and then in grade 3 or 4 they move into a cursive hand. Some ELL/CLD children may come to school with knowledge of cursive writing but no knowledge of manuscript printing because of the way in which they were taught in their former countries/communities. The specific styles of each vary according to region and country. In North America there are a number of popular cursive styles, including D'Nealian (described below). Box 10.15 presents D'Nealian manuscript printing and cursive script.

BOX 10.15

D'NEALIAN MANUSCRIPT PRINTING AND CURSIVE SCRIPT

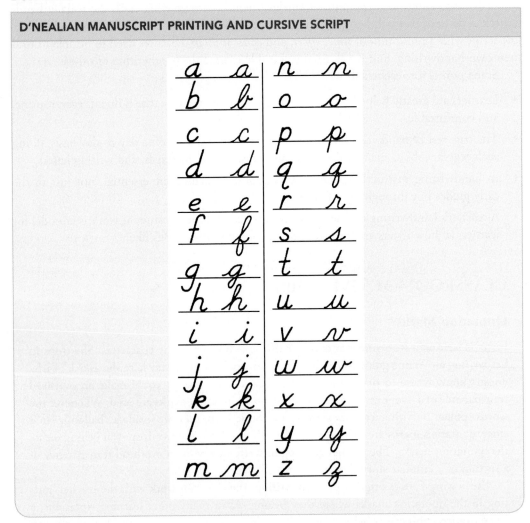

Source: D'Nealian Handwriting is copyrighted by Pearson Education, Inc. or its affiliates(s). Used by permission. All rights reserved. D'Nealian is a registered trademark of Donald Neal Thurber.

While some Canadian provincial curricula contain a model of handwriting, many programs of study no longer include a model script. Curriculum guides and programs of study should be consulted, however, before any handwriting style is taught, as it is important that students have a consistent style across the grades.

Students generally learn manuscript printing in the primary grades because it is believed that the clear circles and horizontal and vertical lines are easier for young writers to control. Manuscript printing is also easy to read and is closer in form to the print learners see in their reading materials. Some learners are eager to begin cursive handwriting and will make the transition on their own. Many others express a preference for continuing to print. There is no particular reason why they should move into cursive handwriting other than that it has become an accepted adult convention.

One advantage of D'Nealian script is that it was developed specifically to make the transition from printing to handwriting easier for learners. It is a form that flows from manuscript to cursive with little change in letter form, and is extremely legible and easy to use. With D'Nealian script, the formation, size, slant, and rhythm learned in kindergarten and grade 1 are continued and built upon in grades 2 and 3. As a result, grades 2 and 3 students don't have to "start over" when they begin learning cursive forms.

Teaching Letter Forms

Handwriting is more than simply a motor skill, fine muscle coordination, and practice. Learners have to remember letter forms, somehow internalizing them. Each learner has to build a mental image of each letter. It's a thinking process as well as a fine motor process. In the early years of schooling, learners must have a clear concept of how each letter appears, saying out loud how each letter is formed, while at the same time drawing it. The same process is used in teaching both manuscript printing and cursive writing. Steps in the instructional process are described in Box 10.16.

Young writers usually benefit from using a lined paper with a dotted mid-line. A guided practice of the manuscript letter *d* might go as follows: Pencil on the midline, go counterclockwise, round to the baseline, back up through the midline, up to the headline, retrace down to the baseline. Stop. This would be repeated a number of times until learners begin to master the letter.

A model of the letter on each learner's desk provides immediate feedback as the individual compares the written letter with the model. An example of one model is presented in Box 10.17. The teacher attends to the number of strokes, the starting and stopping points, the direction of the strokes, and the size of the letters. The process should not be repeated more than five times during each practice session, or handwriting will lose quality.

The approach can be used for teaching cursive writing in much the same way as with printing. In forming capitals, today's learners usually use a simple manuscript form of the letter. In the intermediate grades, the occasional lesson focusing on a certain letter or combination of letters can be effective when the teacher sees learners having difficulty.

BOX 10.16

STEPS IN TEACHING HANDWRITING

1. The teacher models handwriting instruction on the board (or an overhead projector). Clear lines are drawn on the board so that learners can see the spacing of letters and the lines on which they are positioned.

2. The teacher uses a consistent writing vocabulary such as *baseline*, *midline*, *headline*, and *tail-line*.

3. As the teacher draws a letter on the board, he or she describes where the letter begins, the direction in which the hand moves, and the place where the letter ends.

4. Learners describe aloud the strokes the teacher is using as the teacher draws the letter again.

5. Learners draw the letter, saying aloud the description as they write, while being guided by the teacher.

6. After the letter is completed, learners compare the letter they have drawn with a model already on paper at their desks.

BOX 10.17

MODEL OF LETTER WRITING: *S*

"S" starts like "c"   c c c c

Words with "S."
Sky Stars

Sentences with S

Evaluation of handwriting considers

- the form and size of the letters
- the spacing of letters and words
- alignment according to headline and baseline

Many handwriting scales are available for evaluating handwriting, but most do not allow for individuality in writing style. The criteria listed above are usually sufficient for providing feedback to learners and for talking about ways in which handwriting can be improved.

Helping the Left-Handed Writer

Approximately 10 percent of K to 8 learners in North America are left-handed. For these individuals, learning to write can present challenges. These learners have unique instructional needs because of the nature of writing in the English language. English is written from left to right, thus creating a movement of the arm away from the body for right-handed writers. Left-handed writers physically move their arm toward their body as they write. In addition, as left-handed writers move their arm, they cover up what they have just written. Not only do they have no clear visual image of what they have written, but in covering up their writing they are also more likely to smudge their work and have further difficulty in rereading their script. Because they cover their writing, left-handed writers cannot read their writing as they go, but have to stop and move their arm in order to reread their script.

Educators can help left-handed writers to write clearly and legibly without discomfort, developing a hand that requires a minimum of time, effort, and concentration. This is particularly important because, in order to produce clean copy and be able to read their work as they write, left-handed writers frequently develop a "hooked" motion, curling their wrist over the top of the page and distorting the motions necessary to form letters. Left-handed writers may therefore require more one-on-one instruction from the teacher than right-handed writers, but sensitive teachers understand that this is necessary if learners are to be given the opportunity to develop handwriting that is legible, well formed, evenly spaced, and with a uniform slant.

Here are some suggestions to help left-handed writers at school and at home:

- Make sure the writer is holding the pencil correctly—about three to four centimetres from the point and with the correct grasp by the fingers: further away from the point than right-handed writers.

- Position the paper so that it is tilted downward at the right-hand side. Doing this allows for an even slant and lets the writer see what he or she has already written. Some teachers have found it helpful to place a piece of masking tape on the learner's desk to indicate an appropriate tilt.

- Try to prevent the development of a "hooked" wrist—the habit of hooking the wrist around the writing—so as not to cover up what has been written.

- Seat the writer so that light comes over the *right* shoulder and therefore the shadow of the hand does not fall on the writing.

- Provide writers who need it with a lower desk surface to write on or a cushion so that they can be higher in their seat and have a clearer view of their work.

- Do not insist on a slant to the right in letter formation. Many left-handed writers write more effectively with a vertical formation.

KEYBOARDING AND TECHNOLOGY SKILLS

Over the years, there has been debate about when it is appropriate to teach learners basic keyboarding skills. Most Canadian provincial ministries of education have mandated information and communication technology (ICT) programs of study. In Alberta the ICT program of studies (Alberta Learning, 2000b) is not meant to be a stand-alone document. ICT skills are to be infused across the curriculum and learned through their use in purposeful situations. The document lists the following outcomes relevant to writing on the screen for Division 1 (kindergarten to grade 3):

- perform basic computer operations, including moving the cursor, clicking on an icon, using pull-down menus, saving files, retrieving files, printing, and closing down

- use proper keyboarding techniques for the home row, enter, spacebar, tab, backspace, delete, and insertion point arrow keys

- create original text, using word-processing software, to communicate and demonstrate understanding of forms and techniques

- edit complete sentences, using such features as cut, copy, and paste

In Division 2 (grades 4 to 6) the outcomes include these:

- use appropriate keyboarding techniques for the alphabetic and punctuation keys

- create and revise original text to communicate and demonstrate understanding of forms and techniques

- edit and format text to clarify and enhance meaning, using such word-processing features as thesaurus, find/change, text alignment, font size, and font style

In Division 3 (grades 7 to 9) the outcomes include these:

- design a document, using style sheets and with attention to page layout, that incorporates advanced word-processing techniques, including headers, footers, margins, columns, table of contents, bibliography, and index

- use advanced word-processing menu features to accomplish a task; for example, insert a table, graph, or text from another document

- revise text documents based on feedback from others

- use appropriate communication technology to elicit feedback from others

Teaching basic keyboarding skills is no longer an option for teachers. Many learners will learn these skills at home, but many will not. It is especially important that ICT skills are taught to learners who come from homes where computers may not be available for them to play and work on. Computer access remains an issue for learners from lower-income families, and as such, ICT can still privilege some learners over others.

Keyboarding programs for students are numerous, and information about programs and why such programs are valuable can be found on websites such as Typing for Kids Software Review (http://typing-for-kids-software-review.toptenreviews.com). In Wayne McNamara's school, teachers use the program All the Right Type by Ingenuity Works. Learners enjoy it because it incorporates games and a futuristic campus into the lessons that teach sequential keyboarding skills, realistic posture, correct fingering, and speed. Sunburst's Typing to Learn 3 is designed for grades 3 to 12, and includes 25 lessons in an animated program. The free online program Dance Mat Typing on the BBC Schools website is an introduction to touch typing for learners aged 7 to 11 accessible to them at home as well as in school (http://www.bbc.co.uk/schools/typing).

Keyboarding and handwriting habits formed in the early years of schooling frequently persist into adulthood. It is therefore essential that these skills be taught effectively in the elementary grades, with emphasis placed on legibility and comfort in writing. The example teachers set in their own handwriting and keyboarding has an impact on learners. Teachers' writing on the whiteboard/SMART Board should therefore be clear and legible, for, as with spelling and computer use, teachers are the primary models.

SUMMARY

Assessments of writing abilities are undertaken for four purposes: to inform teachers' instructional practices, to inform learners of their progress and the areas on which they need to focus future learning, to inform parents of their children's progress, and to inform school administration and school districts about the competencies of the learners in their schools. Although formal measures provide accountability for educators, assessment is most valuable for the ways in which it helps teachers to meet the needs of individual learners. As teachers assess writing abilities, they gain direct information as to what they need to teach and reteach, and how they might conduct that instruction. Appropriate assessment of writing provides invaluable feedback to educators on what learners need to learn and what teachers need to teach.

Composing a written text is a complex process. The criteria for determining *good* writing vary according to gender, personality, social group, and culture. In their instruction and assessment of writing, teachers show respect for the idiosyncratic nature of the writing process and value both the written products and the writing processes of individual learners. In constructivist classrooms, teachers focus on a wide range of writing abilities and recognize that there is no one way to evaluate writing, nor one mark or grade that adequately represents a learner's writing development or abilities.

Writing assessments can be informal or formal, formative or summative. Informal assessment usually consists of process strategies that attempt to record the writing behaviours and attitudes of learners as well as the written product itself. Data are collected through observations, anecdotal notes, conferences, conversations with parents, portfolios of written work, and writing profiles, as well as through careful reading of writing samples. Educators make informal assessments on the basis of their reviews of collections of writing samples in different

continued

genres—poetry, stories, learning log entries, reports, letters, persuasive pieces, explanations, response journal entries, and more.

More formal assessments of learners' abilities are undertaken through holistic analysis of writing samples or through the more analytic criteria–based scales. Holistic scoring is a guided procedure for sorting and ranking pieces according to general criteria or by matching them with other pieces of writing from the same class of learners. Criteria-based scoring assesses writing according to component parts such as voice, vocabulary, sentence structure, conventions of written language, development, and organization.

Many writers learn to use the conventional transcription tools (including spelling, punctuation, capitalization, and usage) as they engage in the writing process or as teachers provide feedback during editing or writing conferences. Alternatively, these skills can be taught through direct instruction based on learners' own writing and their questions and challenges. Many learners will require multiple lessons using direct instruction: demonstration, guided practice, individual application, and assessment. Teachers use a range of strategies to reteach a concept or skill until they are reasonably certain learners have successfully learned it. Students in kindergarten through grade 2 continue to use invented spelling as they explore the written symbol system and the graphophonic system. Sound–symbol relationships are complex in the English language, and most learners take a number of years to move entirely into standard spelling. Direct instruction in spelling is advised for those who experience particular difficulties in the area, but only in grade 2 or later. Word lists with a study procedure and mastery test remain the most effective means of direct instruction.

Handwriting is taught regularly in the primary grades, but learners in the intermediate grades also require the occasional maintenance lesson. An instructional approach suitable across the grades requires learners to verbalize letter descriptions or say them silently as they draw the letters. A handwriting model at each learner's desk is invaluable. Teachers' own handwriting, particularly their writing on the chalkboard, has a major influence on how learners value handwriting and strive to achieve a legible hand. The aim of handwriting lessons is for each learner to achieve legible handwriting with a minimum of time, effort, and concentration.

An alternative transcription tool is the computer word-processing program. Because so much of our writing is now done on the screen, learners need to be taught basic keyboarding and other computer skills from the primary grades onward. Educators are responsible for teaching the provincial ICT programs of studies, and for infusing digital technologies across the curriculum, including in the language arts.

Learners bring to school a vast store of knowledge about language and how it is used. Teachers plan writing programs that allow learners to use this knowledge to communicate with a wide range of audiences for a variety of purposes. An integral component of that writing program is teaching the conventions of written language. Without a working knowledge of these conventions, compositions cannot be as effective as their writers would wish. Much of the empowerment of writing comes from its precision, clarity, and imagery, whether in a novel, journal, poem, or report.

SELECTED PROFESSIONAL RESOURCES

Alberta Assessment Consortium: http://www.aac.ab.ca

This website is created and maintained by a nonprofit collaboration across a large number of Alberta school boards and the Alberta Teachers' Association. The material presented on this website is dependable—and the links to other sites are excellent. The site connects teachers to a range of assessment materials, professional development opportunities, and networks with other agencies. The site also contains "principles of fair assessment" and how to communicate evaluations to learners, parents, and school districts.

Culham, R. (2003). Theory and practice: 6 + 1 Traits of Writing, the complete guide grades 3 and up. New York, NY: Scholastic.

The book breaks writing into traits and allows teachers and learners to think about one trait at a time as they are teaching/learning and assessing writing. The traits are very similar to the criteria used in the provincial achievement tests. The book contains samples of student writing at different grades and levels, and then presents descriptive assessments of each piece. A scoring guide is included for each trait, which can be very helpful for beginning teachers when they are completing report cards.

Kendall, J., & Khuon, O. (2006). Writing sense: Integrated reading and writing lessons for English language learners, K–8. Portland, ME: Stenhouse.

Because the book is intended primarily for students learning English as a second language, it is applicable across all the grades. It gives a big picture of the conditions necessary for successful writing instruction, including how all the parts fit together and how specific strategies can be used. It includes lesson plans as examples and focuses on best practices. The book presents a three-day writing assessment—what to assess over a three-day period. Applicable to learners at all levels of language learning, it's a very handy book to have.

The Pleasures of Literacy

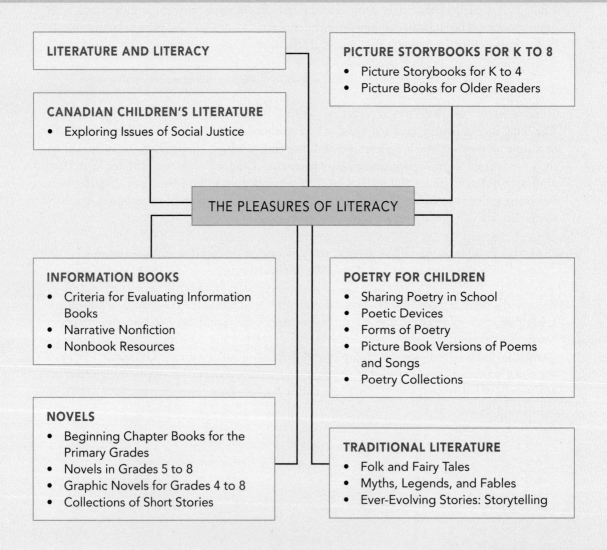

LITERATURE AND LITERACY

CANADIAN CHILDREN'S LITERATURE
- Exploring Issues of Social Justice

PICTURE STORYBOOKS FOR K TO 8
- Picture Storybooks for K to 4
- Picture Books for Older Readers

THE PLEASURES OF LITERACY

INFORMATION BOOKS
- Criteria for Evaluating Information Books
- Narrative Nonfiction
- Nonbook Resources

POETRY FOR CHILDREN
- Sharing Poetry in School
- Poetic Devices
- Forms of Poetry
- Picture Book Versions of Poems and Songs
- Poetry Collections

NOVELS
- Beginning Chapter Books for the Primary Grades
- Novels in Grades 5 to 8
- Graphic Novels for Grades 4 to 8
- Collections of Short Stories

TRADITIONAL LITERATURE
- Folk and Fairy Tales
- Myths, Legends, and Fables
- Ever-Evolving Stories: Storytelling

TEACHER-LIBRARIAN KATHY OSTER

Kathy Oster is a rich source of information on books and other print and online materials that connect to the programs of study in every one of the content areas taught in kindergarten through grade 8. She has lists of books relevant to a wide range of subjects and themes, and she can access them at a few moments' notice. Kathy also knows her school library well. She can take teachers and students directly to the resources they are searching for. She is responsible for selecting and ordering books, both on the recommendation of teachers and from her own browsing of catalogues and websites for the latest high-quality materials (e.g., United Library Services: **http://www .uls.com/ULS/index2.jsp;** and National Book Network: **http://nbnbooks.com**). Knowing the K to 8 curriculum is crucial in her role as a teacher-librarian. She also needs to understand students' reading abilities and interests.

Kathy Oster

Today, there are few teacher-librarians working in public schools. Kathy Oster has seen her time allocation diminish over the years from being a full-time teacher-librarian (1.0) to only 0.2, with 0.8 of her time now dedicated to classroom teaching. This is in spite of research that strongly demonstrates the positive effects on student achievement of well-equipped, well-stocked and professionally staffed school libraries (Haycock, 2011; Lance & Loertscher, 2003).

Kathy has three major roles to fulfill as a teacher-librarian. One is to support teachers in their planning of units across the curriculum and to locate teaching resources for them. Kathy's main responsibility is "to put the right books in the hands of teachers when they need them." A second role is to promote literacy and to encourage a passion for reading among learners. Kathy is in the unique position of meeting and getting to know every student in her school. They all come into the library/resource centre, and she is able to get to know their ways of reading, their reading preferences, and which books might pique their interests. A third role is to bring the teachers up-to-date with new materials available in the library/resource centre and to encourage them to read and experience more **children's literature**—getting high-quality materials into their hands.

Kathy directs teachers' attention to new or relevant books by placing books on the coffee table in the staff room, along with short notes indicating a good curricular fit or reason for recommendation. She also does short book talks at staff meetings, pauses to chat about books with staff in the hallways, and often gives books directly to teachers—a sure way to get books into the hands of students. Kathy finds that all teachers, and especially beginning teachers, are thrilled when she pops a bucket of books related to a current curriculum topic on their desk.

Kathy orders lots of magazines for the school library/resource centre, including *Ranger Rick, Owl, Chirp, Chickadee, Your Big Backyard* (National Wildlife Federation, ages 3 to 7), *Sports Illustrated for Kids, Zoobooks,* and *Highlights.* She orders multiple copies of these magazines, as they go through many hands.

When asked about children's and young adults' favourite books, Kathy says that picture books are enjoyed right across the grades. The most requested novels include *The Tale of Despereaux* by Kate DiCamillo and all of Cornelia Funke's books (especially by the boys). Boys also enjoy **graphic novels** and the girls increasingly request **historical fiction**. Favourite books of historical fiction are *Number the Stars* by Lois Lowry and *Hana's Suitcase* by Karen Levine. Popular titles with grade 7 and 8 learners are *Tangerine* by Edward Bloor and *Double Identity* by Margaret Peterson Haddix.

Kathy suggests that beginning teachers start as many lessons as they can with a book or an oral story that relates directly to the topics and concepts they are teaching. For example, in math in the early grades, they might introduce *The Doorbell Rang* by Pat Hutchins. For social studies, there's *Josepha: A Prairie Boy's Story* by Jim McGugan and for older students, *The Arrival* by Shaun Tan. Starting with a story focuses learners' attention and creates a context for the lessons they are learning. Stories help them to visualize events and settings. ☐

We first need to clarify what a number of terms pertaining to literature mean. In *Constructing Meaning*, we use *children's literature* to refer to those children's books, both fiction and nonfiction, that critics acknowledge to be of high quality; these well-written books provide readers with pleasurable and challenging reading experiences. **Young adult literature** refers to the body of work written specifically for youth in the 14 to 20 age range, with particular attention paid to age-appropriate content and language. As mentioned in Chapter 2, the term **trade books** has a broader definition, including all books that are published for preschoolers, children, and young adults, but *not* as part of a **basal reading series** or as textbooks for use in schools. Trade books encompass many genres of literature, including comics and series books such as *The Maze of Bones* (The 39 Clues series) and *Diary of a Wimpy Kid*, as well as magazines. The term **reading series** refers to a set of materials specifically designed for teaching reading and language arts, and they frequently form the basis for an instructional program in reading. Many current reading series are anthologies of materials taken directly from published works of literature by well-known authors. These series generally consist of teacher guides, student anthologies, workbooks, and supplemental materials, such as assessment resources, big books, correlated trade books, audiovisual aids, and computer software.

Genre, a word borrowed from French, means "literary form." The epic, tragedy, comedy, essay, biography, novel, and poetry are traditional genres. New forms have been added to this list over the years, and now the term is used as a convenient (and somewhat arbitrary) way of classifying literary works. Today, *genre* refers to a body of literature that has certain common elements. The genres usually referred to in children's and young adult literature are picture books, wordless books, concept books, biographies, classics, legends, myths, folk tales, fairy tales, fables, historical fiction, realistic fiction, fantasies, science fiction, graphic novels, poetry, and nonfiction. Each of these may, in turn, be subdivided into a number of different categories, or subgenres.

Many educators have embraced the concept of literature-based reading instruction and have created language arts programs based on trade books of many genres. Educators understand the power of children's literature and have high regard for the authors and illustrators who create literary works for children. Children's literature conferences are met with great enthusiasm by educators and librarians alike. One example is the Kaleidoscope Conference, held every four years in Calgary (sponsored by the Alberta School Library Council of the Alberta Teachers' Association).

Reading or listening to good books is one of the great pleasures in the lives of most children. Students often remember well into adulthood specific books their teachers read to them in the elementary grades. These stories engage the imagination and connect us with people and places that are both like us and different from us. Books help us to be aware of the larger world and provide a context within which we can better understand who we are and the lives we can lead.

Educator and learners at book display

LITERATURE AND LITERACY

With a careful choice of books and appropriate teaching, children learn to read from interesting and well-written, well-illustrated trade books as well as from reading series. Educators must not only know children's books (including their titles, authors, themes, plots, characters, and structures), but also understand how books work, how books teach young readers how to read, and how they assist individuals to become true "readers," not just people able to read. Teaching with literature incorporates all the language arts and may involve such activities as novel studies, Shared Reading, drama (see the online drama chapter available at http://www.constructing meaning6e.nelson.com), art activities, puppetry, journals and other kinds of writing, and book talks by students. It requires a good deal of organization and knowledge of strategies (e.g., literature circles and response groups). It also demands that educators read the books their students are reading and be able to participate with learners as they generate shared meanings from those books. To help you as a beginning teacher, we offer a list of children's and young adult literature, presented by grade level, in the Appendix.

As we noted in Chapter 4, many children entering school already know a great many things about print literacy. They learn from the reading materials they have in their homes, including magazines, games, toys, digital media, and books. Scholars, researchers, and educators have learned that children's literature has a greater likelihood of encouraging learners to take on the four roles of the reader (Freebody & Luke, 1990) described in Chapter 1, than do most school-based reading materials. Reading is more than matching written symbols with sounds, more than acquiring a reading vocabulary, more than understanding word meanings, and more than being able to answer someone else's questions about a text.

In *Me and You* by Anthony Browne, for example, the reader is encouraged not only to decode the text and read the pictures on the right-hand page, but also to read the pictures on the left-hand page—pictures that, at first glance, appear to have nothing to do with the text and pictures on the right. In order to construct a meaningful story in a retelling of "Goldilocks and the Three Bears," the reader has to engage with the book in all four roles of the reader: code breaker, text participant, text user, and text analyst.

There is more than one story being told in these pages. Participating only as a code breaker would create a limited story with little appeal to readers. *Rosie's Walk* by Pat Hutchins provides a further example of this phenomenon. The text *and* the pictures must be read together and with care.

There are times today when a reading series can be very useful to teachers. If a large and varied collection of children's reading material is not available, or when a student has a particular learning need, a reading series may provide the resources necessary for instruction. Children clearly need to learn code-breaking skills early in their lives, but they also deserve to learn how to be text users, text analysts, and text participants. They must, if they are to become independent readers, be capable of constructing meaning from the texts they read. From children's and young adult literature, students are provided with the opportunity to learn both how to read and how to appreciate how texts work. The combination of the two creates rich possibilities for reading for pleasure—and for information—throughout life.

Educators have long known that one of the most important influences in a child's early literacy development is being read to (and with) in the preschool years. In longitudinal studies of language and literacy development, the effects of shared book experiences have been well documented (e.g., Evans & Shaw, 2008; Sénéchal, 2006; Wells, 1986). These studies reached the following conclusions:

- Shared book experiences promote the development of language skills, in particular vocabulary, and also introduce children to the rich structures and phrasing of written language.

- Children who are read to frequently in the preschool years are more likely to read for pleasure and have better reading comprehension abilities in the elementary grades.

- Early reading experiences affect writing as well as reading abilities, and are also influential in developing children's listening skills.

- The more children read and are read to, and the more children talk about what they are reading and writing, the more successful they are likely to be in school and in their literacy endeavours.

DeTemple (2001) wrote, "the book affords an opportunity for complex, explicit language such as explanations, definitions and descriptions. The book is also a starting point for facilitating talk about what is not immediately present: past experiences, predictions and inferences" (p. 35). Furthermore, Dickinson (2001) noted that "book reading supports the development of children's ability to comprehend stories and helps foster a love of books and reading. Growth in comprehension occurs as children learn vocabulary and concepts, become familiar with the language of books, and begin to learn strategies for making meaning from books" (p. 176).

Many preschool children love books. They are fascinated by the pictures on the page, and they enjoy the shared experience of reading, perhaps on a caregiver's lap. A pleasurable anticipation of books gives parents and educators an opportunity to provide quality works of literature for the young. A notable interactive picture book perfect for sharing with children of all ages is *Press Here* by Hervé Tullet. The book is full of surprises as the reader is requested to take action to shape the unfolding events. *Each Peach Pear Plum* by the Ahlbergs is an extension of traditional literature that has become a classic. *Each Peach Pear Plum* contains illustrations rich in the detail of the nursery rhymes, folklore, legends, and fairy tales of Western Europe, and it is a book that can be read on a range of levels. The very young child, still unable to follow the plots of traditional stories, can enjoy the repetition of "each peach pear plum" and the rhyming patterns, as well as the predictability of the language. Older children enjoy the humour derived from their prior knowledge of the fairy tales and nursery rhymes alluded to in the book.

Children learn from books such as these that reading is an active experience. In addition to what they learn about values, culture, and life, they learn about handling and "reading" books. Children learn directionality: the front and back of a book, which way is the right way up, and which way the story moves through the book—in the case of *Each Peach Pear Plum*, with text on the left, pictures on the right, and a "cuing" picture above the text. Children learn that books can be actively responded to and that books are a way into a pleasurable experience.

Children's experiences with books such as *Each Peach Pear Plum*, and the experiences they have with reading throughout their schooling, affect how learners perceive themselves as readers and how they perceive reading: whether it's a relevant activity, whether it's a pleasurable activity, and whether books are worth the time and effort needed to have a truly *satisfying* reading experience. Educators who use literature as a basis for teaching reading demonstrate to children that books *are* worth the time and effort required of a reader, and thus children are more likely to become readers as adults. Educators who clearly enjoy reading—and who demonstrate this joy in their daily life in classrooms—invite children into the world of books with enthusiasm and excitement.

CANADIAN CHILDREN'S LITERATURE

It is well accepted that learners need to see themselves reflected in the books they read. If Canadian children are to know themselves and Canada, they need frequent opportunities to access resources that are Canadian and that depict Canadian culture and identity. In this section, we address the importance of Canadian learners reading Canadian literature in addition to their reading of international literature.

Over the years, Canadians have become accustomed to receiving media largely from the United States. Children's print materials are no exception. However, the stories and experiences of Aboriginal Americans, Hispanic Americans, African Americans, Chinese Americans, and other ethnic and cultural groups do not necessarily parallel those of Canadians. Many excellent books are written and produced in Canada. The Canadian Children's Book Centre (CCBC) in Toronto publishes lists of books and information about authors. More information about the CCBC is presented in Box 11.1.

In Canadian literature, learners read about Canadian people and places from St. John's and Ungava Bay to Yellowknife and Vancouver Island. When they read Canadian materials, learners can imagine the prairies, mountains, cities, or seacoast, and they learn more about what it means to be Canadian. Many scholars and writers have suggested that the land—the environment or physical landscape of Canada—characterizes Canadian literature. *Looking for X* by Deborah Ellis is a realistic novel set in Toronto, *The Red Sash* by Jean Pendziwol is a historical picture book set in Thunder Bay, and *Nana's Cold Days* by Adwoa Badoe is a contemporary picture book set in Canada's winterscape. Each of these books provides different insights into Canada and what it means to be Canadian, and each is profoundly reliant upon the landscape in which it is set.

BOX 11.1

THE CANADIAN CHILDREN'S BOOK CENTRE

The Canadian Children's Book Centre (commonly referred to as the CCBC), located in Toronto, was established in 1976 to encourage, promote, and support the reading, writing, illustrating, and publishing of Canadian books for young readers. With book collections and extensive resources in five cities across Canada, the CCBC provides information to members on current Canadian books, authors, and illustrators. The quarterly magazine *The Children's Book News* highlights what's new and exciting in Canadian children's and young adult books, including information about Canadian Children's Book Week. The semi-annual *Best Books for Kids and Teens* is a guide to the best new Canadian books, magazines, audio, and video. Online resources include a calendar of events, links to publishers' sites, and a complete list of Canadian Children's Book Awards: http://www.bookcentre.ca.

From Canadian books such as those noted above, young readers recognize that authors are real people, and that writing and illustrating are possible professions. Well-known authors and illustrators visit schools on a regular basis, and some of the hard work and the craft of writing and illustrating are demonstrated to learners as they listen to artists speak about and read their published work. Several organizations across Canada, such as the Young Alberta Book Society, exist for the sole purpose of enhancing literacy development and introducing Canadian authors and illustrators to young readers in schools. Because of their importance, Canadian books are included and identified throughout the remainder of this chapter.

Exploring Issues of Social Justice

Official multiculturalism, which was formalized through the *Canadian Multiculturalism Act* of 1988, constitutionally recognized the changing face of Canada as a result of immigration. The Act aimed to promote "tolerance and understanding" for all of Canada's peoples. Multiculturalism has become a significant element of Canadian identity, and Canadians continue their efforts to develop a just society. In order to meet the needs of an increasingly diverse student population, educators must be prepared to develop culturally sensitive curriculum and pedagogy. Children's literature plays a considerable role in helping learners to understand themselves and the society they live in. When educators select books for their classrooms and for their young readers, a key consideration must be a respect for multiple viewpoints, for social justice, and for lives and lifestyles that are different from their own. Literature is a powerful vehicle for the transmission of culture and for the exploration of values and attitudes. Books both mirror cultural attitudes and play a part in acculturating them.

Although Canada prides itself on its "cultural pluralism," for those citizens outside the white mainstream, Canada remains a country where much of the power resides in the hands of those of European descent. There is room in every classroom and library for well-chosen books that address the many faces of marginalization and inequality still experienced by

Canadians and many people around the world. A host of well-written books for readers of all ages explore topics such as sexual orientation, bullying, body image, poverty, war, and racial and linguistic differences. Many books already cited in this chapter deal with these and other social justice issues.

Suitable for learners in grades 4 to 6, *Fatty Legs* by Christy Jordan-Fenton and Margaret Pokiak-Fenton (also in picture book format as *When I Was Eight*) is a memoir that tells the story of Olemaun (Margaret), who desperately wanted to go to school so she could learn to read English. As an Inuk child living on Banks Island, she had to attend the "outsiders'" school far away from home. The nuns took away her name, cut off her long hair, and forced her to do physically strenuous chores, but her dream of learning to read could not be quashed. Olemaun missed her family and endured great hardship, but after two years, when she finally returned home, she could not only read well but had proven to herself that she was brave as well as clever.

In the young adult novel *What World Is Left* by Monique Polak, Anneke and her family are taken from their home in Holland to a German concentration camp at Terezin (Theresienstadt) in Czechoslovakia. The family survives in the camp for two years until liberation by Russian soldiers at war's end. The family eventually returns to Holland, but Anneke has trouble accepting her father's actions and the risks he took to protect and save them all while they were in the camp.

In Box 11.2 we identify some particularly engaging picture books and novels appropriate for exploring issues of social justice with learners in Kindergarten through grade 8.

BOX 11.2

EXPLORING SOCIAL JUSTICE WITH CANADIAN BOOKS

Bannatyne-Cugnet, J. (2000). *From far and wide: A Canadian citizenship scrapbook.* (S. Nan Zhang, Illus.). Toronto, ON: Tundra Books. (pic)

Button, L. (2010). *Willow's whispers.* (T. Howells, Illus.). Toronto, ON: Kids Can Press. (pic)

Curtis, C. P. (2007). *Elijah of Buxton.* New York, NY: Scholastic. (novel)

Day, M. (2002). *Edward the "crazy man."* Toronto, ON: Annick Press. (pic)

Ellis, D. (2006). *I am a taxi.* Toronto, ON: Groundwood Books. (novel)

Fitch, S. (2001). *No two snowflakes.* (J. Wilson, Illus.). Victoria, BC: Orca. (pic)

Gilmore, R. (1998). *A gift for Gita.* (A. Priestley, Illus). Toronto, ON: Second Story Press. (pic)

Hampton, M. J. (2001). *The cat from Kosovo.* (T. Thiébaux-Heikalo, Illus.). Halifax, NS: Nimbus. (pic)

Harrison, T. (2002). *Courage to fly.* (Z.-Y. Huang, Illus). Calgary, AB: Red Deer Press. (pic)

Hof, M. (2006). *Against the odds.* (J. Prins, Trans.). Toronto, ON: Groundwood Books. (novel)

(continued)

Huser, G. (2003). *Stitches*. Toronto, ON: Groundwood Books. (y/a)

Jordan-Fenton, C., & Pokiak-Fenton, M. (2013). *When I was eight.* (G. Grimard, Illus.). Toronto, ON: Annick Press. (pic)

Ka, O. (2009). *My great big mama.* (L. Melanson, Illus.). Toronto, ON: Groundwood Books/House of Anansi. (pic)

Levert, M. (2005). *Eddie Longpants*. Toronto, ON: Groundwood Books. (pic)

Major, K. (2000). *Eh? to zed.* (A. Daniel, Illus.). Red Deer, AB: Red Deer Press. (pic)

McGugan, J. (1994). *Josepha: A prairie boy's story.* (M. Kimber, Illus.). Calgary, AB: Red Deer College Press. (pic)

McMurchy-Barber, G. (2010). *Free as a bird*. Toronto, ON: Dundurn Press. (novel)

Nielsen-Fernlund, S. (2007). *The magic beads.* (G. Cote, Illus.). Vancouver, BC: Simply Read Books. (pic)

Setterington, K. (2004). *Mom and Mum are getting married.* (A. Priestley, Illus.). Toronto, ON: Second Story Press. (pic)

Skrypuch, M. F. (1996). *Silver threads.* (M. Martchenko, Illus.). Toronto, ON: Penguin Books Canada. (pic for older readers)

Skrypuch, M. F. (2010). *Stolen child*. Toronto, ON: Scholastic Canada. (novel)

Steffen, C. (2003). *A new home for Malik.* (J. Stopper, Illus.). Calgary, AB: Calgary Immigrant Women's Association. (pic)

Trilby, K. (2011). *Stones for my father*. Toronto, ON: Tundra Books. (y/a)

Trottier, M. (1999). *Flags.* (P. Morin, Illus.). Toronto, ON: Stoddart Kids. (pic)

Trottier, M. (2011). *Migrant.* (I. Arsenault, Illus.). Toronto, ON: Groundwood Books. (pic)

Uegaki, C. (2003). *Suki's kimono.* (S. Jorisch, Illus.). Toronto, ON: Kids Can Press. (pic)

Upjohn, R. (2007). *Lily and the paper man.* (R. Benoit, Illus.). Toronto, ON: Second Story Press. (pic)

Wang, R. (2008). *Froggy.* (H. Yu, Illus.). Toronto, ON: Kevin & Robin Books. (pic)

Walters, E. (2011). *Shaken*. Toronto, ON: Doubleday Canada. (novel)

Yee, P. (1996). *Ghost train.* (H. Chan, Illus.). Toronto, ON: Douglas & McIntyre/Groundwood Books. (pic for older readers)

Young, B. (2009). *Charlie: A home child's life in Canada*. Toronto, ON: Key Porter Books. (y/a)

Aboriginal Canadian authors and illustrators have contributed greatly to raising an awareness of social justice issues through their books for young readers. The works of George Littlechild, Michael Arvaarluk Kusugak, Thomas King, Richard Van Camp, and Tomson Highway are particularly noteworthy.

George Littlechild's book *This Land Is My Land* is a stunning introduction to Aboriginal literature, with personal stories about Littlechild's family members and ancestors. The short narratives are unforgettable in their intensity and poignancy. Littlechild writes and paints about his experiences in boarding school and recalls memories, many of them tragic, of family members. He speaks excitedly about his first visit to New York City and describes the development of his artwork. The book ends optimistically, with Littlechild telling about the revival of Aboriginal culture and traditions and emphasizing the pride he feels in his ancestry.

Tomson Highway's three books for young readers, *Caribou Song*, *Dragonfly Kite*, and *Fox on the Ice*, make up a trilogy, Songs of the North Wind. The books are superbly illustrated by well-known Canadian artist Brian Deines, and the text is presented in Cree and English. The stories tell of the magical adventures of two brothers, Joe and Cody, as they play together, encountering wildlife and entertaining themselves through the seasons in northern Manitoba. Box 11.3 features a selection of books by Aboriginal Canadian authors and illustrators.

BOX 11.3

BOOKS AUTHORED AND/OR ILLUSTRATED BY ABORIGINAL CANADIANS

Bouchard, D. (2006). *Nokum is my teacher.* (A. Sapp, Illus.). Calgary, AB: Red Deer Press. (pic)

Bruchac, J. (2000). *Crazy Horse's vision.* (S. D. Nelson, Illus.). New York, NY: Lee & Low Books. (pic for older readers)

Campbell, N. (2005). *Shi-shi-etko.* (K. Lafave, Illus.). Toronto, ON: Groundwood Books. (pic)

Campbell, N. (2008). *Shin-chi's canoe.* (K. Lafave, Illus.). Toronto, ON: Groundwood Books. (pic)

Chartrand, J., & Nolan, D. (2009). *I want to be in the show.* (M. Chambers, Illus.). Winnipeg, MB: Pemmican Publications. (pic)

Dumas, P. (2013). *Pīsim finds her miskanow.* (L. Paul, Illus.). Winnipeg, MB: HighWater Press. (pic)

Einarson, E. (2004). *The moccasins.* (J. Flett, Illus.). Penticton, BC: Theytus Books. (pic)

Jordan-Fenton, C., & Pokiak-Fenton, M. (2013). *When I was eight.* (G. Grimard, Illus.). Toronto, ON: Annick Press. (pic)

King, T. (1992). *A coyote Columbus story.* (K. Monkman, Illus.). Toronto, ON: Groundwood Books. (pic for older readers)

Kusugak, M. (1993). *Northern lights: The soccer trails.* (V. Krykorka, Illus.). Toronto, ON: Annick Press. (pic)

Kusugak, M. (1992). *Hide and sneak.* (V. Krykorka, Illus.). Toronto, ON: Annick Press. (pic)

Loewen, I. (1993). *My kookum called today.* (G. Miller, Illus.). Winnipeg, MB: Pemmican. (pic)

Loyie, L. (2013). *The moon speaks Cree: A winter adventure.* (B. Cohen, Illus.). Penticton, BC: Theytus Books. (pic for older readers)

Loyie, L., & Brissenden, C. (2008). *Goodbye Buffalo Bay.* Penticton, BC: Theytus Books. (pic for older readers)

Oliviero, J., & Morrisseau, B. (1993). *The fish skin.* Winnipeg, MB: Hyperion Press. (pic)

(continued)

Slipperjack, R. (2008). *Dog tracks*. Calgary, AB: Fifth House. (novel)

Spalding, A., & Scow, A. (2006). *Secret of the dance*. (D. Gait, Illus.). Victoria, BC: Orca. (pic)

Sterling, J. (1992). *My name is Seepeetza*. Toronto, ON: Groundwood Books. (novel)

Van Camp, R. (1997). *A man called Raven*. (G. Littlechild, Illus.). San Francisco, CA: Children's Book Press. (pic)

Van Camp, R. (1998). *What's the most beautiful thing you know about horses?* (G. Littlechild, Illus.). Markham, ON: Children's Book Press. (pic)

PICTURE STORYBOOKS FOR K TO 8

Every genre of literature is represented in **picture books**. The label "picture book" refers to a general category of books having the same basic format and way of communicating a message. Some books may more appropriately be called "illustrated books." True picture books involve a partnership between text and pictures, with the pictures and text together telling the story or presenting information. The most common genres of picture books are wordless books, concept books (such as counting and alphabet books), **predictable books**, easy-to-read books, and picture storybooks. There is often overlap among the genres within picture books. This section of the chapter focuses on picture storybooks rather than on the other picture book genres, such as alphabet or counting books.

Picture Storybooks for K to 4

Picture storybooks are a powerful vehicle for teaching children both how to read and how to become readers. It is understood that reading should be taught in the context of real texts, but not until we look in detail at books such as *Me and You* by Anthony Browne and *Chester* by Mélanie Watt do we fully understand the reading lessons children receive from picture books. Meek (1988) refers to these as "private lessons," the lessons good readers learn about reading without formal teaching. *Me and You* tells one version of the story through pictures only (from Goldilocks' perspective) and another version of the story through a combination of pictures and text (from Baby Bear's perspective). In *Chester*, about a remarkable cat, storytelling takes on a whole new dimension. Through Mélanie Watt's dialogue with *Chester*, and his frequent hijacking of her story, *Chester* is very much in charge. From the front and back covers of the book to the very last page, this picture book offers multiple stories and multiple points of view, and it does so with a hilarity that both children and adults thoroughly enjoy.

Another example of a picture book that can be read on many levels is the classic *Rosie's Walk* by Pat Hutchins. It contains one sentence, 32 words, and 27 pages of pictures. *Rosie's Walk* is a story that, if told in words alone, would take many paragraphs and lose much of its allure.

It contains at least two stories: the story of Rosie the hen and her barnyard walk, and the story of the fox who silently follows her (not even mentioned in the text, but prominent in the illustrations). The reading lesson, which transfers directly to adult books such as *The Orenda* by Joseph Boyden (2013), is important: that there's more than one story in any book and more in any book than what's written on the page.

In their early reading experiences, children focus strongly on book illustrations and rely heavily on pictures to create meaning from the page. *Wordless books* can make a powerful contribution to reading development in both young children and fluent readers (including adults). By acknowledging the observations children make and the questions they ask, educators enhance readers' responses to the books and help expand their understandings through discussion and interaction.

A selection of wordless books appropriate for children from preschool to grade 3 is presented below.

- *Anno's Spain* by Mitsumasa Anno
- *Home* by Jeannie Baker
- *A Small Miracle* by Peter Collington
- *Sidewalk Circus* by Paul Fleischman
- *Kitten for a Day* by Ezra Jack Keats
- *The Lion and the Mouse* by Jerry Pinkney
- *Dinosaur* by Peter Sis

Young readers understand the way picture books work because they attend to multiple cues, not only to text. They focus on visual cues much more significantly than adults do. Today's young readers are engaging in completely different reading experiences than previous generations of children because they have access to picture storybooks that are more challenging and interactional than in the past, and they engage in video games, television, movies, and websites that are animated, fast paced, and highly visual. While critics might say that children are using their imaginations less than ever before, many observers of young children would say they are more imaginatively involved in various forms of "storytelling" than ever before.

Young readers need experiences with both writerly and readerly texts. In literary terms, books such as *Rosie's Walk* are often called "writerly" texts because readers must use their imaginations to fill in the textual gaps and thus "complete" the writing of the story. "Readerly" texts are those in which the writer has provided most of the information for the reader, and the writer's meanings tend to be clear and direct. The reader has to do less work. As a result of their early reading experiences with writerly texts such as *Chester* and *Me and You,* more children are likely to appreciate novels such as Boyden's *The Orenda* when they grow up. They are also more likely to continue reading for pleasure as well as for information as adults. Educators must provide the instructional support children require if they are to learn how to move with ease from one kind of text to the other.

Box 11.4 lists some picture books that are appropriate for learners in the elementary grades, and Box 11.5 lists specifically Canadian picture books.

BOX 11.4

A SELECTION OF PICTURE STORYBOOKS

Ahlberg, J., & Ahlberg, A. (1986). *The jolly postman*. London, UK: Heinemann.

Base, G. (2001). *The waterhole*. New York, NY: Penguin Putnam.

Brett, J. (1989). *The mitten*. New York, NY: Scholastic.

Briggs, R. (1975). *Father Christmas goes on holiday*. Harmondsworth, UK: Puffin Books.

Browne, A. (1983). *Gorilla*. New York, NY: Alfred A. Knopf.

Carle, E. (1974). *The very hungry caterpillar*. Harmondsworth, UK: Puffin Books.

Fox, M. (2006). *A particular cow*. (T. Denton, Illus.). New York, NY: Harcourt Books.

Graham, B. (2000). *Max*. Cambridge, MA: Candlewick Press.

Matsuoka, M. (2007). *Footprints in the snow*. New York, NY: Henry Holt.

Rathmann, P. (1995). *Officer Buckle and Gloria*. New York, NY: Putnam.

Rosenthal, A., & Lichtenheld, T. (2009). *Duck! Rabbit!* San Francisco, CA: Chronicle Books.

Ross, T. (1993). *The three pigs*. London, UK: Arrow Books.

Waddell, M. (1988). *Can't you sleep, Little Bear?* (B. Firth, Illus.). Cambridge, MA: Candlewick Press.

Waddell, M. (1991). *Farmer Duck*. (H. Oxenbury, Illus.). London, UK: Walker Books.

BOX 11.5

CANADIAN PICTURE BOOKS

Bailey, L. (2007). *Goodnight, Sweet Pig*. (J. Masse, Illus.). Toronto, ON: Kids Can Press.

Croteau, M. D. (2007). *Mr. Gauguin's heart*. (I. Arsenault, Illus.; S. Ouriou, Trans.). Toronto, ON: Tundra Books.

Eyvindson, P. (1996). *Red Parka Mary*. (R. Brynjolson, Illus.). Winnipeg, MB: Pemmican.

Gay, M. L. (1999). *Stella, star of the sea*. Toronto, ON: Groundwood Books.

Harty, N. (1997). *Hold on, McGinty!* (D. Kilby, Illus.). Toronto, ON: Doubleday Canada.

Jam, T. (1997). *The fishing summer*. (A. Zhang, Illus.). Toronto, ON: Groundwood Books.

Lawson, J. (1999). *Bear on the train*. (B. Deines, Illus.). Toronto, ON: Kids Can Press.

Maclear, K. (2012). *Virginia Wolf*. (I. Arsenault, Illus.). Toronto, ON: Groundwood Books.

Mollel, T. (2014). *From the lands of the night*. (D. McCalla, Illus.). Markham, ON: Red Deer Press.

Morin, P. (1998). *Animal dreaming*. (K. Branchflower, Illus.). New York, NY: Silver Whistle Harcourt Brace.

Munsch, R. (2012). *Zoom*. (M. Martchenko, Illus.). Markham, ON: Scholastic Canada.

Oppel, K. (2000). *Peg and the whale*. (T. Widener, Illus.). Toronto, ON: HarperCollins.

Rivard, E. (2011). *Really and truly*. (A.-C. Delisle, Illus.). Toronto, ON: Owlkids Books.

Sobat, G. S.(2011). *In the graveyard*. (S. Yardley-Jones, Illus.). Chester, NS: Bryler.

Wishinsky, F. (2007). *Please, Louise!* (M. L. Gay, Illus.). Toronto, ON: Groundwood Books.

Picture Books for Older Readers

Picture books are not only for pre- and beginning readers, just as wordless books, such as *Sunshine* and *Moonlight* by Jan Ormerod, are not only for children who cannot yet read.

Similar to *Each Peach Pear Plum* in its intertextual references (to "*Red Riding Hood*" and many other folk and fairy tales) is *The Tunnel* by Anthony Browne. Intended for readers in grades 4 to 6, this book requires many readings to unravel its multilayered text and illustrations. There is much reading to be done in the gaps in the turn of a page, or between text and picture. In these gaps readers are invited to take an "inferential walk" (Eco, 1979) or, in other words, to read between the lines. Thus, readers learn the key role that inference plays in reading and in constructing meaning. Some readers may encounter difficulty in following the story depicted in *The Tunnel* and feel that Browne has omitted too much, has left too many inferential gaps, and in general, has created too writerly a text. These readers want the story to be laid out for them more explicitly, so that they receive a direct message from the author and don't have to create the meaning. (Many adults also struggle with the story in the book and with the nature of the illustrations because Browne manages to create allusions to several of the more disturbing aspects of relationships and growing up, leaving readers to relate their own experiences to the story and perhaps respond at deeply personal levels.) In such books, then, educators play an important role, through dialogue and discussion groups, in helping readers take inferential walks, draw inferences, make educated guesses, and understand overall that there is no correct answer when "gap filling" in texts.

Many picture books are aimed at an audience of older readers who can already read well and have had rich experiences in working with text. Students in grades 4 to 8 respond powerfully to books such as *Chester* by Mélanie Watt and *NO BEARS* by Meg McKinlay and Leila Rudge. These are books that are often referred to as **metafiction**, providing a constant and deliberate reminder that a book is something an author and reader create together—something that is not real and is open to many interpretations and structures. Researcher Sylvia Pantaleo (2014) wrote that "post-modern picture books have broadened conventional notions about picture books, as well as what it means to be an engaged reader of these texts" (p. 324). She has written in depth about metafiction, and she explains and describes the importance of these books in a learner's reading development. Some additional titles of metafiction are listed below:

- *Black and White* by David Macaulay
- *Tuesday* by David Wiesner

- *Voices in the Park* by Anthony Browne
- *Wolves* by Emily Gravett
- *Interrupting Chicken* by David Ezra Stein

Pantaleo (2014) noted that fiction is "an elaborate form of play" and that metafiction "can develop visual literacy competence, facilitate higher level thinking skills, and enhance literary and literacy understandings, including the development of a repertoire of narrative structures" (p. 331). In *June 29, 1999*, by David Wiesner, student Holly Evans develops an ambitious and innovative project for her science assignment. While her classmates are sprouting seeds in paper cups, Holly launches seedlings into the sky on tiny air balloons. Although her teacher and fellow students are skeptical, only five weeks later giant vegetables begin to fall from the sky, landing in various parts of the United States. The book displays Wiesner's unconventional artwork and the same dry humour he uses in *Free Fall* and *Tuesday*. In *NO BEARS*, by McKinlay and Rudge, Ruby decides she will make a book that has no bears in it. "You don't need bears for a book," she says. Instead she will have castles and princesses and exciting things—and there could be a monster! However, unbeknownst to Ruby, a kindly bear overhears her comment, and although she remains on the periphery of the story, she plays an important role in it. The running visual joke makes the story humorous as well as engaging.

Picture books created for older readers are not necessarily easy-reading books. Many deal with mature themes and contain illustrations that provide powerful messages supporting and adding to the text. Two books set in Europe during the Second World War are *Rose Blanche* by Roberto Innocenti and *Let the Celebrations Begin!* by Margaret Wild. Where *Rose Blanche* is a story about the darkness of war, *Let the Celebrations Begin!* is a story of hope, a tribute to the human spirit and to the survival of so many innocent people who lived for years in horrific conditions in concentration camps. In addition to these books about Europe during the Second World War, there are a number of powerful picture books about the dropping of the atomic bomb on Hiroshima on August 6, 1945. These include *Hiroshima No Pika* by Toshi Maruki, *My Hiroshima* by Junko Morimoto, *Sadako* by Eleanor Coerr, and *Shin's Tricycle* by Tatsuharu Kodama.

Although many of the books noted above are of a serious nature, many other books for older readers are entertaining, playful, and clever, stimulating the imagination and stretching our notions of reading. Picture storybooks aimed at older readers include *Night in the Country* by Cynthia Rylant, *Piggybook* by Anthony Browne, and *The Widow's Broom* by Chris Van Allsburg. Each of these books creates a sense of wonder and provides challenging perspectives on the reading event and on the nature of the picture book. Additional titles of picture books suitable for older readers are presented in Box 11.6.

Picture books, then, have the potential to teach important concepts about reading that can come only from working with real texts, and they are important in forming the attitudes of young readers toward books in general. There is a wealth of high-quality picture books available for learners from kindergarten through grade 8 and beyond, books containing artistry, excellent writing, and vivid imagery.

BOX 11.6

PICTURE BOOKS FOR OLDER READERS

Barbalet, M. (1992). *The wolf.* (J. Tanner, Illus.). Toronto, ON: Doubleday.

Base, G. (1997). *The eleventh hour: A curious mystery.* New York, NY: Puffin.

Blake, W. (1993). *The tyger.* (Neil Waldman, Illus.). New York, NY: Harcourt Brace Jovanovich.

Briggs, R. (1982). *When the wind blows.* New York, NY: Schocken.

Heffernan, J. (2001). *My dog.* (A. McLean, Illus.). Hunters Hill, NSW: Margaret Hamilton Books.

Hunt, E. (1989). *The tale of three trees.* (T. Jonke, Illus.). Colorado Springs, CO: Lion.

Lemieux, M. (1999). *Stormy night.* Toronto, ON: Kids Can Press.

Macaulay, D. (1995). *Shortcut.* Boston, MA: Houghton Mifflin.

Major, K. (1997). *The house of wooden Santas.* (Woodcarvings by I. George). Red Deer, AB: Red Deer Press.

Marsden, J. (1998). *The rabbits.* (S. Tan, Illus.). Port Melbourne, VC: Thomas Lothian.

Scieszka, J. (1995). *Math curse.* (L. Smith, Illus.). New York, NY: Viking.

Spiegelman, A., & Mouly, F. (Eds.). (2000). *Little lit: Strange stories for strange kids.* New York, NY: HarperCollins.

Tan, S. (2006). *The arrival.* New York, NY: Arthur A Levine Books.

Wild, M. (2000). *Fox.* (R. Brooks, Illus.). La Jolla, CA: Kane/Miller Books.

Yee, P. (1996). *Ghost train.* (H. Chan, Illus.). Toronto, ON: Groundwood Books.

Zhang, A. (2004). *Red land, yellow river: A story from the Cultural Revolution.* Toronto, ON: Douglas & McIntyre.

NOVELS
Beginning Chapter Books for the Primary Grades

As young readers become more familiar with picture books and with story structures, and as their reading abilities become more sophisticated, they move from using pictures as a primary means of creating meaning to an increased reliance on text. Many beginning novels are available for young readers (which children in grades 2 and 3 frequently refer to as **chapter books**), and they fall into all the major genres. It seems that the movement from reading picture books to reading books with chapters denotes a transition in an individual's growth as a reader. Nonetheless, children will still be interested in reading picture books, and picture books will continue to capture their interest and imagination.

The reading levels of many beginning chapter books range from grades 2 to 4. Readability does not depend on the complexity of language alone, however, but has much to do with the structure of the book and the background experience the reader is required to bring to it.

Often, beginning chapter books contain illustrations, and these assist readers in the transition from picture books to novels. The content and writing style of numerous beginning chapter books are equally appropriate for older elementary students whose reading level is below grade level, and for those who simply wish to read a "good" (albeit easier) book.

There are many well-known "entry-level" novels, among them Mordecai Richler's three titles about Jacob Two-Two: *Jacob Two-Two Meets the Hooded Fang*, *Jacob Two-Two and the Dinosaur*, and *Jacob Two-Two's First Spy Case*. These books are a combination of fantasy and **realistic fiction**, and are suitable for reading aloud to a class as well as for independent reading. A recent series of books about Marty McGuire, by Kate Messner, is well written and appeals to both boys and girls. Marty enters grade 3, but in the first book of the series she discovers it's not all she was led to believe. When she's cast as the Frog Princess in the class play, she uses her initiative and improvisation to make it into a very special performance. *Underworlds: The Battle Begins* by Tony Abbott is an action-packed mythological tale that constitutes the first in a four-book series. Owen Brown is an average fourth grader until his friend Dana suddenly disappears before his eyes. Before he knows it, Owen and his friends are in the middle of a deepening mystery. A selection of beginning novels is presented in Box 11.7.

As learners begin to move from picture books to chapter books, their book selections will be determined largely by the encouragement of their teachers, their peers, and their own interests. Teachers help children to grow by making book suggestions on the basis of each child's interests and reading ability. Learners benefit because a novel requires a greater investment of time and effort than a picture storybook. At the same time, young readers need to know that a book they select has the potential to engage their interests as well as being at an appropriate reading level.

BOX 11.7

BEGINNING NOVELS

Cleary, B. (1984). *Ramona forever*. New York, NY: Bantam Doubleday Dell.

Dadey, D., & Thornton Jones, M. (1990–2006). Adventures of the Bailey School Kids Series. Boston, MA: Little Apple.

Dahl, R. (1970). *Fantastic Mr. Fox*. New York, NY: Knopf.

Fleischman, S. (1986). *The whipping boy*. New York, NY: Greenwillow Books.

Gardiner, J. R. (1980). *Stone fox*. New York, NY: Crowell.

Lowry, L. (2001). *Zooman Sam*. New York, NY: Dell Yearling.

MacLachlan, P. (1985). *Sarah, plain and tall*. New York, NY: Harper & Row.

McDonald, M. (2003). *Judy Moody predicts the future*. Cambridge, MA: Candlewick Press.

Park, B. (1982). *Skinnybones*. New York, NY: Alfred A. Knopf.

Paterson, K. (1992). *The king's equal*. New York, NY: HarperCollins. [Originally published in picture book format]

Pilkey, D. (1997). *The adventures of Captain Underpants*. Boston, MA: Little Apple.

Sachar, L. (1991). *The boy who lost his face*. New York, NY: Alfred A. Knopf.

In general, reading materials of high personal interest are more fully comprehended than materials of low interest. A reader's strong interest in a topic can transcend her or his reading abilities. Educators are aware of the importance of reading the books their students are reading, so they can discuss the books with them. Through these discussions, educators may challenge learners to extend their interpretations and to add new dimensions to the meanings they create.

Novels in Grades 5 to 8

Many readers begin their foray into novels with realistic fiction, perhaps because it is one of the avenues through which they can, on the one hand, come to know the world in which they live and, on the other, explore issues with which they have little personal experience. This genre continues to be the most widely read in the intermediate grades.

Gemini Summer by Iain Lawrence is a Governor General's Award winner that has a touch of "magic realism." In the early 1960s, brothers Beau and Danny are following the progress of the Apollo space flight program while at the same time trying to avoid a neighbourhood bully. After Beau's sudden death, Danny makes a journey to Cape Canaveral. Believing that Beau has been reincarnated in the form of a stray dog, Rocket, Danny is able to come to terms with the events that led to his beloved older brother's death.

In *Stargirl*, by Jerry Spinelli, student Leo Borlock describes what happens when an enchanting and spirited new student arrives at his school. At first, the students are smitten by her charms and by her unusual ways of marking birthdays and supporting the school teams. But it's not long before Stargirl is shunned by her peers on account of the very nonconformist attitudes and behaviours that first made her popular. Even Leo is challenged by Stargirl's "difference" and has a hard time accepting her uniqueness.

Other recommended titles of realistic fiction are as follows:

- *Willow and Twig* by Jean Little
- *Maniac Magee* by Jerry Spinelli
- *Walk Two Moons* by Sharon Creech
- *Tangerine* by Edward Bloor
- *Because of Winn-Dixie* by Kate DiCamillo
- *The Princess Diaries* by Meg Cabot
- *Up on Cloud Nine* by Anne Fine
- *The Crazy Man* by Pamela Porter
- *Wild Orchid* by Beverley Brenna
- *Along for the Ride* by Sarah Dessen

Novels such as these encourage students to explore personal and social issues that may help them develop an increased understanding of themselves and of others.

Mystery is a genre much enjoyed by students in the intermediate grades. Mystery stories challenge young readers to become actively engaged in problem solving. They enjoy putting the pieces of the puzzle together, hypothesizing, and making inferences as they act as detectives in solving the mystery. Many young readers discover the genre through series books such as the Hardy Boys, Nancy Drew, or Encyclopedia Brown. As they become familiar with a particular series, they also become increasingly better at predicting solutions and fitting clues together. The result is that readers tend to grow out of these somewhat predictable plots and patterns, becoming ready for something more thrilling, more demanding, and more sophisticated.

There are many excellent mystery stories to recommend. *The Thief Lord* by Cornelia Funke is about orphaned brothers, Prosper and Bo. After running away from their guardian aunt and uncle in Germany, the boys find themselves in Venice, where they decide to hide out. There they meet the Thief Lord, the young leader of a ring of street urchins and petty thieves, who claims to steal from the wealthy to help the poor. A mysterious man hires the Thief Lord to steal a particularly significant item, and the boys' lives suddenly become full of adventure, colourful characters, and deep secrets.

In *Silent to the Bone* by E. L. Konigsburg, Branwell is unable to utter a word after the horrible crime that put his little sister, Nikki, into a coma. While Branwell is retained in a juvenile behavioural centre, accused of perpetrating the crime, his best friend attempts to discover what really happened to Nikki and to clear Branwell's name.

Betsy Byars has authored a series of mystery books about a character named Herculeah Jones. Two titles in the series are *Dead Letter* and *Death's Door*. Other recommended mystery titles include these:

- *The Boundless* by Kenneth Oppel
- *The Metro Dogs of Moscow* by Rachel Delaney
- *Invitation to the Game* by Monica Hughes
- *The Westing Game* by Ellen Raskin
- *Bunnicula: A Rabbit Tale of Mystery* by Deborah Howe and James Howe
- *Crispin: The Cross of Lead* by Avi
- *Bernie Magruder and the Bats in the Belfry* by Phyllis Reynolds Naylor
- *Double Identity* by Margaret Peterson Haddix
- *Nate the Great Talks Turkey* by Marjorie Weinman Sharmat

Historical fiction is a genre that presents new challenges for many young readers, for it typically presents fictional characters in a historically accurate context. The genre sometimes requires that the reader have some prior knowledge of the time period in which the story is set. Historical fiction is a particularly suitable genre for educators to share with their students as a Read-Aloud. It also helps in creating a context and a deeper understanding of many social studies topics, and can inspire themes for work across the curriculum.

The Watsons Go to Birmingham—1963 by Christopher Paul Curtis begins as a humorous romp through family life in Flint, Michigan. Kenny has to put up with his teenage brother, Byron, who is an "official juvenile delinquent." Momma decides the only remedy is to take Byron to stay with his grandmother in Birmingham, Alabama, for the summer. The family piles into the car and heads off to what turns out to be a life-changing experience for the whole family. The book is a warm and wonderful read, but the emotional impact of the events in Birmingham make the book unforgettable. This book is perfect for book clubs and response groups.

Hitler's Daughter by Jackie French is an intriguing Australian novel about Anna, who tells stories to her friends as they wait for the school bus. What if Hitler had a daughter, a child who would have been their age during the war? Anna invents Heidi, a girl who could have lived in Germany and could have been Hitler's daughter. The story causes Anna's friend Mark to ask questions about his own family and about what it means to trust someone. How would you know if your parents were doing something wrong? Would you confront them, or would you go along with it? The book has a disturbing and fast-paced plot that raises questions about relationships, belief systems, and questions of right and wrong. It is a perfect book for literature circles.

Al Capone Does My Shirts by Gennifer Choldenko is set on the island of Alcatraz in 1935. Twelve-year-old Moose Flanagan has recently moved to the Rock because his father is an electrician and guard at the prison. The family hopes that Moose's older sister, Natalie, who is autistic, can go to a special school on the mainland in San Francisco. Moose is very protective of Natalie and distinctly nervous at being so close to such notorious criminals. The warden's daughter, Piper, hatches a scheme to make money from the children at their school on the mainland, and she forces Moose to be her accomplice, using her knowledge of Natalie's condition as "leverage." Although family dilemmas and relationships are central to the story, Choldenko weaves a compelling novel around the history and setting of Alcatraz, and, of course, around one of the most famous inmates, Al Capone.

It's worthwhile checking out books of historical fiction about Canada and by Canadian authors. Titles include *I'll be Watching* by Pamela Porter, set in Saskatchewan shortly after the Great Depression; *That Boy Red* by Rachna Gilmore, set in Prince Edward Island in 1929; and *The Bully Boys* by Eric Walters about the War of 1812.

Two series, *Our Canadian Girl* (Penguin) and *Dear Canada* (Scholastic), have created considerable interest in Canadian history and have won a solid readership in the elementary grades. Both series use the talents of well-known Canadian authors, including Cora Taylor, Julie Lawson, Deborah Ellis, Sharon McKay, Sarah Ellis, Carol Matas, and Kathy Stinson. The *Our Canadian Girl* series covers topics such as the Halifax Explosion, the Frank Slide, and Montreal's smallpox epidemic of the 1880s. The *Dear Canada* series aims to provide a springboard for exploring different periods of Canadian history, and topics include the Battle of the Plains of Abraham, building the Canadian Pacific Railway, the Red River settlement, and the War of 1812. A list of historical fiction is provided in Box 11.8.

BOX 11.8

HISTORICAL FICTION

Canadian

Clark, J. (2002). *The word for home.* New York, NY: Penguin.

Ellis, S. (2001). *A prairie as wide as the sea: The immigrant diary of Ivy Weatherall* (Dear Canada series). Markham, ON: Scholastic Canada.

Haworth-Attard, B. (2009). *Haunted.* Toronto: HarperTrophy Canada.

(continued)

Jocelyn, M. (2010). *Folly.* Toronto, ON: Tundra Books.

Lawson, J. (2001). *Across the James Bay Bridge: Emily* (Our Canadian Girl series). Toronto, ON: Penguin Books Canada.

Lunn, J. (1986). *Shadow in Hawthorn Bay.* Toronto, ON: Lester and Orpen Denys.

McAuley, A. (2012). *Violins of autumn.* New York, NY: Walker.

Paperny, M. (2005). *The Greenies.* Toronto, ON: HarperTrophy Canada.

Pearson, K. (2011). *The whole truth.* Toronto, ON: HarperCollins.

Non-Canadian

Boyne, J. (2006). *The boy in the striped pajamas.* London, UK: David Fickling Books.

Fox, P. (1973). *The slave dancer.* New York, NY: Bradbury.

Greene, B. (1973). *The summer of my German soldier.* New York, NY: Bantam.

Lowry, L. (1989). *Number the stars.* New York, NY: Houghton Mifflin.

McSwigan, M. (1942). *Snow treasure.* New York, NY: E. P. Dutton.

Morpurgo, M. (2003). *Private Peaceful.* London, UK: HarperCollins Children's Books.

O'Dell, S. (1970). *Sing down the moon.* New York, NY: Bantam Doubleday Dell.

Reiss, J. (1972). *The upstairs room.* New York, NY: Scholastic.

Speare, E. G. (1958). *The witch of Blackbird Pond.* New York, NY: Dell.

Uchida, Y. (1978). *Journey home.* New York, NY: Aladdin Paperbacks.

Fantasy literature engages the reader's imagination and gives free rein to endless possibilities. The reader is taken to worlds where animals and toys can speak, and where people can travel across time and into completely fictional worlds. The genre is popular across the K to 8 grades. Young children, for example, enjoy *Charlotte's Web* by E. B. White and *James and the Giant Peach* by Roald Dahl. Older readers enjoy *The Dark Is Rising* by Susan Cooper and *Harry Potter and the Philosopher's Stone* by J. K. Rowling. Although fantasy literature has a devoted following in grades 5 to 8, it can be a challenging genre for learners and teachers alike because of the complexity and sophistication of the ideas embedded within some books of high fantasy.

Books of high fantasy (usually quest stories), such as *The Hobbit* by J. R. R. Tolkien and *The Golden Compass* by Philip Pullman, are often read by both children and adults. Much modern fantasy has its roots in ancient myths and legends, especially in the *Tales from the Mabinogion*, a collection of Welsh myths dating back many hundreds of years.

Skellig by David Almond is an award-winning book that is distinctive in its theme and plot. Ten-year-old Michael has moved into a new house with his parents and new baby sister. The house is being renovated and in the back yard stands an old garage, full of junk and waiting to be torn down. One day, when moving an old tea chest, Michael sees a dark figure beneath the spiderwebs and dead flies. The figure speaks—he needs food, and his name is Skellig. Michael shares his discovery with his new friend, Mina, and through Mina and Skellig, he learns about love, trust, poetry, and art. *Skellig* is as much contemporary realistic fiction as it is fantasy and could be described as "magical realism."

Rachel Hartman's novel *Seraphina* is set in the kingdom of Goredd, where 16-year-old Seraphina, a court musician, is drawn into a murder mystery when the crown prince of Goredd is murdered, apparently by dragons. It is 40 years since the signing of a treaty that ended the war between humans and dragons. Because dragons can take human form, the distrust and hatred between humans and dragons escalates as the mystery unfolds. This is an especially well-written and well-crafted novel that makes compelling reading.

Time-slip fantasy is a genre that has its roots in *Tom's Midnight Garden* by Philippa Pearce. Time-slip stories usually begin in the present and then, through some artifact from the past, the protagonist is transported into a different time, typically a specific period in history. Three high-quality Canadian time-slip fantasy books were published in 1987: *The Doll* by Cora Taylor, *A Handful of Time* by Kit Pearson, and *Who Is Frances Rain?* by Margaret Buffie. In Beverley Brenna's recent time-slip fantasy, *Falling for Henry*, 15-year-old Kate Allen escapes the trials of her own teen existence in central London by travelling back to the court of Henry VII at Greenwich Palace. Here are additional examples of fantasy literature for children and young adults:

- *The Lion, the Witch and the Wardrobe* by C. S. Lewis
- *A Wrinkle in Time* by Madeleine L'Engle
- *Tuck Everlasting* by Natalie Babbitt
- *The Wind in the Willows* by Kenneth Grahame
- *The Keeper of the Isis Light* by Monica Hughes
- *The Hunchback Assignments* by Arthur Slade
- *Plain Kate* by Erin Bow
- *Redwall* by Brian Jacques
- *The Giver* by Lois Lowry
- *Silverwing* by Kenneth Oppel
- *Cirque du Freak* by Darren Shan
- *Merchant of Death* (Pendragon Series No. 1) by D. J. MacHale
- *The Tale of Despereaux* by Kate DiCamillo

Box 11.9 lists a selection of Canadian novels suitable for readers in grades 5 to 8.

Graphic Novels for Grades 4 to 8

In comics and graphic novels, textual and visual information merge and "meaning is constructed through a holistic and simultaneous reading of both the visual and textual elements" (Park, 2010, p. 173). One of the earliest popular graphic novelists was Raymond Briggs, who created *The Snowman* (1978) and *Father Christmas* (1973). Since that time, graphic novels have rapidly increased in popularity with young readers, and there is frequently a wait list for these volumes in school and public libraries. Park wrote, "Reading a comic book or graphic novel is quite different from reading a traditional text because

BOX 11.9

CANADIAN FICTION FOR STUDENTS IN GRADES 5 TO 8
Bass, K. (2008). *Run like Jäger*. Regina, SK: Coteau Books.
Brenna, B. (2005). *Wild orchid*. Calgary, AB: Red Deer Press.
Ellis, S. (2014). *Outside in*. Toronto, ON: Groundwood Books/House of Anansi.
Friesen, G. (2005). *The Isabel factor*. Toronto, ON: Kids Can Press.
Heneghan, J. (2006). *Safe house*. Victoria, BC: Orca.
Johansen, K. V. (2006). *The Cassandra virus*. Victoria, BC: Orca.
Pearson, K. (1996). *Awake and dreaming*. Markham, ON: Viking.
Smith, L. (2004). *The minstrel's daughter*. Regina, SK: Coteau Books.
Walters, E. (2009). *Wave*. Toronto, ON: Doubleday Canada.
Wilson, E. (2001). *The Emily Carr mystery*. Toronto, ON: HarperCollins.

one is decoding and processing both text and images simultaneously. It is a complex, multimodal activity" (p. 178). Graphic novels are now given serious study in schools and universities, and the best of them have sound narrative structure, well-developed characters, and sophisticated plots. The American Library Association provides lists of graphic novels suitable for students in grades 4 to 8 on its website.

Educators would be well advised to read these books and vet titles before introducing them to their classrooms. School and public librarians are a good source of information in selecting suitable material. A range of titles appropriate for classroom use are listed below:

- *This One Summer* by Mariko Tamaki
- *Maus I: A Survivor's Tale* by Art Spiegelman
- *Louis Riel* by Chester Brown
- *Bone, Volume One: Out from Boneville* by Jeff Smith
- *Ramp Rats* by Liam O'Donnell
- *Binky the Space Cat* by Ashley Spires
- *Meanwhile* by Jason Shiga

Many graphic novels are light-hearted stories, while others address serious issues and historical events. *Primates: The Fearless Science of Jane Goodall, Dian Fossey, and Biruté Galdikas* by Jim Ottaviani and Maris Wicks is a superb example of nonfiction in a graphic format. *The Red Rock* by Tomio Nitto is described as a "graphic fable" that addresses the destruction of natural environments. The book appeals to learners in grades 2 to 5. In *Jane, the Fox and Me* by Fanny Britt, Hélène struggles with bullying and its resulting loneliness until she meets a new friend at summer camp. *Good-bye Marianne* by Irene N. Watts, winner of the Geoffrey Bilson Award for Historical Fiction for Young People, is based on historical events in Germany in 1938. When eleven-year-old Marianne's father disappears, her life becomes complicated and she is expelled from school because she is Jewish.

Boys seem to enjoy graphic novels in particular, and these books are often noted as an effective way to get boys (and reluctant readers in general) engaged in reading. The Ontario Ministry of Education has two publications designed to help educators support boys' literacy: *Me Read? No Way!* (2004) and *Me Read? And How?* (2009). Both publications are available online and provide practical and effective strategies for classroom use. Boys generally enjoy reading books that reflect their image of themselves; books that appeal to their sense of mischief; fiction (especially fantasy) that focuses on actions more than emotions; series books (which provide comfort and familiarity); and newspapers, magazines, comic books, and instruction manuals. The *Big Nate* series by Lincoln Peirce is highly popular with boys today, along with the *Amulet* series by Kazu Kibuishi.

Collections of Short Stories

A short story is a brief fictional narrative (though it can be anything from 500 to 15 000 words) that consists of more than just a mere record of an incident. It has a formal structure with unity of time, place, and action. Generally, a short story reveals the true nature of a character. A growing number of well-crafted, high-quality collections of short stories are available for readers in grades 4 to 8 (see Box 11.10). They are frequently both entertaining and thought-provoking narratives. *Guys Read: The Sports Pages* edited by Jon Scieszka is a collection of 10 short stories, each written by a different author. Featuring defeats as well as victories, the stories cover sports from hockey to tennis. Beverley Brenna's collection of stories in *Something to Hang On To* is most appropriate for grades 7 and 8, while readers familiar with Tim Wynne-Jones's novels will appreciate his three books of short stories appropriate for grades 5 and 6: *Some of the Kinder Planets*, which won the Governor General's Award and the Boston Globe–Horn Book Award for Children's Literature; *The Book of Changes*; and *Lord of the Fries*. *Garbage Creek* by W. D. Valgardson and *Back of Beyond* by Sarah Ellis are also excellent collections of short stories suitable for the upper elementary and intermediate grades. *This Family Is Driving Me Crazy*, edited by Jerry and Helen Weiss, consists of 10 stories by well-known authors such as Gordon Korman, Jack Gantos, and Walter Dean Myers. This collection is most suitable for readers in grades 7 and 8.

BOX 11.10

COLLECTIONS OF SHORT STORIES FOR STUDENTS IN GRADES 4 TO 8

Carlson, L. M. (2005). *Moccasin thunder: American Indian stories for today.* New York, NY: HarperCollins.

Coville, B. (1994). *Oddly enough: Stories.* San Diego, CA: Harcourt Brace.

Datlow, E., & Windling, T. (Eds.). (2003). *Swan sister: Fairy tales retold.* New York, NY: Simon & Schuster Books for Young Readers.

French, J. (2002). *Ride the wild wind: The golden pony and other stories.* Sydney, Australia: Angus & Robertson.

(continued)

Gallo, D. R. (Ed.). (2008). *Owning it: Stories about teens with disabilities.* Somerville, MA: Candlewick.

Hughes, S. (1993). *Stories by firelight.* New York, NY: Lothrop, Lee & Shepard.

Khan, R. (1999). *Muslim child: A collection of short stories and poems.* Toronto, ON: Napoleon.

Mackay, C. (Ed.). (1997). *Laughs: Funny stories.* Plattsburgh, NY: Tundra Books.

Mahy, M. (1994). *Tick tock tales: Stories to read around the clock.* New York, NY: Margaret K. McElderry Books.

Pearce, P. (2002). *Familiar and haunting: Collected stories.* New York, NY: Greenwillow Books.

Rylant, C. (2000). *Thimbleberry stories.* San Diego, CA: Harcourt Brace.

San Souci, R. D. (1998). *A terrifying taste of short and shivery: Thirty creepy tales.* New York, NY: Delacorte.

Toten, T. (2010). *Piece by piece: Stories about fitting into Canada.* Toronto, ON: Puffin Canada.

Vande Velde, V. (2000). *The Rumpelstiltskin problem.* Boston, MA: Houghton Mifflin.

Yee, P. (2002). *Dead man's gold and other stories.* Toronto, ON: Groundwood Books.

Yolen, J. (1998). *Here there be ghosts.* San Diego, CA: Harcourt Brace.

TRADITIONAL LITERATURE

Traditional literature remains a staple of the language arts curriculum from kindergarten to grade 8. Today there are many beautifully illustrated retellings of traditional stories, originating from around the world. This section presents a sampling of these books.

The genre of traditional literature, sometimes referred to as "folk literature," includes fairy tales, folk tales, Mother Goose rhymes, legends, myths, proverbs, epics, fables, and more. These are mostly short stories that reflect the values and dreams of a society, and through which societies and their cultures come alive. Traditional literature is, in general, a body of work that was originally passed from generation to generation orally. Scholars and educators agree that traditional literature is a most important genre for children, and it is frequently the first genre with which children become truly familiar.

Folk and Fairy Tales

Many traditional versions of folk and fairy tales are available in picture book format for learners in kindergarten to grade 8. Paul Galdone's version of "Little Red Riding Hood" is particularly appropriate for young children, while Trina Schart Hyman's rendition of the same story is more appropriate for older readers. Michael Morpurgo's *Hansel and Gretel* is a beautifully written version of the Brothers Grimm tale, illustrated by Emma Chichester Clark. "Puss in Boots" has been retold by John Cech and illustrated by Bernhard Oberdieck as one volume in *Sterling's Classic Fairy Tale Collection.* For older readers, Stephen Mitchell's retelling of Hans Christian Andersen's "The Tinderbox," illustrated by Bagram Ibatoulline, is an appropriate choice. Quentin Gréban, one of Europe's most popular illustrators, created a noteworthy rendition of the Brothers Grimm version of "Snow White."

There are also parodies of well-known tales. *The Three Little Wolves and the Big Bad Pig* by Eugene Trivizas and *The True Story of the Three Little Pigs* by Jon Scieszka are both based on "The Three Little Pigs" and depend on intertextual connections for their humour and impact. Bruce Hale has drawn on the traditional story of Sleeping Beauty in his book *Snoring Beauty*, illustrated by Howard Fine. In *Mirror Mirror*, Marilyn Singer and Josée Masse have playfully created "reversible verses" based on fairy tales—the verses can be read from top to bottom or bottom to top.

In a number of clever retellings of fairy tales, the texts deviate little from the original version, but the illustrations create a powerfully different meaning to the story. Anthony Browne's *Hansel and Gretel* is one such book; the traditional story is retold in a contemporary setting. Ian Wallace's rendition of "Hansel and Gretel" also places the story in a contemporary setting, this time in Atlantic Canada.

Modern fairy tales, such as *The Tough Princess* by Martin Waddell (illustrated by Patrick Benson) and *The King's Equal* by Katherine Paterson (illustrated by Vladimir Vagin), play with readers' expectations and knowledge of the fairy-tale genre. These books raise questions about traditional gender roles and the messages implicit in most fairy tales (e.g., that a woman must be rescued by a man and is then dependent on him for living happily ever after). As educators and learners read and interact with these modern versions of fairy tales, readers may discover deeper meanings in the traditional tales. They may also be moved to question them, given the context of current societal beliefs and values.

Myths, Legends, and Fables

Many novels for young readers and for adults are based on the patterns, characters, and plots of the best-known myths and legends, and certain recurring themes in literature can be traced back to myths. Consequently, it is helpful if young readers are introduced to myths and legends as part of the repertoire of reading in school. Greek, Roman, Celtic, and Norse myths are the better known of these stories, though many books are devoted to Aboriginal, Chinese, and South American myths. Joseph Campbell (1988) argued that myths are powerful literature that should be read by everyone to help us understand ourselves as human beings and as social and spiritual creatures.

One beautiful retelling of a Chinese myth, *The Dragon's Pearl* by Julie Lawson, illustrated by Paul Morin, won the Amelia Frances Howard-Gibbon Award for illustrations in 1993. Also illustrated by Paul Morin is Tololwa Mollel's *The Orphan Boy*, based on a Tanzanian myth—the book won the 1990 Governor General's Literary Award for illustration. Priscilla Galloway has retold a number of Greek myths. Her titles include *Aleta and the Queen: A Tale of Ancient Greece*, *Atalanta: The Fastest Runner in the World*, and *Daedalus and the Minotaur*, all illustrated by Normand Cousineau.

Legends are stories told about real people and their feats or accomplishments. Usually the narratives are mixed with superstition, and they expand and enhance the actual exploits of their heroes. Legends are closely related to myths, but they do not contain supernatural deities as myths do. The stories of Beowulf, Robin Hood, William Tell, Davy Crockett, and Johnny Appleseed are legends. A notable retelling of the Arthurian legend is the young adult novel *Arthur, High King of Britain* by Michael Morpurgo, illustrated with black-and-white drawings by Michael Foreman. From reading myths and legends, children and young adults are encouraged to seek explanations for the phenomena in their lives—to ask questions about modern "legendary" figures and heroes and perhaps relate them to the possibilities inherent in their own lives.

Fables are a genre of literature found worldwide. They are fictional tales that are meant to entertain though they also contain a moral. They usually have only two or three characters, frequently talking animals that possess humanlike characteristics. Fables are popular with young children today largely because of the presence of the talking animals and the humour the stories contain. Stories such as "The Town Mouse and the Country Mouse" and "The Tortoise and the Hare" remain particular favourites with children. There are also many variations of "The Lion and the Mouse" and "The Raven and the Fox."

Ever-Evolving Stories: Storytelling

True storytelling is an art that calls upon tales that are part of the tradition of oral literature, stories that have many versions and can be modified to suit audience and purpose. These are the stories that are handed down within families or within cultural groups. The Aboriginal peoples of Canada, the United States, Australia, and New Zealand have a rich fund of stories, some of which are ritual stories that may not be shared with the general public. Families also have their stories and storytellers—stories of early settlement in homesteads on the prairies, stories of great-grandfathers who worked on the trans-Canada railway, stories of hardship, illnesses, long journeys at sea, family treasures, and great adventures. These stories cannot easily be written down and neatly illustrated. They have a special significance to the listener and frequently appeal to a small audience—this is a key difference between storytelling and "performing" a text.

True storytelling demands discipline, so that a story is captured and shaped to suit the audience and the purpose for its telling. A rambling recollection of an event that occurred some years ago is not the same thing as a told story. Thus, educators who wish to engage in storytelling, or to have learners tell stories in the classroom, should hone their storytelling skills. These include perfecting the nuances of chosen vocabulary, intonation, facial expressions, and hand gestures, as well as ensuring that stories have cohesion, development, and appropriate closure, just as a good written tale does. Storytelling must also be rehearsed and known by heart, just like any other performance, before a story is shared with an audience. Children enjoy hearing stories told.

Educators can make full use of storytelling in their classrooms and help learners develop as storytellers by having them read many different versions of a traditional story and then retell it in their own way. In this way they can invest the oral story with their own thoughts and feelings, story and storyteller becoming one.

Two excellent resource books for educators are *And None of It Was Nonsense: The Power of Storytelling in the Classroom* by Betty Rosen (1988) and *Stories to Tell* by Bob Barton (1992). Rosen describes her thinking, preparation, follow-up work, and lessons, also including selections of her students' work. Barton has put together a set of resource materials for story-telling, drawing on his experiences as a Canadian storyteller, teacher, and writer. He encourages educators to tell their own stories, including the songs, rhymes, jingles, chants, and sayings they remember. Barton connects the worlds of storytelling, drama, games, movement, and role-play in the creation of new stories, reminding us that stories can be revisited and remade again and again.

POETRY FOR CHILDREN

The nursery rhymes, songs, and jingles of their infancy constitute a core of literature for most young children, while song lyrics increasingly provide an alternative literature for students in grades 6 to 8. Poetry has a major role to play in the language arts curriculum. This section of the chapter presents a selection of poems, poetic forms, and poetic devices appropriate for kindergarten to grade 8 students. Huck, Hepler, Hickman, and Kiefer (2004) wrote,

> Poetry can both broaden and intensify experience, or it might present a range of experiences beyond the realm of personal possibility for the individual listener. It can also illuminate, clarify, and deepen an everyday occurrence in a way the reader never considered, making the reader see more and feel more than ever before. For poetry does more than mirror life; it reveals life in new dimensions. (p. 350)

Poetry communicates experience by appealing to both the thoughts and feelings of the reader. Every word is carefully chosen by the poet for the nuances and emotive meanings it conveys. Many learners enjoy amusing or playful poems before they appreciate the more aesthetic and philosophical elements of poetry. Learning to understand and appreciate poetry is an ongoing process, as it is with other forms of literature. Learners are more likely to enjoy poetry if they have experienced it from their earliest days, through nursery rhymes, jingles, and songs. Although nursery rhymes and skipping rhymes cannot be considered poetry, they do lay the foundation for later journeys into poetic language.

Defining poetry is a challenge, for many contemporary poets are breaking the traditional expectations of poetry, both in content and in form. Words are placed across the page, at angles, and in bunches. Contemporary poetry is written about subjects not previously dealt with (listening to a fight between parents, dealing with bullying). However, poems continue to make children laugh, ponder, imagine, remember, and see the world in new ways. Indeed, poetry helps to develop insights and new understandings.

As Booth and Moore (1988) wrote, "Children's poetry has a special appeal: the form and language of poetry speaks directly to the child, to their senses, their imaginations, their emotions, their feelings, their experiences of childhood" (p. 22). Young children are interested in poems of action, rhythm, rhyme, and energy that invite them to participate and relate to their everyday experiences. Children are naturally rhythmical. From the earliest nursery rhymes to the poems of Dennis Lee, as well as refrains and particularly humorous stanzas from poems by Ogden Nash, a musical rhythm pervades the text. Children are generally intrigued by the sound of language as they play with it and learn its melody.

For grades 6 to 8, favourites include narrative poems such as "The Highwayman" by Alfred Noyes, "The Road Not Taken" by Robert Frost, "Jabberwocky" by Lewis Carroll,

"Casey at the Bat" by Ernest Thayer, and, in grade 8, "The Raven" by Edgar Allan Poe. Learners in these grades particularly enjoy writing their own poetry, and song lyrics frequently provide inspiration for this work. The exploration of song lyrics is particularly enjoyed in grades 7 and 8. Young readers appreciate making their own selection from among "appropriate" artists and lyrics. Edmonton-area teacher Denise Barrett recommends Savage Garden's "Affirmation" and Garth Brooks's "The River." She also sometimes works with rap. Box 11.11 provides an extended list of song lyrics appropriate for use in grades 7 and 8.

BOX 11.11

RECOMMENDED SONG LYRICS, GRADES 7 AND 8

Educator Denise Barrett suggests the following songs:
As an introduction to hip hop—rhythm/rhyme:

"It's Tricky"—Run DMC

"Rapper's Delight"—Sugarhill Gang

"Fresh Prince of Bel Air"—Will Smith

Example of blank verse:

"Eggman"—The Beastie Boys

Storytelling:

"Hung My Head"—Johnny Cash

"Tom's Diner"—Suzanne Vega

Irony:

"Hero of War"—Rise Against

For the enjoyment of girls:

"Beautiful"—Christina Aguilera

"Just a Girl"—No Doubt

"Unpretty"—TLC

"I Will Survive"—Aretha Franklin

For the enjoyment of boys:

"Pork and Beans"—Weezer

"Creep" (radio edit)—Radiohead

"Hope It Gives You Hell"—The All American Rejects

On the theme of a hard life:

"We Fall"—Emmanuel Jal

"Gangsta's Paradise"—Coolio

"Waterfalls"—TLC

"Fam Jam"—Shad

"Where Is the Love"—Black Eyed Peas

"Same Love"—Macklemore and Ryan

"Don't Speak"—No Doubt
"If I Ruled the World"—Kurtis Blow
Miscellaneous:
"The Devil's Work Day"—Modest Mouse
"Drops of Jupiter"—Train
"Wavin' Flag"—K'naan
"Ignorance"—Paramore

Sharing Poetry in School

Learners come to appreciate poetry by hearing adults enjoy, read, and share poetry with them. The skillfully crafted arrangement of the sounds of a poem read aloud is one of the primary pleasures of poetry. Although enunciation is a fundamental component of any kind of oral sharing of poetry, it is also vital that poetry be read interpretively. This means that a reader must learn to focus on the emotive meanings conveyed by a poem, whether those meanings are playful or wistful. When students hear Sheree Fitch read her poems aloud, they are entranced by her sheer energy and engagement with the words:

I've a yearning
That is burning
A desire for Higher learning
I would like
To go to college
To improve upon
My knowledge....*

Learners in grades 6 through 8 especially enjoy **slam poetry**, a form of poetry performed in front of an audience, often, but not always, in a competitive environment. Audience feedback and response are part of the event. Slam poetry is poetry from the heart. It uses voice, humour, rhythm, exaggeration, and wordplay. Slam poems may use comical exaggerations and surprise twists, and incorporate strong emotions such as love or outrage. They often borrow from hip-hop styles, with lots of rhymes, rhythm, and slang, and tend to be either funny, emotionally powerful, or both of these at once. A key to a successful slam poem is that it evokes a strong and enthusiastic audience response.

One of Canada's best-known slam poets is Boonaa Mohammed, a first-generation Canadian who has written a play as well as poetry. His poem "Under the Armpit of Noah" (published in Teresa Toten's *Piece by Piece: Stories About Fitting into Canada*) is profound and intense. Leaving no reader unmoved, it evokes deep discussion in grades 7 and 8. Part of it reads:

He would come home sore,
his back hurt from all the stabbing and biting.

---

* *If You Could Wear My Sneakers* by Sheree Fitch [poetry] and Darcia Labrosse [illustrations]. © 1997 Sheree Fitch and Darcia Labrosse. Reprinted with the permission of Sheree Fitch.

If it was up to him his name would have been

Christopher or Michael but instead he got a funny African name

that nobody could pronounce,

he blamed his parents

though maybe they didn't care for him enough

why else would they set him up to be the butt of every joke,

he joked about changing his name

but his parents never listened,

thought he was a little strange,

but the strange thing is that he had internalized he was different,

and at that age who wants to be different,

he would have preferred to be like his friends

a quarter Irish, Scottish, Welsh and English.*

In a poetry slam, performers each have three minutes to say their poem. No music, costumes, or props are allowed. Performers memorize the poem, improvise on it, and let it surge and roar through them. The aim is to touch hearts and minds with words, rhymes, or the sheer music of sounds bearing meaning.

There are lots of engaging videos of slam poetry on YouTube. Check the web for a video of educator Taylor Mali with his slam, "What Teachers Make." You can also see various performers in the under 12 and under 15 divisions of the U.K. School Slam Poetry Championship, and read viewers' responses to their poems.

For special insights into working with slam poetry in the classroom, read Brenda Dyck's article "A Poetry Slam Cures the Blahs," where she tells about her experiences with grades 6 and 7 students as they became energized with slam poetry. (See the Education World website: http://www.educationworld.com/a_curr/voice/voice069.shtml.)

Readers of poetry, whether they are adults or children, consider the mood they wish to set when reading a poem aloud. The interpretation of a poem is greatly influenced by how a reader varies its tempo, volume, rhythm, pitch, and juncture. These terms are defined briefly here.

- *Tempo* refers to how slowly or quickly words or lines are read.
- *Volume* refers to loudness.
- *Rhythm* describes emphasis or stress.
- *Pitch* refers to the lowering or raising of the voice.
- *Juncture* describes the location and length of pauses.

Educators and learners may vary these elements when reading poetry and then discuss whether and how the changes affect their interpretations of the poems.

---

* Boonaa Mohammed. "Under the Armpit of Noah." *Piece by Piece*. Edited by Teresa Toten. Penguin Canada. 2010.

Choral reading and the implementation of drama strategies enhance understanding and awareness of poetry. Sound effects, mime, puppets, shadow plays, and role-playing are dramatic techniques that can be used when working with poetry in the classroom.

Poetic Devices

Rhyme is a very common element of poetry. Indeed, some children believe rhyme to be the sole determining feature of poetry. The poems of Michael Rosen, Dennis Lee, Jack Prelutsky, and Shel Silverstein are contemporary works whose use of rhyme, rhythm, and playfulness forms part of their appeal. Although rhyme is a popular device of poets, learners may need to expand their definition of poetry if they are to enjoy more sophisticated poems later in life.

Comparison is another device used by poets. The use of similes, explicitly comparing one thing with another using the words "like" or "as," and the use of *metaphors*, comparing two things by implying that one is like the other, are two common comparison techniques used by poets. A beautifully illustrated picture book of similes is *Quick as a Cricket by Audrey* Wood. A tongue-in-cheek collection of similes for older readers is *A Surfeit of Similes by Norton* Juster. A further poetic device used by writers is *alliteration*—the repeated use of the same initial consonants in consecutive words or the use of words that are in proximity and produce a pattern of the same or similar sounds. Chris Van Allsburg used alliteration in his alphabet book *The Z Was Zapped. Some Smug Slug* by Pamela Duncan Edwards is another example of the use of alliteration to tell a tale.

Onomatopoeia is a device wherein writers use sound words (e.g., *splash*, *slurp*, *boing*) to make the writing more vivid and sensory. The elements of tempo, volume, stress, and pitch can be manipulated in ways to assist in conveying the meaning and imagery of sound words. *Machine Poems,* collected by Jill Bennett, and *Click, Rumble, Roar: Poems About Machines,* edited by Lee Bennett Hopkins, are collections of poems that contain many examples of onomatopoeia. The repetition of words and phrases is another device used by many poets. For example, in *A Dark Dark Tale*, author Ruth Brown repeats the words "dark, dark." As the poem continues, each location described in the text as "dark, dark" is smaller than the one before. The poem begins, "Once upon a time there was a dark, dark moor" and the next dark, dark location is a wood, the next one a house, and then a door, and so on.

Imagery and *figurative language* are other important poetic elements that play a role in poetry for young readers. Langston Hughes's poem "City" creates the image of the city as a bird, and Carl Sandburg likens the fog descending on a city to a cat in his poem "Fog." The language, imagery, and rhythm of poetry interact in creating the emotional force of a poem. Langston Hughes's "Poem" evokes a powerful emotional response in most readers, as does "Listening to Grownups Quarrelling" by Ruth Whitman.

Forms of Poetry

One of the most popular forms of poetry with young readers is *narrative poetry*, poetry that tells a story. One narrative poem that has been reproduced in picture book format is *The Cremation of Sam McGee*, written by Robert Service and illustrated by Ted Harrison.

Lyric and free verse are two other forms of poetry enjoyed in school. Lyric poetry frequently describes a mood or feeling and elicits strong emotions about the subject of the poem. Although free verse poetry generally lacks rhyme, this type of poetry allows poets great freedom in creating their own rules of rhythm. Emotional language and imagery are important elements of free verse. The topics of free verse poetry are often abstract or philosophical.

Haiku and *cinquain* are forms of poetry that have prescribed structures. Haiku is a form of poetry originating in Japan; a haiku is a three-line poem with the first and last lines each having five syllables and the middle line having seven syllables. Traditionally, haiku dealt with topics associated with nature or the seasons, but modern haiku are written about a much broader range of subjects. A cinquain, a five-line stanza, is structured around 22 syllables in a 2-4-6-8-2 syllable pattern.

Rhyme, rhythm, and sound are important poetic elements that influence students' opinions of poems, and children love to chant and move with the words, whether it's *Dirty Dog Boogie by Loris* Lesynski or a limerick by Edward Lear. Lear popularized limericks among children and adults alike with *The Complete Book of Nonsense,* first published in 1846. Two well-known books of limericks are *The Book of Pigericks* by Arnold Lobel and *The Hopeful Trout and Other Limericks* by John Ciardi.

Concrete poems are arranged in a particular manner on a page in order to create an image or visual shape of the poem's subject. For example, in the poetry collection *A Hippopotamusn't,* J. Patrick Lewis has written a concrete poem about the flamingo, cleverly arranging the words in a flamingo shape. Concrete poetry is intended to be seen as much as heard, and it often lacks a rhythm or rhyming pattern. Further examples appear in Robert Froman's *Seeing Things: A Book of Poems.*

Found poems are created by taking text we see around us in our daily lives, and reframing it as poetry by changing the line spacing or by adding or deleting small pieces of text. Found poems can be created from labels, notices, road signs, or advertisements, for example. Most found poetry is published on the Internet. A good resource for educators is the ReadWriteThink site sponsored by the National Council of Teachers of English and the International Literacy Association (http://www.readwritethink.org/parent-afterschool-resources/activities-projects/finding-poetry-pleasure-reading-30301.html?main-tab=2).

A Kick in the Head: An Everyday Guide to Poetic Forms, selected by Paul B. Janeczko, is a must for classroom libraries in kindergarten through grade 8. It contains works that illustrate 29 different forms of poetry, ranging from haiku through odes to elegies, written by well-regarded poets such as Robert Service, Eleanor Farjeon, Gary Soto, and Georgia Heard.

Picture Book Versions of Poems and Songs

There are many picture book versions of single poems and songs. These include Robert Frost's "Stopping by Woods on a Snowy Evening," illustrated by Susan Jeffers, and Eugene Field's "Wynken, Blynken and Nod," also illustrated by Susan Jeffers. Jan Brett illustrated a picture book version of "The Owl and the Pussy Cat" by Edward Lear, and Ed Young illustrated Robert Frost's poem "Birches." Ted Rand illustrated two poems: "My Shadow" by Robert Louis Stevenson and "Arithmetic" by Carl Sandburg.

Two Canadian illustrated songbooks, appropriate for grades 5 to 8, are Gordon Lightfoot's *Canadian Railroad Trilogy* and Stan Rogers' *Northwest Passage*. *Canadian Railroad Trilogy* was illustrated by Ian Wallace, one of Canada's most acclaimed illustrators. The book is "an ode to Canada and its natural beauty," and it includes the music and lyrics for the song as well as notes on the illustrations, a brief history of the building of the railroad, and some suggestions for further reading. Stan Rogers' song "Northwest Passage" was illustrated by the award-winning Matt James. This volume is accompanied by maps, bibliographical information of the key explorers involved, a timeline, and sheet music for the original song.

Diane Siebert created two picture poetry books: *Train Song* and *Motorcycle Song*, written for students in grades 3 to 7. In *Motorcycle Song*, readers follow a motorcyclist on an exhilarating journey through towns, narrow lanes, highways, and open country, with a poetic rhythm that matches the vehicle's movement. Illustrated by Leonard Jenkins, the mixed-media paintings are rich in colour, energy, and movement, capturing the freedom of the open road.

In the picture book *In Flanders Fields: The Story of the Poem*, Linda Granfield not only presents John McCrae's poem but also shares information about the poet and his experiences working in a field hospital during the First World War. She describes the living conditions and daily routines of the soldiers and provides information about the war. She also explains the origin of the symbolic gesture of wearing a poppy.

Poetry Collections

Many books of poetry are collections of one individual's works. Here are some examples:

- *The Sun Is So Quiet* by Nikki Giovanni
- *Face Bug* by J. Patrick Lewis
- *A Light in the Attic* by Shel Silverstein
- *The New Kid on the Block* by Jack Prelutsky
- *If You Could Wear My Sneakers* by Sheree Fitch
- *Something's Drastic* by Michael Rosen
- *Shout: Little Poems That Roar* by Brod Bagert
- *Collected Poems for Children* by Ted Hughes
- *What's the Weather Inside?* by Karma Wilson
- *Messing Around on the Monkey Bars and Other Poems for Two Voices* by Betsy Franco

Many poetry books are specialized collections of poems related to a single theme or topic—for example, snow, dinosaurs, monsters, dragons, magic, festivals, machines, Halloween, and nightmares.

General anthologies of poetry are useful for teachers to have on hand. Notable anthologies include *The Oxford Book of Poetry for Children*, compiled by Edward Blishen; *The Random House Book of Poetry*, compiled by Jack Prelutsky; *Til All the Stars Have Fallen*, selected by David Booth; and *Images of Nature: Canadian Poets and the Group of Seven*, also selected by David Booth. A number of poetry anthologies suitable for use in elementary school classrooms are listed in Box 11.12.

BOX 11.12

POETRY RESOURCES

Balaam, J., & Merrick, B. (1989). *Exploring poetry: 5–8*. Sheffield, UK: National Association for the Teaching of English.

Fleischman, P. (1985). *Joyful noise: Poems for two voices*. New York, NY: Harper and Row.

Harrison, M., & Stuart-Clark, C. (Comps.). (1995). *The new Oxford treasury of children's poems*. Toronto, ON: Oxford University Press.

Hoberman, M. A., & Winston, L. (Comps.). (2009). *The tree that time built: A celebration of nature, science and imagination*. Naperville, IL: Sourcebooks Jabberwocky.

Kennedy, C. (2005). *A family of poems: My favorite poetry for children*. New York, NY: Hyperion.

Lee, D. (1974). *Alligator pie*. Toronto, ON: Macmillan Canada.

Lesynski, L. (2004). *Zigzag: Zoems for zindergarten*. Toronto, ON: Annick.

Martin, B. (2008). *Big book of poetry*. New York, NY: Simon & Schuster Books for Young Readers.

Mayo, M. (2000). *Wiggle waggle fun: Stories and rhymes for the very very young*. Toronto, ON: Random House.

Merrick, B. (1991). *Exploring poetry: 8–13*. Sheffield, UK: National Association for the Teaching of English.

Prelutsky, J. (2005). *Read a rhyme, write a rhyme*. New York, NY: Alfred K. Knopf.

Priest, R. (2002). *The secret invasion of bananas*. Victoria, BC: Cherubim Books.

Rosen, M. (1984). *Quick, let's get out of here*. New York, NY: Dutton.

Silverstein, S. (1974). *Where the sidewalk ends: Poems and drawings*. New York, NY: Harper.

Yolen, J., & Fusek Peters, A. (2007). *Here's a little poem: A very first book of poetry*. Cambridge, MA: Candlewick Press.

INFORMATION BOOKS

Nonfiction or information books are an important learning resource for use across the curriculum as well as for recreational reading. Appropriate nonfiction books must be current, accurate, and appealing to young readers. This section of the chapter addresses various types of nonfiction books, as well as criteria for evaluating nonfiction materials.

Information books (also known as nonfiction literature) play a major role in every elementary classroom. It is this genre that provides much of the resource material for teaching across the curriculum. Through reading about a topic from many sources and from a number of different perspectives, learners are able to construct a fuller understanding of the subject. Each piece of information and each point of view helps a person to create a broader picture of the topic and provides fertile ground for new meanings to develop. Many children in the primary grades (and earlier) thoroughly enjoy reading nonfiction materials, and it is this genre that caters to the special interests of individuals and provides them with the resources they need for pursuing their avocation. Educators recognize learners' interests and pleasure in reading nonfiction materials and they teach young readers how to read expository texts as well as narrative texts (see Chapter 6).

Learners need both narrative and non-narrative reading and writing experiences. Throughout all the grades, learners are encouraged to work on cross-curricular projects using nonfiction materials for information. Educators, even in the early grades, teach their students how to use the index of a book, the glossary, and the table of contents, as well as how to browse through a book quickly to see from the pictures and the headings whether the book would be helpful and interesting or not.

Leaf/Dreamstime.com

Two readers sharing an information book

There are at least eight major types of information books for children:

- photo-documentaries
- how-to books
- question-and-answer formats
- experiment and activity books
- sequential explanation (survey) books
- field guides
- biographies
- narrative nonfiction

Some of these books are designed to be used as reference materials and have a typical expository format. Others are to be read from beginning to end, more like a work of fiction, and consist of narrative text.

Advances in technology, allowing for the superb reproduction of photographs, maps, and other graphics, as well as interesting and accessible page layouts, have helped create a splendid new age of nonfiction. Many awards have been specifically created for information books. These include the Information Book Award, sponsored by the Children's Literature Roundtables of Canada; the Orbis Pictus Award for Outstanding Nonfiction for Children, established by the National Council of Teachers of English (in the United States); the Boston Globe–Horn Book Award, established jointly by *The Boston Globe* and *The Horn Book Magazine* (United States); and the Times Educational Supplement Information Book Awards (United Kingdom).

Criteria for Evaluating Information Books

The information available in any subject area grows rapidly over time, and it is difficult to keep a nonfiction collection up-to-date. Educators as well as learners increasingly use the Internet to access information, as books published 10 years ago could be out-of-date today (depending on the topic). It is therefore essential that nonfiction books be purchased for the school or classroom library with discrimination, and with the aid of library selection tools such as *CM: Canadian Materials*, *The Horn Book Magazine*, *School Library Journal*, *Teacher Librarian*, and *Booklist*. It is also important that the books made available to learners are current and are periodically reviewed. A list of evaluation criteria for information books is presented in Box 11.13.

BOX 11.13

CRITERIA FOR EVALUATING INFORMATION BOOKS

Format

▷ Is the page design uncluttered?

▷ Is the layout visually appealing? Does it invite the reader to browse through it?

▷ Does it pique the reader's interest?

▷ Are there enough visuals and enough colour to make the book appealing?

Organization and Style

▷ Is the material presented in a clear and unambiguous way?

▷ Does the book create a feeling of reader involvement and convey a positive tone?

▷ Does the author use vivid and interesting language?

▷ Is the content structured clearly and logically, with appropriate subheadings?

▷ Are there reference aids, such as a table of contents, index, bibliography, glossary, and appendix?

Content

▷ Is the content presented in a manner that allows learners to connect it with their own experiences?

▷ Where content has been simplified, does it retain accuracy?

▷ Does the book include the author's sources as well as additional information for keen readers who want to learn more?

▷ Does the book provide Internet links?

▷ Is the book current and does it reflect (and mention) current research activity in the field?

▷ Are the qualifications and experiences of the authors presented?

▷ Does the book avoid stereotypes and present differing viewpoints?

▷ Is a distinction made among fact, theory, and opinion?

▷ Does the book foster a scientific method of inquiry?

▷ Are there appropriate and sufficient maps, charts, and diagrams to add to the reader's understanding of the text?

▷ Are the graphics and illustrations an appropriate size?

▷ Are the graphics and illustrations clearly understandable and well labelled?

▷ Do the maps, charts, and diagrams contain appropriate detail?

Source: Based on F. Smardo Dowd, "Trends and evaluative criteria of informational books for children," in E. Freeman and D. Person (eds.), *Using Nonfiction Trade Books in the Classroom: From Ants to Zeppelins.* (Urbana, IL: National Council of Teachers of English), pp. 34–43.

The *accuracy* and *authenticity* of material probably constitute the most difficult criteria for educators to assess. The first thing to look for in any information book is an indication from the author(s) that either they have the necessary expertise or they have consulted with experts in the creation of the book (as in *The Shortest Day* by Wendy Pfeffer). The latter book contains excellent illustrations, clear explanations, and interesting activities for readers to complete either at home or at school. It also provides a list of further reading on the topic and a list of related websites. The author acknowledges assistance provided by a professor of physics at Rhodes College and a history professor at the College of New Jersey. This last piece of information tells the reader that the information featured in the book has come from a reliable source.

Whatever is provided for the reader, however, the main criterion for selecting a book must be compatibility with the reader's own background knowledge of the subject. Educators play a crucial role in assisting learners to select books that are appropriate in content—books that are neither too simple nor conceptually overloaded.

The *format* of information books is an especially important area to evaluate. Some nonfiction books are too "busy" in their layout for young readers. The visual effect is one of overload, as the reader has to attend to too much input at one time. In terms of content and format, an aesthetically appealing and effective book is Nic Bishop's *Forest Explorer: A Life-Size Field Guide*, which presents the wilds of the forest in a unique photographic style. Seven double-page, life-size habitat scenes capture more than 130 animals, from beetles to squirrels. With a superb picture index, the book can be used as a field guide, but it is also a book readers enjoy perusing and reading in depth. This book is highly suitable for a classroom collection.

Information books printed without colour photographs and diagrams may contain lots of interesting information and ideas, but are likely not appealing to today's visually oriented students. Too much information can be presented in a black-and-white format, so that readers cannot easily pick out the chunks of information they are seeking. Colour photographs and drawings help readers move their eyes and attention around the page from one unit of meaning to another more easily.

An exemplary information book for learners age four to eight is *How To* by Julie Morstad. It received the IBBY Canada Elizabeth Mrazik-Cleaver Picture Book Award in 2014. This imaginative "how-to" book explores whimsical ways of doing a host of different tasks, including how to wonder, how to see the breeze, and how to be brave. An example of a well-organized, well-laid-out book for the intermediate grades is *Skin: The Bare Facts*. Not only does author Lori Bergamotto provide clear boxes and diagrams with lots of colour, but she also lists the professionals who helped her gather information for the book. She provides a note reminding readers that they must always read product labels, follow manufacturers' instructions, and heed warnings on labels.

Hugh Brewster's *At Vimy Ridge* is a well-formatted account of the Battle of Vimy Ridge in France during the First World War. The book allows the reader's focus to move smoothly from text to diagram to photograph and back to text. The format helps the reader take in the information and make sense of it. Clear maps, period photographs, excerpts from soldiers' letters home, and excellent text make this book an engaging reading experience for adults as well as children. The story of the battle is grim, but it is told in such a way that readers are helped to understand the nature of gas attacks and life in the trenches. Brewster's careful explanation of a "creeping barrage" is especially well illustrated, and the double-page photograph of the battle at Hill 145 is more eloquent than any text could be on the nature of war and the resulting deaths. The description of Armistice Day, as well as the end photographs and text on the newly restored and stunning memorial at Vimy, adds a deeper layer of meaning to this "war story." A further selection of Canadian information books is presented in Box 11.14.

BOX 11.14

A SELECTION OF CANADIAN INFORMATION BOOKS

Bateman, R. (2008). *Polar worlds: Life at the ends of the Earth*. Toronto, ON: Scholastic/Madison Press.

Berkowitz, J. (2006). *Jurassic poop: What dinosaurs (and others) left behind*. (S. Mack, Illus.). Toronto, ON: Kids Can Press.

Brewster, H. (2007). *Carnation, lily, lily, rose: The story of a painting*. Toronto, ON: Kids Can Press.

Brewster, H. (2009). *Dieppe: Canada's darkest day of World War II*. Toronto, ON: Scholastic.

Dumas, W. (2013). *Pīsim finds her miskanow*. (L. Paul, Illus.). Winnipeg, MB: HighWater Press.

Dyer, H. (2012). *Potatoes on rooftops*. Toronto, ON: Annick Press.

Galat, J. M. (2014). *Dark matters: Nature's reaction to light pollution*. Toronto, ON: Red Deer Press.

Hainnu, R., & Ziegler, A. (2011). *A walk on the tundra*. (Q. Leng, Illus.). Iqaluit, NU: Inhabit Media.

Hodge, D. (2006). *The kids book of Canadian immigration*. (J. Mantha, Illus.). Toronto, ON: Kids Can Press.

Innes, S., & Endrulat, H. (2008). *A bear in war*. (B. Deines, Illus.). Toronto, ON: Key Porter.

Levine, K. (2003). *Hana's suitcase*. Toronto, ON: Second Story Press.

Romanek, T. (2006). *Squirt! The most interesting book you'll ever read about blood*. (R. Cowles, Illus.). Toronto, ON: Kids Can Press.

Ross, V. (2006). *You can't read this: Forbidden books, lost writing, mistranslations and codes*. Toronto, ON: Tundra Books.

Shoveller, H. (2006). *Ryan and Jimmy and the well in Africa that brought them together*. Toronto, ON: Kids Can Press.

Strauss, R. (2009). *One well: The story of water on earth*. (R. Woods, Illus.). Toronto, ON: Kids Can Press.

Swanson, D. (2009). *You are weird: Your body's peculiar parts and funny functions*. (K. Boake, Illus.). Toronto, ON: Kids Can Press.

Thornhill, J. (2006). *I found a dead bird: The kids' guide to the cycle of life and death*. Toronto, ON: Maple Tree Press.

Narrative Nonfiction

Some of the most fascinating nonfiction materials are narrative texts that incorporate details and explanations into a story. The picture book *Locomotive* by Brian Floca, about the building of the railway across the western United States, received the Caldecott Medal in the United States in 2014 as well as being a Sibert Honor Book and *New York Times* bestseller. In the summer of 1869, not long after the golden spike had been driven into the rails at Promontory Summit, a mother and her two children travel westward, riding on the brand-new transcontinental railroad. The family experiences the sounds, speed, and strength of the locomotives. With the hissing steam and the heat of the engine, readers watch the landscape go by and see the work needed to keep the railroads and the enormous locomotives running—up and over the mountains to the coast. Floca includes descriptions of the mechanics of the locomotive, as well as the tasks of crew members. His words (in blank verse), art, and ideas make the book appealing to a wide age range from about grade 3 up.

Snowflake Bentley is a book of narrative nonfiction that won the Caldecott Medal in 1999. Wilson Bentley, a Vermont farmer/photographer, had a special interest in exploring and photographing natural phenomena. During the early part of the 20th century, Bentley created photographs that demonstrated that no two snowflakes are alike and that each one is startlingly beautiful. At the time, Bentley's work with snow was often misunderstood. His book *Snow Crystals* and his "lantern slides" were, however, well respected and were used by many colleges and universities. Author Jacqueline Briggs Martin accompanies the story with sidebars containing snippets of information and explanations of Bentley's work. The woodcuts created by illustrator Mary Azarian bring the story to life.

Bat Loves the Night by Nicola Davies offers vivid descriptions of the pipistrelle bat's nocturnal hunting, flying, and squealing. The book explores the bat's navigational skills and explains how the bat wraps her baby inside her leather wings to keep it safe and to suckle it. Bat facts are presented unobtrusively in a different typeface at some distance from the story itself. The facts can be read along with the story or left for a future reading. The book is beautifully illustrated by Sarah Fox-Davies, and the tone created is tranquil and reflective. The book creates an appreciative space for the reader to meet the pipistrelle bat and understand why "bat loves the night."

Other well-written, well-illustrated nonfiction books for kindergarten to grade 8 are listed in Box 11.15. These books can be read not only for the information they offer but purely for pleasure. Although written for young readers, they make compelling reading for all ages.

BOX 11.15

A SELECTION OF HIGH-QUALITY INFORMATION BOOKS
Anholt, L. (1998). *Stone girl, bone girl: The story of Mary Anning.* (S. Moxley, Illus.). New York, NY: Orchard Books.
Arnold, C. (2006). *A penguin's world.* Minneapolis, MN: Picture Window Books.
Bryant, J. (2013). *A splash of red: The life and art of Horace Pippin.* (M. Sweet, Illus.). New York, NY: Alfred A. Knopf.

(continued)

DeCristofano, C. (2012). *A black hole is NOT a hole*. (M. Carroll, Illus.). Watertown, MA: Charlesbridge.

Krull, K. (2009). *The boy who invented TV: The story of Philo Farnsworth*. (G. Couch, Illus.). New York, NY: Alfred A. Knopf.

Mann, E. (1996). *The Brooklyn Bridge*. (A. Witschonke, Illus.). New York, NY: Mikaya Press.

Martin, R., & Nibley, L. (2009). *The mysteries of Beethoven's hair*. Watertown, MA: Charlesbridge.

Prosek, J. (2009). *Bird, butterfly, eel*. New York, NY: Simon & Schuster.

Rusch, E. (2013). *Eruptions! Volcanoes and the science of saving lives*. (T. Uhlman, Illus.). Boston, MA: Houghton Mifflin Harcourt.

Schubert, L. (2012). *Monsieur Marceau: Actor without words*. (G. DuBois, Illus.). New York, NY: Roaring Book Press.

Sis, P. (1996). *Starry messenger*. New York, NY: Farrar, Straus & Giroux.

Tomacek, S. (2007). *Dirt*. (N. Woodman, Illus.). Washington, DC: National Geographic Society.

Nonbook Resources

In addition to newspapers, magazines, pamphlets, and so on, young readers are increasingly reading material on the Internet. All the magazines listed in Box 11.16 have websites that provide further literacy experiences and activities. Like all other materials, those on the computer are appropriate only if they meet the needs of specific learners in your classrooms.

BOX 11.16

PERIODICALS

Let's Find Out and *Storyworks*

▷ **Let's Find Out** (kindergarten): Mini-books, news stories, classroom photo stories, activity pages

▷ *Storyworks* (grades 3 to 5): Fiction, nonfiction, poetry; and classroom plays, interviews with authors, hands-on activities, student-written book reviews

Scholastic Canada Limited

http://www.scholastic.ca

Your Big Backyard and *Ranger Rick*

▷ *Your Big Backyard* (ages 3 to 7): Photo stories, activities

▷ *Ranger Rick* (ages 7 and up): Nonfiction, fiction, photo stories, activities, environmental tips about wildlife around the world

National Wildlife Federation

> http://www.nwf.org/kids

National Geographic Explorer

▷ Grades 3 to 6: Nonfiction, photo stories, activities for junior members of the National Geographic Society

National Geographic Society

> http://www.nationalgeographic.com

Ladybug, Spider, **and** *Cricket*

▷ *Ladybug* (ages 2 to 6): Stories, poems, activities, games, songs, crafts, some nonfiction

▷ *Spider* (ages 6 to 9): Stories, articles, games, activities, jokes

▷ *Cricket* (ages 9 to 14): Stories, folk tales, biographies, science fiction, cartoons, poems, activities, crafts, crossword puzzles, nonfiction

Cricket **Magazine Group**

> http://www.cricketmag.com/home.asp

Weekly Reader

▷ Children's newspapers at a variety of age and grade levels

▷ Weekly Reader Corporation
http://www.weeklyreader.com

Chirp, Chickadee, **and** *Owl*

▷ *Chirp* (ages 3 to 6): Read-out-loud stories, puzzles, games, crafts

▷ *Chickadee* (ages 6 to 9): Stories, nonfiction, activities, games

▷ *Owl* (ages 9 to 12): Nonfiction, activities, puzzles, news stories, contests

▷ *Chirp, Chickadee,* and *Owl* magazines are Canadian.
http://www.owlkids.com

Sesame Street

▷ Ages 2 to 6: Stories, poems, activities, posters, children's drawing and writing

▷ Children's Television Workshop
http://www.sesameworkshop.org

Highlights **for Children**

▷ Ages 2 to 12: Stories, puzzles, games, activities, jokes, riddles
http://www.highlights.com

As in all other areas of the language arts, when engaging with materials such as those listed here, educators have a responsibility to help students read critically. For example, given that magazines are full of advertising, we might lead learners in grades 6 to 8 in a discussion about representations of bodies in these advertisements. In addition, newspapers and other "factual" sources are never without bias. Educators can help students understand this by, for instance, presenting multiple news sources on the same topic. These sources can be from a variety of modes and media, including print, the Internet, radio, and television.

SUMMARY

Children's and young adult literature is incorporated into most language arts programs in Canada, either to balance a reading series or to serve as the foundation for the literacy program. It is also widely used in teaching across the entire curriculum. Educators understand that readers may identify with the characters, setting, or events of a story, and so it is important to include in school and library collections literature that is written, illustrated, or published in Canada. Canadian literature for children and young adults is now noted and characterized by its multicultural nature, and there are many excellent Aboriginal Canadian authors and illustrators creating books for learners K to 8.

A wide range of top-quality literature is available for learners in kindergarten through grade 8. The picture book genre is especially popular, with many produced for learners in grades 5 through 8. Novels include fantasy, contemporary realistic fiction, historical fiction, and mystery genres. Modern classics—such as E. B. White's *Charlotte's Web* and *The Dark Is Rising* by Susan Cooper—are part of young people's cultural heritage. Traditional stories, poetry, and storytelling all play a role in the repertoire of literary materials and activities with which children engage. Books and media of all genres continue to create opportunities for learners to enhance their reading ability and increase the lifelong pleasures they will gain from reading.

The quality and number of nonfiction books available for the classroom have increased markedly over the years. Current technology has assisted in reproducing colourful, interesting, and understandable diagrams, charts, and maps. Authors of nonfiction material for children must write intelligently for an audience that has access to more information than was ever previously available. Such materials must therefore be current, accurate, well designed, and interesting, for they are competing with the Internet, television, and movies as sources of information for our students. Good nonfiction for K to 8 learners must also be aesthetically appealing to a wide audience, including adults. This is especially the case in books of narrative nonfiction, where information is embedded in a contextualized narrative.

As language arts programs increasingly incorporate works of literature as instructional resources, educators are finding they must be knowledgeable about books, authors, and illustrators—they must be able to talk with their students about the books they are reading. Teachers regularly recommend books of all genres to young readers. Being able to do so relies on reading books written for children and young adults, and being familiar with their reading interests. If educators enjoy books and welcome their students into the world of literature, students will likely also take pleasure in books and become lifelong readers.

SELECTED PROFESSIONAL RESOURCES

CM: Canadian Review of Materials: http://www.umanitoba.ca/cm

CM, published by the Manitoba Library Association since 1995, is an electronic reviewing journal issued weekly from September through June every year. Reviews of materials of interest to children and young adults are provided, with a maple leaf symbol denoting Canadian materials and a globe symbol indicating non-Canadian materials that have a Canadian distributor. Also included are author and illustrator profiles, interviews, and publishing news. Reviewers are teachers, teacher-librarians, public librarians, and university professors who have an interest and expertise in materials for juveniles. Back issues are online from 1995 onward and access is free of charge. The journal provides an archived collection of items from the years 1971 to 1994, when the journal was published by the Canadian Library Association (in print form) under the title *CM: A Reviewing Journal of Canadian Material for Young People.*

Kay Vandergrift's special interest page: http://comminfo.rutgers.edu/professional-development/childlit/ChildrenLit/index.html

This high-quality, non-commercial reference site was developed by Kay Vandergrift, then director of the Information, Technology and Informatics Program in the School of Communication, Information and Library Studies at Rutgers University, New Jersey. The site contains lists of picture books, juvenile novels, and young adult literature, as well as lists of multicultural and multiethnic books, many of them Canadian. The lists include Aboriginal, Islamic, traditional, and feminist literature. The site also has videos about children's authors and illustrators, as well as articles on featured authors and books. Sections of the site are devoted to a history of children's literature, literature applicable to teaching topics across the curriculum, and resources to support teaching.

Kiefer, B. Z., & Huck, C. (2010). *Charlotte Huck's children's literature* (10th ed.). Boston, MA: McGraw-Hill.

This American text remains one of the most encompassing resources on children's literature. It is an excellent source of information on the different genres of literature, the history of children's literature, author and illustrator profiles, and planning for instruction in kindergarten to grade 8. Providing a wealth of background information, the book is a useful reference tool for all educators and librarians. A database on CD-ROM accompanies the text. More than 4000 books can be accessed by author, title, genre, and more. Full bibliographic information, plus the approximate interest level (by grade), is provided for each book. Few Canadian books are listed.

12

Responding to Literature

RESPONDING TO LITERATURE

LITERATURE RESPONSE IN JAN SMITH'S GRADE 6 CLASSROOM

Jan Smith

Jan Smith reads aloud to the learners in her classroom almost every day: fiction and nonfiction, poetry, and magazine articles. In the past, her students' favourite "read-aloud" novels were *Gregor the Overlander* by Suzanne Collins and *Camp X* by Eric Walters. Jan sees series books as being comforting to some learners because they provide continuity and familiarity. Through knowing the characters, readers can develop confidence, especially if they're not strong readers. By reading one of a series to the entire class, Jan feels she hooks some of the more reluctant readers into reading other books in the same series.

Jan organizes part of her reading program around book clubs, which she conducts three or four times a year. At the beginning of the year, she orders multiple copies of a range of novels from the district's learning resources centre: historical fiction, fantasy, and realistic fiction. In the past, her students have read *The Amazing Journey of Adolphus Tips* by Michael Morpurgo, *Maniac Magee* by Jerry Spinelli, *Holes* by Louis Sachar, *Silverwing* by Kenneth Oppel, *Chasing Vermeer* by Blue Balliett, *Escaping the Giant Wave* by Peg Kehret, and *The City of Ember* by Jeanne DuPrau. When the books arrive in the classroom, the students are provided with an extended period of time to browse through them and decide which ones they would like to read. Jan asks her students to scan six to eight books, reading the front and end matter, and making notes about the books. They then rate the books from 1 to 3 in terms of their interest.

Jan organizes learners into groups of six for each book club on the basis of their interest in each of the books. She makes sure that her reluctant readers get their first choice of book, and the book clubs are not organized according to reading ability. Instead Jan tries to balance talkers and shy children, learners who tend to dominate conversations with those she knows can work well together. Sometimes she puts friends together because they need to enjoy this experience and look forward to it. Jan says you must know your students if you're to make successful groupings for book clubs. Sometimes a group will consist entirely of boys or of girls, depending on the topic of the book, and that's okay because these groupings are not long term.

At the beginning of each book club, learners receive a calendar page and they decide which sections of the book they will read for each meeting date. They agree not to read ahead, and they sign an agreement that will make the club work successfully. This agreement is student created and is rewritten each time a new book club is formed. The agreements become more specific (and effective) over time. For example, an agreement might say, "I will read as far as … I agree to let everyone speak. I agree to listen to other people's opinions and ideas. I will come to each meeting with a passage to share." The participants each sign the agreement.

Learners come to each meeting with a passage to share and talk about. They take turns to share their passage and explain why this passage is important or memorable to them. They may make connections to personal experiences (text to self), to another book or movie (text to text), or to events in the local community or globally (text to world). In preparation for this, they can write on sticky notes that Jan gives to each of them or in their notebooks. Sometimes learners illustrate their passage and write a caption below it. Through these activities, they explore the content of the book, the characters, the setting, their predictions, and their questions.

Jan says her students have no problem staying on task in their book clubs. They look forward to them and they don't want to waste any time, so they keep one another focused. They also trust each other and they trust her as an educator to guide them and create a safe space for sharing thoughts and questions. Jan does some teaching and practising beforehand so learners know what is expected of them.

Part of the response process consists of commenting on how well the book club worked. These comments tell Jan what she needs to teach or reinforce. Jan believes strongly that young readers need to be taught some skills before they begin book club and so she does a lot of scaffolding. Sometimes she gives out cards with a topic or question written on each. (Topics might be a favourite holiday or favourite gift; questions might relate to pets or family members.) Individuals are asked to talk for three minutes on the topic, and the others listen without interrupting. At the end of the three minutes, learners can ask questions and have a friendly discussion. This exercise serves as a good reminder to learners about how they need to conduct themselves during book club.

Book club usually lasts three to four weeks. The discussion groups meet twice a week for an hour, and Jan meets with each group for about 15 to 20 minutes during that time. Individuals decide whether to write a journal response before a book club discussion or after it. The choice is theirs—as is their mode of response, most of the time. Jan has found that meeting with one group at a time works best for her, as she gets so much information from the students about their engagement with the text.

Not all learners are engaged in book club at the same time, however. Two groups might meet while the rest work on responses, read assigned book sections, or write poems, journal entries, or conduct other response activities, described later in this chapter.

Jan has learned that not all participants need to talk during book club. Often, a shy person might enjoy a book and the book club discussion, while saying little and thinking a lot. Jan keeps notes about the types of comments learners make and the passages they choose to share. This valuable information directs her teaching in mini-lessons, which she conducts during other blocks of time. Jan generally circulates around book clubs, sitting on the edge and listening. Later she gives feedback to the group. Sometimes she gets more involved in the discussion—but she is very conscious about not taking over. In book club, the participants' voices are more important than hers. ☐

This chapter of *Constructing Meaning* addresses questions about how educators facilitate literature responses in their classrooms and how they go about selecting literature for the classroom. Jan Smith and Carol Walters (whom we met earlier in this book) share their insights and teaching practices to help demonstrate some of the basic principles of reader response. Jan and Carol read children's and young adult books widely, and they plan reader response activities and response groups thoughtfully, always with the aim of enhancing learners' reading abilities and their pleasure in reading and thinking about books.

READER RESPONSE

Reader Response and Reading Comprehension

The title of this book, *Constructing Meaning*, was carefully chosen. Basically the book is about understanding and being understood when we read or view or when we express our thoughts and ideas through a range of modes and media. David Booth (2001) wrote,

> Meaning making with print is developmental and can expand exponentially over time, if we have wise others to support us. Students need to be located in the company of those who are considering similar issues and ideas generated by the text—classmates, critics and reviewers, teachers who share and direct their learning, other authors whose writing connects to their work and references that add to their background knowledge.... Our comprehension alters as our life goes on, as we consider the ideas and opinions of others. Our response to a single text is never frozen in time. (p. 13)

Through responding to literature and visual media, learners strengthen their comprehension. We believe that responding to literature is an essential reading strategy. Readers need to think while they read. They need to construct their own meaning.

Many young readers go through their schooling without opportunities to share, and to benefit from, responding to literature—in other words, to really think about what they are reading. They may word-call and learn how to file a book report or how to answer an educator's questions about a text, but they frequently lack real comprehension or insight into the material they read. They become what Cris Tovani (2000) termed "fake readers." In classrooms, an educator's job is to help learners become true readers: to build bridges between the ideas in the text and their own lived experiences and background knowledge. Learners need opportunities to extend their understandings of texts in deep and engaging ways.

This chapter suggests a range of response strategies for K to 8 learners.

What Is Reader Response?

Reader response refers to the events that occur within a reader when a piece of text is read. Louise Rosenblatt (1978) maintained that text is simply squiggles on a page until a reader reads it. When a reader reads the print, *something* happens within the reader. That "something" is often labelled "response." The response might be boredom, confusion, interest, sadness, empathy, irritation, or joy, but a reading event is never undertaken without a variety of responses. People respond to all kinds of events in their everyday lives—a menu read in a restaurant, a movie seen at the cinema, an email note from a friend, a television show, international news on the radio, a song, a play, an editorial in the newspaper. Response is part of the human condition, part of our interactions with the people and the world around us. It is part of the meaning-making process, and as such, response to literature is an important component of a language arts program.

Rosenblatt (1978) referred to the reading experience as a transaction between *text* and *reader*, a transaction that creates what she called the *poem*, or the "lived-through experience with the text" (Rosenblatt, 1985, p. 35). Readers respond to the "poem" (a term used broadly by Rosenblatt to mean the **transactional reading** experience) as they read, after they read, and when they reflect on or recapture their reading experience. Rosenblatt asserted that a response is dictated to a considerable extent by the purpose for reading or, in other words, by the *stance* from which the reader approaches the text.

A reading stance can be anywhere on a continuum from **efferent** at one end, where the reader seeks information of some kind, to **aesthetic** at the other, where the reader focuses on appreciating what is read. Response fluctuates along this continuum as we read. At one moment a reader may be reading for the pure pleasure and appreciation of a work, and the next moment she or he might be noticing something interesting and memorable in the text, or something that relates to a piece of information received from a different source in the recent past. For example, when reading *The Boy in the Striped Pajamas* by John Boyne, a reader may first appreciate the artistry of the language and the tantalizing nature of the story. Then, suddenly, the reader's attention might shift to focus on Germany during the Second World War—a thought that can be connected to a movie or a magazine article encountered recently. The reading experience thus moves from an aesthetic stance to a more efferent stance.

The extremes of response on this continuum can be demonstrated by two quite different reading events. When someone reads a first-aid manual to treat an injury, the reading has a pragmatic purpose—to allow the reader to gain essential information that will directly affect his or her behaviour in the immediate future. The reading of a first-aid manual is *efferent reading*, at the far end of the continuum. When that same person reads a novel, however, the purpose is likely to be for pleasure, or to allow the reader to gain a deeper understanding of human experience. As readers engage with a novel, they enter into the space of the novel and disconnect themselves from the time of their own existence as well as their own ongoing or chronological time. This is where Rosenblatt (1985) used the term "lived-through experience with the text" to describe an *aesthetic reading* (p. 35). A good book is almost certain to evoke a deep personal engagement, whether that turns out to involve angst or pleasure.

Educators can provide opportunities for learners to have both aesthetic and efferent responses to a text, whether that text is in a reading series or in a trade book. Rosenblatt (1990) maintained that "once the work has been evoked, it can become the object of reflection and analysis, according to the various critical and scholarly approaches" (p. 106). In other words, a text first evokes an aesthetic or "lived-through" response and then evokes a more efferent response as the reader consciously thinks about the text and the reading experience.

For example, a short story such as "Tashkent" (in *Some of the Kinder Planets* by Tim Wynne-Jones) may be read in such a way that the reader enters the story's time, identifying with the protagonist's illness and recuperation, and leaving behind the more immediate concerns of the world. When reflecting on the story, however, the reader constructs meaning (on the basis of the text) that may relate to other stories or poems, to geographical facts, to information the reader already possesses, or to the reader's own life or that of a friend. When readers reflect in this way, they re-enter ongoing chronological time and engage in a more efferent response. A *totally* efferent response to "Tashkent" might include summarizing the story as we retell it to a friend, locating in an atlas the place names mentioned in the story, or comparing the story with a poem that has a similar theme. These transactions form the cornerstone for the creation of possible meanings, as well as for coming to understand how texts work.

What is seen of response to literature in a classroom is like the tip of an iceberg: much of it remains out of sight (Purves & Rippere, 1968). Educators such as Jan and Carol keep the following points in mind as they engage learners with literature:

- The extent to which readers show their responses in a classroom context depends on the reading abilities of the individual learner.

- The depth of response learners demonstrate depends on the level of trust they feel in the classroom environment.

- If they don't feel safe, people in general do not share feelings and thoughts.

- If learners are taught that there is one "right" response to a piece of literature (usually an educator's response or interpretation), they are less likely to express their own responses.

- Through sharing and discussing responses, learners discover that meaning can be negotiated and constructed in a multitude of equally valid ways.

- When learners are encouraged to respond to texts and to engage in dialogue among themselves, their peers, and educators about books, they are more likely to see that meaning is created by the reader, and that multiple ways of knowing and responding to literature are valid and necessary.

- Learners who share their responses to literature and have their responses accepted respectfully are likely to become more thoughtful and critical readers than those who do not experience a fair exchange of responses.

Learning through Response

Young readers learn a great deal through responding to literature. They discover how texts work, what constitutes a good book, how language can be used in different ways to create different meanings and effects—in short, how to become thoughtful readers, not just people able to read. As a result of active responding, learners are likely to take ownership of the reading process and come to understand that literature can be interpreted in many varied ways. However, as Rosenblatt (1978) wrote, some responses are more legitimate or appropriate than others because responses must be based in the text read. Through learning to respect and honour their own interpretations of what they have read, learners gain the confidence to become more critical in their thinking about texts, more creative in their own writing, and much more capable in their ability as language users and language learners. In effect, they take on the four roles of the reader described in Chapter 1: code breaker, text participant, text user, and text analyst (Freebody & Luke, 1990).

Literature can form the basis for an entire language arts program in K to 8 classrooms, for the nature of reading and response encourages learners to integrate their knowledge, make personal sense of it, and express it through movement, the visual arts, music, drama, writing, and dialogue. Thomson (1987) reminded educators that "the development of a mature response to literature involves a progressive movement from close emotional involvement to more distanced reflective detachment, and from an interest in self to an interest in other people and the human condition" (p. 153). In other words, the process of response almost always begins with an aesthetic, personal experience of the text—the very experience that a response activity in the classroom aims to encourage and facilitate.

Educators often speak about literary response in terms of text-to-text, text-to-self, and text-to-world connections. Below are excerpts from responses to literature, written by a student in grade 8, that demonstrate two of these connections:

Text-to-Text Connection ("The Emperor's New Clothes," Hans Christian Andersen)

The text-to-text connection I found between "The Emperor's New Clothes" and another piece of text was the phrase: "There's an elephant in the room." The phrase simply means that something obvious is right in front of you but it is unaddressed or ignored because nobody would like to talk about it. In "The Emperor's New Clothes," the emperor is the elephant that's in the room. His nudity is a clear, obvious topic that people are avoiding simply because they'd like others to think of them as intelligent or successful with their job. Citizens pretend to see the nonexistent clothing to maintain their reputation and status. The elephant in the room is ignored because people do not like to discuss that; they avoid it. The citizens pretended to see the nonexistent clothing to prove they were smart. Are you really an intelligent being if you believe a naked person is clothed? The irony is that a [stereotypically] innocent child points out the obvious to the others. The child did not care (or perhaps know) that others would view him as stupid for saying he was unable to see the clothing.

Some people look past the obvious because they think it doesn't need to be pointed out. Others look past the obvious so they do not stand out next to others. Lastly, some people just ignore the obvious; it could be because they are afraid of the truth, it could be because they do not want to deal with the consequences the truth brings with it. In summary, the connection I found deals with finding the truth in a series of lies and deciding whether or not to ignore it.

Text-to-Self Connection ("The Veldt", Ray Bradbury)

The text-to-self connection I found between "The Veldt" and my own life consisted of an old, recurring nightmare I used to experience at least once a week. I haven't had that nightmare in years but I often think of it. The nightmare took place in my old babysitter's hedge-lined backyard. A soccer ball would be kicked into the hedge and one of us would go get it. When I went to retrieve the ball, I'd have to walk into the hedge to locate it. As soon as I'd step into the hedge it would close behind me and I'd find myself in a never-ending hedge. The nightmare would always end with me being killed by a wolf. In the nightmare I would always scream for help but no one was ever there to hear my cries.

My nightmare and "The Veldt" both have a concept of searching for something and finding yourself in trouble. I would search for the ball then find myself trapped in the hedge; George and Lydia searched for their children and found themselves trapped in the nursery. An obvious connection between the two stories is that in both, the protagonist is killed by a wild animal.

The last similarity between my nightmare and "The Veldt" is that the protagonists both scream for help but nobody was listening. In "The Veldt" George and Lydia cry for their children to open the door, however they refused to listen. In my nightmare, I screamed and screamed but, unlike Bradbury's story, nobody was there to hear me. I was utterly alone.

Response Groups

One important vehicle for exploring a text is the response group, or what Jan Smith calls a "book club." Adult readers have also discovered the pleasures of reading clubs or book clubs, where members read a book in their own time and then come together as a group to discuss the book and explore interpretations of it. Such groups can play a valuable role in K to 8 language arts classrooms, as Jan has described.

Educators and researchers have discovered that learners benefit from *orally* sharing and shaping their responses to books. As they share their own responses and listen to the ways in which other readers have responded to a book, learners become aware that no two readers read in the same way or create meaning in the same way. In the process of discussion, their attention is drawn to details they might have missed, and they are called to think about things that, as individual readers, they might not have thought about.

Taking part in a response group can be a fascinating experience. It can also be a frustrating experience if readers want everyone in the group to respond to a book in the way in which *they* have responded to it. Research conducted by Eeds and Wells formed the foundation for the book *Grand Conversations* (Peterson & Eeds, 1990), a book that underscores the importance of dialogue in constructing meaning from a text. Peterson and Eeds (1990, p. 21) wrote, "The lecture model places knowledge outside the students for them to passively receive; dialogue recognizes that knowledge is something students actively construct." The authors provide many suggestions and insights for educators who work with response groups, including ideas for selecting books, facilitating literature study, and evaluating responses to literature. They also reiterate that learners need time in class just for reading, and they should not be expected to do all their reading outside class time.

Critical to the success of response groups is the respect educators afford each learner's ideas, not imposing their own ideas on the class. There are many occasions when educators have to put their own feelings and opinions aside to listen to the readers' voices. Classroom discussions can be extremely enlightening for an educator and can provide a springboard for choosing and creating alternative ways of responding to books. The role of the educator in literature response groups is that of sensitive guide, helping to create links from the text to life experiences and to other texts, and inserting particular insights about literature at appropriate moments. Peterson and Eeds (1990) maintained that asking a direct question such as "What was your favourite part of the story, and why?" can close down real conversation for learners. The question is artificial and requires a fabricated response.

Carol Walters makes comments such as "Let's think more about that" because open-ended "wondering" comments help readers reflect on their reading and deepen their responses to the reading. Talking with learners about a book can be an effective teaching strategy, because it immediately creates possible connections to the reader's own life and demands a personal engagement with the text.

Stanley Fish (1980) said, "Not only does one believe what one believes, but one teaches what one believes, even if it would be easier and safer and more satisfying to teach something else" (p. 364). If we believe that teaching reading means asking learners questions, requiring them to provide a retelling of almost every story they read, or picking out the main ideas from a chapter in a book, then our teaching of reading will betray those beliefs.

Judith Langer (1994) wrote, "The thought-provoking literature class is an environment where students [and teachers] are encouraged to negotiate their own meanings by exploring possibilities, considering understandings from multiple perspectives, sharpening their own interpretations, and learning through the insights of their own responses" (p. 207). She went on to remind educators that response is based as much on the reader's own personal and cultural experiences as it is on the particular text and its author. Langer also believed that with instructional support, "even the most 'at-risk' learners can engage in thoughtful discussions about literature, develop rich and deep understandings, and enjoy it too" (p. 210).

Literature Response Journals

Literature response journals provide learners with opportunities for reflection on what they are currently reading. They are not the same as personal journals or learning logs, but, as Parsons (2001) explained, they usually consist of a notebook, folder, section of a binder, or electronic file "in which learners record their personal reactions to, questions about, and reflections on what they read, view, write, represent, observe, listen to, discuss, do, and think and how they go about reading, viewing, writing, representing, observing, listening, discussing or doing" (p. 9). Response journals are usually intensely private and personal, for they depict exactly how a reader interprets a text and responds to it. When educators read response journals, they try to be sensitive to the nature of the writing and aware of the privileged position they hold in accessing this material. They do not correct grammar or spelling errors, but try to respond to the content, reading in the role of "fellow reader," not as an "authority" on the text.

Educator Terri Walker's grade 2 learners, who wrote the following journal entries, certainly were not focusing on correct spelling (Walker, 1993, pp. 46–47). In these peer-dialogue journals, the children were encouraged to make text-to-self connections. They wrote an entry, exchanged journals with a partner, and then wrote a response to their partner's entry. Terri did not draw attention to their invented spelling, but instead complimented the pairs on their interesting exchanges and added a personal comment about her own experiences (in this case with birds and their eggs).

MELISSA: This book reminds me when I see bird nests and some have eggs in them. One day a bird floow in my dad's truck and I got to tuch the bird

STUART: Birds are wered when they wot to be!

Another pair wrote:

BROOKE: The story remindid me of when I was at my Gamas and we say a brokin rodine egg. We hid the egg under the deke evre time we go there we go under the deke and see the egg.

PETRA: We have eggs. When we go to feed the cikins sumtimes thare are haf a dusint and sumtimes thare cen be 33.*

Literature response journals work most effectively when they are open-ended and unstructured. However, learners need to know the expectations, requirements, and routines associated with them. For example, they need to know how often they are expected to write in their journal, how their journal writing will be assessed, how often an educator will read the journal, and how they are expected to record the titles and other pertinent information about the books they read. *Response Journals Revisited* by Les Parsons (2001) suggests a number of organizational strategies educators can use in grades 5 to 8. Parsons also emphasizes that educators must make time in the classroom for reading as well as for

* Walker, T. (1993). "Peer Dialogue Journals as Response to Literature in Grade Two." M.Ed Thesis. University of Alberta, Edmonton, AB.

responding, and that learners can respond to read-aloud sessions as well as to their silent reading.

Carol Walters

Directing learners to focus their responses on some specific aspect of the text such as plot, setting, characters, or theme does *not* appear to be as effective as leaving the response options open to them, providing suggestions only where necessary. However, cuing questions can be very effective in getting learners started on writing a response. These are not a prescribed set of questions provided by an educator, but may include such questions as this: "After reading this far, what more do you hope to learn about what these charac-ters plan to do, what they think, feel and believe, or what happens to them?" (Parsons, 2001, p. 37). Response writing, like any other type of writing, is learned. Learners who are not used to writing in the expressive voice (see Chapter 9) may need some time to get used to the idea that this is an acceptable form of writing. It is not a matter of learning *what* to write, but rather of learning what to focus on and *how* to write a response.

Educators keep in mind that a learner's written responses to a text are part of the indi-vidual's meaning making or comprehension. Written responses rely heavily on the learner's ability to comprehend what has been encountered through the reading. For this reason, educa-tors engage learners in strategies that will help them to comprehend the text as well as shape a reflective response to it. Successful response writing is partly about making the invisible "visible." As a first strategy in helping students to write a response, educators assist them in identifying some of the invisible processes of reading.

Experienced educators like Carol Walters explain to their students that successful readers use two types of voices while they are reading. The first can be referred to as the *reciting voice*, which is the voice in the reader's head that says the words found on the page. The second voice can be referred to as the *conversation voice*, which is the voice in the reader's head that responds to what the reader is reading.

Many learners are unaware that their conversation voice needs to be present for good reading to take place. As a result, they use only the reciting voice, and they need to be taught how to develop their conversation voice. One way to aid in this development is to have learners pay attention to their thoughts while watching a television show or a movie. Learners initially seem to find it easier to recognize their conversation voice in this context rather than trying to "hear" it while reading.

INSIDE CLASSROOMS

CHILDREN'S LITERATURE IN CAROL WALTERS'S GRADE 4 CLASSROOM

Carol Walters believes there's nothing like good literature to get learners hooked into reading—and into writing. Good books engage learners like nothing else. Through good literature, educators create motivation for learning and provide models of excel-lent writing. When Carol reads aloud to her grade 4 class, which she does frequently, she

(continued)

uses a think-aloud procedure and she pauses as she reads, talking about what is going through her mind as a reader. "Oh, I wasn't expecting that. I wonder what he's going to do now." "Why do you think she did that?" "Do you notice how the author said that? What does it make you think about?" "What a wonderful description. It's worth reading a second time."

Buddy-reading

Carol has also learned the power of series books, and, like Jan Smith, she sometimes reads aloud a Nancy Drew or other series book, especially near the beginning of the school year. Her students' favourite read-alouds include *The Vicar of Nibbleswicke* by Roald Dahl and *My Name Is Seepeetza* by Shirley Sterling, which connects well with the social studies curriculum and the UN Convention on the Rights of the Child. Grade 4 learners relate easily to the issues raised in *My Name Is Seepeetza* and can connect them to their own family and personal lives. Carol says many of these books demonstrate what is meant by a writer's voice, and she often talks about this and about how learners can develop their own voice in their writing. The main criteria Carol uses for choosing a book to read aloud to the class are that the children will enjoy it and that they will look forward to hearing it.

Carol notes the very wide range of reading abilities in most grade 4 classrooms, with some learners reading at a grade 6/7 level and others at grade 2. She maintains that a wide selection of reading materials, including picture books, novels, and lots of good nonfiction books and magazines, helps to ensure that every one of her students will engage with reading. Open-ended activities allow all the learners to be included successfully in reader response, and they ensure that all learners' reading needs are met and supported. Working with peers in writing, reading, discussion, and other modes of response is essential, in Carol's view. Less-able readers are then supported by their peers, and they can participate fully, even if they are not reading at grade level. Working with a buddy or with a small group enables these children to develop trust and confidence and encourages them to take some risks, which is necessary if they are to become capable, independent readers. Carol knows the importance of developing a safe classroom climate in which learners can take the necessary risks with support and not ridicule.

Carol carefully selects reading buddies for some of the students in her classroom. Having a partner to read and discuss the book with is immeasurably important to struggling readers. The system acknowledges that not all learners read at the same rate or level of competency, and it balances their contributions to the act of reading. Sometimes the pairs take turns reading a paragraph at a time, or they might read a whole page. They help each other with the reading, and they talk about what they're reading as they go along. The buddies can find any comfortable spot in the classroom for their reading, and they often go outside of the classroom into an open area close by, where they can feel cozy and relaxed as they read.

Carol models this process by sharing her thoughts (think-aloud) while she is reading aloud to her class. Learners can join the discussion with Carol by sharing what their conversation voices were saying. Responses in the conversation voice might vary from predicting to questioning or sharing an opinion about something that happened in the story. The think-aloud strategy shows young readers how an expert reader makes sense of text. "By sharing your thinking out loud," said Cris Tovani (2000), "you make the elusive process of comprehension more concrete" (p. 26). If learners are aware of the tools needed to make text meaningful, they will be more able to respond with greater depth in their response journals. The think-aloud strategy is straightforward and requires little planning.

Using Patricia Polacco's picture book *Thank You, Mr. Falker*, for example, an educator might make the following comments during the first two pages of the book: "I wonder why the grandpa is pouring honey on the book. I remember when I learned to read in grade 1. I loved it when my grandma would read to me, because she always read to me in a rocking chair. Why is Trisha not able to read? I think Trisha is going to have trouble learning to read."

After educators model the process, learners can practise their conversation voices while reading instructional-level text. They may record their thoughts on a separate piece of paper or on a sticky note. With the sticky note they can mark the pages in the book that evoked the response. Alternatively, they might write responses in the margin of a photocopied page from the book. Educators can then provide opportunities for learners to share their conversation voices with a partner, teacher, and perhaps the entire class. Educators and students together can begin to identify and record on a class chart the types of conversation voices used during reading. Below are identified some of the conversation voices that successful readers use while reading:

- predicting
- visualizing
- disagreeing
- agreeing
- questioning

- clarifying
- reminding
- summarizing
- inferring
- relating

Educators can also model journal writing using the think-aloud strategy, recording their responses on a SMART Board or on chart paper. Once learners become comfortable writing in their response journals, educators may continue to model written responses but without thinking aloud. Educators write their own responses while learners are writing theirs.

Because writing in a response journal involves the complex processes of reading and writing, some individuals may struggle with the task. Here are some suggestions for providing support to such learners:

- Encourage learners to work at "listening" for one of the conversation voices identified on the class chart and write their response in that voice.

- Encourage struggling writers to record their responses in picture or point form rather than sentences.

- Encourage them to read your modelled responses as a springboard for getting started themselves. Perhaps your response reminds them of something they thought about when they read the text, or that they were confused about and might now write about.

- Before learners begin writing in their response journals, encourage them to share past entries or thoughts they might include in their latest entry.

Any response to literature that young readers might write is shaped by the text itself. Some texts, such as *Gorilla* by Anthony Browne or *The Breadwinner* by Deborah Ellis, invite immediate responses, though the responses will differ significantly from one reader to another. Most readers readily identify with the protagonists of these two stories and can empathize with the situations in which the characters find themselves. Other texts, such as *The Golden Compass* by Philip Pullman, may at first appear strange, complex, or even baffling. The text may generate many questions before a reader can shape a response to it, and the response is likely to change as the reading progresses.

Whether the reader's response to a book is tentative and questioning, or confident and fully engaged, educators and researchers have found that learners' written responses to books demonstrate what they know, what and how they think, and how they have comprehended a text. Thus, there is little need for having a reader retell the story to ascertain whether he or she has understood a book or not. It is clear, for example, that Rob, in grade 5, not only enjoyed *The Dragon Children* by Bryan Buchan, but also understood the complex plot:

> I really liked this book because there were two mysteries in the whole book. One of the mysteries was if the crook would make it out of town in time, and if John, Scott, Cathy and Steven would get the crook or not. The other mystery was to find out who or what Steven really was. I figured out what Steven was by putting all the clues together. At the end of the book I found out who Steven was. At first I thought that Steven was a ghost (even though he was) that the crook had drowned in the river. I was half right about that.
>
> It was a surprise to me when John, Scott, and Cathy found out that the crook wasn't who they thought he was. It surprised me because when Steven told John that the crook was driving a green car with a license plate number 5K-206 it wasn't the crook driving it. Instead it was the man who had come with his family for their vacation. The man did seem like a crook though because when he was walking through the woods with his son, it looked like he had kidnapped the child.
>
> My favorite part, though, was when Scott sneaked up behind the real crook and poked the needle in his back-end. I liked it because it really made me laugh.

Jesper Elgaard/iStockphoto.com

Children sharing a literature response journal

Rob wrote this response about how he played detective as a reader in order to fit all the pieces of the story together, making meaning and solving the two mysteries. The response demonstrates how Rob engaged with the text, and how he experienced a more distanced response to the book rather than a personal identification with the characters and their actions.

Literature response journals provide opportunities for educators to deliver learner-oriented as well as text-oriented teaching support and feedback to readers. Response journals do not replace discussion; they reinforce and support discussion. Response journals provide a place for learners to slow down their thinking and reflect on their reading (and on their group discussions), asking questions, wondering, predicting, and synthesizing. Here they can genuinely work at seeking to understand how literature weaves its magic, how reading is accomplished, and how books work.

Readers' Workshop

A complaint frequently voiced by young readers is that they are given little time in school to *read*. Instead, they are required to devote most of their time to activities *about* reading. Atwell (1998) suggested that if learners are to truly enjoy the reading experience, time for reading, as well as for learning *about* reading, must be established in school. Learners read magazines, website content, and other such material out of school; educators can encourage them to broaden their reading repertoire by selecting novels, poetry, plays, biographies, and works of nonfiction when they are in school. The books, however, should be of interest to the readers and, where appropriate, chosen by them.

In a readers' workshop, most of the in-class time is spent reading, and mini-lessons are used to teach reading and literature. Atwell offered the following guidelines for conducting readers' workshops:

- Have learners come to the workshop with a book that they are ready to read or are already reading. The book should be self-selected from either the classroom or the school library. Readers' workshop is not a time for making book selections.

- Regardless of grade level, ensure that learners have a sustained and uninterrupted time for reading. Suitable timelines for readers' workshops vary from grade level to grade level. Grades 5 to 7 require 20 to 30 minutes for reading. Younger readers require much less, depending on their ability to sustain silent reading. Thus in grades 1 and 2, the reading time might be only 10 minutes.

- Encourage learners not to talk or disturb others during reading time, though they may sit or recline anywhere, depending on the physical constraints of the classroom.

- Help learners understand that quiet time is important when reading. Most readers cannot read fluently if there is noise around them, or if they are trying to attend to more than one activity at once.

Mini-lessons, whether planned or spontaneous, should usually be brief (say, between 5 and 15 minutes) and designed in response to the learners' needs. A mini-lesson may be

- a discussion of a topic (e.g., the need for quiet time during reading, the procedures and agendas for response groups, how the classroom library is organized, classroom literary resources, how to organize a reading folder and keep a record of books read, self-assessment procedures, and goal setting)

- a book-share by an educator (reading part of a book to the class), a book talk by an educator or a group of learners, or some other presentation of activities completed by readers *in response* to a book they have read

- a presentation on a particular author, where an educator shows the class a number of books by that author: information about authors is available online (most authors have their own websites) or in electronic resources such as Something About the Author, or on the web-based catalogues of most public libraries

- a further exploration of a book in response groups, journal writing, or alternative response activities

The key role of the educator in a readers' workshop is to facilitate learning as readers progress from personal interpretations and understandings ("My question is …" "It reminds me of …" "I don't understand why …") to shared meanings ("This story is about …") and on to negotiated meanings ("We think the writer wanted us to understand that …"). Readers' workshop is a place where learners can read, take ownership of their reading, and respond in their own language to the material they have selected to read. They discuss their ideas about a text with other readers and come to shared and negotiated understandings of the meanings of the stories, poems, and plays they are reading.

Purves (1993) emphasized that reading in school can never be like reading out of school, because in school it is the educator's job to facilitate learners' growth in book selection, reading skill, confidence, fluency, and ability to express thoughts and opinions and to engage in critical and creative thought. As Purves wrote, "I urge us to see our task in schools as helping students read literature and understand the culture, to speculate on the ideas and the imaginative vision, and to speculate on the nature and the use of the language that is the medium of the artistic expression" (p. 360). Much of this can be achieved, we believe, in well-handled readers' workshops.

Literature Circles

In his book *Literature Circles: Voice and Choice in Book Clubs and Reading Groups*, Daniels (2002) wrote, "Literature circles are small, temporary discussion groups whose members have chosen to read the same story, poem, article or book. While reading each group-assigned portion of the text (either in or outside of class), members make notes to help them contribute to the upcoming discussion, and everyone comes to the group with ideas to share" (p. 2). In other words, literature circles are reader-led discussion groups. Each literature circle in a classroom is likely to be reading a different book, but the groups meet regularly according to a schedule. The educator acts as a facilitator for the groups.

Role sheets, which give a different role to each group member, are often used at first, as they help to guide learners in the roles they agree to take on. Daniels emphasizes that the aim is to make the role sheets obsolete. After using role sheets once or twice, learners usually opt to work without them as they learn how to tailor the group processes to meet their own needs. Possible roles include the following:

- The *questioner* develops a list of questions the group might like to discuss and generally helps the group to talk over the big ideas.
- The *connector* finds connections between the book and the world outside (the school, the community, events at other times and places).
- The *literary luminary* locates a few special sections of the text the group might like to hear read aloud—emphasis is on interesting, funny, powerful, or puzzling sections.

- The *illustrator* draws some kind of picture or representation related to the text.
- The *summarizer* prepares a brief summary of the day's reading, the essence of it.
- The *researcher* obtains background information on any topic related to the book or the author/illustrator.
- The *word wizard* looks out for a few especially important words—new, interesting, strange, or puzzling.

Daniels's system is highly organized, and can be both interesting and enjoyable for learners. Most educators find that literature circles provide an excellent structure for beginning group work in response to literature. Many educators report that learners no longer need the role sheets after they have participated in the system two or three times. They learn how to organize the groups themselves and understand the possibilities response groups can offer for discussion of innumerable topics and ideas related to their reading. Educators need to be aware that literature circles can become mechanistic and, if due care is not taken, can function from an efferent stance. The greatest learning is likely to take place when learners write in response journals in addition to discussing their reading in a response group, and engage in unstructured grand conversations.

Novel Studies

The term *novel study* is used to describe a range of group activities that encourage and facilitate learners' reading and responding to novels. At the grades 3 to 8 levels, novel studies provide a vehicle for learners to experience a novel in a small-group setting, much like a book club or response group. Novel studies can be conducted with a whole class, though they can usually be separated into small groups for many of the discussions and activities. Novel studies can also be conducted in groups of four to six, as in a literature circle.

Multiple copies of novels are necessary for a novel study, so it is most economical to involve no more than five or six readers with one novel at any one time. Prepared novel study sets are usually packaged in groups of six books. Many educators complete one whole-class novel study at the beginning of the year to set out the expectations for novel studies and to establish guidelines and procedures for novel study activities. After the initial whole-class study, educators usually work with small groups, as in literature circles or the book clubs Jan Smith runs.

Successful novel study requires a classroom community in which reading is valued and where learners and educators are "real readers." As highlighted by both Atwell (1998) and Daniels (2002), learners benefit from opportunities to choose their reading material and from substantial time to read independently. They can be assigned to groups on the basis of their approximate reading speeds, or they can self-select a reading group on the basis of their interest in the novel. The group chooses a book to read, and the group members meet regularly to discuss the book and complete response activities. The activities can be designed by learners or suggested by an educator.

In preparation for the group activity, learners agree to achieve specific goals for each meeting. The goals may include reading a certain number of pages before the meeting, or accomplishing certain tasks such as answering questions raised in the previous meeting. This is a way of "thinking back and thinking ahead." It provides readers with a means of synthesizing their reading, making predictions, asking questions, and negotiating meaning with the group. During the discussion time, an educator circulates about the room, listening to the ongoing conversations and participating where appropriate. Once the discussions are complete, each group sets a new reading goal that can be recorded on a small chart posted at the front of the classroom. An educator can monitor the reading goals to ensure they are appropriate for the various groups. Learners spend the rest of the period reading their novels, writing in their response journals, or engaging in alternative response activities. Educators can either read silently during this time or assist individual learners with their responses.

Journal responses can be written at any time during the reading of a novel: the midpoint, on completion of the texts, or (as more frequently happens) during the reading. Learners can decide on the content of their responses (there is no particular structure or format for the entries), but they are encouraged to select and write in depth about one or two ideas, images, feelings, memories, or thoughts they experienced during or after their reading. Doing this helps them to explore, extend, or develop their reading experiences. Some readers relate the story to other books, movies, or experiences in their lives; some evaluate a situation or a character, or put themselves in a character's position in the book and discuss what they would feel or do and why; and others discuss the author's writing purpose, style, or techniques.

The direct teaching of reading occurs in a novel study when individuals or groups of learners require assistance in dealing with comprehension difficulties, selecting novels, or organizing themselves to meet their goals. Because readers in this activity are largely independent in their work, they need to be aware of the expectations for novel studies, such as when it is appropriate to write in their response journals and when to hand in responses to an educator. It is also important that learners know where to find the novels they are interested in reading, the procedures for signing out books, and any other classroom routines related to this study activity. What educators try to avoid at all cost is turning responses to a work of literature into skill-building exercises (or "dummy runs" as Britton, 1970, called them). Educators keep in mind their own objectives in working with literature in the classroom and the needs of the students they teach.

Alternative Modes of Response

As readers in classrooms begin to read, continue reading, and finish reading novels and picture books, they can engage in many interesting and challenging activities that will help them explore, interpret, and more fully understand the text. The strategies and activities presented in the *Constructing Meaning* chapter on drama (see http://www.constructingmeaning6e.nelson .com) could be included as part of a novel study. Response activities encompass the full spectrum from aesthetic to efferent. Halliday's (1969) functions of language (discussed in Chapter 3) also provide a solid foundation for creating a diverse range of purposeful language activities for learners as they respond to and explore literature. In the rest of this section, more than a dozen examples of response activities are described, using the novel *The Miraculous Journey of Edward Tulane* by Kate DiCamillo. This 2006 novel is unusual in that it has a wide appeal across the grades and is enjoyed by learners from grade 3 up.

In *The Miraculous Journey of Edward Tulane*, a vain, cold-hearted, and proud toy rabbit loves only himself—and resents being referred to as a toy. Edward Tulane is made of china and has wire joints at his knees and elbows. He has the most beautiful and elegant clothes, and even a little pocket watch that works. Abilene, his 10-year-old owner, loves and adores Edward. But one night, Abilene's grandmother tells them a bedtime story about a princess who doesn't know how to love. She whispers to Edward, "You disappoint me." When Edward is separated from Abilene, he is forced into a journey that is long and dangerous, and which takes him on a path that teaches him about love, and eventually brings him great joy.

Here are a number of drama strategies that could be used to facilitate responses to the story:

- *Hot-seating.* One of the characters Edward Tulane meets on his journey is Nellie, an old woman whose husband is a fisher and away from home for most of every day. He has rescued Edward from his fishing net, and now Edward will live with them in their cottage. Nellie adores Edward, but calls him "Susanna" and makes dresses for him. She talks to Edward and sits him on a cupboard in the kitchen each day as she cooks and bakes and sews. In groups of three, students take turns "being" Nellie. What questions do the other learners have for Nellie? What do they want to know about her? Alternatively, at this point in the story, learners might want to hot-seat Edward and find out what he is thinking and what he hopes will happen next. The individual in role as Nellie or Edward draws on personal experiences and prior knowledge to answer the questions in the context of the story. Educators will likely need to model this strategy first, using one of the other characters in the book as an example.

- *Tableaux.* Bryce is a boy who has had a hard and sad life. He has had to work for a living because his family is very poor. Now Bryce's mother and little sister are dead, and his father is hardly ever at home. Bryce hits the road with Edward and makes money as a street performer, attaching strings to Edward's arms and legs so that Edward can dance like a marionette. At the end of the day, with enough money to buy a good meal, they go to Neal's Diner and Bryce orders the meal of his dreams: pancakes, steak, and eggs. But when the bill comes, Bryce does not have enough money to pay. Neal grabs Edward in anger and cracks Edward's head against the counter. In groups of four to six, learners can create tableaux—still pictures of the scenes in the diner. Each group first decides what it wants to include in its tableau and plans who will take the role of each character. Once this is determined, the participants take up their positions, perhaps by acting out a brief portion of the story and freezing the action at a given moment. The learners then orchestrate the tableau so that it becomes an artistic and aesthetically pleasing portrayal of the scene. They can imagine this as either a photograph or as a diorama exhibit in a museum. Each group is given the opportunity to show its tableau to the rest of the class.

- *Thoughts-in-the-head.* While engaged in their tableaux, the facilitator touches each character gently on the shoulder. At the touch, the learners, in role, say what thoughts are going through their minds at that moment. If any participants do not wish to speak, they may remain silent and the facilitator moves on to the next character.

- *Puppets.* Many different kinds of puppets can be created to put on a play of some part of the story. From paper-lunch-bag, sock, or paper-plate puppets to more elaborate creations, learners generally enjoy this activity. Some groups may want to script the play first; others may simply create the dialogue as they go. Either way, all groups should have the opportunity to rehearse before sharing their work.

- *Readers' theatre.* Readers' theatre is a form of oral presentation in which scripts are read aloud rather than memorized. Participants read their parts expressively and use their voices, gestures, and facial expressions to communicate images, events, and actions in the minds of audience members. In readers' theatre, the characters may sit on stools or a high bench to read their parts. Often, to identify themselves, the participants wear an item of clothing typical of the character they are "reading." Thus, Bull, the hobo, might wear a tattered hat and a scarf around his neck. Edward might wear a bow tie. For this dramatic activity, educators may need to rewrite or script portions of the original text or provide learners with instructional assistance as they create the readers' theatre script themselves. The chapters are short in *The Miraculous Journey of Edward Tulane*, and so they lend themselves nicely to this means of interpretation.

- *Character profile.* Learners select a character from the book and dress as that character. Each individual enters the classroom donned in appropriate attire and prepared in role. Drawing on the novel, the learner talks in role as the character and relates what significant events happened to the character. Classmates may ask the character questions.

These activities represent only a few of the many drama strategies that can be used in a literature or language arts program. Drama activities frequently take longer than might be expected and they should not be rushed. Throughout their drama work, participants are encouraged to talk with one another about their interpretations, opinions, likes and dislikes, and personal "pictures" of the characters and setting. This oral processing enhances the learners' personal engagement with the text, and can help them have a more satisfying and memorable experience with a book. Only one or two of the above activities should be selected for use with any one text. A common option is to have groups of learners in a classroom work on different activities, which makes sharing the sessions with one another all the more interesting. Readers or listeners are usually curious about other interpretations of the work under consideration.

Visual activities have the same appeal as the drama strategies suggested above, allowing learners to become actively involved in creating an artifact representative of their responses. Drawing, painting, creating visual images on the web, and making models, dioramas, wall charts, and portraits are just a few of the activities that give learners the opportunity to display their responses to a text. For *The Miraculous Journey of Edward Tulane*, the following activities could be considered:

- *Photograph album.* Learners create a "photograph album" of Edward's journey and the people he met along the way. "Photographs" can consist of pictures taken from magazines, or the participants can create them themselves, either with a camera or with art supplies. A caption can be added beneath each image. Individuals can explain why they chose to include their specific image in their album.

- *Scrapbook.* In a similar manner to the photograph album, learners make a scrapbook of the mementos of Edward's adventures. They can make notes, menus, paw prints, sketches of dresses, and other such memorabilia from Edward's journeys and his encounters with the various characters along the way.

- *Mapping.* Learners create large and colourful maps of the routes Edward may have taken from his first home on Egypt Road in Memphis, to his travel on the *Queen Mary*, the fishing village in which he found himself, and so on. The map is not necessarily intended to be a realistic depiction, but can be created from the descriptions provided in the text. If learners wish to locate a real map of the United States and base their renditions on it, this will also extend their learning and responses to the story.

- *Silhouettes.* Individually or in small groups, learners draw on overhead transparencies a silhouette of a character from the story. The finished drawings can be displayed using the overhead projector. What features have the artists given the various characters? Why are these features important?

- *Drawings.* After reading parts of the book or the entire book, learners draw scenes, characters, or various aspects of their own interpretation of the story. Drawing can elicit some insightful responses that might not otherwise be captured. Individuals may also want to write about their drawings. An opportunity is presented here to use a paint program on the computer and later perhaps have learners in a higher grade animate the painting into short movies (as described in Chapters 9 and 13).

- *Book covers.* Learners usually have very definite ideas about the appropriateness of a book cover. Some may want to design an alternative cover for *The Miraculous Journey of Edward Tulane.* The cover by Bagram Ibatoulline and his illustrations throughout the book are striking, but what do learners think? What might they create as a cover for this book? The graphics used, the positioning of the title and author's name, and the colours are important elements in creating a book's initial appeal. A book cover can invite readers into the text or be a factor in dissuading them from reading the book. An important facet of a learner's response to a book can be found in the alternative cover he or she might design. Covers created by learners can be displayed along with other items profiling the novel.

- *Dioramas.* Any setting from a book can be used as the starting point in creating a diorama. A number of settings in *The Miraculous Journey of Edward Tulane* lend themselves to this kind of interpretation (e.g., the ocean, the garbage dump, Neal's Diner). Dioramas are frequently made from large shoeboxes, and many odds and ends of materials can be carefully put together to create an effective representation of the setting and atmosphere of the novel as a whole. Dioramas can provide an enticement for other learners to read the book.

- *Advertisements.* If a reader had to create a poster advertising *The Miraculous Journey of Edward Tulane,* what would it be like? Most learners are familiar with movie posters, but what would a publishing company look for in a poster designed to promote a book? What would a prospective reader want to know about the book? What ambience could be created through a poster? What colours would be most effective in portraying this story? After learners have read a novel, an advertising poster can be an exciting way to share their responses to the book with the rest of the class.

- *Wall charts.* There are many kinds of wall charts learners can develop to help themselves understand a book. For *The Miraculous Journey of Edward Tulane,* they might consider creating a timeline that tracks the story's events, the characters that enter the adventures, or the settings of each period of Edward's journey.

After completing novels in literature circles, learners in Denise Barrett's grade 7/8 class developed **digital responses.** Denise asked her students to work either individually or in groups. If working in groups, learners were assessed as a group. Here's what the assignment looked like:

There is a saying that a picture is worth a thousand words. Imagine what you could say if you added sound and text to that picture. The possibilities are endless! ☺

Now that you have read a complete narrative in your literature circle, you are going to create a digital representation of the novel.

In order to effectively represent your novel, you must focus on some very important elements of narratives or storytelling:

✓ Theme
✓ Character
✓ Location (not just physical but relational as well)

After watching and hearing your digital representation, viewers should have a clear understanding of your overall impression of the novel. This assignment is not about re-enacting the plot; instead, it is about creating your authentic "experience" of the novel.

Requirements:

• Your (re)presentation should be at least 3 minutes long.
• Your (re)presentation should include a mix of:
  • Images (moving, still, or both)
  • Sound
  • Text

Three of the digital representations created by Denise's students in response to John Boyne's *The Boy In the Striped Pajamas* and Philip Pullman's *The Golden Compass* can be accessed on TeacherTube. Do take a look at these projects online. It is quite clear from these responses that readers were moved by the books and inspired to go beyond the characters and the plot line to probe world events, societal values, and human relationships.

Benton and Fox (1985) suggested that educators, when considering various oral, dramatic, visual, and written response activities, ask themselves two fundamental questions: "Will this activity enable the reader to look back on the text and to develop the meanings he has already made?" and "Does what I plan to do bring reader and text closer together, or does it come between them?" (p. 108). Activities that meet the criteria set by Benton and Fox will extend learners' reading transactions, enhance their meaning making from the text, and avoid any unnecessarily lengthy examination of the text that may detract from the reading experience.

Fan Fiction

Fan fiction is a genre that is authored by readers (fans) and builds upon popular culture and media, including books, movies, video games, music, and comics. Although generally conducted outside of school, there's much educators can learn from it that can apply to classroom contexts. Fan fiction is sometimes written to prolong a deep immersion in the story world, or it can be written to parody or critique that world, but it is always written by and for individuals who are familiar with the original work. Today, most fan fiction is written online. Various websites are devoted to this type of fiction, in particular, http://www.fanfiction.net.

A quick scan of the fan fiction listed on that site reveals many of the book titles mentioned in *Constructing Meaning*, including *Private Peaceful* by Michael Morpurgo, *The Boy in the Striped Pajamas* by John Boyne, and *The Graveyard Book* by Neil Gaimon.

In fan fiction, authors pick up the characters and plotlines of the original work, and creatively deepen them by extending plot and timelines, developing new relationships among characters, and exploring new themes. The audience has the option of publicly posting feedback or reviews of the work. Participation in fan fiction crosses national, linguistic, and socioeconomic boundaries, and researchers (for example, Rebecca Black, 2009) have found fan fiction to be a most appropriate genre for English language learners to engage with. Readers' responses to fan fiction are an important part of the process; they are usually supportive and helpful, and generally aim to help the writer improve his or her writing skills.

Mackey and McClay (2008) maintained, "Using fan fiction as a teaching resource offers an opportunity to help young writers and readers to articulate some of their tacit understandings and subject them to critical scrutiny" (p. 143). By incorporating fan fiction writing strategies into school activities, they believe, learners will experience "congruence between their recreational literacy practices and the literacy practices promoted in their schools" (p. 146).

These researchers also noted that writing good fan fiction is not easy. They urge educators to provide good models of fan fiction writing. Learners are more likely to experience success with fan fiction if they are given a choice of fictional world to focus on and choice of presentation (e.g., narrative or movie script). Mackey and McClay believe that fan fiction writing can provide a scaffold for narrative forms and conventions for young writers; however, they encourage educators to create their own fan sites using school or district websites that provide some control of postings.

Fan fiction is closely allied with "dependent authorship" (Adams, 1987). Learners reading *The Miraculous Journey of Edward Tulane* have written diary entries for Abilene and Nellie; a letter from Maggie to Bryce 10 years after the story ended; a poem Abilene could have written after her visit to Lucius Clarke's shop; a dream that Bull, the hobo, might have had; and a biography of Bryce. This kind of writing from "inside" the literary work can take learners into a deeper understanding of it. It also underscores the intertextual elements of any piece of writing, "recognising that every literary work is a wellspring for others" (Meyers, 1997).

Responding to Information Books

Many readers, especially boys, select nonfiction books for their reading pleasure. When planning opportunities for responding to information books, educators can access many of the activities listed in the sections above. Readers can "play" with both fiction and nonfiction works, and either extend the work or build upon it. Rosenblatt (1978) maintained that all reader responses must be based on the text itself, as a transaction between the reader and the work being read. We suggest, however, that the book's content is of particular importance when learners are responding to information books in school. Learners particularly need opportunities to respond in ways that incorporate and are aligned with the historical timelines, scientific facts, real people, and events that are contained within nonfiction materials.

When responding to fiction and poetry, learners frequently engage in factual discussions about how things work or what happened during certain periods in history, pursuing facts to support their interpretation and appreciation of a text. Janet McConaghy's students (see Chapter 3) engaged in discussions about living conditions in historical times when they discussed Avi's book of fiction *The True Confessions of Charlotte Doyle*. When exploring information books, just as with fiction, learners can respond through creating a map, a scrapbook, an advertising poster, a character's diary entry, a book cover, an interview with a character, and so forth, but the responses must remain true to the factual parameters established in the book. Activities focus more fully on exploring and discovering the content of the text.

Responding to information books can also lead seamlessly into engagements with critical literacy. *Locomotive* by Brian Floca provides intriguing possibilities for extending and enhancing learners' thinking. This Caldecott Medal winner is about the opening of the U.S. transcontinental railway in 1869. The questions presented in Box 2.3 in Chapter 2 (p. 47) can be used as a starting point for engaging learners in critical reflection and inquiry. For example, if learners have access to a hardcover edition with a paper dust jacket, they may address the question, "Why does Floca depict the locomotive on the dust jacket, while beneath it on the hardcover, he presents a vast herd of bison?" More discussion questions might include these:

- How does the opening of the transcontinental railway in the 19th century parallel recent innovations that have changed society and the lives of millions of people?
- What issues do such innovations raise?
- Who are the people who benefit from the events depicted in Floca's book?
- Whose voices are depicted?
- Whose voices are left out?
- Is there another point of view?
- What was the cost (in various terms) associated with the opening of the rail line?
- What was the world like for the people in this book (the family, the crew, the other workers)?
- Which people have power in this book?
- What is the author's underlying message?
- How has the author used language to position the reader?
- What are the design features of this text? Why were they included?

These are questions a sensitive and engaged educator can pose to learners in the elementary grades as well as to older readers. In thinking about these questions, and developing their responses, learners in dialogue groups can engage more deeply with what they are reading. They can connect the reading material to their funds of knowledge and ponder how "this book" makes them think of "other books," how it makes them think of themselves or other people they know, and how it makes them think about the world.

Assessing Response Activities

Response activities are usually conducted in small groups or as individual writing activities. Educators assess learners' growth during these activities on an ongoing basis, and the assessment practices are usually formative—they help the educator to monitor an individual's development and they provide input into instructional planning. When learners are engaged in group activities, assessment is usually completed through an educator's observations: listening to and talking with learners as they discuss books and engage in various response activities—drama, digital media, or written. The listening and speaking assessment practices suggested in Chapter 3 are particularly applicable here. Educators also carefully read or examine the products of group work and engage in conversations with learners about such artifacts and their production.

Educators who work with literature circles and discussion groups have to do a lot of listening in their classrooms. Because well-planned and well-implemented response activities encourage learners to use high-level critical and creative thinking skills, educators try to discover how learners interpret their reading; how they apply their ideas to the world around them, both in and out of school; how they attend to the language of a book; what they learn as a result of their reading; how they dialogue with others in their group; how they listen and acknowledge the ideas of others; what questions they raise; and how they express their own ideas and responses. If educators are to effectively monitor and assess learners' growth as readers through literature circles or novel studies, they need to

- read the books learners are reading
- sit in on the circles or group discussions (some educators take an active role in them)
- keep anecdotal/observational notes on each learner's progress
- use checklists where appropriate
- confer with learners and keep notes
- monitor the work samples and portfolios

One group of educators identified the following criteria for guiding their assessment of learners' responses to literature (Bainbridge, Coleman, & Gellner, 2004):*

1. Growth in responding to literature
   - ❏ responsibility and ownership
   - ❏ personal connections with the book
   - ❏ appreciation of multiple interpretations of a text
   - ❏ critical reading and critical literacy
   - ❏ increase in repertoire of responses to literature

2. Growth as a strategic reader
   - ❏ views self as a successful reader
   - ❏ demonstrates metacognitive awareness of the process of reading
   - ❏ develops knowledge, strategies, and skills

For each of these areas, the educators developed checklists for use in their classrooms. Box 12.1 presents their checklist for the area "Critical reading and critical literacy."

---

* J. Bainbridge, W. Coleman, and J. Gellner. "Assessing children's growth in literature circles and discussion groups." *READ: Reading, Exploration and Discovery. The Journal of the Louisiana Reading Association, Vol. 25*(1), 2004, pp. 21–32.

BOX 12.1

ASSESSMENT CRITERIA FOR CRITICAL READING AND CRITICAL LITERACY

Date: _____

Student's name: _____

In discussions and/or written responses,* the learner:	Rarely	Sometimes	Usually	Frequently	Always
Questions or wonders about points in the text					
Understands that texts reflect a particular historical, cultural, and social context					
Can detect stereotypes, hidden agendas, and so on (No text is neutral.)					
Shows increased awareness of social or ethical issues arising from text					
Analyzes the author's intent or purpose for writing text (e.g., persuasion, ideology, explanation)					
Comments:					

*Indicate on the checklist whether you've seen the characteristic in D (discussion) or in W (written response).

The assessment of response journals is most effective when educators read learners' journals frequently and take the time to respond to the entries, either in brief notes in the journal itself, or on sticky notes on the relevant pages. Educators usually take in four or five journals every few days so that they can respond to learners' ideas regularly, and individuals receive feedback on their entries in a timely fashion. They engage in a brief written conversation with learners, noting interesting comments, applauding thoughtful ideas, and asking questions that encourage deeper thinking about an issue. Educators often write notes to themselves about a learner's work immediately after reading the journal and also provide feedback on how the learner is functioning and how he or she can improve the work.

Educators such as Jan Smith and Carol Walters try to refrain from making summative judgments about journal work, and they do not give grades. Instead they devise simple rubrics based on performance criteria and divided into levels. These rubrics include information that will help learners understand what they do well and how they can improve their work. In his book *Response Journals Revisited*, Les Parsons (2001) presented a number of checklists for educators and learners and some basic rubrics for assessing response journals. These are based on educator expectations and routines agreed upon in the classroom in regard to working with response journals. Box 12.2 presents an assessment guide based on suggestions made by Parsons.

BOX 12.2

Level	Criteria
Noncompliant	Insufficient reading Insufficient number and/or length of responses Content superficial or perfunctory Learner–educator conference required
Functional	Sufficient reading accomplished Sufficient number and length of responses Responses characterized by frequent retelling, likes, and dislikes, occasional relating to personal experience, some prediction
Extended	All routines established as well as some additional reading and responding Responses additionally characterized by brief retelling when necessary, frequent relating to personal experience, prediction, reasons offered for opinions and conclusions
Independent	All routines established as well as considerable additional reading and responding Responses additionally characterized by recognition of characters' motivations, linking of cause and effect, opinions usually supported by evidence from the text, awareness of author/illustrator's purposes

ASSESSMENT GUIDE FOR RESPONSE JOURNALS

BOOK SELECTION

This section of *Constructing Meaning* explores the definition of good literature and who makes that determination. Which awards are devoted to children's and young adult literature? Which books should be selected for use in the classroom, and how are decisions made? The confounding question facing most educators is, Who decides what constitutes "quality" books for children and young adults?

Children, parents, educators, and librarians are all involved in making decisions about purchasing or selecting books for school and home. When it comes to prestigious awards for children's and young adult literature, however, mainly adults on library associations and other committees make the decisions. Examples include the Amelia Francis Howard-Gibbon Award and Governor General's Award in Canada, the Caldecott and Newbery awards in the United States, and the Kate Greenaway and Carnegie medals in the United Kingdom. We know that young readers' choices of "good" literature frequently vary from adult choices. Children and young adults enjoy books that involve mystery, excitement, humour, and adventure. Educators, on the other hand, often think it is more important that the reader be interested in, and able to identify with, the characters in a story (elements, not surprisingly, ranked much lower by learners). Thus educators and librarians sometimes recommend books that may be good from the perspective of the adult reader but which hold less appeal for young readers. The result is that these book suggestions are often ignored.

A number of "Children's Choice" awards exist at the regional level in Canada and at the state level in the United States. Voting for the awards is often conducted through the schools in collaboration with local public libraries. In order to vote, learners must have read a certain number of titles from a list created by educators and librarians. The lists consist of recent books but not necessarily those published in the last year. The Silver Birch Award in Ontario, the Manitoba Young Reader's Choice Award, the Rocky Mountain Book Award in Alberta, and the Red Cedar Award in British Columbia are examples of "Children's Choice" awards in Canada. The awards are highly regarded by authors and illustrators, and they provide young readers with a chance to show their support for the books they like.

We have to ask, If a book is good, what is it good *for*? Is it a challenging reading experience that will delight readers and help them become *better* readers by showing them something new? Is it a good book for taking on vacation and reading on the beach? Is it a good book for teaching more about language arts skills, or for helping readers learn how to do something of special interest to them, such as keeping a healthy tropical aquarium? Is it a good book because it enables the reader to escape from real life or see life differently?

In trying to answer questions such as these, educators, librarians, and scholars of children's and young adult literature are coming to realize how difficult it is to describe the specific characteristics or features of "quality" literature. A book that demonstrates how to create a healthy tropical aquarium will differ enormously from a book of short stories. A book that a person finds so notable that she or he wants to keep a copy for a long time may be very different from the paperback picked up as reading material for a long plane trip. Clearly then, describing quality in each of these cases must vary according to the format of the book, the purpose of the author, and the purpose, interests, and reading experiences of the reader.

Guidelines for Appropriate Selection of Children's Literature

When selecting materials to include in a classroom or school library, educators and librarians make every effort to choose books that meet the needs of both learners and the curriculum. Knowledge of child development and the literary quality of books, as well as knowledge of the provincial programs of study and of curriculum expectations, help educators make appropriate selections. Critics might say that "book selection" is simply a code for a librarian's own brand of censorship, but as Roberts (1996, p. 19) asserts, there are distinct differences between selection and censorship:

> Selection is a positive process that supports intellectual freedom when the selector considers resources in a holistic manner with the intent of including as many as possible in the library collection. Resources are selected objectively, according to set criteria, without regard for a selector's personal biases. Conversely, censorship is a negative process in which the censor searches for reasons, either internal or external, to exclude a resource.

The selection of print materials for use in schools is a complex issue, for it is difficult to say in a public education system who should decide what learners should and should not read. There is also a difference between making book selections for a school library and selecting material that will be used for teaching purposes in a classroom. The debate involves freedom of expression and beliefs about what is appropriate for young readers, what is moral and what is immoral, and what is acceptable and not acceptable in society. It is highly likely that most learners will confront difficult and disturbing ideas as they grow up. Reading and discussing a broad range of literature can help them become critical thinkers and thoughtful human beings capable of making sound judgments, both as individuals and as members of society.

The selection debate relates directly to critical, or emancipatory, literacy, presented in Chapter 1. It is a compelling and difficult issue, and one that educators are frequently required to address.

In 1974, the Canadian Library Association issued a statement on intellectual freedom that was subsequently adopted by the Canadian School Library Association. Two parts of that statement are of particular relevance for educators. The first asserts that it is a person's fundamental right to have access to all expressions of knowledge, creativity, and intellectual activity and to be able to express one's thoughts publicly. The second states that libraries must guarantee and provide access to all expressions of knowledge and intellectual activity, including those elements that conventional society might deem unacceptable or unpopular (Canadian Library Association, 1974). Thus, anyone who endorses this statement, and who thereby advocates selection as opposed to censorship of materials, still has the right to object to certain books if he or she so chooses, but not to insist on their removal from library shelves so that others are denied access to them.

Advocates of book selection respect the learner's intellectual freedom (and innate common sense) and believe that adults have an obligation to be honest with young readers. This approach to selection does not argue that all books for children and young adults are of equal quality and equal value, or that they are even appropriate for learners of all ages, but it does assert that young readers have the right of access to the best literature and learning resources available.

The most important things educators can do when engaged in selecting reading materials are to be aware of their own biases and values; to stay current with issues, themes, and book publications and reviews; and to maintain files of policy statements, useful resources, procedures for dealing with challenges to materials, and guidelines from recognized authorities. ("Challenges" are those occasions where books or other materials are considered by an individual or group to be inappropriate for the audience, and a request is made for the material to be removed from the classroom or library.) As teacher-librarian Kathy Oster mentioned in Chapter 11, many professional resources and tools are available to aid educators and librarians in selecting books. By far the best resources are professional journals. *CM: Canadian Review of Materials* provides book reviews and profiles of Canadian authors and illustrators. *Canadian Children's Literature*, published through the University of Winnipeg, provides reviews of Canadian publications as well as articles about Canadian children's literature. *School Libraries in Canada*, a journal of the Canadian Library Association, contains book reviews, author/illustrator profiles, and well-informed articles on school librarianship in Canada. *Teacher Librarian*, published jointly in Canada and the United States (out of Toronto and Maryland), presents articles that reflect literature-related concerns common to both countries. Other worthy professional journals include *Language Arts*, *The Reading Teacher*, and *The Horn Book*.

In addition to journals, a variety of other resources are available to help educators with book selection. One of these is the *Our Choice* catalogue, which can also be found online, issued annually by the Canadian Children's Book Centre in Toronto. It lists recommended materials published every year in Canada, including fiction and nonfiction books, DVDs, and CDs.

Child selecting a book in library

Canadian Book Review Annual, an evaluative guide to Canadian-authored, English-language publications, is also helpful. It reviews the year's scholarly publications, reference materials, and publications for young readers. The emphasis is on analyzing and evaluating materials, with brief descriptions of the books reviewed.

Selecting books and knowing which new books are available can be overwhelming to a beginning teacher. Educator Carol Walters says, "Language and literacy is a massive subject area, but if you keep literature at the centre of it, you can do a lot. I would advise beginning teachers to get to know their colleagues and talk about books with them. Ask which books are favourites. Get to know the person in charge of the school library and visit the public library as well. Get to know the latest and best information books, because a lot of readers choose those books for free reading, not only for information for a school project. There's a lot to stay on top of, but you can do it if you network with colleagues and ask questions when you need to."

As this section has shown, many book selection tools are available in Canada for learners, beginning teachers, and librarians who want to engage their learners with the very best of children's and young adult literature. Information about book censorship is also available. Since censorship and challenges to books and periodicals in school libraries are unpredictable and usually emotional, it is critical that educators try to remain up-to-date and well informed about processes for dealing with book challenges. We discuss these issues in the next section.

Censorship of Children's Materials

As already noted, there is a clear difference between selecting materials for use in schools and censoring these materials. Where book selection uses positive criteria to determine which books to place in a collection, censorship seeks to remove, suppress, or restrict books *already present* in a collection. Censorship is generally ineffective in ensuring that only the most "appropriate" of books are read by learners, yet it can be extremely disruptive to the life of a school. Occasionally, a **challenged book**, removed from library shelves, will become a best-seller and be read more widely than if it had not been challenged.

School libraries and classrooms encounter far more challenges to books than do public libraries in North America. Educators have a responsibility to fulfill their professional obligations to learners by providing learners with the very best in children's and young adult literature—material that challenges learners to think critically and explore new ideas and perspectives. Educators have a further role, however, which is to help learners become more thoughtful and critical about their choices of reading materials, and to help them develop their abilities to think for themselves and make sound judgments.

Educators are often surprised to see which books have been commonly challenged. *Persepolis* by Marjane Satrapi, *The Giver* by Lois Lowry, *The Paper Bag Princess* by Robert Munsch, and *Harry Potter and the Philosopher's Stone* by J. K. Rowling have all received censorship threats. But in addition to "official" challenges are the indirect instances of censorship, in which books go missing, have pages removed, or are ripped up or defaced. Explicit procedures detailing how book complaints will be received and reviewed can be set up by school boards or by individual schools. Information about past legal rulings, groups behind challenges, and approaches to resisting challenges is available from organizations such as the Book and Periodical Council (Toronto), the Canadian Library Association (Toronto), the National Council of Teachers of English (Urbana, Illinois), and the International Literacy Association (Newark, Delaware). An extremely useful resource is *The Students' Right to Read*, published by the National Council of Teachers of English (http://www.ncte.org/positions/statements/righttoreadguideline). The website contains sample forms for collecting a statement of concern from a complainant, a sample letter to a complainant, instructions for establishing an evaluating committee, and suggestions for evaluating the complaint.

The National Council of Teachers of English and the International Literacy Association have also developed a resource, *Rationales for Challenged Books* (http://www.ncte.org/action/anti-censorship/rationales), which includes rationales for commonly challenged materials for kindergarten through grade 12 (though the emphasis is on publications for grades 7 to 12). Publications are listed both by title and author on this web resource, and information is provided about book challenges and on what schools and libraries can do to counter challenges.

Issues and Controversies

At the present time, challenges and censorship activities are most likely to involve books depicting same-sex family relationships (gay and lesbian couples). All learners have the right of access to these books in the school library, but the issue becomes whether the books should be used in classrooms for teaching purposes. The debate reminds educators how difficult it can be to ensure that all learners have access to books about a range of social and family contexts, while not insisting that all learners read the same books.

No less controversial has been the issue of racial discrimination in literature. In the middle-to-late 20th century, it was not uncommon to find books that were explicitly racist in their treatment of visible ethnic minorities such as Aboriginal people. When many of these books were originally published, society in general was not sensitive to the discrimination portrayed in them. Since the 1948 Universal Declaration of Human Rights by the United Nations General Assembly, book publishers and educators have fought hard to prevent the publication of books that are clearly discriminatory.

Consider the first edition of Laura Lee Hope's *The Bobbsey Twins,* published in 1904. The reader was told what a good mother Flossie was to her dolls, for she protected them from a black doll given to her by one of the servants. Flossie told her friends that the doll didn't really belong in the family. However, since Flossie's mother explained that there were "no asylums for black orphans," the doll was allowed to stay with the others—separated from them by a piece of cardboard. Given the nature of American society at that time, it was hardly surprising to see such blatant racial discrimination in a book for children. What is surprising is that the piece was not removed from the book until the 1950s.

One of the earliest "multicultural" books in North America was *The Story of Little Black Sambo* by Helen Bannerman, first published in 1899. The book was set in India but has illustrations depicting black characters. Although Bannerman's book has received much criticism for its racial stereotyping, the story has remained hugely popular. It has been retold numerous times and has been published in two newer editions. *The Story of Little Babaji by* Bannerman and Marcellino (1996) contains the original text, except that the characters are given authentic Indian names—Fred Marcellino's illustrations place the story clearly in India. *Sam and the Tigers: A New Retelling of Little Black Sambo* was written by Julius Lester and illustrated by Jerry Pinkney. This book, also published in 1996, depicts black characters, but the fantasy setting (Sam-sam-sa-mara) removes it from any specific geographic location.

Stereotypical images abound in literature, from the works of Shakespeare to titles by L. M. Montgomery and Mark Twain. *(Anne of Green Gables* was first published in 1908; *The Adventures of Huckleberry Finn* was first published in 1885.) The central feature of many of the American classics containing racist stereotypes was the presence of "indolent, happy-go-lucky slaves" (Miller-Lachmann, 1992). Other books, such as the 1938 title *The Five Chinese Brothers* by Claire Huchet Bishop, seemed to promote the stereotype that all Chinese people look alike. Such books now provide a springboard for discussing issues such as racism, slavery, social class, and stereotyping in general.

When asked about the way she deals with sensitive issues in books, educator Carol Walters says she has never had a parent complain. She tries to be sensitive about what is appropriate in the community, and she sends book lists home every once in a while so the parents can see which books learners are reading in response groups and which books she is reading aloud to them. If any of the parents want to borrow the books to read themselves, Carol is always delighted to put a copy in their hands.

Literature portrays all aspects of human nature, and children's literature is no exception. Through the library collections that educators make available in schools, students can learn to appreciate the human condition, to discriminate good from bad and just from unjust, and to make sense of the world and their feelings toward it in a new and deeply personal way. As they select literature for children, educators face the challenge of putting their own feelings and biases aside and presenting a balanced and equitable view of our diverse global community.

SUMMARY

"Reader response" refers to the events that occur within a reader when he or she reads a piece of text. That response is part of the meaning-making process, and as such it is an important component of a language arts program. Rosenblatt (1978) maintained that a response to literature is dictated to a considerable extent by the purpose for reading or the *stance* from which the reader approaches the text. A stance can be anywhere on a continuum from efferent at one end, where the reader seeks information of some kind, to aesthetic at the other, where the reader focuses on appreciating what is read. A text first evokes an aesthetic or "lived through" response, and then evokes a more efferent response as the reader consciously thinks about the text and the reading experience.

Through reading works of literature and responding to them, learners come to understand how texts work, what constitutes a good book, how language can be used in different ways to create different meanings and effects—in short, how to become readers, not just people able to read. Learners are more likely to take ownership of the reading process and to understand that there is no right "answer" to literature when they are invited to respond to a text (though, as Rosenblatt says, some responses are more legitimate or appropriate than others). Responses to literature can be captured and represented in written, oral, visual, or dramatic form.

An important vehicle for exploring a text is the response group or book club. Educators and researchers have discovered that learners benefit from orally sharing and shaping their responses to books and that successful group work can enhance their enjoyment of their reading. Literature response journals provide opportunities for written reflection on what learners are currently reading, as do literature circles, novel studies, and readers' workshops, as well as drama, art, and other multimedia activities.

When selecting materials to include in a classroom or school library, educators and librarians make every effort to choose books and web resources that meet learners' needs as well as the needs of the curriculum. The selection of print and media resources for use in schools is a complex issue, for it is difficult to say in a public education system who should decide what learners should and should not read. There is, however, a clear difference between selecting materials for use in schools and censoring these materials. Where book selection uses positive criteria to determine which books to place in a collection, censorship seeks instead to remove, suppress, or restrict books already present in a collection. Guidelines for handling complaints about books can be established by school boards or by individual schools, and many agencies provide guidelines for creating such processes.

SELECTED PROFESSIONAL RESOURCES

Allington, R. (2006). *What really matters for struggling readers: Designing research-based programs* (2nd ed.). Boston, MA: Pearson/Allyn and Bacon.

In this book, Allington raises important issues such as how much time learners are *engaged* with reading in school, and how much time they spend reading at school. The time spent reading, both in and outside of school, is critical. It's also one thing to stress with parents. Allington urges us to encourage parents to read *with* their children, to read *to* their children, and to *listen* to their children reading. Most of all, he says, we can encourage parents to talk with their children and teenagers about what they are reading. The book deals with developing instruction for struggling readers, improving classroom instruction, and making support available for older struggling readers. Teaching reading doesn't stop in grade 6 or in grade 8!

continued

Calkins, L., with McEvoy, M. (2006). *Literary essays: Writing about reading.* Portsmouth, NH: Firsthand/Heinemann.

Lucy Calkins makes the connection between learners' responses to literature and teaching reading. She shows educators how to support learners in reading well, writing well, and reading actively. The key is in demonstration. Calkins models how to help learners to "write inside the story," study characters, develop ideas, use stories as evidence, and write personal essays. She shows how to keep lists, favourite quotations, and other material, and she emphasizes the importance of rereading parts of a text, as well as rereading your own writing. She suggests mini-lessons and focuses on talking about books as well as writing about them. In sum, this book is about teaching learners to become "literary essayists" and thoughtful, reflective readers and writers.

Gear, A. (2006). *Reading power: Teaching students to think while they read.* Markham, ON: Pembroke.

This practical book shows educators how to teach specific strategies for learners to use while they are reading. The book is organized around five reading strategies: connecting, questioning, visualizing, inferring, and transforming. Gear uses quality literature to demonstrate how an educator can model, encourage practice, and foster independent reading. She includes lists of books organized according to grade level and includes tips for developing classroom book collections.

13

New Media

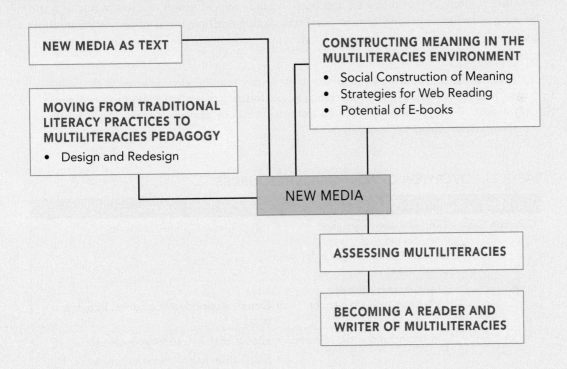

As evidenced throughout *Constructing Meaning*, multiliteracies pedagogies acknowledge that multiple kinds of communication channels and modes of delivery across diverse cultural and social settings are possible. By this point in the book, readers will be aware of the range of ways in which learners may come to and practise literacies, and how multiliteracies pedagogies can offer expanded opportunities for learners to construct meaning. The goal of this chapter is to highlight how new media (such as those described in Table 13.1) in particular can be used in conjunction with a variety of modes to support educators in organizing and preparing to teach from a multiliteracies perspective. Specifically, this chapter explores how new media in a pedagogy of multiliteracies can offer guiding insights to help educators develop their professional wisdom. A multiliteracies approach expands the definition of literacy teaching and learning to include accessing, creating, and redesigning multiple forms of text, using multiple communication modes (e.g., linguistic, oral, visual, and kinesthetic). In particular, a multiliteracies approach will

> enable students to achieve the … twin goals for literacy learning: creating access to the evolving language of work, power, and community, and fostering the critical engagement necessary for them to design their social futures and achieve success through fulfilling employment. (New London Group, 1996, p. 60)

TABLE 13.1 **OVERVIEW OF NEW MEDIA RESOURCES**

Tool	Description	Source
Common Craft	Three-minute videos that explain many of the new media in clear language for most ages	• http://www.commoncraft.com/
Email	Sending and retrieving electronic mail via Internet	Various • Google Apps Education Edition includes email
E-books	Texts rendered in digital form	• eBooks.com: http://www.ebooks.com • Fictionwise: http://www.fictionwise.com • Octavo: http://www.octavo.com
Discussion tools (threaded or non-threaded)	Engender and encourage debate; negotiate meaning	Platforms such as Moodle, WebCt, and Blackboard
Shared document	Shared workspaces for groups; allow sharing, editing	• Googledocs: http://docs.google.com/ • TitanPad: http://titanpad.com/ • Zoho Writer: http://writer.zoho.com/
Interactive whiteboard software	Visual sharable forum for collaborative work	• http://www.groupboard.com/whiteboard.html • http://www.scriblink.com/
Blog	Active learning tool to track and record thoughts, learning, and ideas	• https://www.blogger.com/start • http://edublogs.org/ • http://www.wordpress.com

TABLE 13.1 **OVERVIEW OF NEW MEDIA RESOURCES (*CONTINUED*)**

Tool	Description	Source
Videoblogging		• http://www.freevlog.org • http://www.pbs.org/teachers/ (Video for teachers) • TVO public archive: http://archive.tvo.org/ • National Film Board of Canada: http://www.nfb.ca/
Padlet	Online notice board	• https://padlet.com
Podcasting	Audio file distribution	• Education Podcast Network: http://www.edupodcastnetwork.com • http://www.podcasting-tools.com/
Remixing, DJ culture		• http://techtv.mit.edu/collections/newmedialiteracies:1000
Video, Video Blog, Vlog	Networked public culture	• YouTube: http://www.youtube.com/ • TeacherTube: http://www.teachertube.com/ • An anthropological introduction to YouTube: http://il.youtube.com/watch?v=TPAO-IZ4_hU&feature=related
Wiki	Server software for collaborative creation and sharing of pages:	• http://www.wikispaces.com/site/for/teachers • Wikipedia: http://wikipedia.org • http://www.youtube.com/watch?v=-dnL00TdmLY • Wikipedia for Educators: How K–12 teachers can use Wikipedia in the classroom (Will Richardson): • http://www.archive.org/details/WillRichardsonWikipediaforEducators
Video conferencing	Collaborative video conference	• Skype: http://www.skype.com • Adobe Connect
Slideshare program	Share presentations	• http://www.slideshare.net/
Peer-to-peer messaging	Instant message tool	• MSN • Twitter • Google Chat
Classroom communication systems	Interactive, graphic response	• Classtalk; EduCue PRS; eInstruction CPS; Clickers
Group communication around image, document, or video	"Talk" or "write" about a shared artifact	• VoiceThread: http://voicethread.com/#home • Sketchlot: http://www.sketchlot.com • Glogster: http://edu.glogster.com/

(continued)

TABLE 13.1 **OVERVIEW OF NEW MEDIA RESOURCES (*CONTINUED*)**

Tool	Description	Source
CoSketch.com	Multi-user online whiteboard	• http://www.cosketch.com/
Creating comics in the classroom		• Bitstrips for Schools: http://www .bitstripsforschools.com/
Assessment tools	Exam tools Rubric generator	• SurveyMonkey, EasyTestMaker, Quia RubiStar: rubric maker
Forming groups	Conveners	• http://www.Googlegroups.com • http://www.Facebook.com
Teacher connections	Cross-classroom collaboration connections	• http://www.teachersconnecting.com/
Resource sharing	Multiliteracies—across grades, subject areas	• The Salty Chip: A Canadian Multiliteracies Collaborative: http://www.saltychip .com/
Social network sites	Socializing, sharing artifacts, developing support networks	• http://www.ning.com • Facebook: http://www.facebook.com/ • MySpace: http://www.myspace.com/ • Bebo: http://www.bebo.com/ • Google+: https://plus.google.com • Twiducate—free resource for educators: http://twiducate.com/about.php
Image sharing	Photo-sharing network	• Pics4Learning—copyright-friendly images: http://pics4learning.com/index .php?view=about • Flikr: http://www.flickr.com/ • Google Images: http://www.google .com/imghp
Virtual worlds		• Second life: http://secondlife.com/
Remix		• Total Recut: http://www.totalrecut.com • Political Remix: http://www .politicalremixvideo.com • Anime Music Videos: http://www .animemusicvideos.org/home/home.php • Machinima: http://www.machinima.com • FanFiction: http://www.fanfiction.net • Storybird—Collaborative Storytelling: http://storybird.com/ • PinkyDinkyDo: http://www .pinkydinkydoo.com/storybox.html • StoryMaker: http://www.carnegielibrary .org/kids/storymaker/storymaker .swf

NEW MEDIA AS TEXT

Further to the earlier discussions of critical literacy in *Constructing Meaning*, it is understood that a pedagogy of multiliteracies includes helping learners understand that the ways in which knowledge is generated, categorized, given value, and made available (or not) reflect the choices of those with power over information. In the current context, what are described as **web 2.0 tools** reflect a significant shift into a **participatory culture** in which users are trusted co-developers with increasing influence on communication, design, and development.

With these additional opportunities come responsibilities. Learners and educators need to bring a critical perspective to all media, new or old. Paul Clark (1999) explained this, using pictures as an example:

> Students need to learn to examine pictures from a critical perspective. They are not only a rich source of information and insights, but deliberate constructions, rather than mere reflections of reality; and as constructions, they represent the purposes and perspectives of their creators. Coupled with this is the need to actively examine visuals for the meanings which underlie their surface images. In order to make them yield all that they have to offer, students spend much time studying them and learn to ask compelling questions of them. (p. 361)

Similarly, we need to understand the ways in which commercial web search engines are driven by a corporate "for profit" ideology. Educators can use publicly available, non-profit digital archives such as these:

- ibiblio: http://www.ibiblio.org
- OAIster: http://www.oclc.org/oaister.en.html
- LibriVox: https://librivox.org/
- CBC Digital Archives: http://www.cbc.ca/archives/teachers/
- Library and Archives Canada: http://www.bac-lac.gc.ca/eng/Pages/home.aspx
- Open Education Resources (OER) Commons: https://www.oercommons.org/
- Images Canada: http://www.imagescanada.ca/index-e.html

In addition to the necessary cautions and ongoing need for critical information literacy, new media open up multiple, accessible avenues to make meaning with a variety of texts, across cultures, for various purposes that bring significant implications for reading and writing into the classroom. In the following sections, I explore some examples of **new media**, and the considerations that such technologies bring to bear on the learner.

A group of researchers (Ito, Horst, Bittanti, boyd, Herr-Stephenson, Lange, Pascoe, and Robinson) engaged in the Digital Youth Project. In their 2008 report, *Living and Learning with New Media: Summary of Findings from the Digital Youth Project*, they noted four areas of focus: genres of participation, networked publics, peer-based learning, and new media literacy. In the genres of participation category, Ito et al. (2008) further delineated the subcategories of friendship-driven (e.g., Facebook) and interest-driven (e.g., Twitter). *Networked publics* is the term that was selected to describe youth participation in "public culture that is supported by online networks … to connect, communicate and develop public identities" (pp. 10–11). Peer-based learning intersects with both, and draws attention to the "opportunit[ies] for learning" that exist outside of schools and that result from interactions with peers. Finally, the category of new media literacy relates to examining the types of literacies youth are engaged with in their everyday lives.

Not surprisingly, it is clear that while new literacies have emerged with some familiar conventions and rules of traditional literacy, many have been modified to suit a changing context, purpose, and audience. Just as shorthand developed out of a need for stenographers to take notes in meetings, the instant message culture has responded to the affordances and constraints of having mobile devices for communication with limited character input. These adaptations and redesigns are spawning hybrid genres of discourse familiar to regular users in the community, but often disconcerting to the public. Box 13.1 provides an overview of some of the new literacies that youth are engaging with.

BOX 13.1

NEW LITERACIES IN WHICH YOUTH ENGAGE

The read/write web	A website is a collection of related pages that address particular topics or areas of interest. The designer of the site might author, select, and arrange a series of texts (including images, sound, hyperlinks, and video) according to the perceived interests of an imagined audience or to express knowledge in nonlinear ways. Hypertext is the form of text used in websites. The use of multimodal texts as well as hypertexts allows readers much more control and decision making about how they will engage with the text. The ability to easily publish and share knowledge, to collaborate with an unlimited audience, and to access information from a vast array of sources is changing the teaching and learning environment. Douglas Rushkoff (2004) predicted that such shifts are providing everyone with an opportunity to contribute to a "society of authorship" that invites us to participate in ways that were previously unimaginable. Within this culture of sharing and collaboration comes the requirement to re-examine issues of privacy, safety, connectivity, and authorship.
Video games	Researchers who have studied video games suggest that the process of engaging in them leads to narrative making and therefore has pedagogical value (Gee, 2007; Squire, 2008). Researcher James Paul Gee argued that video games can teach us important lessons about learning because they provide the player with the scaffolding needed to learn complex skills and to "read" a new setting and set of challenges. Immersion in a video game (or learning activity) prior to being required to learn the technical skills involved, Gee argued, fosters both engagement and situates the learning, making it easier for the learner to make connections. For example, some teachers use video games as a context to teach literary concepts (e.g., describe/explain character, setting, conflict, theme). Another important lesson from video games is that the most powerful learning experiences are social—people prefer to play video games with at least one other person because they learn more about how to play the game and the experience becomes much more enjoyable.

Real-time text-based communication	We live in a connected world. Our interest in communicating with new media has led to the development of a range of ways that many of us use to chat, send and receive messages, and express ourselves. The speed with which we type in a virtual chat (such as MSN or "Messenger") or the limited characters permitted in Twitter (140) have led to a new form of shorthand where normal conventions do not apply. For example, when using IM (Instant Message), SMS (Short Message Service), or Twitter, it is common to see shortcuts with language. Take a look at the left-hand column below and see what you can identify before checking your response in the right-hand column:
	Cul8tr See you later Brb Be right back Fotfl Falling on the floor laughing Cyo See you online Gbtw Get back to work!
	Learners also need to understand practical matters, such as the fact that digital communications are easily shared and information that they provide in social media environments usually becomes the property of another entity (such as Facebook); it may be archived permanently (Clifford, 2010) or shared with unintended audiences. What skills are required to both produce and read such unconventional text? Several educators began experimenting with the new tools after the Royal Shakespeare Company's retelling of *Romeo and Juliet* through the microblogging of six characters on Twitter.
Image/Video sharing	Access to high-quality digital cameras in daily personal devices such as phones have made capturing and sharing images and video one of the most popular web activities in recent years. Websites such as Flickr, YouTube, Vimeo, and TeacherTube provide space to upload, manage, and share video content. The popularity of these tools has spawned numerous applications that make it easy for even young students to capture, upload, and share images and video to a shared site using a single device. Activities such as Vlogging (videoblogging) and Digital Storytelling allow learners to tell stories through the sophisticated manipulation of photographs, digital images, video segments, maps, and drawings, along with sound effects, music, and narration. (For more ideas, see the Flickr Toolbox: http://mashable.com/2007/08/04/flickr-toolbox/.) Some inspired teachers have combined a number of forms for new purposes. Consider, for example, engaging your learners in a *90-Second Newbury Competition* to abridge children's literature into a 90-second video. For an illustration, check out *A Wrinkle in Time in 90 Seconds* at http://jameskennedy.com/90-second-newbery/.

(continued)

Podcasts	Podcasts are portable audio files that allow learners to do basic things, such as listen to audio books or music, or more sophisticated projects that engage them in downloading and following a series of talks or producing their own classroom talk-shows or community radio programs. Programs that teachers can use to index, search, or receive podcasts include
	• iTunes: http://www.itunes.com • Juice: http://juicereceiver.sourceforge.net • FireAnt: http://www.getfireant.com • Mediafly.com: http://www.mediafly.com • PodBean: http://podbean.com
	When students engage in the production of podcasts, they are able to learn about the power of language and the need to communicate clearly and coherently. The basic podcast has three key parts: an introduction, a body, and an "outro." Many are fully scripted and include an introductory music clip fading in and fading out at the end. Consider having students bring their music to class and examine the song lyrics as an introduction to poetry or as an introduction to discussions about gender roles. Classroom applications often include one of the following designs: *Interview:* One person or more is invited to participate in a podcast. Interviews may be conducted in person, via telephone, or via the Internet. *Group talk:* Here, two or more co-hosts may share leadership of the podcast. *Recorded event:* An event, such as a school play, can be recorded for broadcast. *Newscast:* Reflecting a journalistic format, the podcast includes news anchors, special reports, and regular features. *Dramatic reading:* A recording of a dramatic reading of a text is made for audio production and sharing. *Audio guide:* Audio direction or interpretation of a location, cultural artifacts, or an event is provided. *Monologue:* The podcast consists of an individual narration, audioblog, or dramatic reading. *Panelcast:* In a panelcast, a session conducted with a live audience is recorded. (Adapted from King & Gura, 2009, p. 120) For a rich example of educational podcasts, see • http://edtechtalk.com/TeachersTeachingTeachers
Social networks	The proliferation of social networking systems has created numerous opportunities for people to come together in virtual spaces. Facebook, one of the most popular network tools to date, is used by millions of people young and old to share and access new media and information, and stay connected with friends and family. Educators have created classroom networks (such as Nings) that allow them to create virtual communities accessible only to their students or collaborating classrooms around the globe. They talk about literary works, exchange ideas about social justice issues they are championing, or role-play and redesign texts. For an example of an educator who is using social networking in the classroom, see • http://coolcatteacher.blogspot.com/

Blogging	Many educators have found that blogging has motivated their learners to both read and write. Since blogging includes producing text for a broad audience, learners find more pleasure in playing with language. Penrod (2007) reported that a clear purpose, immediacy of feedback, balance of challenge and skill, focused concentration, and creativity are some of the reasons that contribute to increased interest and engagement with blogging as a form of literacy. She noted that blogs reinforce the idea that information and knowledge are not static, and that everyone can participate in the construction of knowledge. Blogs offer a way to integrate many of the new media into one location and provide multidimensional spaces in which to participate in identity formation. As learners gain experience, they learn that they must become more adept "at both writing and critiquing the English language in order to reach their desired audience" (p. 19). Blogging requires students to "select, evaluate and manipulate information ... as well as media in order to highlight important data" (p. 20).

Burke and Rowsell (2008) reminded us to think about the ways in which new textual genres can subtly influence identity formation. All texts engage a variety of devices that may serve to mediate and contribute to the meaning-making process. New media hold great appeal for learners, and in many cases learners have a fairly sophisticated set of skills that allow them to use the technology. Less well developed is an understanding of the textual features that various forms of text present: their affordances and constraints, and how they contribute to meaning making across contexts.

CONSTRUCTING MEANING IN THE MULTILITERACIES ENVIRONMENT

Social Construction of Meaning

The Internet is an ideal environment for the social construction of meaning. As learners navigate through a wide variety of information sources, they discriminate between important and unimportant information, respond to email, blog, and engage with others in electronic chat sessions. In this process, what counts as knowledge is under constant construction, as the "knowledge base on the Internet becomes a function of social interaction among its users" (El-Hindi, 1999, n.p.).

Learning on and with the Internet promotes the active construction of meaning in several ways:

- *Currency.* Learners have immediate access to current information. Nearly all major newspapers publish online versions, and research findings in most fields are now available. Most websites are continuously upgraded.

- *Relevancy.* Learners can choose lines of inquiry and pursue personal interests. Topics are linked and cross-referenced to enable web surfers to navigate their own inquiry pathways.
- *Immediacy.* Readers can learn about events almost as they happen.
- *Multiple perspectives.* Learners using weblinks can view and appraise the same information from a number of viewpoints.
- *Multiple dimensions.* The same event, concept, or topic is often available in multiple formats—text, chart, video, and sound.

The very currency and immediacy of the Internet, however, causes both learners and educators their greatest frustration as sites can appear and disappear overnight. By the time this book is published, several of the websites we reference may have changed their web addresses.

In addition, educators must be responsible for the material learners encounter on the Internet during school time. Educators must work together with learners to teach them the critical skills necessary to evaluate which sites are reputable and useful, how information is represented and presented for a variety of purposes, and how reading only selective pieces we are interested in can reduce our understanding of the "whole." Educators must therefore become web savvy themselves so that they can connect to the experiences their students will encounter.

Strategies for Web Reading

Navigating the web is easy, fun, and time consuming! "Reading" on the web, however, requires a complex set of literacy practices if learners are to develop the level of critical comprehension necessary for deep learning. Within traditional texts, the organization of writing is governed by the logic of time and the sequence of its constituent parts, arranged according to timelines; the organization of the image, however, is governed by the logic of space (Kress, 2003). Our challenge as educators, then, is to reconsider what it means to read and be literate in a digital space.

Most of the learners in K to 8 classrooms today have grown up with computers and access to powerful hand-held digital devices. They bring certain web-based skills into classrooms with them:

- Ability to read visual images—they are intuitive visual communicators;
- Visual-spatial skills—perhaps because of their expertise with games they can integrate the virtual and physical;
- Inductive discovery—they learn better through discovery than by being told;
- Attentional deployment—they are able to shift their attention rapidly from one task to another, and may choose not to pay attention to things that don't interest them;
- Fast response time—they are able to respond quickly and expect rapid responses in return. (Oblinger & Oblinger, 2005, p. 25)

Although we cannot assume that all students arriving in schools today are digitally experienced, most learners possess a relatively sophisticated set of user skills. Often their knowledge and understanding of these skills is implicit and decontextualized. If we think about these skills as a type of "functional grammar" of learning to read digital texts, we can consider strategies to help those less experienced, including many educators, to understand; we can also articulate some basic strategies to scaffold and translate practices into learning. For example, Sutherland-Smith (2002) recommended several strategies for teaching web reading, adapted here:*

1. *Use the "snatch-and-grab" reading technique.* Learners do not read web texts in the same linear fashion as traditional texts. Often, they do not read every web text available. Educators can help readers understand that texts are situated in particular contexts, and that when they read selectively, they are reading a part of the whole. Educators can help readers understand how to skim text to identify a key word or phrase, and copy the required material to another document. Once they have compiled these texts, learners read them in a more detailed manner and cull unwanted material. This technique emphasizes the broad nature of searching and helps individuals obtain a great deal of material in a limited time. (Of course, educators will also model and teach students about the ethical use of texts, and the adherence to appropriate referencing and citation rules. See the slideshare "Creative Commons: What Every Educator Needs to Know" by educator and consultant Rodd Lucier in Table 13.3.)

2. *Focus on refining keyword searches.* Educators explicitly teach readers to narrow the scope of their keyword search to find information more efficiently. For example, narrowing a search from the phrase *printing press* to *invention of* or *history of the printing press* will result in a more manageable and focused list of usable sites.

3. *Use the "chunking technique."* Sutherland-Smith coined this term to show learners ways to break down a complex topic into manageable sections or chunks. For example, when researching the creation of a national airline such as Qantas, the educator can explain how students can think about the topic in chunks, such as when and why the airline was created, and its effects on remote communities. Learners then brainstorm words to use as a search focus.

4. *Provide shortcut lists to sites or search engines.* Educators can provide shortcuts or bookmarks to reliable sites and hints for learners to effectively organize their lists of web addresses.

5. *Limit links.* One strategy to assist learners is to limit the number of links they follow. Doing this helps them refocus on key words or questions and keep on track.

6. *Evaluate nontextual features (images, graphics).* Readers need to learn how to decode visual images and not regard them merely as illustrations. They also need to learn to evaluate visual images and to discern discrepancies between visual images and text information.

In a case study that examined the literacy practices of middle-school students, Burke and Rowsell (2008) observed that readers appeared to move along reading paths governed by their interests, the content of the web, the level of interactivity, and the functionality of the site (e.g., speed and access). Although learners appeared to frequently compare the digital texts to traditional texts, they seemed to focus little on thinking critically about the content as a whole.

---

* W. Sutherland-Smith. Weaving the literacy web: Changes in reading from page to screen. *The Reading Teacher, Vol. 55*(7), 2002, pp. 662–668.

Potential of E-books

E-books have been available for many years, but the introduction of portable e-readers such as the Amazon Kindle and Apple's iPad led to a greater demand for books to be available electronically (and at a reduced cost). As school boards explore the potential cost savings involved in the paper-free environment, educators, researchers, and publishers are exploring opportunities to customize classroom texts and develop greater interactivity and multimodal supports for the reading experience.

For example, although most e-books include standard multimodal features such as images, hyperlinks, and embedded video or audio clips, the newest e-readers allow readers to interact with their text by highlighting, annotating on digital sticky notes (or inserting/deleting text), looking up unfamiliar words as they come to them, selecting viewer preferences, choosing an audio format, and so on.

E-books offer a rich opportunity to develop a complex and shared language for talking about the various textual features that contribute to the process of making meaning. Developing a "metalanguage, allows readers to take a more critical reading position and interrogate the structures and components that authors, illustrators, and designers use to convey meanings" (Zammit, as cited in Serafini, 2011, p. 344).

INSIDE CLASSROOMS

BEN HAZZARD

Educator Ben Hazzard says that using new media within his language arts classroom has provided the context for instruction, while the content and reflective focus of his teaching remain the same. Since the context of digital technologies permeates everyday interaction, Ben believes students need critical thinking skills in order to understand, evaluate, and make judgments about the messages embedded within the media. The new media of today will quickly become the old media of tomorrow.

Ben Hazzard

In Ben's classroom new media are used to facilitate engagement, collaboration, and community. He engages learners through using video clips from websites such as YouTube. Learners write, plan, film, and edit digital video segments based on song lyrics, commercials, and creative holiday segments. Here, they write for a true purpose and audience. The focus is on the content, on the message they wish to communicate.

New media have also provided Ben and his students with opportunities for collaboration with other educators and to connect learners across classrooms. Tools such as blogging software allow students to publish their writing on the web for another classroom of students to read and comment on. Reading and writing are linked together through the creation of blog posts and making connections to the posts of others. Moderated forums between students also allow students to interact with each other about science concepts using a style of interaction that they are very comfortable communicating with, that is, informal digital communication. The key to each of these examples of collaboration is the ability to interact socially with other students, educators, and classrooms. The response and feedback are timely, relevant, and connected to classroom instructional content.

Through the use of new media, students become part of a larger community. The audience for their work extends beyond the classroom to parents, school, and local community. Parents can have more meaningful discussions with their children about their studies; students often download photos of classroom activities; and community members are aware of work being done within the school.

MOVING FROM TRADITIONAL LITERACY PRACTICES TO MULTILITERACIES PEDAGOGY

In Ben Hazzard's classroom, new media were integrated into the teaching/learning culture, and learners moved seamlessly from one text form to another. The learning community was extended to the geographic community at large and also included members of a strong virtual network, what we might call the global village. Here, learners explored how texts work, what effects they have, and how power is exercised (Comber, 2001). Learners worked across classrooms in support of one another—even in support of learners they had never met. In return, they received support from their virtual acquaintances. As Jenkins, Clinton, Purushotma, Robison, and Weigel (2006, p. 5) identified, the resultant participatory culture opens up the following opportunities for learners:*

- *affiliations*—gaining memberships, formal and informal, including online communities centred around various forms of media

- *expressions*—producing new creative forms, such as digital sampling, video making, fan fiction writing, zines, and mash-ups

- *collaborative problem-solving*—working together in teams, formal and informal, to complete tasks and develop new knowledge

- *circulations*—shaping the flow of media (such as podcasting and blogging)

Understanding how texts operate is an important part of constructing meaning. It is helpful for educators to pay attention to the texts they interact with on a daily basis to see what and how they operate in their own lives as a means of building a foundation of understanding for their classrooms. We must recognize the emergence of hybrid forms of text that necessitate an overlap of conventions while potentially generating new ones in their assemblage.

---

* H. Jenkins, K. Clinton, R. Purushotma, A.J. Robison, & M. Weigel. *Confronting the challenges of participatory culture: Media education for the 21st century.* The MacArthur Foundation, 2006, p. 3.

For many educators, figuring out how to begin to move from what has been termed traditional literacy pedagogy to a multiliteracies pedagogy can be daunting. Revisiting their 1996 *A Pedagogy of Multiliteracies*, Cope and Kalantzis (2009) offered a revised set of essential elements, or "knowledge processes" that they believe compose a multiliteracies pedagogy:

Experiencing (Situated Practice): grounding or situating learning in meaningful and authentic experiences, actions, and subjective interests
  Experiencing the known: reflecting upon our own experiences, interests and perspectives
  Experiencing the new: observing or reading the unfamiliar

Conceptualizing (Overt Instruction): teaching learners about the available patterns of meaning and the resources we can find and use to design, redesign, and make meaning
  Conceptualizing by naming: similarity and difference
  Conceptualizing with theory, using interpretive frameworks and disciplinary schemas

Analyzing (Critical Framing): interpreting meaning, attending, in particular, to the social and cultural context
  Analyzing functionally: reasoning, inference, deductive conclusions, cause/effect, logical and textual conclusions
  Analyzing critically: evaluating your own and others' perspectives interests and motives

Applying (Transformed Practice): students applying their knowledge and designs in a different context, redesigning it and their learning in the process
  Applying appropriately—applying knowledge in real-world situations in expected ways
  Applying creatively—applying knowledge in innovative and unexpected ways
  (pp. 184–186)

Multiliteracies pedagogy is an emerging field, and researchers and educators are working out "multiliteracies in use" in a changing environment. It is one of the reasons why I created *The Salty Chip: A Canadian Multiliteracies Collaborative* (http://www .saltychip.com). This freely accessible network allows educators and learners across content areas and grades to share and build upon their work as they develop their knowledge and use of multiliteracies. It seeks to capture cultural and linguistic diversity and to make use of new and emerging communication technologies that consider pedagogy in a participatory culture. Educators and learners produce and exchange multimodal uses of text at home or at school and share them on the network. Carefully selected tags allow users to collectively classify and locate information contributed (often referred to as "folksonomies"). Educators and students can then upload, download, design, modify, and redesign their activities in use. The community rates submissions through a process of "upvoting." Users may choose to follow other users, comment on contributions, and through their participation, learn about some of the features of web 2.0 tools in a non-threatening environment. In addition, the works submitted are licensed under Creative Commons, thereby allowing participants to learn about the ethical use of digital materials and proper citation and attribution.

Table 13.2 outlines some examples of how literacy practices have changed as a multiliteracies approach is adopted. It is important to note that traditional literacy practices are included in a multiliteracies approach and are separated out here only as an illustration.

TABLE 13.2 **A CONTINUUM OF PRACTICE: FROM TRADITIONAL LITERACY PRACTICES TO MULTILITERACIES PEDAGOGY**

Traditional Literacy	Multiliteracies
Text is generally considered to be either oral or print on paper.	Text involves all sign systems, including print, graphic, animated, and electronic. For example, text can be developed into a storyboard to become a visual story, a digital story, a video, a movie, a documentary, a comic strip, or a photo essay.
Meaning making involves learning the code and understanding the orthographic (visual) or phonological (spoken) units.	Meaning making occurs as the reader engages with all forms of text through cultural practices (through writing, designing, illustrating, storytelling, remixing, and so on). **Anime, fan sites, webquests**, and **zines** are included.
Meaning is embedded in the text.	Meaning varies depending on the context, the audience, and the way in which the text is read.
Learners write their own text to create meaning.	New meanings are created when learners design a text or take an idea from a text and create a new text (design and redesign). Learners "rewrite" the story (e.g., **fan fiction**).
Learners create a "mixed tape."	Learners make a "play list" or a podcast, or engage in **relay writing** using microblogging platforms such as Twitter.
Learners record music from the radio or CD.	Learners download and remix music from various artists or computer-generated music from Internet sites.
Learners learn skills (dance, piano, cooking) from family, friends, movies, or classes.	Learners learn from YouTube or video-game applications—or share their own original creations with the world via the web.
Learners listen to tapes and Walkmans.	Learners listen to iPods or MP3 players.
Learners have air guitar contests.	Learners play along with a virtual band or cartoon band, or through video games such as Guitar Hero.
Youth hang posters of idols on bedroom walls.	Youth use idol images as screen savers and the songs of idols as ring tones or lyrics in profiles.
Learners read a book.	Learners read a **transmedia** story.
Learners write individually and work with a classroom peer or teacher to revise and edit before writing a final version.	Learners network and collaborate with multiple partners on writing activities using web 2.0 tools and publish to a global audience, participate in relay writing (a group activity where everyone takes a turn writing to generate a composition), and so on.
Learners memorize formulas.	Learners research and apply strategies, and see "gaming" as problem solving.

Sources: Adapted in part from: Baker, E. (Ed.), *The new literacies: Multiple perspectives on research and practice*, (New York: Guilford Press) 2010; Parker J., *Teaching tech-savvy kids: Bringing digital media into the classroom, grades 5–12*, (Thousand Oaks, CA: Corwin Sage) 2010; Richardson, W. *Blogs, wikis, podcasts and other powerful web tools for classrooms, 3rd Edition*, (Thousand Oaks, CA: Corwin) 2010.

Design and Redesign

Sheridan and Rowsell (2010) suggested that "reading and composing in today's digitally mediated age requires a whole new way of learning" (p. 1). They viewed literacy as enabling and argued that for many educators,

> preparing students to be leaders within these multimodal, networked environments is an issue of social justice.... Those who have not developed the skills, attitudes, and comfort gained by critically engaging in the "new form of the hidden curriculum" (Jenkins, 2006, p. 3) will be at a disadvantage in their future. (p. 11)*

They advocated for learners to take on the role of producers, arguing that producers share "striking patterns that reflect an expanded understanding of the places and practices of literacy learning" and that producing "helps people develop the dispositions to problem solve in innovative ways" (p. 3). In addition, we can see the hybridization of genres, textual features, vocabulary, and practices.

Table 13.3 outlines an activity that draws on traditional literacy and gradually makes the shift to a multiliteracies approach in which learners also shift from consumer to producer.

TABLE 13.3 **CLASSROOM ACTIVITY: "READING A DYNAMIC CANADA"**

Print Literacy	Decoding	Analyze
Find written information about your own local community from books, brochures, newspapers, historical plaques, and so on.	Teachers and learners work together to deconstruct the print text (using, for example, Freebody and Luke's "Four Resources Model"). What appeals to you? What makes it so effective? Consider the codes used in the various texts: dialogue, framing, images, perspective, and so on.	Think about what message is being communicated from the culmination of print sources you have collected.
Community Walk	**Redesigning the Message**	**Planning**
Encourage learners to collect artifacts as they move about their community: sights, (images, video), sounds (audio recordings), and feelings (e.g., displays, artistic representations, pollution, graffiti) and to consider what these artifacts are communicating about their home. Encourage learners to select an issue that they want to highlight or anchor their message to. It should be something they feel passionate about.	Think about how you might redesign the story from your community by drawing on language modes that will work best to convey your intended meaning and organize your time according to • planning • scripting • actualizing • evaluating The three-minute Common Craft videos produced to clearly explain complex subjects in simple terms are a useful tool for design. Check them out: http://www.commoncraft.com/. (To assist you with your redesign, consider Figure 13.1: Using the Multiliteracies Map.)	What text(s) will most powerfully and successfully communicate the message to the intended audience? Actively search for rich examples and again deconstruct the examples to learn what makes them effective or ineffective. It is important at this stage to review the ethical use of resources on the web. Take a look at the slide-deck presentation developed by leading Ontario Educator Rodd Lucier: http://www.slideshare.net/ thecleversheep/ creative-commons-what-every-educator-needs-to-know.

---

* Sheridan, M.P. & Rowsell, J. *Design literacies: Learning and innovation in the digital age.* (London: Routledge) 2010, p. 11.

TABLE 13.3 **CLASSROOM ACTIVITY: "READING A DYNAMIC CANADA"** (*CONTINUED*)

Scripting	Actualizing	Evaluating
Working with multiliteracies often requires that you script your work using a storyboard that allows you to include a visual layout. It is important at this stage to include whatever dialogue and rough soundtracks you may have developed to get a sense of flow, timing, and sequence with your dialogue; work out visual issues such as lighting, backgrounds, and camera angles. Be sure to share your work with peers at this stage to get feedback on its clarity, coherence, and conciseness.	How will you generate your work? How will you delegate tasks in a group, or draw on particular strengths that individuals may bring to production? How do you keep purpose, awareness of audience, and critical literacy skills at the forefront of the process? What tools might you need? MS Paint: http://windows.microsoft.com/en-ca/windows7/products/features/paint Screen capture: http://en.wikipedia.org/wiki/Screenshot Audacity (Free cross-platform sound editor): http://audacity.sourceforge.net/ Windows Movie Maker: http://windows.microsoft.com/en-ca/windows-live/movie-maker	Evaluation of a project like this involves an evaluation of what was learned throughout the process, as well as an evaluation of the end product and how it may have been received by the community it was designed for. Opportunities for screenings or showcasing the work are useful for allowing the end product to be viewed through the eyes of an audience outside of the classroom. Additional components could include these: • Reflection—A multimedia study guide documenting the learning journey and serving as a resource for others (dual/multiple languages) • A progress report that focuses on challenges and successes encountered and strategies for overcoming them

ASSESSING MULTILITERACIES

Recognizing the important role of accountability in education and "that assessment powerfully influences pedagogy" (Asselin, Early, & Filipenko, 2005, p. 822), it is encouraging to see there is a growing awareness of the need to develop multiple means of assessment in the area of multiliteracies. A multiliteracies approach acknowledges and allows "alternative starting points for learning ... alternative forms of engagement ... different conceptual bents of learners, ... different analytical perspectives ... divergent learning orientations ... and different modalities in meaning making" (Cope & Kalantzis, 2009, p. 188). We must take an equally diverse approach to assessment of these practices. It is critical for educators to develop a sound understanding of how to not only assess their learners, but also assess the materials available for their consumption on the web.

Educators can observe learners keenly and consider learning in terms of the following:*

- project assessment, based on in-depth tasks that involve planning, complex collation of material, and presentation to measure breadth of knowledge and flexible solutions orientation to knowledge; enables some measurement of multiple intelligences, communicative, analytical, or creative
- performance assessment, based on task planning, doing, and problem solving

* "Assessing Multiliteracies and the New Basics," by Mary Kalantzis, Bill Cope & Andrew Harvey, published in *Assessment in Education: Principles, Policy & Practice, Vol. 10*:1, pp. 15–26 (2003) reprinted by permission of Taylor & Francis Ltd, www.tandfonline.com.

FIGURE 13.1

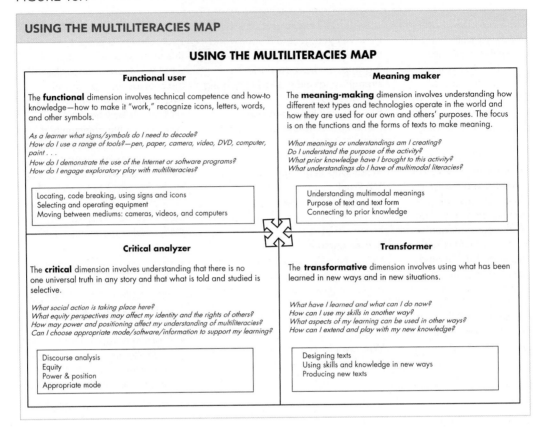

USING THE MULTILITERACIES MAP

USING THE MULTILITERACIES MAP

Functional user

The **functional** dimension involves technical competence and how-to knowledge—how to make it "work," recognize icons, letters, words, and other symbols.

As a learner what signs/symbols do I need to decode?
How do I use a range of tools?—pen, paper, camera, video, DVD, computer, paint . . .
How do I demonstrate the use of the Internet or software programs?
How do I engage exploratory play with multiliteracies?

Locating, code breaking, using signs and icons
Selecting and operating equipment
Moving between mediums: cameras, videos, and computers

Meaning maker

The **meaning-making** dimension involves understanding how different text types and technologies operate in the world and how they are used for our own and others' purposes. The focus is on the functions and the forms of texts to make meaning.

What meanings or understandings am I creating?
Do I understand the purpose of the activity?
What prior knowledge have I brought to this activity?
What understandings do I have of multimodal literacies?

Understanding multimodal meanings
Purpose of text and text form
Connecting to prior knowledge

Critical analyzer

The **critical** dimension involves understanding that there is no one universal truth in any story and that what is told and studied is selective.

What social action is taking place here?
What equity perspectives may affect my identity and the rights of others?
How may power and positioning affect my understanding of multiliteracies?
Can I choose appropriate mode/software/information to support my learning?

Discourse analysis
Equity
Power & position
Appropriate mode

Transformer

The **transformative** dimension involves using what has been learned in new ways and in new situations.

What have I learned and what can I do now?
How can I use my skills in another way?
What aspects of my learning can be used in other ways?
How can I extend and play with my new knowledge?

Designing texts
Using skills and knowledge in new ways
Producing new texts

Source: Built from the work of the Children of the New Millennium Research Project, University of South Australia and Department of Education and Children's Services (2003–2004).

- group assessment, either of the whole group's collective work or the collaborative capacities of individual group members—an important means of measuring the collaborative skills so important now
- portfolio assessment, through documenting the body of works undertaken, unique life experiences, and other learning achievements, thereby enabling open sensibilities to be measured as well as the strengths of individuals

Educators can also learn a great deal about learners' *funds of knowledge* by attending to the ways in which students engage in participatory texts and affinity spaces such as fan fiction, zines, blogging, and interactive gaming (Burke & Hammett, 2009; Moll, Amanti, Neff, & Gonzalez, 1992). However, as Bearne (2009a) noted, the processes and descriptors that have been traditionally used to assess writing are inappropriate to use with multimodal texts. She offered an alternative way to note progress as follows:

(i) *Decide on mode and content for specific purpose(s) and audience(s).* *

☐ Choose which mode(s) will best communicate meaning for specific purposes (deciding on words rather than images, or gesture/music rather than words).

* Bearne, E. (2009b). "Assessing multimodal texts." In A. Burke & R. Hammett (Eds.), *Assessing new literacies: Perspectives from the classroom* pp. 22–23. New York, NY: Peter Lang.

- Use perspective, colour, sound, and language to engage and hold a reader's/viewer's attention.
- Select appropriate content to express personal intentions, ideas, opinions.
- Adapt, synthesise, and shape content to suit personal intentions and communication.

(ii) *Structure texts.*
- Pay conscious attention to design and layout of texts, use structural devices (pages, sections, frames, paragraphs, blocks of text, screens, sound sequences) to organise texts.
- Integrate and balance modes for design purposes.
- Structure longer texts with visual, verbal, and sound cohesive devices.
- Use background detail to create mood and setting.

(iii) *Use technical features for effect.*
- Handle technical aspects and conventions of different kinds of multimodal texts, including line, colour, perspective, sound, camera angles, movement, gesture, facial expression and language.
- Choose language, punctuation, font, typography, and presentational techniques to create effects and clarify meaning.
- Choose and use a variety of sentence structures for specific purposes.

(iv) *Reflect.*
- Explain choices of mode(s) and expressive devices, including words.
- Improve own composition or performance, reshaping, redesigning, and redrafting for purpose and readers'/viewers' needs.
- Comment on the success of a composition in fulfilling the design aims.
- Comment on the relative merits of teamwork and individual contribution for a specific project. (Bearne, 2009a, pp. 22–23)

Educators can review their practices to think about whether their approach invites creativity and engagement, or simply compliance and following direction.

BECOMING A READER AND WRITER OF MULTILITERACIES

As outlined earlier in *Constructing Meaning*, Freebody and Luke (1990) developed the Four Resources Model to explain how learners can develop their reading and writing abilities in four interrelated areas: as code breaker, with the ability to decode text largely through phonics; as meaning maker, with the ability to make meaning in context drawing on semantics; as text user, with the ability to use text in everyday life to read, write, complete forms, and so on; and as text critic, with the ability to critically review and analyze texts. This model also serves as a basis to begin to read and write across multiliteracies texts.

As you begin working with your learners, you may find it helpful to use the following prompts to orient them into a way of reading multiple forms of text. Table 13.4, which provides prompts for reading a transmedia text, offers a beginning. Transmedia texts not only integrate multiple modes, but reflect the desire of a reader or viewer to participate more fully in the experience or affect the outcomes of the experience. Adapt the prompts to the various modes of communication that you are interacting with. The questions can be used (as appropriate) to tease out and locate power, decision making, purpose, effect, and more.

TABLE 13.4 **PROMPTS FOR READING TRANSMEDIA TEXT**

People	Describe what you see [in the picture, on the screen, on the stage]. Who are the main characters? How do you know? What can you tell about them from the way they look or are dressed? Who or what do the people represent? Why has the artist, producer, or author chosen to include them in this representation in this way? How might their appearance or disappearance affect the overall meaning communicated? What would you change if you could and why?
Activities	What activities do you see represented? What do the activities tell you about the people or events before you? What story is being told?
Objects	What objects do you see before you—natural objects or objects made by people? When do the objects appear? Why at those times? What do they communicate? What is prevalent? What is missing?
Appeal	What draws your eye? Who (if anyone) captures the attention of people in the text? Do the characters look directly at you? At the audience? What angle is the camera, artist, producer, or director assuming most of the time? If the angle changes, why does it change? After viewing, what images stay in your mind? How did the artist or producer achieve this?
Setting	What people or objects are in the foreground? In the background? What does the landscape, background, or conditions look like? Where do you think this text is set? How would setting the text, story, or production somewhere else affect the meaning?
Layout	Do images or scenes move from one place to another in any particular sequence? Why do you suppose this has been done in this way? How does the producer or artist ensure that you understand the text as a whole? How are the texts connected? How would you describe any accompanying audio or music? Does it change from beginning to end? If so, why? How does the inclusion or choice of audio affect you and your response to the text? Does the text change from beginning to end? Why would these choices have been made?
Emotional content	What words would you use to describe the feelings you experience when engaging with this text? What changes would make you feel differently?
Aesthetic qualities	How has the photographer, artist, or producer made the texts pleasing [or disturbing, shocking, interesting …] to look at? (Ways may include use of light, colour, composition, line, sound, volume, costume, and gesture.)
Perspective and purpose: Becoming a critical viewer	Who do you think made this? Why do you think it was made? What was the intended message and how was it constructed? Do you agree with the message being conveyed? Why? Can you think of any groups of people who will like or object to the messages constructed in this text? Why? If you could add or remove something from the text, what would it be? On the whole, do you consider this an effective text? Why?

Sources: Adapted from: Clark, 1999; Education Staff, National Archives, Washington, D.C.; Tan, L., Guo, L., & Chia, A.L. (2009) "Teaching English in new times." P. Teo, T.M. Yin, & C. Ho (Eds). *Exploring new frontiers: Challenging students in the language and literature classroom.* (Toronto: Pearson), pp. 15–29; Kress & Van Leeuwen, 1996. "Reading images: The grammar of visual design." *English in Australia*, pp. 92–100.

SUMMARY

It is important for educators to be aware of the full range of ways that learners may come to literacy. As our conceptions about what it means to be literate in the 21st century have expanded, so too must our understandings and practices change. Achieving this can be challenging in an environment where we must straddle accountability standards that reflect traditional forms of literacy while meeting society's expectations that we are engaging our students in literacy experiences that will prepare them for a rapidly changing future.

A community of learners in new media environments usually includes peer-based learning, collaboration, creativity, interest-driven practices, and friendship-driven practices. As educators transition to a pedagogy of multiliteracies, they will need to engage in multiliteracies practices themselves in order to effectively and purposefully engage in the education of today's youth.

Technology is a means of affording new practices and not an end in itself. Therefore the particular technologies used are less important than the purpose and meaning derived from using them appropriately. Technological advances have outpaced the abilities of policy-makers, legislators, and school district personnel to set appropriate guidelines. It thus becomes even more critical that educators are well-informed, savvy users of multiliteracies so that they can lead the necessary changes and functions as responsible stewards in uncharted territory.

Selected Professional Resources lists, among other things, include the professional blogs of a few Canadian educators who have been actively engaging in the participatory culture afforded by technology. Following their blogs is one way to learn about the experiences of professionals with similar challenges and interests. Professional Learning Networks (PLNs) offer a great way to exchange ideas with a community driven initially by interest, but often leading to friendship. PLNs are opportunities for professionals to form informal or formal groups (small and large) around issues that are shared or valued in a global network. One is identified under Selected Professional Resources.

Get involved. Expand your own horizons and quite possibly your worlds!

SELECTED PROFESSIONAL RESOURCES

The Salty Chip—A Canadian Multiliteracies Collaborative: http://www.saltychip.com/

The Salty Chip is a space for educators and students to share and build upon their work as they develop their use of multiliteracies. It seeks to capture cultural and linguistic diversity and to make use of new and emerging communication technologies that consider pedagogy in a participatory culture.

The Clever Sheep Podcasts: http://canadapodcasts.ca/podcasts/Teacher

The Clever Sheep, developed by Rodd Lucier, aims to assist educators in harnessing evolving e-learning tools, Internet sites, and web 2.0 technologies to engage learners of all ages. Podcasts generally run 7 to 10 minutes.

continued

Weblogg-ed: http://weblogg-ed.com/

This blog has been developed by Will Richardson, author of *Blogs, Wikis, Podcasts and Other Powerful Web Tools for Classrooms (2010)*.

Burke, A., & Hammett, R. (2009). *Assessing new literacies: Perspectives from the classroom.* New York, NY: Peter Lang.

Written by two Canadian scholars, this book explores numerous practical examples of what it means to assess new literacies.

The John D. and Catherine T. MacArthur Foundation Reports on Digital Media and Learning: https://mitpress.mit.edu/books/series/john-d-and-catherine-t-macarthur-foundation-reports-digital-media-and-learning

The MacArthur Reports summarize research findings drawn from MacArthur's digital media and learning initiative. They are available for download at the above website.

Sample Educator Blogs

Thinking in Mind: http://www.teachinquiry.com/index/Introduction.html

Neil Stephenson is the professional development and outreach coordinator at the Calgary Sciences School. His engagement with inquiry-based projects offers him numerous opportunities to work with multiliteracies across subject areas.

Open Thinking: http://educationaltechnology.ca/couros/about

Open Thinking and Digital Pedagogy is the personal and professional blogging space of Dr. Alec Couros, a professor of educational technology and media at the Faculty of Education, University of Regina. Dr. Couros wrote, "I created this space in early 2004 as I pondered the educational uses of blogging and podcasting. This space is a growing collection of personal reflections and resources related to teaching and learning, democratic media, critical media literacy, digital citizenship, openness, and social justice."

Mrs. Cassidy's Classroom Blog: http://staff.prairiesouth.ca/sites/kcassidy/

Kathy Cassidy, a grade 1 educator and award-winning blogger, shares resources and examples of her experiences.

Professional Learning Network

Canadian Mashup at Classroom 2.0: http://www.classroom20.com/group/canadianmashup

APPENDIX

CHILDREN'S LITERATURE BY GRADE LEVEL: FICTION AND NONFICTION FOR RECREATIONAL READING

Preschool to Grade 1

FICTION

Adler, D. A. (2004). *Bones and the dog gone mystery.* (B. J. Newman, Illus.). New York, NY: Viking.

Ahlberg, J., & Ahlberg, A. (1978). *Each peach pear plum.* London, UK: Kestrel Books.

Alborough, J. (1992). *Where's my teddy?* Cambridge, MA: Candlewick Press.

❦ Badoe, A. (2002). *Nana's cold days.* (B. Junaid, Illus.). Toronto, ON: Groundwood Books.

Baker, K. (1990). *Who is the beast?* New York, NY: Harcourt Brace & Company.

❦ Bailey, L. (2006). *The farm team.* (B. Slavin, Illus.). Toronto, ON: Kids Can Press.

❦ Bailey, L. (2007). *Goodnight, sweet pig.* (J. Masse, Illus.). Toronto, ON: Kids Can Press.

Brett, J. (1999). *Gingerbread baby.* New York, NY: G. P. Putnam's Sons.

Brown, K. (2001). *The scarecrow's hat.* London, UK: Andersen Press.

Brown, M. W. (2007). *Goodnight Moon 1 2 3: A counting book/Buenas noches, luna 1 2 3: Un libro para contar* [Text in English and Spanish]. (C. Hurd, Illus.). New York, NY: Rayo.

Brown, R. (1985). *The big sneeze.* New York, NY: Mulberry Books.

Browne, A. (1985). *Willy the champ.* New York, NY: Knopf.

Campbell, R. (2007). *Dear zoo.* New York, NY: Little Simon.

Carle, E. (1968). *The very hungry caterpillar.* New York, NY: World Books.

Carle, E. (1997). *From head to toe.* New York, NY: HarperCollins.

Carle, E. (2003). *Where are you going? To see my friend: A story of friendship in two languages* [Text in English and Japanese]. (K. Iwamura, Illus.). New York, NY: Orchard Books.

Cheng, A. (2000). *Grandfather counts.* (A. Zheng, Illus.). New York, NY: Lee & Low Books.

Cowley, J. (1983). *The jigaree.* Auckland, NZ: Shortland Publications.

Cranstoun, M. (1967). *1, 2, buckle my shoe.* New York, NY: Holt, Rinehart & Winston.

Dann, P. (2000). *Five in the bed.* London, UK: Little Orchard Books.

Day, A. (1985). *Good dog, Carl.* New York, NY: Simon and Schuster.

Dragonwagon, C. (2012). *All the awake animals are almost asleep.* (D. McPhail, Illus.). New York, NY: Little Brown.

Emberley, R. (1989). *City sounds.* New York, NY: Little Brown and Company.

❦ Gay, M. (2002). *Stella, fairy of the forest.* Toronto, ON: Douglas and McIntyre.

Harter, D. (2003). *Walking through the jungle* [Text in English and Arabic]. London, UK: Mantra Lingua.

Hoberman, M. A. (2001). *It's simple, said Simon.* (M. So, Illus.). New York, NY: Alfred A. Knopf.

Hutchins, P. (1969). *Rosie's walk.* London, UK: Bodley Head Press.

Martin, B., Jr. (1972). *Brown bear, brown bear, what do you see?* (E. Carle, Illus.). New York, NY: Holt, Rinehart & Winston.

Martin, B., Jr. (1991). *Polar bear, polar bear, what do you hear?* (E. Carle, Illus.). New York, NY: Henry Holt & Company.

McKee, D. (2006). *Tusk tusk.* London, UK: Beaver Books.

Melser, J. (1980). *Lazy Mary.* (J. Shanahan, Illus.). Auckland, NZ: Shortland Publications.

Melser, J. (1980). *Sing a song.* (D. Gardiner, Illus.). Auckland, NZ: Shortland Publications.

❦ Morgan, A. (2001). *Matthew and the midnight wrecker.* (M. Martchenko, Illus.). Toronto, ON: Stoddart Kids.

Morris, W. B. (1970). *The longest journey in the world.* (B. Fraser, Illus.). New York, NY: Holt, Rinehart & Winston.

Ormerod, J. (1981). *Sunshine.* Harmondsworth, UK: Puffin/Penguin.

Ormerod, J. (1982). *Moonlight.* Harmondsworth, UK: Puffin/Penguin.

Paye, W., & Lippert, M. H. (2002). *Head, body, legs: A story from Liberia.* (J. Paschkis, Illus.). New York, NY: Henry Holt & Co.

Pichon, L. (2008). *The three horrid little pigs.* Wilton, CT: Tiger Tales.

Polacco, P. (2004). *Oh, look!* New York, NY: Philomel Books.

Root, P. (2001). *Rattletrap car.* (J. Barton, Illus.). Cambridge, MA: Candlewick Press.

Rosen, M., & Oxenbury, H. (1989). *We're going on a bear hunt.* London, UK: Walker Books.

❦ Schwartz, R. (2001). *The mole sisters and the moonlit night.* Toronto, ON: Annick Press.

Sis, P. (1998). *Fire truck.* New York, NY: Greenwillow Books.

Tullet, H. (2011). *Press here.* San Francisco, CA: Chronicle Books.

❦ Vaage, C. (1995). *Bibi and the bull.* (G. Graham, Illus.). Edmonton, AB: Dragon Hill Press.

Van Leeuwen, J. (2007). *Amanda pig and the really hot day.* (A. Schweninger, Illus.). New York, NY: Puffin Books.

Waddell, M. (1992). *Can't you sleep, Little Bear?* (B. Firth, Illus.). Cambridge, MA: Candlewick Press.

Waddell, M. (1992). *Owl babies.* (P. Benson, Illus.). Cambridge, MA: Candlewick Press.

Williams, S. (1994). *I went walking.* (J. Vivas, Illus.). New York, NY: Harcourt Brace & Company.

Wise Brown, M. W. (1982). *Goodnight moon.* (C. Hurd, Illus.). New York, NY: HarperCollins.

Wood, A. (1984). *The napping house.* (D. Wood, Illus.). New York, NY: Harcourt Brace & Company.

Wood, A. (1992). *Silly Sally.* New York, NY: Harcourt Brace Jovanovich.

Yolen, J., & Peters, A. (2007). *Here's a little poem: A very first book of poetry.* (P. Dunbar, Illus.). Cambridge, MA: Candlewick Press.

NONFICTION

Bradley, K. B. (2001). *Pop! A book about bubbles.* (M. Miller, Illus.). New York, NY: HarperCollins Children's Books.

Brown, R. (2001). *Ten seeds*. New York, NY: Alfred A. Knopf/Random House Children's Books.

Campbell, S. (2008). *Wolfsnail: A backyard predator*. (R. P. Campbell, Photo.). Honesdale, PA: Boyds Mill Press.

❧ Jocelyn, M. (2005). *ABC × 3: English, Español, Français*. (T. Slaughter, Illus.). Toronto, ON: Tundra Books.

❧ Morstad, J. (2013). *How to*. Vancouver, BC: Simply Read Books.

❧ Swanson, D. (2001). *Animals can be so sleepy*. Vancouver, BC: Greystone Books.

Tafuri, N. (1999). *Snowy flowy blowy*. New York, NY: Scholastic Press.

Kindergarten to Grade 2

FICTION

❧ Argueta, J. (2010). *Arroz con leche/ Rice pudding* [Text in English and Spanish]. (F. Vilela, Illus.). Toronto, ON: Groundwood Books.

Arnold, T. (2006). *Hi! Fly Guy*. New York, NY: Scholastic.

❧ Bailey, L. (2007). *Goodnight, Sweet Pig*. (J. Masse, Illus.). Toronto, ON: Kids Can Press.

Banks, K. (2006). *Max's words*. (B. Kulikov, Illus.). New York, NY: Farrar, Straus & Giroux.

Beaton, C. (2001). *There's a cow in the cabbage patch*. (C. Beaton, Illus.). Bristol, UK: Barefoot Books.

Bennett, J. (1993). *Machine poems*. (N. Sharratt, Illus.). Don Mills, ON: Oxford University Press.

Berenstain, S., & Berenstain, J. (1964). *The bike lesson*. New York, NY: Beginner Books.

Bogart, J. (1997). *Jeremiah learns to read*. (L. Fernandez & R. Jacobson, Illus.). Richmond Hill, ON: North Winds Press.

Brown, M. W. (1977). *The important book*. (L. Weisgard, Illus.). New York, NY: HarperCollins.

Brown, R. (1981). *A dark, dark tale*. New York, NY: Scholastic.

Bunting, E. (1999). *Butterfly house*. (G. Shed, Illus.). New York, NY: Scholastic Press.

❧ Campbell, N. (2005). *Shi-shi-etko*. (K. LaFave, Illus.). Toronto, ON: Groundwood Books.

Cowley, J. (1983). *Who will be my mother?* Auckland, NZ: Shortland Publications.

❧ Davis, A. (2003). *Bagels from Benny*. (D. Petricic, Illus.). Toronto, ON: Kids Can Press.

❧ Delaronde, D. (2000). *Little Métis and the Métis sash*. (K. Flamand, Illus.). Winnipeg, MB: Pemmican Publications.

Edwards, P. (1996). *Some smug slug*. (H. Cole, Illus.). New York, NY: HarperCollins.

❧ Flett, J. (2013). *Wild berries* [Text in English and Cree]. (E. N. Cook, Trans.). Vancouver, ON: Simply Read Books.

Galdone, P. (1974). *Little Red Riding Hood*. New York, NY: McGraw-Hill.

Giovanni, N. (2014). *The sun is so quiet: Poems*. (A. Bryan, Illus.). New York, NY: Henry Holt.

❧ Gillard, D. (2001). *Music from the sky*. (S. Taylor, Illus.). Toronto, ON: Groundwood Books.

❧ Gilman, P. (1992). *Something from nothing*. Richmond Hill, ON: North Winds Press.

Gramatky, H. (1939). *Little Toot*. New York, NY: G. P. Putnam's Sons.

❧ Hartry, N. (2000). *Jocelyn and the ballerina*. (L. Hendry, Illus.). Markham, ON: Fitzhenry and Whiteside.

Hoffman, M. (1991). *Amazing Grace*. (C. Binch, Illus.). New York, NY: Dial.

Hutchins, P. (1986). *The doorbell rang*. New York, NY: Greenwillow Books.

Isadora, R. (1991). *At the crossroads.* New York, NY: Greenwillow Books.

Isadora, R. (2010). *Say hello!* New York, NY: G. P. Putnam's Sons.

♣ Kusugak, M. (1998). *Arctic stories.* (V. Krykorka, Illus.). Toronto, ON: Annick Press.

Lear, E. (1991). *The owl and the pussycat.* (J. Brett, Illus.). New York, NY: G. P. Putnam's Sons.

♣ Lesynski, L. (1999). *Dirty dog boogie.* Toronto, ON: Annick Press.

♣ London, J. (2001). *What the animals were waiting for.* (P. Morin, Illus.). Markham, ON: Scholastic Canada.

♣ Manuel, L. (1997). *Lucy Maud and the Cavendish cat.* (J. Wilson, Illus.). Toronto, ON: Tundra Books.

Martin, B., Jr. (1970). *The haunted house.* (B. Martin & P. J. Lippman, Illus.). New York, NY: Holt, Rinehart & Winston.

Martin, B., Jr. (1989). *Monday, Monday, I like Monday.* (D. Leder, Illus.). New York, NY: Holt, Rinehart & Winston.

Mayer, M. (1975). *Just for you.* New York, NY: Golden Press.

Moser, B. (2001). *The three little pigs.* Boston, MA: Little, Brown and Company.

♣ Munsch, R. (2010). *Put me in a book!* (M. Martchenko, Illus.). Toronto, ON: North Winds Press.

♣ Oberman, S. (1997). *By the Hanukkah light.* (N. Waldman, Illus.). Toronto, ON: McClelland and Stewart.

♣ Oppel, K. (2001). *Peg and the whale.* (T. Widener, Illus.). Toronto, ON: HarperCollins Canada.

Pilon, A. (1972). *Concrete is not always hard.* New York, NY: Xerox Education.

Pinkney, J. (2009). *The lion and the mouse.* New York, NY: Little, Brown.

Rylant, C. (2006). *Henry and Mudge and the great grandpas.* (S. Stevenson, Illus.). New York, NY: Aladdin Paperbacks.

Sanderson, R. (2001). *Cinderella.* Boston, MA: Little, Brown and Company.

♣ Simard, D. (2007). *The little word catcher.* (G. Cote, Illus.). Toronto, ON: Second Story Press.

♣ Setterington, K. (2004). *Mom and Mum are getting married!* (A. Priestley, Illus.). Toronto, ON: Second Story Press.

Seuss, D. (1960). *Green eggs and ham.* New York, NY: Random House.

Silverman, E. (2005). *Cowgirl Kate and cocoa.* (B. Lewin, Illus.). Orlando, FL: Harcourt.

Stevenson, R. L. (1990). *My shadow.* (T. Rand, Illus.). (Poem by Robert Louis Stevenson). New York, NY: G. P. Putnam's Sons.

Teague, K. (1991). *Anna goes to school* [Text in English and Chinese]. London, UK: Magi Publications.

♣ Thompson, R. (2000). *The follower.* (M. Springett, Illus.). Markham, ON: Fitzhenry and Whiteside.

♣ Tibo, G. (2000). *The cowboy kid.* (T. Kapas, Illus.). Toronto, ON: Tundra Books.

♣ Villeneuve, A. (2010). *The red scarf.* Toronto, ON: Tundra Books.

Waddell, M., (1991). *Farmer duck.* (H. Oxenbury, Illus.). London, UK: Walker Books.

Ward, H. (2001). *The animals' Christmas carol.* Brookfield, CN: The Millbrook Press. (All ages)

NONFICTION

Baker, J. (1987). *Where the forest meets the sea.* New York, NY: Greenwillow Books.

Bernard, R. (2001). *Insects.* Washington, DC: National Geographic Society.

Bunting, E. (1993). *Red fox running*. (W. Minor, Illus.). New York, NY: Houghton Mifflin.

Cowley, J. (1999). *Red-eyed tree frog*. (N. Bishop, Photo.). New York, NY: Scholastic.

Davies, N. (2001). *Bat loves the night*. (S. Fox-Davies, Illus.). Cambridge, MA: Candlewick Press.

Demarest, C. L. (1939). *Firefighters A to Z*. Eau Clair, WI: E. M. Hale.

❧ Douglas, A. (2000). *Before you were born: The inside story!* (E. Fernandes, Illus.; G. Duclos, Photo.). Toronto, ON: Owl Books.

George, T. C. (2000). *Jellies: The life of jellyfish*. Brookfield, CN: Millbrook Press.

Horenstein, H. (1999). *A is for...? A photographer's alphabet of animals*. San Diego, CA: Gulliver/Harcourt Brace.

Kessler, C. (2001). *Jubela*. (J. McAllister Stammen, Illus.). New York, NY: Simon and Schuster.

❧ K'naan, & Guy, S. (2012). *When I get older: The story behind "Wavin' Flag."* (R. Gutierrez, Illus.). Toronto, ON: Tundra Books.

❧ Kusugak, M. (1996). *My Arctic 1, 2, 3*. (V. Krykorka, Illus.). Toronto, ON: Annick Press.

Pfeffer, W. (2003). *The shortest day: Celebrating the winter solstice*. (J. Reisch, Illus.). New York, NY: Dutton Children's Books.

Posada, M. (2000). *Dandelions: Stars in the grass*. Minneapolis, MN: Carolrhoda Books/Lerner.

❧ Serafini, F. (2008). *Looking closely along the shore*. Toronto, ON: Kids Can Press.

Shea, S. (2012). *Do you know which ones will grow?* (T. Slaughter, Illus.). New York, NY: Roaring Brook Press.

Grade 2 to Grade 3

FICTION

❧ Ahlberg, A. (2001). *The adventures of Bert*. (R. Briggs, Illus.). Toronto, ON: Penguin Books.

Bagert, B. (2007). *Shout! Little poems that roar*. (S. Yoshikawa, Illus.). New York, NY: Dial Books for Young Readers.

Bannerman, H. (1996). *The story of Little Babaji*. (F. Marcellino, Illus.). New York, NY: HarperCollins.

Briggs, R. (1973). *Father Christmas*. London, UK: Hamish Hamilton.

Brownridge, W. (1995). *The moccasin goalie*. Victoria, BC: Orca.

Bunting, E. (1994). *Smoky night*. (D. Diaz, Illus.). New York, NY: Harcourt Brace.

Cech, J. (2010). *Puss in Boots*. (B. Oberdieck, Illus.). New York, NY: Sterling.

DiCamillo, K. (2003). *The tale of Despereaux: Being the story of a mouse, a princess, some soup, and a spool of thread*. (T. B. Ering, Illus.). Cambridge, MA: Candlewick Press.

❧ Eyvindson, P. (1996). *Red Parka Mary*. (R. Brynjolson, Illus.). Winnipeg, MB: Pemmican Publications.

Falconer, I. (2000). *Olivia*. New York, NY: Atheneum.

Fox, M. (1989). *Wilfrid Gordon McDonald Partridge*. (J. Vivas, Illus.). New York, NY: Kane Miller.

❧ Gilmore, R. (1999). *A screaming kind of day*. (G. Sauve, Illus.). Markham, ON: Fitzhenry and Whiteside.

Gréban, Q. (2009). *Snow White*. New York, NY: NorthSouth.

Hoberman, M. A. (1978). *A house is a house for me*. (B. Fraser, Illus.). New York, NY: Viking Press.

Howe, D., & Howe, J. (1996). *Bunnicula: A rabbit tale of mystery.* (A. Daniel, Illus.). New York, NY: Simon and Schuster.

✤ Hume, S. E. (2001). *Red moon follows truck.* (L. E. Watts, Illus.). Victoria, BC: Orca.

✤ Hundal, N. (2001). *Number 21.* (B. Deines, Illus.). Markham, ON: Fitzhenry and Whiteside.

✤ Jam, T. (1998). *The stoneboat.* (A. Zhang, Illus.). Toronto, ON: Groundwood Books.

✤ King, T. (1992). *A coyote Columbus story.* (K. Monkman, Illus.). Toronto, ON: Groundwood Books.

✤ Lawson, J. (1992). *The dragon's pearl.* (P. Morin, Illus.). Toronto, ON: Stoddart.

✤ Lawson, J. (1999). *Bear on the train.* (B. Deines, Illus.). Toronto, ON: Kids Can Press.

✤ Maclear, K. (2010). *Spork.* (I. Arsenault, Illus.). Toronto, ON: Kids Can Press.

Matsuoka, M. (2007). *Footprints in the snow.* New York, NY: Henry Holt.

✤ McNicoll, S. (1996). *The big race.* Richmond Hill, ON: Scholastic Canada.

Medina, J. (1999). *My name is Jorge: On both sides of the river.* (F. Vanden Broeck, Illus.). Honesdale, PA: Wordsong, Boyds Mills Press.

Messner, K. (2011). *Marty McGuire.* (B. Floca, Illus.). New York, NY: Scholastic.

✤ Miller, R. (2002). *The bear on the bed.* (B. Slavin, Illus.). Toronto, ON: Kids Can Press.

✤ Mollel, T. M. (1999). *My rows and piles of coins.* (E. B. Lewis, Illus.). Markham, ON: Clarion Books.

✤ Morck, I. (1996). *Tiger's new cowboy boots.* (G. Graham, Illus.). Red Deer, AB: Red Deer College Press.

✤ Munsch, R. (1980). *The paper bag princess.* (M. Martchenko, Illus.). Toronto, ON: Annick Press.

Myers, C. (2000). *Wings.* New York, NY: Scholastic.

Osborne, M. P. (2011). *A crazy day with cobras.* New York, NY: Random House.

Polacco, P. (1988). *Thank you, Mr. Falker.* New York, NY: Philomel Books.

✤ Richler, M. (1975). *Jacob Two-Two meets the hooded fang.* (F. Wegner, Illus.). Toronto, ON: Puffin Books.

✤ Richler, M. (1987). *Jacob Two-Two and the dinosaur.* (N. Eyolfson, Illus.). Toronto, ON: Puffin Books.

✤ Richler, M. (1995). *Jacob Two-Two's first spy case.* (D. Petricic, Illus.). Toronto, ON: McClelland and Stewart.

Rosenthal, A., & Lichtenheld, T. (2009). *Duck! Rabbit!* San Francisco, CA: Chronicle Books.

Siebert, D. (1991). *Sierra.* (W. Minor, Illus.). New York, NY: HarperCollins.

Singer, M. (2010). *Mirror mirror: A book of reversible verse.* (J. Masses, Illus.). New York, NY: Dutton.

✤ Spalding, A. (1999). *Me and Mr. Mah.* (J. Wilson, Illus.). Victoria, BC: Orca.

Tolstoy, A. (1968). *The great big enormous turnip.* (H. Oxenbury, Illus.). New York, NY: Franklin Watts.

Trivizas, E. (1993). *The three little wolves and the big bad pig.* (H. Oxenbury, Illus.). London, UK: William Heinemann.

✤ Upjohn, R. (2007). *Lily and the paper man.* (R. Benoit, Illus.). Toronto, ON: Second Story Press.

✤ Van Camp, R. (1998). *What's the most beautiful thing you know about horses? (G. Littlechild, Illus.).* Markham, ON: Children's Book Press.

Waddell, M. (1986). *The tough princess.* (P. Benson, Illus.). London, UK: Walker Books.

✤ Watt, M. (2007). *Chester.* Toronto, ON: Kids Can Press.

NONFICTION

Adler, D. A. (1999). *How tall, how short, how faraway?* (N. Tobin, Illus.). New York, NY: Holiday House.

❀ Bannatyne-Cugnet, J. (2000). *From far and wide: A citizenship scrapbook.* (S. N. Zhang, Illus.). Toronto, ON: Tundra Books.

❀ Bateman, R., & Archbold, R. (1998). *Safari.* Toronto, ON: Penguin Books Canada/Madison Press.

❀ Berkowitz, J. (2006). *Jurassic poop: What dinosaurs (and others) left behind.* (S. Mack, Illus.). Toronto, ON: Kids Can Press.

Bishop, N. (2004). *Forest explorer: A life-size field guide.* New York, NY: Scholastic.

❀ Hodge, D. (2000). *The kids book of Canada's railway and how the CPR was built.* (J. Mantha, Illus.). Toronto, ON: Kids Can Press.

❀ Innes, S., & Endrulat, H. (2008). *A bear in war.* (B. Deines, Illus.). Toronto, ON: Key Porter.

❀ Jordan-Fenton, C., & Pokiak-Fenton, M. (2013). *When I was eight.* (G. Grimard, Illus.). Toronto, ON: Annick Press.

Kalman, B., & Everts, T. (1994). *Butterflies and moths.* New York, NY: Crabtree.

Lipsey, J. (2007). *I love to draw cartoons!* New York, NY: Lark Books.

Lock, F. (2009). *Ponies and horses.* New York, NY: DK Publishing.

London, J. (1999). *Baby whale's journey.* (J. Van Zyle, Illus.). San Francisco, CA: Chronicle Books.

Loyie, L., & Brissenden, C. (2005). *The gathering tree.* (H. Holmlund, Illus.). Penticton, BC: Theytus Books.

❀ Mackin, B. (2001). *Soccer the winning way.* Vancouver, BC: Greystone Books.

❀ Milich, Z. (2001). *The city ABC book.* Toronto, ON: Kids Can Press.

Montgomery, S. (1999). *The snake scientist.* (N. Bishop, Photo.). Boston, MA: Houghton Mifflin.

❀ Morton, A. (1993). *In the company of whales: From the diary of a whale watcher.* Victoria, BC: Orca.

Pratt-Serafini, K. J. (2001). *Salamander rain: A lake and pond journal.* Nevada City, CA: Dawn Publications.

Pulley Sayre, A. (2001). *Dig, wait, listen: A desert toad's tale.* (B. Bash, Illus.). New York, NY: Greenwillow Books.

Schlaepfer, G. (2006). *Animal ways: Butterflies.* New York, NY: Marshall Cavendish.

Shapiro, N., & Adelson-Goldstein, J. (2009). *The Oxford picture dictionary: English–Arabic.* New York, NY: Oxford University Press.

Walker, A. M. (2001). *Fireflies.* Minneapolis, MN: Lerner Publications.

Yolen, J. (2001). *Welcome to the river of grass.* (L. Regan, Illus.). New York, NY: G. P. Putnam's Sons.

Grade 3 to Grade 4

FICTION

Abbott, T. (2011). *Underworlds: The battle begins.* (A. J. Caparo, Illus.). New York, NY: Scholastic.

Ahlberg, J., & Ahlberg, A. (1993). *It was a dark and stormy night.* London, UK: Viking.

Baker, J. (1995). *The story of Rosy Dock.* New York, NY: Greenwillow Books.

Blishen, E. (Comp.). (1963). *The Oxford book of poetry for children.* (B. Wildsmith, Illus.). London, UK: Oxford University Press.

Browne, A. (1983). *Gorilla.* New York, NY: Alfred A. Knopf.

❦ Carrier, R. (1985). *The hockey sweater.* (S. Cohen, Illus.; S. Fischman, Trans.). Montreal, QC: Tundra Books.

Cassedy, S. (1987). *Roomrimes.* (M. Chessare, Illus.). New York, NY: Thomas Crowell.

Ciardi, J. (1989). *The hopeful trout and other limericks.* (S. Meddaugh, Illus.). New York, NY: Houghton Mifflin.

Cooney, B. (1982). *Miss Rumphius.* New York, NY: Viking Penguin.

Cowen-Fletcher, J. (1994). *It takes a village.* New York, NY: Scholastic.

Dahl, R. (1961). *James and the giant peach.* (N. Ekholm Burkert, Illus.). New York, NY: Puffin Books.

Dahl, R. (1982). *Revolting rhymes.* (Q. Blake, Illus.). London, UK: Jonathan Cape.

Dahl, R. (1991). *The vicar of Nibbleswicke.* (Q. Blake, Illus.). New York, NY: Viking.

Denslow, S. P. (2002). *Georgie Lee.* (L. R. Perkins, Illus.). New York, NY: Greenwillow Books.

❦ Elwin, R., & Paulse, M. (1990). *Asha's mums.* (D. Lee, Illus.). Toronto, ON: Women's Press.

❦ Fitch, S., & Labrosse, D. (1997). *If you could wear my sneakers!* Toronto, ON: Doubleday.

❦ Gilmore, R. (2000). *Mina's spring of colours.* Markham, ON: Fitzhenry and Whiteside.

Hale, B. (2008). *Snoring Beauty.* (H. Fine, Illus.). Orlando, FL: Harcourt.

❦ Highway, T. (2001). *Caribou song* [Text in English and Cree]. (J. Rombough, Illus.). Toronto, ON: HarperCollins.

❦ Highway, T. (2002). *Dragonfly kites* [Text in English and Cree]. (B. Deines, Illus.). Toronto, ON: HarperCollins.

❦ Highway, T. (2003). *Fox on the ice* [Text in English and Cree]. (B. Deines, Illus.). Toronto, ON: HarperCollins.

Hope, L. L. (1904). *The Bobbsey twins.* New York, NY: Grosset and Dunlap.

Hopkins, L. B. (1987). *Click, rumble, roar: Poems about machines.* New York, NY: Thomas Y. Crowell.

Hyman, T. S. (1983). *Little Red Riding Hood.* New York, NY: Holiday House.

❦ Jam, T. (1997). *The fishing summer.* (A. Zhang, Illus.). Toronto, ON: Groundwood Books/ Douglas and McIntyre.

Janeczko, P. (2005). *A kick in the head: An everyday guide to poetic forms.* (D. Raschka, Illus.). Cambridge, MA: Candlewick Press.

❦ Jocelyn, M. (2005). *ABC × 3: English, Español, Français.* (T. Slaughter, Illus.). Toronto, ON: Tundra Books.

Juster, N. (1989). *As: A surfeit of similes.* (D. Small, Illus.). New York, NY: William Morrow.

Keats, E. J. (1971). *Over in the meadow.* New York, NY: Scholastic.

❦ Keens-Douglas, R. (1992). *The nutmeg princess.* (A. Galouchko, Illus.). Toronto, ON: Annick Press.

❦ Kusugak, M. (1990). *Baseball bats for Christmas.* (V. Krykorka, Illus.). Toronto, ON: Annick Press.

❦ Kusugak, M. (1992). *Hide and sneak.* (V. Krykorka, Illus.). Toronto, ON: Annick Press.

❦ Kusugak, M. (1993). *Northern lights: The soccer trails.* (V. Krykorka, Illus.). Toronto, ON: Annick Press.

❦ Laurence, M. (1979). *The olden days coat.* (M. Wood, Illus.). Toronto, ON: McClelland and Stewart.

Lear, E. (1964). *The complete book of nonsense.* New York, NY: Dodd, Mead.

Lester, J. (1996). *Sam and the tigers: A new retelling of Little Black Sambo.* (J. Pinkney, Illus.). New York, NY: Dial Books for Young Readers.

Lewis, J. P. (2013). *Face bug: Poems.* (K. Murphy, Illus.; F. B. Siskind, Photo.). Honesdale, PA: Wordsong.

❦ McGugan, J. (1994). *Josepha: A prairie boy's story.* (M. Kimber, Illus.). Red Deer, AB: Red Deer College Press.

Morpurgo, M. (2006). *The amazing journey of Adolphus Tips.* New York, NY: Scholastic.

Morpurgo, M. (2008). *Hansel and Gretel.* (E. Chichester Clark, Illus.). Cambridge, MA: Candlewick.

❦ Munsch, R. (1989). *Giant: Or, waiting for the Thursday boat.* (G. Tibo, Illus.). Toronto, ON: Annick Press.

❦ Nitto, T. (2006). *The red rock.* Toronto, ON: Groundwood Books.

Norton, M. (1952). *The borrowers.* (D. L. Stanley, Illus.). San Diego, CA: Harcourt.

Pierce, L. (2014). *Big Nate.* New York, NY: Harper.

Prelutsky, J. (2009). *Read a rhyme, write a rhyme.* (M. So, Illus.). New York, NY: Dragonfly Books.

❦ Provensen, A. (2001). *The master swordsman and the magic doorway: Two legends from ancient China.* Toronto, ON: Simon and Schuster Books for Young Readers.

❦ Roberts, K. (2001). *The thumb in the box.* (L. Franson, Illus.). Toronto, ON: Groundwood Books.

❦ Sanderson, E. (1990). *Two pairs of shoes.* (D. Beyer, Illus.). Winnipeg, MB: Pemmican Publications.

Scieszka, J. (1989). *The true story of the three little pigs.* (L. Smith, Illus.). New York, NY: Scholastic.

Van Camp, R. (1999). *A man called raven.* (G. Littlechild, Illus.). San Francisco, CA: Children's Book Press.

❦ Wallace, I. (1994). *Hansel and Gretel.* Toronto, ON: Douglas and McIntyre.

❦ Wallace, I. (1999). *Boy of the deeps.* Toronto, ON: Groundwood Books.

❦ Watts, I. M. (2000). *Remember me.* Toronto, ON: Tundra Books.

White, E. B. (1952). *Charlotte's web.* (G. Williams, Illus.). New York, NY: Harper and Row.

White, E. B. (1970). *Trumpet of the swan.* (E. Frascino, Illus.). New York, NY: Harper and Row.

Wiesner, D. (1988). *Free fall.* New York, NY: Lothrop, Lee and Shepard Books.

NONFICTION

Baker, J. (1991). *Window.* New York, NY: Greenwillow Books.

Chin, J. (2009). *Redwoods.* New York, NY: Roaring Book Press.

Collard, S. B. (2000). *The forest in the clouds.* (M. Rothman, Illus.). Watertown, MA: Charlesbridge.

Dewey, J. O. (1999). *Antarctic journal: Four months at the bottom of the world.* New York, NY: HarperCollins.

Floca, B. (2013). *Locomotive.* New York, NY: Atheneum/Simon and Schuster.

♣ Galloway, P. (2003). *Archers, alchemists and 98 other medieval jobs you might have loved or loathed.* (M. Newbigging, Illus.). Toronto, ON: Annick Press.

♣ Godkin, C. (1989). *Wolf Island.* Markham, ON: Fitzhenry and Whiteside.

♣ Granfield, L. (1997). *Silent night.* (N. Hofer & E. Hofer, Illus.). Toronto, ON: Tundra Books.

♣ Greenwood, B. (2001). *Gold rush fever: A story of the Klondike, 1898.* (H. Collins, Illus.). Toronto, ON: Kids Can Press.

♣ Harrison, T. (1992). *O Canada.* Toronto, ON: Kids Can Press.

Hurst, C. O. (2001). *Rocks in his head.* (J. Stevenson, Illus.). New York, NY: Greenwillow Books.

Levine, S., & Johnston, L. (2000). *The science of sound and music.* New York, NY: Sterling.

♣ MacLeod, E. (2004). *Helen Keller: A determined life.* Toronto, ON: Kids Can Press.

Martin, J. B. (1998). *Snowflake Bentley.* (M. Azarian, Illus.). Boston, MA: Houghton Mifflin.

Maydak, M. (2001). *Salmon stream.* (M. S. Maydak, Illus.). Nevada City, CA: Dawn Publications.

♣ Rhodes, R. (2001). *A first book of Canadian art.* Toronto, ON: Owl Books/Greey de Pencier Books. (All ages)

♣ Swanson, D. (2009). *You are weird: Your body's peculiar parts and funny functions.* (K. Boake, Illus.). Toronto, ON: Kids Can Press.

♣ Szpirglas, J. (2004). *Gross universe: Your guide to all disgusting things under the sun.* (M. Cho, Illus.). Toronto, ON: Maple Tree Press.

Truss, L. (2006). *Eats, shoots and leaves: Why, commas really do make a difference!* (B. Timmons, Illus.). New York, NY: G. P. Putnam's Sons.

Wetherford, C. B. (2008). *Before John was a jazz giant: A song by John Coltrane.* (S. Qualls, Illus.). New York, NY: Henry Holt.

Grade 4 to Grade 5

FICTION

Avi. (2000). *Crispin: The cross of lead.* New York, NY: Hyperion.

Babbitt, N. (1975). *Tuck everlasting.* New York, NY: Farrar, Straus and Giroux.

Balliett, B. (2004). *Chasing Vermeer.* (B. Helquist, Illus.). New York, NY: Scholastic.

Bauer, M. D. (1986). *On my honor.* New York, NY: Bantam Doubleday Dell.

♣ Booth, D. (Ed.). (1995). *Images of nature: Canadian poets and the Group of Seven.* Toronto, ON: Kids Can Press.

Browne, A. (1981). *Hansel and Gretel.* London, UK: Julia MacRae Books.

Browne, A. (1989). *The tunnel.* London, UK: Julia MacRae Books.

Browne, A. (1998). *Voices in the park.* New York, NY: DK Publishing.

Browne, A. (2010). *Me and you.* London, UK: Doubleday.

♣ Butler, G. (1998). *The Hangashore.* Toronto, ON: Tundra Books.

Byars, B. (1996). *Dead letter.* New York, NY: Viking.

Choldenko, G. (2004). *Al Capone does my shirts.* New York, NY: G. P. Putnam's Sons.

Coerr, E. (1977). *Sadako and the thousand paper cranes*. (R. Himler, Illus.). New York, NY: G. P. Putnam's Sons.

Coerr, E. (1993). *Sadako*. (E. Young, Illus.). New York, NY: G. P. Putnam's Sons.

Collington, P. (1997). *A small miracle*. New York, NY: Alfred Knopf.

Cowell, C. (2003). *How to train your dragon*. New York, NY: Little Brown.

Creech, S. (2009). *The unfinished angel*. New York, NY: HarperCollins.

❧ Croteau, M. D. (2007). *Mr. Gauguin's heart*. (I. Arsenault, Illus.). Toronto, ON: Tundra Books.

Curtis, C. P. (1995). *The Watsons go to Birmingham—1963*. New York, NY: Bantam Doubleday Dell/Delacorte.

❧ Delaney, R. (2013). *The metro dogs of Moscow*. Toronto, ON: Penguin.

DiCamillo, K. (2006). *The miraculous journey of Edward Tulane*. (B. Ibatoulline, Illus.). Cambridge, MA: Candlewick Press.

Field, E. (1982). *Wynken, Blynken and Nod*. (S. Jeffers, Illus.). New York, NY: E. P. Dutton.

Frost, R. (1976). *Stopping by woods on a snowy evening*. (S. Jeffers, Illus.). New York, NY: Dutton Books.

Frost, R. (1988). *Birches*. (E. Young, Illus.). New York, NY: Henry Holt and Company.

Giff, P. R. (1997). *Lily's crossing*. New York, NY: Delacorte Press.

Graham, K. (1908). *The wind in the willows*. New York, NY: Charles Scribner's Sons.

Hoberman, M. A., & Winston, L. (Comp.). (2009). *The tree that time built: A celebration of nature, science, and imagination*. Naperville, IL: Sourcebooks Jabberwocky.

Hughes, T. (1968). *The iron man*. London, UK: Faber and Faber.

Hughes, T. (2007). *Collected poems for children*. (R. Briggs, Illus.). New York, NY: Farrar, Straus and Giroux.

Jacques, B. (1987). *Redwall*. New York, NY: Philomel.

Kinney, J. (2007). *Diary of a wimpy kid*. New York, NY: Amulet Books.

Macaulay, D. (1995). *Shortcut*. Boston, MA: Houghton Mifflin.

❧ MacGregor, R. (1997–2013). *The Screech Owls series*. Toronto, ON: McClelland and Stewart.

❧ Major, K. (2000). *Eh? to Zed: A Canadian ABeCedarium*. (A. Daniel, Illus.). Calgary, AB: Red Deer Press.

Martin, B. (2008). *Big book of poetry*. (E. Carle, Illus.). New York, NY: Simon and Schuster Books for Young Readers.

❧ Mollel, T. (1990). *The orphan boy*. (P. Morin, Illus.). Toronto, ON: Oxford University Press.

❧ Morin, P. (1998). *Animal dreaming: An Aboriginal dreamtime story*. Toronto, ON: Stoddart Kids.

Naylor, P. R. (2003). *Bernie Magruder and the bats in the belfry*. New York, NY: Atheneum Books for Young Readers.

Oberman, S. (1994). *The always prayer shawl*. (T. Lewin, Illus.). Honesdale, PA: Boyds Mills Press.

Paterson, K. (1992). *The king's equal*. New York, NY: HarperCollins.

Pearce, P. (1958). *Tom's midnight garden*. London, UK: Oxford University Press.

❧ Pendziwol, J. (2005). *The red sash*. (N. Debon, Illus.). Toronto, ON: Groundwood Books.

Prelutsky, J. (1983). *The Random House book of poetry*. (A. Lobel, Illus.). New York, NY: Random House.

Prelutsky, J. (1984). *The new kid on the block*. (J. Stevenson, Illus.). New York, NY: Greenwillow Books.

Rosen, M. (2007). *Something's drastic.* (T. Archbold, Illus.). London, UK: Collins.

Sandburg, C. (1944). Fog. In *Chicago poems.* New York, NY: Harcourt Brace.

Sharmat, M. W., & Sharmat, M. (2006). *Nate the Great talks turkey.* (J. Wheeler, Illus.). New York, NY: Delacorte Press.

Siebert, D. (2002). *Motorcycle song.* (L. Jenkins, Illus.). New York, NY: HarperCollins.

Silverstein, S. (1981). *A light in the attic.* New York, NY: Harper and Row.

Stein, D. E. (2010). *Interrupting chicken.* Somerville, MA: Candlewick.

🍁 Taylor, C. (1987). *The doll.* Toronto, ON: Douglas and McIntyre.

Valentine, J. (1994). *One dad, two dads, brown dad, blue dad.* (M. Sarecky, Illus.). Boston, MA: Alyson Wonderland.

🍁 Valgardson, W. D. (1997). *Garbage Creek.* Toronto, ON: Groundwood Books.

Van Allsburg, C. (1992). *The widow's broom.* New York, NY: Houghton Mifflin.

Whitman, R. (1968). Listening to grownups quarrelling. In *The marriage wig and other poems.* New York, NY: Harcourt Brace.

Wiesner, D. (1991). *Tuesday.* New York, NY: Clarion.

Wilson, K. (2009). *What's the weather inside?* (B. Blitt, Illus.). New York, NY: Margaret McElderry Books.

NONFICTION

Anholt, L. (1999). *Stone girl, bone girl: The Story of Mary Anning.* (S. Moxley, Illus.). New York, NY: Orchard Books.

Atkins, J. (1999). *Mary Anning and the sea dragon.* (M. Dooling, Illus.). New York, NY: Farrar, Straus and Giroux.

🍁 Bateman, R. (2008). *Polar worlds: Life at the ends of the Earth.* Toronto, ON: Scholastic/Madison Press.

🍁 Bowers, V. (2004). *That's very Canadian! An exceptionally interesting report about all things Canadian.* (D. Eastman, Illus.). Toronto, ON: Maple Tree Press.

🍁 Brewster, H. (2004). *On Juno Beach: Canada's D-Day heroes.* Markham, ON: Scholastic Canada/ Madison Press.

🍁 Brewster, H. (2006). *At Vimy Ridge: Canada's greatest World War I victory.* Toronto, ON: Scholastic.

Goodman, S. E. (2001). *Claws, coats and camouflage: The ways animals fit into their world.* (M. J. Doolittle, Photo.). Brookfield, CN: Millbrook Press.

🍁 Granfield, L. (1995). *In Flanders fields: The story of the poem by John McCrae.* (J. Wilson, Illus.). Toronto, ON: Lester.

🍁 Hegedus, A., & Rainey, K. (1999). *Shooting hoops and skating loops: Great inventions in sports.* (B. Slavin, Illus.). Toronto, ON: Tundra Books.

🍁 Jordan-Fenton, C., & Pokiak-Fenton, M. (2010). *Fatty legs: A true story.* (L. Amini-Holmes, Illus.). Toronto, ON: Annick Press.

🍁 Kaplan, W., & Tanaka, S. (1998). *One more border: The true story of one family's escape from war-torn Europe.* (S. Taylor, Illus.). Toronto, ON: Groundwood Books.

🍁 Kuitenbrouwer, P. (2004). *Our song: The story of O Canada.* (A. Spires, Illus.). Montreal, QC: Lobster Press.

🍁 Levine, K. (2002). *Hana's suitcase.* Toronto, ON: Second Story Press.

❧ Macleod, E. (2003). *Albert Einstein: A life of genius.* Toronto, ON: Kids Can Press.

Napier, M. (2002). *Z is for Zamboni: A hockey alphabet.* (M. Rose, Illus.). Chelsea, MI: Sleeping Bear Press.

❧ Smith, D. (2011). *This child, every child: A book about the world's children.* (S. Armstrong, Illus.). Toronto, ON: Kids Can Press.

❧ Suzuki, D., & Vanderlinden, K. (1999). *You are the earth.* (W. Edwards, Illus.). Vancouver, BC: Greystone Books.

❧ Tanaka, S. (1997). *The buried city of Pompeii: What it was like when Vesuvius exploded (I was there).* (G. Ruhl, J. McMaster, & P. Christopher, Illus.). Richmond Hill, ON: Scholastic Canada/Madison Press.

❧ Thornhill, J. (2006). *I found a dead bird: The kids' guide to the cycle of life and death.* Toronto, ON: Maple Tree Press.

Tripp, N. (1994). *Thunderstorm!* (J. Wijngaard, Illus.). New York, NY: Dial Books.

Ulmer, M. (2001). *M is for maple: A Canadian alphabet.* (M. Rose, Illus.). Chelsea, MI: Sleeping Bear Press.

Grade 5 to Grade 6

FICTION

❧ Bastedo, J. (2001). *Tracking triple seven.* Calgary, AB: Red Deer Press.

❧ Buffie, M. (1987). *Who is Frances Rain?* Toronto, ON: Kids Can Press.

Creech, S. (1994). *Walk two moons.* New York, NY: HarperCollins.

Creech, S. (2001). *Love that dog.* New York, NY: HarperCollins.

DuPrau, J. (2003). *The city of Ember.* New York, NY: Random House.

❧ Ellis, D. (1999). *Looking for X.* Toronto, ON: Groundwood Books.

❧ Ellis, D. (2000). *The breadwinner.* Toronto, ON: Douglas and McIntyre.

❧ Ellis, S. (1997). *Back of beyond.* Toronto, ON: Groundwood Books.

Fenner, C. (1991). *Randall's wall.* New York, NY: HarperCollins.

Fine, A. (2002). *Up on cloud nine.* London, UK: Doubleday.

Fletcher, R. (1998). *Flying solo.* New York, NY: Clarion Books.

Florian, D. (2010). *Poetrees.* New York, NY: Beach Lane Books.

Franco, B. (2009). *Messing around on the monkey bars and other school poems for two voices.* (J. Hartland, Illus.). Cambridge, MA: Candlewick Press.

French, J. (2001). *Hitler's daughter.* London, UK: Collins.

Funke, C. (2001). *The thief lord.* (C. Funke, Illus.). New York, NY: Scholastic.

❧ Galloway, P. (1995). *Aleta and the queen: A tale of ancient Greece.* (N. Cousineau, Illus.). Toronto, ON: Annick Press.

❧ Galloway, P. (1995). *Atalanta: The fastest runner in the world.* (N. Cousineau, Illus.). Toronto, ON: Annick Press.

❧ Galloway, P. (1997). *Daedalus and the minotaur.* (N. Cousineau, Illus.). Toronto, ON: Annick Press.

Gaiman, N. (2008). *The graveyard book.* (D. McKean, Illus.). New York, NY: HarperCollins.

❧ Gilmore, R. (2011). *That boy Red.* Toronto, ON: HarperTrophy Canada.

Gravett, E. (2005). *Wolves.* London, UK: MacMillan.

Harrison, T. (1987). *The cremation of Sam McGee.* (Poem by Robert W. Service). New York, NY: Greenwillow Books.

Hesse, K. (1998). *Just juice.* New York, NY: Scholastic.

❧ Horrocks, A. (2000). *Topher.* Toronto, ON: Stoddart.

Hughes, L. (1950). City. In *The Langston Hughes reader.* New York, NY: Harold Ober Associates.

Hughes, L. (1960). Poem. In L. B. Hopkins (Ed.), *Don't you turn back: Poems by Langston Hughes.* New York, NY: Knopf.

Hughes, M. (1980). *The keeper of the Isis light.* London, UK: Mammoth.

Innocenti, R. (1985). *Rose Blanche.* Mankato, MN: Creative Education.

❧ Jocelyn, M. (2000). *Earthly astonishments.* Toronto, ON: Tundra Books.

Kehret, P. (2003). *Escaping the giant wave.* New York, NY: Simon and Schuster Books for Young Readers.

Kennedy, C. (2005). *A family of poems: My favorite poetry for children.* (J. J. Muth, Illus.). New York, NY: Hyperion.

Kibuishi, K. (2011). *Amulet: The last council.* New York, NY: Graphix.

L'Engle, M. (1962). *A wrinkle in time.* New York, NY: Farrar, Straus and Giroux.

❧ Little, J. (2001). *Willow and Twig.* Toronto, ON: Puffin Books.

Lowry, L. (1993). *The giver.* Boston, MA: Houghton Mifflin.

Lunn, J. (1981). *The root cellar.* New York, NY: Charles Scribner's Sons.

Macaulay, D. (1990). *Black and white.* New York, NY: Houghton Mifflin.

Mitchell, S. (Adapter). (2007). *The tinderbox.* (B. Ibatoulline, Illus.). Cambridge, MA: Candlewick.

Newman, L. (1998). *Belinda's bouquet.* (M. Willhoite, Illus.). Anola, MB: Blue Heron Enterprises.

❧ Oppel, K. (1997). *Silverwing.* Scarborough, ON: HarperCollins.

Paterson, K. (1977). *Bridge to Terabithia.* New York, NY: HarperCollins.

❧ Pearson, K. (1987). *A handful of time.* Markham, ON: Viking Kestrel.

❧ Pearson, K. (1996). *Awake and dreaming.* Toronto, ON: Viking.

❧ Pratt, E. J. (1923). The shark. In *Newfoundland verse.* (F. Varley, Illus.). Toronto, ON: Ryerson Press.

Rowling, J. K. (1998). *Harry Potter and the sorcerer's stone.* New York, NY: A. A. Levine Books.

Sachar, L. (2000). *Holes.* New York, NY: Dell Yearling.

Scieszka, J. (Ed.). (2012). *Guys read: The sports pages.* New York, NY: Walden Pond Press.

Shreve, S. (1987). *Lucy Forever and Miss Rosetree, shrinks.* New York, NY: Alfred A. Knopf.

❧ Smucker, B. (1977). *Underground to Canada.* Toronto, ON: Clarke, Irwin.

Spinelli, J. (1990). *Maniac Magee.* New York, NY: Little, Brown.

❧ Sterling, S. (1992). *My name is Seepeetza.* Vancouver, BC: Groundwood Books.

❧ Taylor, C. (1987). *The doll.* Toronto, ON: Douglas and McIntyre.

Thayer, E. L. (2000). *Casey at the bat: A ballad of the republic sung in the year 1888.* (C. Bing, Illus.). New York, NY: Handprint Books.

Twain, M. (1963). *The adventures of Huckleberry Finn.* New York, NY: Washington Square Press. (Original work published 1885)

Van Allsburg, C. (1986). *The stranger.* Boston, MA: Houghton Mifflin.

❧ Walters, E. (2002). *Camp X.* Toronto, ON: Viking.

Wild, M. (1991). *Let the celebrations begin!* (J. Vivas, Illus.). Adelaide, Australia: Omnibus Books.

❉ Wilson, E. (1995). *The Inuk Mountie adventure.* Toronto, ON: HarperCollins Canada.

❉ Withrow, S. (1998). *Bat summer.* Toronto, ON: Groundwood Books.

❉ Wynne-Jones, T. (1993). *Some of the kinder planets.* Toronto, ON: Douglas and McIntyre.

❉ Wynne-Jones, T. (1994). *The book of changes.* Toronto, ON: Douglas and McIntyre.

❉ Wynne-Jones, T. (1999). *Lord of the fries and other stories.* Toronto, ON: Douglas and McIntyre.

❉ Yee, P. (1996). *Ghost train.* (H. Chan, Illus.). Toronto, ON: Groundwood Books.

York, C. B. (1986). *Secrets in the attic.* New York, NY: Scholastic.

NONFICTION

❉ Bogart, J. (2003). *Emily Carr: At the edge of the world.* (M. Newhouse, Illus.). Toronto, ON: Tundra Books.

❉ Brewster, H. (2007). *Carnation, Lily, Lily Rose: The story of a painting.* Toronto, ON: Kids Can Press.

❉ Brewster, H. (2009). *Dieppe: Canada's darkest day of World War II.* Toronto, ON: Scholastic.

❉ Dumas, P. (2013). *Pīsim finds her miskanow.* (L. Paul, Illus.). Winnipeg, MB: HighWater Press.

❉ Granfield, L. (2001). *Where poppies grow: A World War I companion.* Toronto, ON: Stoddart Kids.

❉ Graydon, S. (2003). *Made you look: How advertising works and why you should know.* (W. Clark, Illus.). Toronto, ON: Annick Press.

❉ Greenwood, B. (1998). *The last safe house: A story of the underground railway.* (H. Collins, Illus.). Toronto, ON: Kids Can Press.

❉ Hodge, D. (2006). *The kids book of Canadian immigration.* (J. Mantha, Illus.). Toronto, ON: Kids Can Press.

Holler Aulenbach, N., & Barton, H. A. (2001). *Exploring caves: Journeys into the earth.* Washington, DC: National Geographic Society.

Kodama, T. (1995). *Shin's tricycle.* (N. Ando, Illus.). New York, NY: Walker.

Littlechild, G. (1993). *This land is my land.* Emeryville, CA: Children's Book Press.

Martin, R., & Nibley, L. (2009). *The mysteries of Beethoven's hair.* Watertown, MA: Charlesbridge.

Maruki, T. (1980). *Hiroshima no pika.* New York, NY: Lothrop, Lee and Shepard Books.

Ottaviani, J. (2013). *Primates: The fearless science of Jane Goodall, Dian Fossey, and Biruté Galdikas.* (M. Wicks, Illus.). New York, NY: First Second.

❉ Ross, V. (2006). *You can't read this: Forbidden books, lost writing, mistranslations, and codes.* Toronto, ON: Tundra Books.

❉ Savage, C. (2001). *Born to be a cowgirl.* Vancouver, BC: Greystone Books.

❉ Shoveller, H. (2006). *Ryan and Jimmy and the well in Africa that brought them together.* Toronto, ON: Kids Can Press.

❉ Trottier, M. (2005). *Terry Fox: A story of hope.* Markham, ON: Scholastic Canada.

Grade 6 to Grade 8

FICTION

Almond, D. (1999). *Skellig.* New York, NY: Delacorte Press.

Almond, D. (2000). *Kit's wilderness*. New York, NY: Delacorte Press.

❀ Barwin, G. (2001). *Seeing stars*. Toronto, ON: Stoddart Kids.

❀ Bass, K. (2008). *Run like Jäger*. Regina, SK: Coteau Books.

❀ Bow, E. (2010). *Plain Kate*. Toronto, ON: Scholastic.

Bloor, E. (1997). *Tangerine*. Orlando, FL: Harcourt.

❀ Brenna, B. (2005). *Wild orchid*. Calgary, AB: Red Deer Press.

❀ Brenna, B. (2009). *Something to hang on to*. Saskatoon, SK: Thistledown Press.

❀ Brenna, B. (2011). *Falling for Henry*. Calgary, AB: Red Deer Press.

❀ Britt, F. (2012). *Jane, the fox and me*. (I. Arsenault, Illus.). Toronto, ON: Groundwood Books/ House of Anansi.

❀ Buchan, B. (1975). *The dragon children*. (K. Cole, Illus.). Richmond Hill, ON: Scholastic-TAB.

Byars, B. (1997). *Death's door*. New York, NY: Viking.

Collins, S. (2003). *Gregor the Overlander*. New York, NY: Scholastic Press.

Cooney, C. (1990). *The face on the milk carton*. New York, NY: Bantam.

Cooney, C. (1995). *Both sides of time*. New York, NY: Dell Laurel-Leaf.

Cooper, S. (1969). *The dark is rising*. New York, NY: Collier Macmillan.

Dessen, S. (2009). *Along for the ride*. New York, NY: Viking.

❀ Doyle, B. (2001). *Mary Ann Alice*. Toronto, ON: Groundwood Books.

Frank, A. (1952). *The diary of a young girl: Anne Frank*. New York, NY: Doubleday.

❀ Friesen, G. (2000). *Men of stone*. Toronto, ON: Kids Can Press.

Gallo, D. (Ed.). (2008). *Owning it: Stories about teens with disabilities*. Somerville, MA: Candlewick.

Haddix, M. P. (2005). *Double identity*. New York, NY: Aladdin Paperbacks.

❀ Hartman, R. (2012). *Seraphina*. Toronto, ON: Random House.

❀ Heneghan, J. (2006). *Safe house*. Victoria, BC: Orca.

Herrick, S. (1999). *The spangled drongo*. St. Lucia, Australia: University of Queensland Press.

Herrick, S. (2002). *Tom Jones saves the world*. St. Lucia, Australia: University of Queensland Press.

Hesse, K. (1997). *Out of the dust*. New York, NY: Scholastic Press.

❀ Huser, G. (2003). *Stitches*. Toronto, ON: Groundwood Books.

❀ Jocelyn, M. (2010). *Folly*. Toronto, ON: Tundra Books.

Konigsburg, E. L. (2002). *Silent to the bone*. New York, NY: Aladdin Paperbacks.

Korman, G. (2003). *The discovery*. Dive, Book 1. New York, NY: Scholastic.

❀ Lawrence, I. (2006). *Gemini summer*. New York, NY: Delacorte Press.

❀ Lightfoot, G. (2010). *Canadian Railroad Trilogy*. (I. Wallace, Illus.). Toronto, ON: Groundwood Books.

❀ Lottridge, C. B. (2010). *Home is beyond the mountains*. Toronto, ON: Groundwood Books/ House of Anansi Press.

Lowry, L. (2000). *Gathering blue*. Boston, MA: Houghton Mifflin.

❀ Lunn, J. (1997). *The hollow tree*. Toronto, ON: Alfred A. Knopf Canada.

MacHale, D. J. (2002). *The merchant of death*. Pendragon, Book 1. New York, NY: Aladdin Paperbacks.

❀ Martel, S. (1980). *The king's daughter*. Vancouver, BC: Douglas and McIntyre.

❀ Matt, J. (2013). *Northwest Passage: Stan Rogers*. Toronto, ON: Groundwood Books.

Morimoto, J. (1987). *My Hiroshima*. Sydney, Australia: Collins.

Morpurgo, M. (2008). *Arthur, high king of Britain*. London, UK: Egmont UK.

Muth, J. (2002). *The three questions*. New York, NY: Scholastic.

❦ Oppel, K. (2014). *The Boundless*. Toronto, ON: HarperCollins.

O'Roark Dowell, F. (2000). *Dovey Coe*. New York, NY: Atheneum Books for Young Readers.

❦ Pearson, K. (2007). *A perfect gentle knight*. Toronto, ON: Puffin Canada.

❦ Polak, M. (2008). *What world is left*. Victoria: Orca. (y/a)

❦ Porter, P. (2005). *The crazy man*. Toronto, ON: Groundwood Books.

❦ Porter, P. (2011). *I'll be watching*. Toronto, ON: Groundwood Books.

Pullman, P. (1995). *The golden compass*. New York, NY: Ballantine Books.

Rees, C. (2001). *Witch child*. Cambridge, MA: Candlewick Press.

Riordan, R. (2008). *The maze of bones*. The 39 Clues, Book 1. New York, NY: Scholastic.

Rowling, J. K. (2005). *Harry Potter and the half-blood prince*. Vancouver, BC: Raincoast Books.

Shan, D. (2000). *Cirque du Freak*. The Saga of Darren Shan, Book 1. London, UK: Collins.

Shiga, J. (2010). *Meanwhile*. New York, NY: Amulet Books.

Silverstein, S. (1964). *The giving tree*. New York, NY: Harper and Row.

❦ Slade, A. (2001). *Dust*. Toronto, ON: HarperCollins.

Spiegelman, A. (1986). *Maus I: A survivor's tale*. New York, NY: Pantheon Books.

Spinelli, J. (2000). *Stargirl*. New York, NY: Dell Laurel-Leaf.

❦ Tamaki, M. (2008). *Skim*. (J. Tamaki, Illus.). Toronto, ON: Groundwood Books.

❦ Tamiki, M. (2014). *This one summer*. (J. Tamaki, Illus.). Toronto, ON: Groundwood Books.

Tan, S. (2006). *The arrival*. New York, NY: Arthur A Levine Books.

❦ Thayer, E. L. (2006). *Casey at the bat*. (J. Morse, Illus.). Toronto, ON: Kids Can Press.

Thomas, G., & Crossley-Holland, K. (1985). *Tales from the Mabinogion*. New York, NY: Overlook Press.

Tolkien, J. R. R. (1937). *The hobbit*. Boston, MA: Houghton.

❦ Toten, T. (Ed.). (2010). *Piece by piece: Stories about fitting into Canada*. Toronto, ON: Penguin Canada.

❦ Tullson, D. (2005). *Red sea*. Victoria, BC: Orca.

Walliams, D. (2008). *The boy in the dress*. (Q. Blake, Illus.). London, UK: HarperCollins.

❦ Walters, E. (2009). *Wave*. Toronto, ON: Doubleday Canada.

❦ Walters, E. (2012). *The bully boys*. Toronto, ON: Puffin.

❦ Watts, I. N. (2008). *Good-bye Marianne: The graphic novel*. (K. E. Shoemaker, Illus.). Toronto, ON: Tundra Books.

Weiss, M. J., & Weiss, H. S. (Eds.). (2009). *This family is driving me crazy*. New York, NY: Putnam's.

Westerfeld, S. (2005). *Uglies*. New York, NY: Simon Pulse.

Wrede, P. (1990). *Dealing with dragons*. The Enchanted Forest Chronicles, Book 1. San Diego, CA: Magic Carpet Books.

❦ Wynne-Jones, T. (1995). *The maestro*. Toronto, ON: Groundwood Books.

❦ Wynne-Jones, T. (2006). *Rex Zero and the end of the world*. Toronto, ON: Groundwood Books.

NONFICTION

Bergamotto, L. (2009). *Skin: The bare facts*. San Francisco, CA: Zest Books.

❦ Ellis, D. (2005). *Our stories, our songs: African children talk about AIDS*. Markham, ON: Fitzhenry and Whiteside.

❦ Graydon, S. (2004). *In your face: The culture of beauty and you*. (K. Klassen & K. Lemay, Illus.). Toronto, ON: Annick Press.

Satrapi, M. (2003). *Persepolis*. New York, NY: Pantheon Books.

GLOSSARY

aesthetic response describes the enjoyment or appreciation a reader feels while reading a text or viewing an image. An aesthetic response is concerned not with comprehension, word meanings, recall, or learning, but with the deep personal engagement of reader and text/image. Aesthetic responses are not necessarily pleasurable; some texts/images can be deeply moving and cause stress or discomfort rather than pleasure, but such responses are still considered to be aesthetic. p. 159, 414

anime refers to Japanese cartoon or animation. p. 457

assessment involves collecting and analyzing information about learners to help make decisions about what they know, value, and are able to do. The end goal of assessment is to inform future decisions about instruction. p. 6, 54, 117, 153, 196, 222

automaticity is the ability to carry out a complex act rapidly and without conscious awareness or control. An important characteristic of automaticity is that an individual can perform a complex skill or act while performing another that may not be automatic. As readers become proficient and are able to identify most of the words in texts automatically, they can direct their mental resources to constructing meaning. Most experts feel that readers need to engage in extensive reading to achieve automaticity. p. 196

basal reading series or **basal readers** are grade-levelled series of textbooks and related materials for teaching reading and other dimensions of literacy. These series generally consist of teacher guides, student anthologies, workbooks, and supplemental materials such as assessment materials, big books, correlated **trade books**, audiovisual aids, and computer software. Basal series derive their name from the original intention that they form the basis of a program of instruction in reading. p. 7, 44, 228, 368

basic interpersonal communication skills (BICS) refers to context-specific social language, such as what happens in the lunchroom or on the playground. This language is usually developed among second language learners within two years. p. 14, 64

capital is a term coined by sociologist Pierre Bourdieu. There are three kinds of capital: economic (referring to financial resources), social (referring to social connections), and cultural (referring to academic and other qualifications). p. 33

challenged books are those books that groups or individuals have attempted to censor by having them removed from the shelves of libraries, especially in schools. Not all challenges result in the removal of a book. Specific procedures are usually followed in dealing with a challenge to a book, and a committee of parents and teachers usually makes the final decision on whether a book should be removed from a school library. p. 438

chapter books are beginning novels for children that are designed to facilitate the reader's transition from a reliance on illustrations for creating meaning (as is done with **picture books**) to a stronger reliance on text. Many chapter books are available for young readers. Like **picture books**, chapter books include all the major **genres** of literature. An example of a chapter book is *Marty McGuire*, by Kate Messner. p. 208, 381

children's literature is a term used in this book to refer to those print materials (fiction, nonfiction, magazines, and poetry) that possess an aesthetic quality, that are written primarily with an audience of young readers in mind, that provide children with pleasurable and challenging reading experiences, that are acknowledged by critics to meet high standards, and that are well written and illustrated. p. 44, 170, 367

cognitive academic language proficiency (CALP) refers to the academic language that students need in order to understand content-area lessons and/or texts. English language learners usually take five to seven years to develop this level of linguistic proficiency. p. 14, 64

comprehensible input is used with regard to second language learning and refers to exposure to the new language that is only slightly above what the learner can already understand and use. p. 62

context cues are knowledge and linguistic cues that help a reader construct meaning when reading. Linguistic cues involve both syntactic (**grammar** or word order) and semantic (meaning) aspects of language. When readers use context cues, they make predictions and monitor their reading in terms of what sounds right and makes sense. p. 133, 241

critical literacy goes beyond providing students with conventional literacy skills to equipping them to critically examine how texts reflect power structures and inequalities. It involves examining texts from different perspectives and taking action to promote social justice. p. 7, 159, 209

cuing systems are the systems of **semantics**, **syntax**, **pragmatics,** and **graphophonics** that readers and writers use to make meaning from printed symbols. Pictures, diagrams, and charts also act as cues for readers to construct meaning, but *cuing systems* usually refers to the text-based systems discussed in this book. p. 72, 158, 192, 225

culturally and linguistically diverse (CLD) refers to students who are learning in a language that is not their first language. This grouping includes students coined as ESL (English as a second language), EAL (English as an additional language), and ELL (English language learner). The term *CLD* recognizes the ties between language and culture, and acknowledges that these learners bring an already acquired language and culture to their learning. p. 3, 59, 112, 165, 201, 224

cursive writing is handwriting in which the letters are connected to one another with a continuous flow from one stroke to another. The most prevalent form of handwriting today is a combination of printing and cursive writing, with printed uppercase letters and cursive lowercase letters. p. 358

dialect is a variety of a spoken language used in a geographic region or by members of a social class. Every dialect has distinctive patterns, rules, and features. p. 78, 134, 226

differentiation in a lesson or activity can allow for learners to perform differently on the same learning task. Educators will not expect all students to make the same learning connections, as they are learning in different ways and at different rates. p. 38, 202

directionality refers to the way print is written and read. More specifically, students learning to read English learn that (1) print begins at the top of a page and continues to the bottom, (2) text is read and written from left to right on the page, (3) the front of a book opens on the right, and (4) directionality is important to the identification of letters. p. 114

discourse is a linguistics term used to describe a continuous stretch of spoken or written language longer than one sentence. Frequently, *discourse* is reserved for spoken language and *text* for written language. Discourse is also used to refer to specific topics or types of language (e.g., the discourse of high finance). Discourse can be perceived as process and text as product. p. 12, 113

domain is a concept referring to the space (e.g., an academic space or the world of the mosque) where the dimensions of language and literacy are practised and where what gets practised as language and literacy is related to the domain (e.g., essay writing or reading a religious text). p. 5, 111

early literacy refers to the specific form of literacy practised by young children. This term respects the fact that young children communicate in various ways; it also views this communication as meaningful in its own right, not just a lesser form of adult communication. p. 7, 110

efferent response describes a response to literature, movies, etc., in which the intent is to focus on what can be learned, observed, and taken away from the reading/viewing. Focused on gaining information, an efferent response is at the opposite end of the continuum from an aesthetic response. p. 159, 414

emergent literacy is a term developed during the early 1980s to refer to the literacy development of young children. Sulzby (1985) defined emergent literacy as the reading and writing concepts, attitudes, and behaviours that precede and develop into conventional literacy. Emergent literacy begins early in children's lives at home, involves interactions with print, and is part of, rather than separate from, reading and writing development. p. 110

English as a second language (ESL) is an official term often used by governments or school boards in relation to learners whose first language is not English. p. 3

English language learner (ELL) refers to a learner learning English in addition to his or her first language(s). p. 3, 43

evaluation is a measurement of learner performance on a particular skill or set of skills in order to make a judgment about a learner's ability. p. 8, 27, 59, 153

expository writing is a form of writing that provides information, detailed explanations, judgments, and supporting examples. It may also be persuasive or argumentative. p. 275, 295

expressive writing is found in diaries, journals, and personal letters; the writer's intent is to share personal points of view, ideas, thoughts, and questions. Expressive writing aims to communicate the personal identity of the writer. p. 275, 293

fan fiction is a text created as a response to an admired text (e.g., a web show, movie, comic book, novel) wherein the new text includes elements (e.g., characters, plot features) of the original admired text. p. 45

fan sites are websites that allow fans to interact and engage with the object of their affection and engage with others who share a common passion. It can include video clips, images, latest news, and discussion boards. p. 457

fantasy is a **genre** of literature that engages and stimulates the reader's imagination and gives free rein to endless possibilities. The reader is taken to worlds where animals and toys can speak, where people can travel across time and into completely fictional worlds. Modern fantasy is rooted in folk tales, myths, and dreams. Examples of modern fantasy literature include *Charlotte's Web* by E. B. White and *Harry Potter and the Philosopher's Stone* by J. K. Rowling. p. 208, 386

formative assessment is ongoing assessment that considers learners' progress and provides feedback as learners work toward a goal. p. 222

funds of knowledge are the various resources learners bring with them to school. They include cultural, intellectual, and physical resources. p. 11, 38, 111, 159, 193, 225

genre refers to the different literary and linguistic forms and functions of various texts. **Narrative**, for example, is different in form and function from expository text, which is different again from persuasive or descriptive text. Genre also refers to categories of literature such as myth, fable, poetry, **fantasy**, and **realistic fiction**. Each of these genres meets different functions and uses a variety of different forms to achieve the intentions of the text. p. 31, 40, 113, 161, 206, 368

grammar is a term that has been largely replaced by the term **syntax**. However, where "grammar" is used, it refers to three distinct perspectives on language: (1) systemic-functional grammar, a description of the choices made by language users based on context and intention in order to create meaning; (2) generative-transformational grammar, a description of how language works as a process based on language universals; and (3) prescriptive grammar, focused on the rules of language and how language *should* work. Most grammar taught today is descriptive and functional, and more like perspective 1 or 2. p. 5, 53, 76, 147

graphic novels are narratives that merge textual and visual information (like a comic book) through sequential art. They can be fictional or nonfiction works, but they are usually longer than the typical comic book and are bound in book format. Graphic novels are increasingly popular with both young readers and adults. p. 33, 56, 368

graphophonics refers to the print–sound relationship of text. Graphic cues generally include letters, letter clusters, words, and parts of words. **Phonics** refers to the relationships between graphic cues and sounds. Graphophonic cues are one of the **cuing systems** that help readers identify words as they read. They identify words by relating speech sounds to letters and letter clusters. p. 77, 226

historical fiction is a **genre** of literature set in a specific place and time in the past. It requires a great deal of research, descriptive detail, and authentic language to be credible. Good historical fiction is both an aesthetic and an efferent reading experience. Readers can learn history from it, as well as identify with the lives and concerns of the characters. p. 208, 368

holistic scoring of writing assesses what learners do well rather than what they cannot yet do. Teachers are encouraged to focus on the specifics they have in mind for rating pieces of writing, e.g., the writer's attention to purpose and audience, the learner's developmental capabilities, or the writer's attention to the specifics of the assignment. p. 332

hypertext is nonlinear writing. Text is linked so that the reader can go through a topic in any order. Readers of hypertext have greater control over what they read and the sequence in which they read it than with traditional texts. p. 33, 161, 215

instructional reading level is the level of reading instruction a learner needs in order to make maximum progress learning to read. Texts at this level must be just difficult enough to help learners develop reading strategies with the support of instruction. On an informal reading inventory, this is the highest level at which a learner is able to accurately identify 90 percent of the words and answer 70 percent of the comprehension questions. p. 31, 178

invented spelling refers to a learner's first attempts at transcribing spoken language into print symbols before learning the conventions of standard spelling. Learners pay particular attention to the sounds of language; invented spelling is a reflection of this focus. p. 126, 343

levelled text refers to reading materials that represent a progression from more simple to more complex and challenging texts. Some text progressions are based on readability formulas, others on letter–sound relationships, and still others on multiple criteria related to language predictability, text format, and content. p. 214

literacy is a term generally associated with reading and writing, but it has been defined in many different ways. *Basic* literacy is the ability to read and write. *Functional* literacy is frequently defined as those reading and writing skills needed by people to do everyday tasks such as writing cheques and reading instructions on a medicine bottle. **Critical literacy** goes beyond conventional reading and writing to an examination of texts and taking action to promote social justice. In recent years, *literacy* has been extended to other forms of representation, such as *media literacy* and *computer literacy*. p. 2, 152, 194

manuscript printing sometimes called *manuscript writing*, is usually the first form of written language taught to children; it consists of individual letters that are not connected. There are a number of styles of manuscript writing, but all of them are plain and easy to recognize. p. 358

media (plural; singular *medium*) are the resources one uses to communicate meaning (e.g., pencil and paper, computer). p. 28, 39, 114, 188

metacognition is awareness and control of the thinking processes involved in developing an ability. In reading, metacognition includes knowledge of factors that affect reading, of reading tasks, and of reading strategies. The regulative or control dimension of metacognition in reading involves planning and monitoring. p. 4, 49, 252

metafiction is a **narrative** mode used by authors to provide a constant and deliberate reminder that a book is something an author and reader create together, something that is not real but fictional and open to many interpretations. By drawing attention to how texts are structured, works of metafiction can show readers how texts "mean." Techniques used to this end include obtrusive narrators who directly address the reader, the insertion of parodies of other texts, typographic experimentation, and the mixing of **genres** and **discourses**. Works of metafiction usually employ any number of these techniques in combination. *Black and White* by David Macaulay and *Piggybook* by Anthony Browne are examples. p. 379

metalinguistic awareness is the growing awareness and ability we have to think and talk about language as a formal code. With learners, it can refer to understanding terms such as *letter*, *word*, *sentence*, and *sound*. p. 115

miscue is a term coined by Goodman (1969) for errors made during oral reading. Goodman purported that analyzing oral miscues gives insights into the reading process, since miscues result from the same cues and processes as correct responses. p. 133, 175

miscue analysis is a term originally developed by Goodman. It is a tool that includes an examination of oral reading followed by a retelling. Miscue analysis allows educators to analyze why miscues in reading occur. Miscue analysis can be used as a diagnostic tool for individual students' oral reading. It also helps teachers to gain insight into the reading process. p. 132

modes are a set of resources that people in a given culture can use to communicate. Examples of modes include print, image, music, and speech. All modes relate to at least one dimension of the six language arts. p. 5, 39, 110, 160, 215

monolingualism is the condition of being able to speak only one language. It may also refer to language policies that enforce one official or national language over others. p. 25

morphology is the study of the structure of words, specifically the ways in which morphemes (the smallest units of meaning in a language) combine to create meanings. An example of a morpheme is *s*, which denotes plural in English; hence, *dog* means one creature, and *dogs* means more than one. Suffixes and prefixes are also morphemes. Morphology is one of the essential **cuing systems** readers use to make sense of the printed word. p. 76

multimodal literacy refers to the myriad ways in which people can construct meaning (e.g., through visual, auditory, spatial, and gestural modes). p. 5

multimodal text is the use or integration of two or more **modes** of communication. p. 292

narrative consists of a story or a succession of related events. These events are frequently organized according to cause and effect or chronology. Narratives include descriptions of settings, events, and characters, as well as comments and observations. Narratives can have the structure of a story or a much looser structure without opening and closing sequences. p. 33, 197, 268, 292

native-like speech is the ability to use language in many situations to accomplish a wide range of purposes. Idiomatic language, **pragmatics**, and **dialect** are all important in native speaker ability. p. 73

New Literacies refers to literacies that have recently emerged with the era of digitalization and the Internet. Being able to navigate a video game, surf the Internet, shop on eBay, or chat online all require particular literacy skills. p. 44

new media standing in contrast to print media, is a broadened term for all forms of electronic communication. Emerging in the latter part of the 20th century, this catch-all term includes online news, streaming video and streaming audio, 3-D and virtual reality environments and effects, highly interactive user interfaces, mobile presentation, telephone and digital data integration, online communities, and live Internet broadcasting. p. 2, 44, 136, 292

oracy refers to the ability to express oneself fluently and grammatically in, and to understand, spoken language. Oral skills are especially important at all levels of learning and teaching. Emphasis is today placed on K to 8 learners talking and reasoning together as they think and learn. p. 90

participatory culture refers to the shift from a culture in which persons acted only as consumers to one in which they are seen as actively engaged in contributing to production (often referred to as *prosumers*). p. 447

performance assessment refers to assessment in which students demonstrate what they can do by doing it. Rather than using paper-and-pencil tests, teachers use their best judgment to evaluate performance along a continuum defined by increasingly demanding performance criteria. These criteria are written descriptions that capture quality performance at various levels of achievement. This form of assessment is frequently used for learners' writing. p. 172, 326

phonemes are the smallest units of meaningful sound in a language (e.g., /a/ as in *cat*. See also **phonemic awareness, phonetics, phonics, phonological awareness,** and **phonology.** p. 115

phonemic awareness is the ability to segment spoken words into their distinct sounds, or phonemes. The spoken word *dog* consists of three separate phonemes, one for each letter in the written word, D-O-G. The spoken word *chin* has three phonemes, the two letters in /ch/ representing one phoneme. See also **phonemes, phonetics, phonics, phonological awareness,** and **phonology.** p. 115, 175, 232

phonetics refers to the way sounds are articulated and produced. The term is often used to describe the way children spell, sounding out a word so they can articulate individual sounds (phonemes) within a word and transcribe them into print symbols. See also **phonemes, phonemic awareness, phonics, phonological awareness,** and **phonology.** p. 77

phonics is the relationship between letters and their spoken sounds. **Analytic** phonics is the association of sounds with larger clusters of letters such as phonograms or word families (e.g., *ight*). **Synthetic** phonics is the association of sounds with individual letters or letter clusters and the blending of these sounds to identify words. See also **phonemes, phonemic awareness, phonetics, phonological awareness,** and **phonology.** p. 7, 115, 227

phonological awareness is an awareness of patterns of sound that create meaning in language. See also **phonemes, phonemic awareness, phonetics, phonics,** and **phonology.** p. 32, 115, 197

phonology sometimes called *phonemics,* is the study of the patterns of sound that create meaning in language. In any one language, a number of sounds (phonemes) combine to produce words and meanings. See also **phonemes, phonemic awareness, phonetics, phonics,** and **phonological awareness.** p. 72

picture books are books in which illustrations play an integral role in creating meaning. Picture books are not the same as illustrated books, in which meaning does not depend on illustrations. In a picture book, text and pictures work together. Good examples of picture books are *Each Peach Pear Plum* by Janet and Allan Ahlberg and *The Tunnel* by Anthony Browne. p. 33, 376

poetic writing refers to the aesthetic element of writing. It consists of poetry and also fictional writing, including **narrative** and description. The purpose of poetic writing is purely pleasure or satisfaction on the part of the writer and audience. p. 303

portfolio assessment uses a compilation of work done by a learner over a period of time. Frequently, the portfolio items are selected by the learner or by the educator and learner together. Items included in a portfolio are chosen with deliberation in order to demonstrate what a learner can do. Educators find portfolios useful in demonstrating a student's learning to parents and administrators, and in explaining to learners what they need to focus on and what learning must be accomplished next. Portfolios also give educators an opportunity to reflect on their teaching and the learning their learners are engaged in. Portfolios provide learners with an opportunity to see the range of work they have done over time and to assess what they are accomplishing. p. 187, 327

pragmatics is the study of how speakers create meaning. The emphasis in pragmatics is on the context of language use and on the intentions and presuppositions of the speakers. The focus is on what an individual speaker means and on how that meaning is communicated. Pragmatics examines relatively short stretches of language compared with **discourse** analysis, which studies linguistic patterns in longer stretches of language. p. 72

predictable books are books that make reading easier for beginning readers. They have the following characteristics: the pictures support the text; large chunks of text are repeated; and the language has cadence, rhythm, or rhyme that supports the reading of the text. *Brown Bear, Brown Bear, What Do You See?* by Bill Martin *Jr.* and *Each Peach Pear Plum* by Janet and Allan Ahlberg are examples of predictable books. p. 142, 376

print literacy refers to the construction of meaning through written language. Definitions of literacy have recently expanded to include the multiple modes and media through which people may communicate. The term "print literacy" emerged to respond to this expansion and distinguish the decoding and encoding of print from other forms of literacy. p. 7, 45

reading series (See **basal reading series**.)

realistic fiction is imaginative writing that accurately reflects life as it is lived today or in the recent past. Events and situations in such stories might conceivably happen to people living in the real world. Young readers consistently select contemporary realistic fiction as their preferred **genre**. Stories are often about characters growing up in the world and their manner of coping with the problems and dilemmas of the human condition. An example of realistic fiction is *Stargirl* by Jerry Spinelli. p. 382

relay writing is the process of writing parts of an overall text and passing it along to others to continue, thus shaping the meaning in response to the interpretation and ideas generated by a number of authors. p. 457

retellings are an assessment strategy in which learners are invited to retell their understanding of a text. p. 175

running records are an assessment strategy that involves learners reading aloud a short passage to the educator. The educator takes note of all reading miscues and calculates an oral reading accuracy percentage, which is used to place learners in reading levels. Running records can also help to determine learner strengths and weaknesses by noting trends in the types of miscues they make when reading. p. 129, 177, 213, 222

scaffolding refers to the temporary supports educators give to learners to help them extend their skills and knowledge to a higher level of competence. p. 27, 38, 203, 252, 264

schemata (plural; singular **schema**) are organized mental frameworks that develop through repeated exposure to ritualized experiences such as playing baseball, eating in restaurants, or singing on car trips. Schemata influence our expectations and impose structure on the information we receive. p. 110

semantic map or web is a diagram that shows relationships among ideas. It consists of nodes containing key words, with connecting lines between the nodes. Educators and learners use semantic maps or webs to organize ideas about concepts, texts, or units of study. p. 255

semantics is the meaning component of language. It does not refer simply to the denotational meanings of words but also to the ways in which words are used, in both the choice of one word rather than another and the connotations created by those words. A semantic system includes idioms and compound words and the unique ways that words are used in different situations. p. 72, 73, 133

slam poetry is spoken poetry where the artist engages directly with the audience. Along with rap and hip-hop, slam poetry was influenced by jazz. It is often performed as part of a slam competition. Props, costumes, and music are generally forbidden. Most slam poems stay within a time limit of three minutes. p. 395

social constructivism is a model of learning based in the theoretical work of Vygotsky (1978). This model postulates that the ways in which people think are learned primarily through social interactions and that the ways in which we learn language develop as a result of our use of language in social contexts. p. 8, 111, 157, 195

strategy is an overall, conscious plan for performing a task. One strategy can be used in several learning situations. In contrast, skills are more context specific and are used in the service of a strategy. Examples of strategies include predicting meanings, summarizing, and monitoring. p. 9, 53, 187, 222

syntax (formerly *grammar*) is a linguistic term that refers to the structure of sentences. In the English language, syntax consists largely of word order. English is a non-inflected language; it does not depend on specific inflectional word endings to denote the role of a word in a sentence. p. 75

text structure is the pattern or organization of ideas in a text. There are two major types of texts: **narrative** (story) and **expository** (informational). Knowledge of text structure helps learners to construct meaning when reading and writing. p. 161, 266

trade books are books published by publishing companies as works of literature and not as educational texts. Books published as part of an educational program and intended for use in schools are usually referred to as *textbooks*. p. 368

transactional reading theory also called *transactive theory*, is based on the work of Louise Rosenblatt (1978). It posits that meaning comes from a transaction between a reader and a text in a specific context. Readers rely on the text itself and on their background knowledge, experiences, and worldview to construct meaning while reading. The focus is on the reader's response to texts. p. 158, 414

transmedia is a term meaning across multiple texts and formats. p. 457

voice is a term used in writing to refer to the combined effects of the writer's purpose, style, tone, and other intangibles, such as commitment, energy, conviction, and personality. p. 292

web 2.0 tools are features or practices of web-based applications that allow users to engage in the use or redesign of the systems in ways that are interactive and that permit increased control over their data. p. 447

webquest refers to structured, inquiry-based lessons that take learners through guided research and activities almost entirely based on the web. p. 457

young adult (YA) literature is fiction created especially for teens and young adults (usually aged 14 to 20); themes often focus on the challenges of youth. Whether in the form of novels or short stories, most YA stories feature an adolescent as the protagonist; the subject matter and story lines are typically consistent with the age and experience of the main character. p. 44, 368

zines are self-published fan magazines in a variety of formats, including print and digital versions. p. 457

zone of proximal development, a term coined by Vygotsky (1978), refers to a level of difficulty just beyond that which a child can handle independently but at which he or she can manage with help from others. Providing children with the opportunity to work with others on problems or tasks at this level maximizes learning. p. 132, 203

REFERENCES

Aboriginal Affairs and Northern Development Canada. (2013). *Aboriginal peoples and communities*. Retrieved from http://www.aadnc-aandc.gc.ca/eng/1100100013785/1304467449155

Aceves, T. C., & Orosco, M. J. (2014). *Culturally responsive teaching* (Document No. IC-2). Retrieved from University of Florida, Collaboration for Effective Educator, Development, Accountability, and Reform Center website: http://ceedar.education.ufl.edu/wp-content/uploads/2014/08/culturally-responsive.pdf

Adams, M. J. (1990). *Beginning to read: Thinking and learning about print*. Cambridge, MA: MIT Press.

Adams, M. J. (1998). *What children need in order to read: Preparing young children for reading success* [Videorecording]. Bellingham, WA: DeBeck Educational Video.

Adams, M. J. (2002). Alphabetic anxiety and explicit, systematic phonics instruction: A cognitive science perspective. In S. B. Neuman & D. K. Dickinson (Eds.), *Handbook of early literacy research* (pp. 66–80). New York, NY: Guilford Press.

Adams, M. J., Anderson, R. C., & Durkin, D. (1978). Beginning reading: Theory and practice. *Language Arts, 55*, 19–25.

Adams, P. (1987). Writing from reading: "Dependent authorship" as a response. In B. Corcoran & E. Evans (Eds.), *Readers, texts, teachers*. Portsmouth, NH: Boynton/Cook.

Albers, P. (2007). *Finding the artist within: Creating and reading visual texts in the English language arts classroom*. Newark, DE: International Reading Association.

Albers, P., & Murphy, S. (2000). *Telling pieces: Art as literacy in middle school classes*. Mahwah, NJ: Lawrence Erlbaum Associates.

Alberta Education. (1993). *Diagnostic teaching in a language learning framework 5*. Edmonton, AB: Student Evaluation Branch.

Alberta Learning. (2000a). *English language arts, K–9*. Retrieved from https://education.alberta.ca/media/450519/elak-9.pdf

Alberta Learning. (2000b). *Information and communication technology program of studies (K–12)*. Retrieved from http://education.alberta.ca/teachers/program/ict/programs.aspx

Alford, J. (2001). Learning language and critical literacy: Adolescent ESL students. *Journal of Adolescent and Adult Literacy, 45*(3), 238–242.

Allen, J. (2004). *Tools for teaching content literacy*. Markham, ON: Pembroke.

Allington, R. L. (2001). *What really matters for struggling readers* (1st ed.). New York, NY: Longman.

Allington, R. L. (2006). *What really matters for struggling readers* (2nd ed.). Boston, MA: Pearson/Allyn and Bacon.

Allington, R. L. (2009a). *What really matters in fluency: Research-based practices across the curriculum*. Boston, MA: Allyn and Bacon.

Allington, R. L. (2009b). *What really matters in response to intervention: Research-based designs*. Boston, MA: Pearson.

Allington, R. (2012). *What really matters for struggling readers: Designing research-based programs* (3rd ed.). Boston, MA: Pearson.

Allington, R. L., & Baker, K. (2007). Best practices for struggling readers. In L. B. Gambrell, L. M. Morrow, & M. Pressley (Eds.), *Best practices in literacy instruction* (3rd ed., pp. 83–103). New York, NY: Guilford Press.

Allington, R., & Gabriel, R. E. (2012). Every child, every day. *Educational Leadership, 69*(6), 10–15.

Allington, R., & Walmsley, S. A. (Eds.). (1995). *No quick fix: Rethinking literacy programs in America's elementary schools*. New York, NY: Teachers College Press.

Anderson, J., Moffatt, L., & Shapiro, J. (2006). Reconceptualizing language education in early childhood: Socio-cultural perspectives. In B. Spodek & O. N. Saracho (Eds.), *Handbook of research on the education of young children* (pp. 135–151). Mahwah, NJ: Lawrence Erlbaum Associates.

Anstey, M., & Bull, G. (2006). *Teaching and learning multiliteracies: Changing times, changing literacies*. Kensington Gardens, Australia: Australian Literacy Educators' Association and the International Reading Association.

Antone, E. (2003). Culturally framing aboriginal literacy and learning. *Canadian Journal of Native Education, 27*(1), 7–15.

Applebee, A. (1978). *The child's concept of story*. Chicago, IL: University of Chicago Press.

Armbruster, B. B., & Osborn, J. H. (2002). *Reading instruction and assessment: Understanding the IRA standards*. Boston, MA: Allyn and Bacon.

Arnold, B., DeBlois, D., & Sanders, C. (2010). *How to train your dragon* [Motion picture]. USA: Paramount Studios.

Ashton-Warner, S. (1986). *Teacher*. New York, NY: Touchstone Books.

Asselin, M., Early, M., & Filipenko, M. (2005). Accountability, assessment, and the literacies of information and communication technologies. *Canadian Journal of Education, 28*(4), 802–923.

Atwell, N. (1987). *In the middle: Writing, reading, and learning with adolescents*. Portsmouth, NH: Heinemann.

Atwell, N. (1998). *In the middle: New understandings about writing, reading and learning* (2nd ed.). Portsmouth, NH: Boynton/Cook.

Au, K., & Valencia, S. (2010). Fulfilling the potential of standards-based education: Promising policy principles. *Language Arts, 87*(5), 373–380.

Au, W. (2007). High-stakes testing and curricular control: A qualitative metasynthesis. *Educational Researcher, 36*(5), 258–267.

Baghban, M. (2007). Scribbles, labels, and stories: The role of drawing in the development of writing. *YC Young Children, 62*(1), 20–26.

Bainbridge, J., Coleman, W., & Gellner, J. (2004). Assessing children's growth in literature circles and discussion groups. *READ: Reading, Exploration and Discovery. The Journal of the Louisiana Reading Association, 25*(1), 21–32.

Baines, E., Blatchford, P., & Kutnick, P. (2007). Pupil grouping for learning: Developing a social pedagogy of the classroom. In R. M. Gillies, A. F. Ashman, & J. Terwel (Eds.), *The teacher's role in implementing cooperative learning in the classroom* (pp. 56–72). New York, NY: Springer.

Baker, C. (2006). *Foundations of bilingual education and bilingualism*. Clevedon, UK: Multilingual Matters.

Baker, E. (Ed.). (2010). *The new literacies: Multiple perspectives on research and practice*. New York, NY: Guilford Press.

Ball, J. (2007). *Aboriginal young children's language and literacy development: Research evaluating progress, promising practices, and needs*. Retrieved from http://www.afn.ca/uploads/files/education2/aboriginal_young_childrens_language_%26_literacy_development,_j._ball,_2007.pdf

Ball, J., & Bernhardt, B. M. (2008). First Nations English dialects in Canada: Implications for speech-language pathology. *Clinical Linguistics & Phonetics, 22*(8), 570–588.

Ball, J., Bernhardt, B., & Deby, J. (2005). *Implications of First Nations English dialects for supporting children's language development*. Paper presented at the World Indigenous Peoples Conference on Education, University of Waikato, Hamilton, New Zealand.

Ball, J., & Lewis, M. (2005). *Using Indigenous parents' goals for children's language to guide speech-language practice and policy*. Paper presented at the World Indigenous Peoples Conference on Education, University of Waikato, Hamilton, New Zealand. Retrieved from http://www.ecdip.org/docs/pdf/WIPCE%20Talking%20Points.pdf

Ball, J., & Mcivor, O. (2013). Canada's big chill: Indigenous languages in education. In C. Benson & K. Kosonen (Eds.), *Language issues in comparative education: Inclusive teaching and learning in non-dominant languages and cultures* (Vol. 24, pp. 19–38). Rotterdam, Netherlands: Sense Publishers.

Bannerman, H. (1899). *The story of Little Black Sambo*. New York, NY: Frederick A. Stokes.

Barnes, D. (1976). *From communication to curriculum*. Harmondsworth, UK: Penguin Books.

Barone, D., & Taylor, J. M. (2007). *The practical guide to classroom literacy assessment*. Thousand Oaks, CA: Corwin Press.

Barrs, M. (2000). Gendered literacy? *Language Arts, 77*(4), 287–293.

Barton, B. (1992). *Stories to tell*. Markham, ON: Pembroke.

Bassetti, B. (n.d.). *Learning second language writing systems*. Subject Centre for Languages, Linguistics and Area Studies Good Practice Guide. Retrieved from http://www.llas.ac.uk/resources/gpg/2662#

Bear, D., Invernizzi, M., Templeton, S., & Johnston, F. (2004). *Words their way: Word study for phonics, vocabulary, and spelling instruction* (3rd ed.). Upper Saddle River, NJ: Pearson/Merrill Prentice Hall.

Bearne, E. (2009a). Assessing multimodal texts. In A. Burke & R. Hammett (Eds.), *Assessing new literacies: Perspectives from the classroom* (pp. 16–32). New York, NY: Peter Lang.

Bearne, E. (2009b). Multimodality, literacy and texts: Developing a discourse. *Journal of Early Childhood Literacy, 9*(2), 156–187.

Beaver, J. (2001). *Developmental Reading Assessment* [Kit]. Parsippany, NJ: Celebration Press.

Beaver, J. M. (2006). *Teacher guide: Developmental Reading Assessment, grades K–3* (2nd ed.). Parsippany, NJ: Pearson Education.

Beck, I., McKeown, M., Hamilton, R., & Kucan, L. (1997). *Questioning the author: An approach for enhancing student engagement with text*. Newark, DE: International Reading Association.

Beck, I. L. (2006). *Making sense of phonics: The hows and whys*. New York, NY: Guilford Press.

Beck, I. L., McKeown, M. G., & Kucan, L. (2008). *Creating robust vocabulary: Frequently asked questions and extended examples*. New York, NY: Guilford Press.

Bender, W. N., & Larkin, M. J. (2003). *Reading strategies for elementary students with learning difficulties*. Thousand Oaks, CA: Corwin.

Benton, M., & Fox, G. (1985). *Teaching literature: Nine to fourteen*. London, UK: Oxford University Press.

Biancarosa, G., & Snow, C. E. (2004). *Reading next—A vision for action and research in middle and high school literacy: A report to Carnegie Corporation of New York*. Washington, DC: Alliance for Excellent Education.

Biemiller, A. (2006). An effective method for building meaning vocabulary in primary grades. *Journal of Educational Psychology, 98*(1), 44–62.

Binks-Cantrell, E., Joshi, R. M., & Washburn, E. K. (2012). Validation of an instrument for assessing teacher knowledge of basic language constructs of literacy. *Annals of Dyslexia, 62*(3), 153–171. doi:http://dx.doi.org/10.1007/s11881-012-0070-8

Bishop, C. (1938). *The five Chinese brothers*. (K. Wiese, Illus.). New York, NY: Coward, McCann and Geoghegan.

Black, R. W. (2005). Access and affiliation: The literacy and composition practices of English-language learners in an online fanfiction community. *Journal of Adolescent and Adult Literacy, 49*(2), 118–128.

Black, R. (2009). English language learners, fan communities, and 21st-century skills. *Journal of Young Adolescent and Adult Literacy, 52*(8), 688–697.

Blair, H., & Sanford, H. (2003, November 26–29). *Rethinking literacy for boys*. Paper presented at the International Conference on Language, Education and Diversity, University of Waikato, Hamilton, New Zealand. Retrieved from http://www.education.ualberta.ca/boysandliteracy/publications.html

Blair, H., & Sanford, K. (2004). Morphing literacy: Boys reshaping their school-based literacy practices. *Language Arts, 81*(6), 452–460.

Blessing, C. (2005). Reading to kids who are old enough to shave. *School Library Journal, 51*(4), 44–45.

Booth, D. (1996). *Literacy techniques for building successful readers and writers*. Markham, ON: Pembroke.

Booth, D. (2001). *Reading and writing in the middle years*. Markham, ON: Pembroke.

Booth, D., & Moore, B. (1988). *Poems please! Sharing poetry with children*. Markham, ON: Pembroke.

Boushey, G., & Moser, J. (2014). *The daily five: Fostering literacy independence in the elementary grades* (2nd ed.). Portland, ME: Stenhouse.

Bowen, L. (2006). Attracting, addressing, and amusing the teen reader. *ALAN Review, 34*(1), 17–23.

Bowers, P. N., & Cooke, G. (2012). Morphology and the common core: Building students' understanding of the written word. *Perspectives on Language and Literacy, 38*(4), 31–35.

Bowman-Perrott, L., Davis, H., Vannest, K., Williams, L., Greenwood, C., & Parker, R. (2013). Academic benefits of peer tutoring: A meta-analytic review of single-case research. *School Psychology Review, 42*(1), 39–55.

Boyden, J. (2013). *The orenda*. Toronto, ON: Hamish Hamilton.

Brabham, E. G., & Villaume, S. K. (2001). Building walls of words. *Reading Teacher, 54*(7), 700–702.

Braxton, B. (2007). Read-alouds: Choosing the right book. *Teacher Librarian, 34*(3), 52–53.

British Columbia Ministry of Education. (1988). *Enhancing and evaluating oral communication in the primary grades: Teacher's resource package*. Victoria, BC: Author.

British Columbia Ministry of Education. (2006). *English language arts, kindergarten to grade 7: Integrated resource package*. Victoria, BC: Author. Retrieved from http://www.bced.gov.bc.ca/irp/pdfs/english_language_arts/2006ela_k7.pdf

British Columbia Ministry of Education. (2010a). *Grade 6 curriculum package*. Retrieved from https://www.bced.gov.bc.ca/irp/curric_grade_packages/gr6curric_req.pdf

British Columbia Ministry of Education. (2010b, September). *Kindergarten curriculum package*. Retrieved from http://www.bced.gov.bc.ca/irp

British Columbia Teacher-Librarians' Association. (2001). *The research quest: A student guide*. Retrieved from https://bctf.ca/bctla/pub/documents/libraryprogram/RQ%20English.pdf

Britton, J. (1970). *Language and learning*. Harmondsworth, UK: Penguin Books.

Britton, J. (1972). Writing to learn and learning to write. In National Council of Teachers of English (Ed.), *The humanity of English: NCTE 1972 distinguished lectures* (pp. 31–53). Urbana, IL: NCTE.

Britton, J. (1982). *Prospect and retrospect: Selected essays of James Britton* (G. Pradl, Ed.). Montclair, NJ: Boynton Cook.

Britzman, D. (1998). *Lost subjects, contested objects: Toward a psychoanalytic inquiry*. Albany, NY: State University of New York Press.

Britzman, D. (2003). *Practice makes practice: A critical study of learning to teach*. Albany, NY: State University of New York Press.

Brown, D. (2007). *Teaching by principles: An interactive approach to language pedagogy* (3rd ed.). White Plains, NY: Longman.

Brown, J., & Fisher, P. (2006). Balanced literacy: One middle school's experience. *Principal Leadership, 7*(1), 38–40.

Brozo, W. G. (2010). *To be a boy, to be a reader: Engaging teen and preteen boys in active literacy* (2nd ed.). Newark, DE: International Reading Association.

Bruner, J. S. (1975). The ontogenesis of speech acts. *Journal of Child Language, 2*, 1–40.

Burke, A. (2010). *Ready to learn: Using play to build literacy skills in young learners.* Markham, ON: Pembroke.

Burke, A., & Hammett, R. F. (2009). *Assessing new literacies: Perspectives from the classroom.* New York, NY: Peter Lang.

Burke, A., & Rowsell, J. (2008). Screen pedagogy: Challenging perceptions of digital reading practice. *Changing English, 15*(4), 445–456.

Burns, M. (2004a). *Math and literature (K–1).* Sausalito, CA: Marilyn Burns Education Associates.

Burns, M. (2004b). *Math and literature (2–3).* Sausalito, CA: Marilyn Burns Education Associates.

Burns, P. C., & Roe, B. D. (2007). *Informal reading inventory* (7th ed.). Boston, MA: Houghton Mifflin.

Butler, A. (1993). *Phonics and spelling* [Videorecording]. Crystal Lake, IL: Rigby.

Cadiero-Kaplan, K. (2002). Literacy ideologies: Critically engaging the language arts curriculum. *Language Arts, 79*(5), 372–381.

Calkins, L. (2006). *Units of study for teaching writing, grades 3–5.* Portsmouth, NH: Firsthand Heinemann.

Cambourne, B. (1988). *The whole story: Natural learning and the acquisition of literacy in the classroom.* New York, NY: Scholastic.

Cambourne, B. (2000/2001). Conditions for literacy learning. *The Reading Teacher, 54*(4), 414–417.

Cambourne, B. (2002). The conditions of learning: Is learning natural? *The Reading Teacher, 55*(8), 758–762.

Cambourne, B. (2009). Revisiting the concept of "natural learning." In J. V. Hoffman & Y. Goodman (Eds.), *Changing literacies for changing times: An historical perspective on the future of reading research, public policy, and classroom practices* (pp. 125–145). New York, NY: Routledge.

Campbell, J. (1988). *The power of myth.* New York, NY: Doubleday.

Canadian Council on Learning. (2009). *Why boys don't like to read: Gender differences in reading achievement.* Retrieved from http://www.ccl-cca.ca/pdfs/LessonsInLearning

Canadian Library Association. (1974). *Statement on intellectual freedom.* Presented at the 29th annual conference, Winnipeg, MB.

Carlo, M. S. (2007). Best practices for literacy instruction for English language learners. In L. B. Gambrell, L. M. Morrow, & M. Pressley (Eds.), *Best practices in literacy instruction* (3rd ed., pp. 104–126). New York, NY/London, UK: Guilford Press.

Carroll, J., Davies, P., & Richman, B. (1971). *Word frequency book.* Boston, MA: Houghton Mifflin.

Castagno, A., & McKinley, B. (2012). Culturally responsive schooling for Indigenous youth: A review of the literature. *Review of Educational Literature, 78*(4), 941–993.

Castellano, M. B., Archibald, L., & DeGagné, M. (2008). *From truth to reconciliation: Transforming the legacy of residential schools.* Ottawa, ON: Aboriginal Healing Foundation.

Cazden, C. B. (1988). *Classroom discourse: The language of teaching and learning.* Portsmouth, NH: Heinemann.

Cazden, C. B., Michaels, S., & Tabor, P. (1985). Self-repair in Sharing Time narratives: The intersection of metalinguistic awareness, speech event and narrative style. In S. W. Freedman (Ed.), *The acquisition of writing: Revision and response* (pp. 51–64). Norwood, NJ: Ablex.

CBS Interactive. (n.d.). K'naan Wavin' Flag. Last.fm. Retrieved from http://www.last.fm/music/K%27naan/_/Wavin%2B+Flag

Cervetti, G., Pardales, M. J., & Damico, J. S. (2001). A tale of differences: Comparing the traditions, perspectives, and educational goals of critical reading and critical literacy. *Reading online 4*(9). Retrieved from http://www.readingonline.org/articles/cervetti

Chakraborty, B., & Stone, S. J. (2009). Language and literacy: Development through primary sociodramatic play. *Childhood Education, 86*(2): 96G–J.

Chapin, S., O'Connor, M., & Anderson, N. (2013). *Classroom discussions in math: A teacher's guide for using talk moves to support the common core and more, grades K–6* (3rd ed.). Sausalito, CA: Scholastic.

Chiefs Assembly on Education. (2012). *A portrait of First Nations and education.* Retrieved from http://www.afn.ca/uploads/files/events/fact_sheet-ccoe-3.pdf

Chipman, M., & Roy, N. (2006, November). The peer tutoring literacy program: Achieving reading fluency and developing self-esteem in elementary school students. *ACIE Newsletter, 10*(1), 1–8. Retrieved from http://www.carla.umn.edu/-immersion/acie/vol10/Bridge_Nov06.pdf

Chorzempa, B. F., & Graham, S. (2006). Primary-grade teachers' use of within-class ability grouping in reading. *Journal of Educational Psychology, 98*(3), 529–541.

Christie, J., Enz, B., & Vukelich, C. (2003). *Teaching language and literacy: Preschool through the elementary grades.* Boston, MA: Allyn and Bacon.

Christie, J. F., & Roskos, K. A. (2009). Play's potential in early literacy development. In R. E. Tremblay, R. G. Barr, R. D. V. Peters, & M. Boivin (Eds.), *Encyclopedia on early childhood development* (pp. 1–6). Montreal, QC: Centre of Excellence for Early Childhood Development. Retrieved from http://www.child-encyclopedia.com/documents/Christie-RoskosANGxp.pdf

Clark, P. (1999). Training the eye of the beholder: Using visual resources thoughtfully. In R. Case & P. Clark (Eds.), *The Canadian anthology of social studies: Issues and strategies for teachers* (pp. 361–375). Vancouver, BC: Pacific Educational Press.

Clausen-Grace, N., & Kelley, M. (2007). You can't hide in R5: Restructuring independent reading to be more strategic and engaging. *Voices from the Middle, 14*(3), 38–49.

Clay, M. M. (1972). *Reading: The patterning of complex behaviour.* Auckland, New Zealand: Heinemann.

Clay, M. M. (1975). *What did I write?* Portsmouth, NH: Heinemann.

Clay, M. M. (1993a). *An observation survey of early literacy achievement.* Portsmouth, NH: Heinemann.

Clay, M. M. (1993b). *Reading recovery: A guidebook for teachers in training.* Portsmouth, NH: Heinemann.

Clay, M. (2000). *Running records for classroom teachers.* Auckland, New Zealand: Heinemann.

Clay, M. M. (2002). *An observation survey of early literacy achievement* (2nd ed.). Portsmouth, NH: Heinemann.

Cleary, L., & Peacock, T. (1998). *Collected wisdom: American Indian education.* Needham Heights, MA: Allyn and Bacon.

Clifford, S. (2010). Web start-ups offer bargains for users' data. *The New York Times,* p. A1.

Clymer, T. (1963). The utility of phonic generalizations in the primary grades. *The Reading Teacher, 16,* 252–258.

Comber, B. (2001). Critical literacy and local action: Teacher knowledge and a "new" research agenda. In B. Comber & A. Simpson (Eds.), *Negotiating critical literacies in classrooms* (pp. 271–282). Mahwah, NJ: Lawrence Erlbaum Associates.

Cook, V. J., & Bassetti, B. (2005). An introduction to researching second language writing systems. In V. J. Cook & B. Bassetti (Eds.), *Second language writing systems* (pp. 1–67). Clevedon, UK: Multilingual Matters.

Cooper, J. D., & Kiger, N. D. (2001). *Literacy assessment: Helping teachers plan instruction.* Boston, MA: Houghton Mifflin.

Cooper, J. D., & Kiger, N. D. (2005). *Literacy assessment: Helping teachers plan instruction* (2nd ed.). Boston, MA: Houghton Mifflin.

Cope, B., & Kalantzis, M. (2009). Multiliteracies: New literacies, new learning. *Pedagogies, 4*(3), 164–195.

Council of Chief State School Officers. (n.d.). *The words we use: A glossary of terms for early childhood education standards and assessment.* Retrieved from http://www.ccsso.org/projects/SCASS/projects/early_childhood_education_assessment_consortium/publications_and_products/2926.cfm

Cowell, C. (2010). *How to train your dragon.* London, UK: Hachette Children's Books.

Cox, C. (1999). *Teaching language arts: A student- and response-centered classroom.* Boston, MA: Allyn and Bacon.

Culham, R. (2003). *6+1 traits of writing: The complete guide grades 3 and up.* Toronto, ON: Scholastic Professional Books.

Cummins, J. (1979). Cognitive/academic language proficiency, linguistic interdependence, the optimum age question and some other matters. *Working Papers on Bilingualism, 19,* 121–129.

Cummins, J. (1994). The acquisition of English as a second language. In K. Spangenberg-Urbschat & R. Pritchard (Eds.), *Kids come in all languages: Reading instruction for ESL students* (pp. 36–62). Newark, DE: International Reading Association.

Cummins, J. (2000). *Language, power and pedagogy: Bilingual children in the crossfire.* Clevedon, UK: Multilingual Matters.

Cummins, J. (2001, February). Bilingual children's mother tongue: Why is it important for education? *Sprogforum, 7*(19), 15–20.

Cummins, J. (2005, April). *Diverse futures: Rethinking the image of the child in Canadian schools.* Presented at the Joan Pederson Distinguished Lecture Series, University of Western Ontario, London, ON.

Cummins, J. (2006, Spring). Multiliteracies and equity: How do Canadian schools measure up? *Education Canada, 46*(2), 4–7.

Cummins, J. (2007). Pedagogies for the poor? Realigning reading instruction for low-income students with scientifically based reading research. *Educational Researcher, 35*(9), 564–572.

Cummins, J., Bismilla, V., Chow, P., Cohen, S., Giampapa, F., Leoni, L., … Sastri, P. (2005). Affirming identity in multilingual classrooms.

Educational Leadership, 63(1), 38–42. Retrieved from http://www.ascd.org/authors/ed_lead/el200509_cummins.html

Cunningham, P. M. (2007). Best practices in teaching phonological awareness and phonics. In L. B. Gambrell, L. M. Morrow, & M. Pressley (Eds.), *Best practices in literacy instruction* (3rd ed., pp. 159–177). New York, NY/London, UK: Guilford Press.

Cunningham, P. M., & Allington, R. L. (2007). *Classrooms that work: They can all read and write* (4th ed.). Boston, MA: Pearson/Allyn and Bacon.

Cunningham, P. M., & Allington, R. L. (2011). *Classrooms that work: They can all read and write* (5th ed.) New York, NY: Longman.

Cunningham, P. M., & Hall, D. (2007). *Making words first grade: 100 hands-on lessons for phonemic awareness, phonics and spelling.* Toronto, ON: Pearson.

Cunningham, P. M., & Hall, D. (2008). *Making words fifth grade: 50 hands-on lessons for teaching prefixes, suffixes, and roots.* Toronto, ON: Pearson.

Cunningham, P. M., Hall, D. P., & Gambrell, L. B. (2002). *Self-selected reading the Four-Blocks way.* Greensboro, NC: Carson-Dellosa.

Cunningham, P. M., Hall, D. P., & Heggie, T. (2001). *Making big words, grades 3–6: Multilevel, hands-on spelling and phonics activities.* New York, NY: Good Apple.

Daniels, H. (2002). *Literature circles: Voice and choice in book clubs and reading groups.* Portland, ME: Stenhouse.

Davey, B. (1983). Think aloud—modeling the cognitive processes of reading comprehension. *Journal of Reading, 27*(1), 44–47.

David, T., Raban, B., Ure, C., Goouch, K., Jago, M., & Barriere, I. (2000). *Making sense of early literacy: A practitioner's perspective.* Stoke on Trent, UK: Trentham.

DeFord, D. E. (1985). Validating the construct of theoretical orientation in reading instruction. *Reading Research Quarterly, 20*(3), 351–367.

Delpit, L. (1995). *Other people's children: Cultural conflict in the classroom.* New York, NY: The New Press.

Delpit, L. (2006). *Other people's children: Cultural conflict in the classroom.* New York, NY: The New Press.

Department of Education and Training in Western Australia. (2006a). *First steps* (2nd ed.). *Writing map of development.* Toronto, ON: Pearson Professional Learning.

Department of Education and Training in Western Australia. (2006b). *First steps* (2nd ed.). *Writing resource book.* Toronto, ON: Pearson Professional Learning.

DeTemple, J. M. (2001). Parents and children reading books together. In D. Dickinson & P. Tabors (Eds.), *Beginning literacy with language: Young children learning at home and at school* (pp. 31–51). Baltimore, MD: Paul H. Brookes.

DiCamillo, K. (2003). *The tale of Despereaux: Being the story of a mouse, a princess, some soup, and a spool of thread.* (T. B. Ering, Illus.). Cambridge, MA: Candlewick Press.

Dickinson, D. (2001). Book reading in preschool classrooms: Is recommended practice common? In D. Dickinson & P. Tabors (Eds.), *Beginning literacy with language: Young children learning at home and at school* (pp. 175–203). Baltimore, MD: Paul H. Brookes.

Dickinson, D., & Tabors, P. (Eds.). (2001). *Beginning literacy with language: Young children learning at home and at school.* Baltimore, MD: Paul H. Brookes.

Dickinson, D., & Tabors, P. (2002). Fostering language and literacy development in classrooms and homes. *Young Children, 57*(2), 10–18.

Dillon, D. (1985). Editorial. *Language Arts, 62*(1), 9.

Doake, D. B. (1981). *Book experience and emergent reading behaviour in preschool children* (Unpublished doctoral dissertation). University of Alberta, Edmonton, AB.

Doake, D. B. (1988). *Reading begins at birth.* Richmond Hill, ON: Scholastic-TAB Publications.

Doctorow, R., Bodiam, M., & McGowan, H. (2009). *CASI reading assessment [kit]: Comprehension, attitude, strategies, interests.* Toronto, ON: Thomson Nelson.

Doiron, R. (2002). *Lesson planning* [Unpublished paper presentation]. University of Prince Edward Island, Charlottetown, PE.

Doiron, R. (2003a). Boy books, girl books: Should we re-organize our school library collections? *Teacher Librarian, 30*(3), 14–16.

Doiron, R. (2003b). Motivating the lifelong reading habit through a balanced use of children's information books. *School Libraries Worldwide, 9*(1), 39–49.

Donald, D., & Krahn, M. (2014). Abandoning pathologization: Conceptualizing Indigenous youth identity as flowing from communitarian understandings. In S. Steinberg & A. Ibrahim (Eds.), *Critical youth studies reader* (pp. 114–129). New York, NY: Peter Lang.

Donnelly, A., Morgan, D. N., DeFord, D. E., Files, J., Long, S., Mills, H., … Styslinger, M. (2005). Transformative professional development: Negotiating knowledge with an inquiry stance. *Language Arts, 82*(5), 336–346.

Dorn, L. J., & Soffos, C. (2001). *Shaping literate minds: Developing self-regulated learners.* Portland, ME: Stenhouse.

Dudley-Marling, C., & Paugh, P. C. (2004). *A class-room teacher's guide to struggling readers.* Portsmouth, NH: Heinemann.

Duffy, G. G. (2002). Visioning and the development of outstanding teachers. *Reading Research and Instruction, 41*(4), 331–343.

Duffy, G. G., Webb, S. M., & Davis, S. (2009). Literacy education at crossroad: Can we counter the trend to marginalize quality teacher education? In J. V. Hoffman & Y. Goodman (Eds.), *Changing literacies for changing times: An historical perspective on the future of reading research, public policy, and classroom practices* (pp. 189–197). New York, NY: Routledge.

Dzaldov, B. S., & Peterson, S. (2005). Book leveling and readers. *The Reading Teacher, 59*(3), 222–229.

Easley, S., & Mitchell, K. (2003). *Portfolios matter: What, where, when, why and how to use them.* Markham, ON: Pembroke.

Eco, U. (1979). *The role of the reader: Explorations in the semiotics of texts.* Bloomington, IL: Indiana University Press.

Education Department of Western Australia. (1997). *First steps: Reading: Developmental continuum.* Melbourne, Australia: Rigby Heinemann.

Edwards, P. A. (2004). *Children's literacy development: Making it happen through school, family, and community involvement.* Boston, MA: Pearson.

El-Hindi, A. (1999). Beyond classroom boundaries: Constructivist teaching with the Internet. *Reading online.* Retrieved from http://www.readingonline.org/electronic/elec_index.asp?HREF=/electronic/RT/constructivist.html

Elkonin, D. B. (1973). USSR. In J. Downing (Ed.), *Comparative reading: Cross-national studies of behavior and processes in reading and writing* (pp. 551–579). New York, NY: Macmillan.

Evans, M. E., & Shaw, D. (2008). Home grown for reading: Parental contributions to young children's emergent literacy and word recognition. *Canadian Psychology, 49*(2), 89–95.

Evans, M. J., & Moore, J. S. (2013). Peer tutoring with the aid of the Internet. *British Journal of Educational Technology, 44*(1), 144–155.

Fairbanks, C. M., Cooper, J. E., Masterson, L., & Webb, S. (2009). Culturally relevant pedagogy and reading comprehension. In S. E. Israel & G. G. Duffy (Eds.), *Handbook of research on reading comprehension* (pp. 587–606). New York, NY: Routledge.

Farr, R., & Tone, B. (1998). *Portfolio and performance assessment: Helping students evaluate their progress as readers and writers* (2nd ed.). Fort Worth, TX: Harcourt Brace College.

Farrell, T. S. C. (2009). *Teaching reading to English language learners: A reflective guide.* Thousand Oaks, CA: Corwin.

Ferreiro, E., & Teberosky, A. (1993). *Sistemas de escritura en el desarrollo del niño [Literacy before schooling].* (K. Goodman Castro, Trans.). Thousand Oaks, CA: Corwin.

Field, J. C. (1990). *Educators' perspectives on assessment: Tensions, contradictions and dilemmas* (Unpublished doctoral dissertation). University of Victoria, Victoria, BC.

Fischer, D., Brozo, W. G., Frey, N., & Ivey, G. (2007). *50 Content area strategies for adolescent literacy.* Upper Saddle River, NJ: Merrill Prentice Hall.

Fish, S. (1980). *Is there a text in this class? The authority of interpretive communities.* Cambridge, MA: Harvard University Press.

Flippo, R. F. (2012). About the "expert study": Report and original findings. In R. F. Flippo (Ed.), *Reading researchers in search of common ground: The expert study revisited* (2nd ed., pp. 3–23). New York, NY: Routledge.

Flurkey, A. D. (2008). Reading flow. In A. D. Flurkey, E. Paulson, & K. Goodman (Eds.), *Scientific realism in studies of reading* (pp. 266–304). New York, NY: Lawrence Earlbaum Associates.

Fountas, I. C., & Pinnell, G. S. (1996). *Guided reading: Good first teaching for all children.* Portsmouth, NH: Heinemann.

Fountas, I. C., & Pinnell, G. S. (2006). *Leveled books (K–8): Matching texts to readers for effective teaching.* Portsmouth, NH: Heinemann.

Frager, A. (1994). Teaching, writing and identity. *Language Arts, 71*(4), 274–242.

Frank, C. B., Grossi, J. M., & Stanfield, D. J. (2006). *Applications of reading strategies within the classroom: Explanations, models, and teacher templates for content areas in grades 3–12.* Boston, MA: Pearson.

Freebody, P., & Luke, A. (1990). Literacies programs: Debates and demands in cultural context. *Prospect: Australian Journal of TESOL, 5*(3), 7–16.

Frey, N., Allington, R., & Fisher, D. (2010). *RTI and students with disabilities: A research synthesis and qualitative exploration.* Presented at the 2010 annual meeting of National Reading Conference, Fort Worth, TX.

Gallagher, K. (2009). *Readicide: How schools are killing reading and what you can do about it.* Portland, ME: Stenhouse.

Gallant, R. (1970). *Handbook in corrective reading.* Columbus, OH: Charles E. Merrill.

Gambell, T., & Hunter, D. (2000). Surveying gender differences in Canadian school literacy. *Journal of Curriculum Studies, 32*(5), 689–719.

Gambrell, L. B., & Gillis, V. R. (2007). Assessing children's motivation for reading and writing. In J. R. Paratore & R. L. McCormack (Eds.), *Classroom literacy assessment: Making sense of what students know and do* (pp. 50–61). New York, NY: Guilford Press.

Gambrell, L. B., Malloy, J. A., & Mazzoni, S. A. (2007). Evidence-based best practices for comprehensive literacy instruction. In L. B. Gambrell, L. M. Morrow, & M. Pressley (Eds.), *Best practices in literacy instruction* (3rd ed., pp. 11–29). New York, NY: Guilford Press.

Gammill, D. M. (2006). Learning the write way. *The Reading Teacher, 59*(8), 754–762.

Gandy, S. E. (2013). Informal reading inventories and ELL Students. *Reading & Writing Quarterly, 29,* 271–287. doi:10.1080/10573569.2013.789782

Gangi, J. M. (2004). *Encountering children's literature: An arts approach.* Boston, MA: Pearson.

Garcia, C. L. (1998). No fun with Dick and Jane. *The Reading Teacher, 51*(7), 606–607.

Gay, G. (2010). *Culturally responsive teaching: Theory, research, and practice* (2nd ed.). New York, NY: Teachers College Press.

Gee, J. P. (2007). *What video games have to teach us about learning and literacy* (2nd ed.). Basingstoke, UK: Palgrave Macmillan.

Gee, J. P. (2013). *The anti-education era: Creating smarter students through digital learning* (1st ed.). New York, NY: Palgrave Macmillan.

Giambo, D. A. (2010). American secondary education. *Bowling Green, 38*(2), 44–57.

Gichuru, W. J. (2013). *A case study mapping literacy learning opportunities and identity construction among African immigrant youth in a Canadian secondary school* (Doctoral dissertation). Retrieved from University of Western Ontario Electronic Thesis and Dissertation Repository. (Document ID Paper 1564)

Gillen, J., & Hall, N. (2003). The emergence of early childhood literacy. In N. Hall, J. Larson, & J. Marsh (Eds.), *Handbook of early childhood literacy* (pp. 3–12). London, UK: Sage.

Gillet, J. W., & Temple, C. (1994). *Understanding reading problems: Assessment and instruction.* New York, NY: HarperCollins.

Gillies, R. M., & Boyle, M. (2006). Ten Australian elementary teachers' discourse and reported pedagogical practices during cooperative learning. *The Elementary School Journal, 106*(5), 429–451.

Golub, J. N. (1994). Cooperative learning. In A. C. Purves (Ed.), *Encyclopedia of English studies and language arts* (pp. 298–299). New York, NY: Scholastic.

Gonzalez, N., Moll, L. C., Floyd-Tenery, M., Rivera, A., Rendon, P., Gonzales, R., & Amanti, C. (1993). *Teacher research on funds of knowledge: Learning from households.* Tucson, AZ: National Center for Research on Cultural Diversity and Second Language Learning. Retrieved from http://www.ncela.gwu.edu/pubs/ncrcdsll/epr6.htm

Gonzalez-Ramos, G., & Sanchez-Nester, M. (2001). Responding to immigrant children's mental health needs in the schools: Project mi tierra/my country. *Children and Schools, 23*(1), 49–62.

Goodman, K. (1969). Analysis of oral reading miscues: Applied psycholinguistics. *Reading Research Quarterly, 5*(1), 9–30.

Goodman, K. S. (1970). Behind the eye: What happens in reading. In K. S. Goodman & O. Niles (Eds.), *Reading: Process and program* (pp. 3–38). Urbana, IL: National Council of Teachers of English.

Goodman, K. S., Watson, D. J., & Burke, C. L. (1987). *Reading miscue inventory: Alternative procedures.* New York, NY: Macmillan.

Goodman, Y. M. (1991). Informal methods of evaluation. In J. Flood, J. M. Jensen, D. Lapp, & J. R. Squire (Eds.), *Handbook of research on teaching the English language arts* (pp. 502–509). New York, NY: Macmillan.

Gordon, E. E. (2005). *Peer tutoring: A teacher's resource guide.* Lanham, MD: Scarecrow Education.

Gouvernement du Québec Ministère de l'Éducation. (2001). *Québec education program: Preschool education, elementary education.* Quebec, QC: Author.

Government of the Northwest Territories. (n.d.). *Revitalizing, enhancing, and promoting Aboriginal languages: Strategies for supporting Aboriginal languages.* Retrieved from https://www.ece.gov.nt.ca/files/T4.02.02_Strategies%20for%20Supporting%20Aboriginal%20Languages.pdf

Gregory, E. (2008). *Learning to read in a new language: Making sense of words and worlds* (2nd ed.). Los Angeles, CA: Sage.

Gregory, E., Long, S., & Volk, D. (Eds.). (2004). *Many pathways to literacy: Young children learning with siblings, grandparents, peers, and communities.* New York, NY/London, UK: RoutledgeFalmer.

Gummersall, D. M., & Strong, C. J. (1999). Assessment of complex sentence production in a narrative context. *Language, Speech, and Hearing Services in Schools, 30*(2), 152–164.

Guthrie, J. T., & Klauda, S. L. (2014). Effects of classroom practices on reading comprehension, engagement, and motivations for adolescents. *Reading Research Quarterly, 49*(4), 387–416.

Halliday, M. A. K. (1969). Relevant models of language. *Educational Review, 22*(1), 26–37.

Halliday, M. A. K. (1975). *Learning how to mean: Explorations in the functions of language*. London, UK: Edward Arnold.

Handsfield, L. (2006). Being and becoming American: Triangulating habitus, field, and literacy instruction in a multilingual classroom. *Language and Literacy, 8*(2). Retrieved from http://www.langandlit.ualberta.ca/current.html

Hardy, B. (1975). *Tellers and listeners: The narrative imagination*. Dover, NH: Longwood.

Haycock, K. (2011). Connecting British Columbia (Canada) school libraries and student achievement: A comparison of higher and lower performing schools with similar overall funding. *School Libraries Worldwide, 17*(1), 37–50.

Heath, S. B. (1983). *Ways with words: Language, life and work in communities and classrooms*. Cambridge, MA: Cambridge University Press.

Hedrick, W. (2006). Reading incentives don't necessarily grow readers. *Voice from the Middle, 14*(2), 77–78.

Heydon, R. (2007). Making meaning together: Multimodal literacy learning opportunities in an intergenerational art program. *Journal of Curriculum Studies, 39*(1), 35–62.

Heydon, R. (2013). Learning opportunities: A study of the production and practice of kindergarten literacy curricula. *Journal of Curriculum Studies, 45*(4), 481–510.

Heydon, R., Crocker, W., & Zheng, Z. (2014). Nests, novels, and other provocations: Emergent literacy curricula in a child care centre. *Journal of Curriculum Studies, 46*(1), 1–32.

Heydon, R., & Hibbert, K. (2006). [Pre-service language arts teaching and learning]. Unpublished raw data.

Heydon, R., & Hibbert, K. (2010). A case study examining the complex interplay between teacher candidates' beliefs and practices in a pre-service language arts course. *Teaching and Teacher Education, 26*, 796–804.

Heydon, R., Hibbert, K., & Iannacci, L. (2004). Strategies to support balanced literacy approaches in pre- and inservice teacher education. *Journal of Adolescent and Adult Literacy, 48*(4), 312–319.

Heydon, R., & Iannacci, L. (2005). Biomedical literacy: Two curriculum teachers challenge the treatment of dis/ability in contemporary literacy education. *Language and Literacy, 7*(2). Retrieved from http://www.langandlit.ualberta.ca

Heydon, R., & Iannacci, L. (2008). The biomedical approach to literacy: Pathologizing practices within early literacy. In R. Heydon & L. Iannacci, *Early childhood curricula and the de-pathologizing of child-hood* (pp. 32–45). Toronto, ON: University of Toronto Press.

Heydon, R., & Rowsell, J. (in press). Phenomenology and literacy studies. In K. Pahl & J. Rowsell (Eds.), *Routledge handbook of literacy studies*. London, UK: Routledge.

Hibbert, K. (n.d.). The Salty Chip: A Canadian multi-literacies collaborative. Retrieved from http://www.saltychip.com

Hibbert, K. (2005). [Students' perceptions of assessment and evaluation]. Unpublished raw data.

Hibbert, K. (2006). *Assessment strategies*. Unpublished course material, University of Western Ontario, London, ON.

Hibbert, K. (2008). Virtual communities of practice: A vehicle for meaningful professional development. In C. Kimble & P. Hildreth (Eds.), *Communities of practice: Creating learning environments for educators* (pp. 127–148). London, UK: Idea Group.

Hibbert, K. (2015). The secret of "Will" in new times: The affordances of a cloud curriculum. In M. Hamilton, R. Heydon, K. Hibbert, & R. Stooke (Eds.), *Negotiating spaces for literacy learning: Multimodality and governmentality*. London, UK: Bloomsbury. Manuscript in preparation.

Hibbert, K., & Heydon, R. (2010). "Relocating the personal" to engender critically reflective practice in pre-service literacy teachers. *Teaching and Teacher Education, 26*, 796–804.

Hibbert, K., Heydon, R., & Rich, S. (2008). Beacons of light, rays, or sun catchers? A case study of the positioning of lead literacy teachers and their knowledge in neoliberal times. *Teaching and Teacher Education, 24*(2), 303–315.

Hibbert, K., Ott, M., & Iannacci, L. (2015). Co-constructed by design: "Knowledge processes" in a fluid "cloud curriculum." In B. Cope & M. Kalantzis (Eds.), *Learning by design: Reflexive pedagogy in the new media age*. Manuscript submitted for publication.

Hicks, D. (2002). *Reading lives: Working-class children and literacy learning*. New York, NY: Teachers College Press.

Hill, S. E., & Nichols, S. (2006). Emergent literacy: Symbols at work. In B. Spodek & O. N. Saracho (Eds.), *Handbook of research on the education of young children* (pp. 153–165). Mahwah, NJ: Lawrence Erlbaum Associates.

Holdaway, D. (1979). *The foundations of literacy*. Gosford, Australia: Ashton Scholastic.

Holland, H. (2007). Can educators close the achievement gap? *Journal of Staff Development, 28*(1), 54–75.

Huck, C. S., Hepler, S., Hickman, J., & Kiefer, B. Z. (2004). *Children's literature in the elementary school* (8th ed.). Dubuque, IA: McGraw-Hill.

Hudson, R. F., Isakson, C., Richman, T., Lane, H. B., & Arriaza-Allen, S. (2011). An examination of a small-group decoding intervention for struggling readers: Comparing accuracy and automaticity criteria. *Learning Disabilities Research & Practice, 26*(1), 15–27.

Huss, J. (2006). Gifted education and cooperative learning: A miss or a match? *Gifted Child Today, 29*(4), 19–23.

Iannacci, L. (2005). *Othered among others: A critical narrative of culturally and linguistically diverse (CLD) children's literacy and identity in early childhood education (ECE)* (Unpublished doctoral dissertation). University of Western Ontario, London, ON.

Iannacci, L. (2008a). Asset-oriented approaches to cultural and linguistic diversity in early childhood education. In R. Heydon & L. Iannacci, *Early childhood curricula and the de-pathologizing of childhood* (pp. 130–153). Toronto, ON: University of Toronto Press.

Iannacci, L. (2008b). The pathologizing of culturally and linguistically diverse students in early years classrooms. In R. Heydon & L. Iannacci, *Early childhood curricula and the de-pathologizing of childhood* (pp. 46–81). Toronto, ON: University of Toronto Press.

Indrisano, R., & Paratore, J. R. (1991). Classroom contexts for literacy learning. In J. Flood, J. M. Jensen, D. Lapp, & J. R. Squire (Eds.), *Handbook of research on teaching the English language arts* (pp. 477–487). New York, NY: Macmillan.

International Literacy Association. (n.d.). *Using multiple methods of beginning reading instruction.* Retrieved from http://www.reading.org/General/AboutIRA/PositionStatements/MultipleMethodsPosition.aspx

International Reading Association. (1998). *Phonemic awareness and the teaching of reading: A position statement from the board of directors of the International Reading Association.* Retrieved from http://www.readwritethink.org/resources/resource-print.html?id=20977

International Reading Association. (1999). *Position statement: High-stakes assessments in reading.* Retrieved from http://www.reading.org/resources/issues/positions_high_stakes.html

International Reading Association. (2002). *What is evidence-based reading instruction? A position statement.* Retrieved from http://www.reading.org/downloads/positions/ps1055_evidence_based.pdf

Invernizzi, M. (2003). Concepts, sounds, and the ABCs: A diet for a very young reader. In D. M. Barone & L. M. Morrow (Eds.), *Literacy and young children: Research-based practices* (pp. 140–156). New York, NY/London, UK: Guilford Press.

Irvin, J. J., Buehl, D. R., & Radcliffe, B. J. (2007). *Strategies to enhance literacy and learning in middle school content area classrooms* (3rd ed.). Boston, MA: Pearson Education.

Iser, W. (1974). *The implied reader: Patterns of communication in prose fiction from Bunyan to Beckett.* Baltimore, MD: Johns Hopkins University Press.

Israel, S., & Massey, D. D. (2005). Metacognitive think-alouds: Using a gradual release model with middle school students. In S. E. Israel, C. C. Block, S. Israel, K. L. Bauserman, & K. Kinnucan-Welsch (Eds.), *Metacognition in literacy learning: Theory, assessment, instruction, and professional development* (pp. 183–198). Mahwah, NJ: Lawrence Erlbaum Associates.

Ito, M., Horst, H., Bittanti, M., boyd, d., Herr-Stephenson, B., Lange, P. G., Robinson, L. (2008). *Living and learning with new media: Summary of findings from the Digital Youth Project* (John D. and Catherine T. MacArthur Foundation Reports on Digital Media and Learning). Cambridge, MA: MIT Press.

Jalongo, M. R. (2007). *Early childhood language arts.* Boston, MA: Pearson.

Jenkins, H., Clinton, K. Purushotma, R., Robison, A. J., & Weigel, M. (2006). *Confronting the challenges of participatory culture: Media education for the 21st century.* Retrieved from https://mitpress.mit.edu/sites/default/files/titles/free_download/9780262513623_Confronting_the_Challenges.pdf

Jewitt, C., & Kress, G. (2003). Introduction. In C. Jewitt & G. Kress (Eds.), *Multimodal literacy* (pp. 1–18). New York, NY: Peter Lang.

Johnston, F. P. (2001). The utility of phonic generalizations: Let's take another look at Clymer's conclusions. *The Reading Teacher, 55*(2), 132–142.

Jones, B. D. (2007). The unintended outcomes of high-stakes testing. *Journal of Applied School Psychology, 23*(2), 65–86.

Jones, J., & Leahy, S. (2006). Developing strategic readers. *Science and Children, 44*(3), 30–34.

Jordan-Fenton, C., & Pokiak-Fenton, M. (2010). *Fatty legs: A true story.* (L. Amini-Holmes, Illus.). Toronto, ON: Annick Press.

Juel, C. (1988). Learning to read and write: A longitudinal study of 54 children from first through fourth grades. *Journal of Educational Psychology, 80*, 437–447.

Kaufman, M. (2002). Putting it all together: From one first-grade teacher to another. *The Reading Teacher, 55*(8), 722–726.

Kavanagh, B. (2006). *Teaching in a First Nations school: An information handbook for teachers new to First Nations schools.* Vancouver, BC: First Nations Schools Association.

Kendrick, M. (2003). *Converging worlds: Play, literacy, and culture in early childhood.* New York, NY: Peter Lang.

Kincheloe, J. (2004). The knowledges of teacher education: Developing a critical complex epistemology. *Teacher Education Quarterly, 31*(1), 49–67.

King, A. (2007). Structuring peer interaction to promote higher-order thinking and complex learning in cooperating groups. In R. M. Gillies, A. F. Ashman, & J. Terwel (Eds.), *The teacher's role in implementing cooperative learning in the classroom* (pp. 73–91). New York, NY: Springer.

King, K., & Gura, M. (2009). *Podcasting for teachers: Using a new technology to revolutionize teaching and learning* (Rev. 2nd ed.). Charlotte, NC: Information Age.

Klinger, D., DeLuca, C., & Miller, T. (2008). The evolving culture of large-scale assessments in Canadian education. *Canadian Journal of Educational Administration and Policy, 76*, 1–34.

K'naan & Guy, S. (2012). *When I get older: The story behind "Wavin' Flag."* Toronto, ON: Tundra Books.

Knobel, M., & Lankshear, C. (Eds.). (2007). *A new literacies sampler.* New York, NY: P. Lang.

Kohn, A. (2002). Poor teaching for poor kids. *Language Arts, 79*(3), 251–255.

Kong, A., & Pearson, P. D. (2003). The road to participation: The construction of a literacy practice in a learning community of linguistically diverse learners. *Research in the Teaching of English, 38*(1), 85–124.

Krashen, S. D. (1982). *Principles and practice in second language acquisition.* Oxford, UK/New York, NY: Pergamon.

Kress, G. (1997). *Before writing: Rethinking the paths to literacy.* New York, NY/London, UK: Routledge.

Kress, G. (2003). *Literacy in the new media age.* London, UK: Routledge.

Kress, G., & Jewitt, C. (2003). Introduction. In C. Jewitt & G. Kress (Eds.), *Multimodal literacy* (pp. 1–18). New York, NY: Peter Lang.

Kress, G., & Van Leeuwen, T. (1996a). *Reading images: The grammar of visual design.* London, UK: Routledge.

Kress, G., & Van Leeuwen, T. (1996b). Reading images: The grammar of visual design. *English in Australia,* 92–100.

Kuhn, M., Rasinski, T., & Zimmerman, B. N. (2014). Integrated fluency instruction: Three approaches for working with struggling readers. *International Electronic Journal of Elementary Education, 7*(1), 71–82.

Kuiper, E., Volman, M., & Terwel, J. (2009). Developing Web literacy in collaborative inquiry activities. *Computers & Education, 52*(3), 668–680.

Lance, K. C., & Loertscher, D. V. (2003). *Powering achievement: School library media programs make a difference: The evidence.* San Jose, CA: Hi Willow Research and Publishing.

Langer, J. (1994). Focus on research: A response-based approach to teaching literature. *Language Arts, 71*(3), 203–211.

Language and Literacy Researchers of Canada. (2008, May). *Language and literacy, research, education practice and policy in Canada* [Position paper]. Retrieved from http://www.csse-scee.ca/cacs/LLRC/docs/LLRCPositionStatement.pdf

Lankshear, C., & Knobel, M. (2003). *New literacies: Changing knowledge and classroom learning.* Buckingham, UK: Open University Press.

Larson, J. (Ed.). (2001). *Literacy as snake oil: Beyond the quick fix.* New York, NY: Peter Lang.

Laufer, B. (2013). Lexical thresholds for reading comprehension: What they are and how they can be used for teaching purposes. *TESOL Quarterly, 47*(4), 867–872.

Leland, C., Harste, J., Ociepka, A., Lewison, M., & Vasquez, V. (1999). Exploring critical literacy: You can hear a pin drop. *Language Arts, 77*(1), 70–77.

Lesesne, T. S. (2006). Reading aloud: A worthwhile investment? *Voices from the Middle, 13*(4), 50–54.

Leslie, L., & Caldwell, J. S. (2011). *Qualitative reading inventory* (5th ed.). New York, NY: Pearson Allyn and Bacon.

Lewis, C. (1989). *Partnership writing: Ten-year-olds talking and writing together* (Master of education thesis). University of Alberta, Edmonton, AB.

Lewis, M., & Wray, D. (1995). *Developing children's non-fiction writing.* Leamington Spa, UK: Scholastic.

Lewison, M., Flint, A. S., & Van Sluys, K. (2002). Taking on critical literacy: The journey of newcomers and novices. *Language Arts, 79*(5), 382–392.

Lietz, P. (2006). Meta-analysis of gender differences in reading achievement at the secondary school level. *Studies in Educational Evaluation, 32*, 317–344.

Lindfors, J. W. (1987). *Children's language and learning* (2nd ed.). Englewood Cliffs, NJ: Prentice Hall.

Lipson, M. Y., & Wixson, K. K. (1991). *Assessment and instruction of reading disability: An interactive approach.* New York, NY: HarperCollins.

Lipson, M. Y., & Wixson, K. K. (2003). *Assessment and instruction of reading and writing difficulty: An interactive approach* (3rd ed.). Boston, MA: Allyn and Bacon.

Lipson, M. Y., & Wixson, K. K. (2009). *Assessment and instruction of reading and writing difficulties: An interactive approach* (4th ed.). Boston, MA: Pearson.

Little, D. (2007). Language learner autonomy: Some fundamental considerations revisited. *Innovation in Language Learning and Teaching, 1*(1), 14–29.

Lleras, C. (2008). Race, racial concentration, and the dynamics of educational inequality across urban and suburban schools. *American Educational Research Journal, 45*(4), 886–913.

Lleras, C., & Rangel, C. (2009). Ability grouping practices in elementary school and African American/Hispanic achievement. *American Journal of Education, 115*(2), 279–305.

Luke, A., & Freebody, P. (1997). Shaping the social practices of reading. In S. Muspratt, A. Luke, & P. Freebody (Eds.), *Constructing critical literacies* (pp. 1–18). Cresshill, NJ: Hampton.

Macdonald, D., & Wilson, D. (2013). *Poverty or prosperity: Indigenous children in Canada*. Retrieved from Canadian Centre for Policy Alternatives website: https://www.policyalternatives.ca/sites/default/files/uploads/publications/National%20Office/2013/06/Poverty_or_Prosperity_Indigenous_Children.pdf

Mackey, M., & McClay, J. (2008). Pirates and poachers: Fan fiction and the conventions of reading and writing. *English in Education, 42*(2), 131–147.

Malloy, J. A., & Gambrell, L. B. (2006). Approaching the unavoidable: Literacy instruction and the Internet. *The Reading Teacher, 59*(5), 482–484.

Mariconda, B., & Auray, D. P. (2014). *Empowering writers*. Monroe, CT: Empowering Writers LLC.

Mason, J. M. (1984). A schema-theoretical view of the reading process as a basis for comprehension instruction. In G. G. Duffy, L. R. Roehler, & J. Mason (Eds.), *Comprehension instruction perspectives and suggestions* (pp. 26–38). New York, NY: Longman.

Massey, D. (2002). Personal journeys: Teaching teachers to teach literacy. *Reading Research and Instruction, 41*(2), 103–125.

Mayer, K. (2007). Emerging knowledge about emergent writing. *YC Young Children, 62*(1), 34–40.

McCarrier, A., Pinnell, G. S., & Fountas, I. C. (2000). *Interactive writing: How language and literacy come together, K–2*. Portsmouth, NH: Heinemann.

McCoach, D., O'Connell, A., & Levitt, H. (2006). Ability grouping across kindergarten using an early childhood longitudinal study. *The Journal of Educational Research, 99*(6), 339–347.

McConaghy, J. (2014). *The centrality of exploratory talk in dialogic teaching and learning* (Doctoral dissertation). University of Alberta, Edmonton, AB.

McCormack, R. L., & Pasquarelli, S. L. (2010). *Teaching reading: Strategies and resources for grades K–6*. New York, NY: Guilford Press.

McGee, L. M., & Richgels, D. J. (1996). *Literacy's beginnings: Supporting young readers and writers*. Boston, MA: Allyn and Bacon.

McKee, L., & Heydon, R. (2014). Orchestrating literacies: Print literacy learning opportunities within multimodal intergenerational ensembles. *Journal of Early Childhood Literacy*. Advance online publication. doi:10.177/1468798414533562

McKenna, M. C., & Stahl, S. A. (2009). *Assessment for reading instruction* (2nd ed.). New York, NY: Guilford Press.

McKeown, M. G., & Curtis, M. E. (Eds.). (1987). *The nature of vocabulary acquisition*. Hillsdale, NJ: Lawrence Erlbaum Associates.

McLaughlin, M., & Allen, M. B. (2002). *Guided comprehension: A teaching model for grades 3–8*. Newark, DE: International Reading Association.

McNamara, D. S. (Ed.). (2007). *Reading comprehension strategies: Theories, interventions, and technologies*. New York, NY: Lawrence Erlbaum and Associates.

McTavish, M. (2007). Constructing the big picture: A working class family supports their daughter's pathways to literacy. *The Reading Teacher, 60*(5), 476–484.

Mead, S. (2006). *The evidence suggests otherwise: The truth about boys and girls*. Washington, DC: Education Sector.

Media Awareness Network. (2010). *Media education in Canada: Introduction*. Retrieved from http://www.media-awareness.ca/english/teachers/media_education/index.cfm

Medina, J. (1999). *My name is Jorge: On both sides of the river*. Honesdale, PA: Boyds Mills.

Meek, M. (1988). *How texts teach what readers learn*. Stroud, UK: Thimble Press.

Mendelsohn, D. J. (1989). Testing should reflect teaching. *TESL Canada Journal, 7*(1), 95–108.

Merchant, G. (2005). Barbie meets Bob the Builder at the workstation: Learning to write on screen. In J. Marsh (Ed.), *Popular culture, new media and digital literacy in early childhood* (pp. 183–200). London, UK: RoutledgeFalmer.

Merriman, E. (1999). A lazy thought. In J. Simon (Ed.), *Days like this*. Cambridge, MA: Candlewick Press.

Meyers, D. (1997, Fall). Dependent authorship: A dependable teaching activity for reading and writing critically and creatively. *Statement*, 20–22.

Michaels, S. (1981). "Sharing time": Children's narrative styles and differential access to literacy. *Language in Society, 10*, 423–442.

Michaels, S., & Cazden, C. B. (1986). Teacher/child collaboration as oral preparation for literacy. In B. B. Schieffelin (Ed.), *The acquisition of literacy:*

Ethnographic perspectives (pp. 132–154). Norwood, NJ: Ablex.

Miller, D., Topping, K., & Thurston, A. (2010). Peer tutoring in reading: The effects of role and organization on two dimensions of self-esteem. *British Journal of Educational Psychology, 80*(3), 417–433.

Miller-Lachmann, L. (1992). *Our family, our friends, our world.* New Providence, NJ: R. R. Bowker.

Moffett, J. (1979). Integrity in the teaching of writing. *Phi Delta Kappa, 61*(4), 276–279.

Moje, E. B., Ciechanowski, K. M., & Kramer, K. (2004). Working toward third space in content area literacy: An examination of everyday funds of knowledge and discourse. *Reading Research Quarterly, 39*(1), 38–70.

Moll, L., Amanti, C., Neff, D., & Gonzalez, N. (1992). Funds of knowledge for teaching: Using a qualitative approach to connect homes and classrooms. *Theory into Practice, 31*(2), 132–141.

Monaghan, D. (2006). *Components of a successful student tutor and classroom aide program.* Retrieved from Homestead website: http://www.teachtutors.com/successful_peer_tutoring_program.html

Montgomery, A., & Smith, K. M. (2014). Together in song: Builidng literacy relationships with song-based picture books. *Language & Literacy, 16*(3), n.p. Retrieved from http://ejournals.library.ualberta.ca/index.php/langandlit/article/view/23435

Morrow, L. M. (1989). Designing the classroom to promote literacy development. In D. S. Strickland & L. M. Morrow (Eds.), *Emerging literacy: Young children learn to read and write* (pp. 121–134). Newark, DE: International Reading Association.

Moss, G. (2000). Raising boys' attainment in reading: Some principles for intervention. *Reading, 34,* 101–106.

Mullis, I. V. S., Martin, M. O., Foy, P., & Drucker, K. T. (2012). *PIRLS 2011 international results in reading.* Retrieved from http://timssandpirls.bc.edu/pirls2011/international-results-pirls.html

Murphy, S. (2010, May). About the project [Multiliteracy Project]. In *Reclaiming pleasure in the teaching of reading.* Paper presented at the OTF/OADE conference, York University, Toronto, ON. Retrieved from http://www.multiliteracies.ca/index.php/index/showAbout

NAEYC (National Association for the Education of Young Children). (2009). *Developmentally appropriate practice in early childhood programs serving children from birth through age 8.* Retrieved from http://www.naeyc.org/files/naeyc/file/positions/position%20statement%20Web.pdf

Nagle, J. (2009). *Multimodal literacy practices: Fostering interest and identity for meaning-making in the intermediate classroom* (Unpublished master's thesis). University of Western Ontario, London, ON.

National Center for Education Statistics. (n.d.). *The nation's report card: 2013 mathematics and reading.* Washington, DC: Institute of Education Sciences, U.S. Department of Education. Retrieved from http://www.nationsreportcard.gov/reading_math_2013/#/

National Council of Teachers of Mathematics. (2000). *Principles and standards for school mathematics.* Reston, VA: Author.

National Reading Panel. (2000). *Teaching children to read: An evidence-based assessment of the scientific research literature on reading and its implications for reading instruction.* Washington, DC: National Institute of Child Health and Human Development. Retrieved from http://www.nationalreadingpanel.org

Nelson Language Arts. (1999 & 2000). Scarborough, ON: Nelson Thomson Learning.

New Brunswick Department of Education and Culture. (1998). *Atlantic Canada English language arts curriculum grades 4–6.* Retrieved from https://www.gnb.ca/0000/publications/curric/englangarts4-6.pdf

New London Group. (1996). A pedagogy of multiliteracies: Designing social futures. *Harvard Educational Review, 66*(1). Retrieved from http://wwwstatic.kern.org/filer/blogWrite44ManilaWebsite/paul/articles/A_Pedagogy_of_Multiliteracies_Designing_Social_Futures.htm

New London Group. (2000). A pedagogy of multiliteracies: Designing social futures. In B. Cope & M. Kalantzis (Eds.), *Multiliteracies: Literacy learning and the design of social futures* (pp. 9–38). London, UK: Routledge.

Nichols, M. (2006). *Comprehension through conversation: The power of purposeful talk in the reading workshop.* Portsmouth, NH: Heinemann.

Nomi, T. (2010). The effects of within-class ability grouping on academic achievement in early elementary years. *Journal of Research on Educational Effectiveness, 3,* 56–92. doi:10.1080/19345740903277601

Oblinger, D., & Oblinger, J. (Eds.). (2005). *Educating the net generation.* Retrieved from http://www.educause.edu/educatingthenetgen

Oczkus, L. D. (2003). The four reciprocal teaching strategies. In L. D. Oczkus, *Reciprocal teaching at work* (pp. 13–28). Newark, DE: International Reading Association.

Ogle, D. M. (1986). KWL: A teaching model that develops active reading of expository text. *Reading Teacher, 39*(6), 564–570.

Ontario Ministry of Education. (2003a). *Early reading strategy: The report of the expert panel on early reading in Ontario*. Toronto, ON: Queen's Printer for Ontario.

Ontario Ministry of Education. (2003b). *A guide to effective instruction in reading, Kindergarten to Grade 3*. Retrieved from http://www.eworkshop.on.ca/edu/resources/guides/Reading_K_3_English.pdf

Ontario Ministry of Education. (2004). *Me read? No way! A practical guide to improving boys' literacy skills*. Toronto, ON: Queen's Printer for Ontario.

Ontario Ministry of Education. (2006). *The Ontario curriculum, grades 1–8: Language* (Rev. ed.). Toronto, ON: Queen's Printer for Ontario.

Ontario Ministry of Education. (2009). *Me read? And how! Ontario teachers report on how to improve boys' literacy skills*. Toronto, ON: Queen's Printer for Ontario.

Ontario Ministry of Education. (2010–2011). *The full-day early learning–kindergarten program* [Draft version]. Retrieved from https://www.edu.gov.on.ca/eng/curriculum/elementary/kindergarten_english_june3.pdf

Opitz, M. F. (2000). *Rhymes and reason: Literature and language play for phonological awareness*. Portsmouth, NH: Heinemann.

Opitz, M. F., & Ford, M. (2001). *Reaching readers: Flexible and innovative strategies for guided reading*. Portsmouth, NH: Heinemann.

Osborne, M. P. (2011). *A crazy day with cobras*. New York, NY: Random House.

Owicki, G., & Goodman, Y. (2002). *Kidwatching: Documenting children's literacy development*. Portsmouth, NH: Heinemann.

Pahl, K. (1999). *Transformations: Children's meaning making in a nursery*. Oakhill, UK: Trentham Books.

Pahl, K., & Rowsell, J. (2005). *Literacy and education: Understanding the new literacy studies in the classroom*. London, UK: Paul Chapman.

Pahl, K., & Rowsell, J. (2006). *Travel notes from the new literacy studies: Instances of practice*. Toronto, ON: Multilingual Matters.

Palincsar, A. S. (1986). Metacognitive strategy instruction. *Exceptional Children, 53*(2), 118–124.

Palmer, B. C., Chen, C., Chang, S., & Leclere, J. T. (2006). The impact of biculturalism on language and literacy development: Teaching Chinese English language learners. *Reading Horizons, 46*(4), 239–265.

Pantaleo, S. (2014). The metafictive nature of postmodern picture books. *The Reading Teacher, 67*(5), 324–332.

Paratore, J. R., Melzi, G., & Krol-Sinclair, B. (2003). Learning about the literate lives of Latino families.

In D. M. Barone & L. M. Morrow (Eds.), *Literacy and young children: Research-based practices* (pp. 101–118). New York, NY: Guilford Press.

Paris, S. G., & Hoffman, J. V. (2004). Reading assessments in kindergarten through third grade: Findings from the Center for the Improvement of Early Reading Achievement. *The Elementary School Journal, 105*(2), 199–217.

Park, J. (2010). Graphic novels in the modern English language arts classroom. In M. C. Courtland & T. Gambell (Eds.), *Literature, media and multiliteracies in adolescent language arts*. Vancouver, BC: Pacific Educational Press.

Parker, J. (2010). *Teaching tech-savvy kids: Bringing digital media into the classroom, grades 5–12*. Thousand Oaks, CA: Corwin Sage.

Parsons, L. (2001). *Response journals revisited: Maximizing learning through reading, writing, viewing, discussing, and thinking*. Markham, ON: Pembroke.

Pearson, P. D., & Johnson, D. D. (1978). *Teaching reading comprehension*. New York, NY: Holt, Rinehart and Winston.

Peltier, S. (2009). *First Nations English dialects in young children: Assessment issues and supportive interventions*. London, ON: Canadian Language and Literacy Research Network. Retrieved from http://www.literacyencyclopedia.ca/pdfs/topic.php?topId=276

Penrod, D. (2007). *Using blogs to enhance literacy: The next powerful step in 21st century learning*. New York, NY: Rowman & Littlefield Education.

Peregoy, S. F., & Boyle, O. F. (2000). English learners reading English: What we know, what we need to know. *Theory into Practice, 39*(4), 237–247.

Peregoy, S. F., & Boyle, O. F. (2004). English learners reading English: What we know, what we need to know. In R. D. Robinson, M. C. McKenna, & J. M. Wedman (Eds.), *Issues and trends in literacy education* (3rd ed., pp. 103–118). Boston, MA: Pearson/Allyn and Bacon.

Perez, I. R. (2008). *Phonemic awareness*. Plymouth, UK: Rowman and Littlefield Education.

Peterson, R., & Eeds, M. (1990). *Grand conversations*. Richmond Hill, ON: Scholastic-TAB.

Peterson, S. (2001). Teachers' perceptions of gender equity in writing assessment. *English Quarterly, 33*(1 & 2), 22–30.

Peterson, S. S., & McClay, J. K. (2010). Assessing and providing feedback for student writing in Canadian classrooms. *Assessing Writing 15*(2), 86–99.

Petite Rivière Elementary School. (1993). *History of Crousetown*. Lunenburg County, NS: Petite Rivière Publishing.

Phenix, J. (2001). *The spelling teacher's handbook.* Markham, ON: Pembroke.

Pikulski, J. J., & Chard, D. J. (2005). Fluency: Bridge between decoding and reading comprehension. *The Reading Teacher, 58*(6), 510–519.

Pinnell, G. S., & Fountas, I. C. (1998). *Word matters: Teaching phonics and spelling in the reading/writing classroom.* Portsmouth, NH: Heinemann.

Pinnell, G. S., & Fountas, I. C. (2009). *When readers struggle: Teaching that works (K–3).* Portsmouth, NH: Heinemann.

Pinnell, G. S., & Scharer, P. L. (2003). *Teaching for comprehension and reading in grades K–2: Strategies for helping children read with ease, confidence, and understanding.* New York, NY: Scholastic.

Pogrow, S. (2006). Restructuring high-poverty elementary schools for success: A description of the hi-perform school design. *Phi Delta Kappan, 88*(3), 223–230.

Prasad, G. L. (2009). *Alter(n)ative literacies: Elementary teachers' practices with culturally and linguistically diverse students in one French-language school in Ontario* (Unpublished master's thesis). Ontario Institute for Studies in Education/University of Toronto, ON.

Pressley, M. (2006). *Reading instruction that works: The case for balanced teaching.* New York, NY: Guilford Press.

Prince Edward Island Department of Education and Early Childhood Development. (2008). *Prince Edward Island kindergarten integrated curriculum document.* Retrieved from http://www.gov.pe.ca/photos/original/k_doc.pdf

Pugh, K. H. (2005). Peer tutoring dos and don'ts. *Phi Delta Kappa, 528*, 5–31.

Puranik, C. S., Lonigan, C. J., & Kim, Y. S. (2011). Contributions of emergent literacy skills to name writing, letter writing, and spelling in preschool children. *Early Childhood Research Quarterly, 26*(4), 465–474.

Purcell-Gates, V. (1996). Stories, coupons, and the TV guide: Relationships between home literacy experiences and emergent literacy knowledge. *Reading Research Quarterly, 31*(4), 406–428.

Purcell-Gates, V. (1998). Growing successful readers: Homes, communities, and schools. In J. Osborn & F. Lehr (Eds.), *Literacy for all: Issues in teaching and learning* (p. 54). New York, NY: Guilford Press.

Purcell-Gates, V. (2001). What we know about readers who struggle. In R. Flippo (Ed.), *Reading researchers in search of common ground* (pp. 118–128). Newark, DE: International Reading Association.

Purcell-Gates, V., Jacobson, E., & Degener, S. (2004). *Print literacy development: Uniting cognitive and social practice theories.* Cambridge, MA: Harvard University Press.

Purcell-Gates, V., & Waterman, R. A. (2000). *Now we read, we see, we speak.* New York, NY: Routledge.

Purves, A. (1993). Toward a re-evaluation of reader response and school literature. *Language Arts, 70*(5), 348–361.

Purves, A., & Rippere, V. (1968). *Elements of writing about a literary work: A study of response to literature* (NCTE Research Report No. 9). Urbana, IL: National Council of Teachers of English.

Quebec Ministry of Education. (2001). *English language arts program of study.* Retrieved from http://www.mels.gouv.qc.ca/dfgj/dp/programme_de_formation/primaire/pdf/educprg2001bw/educprg2001bw.pdf

Raphael, T. E. (1986). Teaching question–answer relationships. *The Reading Teacher, 39*(6), 516–522.

Raphael, T. E., George, M. A., Weber, C. M., & Nies, A. (2009). Approaches to teaching reading comprehension. In G. G. Duffy & S. E. Israel (Eds.), *Handbook of research on reading comprehension* (pp. 449–469). New York, NY: Lawrence Erlbaum Associates, Taylor and Francis Group.

Rasinski, T. V., & Padak, N. D. (2001). *From phonics to fluency.* New York, NY: Longman.

Reid, R. (2006). Comedy club: Read-aloud passages that young teens will find funny. *Book Links, 16*(2), 20–21.

Reid, R. (2007). Flying under the radar: Great read-alouds you may have missed. *Book Links, 16*(3), 32–33.

Rennie, J., & Patterson, A. (2010). Young Australians reading in a digital world. In D. R. Cole & D. L. Pullen (Eds.), *Multiliteracies in motion: Current theory and practice* (pp. 207–223). New York, NY: Routledge.

Rhodes, L. K., & Shanklin, N. L. (1993). *Windows into literacy: Assessing learners, K–8.* Portsmouth, NH: Heinemann.

Richardson, W. (2010). *Blogs, wikis, podcasts and other powerful web tools for classrooms* (3rd ed.). Thousand Oaks, CA: Corwin Sage.

Riley, J. (2006). *Language and literacy 3–7: Creative approaches to teaching.* Thousand Oaks, CA: Sage.

Ritchey, K. D. (2006). Learning to write: Progress-monitoring tools for beginning and at-risk writers. *Teaching Exceptional Children, 39*(2), 22–26.

Roberts, E. A. (1996). *A survey of censorship practices in public school libraries in Saskatchewan* (Master of library and information studies thesis). University of Alberta, Edmonton, AB.

Rog, L. J. (2003). *Guided reading basics: Organizing, managing, and implementing a balanced literacy program in K–3.* Portland, ME/Markham, ON: Stenhouse/Pembroke.

Rose, D. (2015). Myth making and meaning making: The school and indigenous children. In M. Hamilton, R. Heydon, K. Hibbert, & R. Stooke (Eds.), *Negotiating spaces for literacy learning: Multimodality and governmentality* (pp. 167–184). London, UK: Bloomsbury.

Rosen, B. (1988). *And none of it was nonsense: The power of storytelling in the classroom.* Richmond Hill, ON: Scholastic-TAB.

Rosenblatt, L. (1978). *The reader, the text, the poem: The transactional theory of the literary work.* Carbondale, IL: Southern Illinois University Press.

Rosenblatt, L. (1985). The transactional theory of the literary work. In C. Cooper (Ed.), *Researching response to literature and the teaching of literature* (pp. 33–53). Norwood, NJ: Ablex.

Rosenblatt, L. (1990). Retrospect. In E. Farrell & J. Squire (Eds.), *Transactions with literature: A fifty year perspective* (pp. 97–107). Urbana, IL: National Council of Teachers of English.

Rothenberg, C., & Fisher, D. (2007). *Teaching English language learners: A differentiated approach.* Upper Saddle River, NJ: Pearson.

Rothstein, R. (2004). *Class and schools: Using social, economic, and educational reform to close the black–white achievement gap.* New York, NY/Washington, DC: Teachers College, Columbia University/Economic Policy Institute.

Routman, R. (1991). *Invitations: Changing as teachers and learners K–12.* Toronto, ON: Irwin.

Routman, R. (2000). *Conversations: Strategies for teaching, learning and evaluating.* Portsmouth, NH: Heinemann.

Routman, R. (2003). *Reading essentials: The specifics you need to teach reading well.* Portsmouth, NH: Heinemann.

Rowan, L., Knobel, M., Bigum, C., & Lankshear, C. (2002). *Boys, literacies and schooling: The dangerous territories of gender-based literacy reform.* Buckingham, UK: Open University Press.

Rowsell, J. (2006). *Family literacy experiences: Creating reading and writing opportunities that support classroom learning.* Markham, ON: Pembroke.

Rubin, B. C. (2006). Tracking and detracking: Debates, evidence, and best practices for a heterogeneous world. *Theory into Practice, 45*(1), 4–14.

Ruiz, N. T., Vargas, E., & Beltran, A. (2002). Becoming a reader and writer in a bilingual special education classroom. *Language Arts, 79*(4), 297–309.

Rumelhart, D. E. (1977). *Introduction to human information processing theory.* New York, NY: John Wiley and Sons.

Rushkoff, D. (2004). *Renaissance prospects.* Retrieved from http://www.itconversations.com/shows/detail243.html

Rycik, M., & Rycik, J. (2007). *Phonics and word identification: Instruction and intervention K–8.* Columbus, OH: Pearson.

Saccomano, D. T. (2006). *A descriptive study of a classroom teacher and the conditions of learning and the dimensions of teaching reflected in practice with intermediate-level literacy students* (Unpublished doctoral dissertation). Central Connecticut State University, New Britain, CT.

Salahu-Din, D., Persky, H., & Miller, J. (2008). *The nation's report card: Writing 2007.* Washington, DC: National Center for Education Statistics, Institute of Education Sciences, U.S. Department of Education. Retrieved from http://nces.ed.gov/nationsreportcard/pdf/main2007/2008468.pdf

Sampson, M. B. (2002). Confirming a K-W-L: Considering the source. *The Reading Teacher, 55*(6), 528–532.

Sanford, K. (2005/2006). Gendered literacy experiences: The effects of expectation and opportunity for boys' and girls' learning. *Journal of Adolescent and Adult Literacy, 49*(4), 302–315.

Sanford, K., & Blair, H. (n.d.). *Boys and literacy.* Retrieved from http://www2.education.ualberta.ca/boysandliteracy/

Sanford, K., & Madill, L. (2006). Resistance through video game play: It's a boy thing. *Canadian Journal of Education, 29*(1), 287–306.

Saracho, O. N. (2001). Exploring young children's literacy development through play. *Early Childhood Development and Care, 167*(1), 103–114.

Saskatchewan Education. (2000). *Early literacy: A resource for teachers.* Regina, SK: Author. Retrieved from http://www.sasked.gov.sk.ca/docs/ela/e_literacy/index.html

Saskatchewan Learning. (1994, August). *Aboriginal languages: A curriculum guide for Kindergarten to Grade 12.* Retrieved from https://www.edonline.sk.ca/bbcswebdav/library/curricula/English/More/Aboriginal_Languages_K-12_1994.pdf

Sastri, P. (2005). Affirming identity in multilingual classrooms. *Educational Leadership, 63*(1), 38–42. Retrieved from http://www.ascd.org/authors/ed_lead/el200509_cummins.html

Scanlon, D. M., Anderson, K. L., & Sweeney, J. M. (2010). *Early intervention for reading difficulties: The interactive strategies approach.* New York, NY: Guilford Press.

Schirmer, B. R. (2010). *Teaching the struggling reader.* Boston, MA: Pearson.

Schwartz, S., & Bone, M. (1995). *Retelling, relating, reflecting: Beyond the 3 R's.* Concord, ON: Irwin.

Scollon, R., & Scollon, S. B. K. (1981). *Narrative, literacy and face in interethnic communication.* Norwood, NJ: Ablex.

Scollon, R., & Scollon, S. B. K. (1983). *Narrative, literacy, and face in interethnic communication.* Norwood, NJ: Ablex.

Sénéchal, M. (2006). Testing the Home Literacy Model: Parent involvement in kindergarten is differentially related to grade 4 reading comprehension, fluency, spelling, and reading for pleasure. *Scientific Studies of Reading, 10*(1), 59–87.

Serafini, F. (2001). Three paradigms of assessment: Measurement, procedure and inquiry. *The Reading Teacher, 54*(4), 384–393.

Serafini, F. (2011). Expanding perspectives for comprehending visual images in multimodal texts. *Journal of Adolescent & Adult Literacy, 54*(5), 342–350.

Sheridan, M. P., & Rowsell, J. (2010). *Design literacies: Learning and innovation in the digital age.* London, UK: Routledge.

Shields, C. M., Bishop, R., & Mazawi, A. E. (2005). *Pathologizing practices: The impact of deficit thinking on education.* New York, NY: Peter Lang.

Silver, A. (1999). A fundamental equalizer for ESL children. *TESL Canada Journal/La Revue TESL du Canada, 16*(2), 62–69.

Simon, R. I., & Armitage-Simon, W. (1995). Teaching risky stories: Remembering mass destruction through children's literature. *English Quarterly, 28*(1), 27–31.

Simpson, C. (1980). *The Scott, Foresman word study for spelling.* Glenview, IL: Scott, Foresman and Company.

Sinatra, R. C., Stahl-Gemake, J., & Berg, D. N. (1984). Improving the reading comprehension of disabled readers through semantic mapping. *The Reading Teacher, 38*(1), 22–29.

Skutnabb-Kangas, T. (2000). Linguistic human rights and teachers of English. In J. K. Hall & W. G. Eggington (Eds.), *The sociopolitics of English language teaching* (pp. 22–44). Clevedon, UK: Multilingual Matters.

Slavin, R. E. (1980). Cooperative learning. *Review of Educational Research, 50*, 315–342.

Sloan, K. (2007). High-stakes accountability, minority youth, and ethnography: Assessing the multiple effects. *Anthropology and Education Quarterly, 38*(1), 24–41.

Smith, F. (1988). *Joining the literacy club: Further essays into education.* London, UK: Heinemann.

Smith, F. (2007). *Reading: FAQ.* New York, NY: Teachers College Press.

Snow, C. E., Burns, M. S., & Griffin, P. (Eds.). (1998). *Preventing reading difficulties in young children.* Ottawa, ON: National Research Council.

Something about the author. (Published annually since 1971). Detroit, MI: Gale Research.

Spence, C. M. (2006). *Creating a literacy environment for boys: Ideas for administrators, teachers, and parents.* Toronto, ON: Nelson.

Spinelli, C. G. (2006). *Classroom assessment for students in special and general education* (2nd ed.). Upper Saddle River, NJ: Pearson Education.

Squire, K. D. (2008). Video-game literacy: A literacy of expertise. In J. Coiro, M. Knobel, C. Lankshear, & D. Leu (Eds.), *Handbook of research on new literacies* (pp. 635–669). New York, NY: Lawrence Erlbaum Associates.

Starnes, B. (2006). What we don't know can hurt them: White teachers, Indian children. *Phi Delta Kappan, 87*(5), 384–392.

Starrett, E. V. (2007). *Teaching phonics for balanced reading.* Thousand Oaks, CA: Corwin Press.

Statistics Canada. (2012). *Linguistic characteristics of Canadians: Language, 2011 Census of Population* (Catalogue No. 98-314-X2011001). Retrieved from http://www12.statcan.gc.ca/census-recensement/2011/as-sa/98-314-x/98-314-x2011001-eng.pdf

Statistics Canada. (2013a). *Aboriginal peoples in Canada: First Nations people, Métis and Inuit: National Household Survey, 2011* (Catalogue No. 99-011-X2011001). Retrieved from http://www12.statcan.gc.ca/nhs-enm/2011/as-sa/99-011-x/99-011-x2011001-eng.pdf

Statistics Canada. (2013b). *Immigration and ethnocultural diversity in Canada: National Household Survey, 2011* (Catalogue No. 99-010-X2011001). Retrieved from http://www12.statcan.gc.ca/nhs-enm/2011/as-sa/99-010-x/99-010-x2011001-eng.pdf

Stauffer, R. G. (1975). *Directing the reading-thinking process.* New York, NY: Harper & Row.

Stein, P. (2008). *Multimodal pedagogies in diverse classrooms: Representation, rights and resources.* New York, NY: Routledge.

Stevens, R. J. (2007). Cooperative learning and literacy instruction in middle level education. In R. M. Gillies, A. F. Ashman, & J. Terwel (Eds.), *The teacher's role in implementing cooperative learning in the classroom* (pp. 92–109). New York, NY: Springer.

Stone, S. J. (1993). *Playing: A kid's curriculum.* Parsippany, NJ: Goodyear Books.

Straw, S. B. (1990). The actualization of reading and writing: Public policy and conceptualizations of literacy. In S. P. Norris & L. M. Phillips (Eds.), *Literacy policy in Canada* (pp. 165–181). Calgary, AB: Detselig Enterprises.

Street, B. (1984). *Literacy in theory and practice.* Cambridge, MA: Cambridge University Press.

Strickland discusses proper role of phonics. (2011). *Reading Today, 28*(4), 6. Retrieved from http://web.b.ebscohost .com.proxy1.lib.uwo.ca/ehost/pdfviewed/ pdfviewer?sid=7f97d705-5952-46ce-8dd5-9cdf873ef4 f3%40sessuinmgr114&vid=6&hid=118

Sullivan, M. (2004). Why Johnny won't read. *School Library Journal, 50*(8), 36–39.

Sulzby, E. (1985). Children's emergent reading of favorite storybooks: A developmental study. *Reading Research Quarterly, 20,* 458–481.

Sulzby, E. (1991). The development of the young child and the emergence of literacy. In J. Flood, J. M. Jensen, D. Lapp, & J. R. Squire (Eds.), *Handbook of research on teaching the English language arts* (pp. 273–285). New York, NY: Macmillan.

Sutherland-Smith, W. (2002). Weaving the literacy web: Changes in reading from page to screen. *The Reading Teacher, 55*(7), 662–668.

Swadener, B. B., & Lubeck, S. (Eds.). (1995). *Children and families "at promise": Deconstructing the discourse of risk.* Albany, NY: Albany State University of New York Press.

Swearingen, R., & Allen, D. (2000). *Classroom assessment of reading* (2nd ed.). Boston, MA: Houghton Mifflin Company.

Taberski, S. (1996). *A close-up look at teaching reading: Focusing on children and our goals* [Videorecording]. Portsmouth, NH: Heinemann.

Taberski, S. (2000). *On solid ground: Strategies for teaching reading K–3.* Portsmouth, NH: Heinemann.

Tan, L., Guo, L, & Chia, A. L. (2009). Teaching English in new times. In P. Teo, T. M. Yin, & C. Ho (Eds.), *Exploring new frontiers: Challenging students in the language and literature classroom* (pp. 15–29). Toronto, ON: Pearson.

Teachers' resources. (n.d.). Retrieved from National Archives website: http://www.archives.gov/education/

Temple, C. A., & Gillet, J. W. (1989). *Language arts: Learning processes and teaching practices* (2nd ed.). Glenview, IL: Scott, Foresman and Company.

Thomas, V. (1979). *Teaching spelling: Canadian word lists and instructional techniques.* Toronto, ON: Gage.

Thomson, J. (1987). *Understanding teenagers' reading: Reading processes and the teaching of literature.*

Norwood, Australia: Australian Association for the Teaching of English.

Tizard, B., & Hughes, M. (1984). *Young children learning.* Cambridge, MA: Harvard University Press.

Tompkins, G. (2007). *Teaching writing: Balancing process and product* (5th ed.). Upper Saddle River, NJ: Prentice Hall.

Tovani, C. (2000). *I read it, but I don't get it: Comprehension strategies for adolescent readers.* Portland, ME: Stenhouse.

Tsao, Y.-L. (2008). Using guided play to enhance children's conversation, creativity and competence in literacy. *Education, 128*(3), 515–520.

Tse, L., & Nicholson, T. (2014). The effect of phonics-enhanced Big Book reading on the language and literacy skills of 6-year-old pupils of different reading ability attending lower SES schools. *Frontiers in Psychology, 5,* 1–20. doi:10.3389/fpsyg.2014.01222

University of Oregon. (n.d.). *Phonemic awareness in beginning reading.* Retrieved from http://reading .uoregon.edu/pa/pa_features.php

Unrau, N., & Schlackman, J. (2006). Motivation and its relationship with reading achievement in an urban middle school. *The Journal of Educational Research, 100*(2), 81–101.

Vacca, J. L., Vacca, R. T., & Gove, M. K. (2006). *Reading and learning to read* (6th ed.). Boston, MA: Pearson/Allyn and Bacon.

Vacca, R. T., Vacca, J. L., & Begorary, D. L. (2005). *Content area reading: Literacy and learning across the curriculum* (Canadian ed.). Toronto, ON: Pearson/ Allyn and Bacon.

Valencia, S. W., Hiebert, E. H., & Afflerbach, P. P. (Eds.). (1994). *Authentic reading assessment: Practices and possibilities.* Newark, DE: International Reading Association.

Valli, L., & Chambliss, M. (2007). Creating classroom cultures: One teacher, two lessons, and a high-stakes test. *Anthropology and Education Quarterly, 38*(1), 57–75.

Venn, J. J. (2007). *Assessing students with special needs* (4th ed.). Upper Saddle River, NJ: Pearson Education.

Villaume, S. K., & Brabham, E. G. (2001). Guided reading: Who is in the driver's seat? *The Reading Teacher, 55*(3), 260–263.

Voke, H. (2002). What do we know about sanctions and rewards? *Infobrief, 31,* 1–10.

Vygotsky, L. S. (1978). *Mind in society: The development of higher psychological processes* (M. Cole, V. John-Steiner, S. Sribner, & E. Souberman, Eds.). Cambridge, MA: Harvard University Press.

Walker, B. J. (2005). Thinking aloud: Struggling readers often require more than a model. *The Reading Teacher, 58*(7), 688–692.

Walker, T. (1993). *Peer dialogue journals as response to literature in grade two* (Master of education thesis). University of Alberta, Edmonton, AB.

Walker-Dalhouse, D., & Risko, V. J. (2008, September). Homelessness, poverty, and children's literacy development. *The Reading Teacher, 62*(1), 84–86.

Washburn, E. K., & Mulcahy, C. A. (2014). Expanding preservice teachers' knowledge of the English language: Recommendations for teacher educators. *Reading and Writing Quarterly: Overcoming Learning Difficulties, 30*(4), 328–347.

Wason-Ellam, L. (2002). Interwoven responses to critically conscious stories. *Query, 31*(1), 21–26.

Wassermann, S. (1992). Serious play in the classroom. *Childhood Education, 68*, 133–139.

Watts-Taffe, S., & Truscott, D. M. (2000). Using what you know about language and literacy development for ESL students in the mainstream classroom. *Language Arts, 77*(3), 258–264.

Weaver, C. (1996). *Teaching grammar in context.* Portsmouth, NH: Boynton/Cook.

Weaver, C., Gillmeister-Krause, L., & Vento-Zogby, G. (1996). *Creating support for effective literacy education.* Portsmouth, NH: Heinemann.

Weber-Pillwax, C. (2001). Orality in Northern Cree Indigenous worlds. *Canadian Journal of Native Education, 25*(2), 149–165.

Wells, G. (1986). *The meaning makers.* Portsmouth, NH: Heinemann.

Welsch, J. G. (2008). Playing within and beyond the story: Encouraging book-related pretend play. *The Reading Teacher, 62*(2), 138–148.

Western Canadian Protocol for Collaboration in Basic Education. (1998). *The common curriculum framework for English language arts in western Canada, kindergarten to grade 12.* Retrieved from http://www.wncp.ca/media/40977/wcpla.pdf

Western Canadian Protocol for Collaboration in Basic Education. (2001, June). *Kindergarten to grade 9 English language arts resources: Annotated bibliography.* Retrieved from http://www.edu.gov.mb.ca/k12/cur/ela/wcpelak-9.pdf

What is balanced literacy? (n.d.). Retrieved from http://www.harcourtcanada.com/rigby/bal-lit.htm

White, E. B. (1952). *Charlotte's web.* New York, NY: Harper & Row.

Whitin, P., & Whitin, D. (2000). *Math is language too: Talking and writing in the mathematics classroom.* Reston, VA: NCTM.

Widdowson, F., & Howard, A. (2013). *Approaches to Aboriginal education in Canada.* Edmonton, AB: Brush Education.

Wiener, R. B., & Cohen, J. H. (1997). *Literacy portfolios: Using assessment to guide instructions.* Des Moines, IA: Merrill Prentice Hall.

Wilkinson, L. C., & Silliman, E. R. (2000). Classroom language and literacy learning. In M. L. Kamil, P. B. Mosenthal, P. D. Pearson, & R. Barr (Eds.), *Handbook of reading research* (Vol. 3, pp. 337–360). Mahwah, NJ: Lawrence Erlbaum Associates.

Wink, J. (2011). *Critical pedagogy: Notes from the real world* (4th ed.). Boston, MA: Pearson/Allyn and Bacon.

Young, J. P., & Brozo, W. G. (2001). Boys will be boys, or will they? Literacy and masculinities. *Reading Research Quarterly, 36*(3), 316–325.

Zajda, J. I., Majhanovich, S., & Rust, V. (2006). *Education and social justice.* Dordrecht, Netherlands: Springer.

INDEX